Worlds of History

A Comparative Reader

Volume Two: Since 1400

Fifth Edition

Kevin Reilly
Raritan Valley College

Bedford/St. Martin's
Boston • New York

For Bedford/St. Martin's

Publisher for History: Mary Dougherty
Executive Editor for History: Traci M. Crowell
Director of Development for History: Jane Knetzger
Senior Developmental Editor: Laura Arcari
Production Editor: Katherine Caruana
Production Supervisor: Samuel Jones
Senior Marketing Manager: Paul Stillitano
Editorial Assistant: Victoria Royal
Copyeditor: Susan Moore
Cartography: Mapping Specialists, Ltd.
Photo Researcher: Naomi Kornhauser
Permissions Manager: Kalina K. Ingham
Senior Art Director: Anna Palchik
Text Designer: Janis Owens
Cover Designer: Marine Miller
Cover Art: Top: *Spring Scything*, 1974 (color litho). Chinese School
    (20th Century). © Private Collection/DaTo Images/The Bridgeman Art
    Library. Bottom: Candido Portinari, *Coffee*, 1935. © Art Resource, NY.
Composition: Cenveo Publisher Services
Printing and Binding: RR Donnelley and Sons

President, Bedford/St. Martin's: Denise B. Wydra
Presidents, Macmillan Higher Education: Joan E. Feinberg and Tom Scotty
Director of Marketing: Karen R. Soeltz
Director of Production: Susan W. Brown
Associate Director, Editorial Production: Elise S. Kaiser
Managing Editor: Elizabeth M. Schaaf

Manufactured in the United States of America.

3   4   5   16   15   14   13

For information, write: Bedford/St. Martin's, 75 Arlington Street,
Boston, MA 02116 (617-399-4000)

ISBN 978-1-4576-1782-9 (Volume 1)
ISBN 978-1-4576-1783-6 (Volume 2)
ISBN 978-1-4576-1785-0 (High School Edition)

Acknowledgments

Preface

Teaching introductory world history to college students for forty years has helped me appreciate the enduring truths that have governed the framework of this book since its inception. When asked what has made *Worlds of History* such a successful supplemental or stand-alone text for their world history courses, adopters point to the accessible and engaging selections; the choice of interesting themes and topics presented comparatively that address the interests of students while respecting the integrity of the field; and the inclusion of "Thinking Historically" sections that show teachers and students how the study of history can not only teach broad trends and comparative experiences but also develop critical thought. I have continued all of these features in this fifth edition.

To engage students who are not only new to the college experience but new to reading source material as well, I have continued my efforts to provide accessible readings that pique student interest. This new edition aims to maintain that high level of reader interest with new selections that are real page-turners, like the diary of a young man on a doomed slave ship and Pu Songling's story of a mysterious "Lady Knight," along with some new, more accessible translations of established classical sources like *The Tale of Genji*. As in previous editions, I have also included secondary as well as primary texts. In some chapters the secondary text introduces an issue that the primary sources address, while at other times the secondary source offers a summary or suggestions for new directions. My strategy is that students will learn how texts, whether primary or secondary, talk to each other—and without having to buy separate books of each.

As a framework, the reader continues to have a **thematic and topical organization** that also proceeds chronologically, with each chapter focusing on a captivating topic within a particular time period. I have long found a **comparative approach** to be a useful tool for approaching world history, and for the fifth edition, I have continued to use this tool, examining two or more cultures at a time. In some chapters students can trace parallel developments in separate regions, such as the development of society in ancient Greece and India in Chapter 3, or the advent of nationalism in Japan and India in Chapter 23. In other cases students examine the enduring effects of contact and exchange between cultures, as in the chapter on Mongol and Viking raiding and settlements from the tenth to the fourteenth centuries, or Volume Two's chapter on the scientific revolution in Europe, the Ottoman Empire, China, Japan, and the Americas. Even the normally bipolar study of the Cold War in Chapter 26 can be opened up to more comparisons with new documents relating to the fight to control the emerging "Third World."

I have long felt that we should teach "habits of mind" as much as subject matter. This view is becoming more pervasive in recent years, emphasized by the College Board in its AP World History course, and as evidenced by the spreading appeal of assessing common goals for the study of history that is currently winning the endorsement of the American Historical Association. To encourage these "habits of mind," I continue to include a wealth of **pedagogical tools** to help students unlock the readings and hone their criticalthinking skills. Each chapter begins with **"Historical Context,"** an introduction to the chapter's topic that sets the stage for directed comparisons among the readings. A separate **"Thinking Historically"** section follows, which introduces a particular critical thinking skill—such as asking about author, audience, and agenda or distinguishing causes of change—that is designed to mine the chapter's selections. Headnotes preceding each selection provide additional context, while document-specific "Thinking Historically" paragraphs pose questions to encourage close analysis of the selections using the critical thinking skill introduced at the beginning of the chapter. **Explanatory gloss notes** and **pronunciation guides** throughout ensure comprehension of the readings. A set of **"Reflections"** that both summarizes and extends the chapter's lessons concludes each chapter.

To enrich the instructor's experience teaching with this reader, I have written an **instructor's resource manual**. Available online at **bedfordstmartins.com/reilly/catalog**, this manual provides the rationale for the selection and organization of the readings, suggestions for teaching with the documents, an alternate table of contents organized by topics, and information about additional resources, including films and Internet sites. At the same site, instructors can also access and download all of the maps and images from this book, many in color, for presentation. All of the maps from the book are also available for download in Make History at **bedfordstmartins.com/makehistory**.

■ NEW TO THIS EDITION

While I am continually testing selections in my own classroom, I appreciate input from readers and adopters, and I want to thank them for their many suggestions for exciting new chapters and selections. Having incorporated some of this feedback, I think those who have used the reader previously will find the fifth edition even more geographically and topically comprehensive, interesting, and accessible to students. More than a quarter of the selections are new, which has allowed me to introduce fresh material into almost every chapter. In addition, I have included three new chapters, which explore empire and government in China and Rome (Chapter 4); trade, travel, and migrations in Eurasia,

Africa, and the Pacific (Chapter 8); and New Democracy movements from 1977 to the present (Chapter 27).

One more change to this edition of *Worlds of History* has, I hope, made the book more accessible. I significantly expanded the Introduction for Students to give students an idea of how I conceive the purpose of this reader, how it might work with a textbook, if they use one, and how they might read primary sources without abject fear. For instance, I encourage them to ask the basic who, what, where, when, why questions of each source—keeping in mind that it is their understanding of the source that matters most, not what the author of the source may have wanted them to learn.

I am not a believer in change for its own sake; when I have a successful way of teaching a subject, I am not disposed to jettison it for something new. Consequently, many of my most satisfying changes are incremental: a better translation of a document, the addition of a newly discovered source, or additional questions to further inspire critical thinking. In some cases I have been able to further edit a useful source, retaining its muscle, but providing room for a precious new find. I begin each round of revision with the conviction that the book is already as good as it can get. And I end each round with the surprising discovery that it is much better than it was.

■ ACKNOWLEDGMENTS

A book like this cannot be written without the help and advice of a vast army of colleagues and friends. I consider myself enormously fortunate to have met and known such a large group of gifted and generous scholars. Some were especially helpful in the preparation of this new edition. They include: William Baller, Worcester Polytechnic Institute; Peter Burkholder, Fairleigh Dickinson University; Jessica A. Coope, University of Nebraska–Lincoln; Matthew Crawford, Kent State University; Eric Cunningham, Gonzaga University; Paul Droubie, Manhattan College; Vefa Erginbas, The Ohio State University; Ken Faunce, Washington State University; Alan W. Fisher, Michigan State University; Judy Ann Ford, Texas A&M University; Dana Goodrich, Northwest Vista College; Andrew Goss, University of New Orleans; Candace Gregory-Abbott, California State University–Sacramento; Kyle Griffith, California State University–San Marcos; Andrew Hamilton, Viterbo University; Jesse Hingson, Jacksonville University; David M. Kalivas, Middlesex Community College; Sandra LeBeau, Colby-Sawyer College; Luke Kelly, University of Utah; Jonathan Lee, San Antonio College; George E. Longenecker, Vermont Technical College; Erik C. Maiershofer, Hope International University; Michael S. Mangus, The

Ohio State University; Deena C. McKinney, East Georgia College; Heather McNamee, Arkansas State University; Craig Miller, Pennsylvania College; Dayo Nicole Mitchell, University of Oregon; Jason Neidleman, University of La Verne; Kenneth W. Noe, Auburn University; Patrick M. Patterson, Honolulu Community College; Mark Peach, Southern Adventist University; Laura Ryan, Southwestern College; Steven Seegel, University of Northern Colorado; Jonathan Seitz, Drexel University; Matthew G. Stanard, Berry College; Lisa Tran, California State Fullerton; Teresa Fava Thomas, Fitchburg State University; Doug Tompson, Columbus State University; Karen M. Teoh, Stonehill College; Sally West, Truman State University.

I'd also like to thank the following high school instructors who provided guidance and expertise: Jeffrey Filson, Glen Burnie High School; Deborah Johnston, Lakeside School; Dana Ann Landesman, Bronxville High School; Drew H. Maddock, Harvard-Westlake School; and Kaylene Schliesser, Clements High School.

Over the years I have benefited from the suggestions of innumerable friends and fellow world historians. Among them: Michael Adas, Rutgers University; the late Jerry Bentley, University of Hawai'i; David Berry, Essex County Community College; Edmund (Terry) Burke III, University of California–Santa Cruz; Catherine Clay, Shippensburg University; the late Philip Curtin, Johns Hopkins University; S. Ross Doughty, Ursinus College; Ross Dunn, San Diego State University; Marc Gilbert, Hawai'i Pacific University; Steve Gosch, University of Wisconsin–Eau Claire; Sue Gronewold, Kean University; Gregory Guzman, Bradley University; Brock Haussamen, Raritan Valley College; Allen Howard, Rutgers University; Sarah Hughes, Shippensburg University; Karen Jolly, University of Hawai'i; Stephen Kaufman, Raritan Valley College; Maghan Keita, Villanova University; Craig Lockard, University of Wisconsin–Green Bay; Pat Manning, University of Pittsburgh; Adam McKeown, Columbia University; John McNeill, Georgetown University; William H. McNeill, University of Chicago; Gyan Prakash, Princeton University; Lauren Ristvet, University of Pennsylvania; Robert Rosen, University of California–Los Angeles; Heidi Roupp, Aspen High School; John Russell-Wood, Johns Hopkins University; Lynda Shaffer, Tufts University; Ira Spar, Ramapo College; Robert Strayer, California State University–Monterey Bay; George Sussman, LaGuardia Community College; Robert Tignor, Princeton University; John Voll, Georgetown University; and Peter Winn, Tufts University.

I also want to thank the people at Bedford/St. Martin's. Joan Feinberg and Denise Wydra remained involved and helpful throughout, as did Mary Dougherty, Traci Crowell, and Jane Knetzger. Victoria Royal provided invaluable help in reviewing the previous edition, and she coordinated the development of the instructor's manual, ensured the book's images and maps all appeared online for download, and provided invaluable behind-the-scenes support for the reader. I want to thank my production editor, Katherine Caruana, for overseeing the entire production process of design, copyediting, and page composition. I would also like to thank Susan Moore for copyediting, Marine Miller for the cover design, Sara Hillman for designing promotional materials, and Paul Stillitano, Katherine Bates, and Dan McDonough for expertly marketing the book. Thanks also to photo researcher Naomi Kornhauser and to Heather Salus for clearing the text permissions. Finally, my deepest appreciation goes to Senior Editor Laura Arcari for her editorial guidance, forcing me to make it a better book than I had any right to expect. None of this would have been possible if I had not been blessed in my own introduction to history and critical thinking at Rutgers in the 1960s with teachers I still aspire to emulate. Eugene Meehan taught me how to think and showed me that I could. Traian Stoianovich introduced me to the world and an endless range of historical inquiry. Warren Susman lit up a room with more life than I ever knew existed. Donald Weinstein guided me as a young teaching assistant to listen to students and talk with them rather than at them. And Peter Stearns showed me how important and exciting it could be to understand history by making comparisons. I dedicate this book to them.

Finally, I want to thank my own institution, Raritan Valley College, for nurturing my career, allowing me to teach whatever I wanted, and entrusting me with some of the best students one could encounter anywhere. I could not ask for anything more. Except, of course, a loving wife like Pearl.

Kevin Reilly

Introduction for Students

When most people think of history books, they think of books that tell a story about the past. It may be a small part of the past, like a presidential election or the making of the atomic bomb, or a large chunk of the past like the history of China or the history of warfare. In either case, these are books that tell a continuous story from beginning to end. The story might evolve gradually or reveal a conclusion at the start. It might be dramatic or plodding. There may be quotations from various people scattered throughout or indented in long paragraphs, but the book is written by a single author (or sometimes a few who agree on what to say) and presented with a single voice. The voice of a single storyteller gives this kind of history book a strong sense of authority. The reader is not invited to question anything, much less disagree. Any doubts are met by an implicit: "Wait, let me finish," and the author's conclusions follow inevitably from the facts that he or she has determined best fit the story.

The book you are holding in your hands is a different kind of history book. It does not tell a single story, but many. And while these selections are gathered by a single editor (a not unimportant matter), they were originally crafted by hundreds of different people. These people came from various places throughout the world, lived at different times, and were addressing different subjects, often with no awareness of what any of the other authors in this book said—or even of their existence.

This book contains many different stories. But it contains much more. Most of the selections are not stories in the way that history books are. First of all, most were not written by historians. Some of the stories in this book are literary or imaginary, while others come from personal letters or diaries. And many are not even stories. There are selections from treaties, philosophy books, scientific treatises, holy books, telegrams, and posts from Facebook. Further, some of the selections are not even writings. There are paintings, art works, photographs, pictures of things, and cartoons. There would be music too, if it could fit into a book.

The point is that this book contains what are called **historical sources** rather than histories. Historical sources are the raw materials that historians use to construct histories. Of course, when you think of all the possible sources available to historians, you realize that even a book of this size can contain only a miniscule number of sources. There are in fact whole libraries devoted to archiving historical sources—from presidential libraries that contain the papers of a president to the archives of government offices. In addition, museums, university libraries, film archives, and ever-expanding online collections include sources ranging from newspapers, magazines, and books to images, letters, e-mails, and more.

Historians use these collections in order to find the sources they need to tell a particular story. The sources are as varied as the questions historians ask. Say, for instance, you are studying the history of individuality and you want to see if the use of the pronoun *I* increased in the late Middle Ages. There happens to be an archive that includes every scrap of writing from a medieval Jewish community in Cairo that saved everything on the chance that a piece of paper might contain the word for God, and therefore, under Jewish tradition, could not be destroyed. With this archive, tedious work, and a good computer, you could chart the use of a single word like *I* over the hundreds of years in which these papers were gathered. It would be within one community, to be sure; but there are few, if any, comparable source collections for this period. Someday a historian may even try to figure out what college students were thinking in the last years of the Age of Reading by a study of your e-mail, essays, or other personal possessions.

This book, then, is one of the two types of books most often used in a history course. The first type is the survey textbook. This book is the second type. It is variously called a "reader," "source book," or an anthology, and it collects a variety of sources in one book. It is designed to introduce you to working with historical sources. The reason for using a reader in addition to, or instead of, a survey text is that it allows us to do those things that the text makes so difficult. It allows us to interpret sources on our own, ask questions, solve problems, and actively build our understanding. Sources can engage our minds in ways that narrative textbooks, with their sense of authority and finality, do not.

Many source books contain only what are called **primary sources**, pieces from the past that were created in the period we are studying. This book contains some **secondary sources** as well. Secondary sources are pieces *about* the period we are studying. They are usually written by scholars. Most of the secondary sources in this book were written fairly recently by modern historians. My reason for including secondary sources is to provide some context or perspective to consider the primary sources (which make up most of the selections in each chapter). Historians read and write secondary sources, continually checking and revising them to conform to primary sources—the actual evidence from the past.

Primary sources can be difficult to interpret because they were often written in a time that is not familiar to us, and the context specific to their creation may be unknown. They use funny words, address weird issues, say strange things, and are sometimes written in a language that we have to struggle to make sense of. I have tried to minimize some of these problems with footnotes, pronunciation help, and some modernization of the language.

I've also included headnotes before each source that give you some historical background about the author and the source. But I can't do too much of that because it is important for you to appreciate the unfamiliarity of these sources in order to do your own analysis. A wise novelist once said: "The past is a foreign country: They do things differently there."[1] These sources were created in a different time, which often makes them seem foreign and remote. So it is precisely this context of a different time that we have to immerse ourselves in to understand the source and the world from which it came. Primary sources require and enable a kind of time travel to knowledge in which we have to leave many of our assumptions behind as excess baggage.

Because the authors of primary sources were not writing for us, and indeed had no idea we'd ever exist, they can't lie to us (at least as they might have, had they been given the opportunity). They tell us so much more than they intended. Primary sources can also be full of deceit, based on illusion, and riddled with error. They can even seem bonkers—and by those very characteristics, tell us much. Working with primary sources is like being a fly on the wall or being able to see things while remaining invisible. It is like having a superpower—gained from the study of history.

Throughout both volumes of this reader you have chapters in world history, which deal with particular historical periods and topics. Some topics cover long periods, like the rise of civilization and patriarchy (Chapter 1) or migrations, travel, and trade from 3000 B.C.E to 1350 C.E. (Chapter 8). Some topics cover brief periods, like the First Crusade from 1095–1099 (Chapter 10) and the Black Death from 1346–1350 (Chapter 12). Most fall in between these extremes. There are, for example, chapters on the topics of women, marriage, and family in most of the large periods that divide the book, i.e., ancient, classical, medieval, and early modern. There are also chapters that compare different societies: classical India and Greece, the Roman and Chinese empires, and Mongols and Vikings. There are chapters on such conventionally defined topics as the Atlantic Slave Trade, the Scientific Revolution, the Enlightenment, the First and Second World Wars, and the Cold War. There are also chapters that pose new historical frameworks like secularization, democratization, and globalization.

As you learn about historical periods and topics, you will also be learning to explore history by analyzing primary and secondary sources systematically. The "Thinking Historically" exercises in each chapter encourage habits of mind that I associate with my own study of history. They are not necessarily intended to turn you into historians, but rather, to give you skills that will help you in all of your college courses. Indeed, these are skills for life: for jury duty and the voting booth; for writing letters or drafting memos on the job; for weighing options and making smart decisions. Hopefully these new habits of mind will also expand your interests and nourish your self-confidence.

---

[1] L. P. Hartley, *The Go-Between* (New York: NYRB Classics, 2002), 17. First published in London in 1953.

These skills are organized from the simple to the more complex. Since skill building is cumulative, your ability to understand, analyze, and use sources will become increasingly sophisticated as you read through this text. But you need not wait for the end of the course to begin your analysis of these sources. Rather, it would be useful to develop the habit of asking the basic questions that journalists are trained to ask whenever they are assigned a story: who, what, where, when, and why?

Whether the source is primary or secondary, a piece of writing or a work of art, a run-through of these basic "w" questions is a good place to start when analyzing sources:

- **Who** wrote or created the source? If the author is unknown or anonymous, what sort of person does the author appear to be? An observer, participant, or eyewitness? A later historian? This will establish whether it is a primary or secondary source. Are there any clues to the identity of the author in the source itself? Are there signs of the author's social class, political position, and attitudes toward the subject of the source?
- **What** is the source? Is it a history by a modern historian and, therefore, a secondary source? Or is it a primary source from the past? If so, what kind of primary source? Is it an engraved stone, a poem, a love letter, a diary entry, a chapter from an ancient book of philosophy, a prayer?
- **Where** does it come from? China? Ancient Mesopotamia? France? Paris? Has it traveled from one place to another, or has it always been in the same place?
- **When** was it created? If it is writing, was it revised? Was there an earlier written or oral version? Is it an example of an older style? How new is it?
- **Why** was it created? To entertain, exorcise, instruct, persuade? **What** was the purpose? **Who** was the audience?

Ultimately, our answers to these questions might help us answer the most important question of all: **What** does this source tell us about the world from which it came?

World history is nothing less than everything ever done or imagined, so we cannot possibly cover it all; we are forced to choose among different places and times in our study of the global past. Our choices do include some particular moments in time, like the one in 111 C.E. in the first half of this reader, when the Roman governor of Bithynia consulted Emperor Trajan about proper treatment of Christians. But our attention will be directed toward much longer periods as well. While we will visit particular places in time like Imperial Rome in the second century or Africa in the nineteenth century, typically we will study more than one place at a time by using a comparative approach.

Comparisons can be enormously useful in studying world history. When we compare the raiding and trading of Vikings and Mongols, the scientific revolution in Europe and Japan, and the Cold War in Cuba and Afghanistan, we learn about the general and the specific at the same time. My hope is that by comparing some of the various worlds of history, a deeper and more nuanced understanding of our global past will emerge. With that understanding, we are better equipped to make sense of the world today and to confront whatever the future holds.

Contents

15. Overseas Expansion in the Early Modern Period: Asia, Africa, Europe, and the Americas, 1400–1600 560

Both China and Europe set sail for global expansion in the fifteenth century, but China's explorations ended just as Europe's began. What were the factors that led to their similar efforts yet different outcomes? We examine primary and secondary sources in search of clues.

HISTORICAL CONTEXT 560

THINKING HISTORICALLY: Reading Primary and Secondary Sources 562

REFLECTIONS 607

16. Atlantic World Encounters: Europeans, Americans, and Africans, 1500–1850 609

European encounters with Africans and Americans were similar in some ways, yet markedly different in others. The cultural clash created a new Atlantic world that integrated and divided these indigenous peoples. We compare primary sources, including visual evidence, to understand these first contacts and conflicts.

HISTORICAL CONTEXT 609

THINKING HISTORICALLY: Comparing Primary Sources 611

17. State and Religion: Asian, Islamic, and Christian States, 1500–1800 657

In this chapter, we view the relationship between religion and political authority through the prism of Chinese, Japanese, South Asian, and Western experience in the early modern period. By examining the competing and sometimes cooperating dynamics between church and state in the past, we explore the history of an issue much debated in our own time and gain new insights on church-state relations today.

18. Women, Marriage, and Family: China and Europe, 1550–1700 684

With the blinds drawn on the domestic lives of our ancestors, one might assume their private worlds were uneventful and everywhere the same. By comparing different cultures, we see historical variety in family and economic life and the roles of both men and women.

Historical Context *684*

Thinking Historically: **Making Comparisons** *685*

19. The Scientific Revolution: Europe, the Ottoman Empire, China, Japan, and the Americas, 1600–1800 726

The scientific revolution of the seventeenth and eighteenth centuries occurred in Europe, but it had important roots in Asia and its consequences reverberated throughout the world. In this chapter we seek to understand what changed and how. How "revolutionary" was the scientific revolution, and how do we distinguish between mere change and "revolutionary" change?

20. Enlightenment and Revolution: Europe, the Americas, and India, 1650–1850 768

The eighteenth-century Enlightenment applied scientific reason to
politics, but reason meant different things to different people and
societies. What were the goals of the political revolutions produced by the
Enlightenment? A close reading of the period texts reveals disagreement
and shared dreams.

21. Capitalism and the Industrial Revolution: Europe and the World, 1750–1900 799

Modern society has been shaped dramatically by capitalism and the industrial revolution, but these two forces are not the same. Which one is principally responsible for the creation of our modern world: the economic system of the market or the technology of the industrial revolution? Distinguishing different "causes" allows us to gauge their relative effects and legacies.

24. World War I and Its Consequences: Europe and the World, 1914–1929 918

The First World War brutally ended an era—the world would never be the same after such death and destruction. We read historical accounts and analyze images from the era so that we can begin to understand the war's far-reaching chain of causes and consequences.

27. New Democracy Movements: The World, 1977 to the Present 1038

Demands for democracy are on the rise, challenging and sometimes sweeping away old empires, petty tyrants, military dictatorships, and one-party states. Even "old" democracies are pushed to raise the bar to include social justice, economic opportunity, and a right to education. Where are these movements coming from? Are they connected or coincidental? Are they for real?

28. Globalization: The World, 1990 to the Present 1089

Globalization is a word with many meanings and a process with many causes. What are the forces most responsible for the shrinking of the world into one global community? Do the forces of globalization unite or divide us? Do they impoverish or enrich us? We undertake the study of process to answer these questions.

LIST OF MAPS

Geographic Contents

Central Asia

South Asia

East Asia

The Americas

Interregional Contacts

Worlds of History

A Comparative Reader

Volume Two: Since 1400

15

Overseas Expansion in the Early Modern Period

Asia, Africa, Europe, and the Americas, 1400–1600

■ HISTORICAL CONTEXT

Between 1400 and 1500, the balance between Chinese and European sea power changed drastically. Before 1434, Chinese shipbuilding was the envy of the world. Chinese ships were larger, more numerous, safer, and better outfitted than European ships. The Chinese navy made frequent trips through the South China Sea to the Spice Islands, through the Indian Ocean, and as far as East Africa and the Persian Gulf (see Map 15.1). Every island, port, and kingdom along the route was integrated into the Chinese system of tributaries. Goods were exchanged, marriages arranged, and princes taken to visit the Chinese emperor.

In the second half of the fifteenth century, the Chinese navy virtually disappeared. At the same time, the Portuguese began a series of explorations down the coast of Africa and into the Atlantic Ocean. In 1434 Portuguese ships rounded the treacherous Cape Bojador, just south of Morocco, and in 1498 Bartolomeu Dias rounded the Cape of Good Hope. Vasco da Gama sailed into the Indian Ocean, arriving in Calicut the following year. And in 1500 a fortuitous landfall in Brazil by Pedro Cabral gave the Portuguese a claim from the western Atlantic to the Indian Ocean. By 1512 Portuguese ships had reached the Bandas and Moluccas—the Spice Islands of what is today eastern Indonesia.

Beginning in 1492, after the defeat of the Moors (Muslims) and the voyages of Columbus, the Spanish claimed most of the Western Hemisphere until challenged by the Dutch, English, and French. European control in the Americas penetrated far deeper than in Asia, where it was limited to enclaves on the coast and where European nations were in an almost

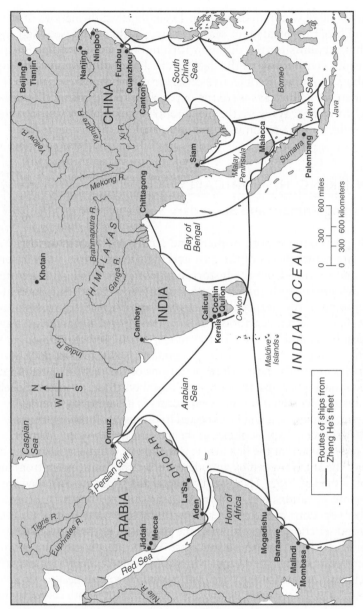

Map 15.1 Chinese Naval Expeditions, 1405–1433.

perpetual state of war with each other. Taken together, the nations of Western Europe dominated the seas of the world after 1500 (see Map 15.2).

What accounts for the different fortunes of China and Europe in the fifteenth century? Were the decline of China and the rise of Europe inevitable? Probably no objective observer of the time would have thought so. In what ways were the expansions of China and Europe similar? In what ways were they different? Think about these questions as you reflect on the readings in this chapter.

■ THINKING HISTORICALLY

Reading Primary and Secondary Sources

This chapter contains both primary and secondary sources. *Primary sources* are actual pieces of the past and include anything—art, letters, essays, and so on—from the historical period being studied. If a future historian were to study and research students in American colleges at the beginning of the twenty-first century, some primary sources might include diaries, letters, cartoons, music videos, posters, paintings, e-mail messages, blogs and Web sites, class notes, school newspapers, tests, and official and unofficial records. *Secondary sources* are usually books and articles *about* the past—interpretations of the past. These sources are "secondary" because they must be based on primary sources; therefore, a history written after an event occurs is a secondary source.

In your studies, you will be expected to distinguish primary from secondary sources. A quick glance at the introductions to this chapter's selections tells you that the first article is written by a modern journalist in 1999 and the last is written by a modern environmentalist, taken from his book published in 1991. These are both secondary sources since they are modern interpretations of the past rather than documents from the past. The other selections in this chapter are such documents, or primary sources. The second selection is an account of the great fifteenth-century Chinese admiral Zheng He's* voyage to Southeast Asia written by someone who was there, Ma Huan, a member of the crew. The third selection is similarly a participant's account of the voyage of the first European fleet to reach South Asia, that of Vasco da Gama at the end of the fifteenth century. These and the fourth selection, a letter penned by Christopher Columbus more than five hundred years ago, are firsthand accounts of worlds long past.

Having determined whether selections are primary or secondary sources, we also explore some of the subtle complexities that are overlooked by such designations.

* jung HUH

Note: Pronunciations of difficult-to-pronounce terms will be given throughout the book. The emphasis goes on the syllable appearing in all capitals. [Ed.]

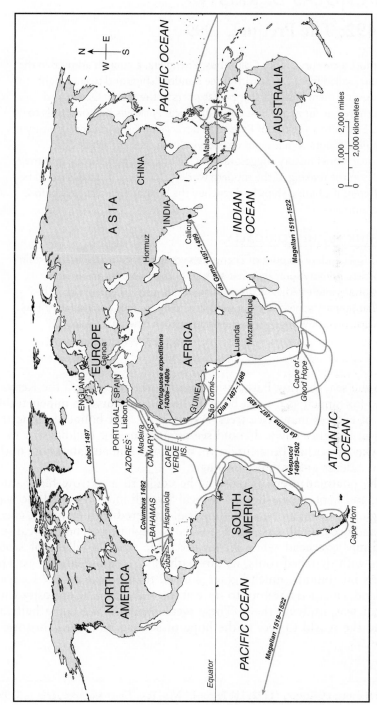

Map 15.2 European Overseas Exploration, 1430s–1530s.

1

NICHOLAS D. KRISTOF

1492: The Prequel, 1999

Almost a century before Columbus, Zheng He, a eunuch admiral in the court, sailed from China with three hundred ships and twenty-eight thousand men. His fleet stopped at ports in the Indian Ocean and journeyed as far as the east coast of Africa. Nicholas Kristof travels to the East African island of Pate to find traces of these fifteenth-century Chinese sailors. What types of evidence is he seeking? What does Kristof's brief history suggest about China, India, and Europe and their roles in the making of the modern world? How would today's world be different if Chinese ships had reached the Western Hemisphere before Columbus?

THINKING HISTORICALLY

In his secondary account of Zheng He's voyages, Kristof alludes to certain possible primary sources. What sorts of primary sources are available to historians interested in reconstructing the life and voyages of Zheng He? What primary sources are not available? Why are they not available? Has Kristof's recent voyage led to the discovery of a new primary source?

From the sea, the tiny East African island of Pate, just off the Kenyan coast, looks much as it must have in the 15th century: an impenetrable shore of endless mangrove trees. As my little boat bounced along the waves in the gray dawn, I could see no antennae or buildings or even gaps where trees had been cut down, no sign of human habitation, nothing but a dense and mysterious jungle.

The boatman drew as close as he could to a narrow black-sand beach, and I splashed ashore. My local Swahili interpreter led the way through the forest, along a winding trail scattered with mangoes, coconuts, and occasional seashells deposited by high tides. The tropical sun was firmly overhead when we finally came upon a village of stone houses with thatched roofs, its dirt paths sheltered by palm trees. The village's inhabitants, much lighter-skinned than people on the Kenyan mainland, emerged barefoot to stare at me with the same curiosity with which I was studying them. These were people I had come halfway around the world to see, in the hope of solving an ancient historical puzzle.

Source: Nicholas D. Kristof, "1492: The Prequel," *New York Times Magazine*, June 6, 1999, 6, 80:1.

"Tell me," I asked the first group I encountered, "where did the people here come from? Long ago, did foreign sailors ever settle here?" The answer was a series of shrugs. "I've never heard about that," one said. "You'll have to ask the elders."

I tried several old men and women without success. Finally the villagers led me to the patriarch of the village, Bwana Mkuu Al-Bauri, the keeper of oral traditions. He was a frail old man with gray stubble on his cheeks, head, and chest. He wore a yellow sarong around his waist; his ribs pressed through the taut skin on his bare torso. Al-Bauri hobbled out of his bed, resting on a cane and the arm of a grandson. He claimed to be 121 years old; a pineapple-size tumor jutted from the left side of his chest.

"I know this from my grandfather, who himself was the keeper of history here," the patriarch told me in an unexpectedly clear voice. "Many, many years ago, there was a ship from China that wrecked on the rocks off the coast near here. The sailors swam ashore near the village of Shanga—my ancestors were there and saw it themselves.

"The Chinese were visitors, so we helped those Chinese men and gave them food and shelter, and then they married our women. Although they do not live in this village, I believe their descendants still can be found somewhere else on this island."

I almost felt like hugging Bwana Al-Bauri. For months I had been poking around obscure documents and research reports, trying to track down a legend of an ancient Chinese shipwreck that had led to a settlement on the African coast. My interest arose from a fascination with what to me is a central enigma of the millennium: Why did the West triumph over the East?

For most of the last several thousand years, it would have seemed far likelier that Chinese or Indians, not Europeans, would dominate the world by the year 2000, and that America and Australia would be settled by Chinese rather than by the inhabitants of a backward island called Britain. The reversal of fortunes of East and West strikes me as the biggest news story of the millennium, and one of its most unexpected as well.

As a resident of Asia for most of the past thirteen years, I've been searching for an explanation. It has always seemed to me that the turning point came in the early 1400s, when Admiral Zheng He sailed from China to conquer the world. Zheng He (pronounced JUNG HUH) was an improbable commander of a great Chinese fleet, in that he was a Muslim from a rebel family and had been seized by the Chinese Army when he was still a boy. Like many other prisoners of the time, he was castrated, his sexual organs completely hacked off, a process that killed many of those who suffered it. But he was a brilliant and tenacious boy who grew up to be physically imposing. A natural leader, he had the good fortune to be assigned, as a houseboy, to the household of a great prince, Zhu Di.

In time, the prince and Zheng He grew close, and they conspired to overthrow the prince's nephew, the Emperor of China. With Zheng He as one of the prince's military commanders, the revolt succeeded and the prince became China's Yongle Emperor. One of the emperor's first acts (after torturing to death those who had opposed him) was to reward Zheng He with the command of a great fleet that was to sail off and assert China's pre-eminence in the world.

Between 1405 and 1433, Zheng He led seven major expeditions, commanding the largest armada the world would see for the next five centuries. Not until World War I did the West mount anything comparable. Zheng He's fleet included twenty-eight thousand sailors on three hundred ships, the longest of which were four hundred feet. By comparison, Columbus in 1492 had ninety sailors on three ships, the biggest of which was eighty-five feet long. Zheng He's ships also had advanced design elements that would not be introduced in Europe for another 350 years, including balanced rudders and watertight bulwark compartments.

The sophistication of Zheng He's fleet underscores just how far ahead of the West the East once was. Indeed, except for the period of the Roman Empire, China had been wealthier, more advanced, and more cosmopolitan than any place in Europe for several thousand years. Hangzhou, for example, had a population in excess of a million during the time it was China's capital (in the twelfth century), and records suggest that as early as the seventh century, the city of Guangzhou had 200,000 foreign residents: Arabs, Persians, Malays, Indians, Africans, and Turks. By contrast, the largest city in Europe in 1400 was probably Paris, with a total population of slightly more than 100,000.

A half-century before Columbus, Zheng He had reached East Africa and learned about Europe from Arab traders. The Chinese could easily have continued around the Cape of Good Hope and established direct trade with Europe. But as they saw it, Europe was a backward region, and China had little interest in the wood, beads, and wine Europe had to trade. Africa had what China wanted—ivory, medicines, spices, exotic woods, even specimens of native wildlife.

In Zheng He's time, China and India together accounted for more than half of the world's gross national product, as they have for most of human history. Even as recently as 1820, China accounted for 29 percent of the global economy and India another 16 percent, according to the calculations of Angus Maddison, a leading British economic historian.

Asia's retreat into relative isolation after the expeditions of Zheng He amounted to a catastrophic missed opportunity, one that laid the groundwork for the rise of Europe and, eventually, America. Westerners often attribute their economic advantage today to the intelligence, democratic habits, or hard work of their forebears, but a more important reason may well have been the folly of fifteenth-century Chinese rulers. That is why I came to be fascinated with Zheng He and set out earlier this year to retrace his journeys. I wanted to see what legacy, if any, remained of his achievement, and to figure out why his travels did not remake the world in the way that Columbus's did.

Zheng He lived in Nanjing, the old capital, where I arrived one day in February. Nanjing is a grimy metropolis on the Yangtze River in the heart of China. It has been five centuries since Zheng He's death, and his marks on the city have grown faint. The shipyards that built his fleet are still busy, and the courtyard of what had been his splendid seventy-two-room mansion is now the Zheng He Memorial Park, where children roller-skate and old couples totter around for exercise. But though the park has a small Zheng He museum, it was closed—for renovation, a caretaker told me, though he knew of no plans to reopen it.

I'd heard that Zheng He's tomb is on a hillside outside the city, and I set out to find it. It wasn't long before the road petered out, from asphalt to gravel to dirt to nothing. No tomb was in sight, so I approached an old man weeding a vegetable garden behind his house. Tang Yiming, seventy-two, was still lithe and strong. His hair was gray and ragged where he had cut it himself, disastrously, in front of a mirror. Evidently lonely, he was delighted to talk, and offered to show me the path to the tomb. As we walked, I mentioned that I had read that there used to be an old Ming Dynasty tablet on Zheng He's grave.

"Oh, yeah, the old tablet," he said nonchalantly. "When I was a boy, there was a Ming Dynasty tablet here. When it disappeared, the Government offered a huge reward to anyone who would return it—a reward big enough to build a new house. Seemed like a lot of money. But the problem was that we couldn't give it back. People around here are poor. We'd smashed it up to use as building materials."

A second mystery concerned what, if anything, is actually buried in Zheng He's tomb, since he is believed to have died on his last voyage and been buried at sea. So I said in passing that I'd heard tell the tomb is empty, and let my voice trail off.

"Oh, there's nothing in there," Tang said, a bit sadly. "No bones, nothing. That's for sure."

"How do you know?"

"In 1962, people dug up the grave, looking for anything to sell. We dug up the ground to one and a half times the height of a man. But there was absolutely nothing in there. It's empty."

The absence of impressive monuments to Zheng He in China today should probably come as no surprise, since his achievement was ultimately renounced. Curiously, it is not in China but in Indonesia where his memory has been most actively kept alive. Zheng He's expeditions led directly to the wave of Chinese immigration to Southeast Asia, and in some countries he is regarded today as a deity. In the Indonesia city of Semarang, for example, there is a large temple honoring Zheng He, located near a cave where he once nursed a sick friend. Indonesians still pray to Zheng He for a cure or good luck.

Not so in his native land. Zheng He was viewed with deep suspicion by China's traditional elite, the Confucian scholars, who made sure to destroy the archives of his journey. Even so, it is possible to learn something about his story from Chinese sources—from imperial archives and even the memoirs of crewmen. The historical record makes clear, for example, that it was not some sudden impulse of extroversion that led to Zheng He's achievement. It grew, rather, out of a long sailing tradition. Chinese accounts suggest that in the fifth century a Chinese monk sailed to a mysterious "far east country" that sounds very much like Mayan Mexico, and Mayan art at that time suddenly began to include Buddhist symbols. By the thirteenth century, Chinese ships regularly traveled to India and occasionally to East Africa.

Zheng He's armada was far grander, of course, than anything that came before. His grandest vessels were the "treasure ships," 400 feet long and 160 feet wide, with nine masts raising red silk sails to the wind, as well as multiple decks and luxury cabins with balconies. His armada included supply ships to carry horses, troop transports, warships, patrol boats, and as many as twenty tankers to carry fresh water. The full contingent of 28,000 crew members included interpreters for Arabic and other languages, astrologers to forecast the weather, astronomers to study the stars, pharmacologists to collect medicinal plants, ship-repair specialists, doctors, and even two protocol officers to help organize official receptions.

In the aftermath of such an incredible undertaking, you somehow expect to find a deeper mark on Chinese history, a greater legacy. But perhaps the faintness of Zheng He's trace in contemporary China is itself a lesson. In the end, an explorer makes history but does not necessarily change it, for his impact depends less on the trail he blazes than on the willingness of others to follow. The daring of a great expedition ultimately is hostage to the national will of those who remain behind.

In February I traveled to Calicut, a port town in southwestern India that was (and still is) the pepper capital of the world. The evening I arrived, I went down to the beach in the center of town to look at the coastline where Zheng He once had berthed his ships. In the fourteenth and fifteenth centuries, Calicut was one of the world's great ports, known to the Chinese as "the great country of the Western ocean." In the early fifteenth century, the sight of Zheng He's fleet riding anchor in Calicut harbor symbolized the strength of the world's two greatest powers, China and India.

On this sultry evening, the beach, framed by long piers jutting out to sea, was crowded with young lovers and ice-cream vendors. Those piers are all that remain of the port of Calicut, and you can see at a glance that they are no longer usable. The following day I visited the port offices, musty with handwritten ledgers of ship visits dating back nearly a century. The administrator of the port, Captain E. G. Mohanan, explained matter-of-factly what had happened. "The piers got old and no proper maintenance was ever carried out," he said, as a ceiling fan whirred tiredly overhead. "By the time we thought of it, it was not economical to fix it up." So in 1989, trade was halted, and one of the great ports of the world became no port at all.

The disappearance of a great Chinese fleet from a great Indian port symbolized one of history's biggest lost opportunities—Asia's failure to dominate the second half of this millennium. So how did this happen?

While Zheng He was crossing the Indian Ocean, the Confucian scholar-officials who dominated the upper echelons of the Chinese Government were at political war with the eunuchs, a group they regarded as corrupt and immoral. The eunuchs' role at court involved looking after the concubines, but they also served as palace administrators, often doling out contracts in exchange for kickbacks. Partly as a result of their legendary greed, they promoted commerce. Unlike the scholars—who owed their position to their mastery of two thousand-year-old texts—the eunuchs, lacking any such roots in a classical past, were sometimes outward-looking and progressive. Indeed, one can argue that it was the virtuous, incorruptible scholars who in the mid-fifteenth century set China on its disastrous course.

After the Yongle Emperor died in 1424, China endured a series of brutal power struggles; a successor emperor died under suspicious circumstances and ultimately the scholars emerged triumphant. They ended the voyages of Zheng He's successors, halted construction of new ships, and imposed curbs on private shipping. To prevent any backsliding, they destroyed Zheng He's sailing records and, with the backing of the new emperor, set about dismantling China's navy.

By 1500 the Government had made it a capital offense to build a boat with more than two masts, and in 1525 the Government ordered the destruction of all oceangoing ships. The greatest navy in history, which a century earlier had 3,500 ships (by comparison, the United States Navy today has 324), had been extinguished, and China set a course for itself that would lead to poverty, defeat, and decline.

Still, it was not the outcome of a single power struggle in the 1440s that cost China its worldly influence. Historians offer a host of reasons for why Asia eventually lost its way economically and was late to industrialize; two and a half reasons seem most convincing.

The first is that Asia was simply not greedy enough. The dominant social ethos in ancient China was Confucianism and in India it was caste, with the result that the elites in both nations looked down their noses at business. Ancient China cared about many things—prestige, honor, culture, arts, education, ancestors, religion, filial piety—but making money came far down the list. Confucius had specifically declared that it was wrong for a man to make a distant voyage while his parents were alive, and he had condemned profit as the concern of "a little man." As it was, Zheng He's ships were built on such a grand scale and carried such lavish gifts to foreign leaders that the voyages were not the huge money spinners they could have been.

In contrast to Asia, Europe was consumed with greed. Portugal led the age of discovery in the fifteenth century largely because it wanted spices, a precious commodity; it was the hope of profits that drove its ships steadily farther down the African coast and eventually around the Horn to Asia. The profits of this trade could be vast: Magellan's crew once sold a cargo of twenty-six tons of cloves for ten thousand times the cost.

A second reason for Asia's economic stagnation is more difficult to articulate but has to do with what might be called a culture of complacency. China and India shared a tendency to look inward, a devotion to past ideals and methods, a respect for authority, and a suspicion of new ideas. David S. Landes, a Harvard economist, has written of ancient China's "intelligent xenophobia"; the former Indian Prime Minister Jawaharlal Nehru referred to the "petrification of classes" and the "static nature" of Indian society. These are all different ways of describing the same economic and intellectual complacency.

Chinese elites regarded their country as the "Middle Kingdom" and believed they had nothing to learn from barbarians abroad. India exhibited much of the same self-satisfaction. "Indians didn't go to Portugal not because they couldn't but because they didn't want to," mused M. P. Sridharan, a historian, as we sat talking on the porch of his home in Calicut.

The fifteenth-century Portuguese were the opposite. Because of its coastline and fishing industry, Portugal always looked to the sea, yet rivalries with Spain and other countries shut it out of the Mediterranean trade. So the only way for Portugal to get at the wealth of the East was by conquering the oceans.

The half reason is simply that China was a single nation while Europe was many. When the Confucian scholars reasserted control in Beijing and banned shipping, their policy mistake condemned all of China. In contrast, European countries committed economic suicide selectively. So when Portugal slipped into a quasi-Chinese mind-set in the sixteenth century, slaughtering Jews and burning heretics, and driving astronomers and scientists abroad, Holland and England were free to take up the slack.

When I first began researching Zheng He, I never thought I'd be traveling all the way to Africa to look for traces of his voyages. Then I came across a few intriguing references to the possibility of an ancient Chinese shipwreck that might have left some Chinese stranded on the island of Pate (pronounced PAH-tay). One was a skeptical reference in a scholarly journal, another was a casual conversation with a Kenyan I met a few years ago, and the third was the epilogue of Louise Levathes's wonderful 1994 book about China's maritime adventures, "When China Ruled the Seas." Levathes had traveled to Kenya and found people who believed they were descended from survivors of a Chinese shipwreck. So, on a whim and an expense account, I flew to Lamu, an island off northern Kenya, and hired a boat and an interpreter to go to Pate and see for myself.

Pate is off in its own world, without electricity or roads or vehicles. Mostly jungle, it has been shielded from the twentieth century largely because it is accessible from the Kenyan mainland only by taking a boat through a narrow tidal channel that is passable only at high tide. Initially I was disappointed by what I found there. In the first villages I visited, I saw people who were light-skinned and had hair that was not tightly curled, but they could have been part Arab or European rather than part Chinese. The remote villages of Chundwa and Faza were more promising, for there I found people whose eyes, hair, and complexion hinted at Asian ancestry, though their background was ambiguous.

And then on a still and sweltering afternoon I strolled through the coconut palms into the village of Siyu, where I met a fisherman in his forties named Abdullah Mohammed Badui. I stopped and stared at the man in astonishment, for he had light skin and narrow eyes. Fortunately, he was as rude as I was, and we stared at each other in mutual surprise before venturing a word. Eventually I asked him about his background and appearance.

"I am in the Famao clan," he said. "There are fifty or one hundred of us Famao left here. Legend has it that we are descended from Chinese and others.

"A Chinese ship was coming along and it hit rocks and wrecked," Badui continued. "The sailors swam ashore to the village that we now call Shanga, and they married the local women, and that is why we Famao look so different."

Another Famao, with the same light complexion and vaguely Asian features, approached to listen. His name was Athman Mohammed Mzee, and he, too, told of hearing of the Chinese shipwreck from the elders. He volunteered an intriguing detail: The Africans had given giraffes to the Chinese.

Salim Bonaheri, a fifty-five-year-old Famao man I met the next day, proudly declared, "My ancestors were Chinese or Vietnamese or something like that." I asked how they had got to Pate.

"I don't know," Bonaheri said with a shrug. Most of my conversations were like that, intriguing but frustrating dead ends. I was surrounded by people whose appearance seemed tantalizingly Asian, but who had only the vaguest notions of why that might be. I kept at it, though, and eventually found people like Khalifa Mohammed Omar, a fifty-five-year-old Famao fisherman who looked somewhat Chinese and who also clearly remembered the stories passed down by his grandfather. From him and others, a tale emerged.

Countless generations ago, they said, Chinese sailors traded with local African kings. The local kings gave them giraffes to take back to China. One of the Chinese ships struck rocks off the eastern coast of Pate, and the sailors swam ashore, carrying with them porcelain and other goods from the ship. In time they married local women, converted to Islam, and named the village Shanga, after Shanghai. Later, fighting erupted among Pate's clans, Shanga was destroyed, and the Famao fled, some to the mainland, others to the village of Siyu.

Every time I heard the story about the giraffes my pulse began to race. Chinese records indicate that Zheng He had brought the first giraffes to China, a fact that is not widely known. The giraffe caused an enormous stir in China because it was believed to be the mythical qilin, or Chinese unicorn. It is difficult to imagine how African villagers on an island as remote as Pate would know about the giraffes unless the tale had been handed down to them by the Chinese sailors.

Chinese ceramics are found in many places along the east African coast, and their presence on Pate could be the result of purchases from Arab traders. But the porcelain on Pate was overwhelmingly concentrated among the Famao clan, which could mean that it had been inherited rather than purchased. I also visited some ancient Famao graves that looked less like traditional Kenyan graves than what the Chinese call "turtle-shell graves," with rounded tops.

Researchers have turned up other equally tantalizing clues. Craftsmen on Pate and the other islands of Lamu practice a kind of basket-weaving that is common in southern China but unknown on the Kenyan mainland. On Pate, drums are more often played in the Chinese than the African style, and the local dialect has a few words that may be Chinese in origin. More startling, in 1569 a Portuguese priest named Monclaro wrote that Pate had a flourishing silk-making industry — Pate, and no other place in the region. Elders in several villages on Pate confirmed to me that their island had produced silk until about half a century ago.

When I asked my boatman, Bakari Muhaji Ali, if he thought it was possible that a ship could have wrecked off the coast near Shanga, he laughed. "There are undersea rocks all over there," he said. "If you don't know exactly where you're going, you'll wreck your ship for sure."

If indeed there was a Chinese shipwreck off Pate, there is reason to think it happened in Zheng He's time. For if the shipwreck had predated him, surviving sailors would not have passed down stories of the giraffes. And if the wreck didn't occur until after Zheng He, its survivors could not have settled in Shanga, since British archeological digs indicate that the village was sacked, burned, and abandoned in about 1440 — very soon after Zheng He's last voyage.

Still, there is no hard proof for the shipwreck theory, and there are plenty of holes in it. No ancient Chinese characters have been found on tombs in Pate, no nautical instruments have ever turned up on the island, and there are no Chinese accounts of an African shipwreck. This last lacuna might be explained by the destruction of the fleet's records. Yet if one of Zheng He's ships did founder on the rocks off Pate, then why didn't some other ships in the fleet come to the sailors' rescue?

As I made my way back through the jungle for the return trip, I pondered the significance of what I'd seen on Pate. In the faces of the Famao, in those bits of pottery and tantalizing hints of Chinese culture, I felt as though I'd glimpsed the shadowy outlines of one of the greatest might-have-beens of the millennium now ending. I thought about the Columbian Exchange, the swap of animals, plants, genes, germs, weapons, and peoples that utterly remade both the New World and the Old, and I couldn't help wondering about another exchange — Zheng He's — that never took place, yet could have.

If ancient China had been greedier and more outward-looking, if other traders had followed in Zheng He's wake and then continued on, Asia might well have dominated Africa and even Europe. Chinese might have settled in not only Malaysia and Singapore, but also in East Africa, the Pacific Islands, even in America. Perhaps the Famao show us what the mestizos of such a world might have looked like, the children of a hybrid culture that was never born. What I'd glimpsed in Pate was the highwater mark of an Asian push that simply stopped — not for want of ships or know-how, but strictly for want of national will.

All this might seem fanciful, and yet in Zheng He's time the prospect of a New World settled by the Spanish or English would have seemed infinitely more remote than a New World made by the Chinese. How different would history have been had Zheng He continued on to America? The mind rebels; the ramifications are almost too overwhelming to contemplate. So consider just one: This magazine would have been published in Chinese.

2

MA HUAN

On Calicut, India, 1433

Ma Huan was a Chinese Muslim who acted as an aide and interpreter on Zheng He's expeditions to Southeast Asia. In 1433 he wrote *The Overall Survey of the Ocean Shores,* a travel account of the lands he visited. This selection, taken from that account, describes his visit to Calicut on the Malabar, or southwest, coast of India. Note that Ma Huan is not always an accurate observer. More familiar with Buddhists than Hindus, for example, he mistakes the latter for the former. Nevertheless, he provides some useful information about

Source: Ma Huan, "On Calicut, India," in *Ma Huan, Ying-yai Sheng-lan: The Overall Survey of the Ocean's Shores,* ed. and trans. by Feng Ch'eng-Chun with an introduction by J. V. G. Mills (Bangkok: The White Lotus Press, 1970), 137–44.

Hindu-Muslim relations, the spread of the Abrahamic religions (note the story about Moses), the vitality of Indian trade, and the variety of Indian plants, animals, and manufactures. In addition to describing Calicut, what does Ma Huan tell us about the reasons for these expeditions?

THINKING HISTORICALLY

Ma Huan's account of Zheng He's expedition does not seem to have had an official purpose, but it was probably published instead to satisfy the growing interests of a Chinese public hungry for information about foreign lands and peoples. What sorts of things are of interest to Ma Huan? What does this tell us about his audience? How are his interests similar to, or different from, those of a modern traveler? What might be Ma Huan's strengths and weaknesses as a primary source?

The Country of Ku-Li
[Calicut]

[This is] the great country of the Western Ocean.

Setting sail from the anchorage in the country of Ko-chih,[1] you travel north-west, and arrive [here] after three days. The country lies beside the sea. [Travelling] east from the mountains for five hundred, or seven hundred, *li*, you make a long journey through to the country of K'an-pa-i.[2] On the west [the country of Ku-li] abuts on the great sea; on the south it joins the boundary of the country of Ko-chih; [and] on the north side it adjoins the territory of the country of Hen-nu-erh.[3]

"The great country of the Western Ocean" is precisely this country.

In the fifth year of the Yung-lo [period] the court ordered[4] the principal envoy the grand eunuch Cheng Ho and others to deliver an imperial mandate to the king[5] of this country and to bestow on him a patent conferring a title of honour, and the grant of a silver seal, [also] to

---

[1] Cochin, a city in southwest India along the Arabian Sea, 80 miles south of Calicut; Ma Huan made a very slow voyage.

[2] Koyampadi, modern Coimbatore, situated in about 11° N, 77° E, 76 miles nearly due east of Calicut. In giving the distance as 500 *li*, nearly 200 miles, Ma Huan was guilty of an exaggeration.

[3] Now called Honavar, situated in 14° 16' N, 74° 27' E; it is on the coast, 199 miles northward from Calicut.

[4] The order was made in October 1407; but, although in nominal command of this, the second expedition, Cheng Ho did not accompany it.

[5] A new king, Mana Vikraman, had evidently succeeded since Cheng Ho was at Calicut in 1406–7 during the course of his first expedition.

promote all the chiefs and award them hats and girdles of various grades.

[So Cheng Ho] went there in command of a large fleet of treasure-ships, and he erected a tablet with a pavilion over it and set up a stone which said "Though the journey from this country to the Central Country is more than a hundred thousand *li*, yet the people are very similar, happy and prosperous, with identical customs. We have here engraved a stone, a perpetual declaration for ten thousand ages."[6]

The king of the country is a Nan-k'un[7] man; he is a firm believer in the Buddhist religion;[8] [and] he venerates the elephant and the ox.

The population of the country includes five classes, the Muslim people, the Nan-K'un people, the Che-ti people, the Ko-ling people, and the Mu-kua people.

The king of the country and the people of the country all refrain from eating the flesh of the ox.[9] The great chiefs are Muslim people; [and] they all refrain from eating the flesh of the pig.[10] Formerly there was a king who made a sworn compact with the Muslim people, [saying] "You do not eat the ox; I do not eat the pig; we will reciprocally respect the taboo,"[11] [and this compact] has been honoured right down to the present day.

The king has cast an image of Buddha in brass; it is named Nai-na-erh;[12] he has erected a temple of Buddha and has cast tiles of brass and covered the dais of Buddha with them; [and] beside [the dais] a well has been dug. Every day at dawn the king goes to [the well], draws water, and washes [the image of] Buddha; after worshipping, he orders men to collect the pure dung of yellow oxen; this is stirred with water in a brass basin [until it is] like paste; [then] it is smeared all over the surface of the ground and walls inside the temple. Moreover, he has given orders that the chiefs and wealthy personages shall also smear and scour themselves with ox-dung every morning.

He also takes ox-dung, burns it till it is reduced to a white ash, and grinds it to a fine powder; using a fair cloth as a small bag, he fills it with the ash, and regularly carries it on his person. Every day at dawn, after he has finished washing his face, he takes the ox-dung ash, stirs it up with water, and smears it on his forehead and between his two

---

[6] Translated "May the period Yung-lo last for ever."

[7] Probably Ma Huan wrote "Nan-p'i" and meant the upper classes consisting of Brahmans and Kshatriyas.

[8] Ma Huan is mistaken; the king was a Hindu.

[9] Detestation of cow-slaughter is the most prominent outward mark of Hinduism.

[10] It is noteworthy that a Hindu ruler was employing Muslims as great officers.

[11] Since it was the king who made the compact, it would seem reasonable to prefer, "You do not eat the pig; I do not eat the ox"; thus, they agreed to respect each others' convictions in the matter of diet. It scarcely needs to be said that the pig is anathema to Muslims.

[12] The name might be a corruption of Narayana, a name for Vishnu. All these references to Buddha, then, must be construed as references to a Hindu deity.

thighs—thrice in each [place]. This denotes his sincerity in venerating Buddha[13] and in venerating the ox.

There is a traditional story that in olden times there was a holy man named Mou-hsieh,[14] who established a religious cult; the people knew that he was a true [man of] Heaven, and all men revered and followed him. Later the holy man went away with [others] to another place, and ordered his younger brother named Sa-mo-li[15] to govern and teach the people.

[But] his younger brother began to have depraved ideas; he made a casting of a golden calf and said "This is the holy lord; everyone who worships it will have his expectations fulfilled." He taught the people to listen to his bidding and to adore the golden ox, saying "It always excretes gold." The people got the gold, and their hearts rejoiced; and they forgot the way of Heaven; all took the ox to be the true lord.

Later Mou-hsieh the holy man returned; he saw that the multitude, misled by his younger brother Sa-mo-li, were corrupting the holy way; thereupon he destroyed the ox and wished to punish his younger brother; [and] his younger brother mounted a large elephant and vanished.

Afterwards, the people thought of him and hoped anxiously for his return. Moreover, if it was the beginning of the moon, they would say "In the middle of the moon he will certainly come," and when the middle of the moon arrived, they would say once more "At the end of the moon he will certainly come"; right down to the present day they have never ceased to hope for his return.

This is the reason why the Nan-k'un[16] people venerate the elephant and the ox.

The king has two great chiefs who administer the affairs of the country; both are Muslims.

The majority of the people in the country all profess the Muslim religion. There are twenty or thirty temples of worship, and once in seven days they go to worship. When the day arrives, the whole family fast and bathe, and attend to nothing else. In the *ssu* and *wu* periods,[17] the menfolk, old and young, go to the temple to worship. When the *wei* period[18] arrives, they disperse and return home; thereupon they carry on with their trading, and transact their household affairs.

---

[13] Again, a Hindu deity.

[14] "Musa" (Moses). Ma Huan alleges that the incidents occurred at Calicut. Presumably he learnt the story of Aaron and the golden calf from Arab informants. A number of Old Testament characters, including Moses, figure prominently in the Koran.

[15] "Al-Sameri" (the Samaritan), the name appearing in the Koran.

[16] Probably Ma Huan wrote "Nan-p'i," and referred to the upper classes of Brahmans and Kshatriyas.

[17] 9 A.M. to 11 A.M., and 11 A.M. to 1 P.M., respectively.

[18] 1 P.M. to 3 P.M.

The people are very honest and trustworthy. Their appearance is smart, fine, and distinguished.

Their two great chiefs received promotion and awards from the court of the Central Country.

If a treasure-ship goes there, it is left entirely to the two men to superintend the buying and selling; the king sends a chief and a Che-ti Wei-no-chi[19] to examine the account books in the official bureau; a broker comes and joins them; [and] a high officer who commands the ships discusses the choice of a certain date for fixing prices. When the day arrives, they first of all take the silk embroideries and the openwork silks, and other such goods which have been brought there, and discuss the price of them one by one; [and] when [the price] has been fixed, they write out an agreement stating the amount of the price; [this agreement] is retained by these persons.

The chief and the Che-ti, with his excellency the eunuch, all join hands together, and the broker then says "In such and such a moon on such and such a day, we have all joined hands and sealed our agreement with a hand-clasp; whether [the price] be dear or cheap, we will never repudiate it or change it."

After that, the Che-ti and the men of wealth then come bringing precious stones, pearls, corals, and other such things, so that they may be examined and the price discussed; [this] cannot be settled in a day; [if done] quickly, [it takes] one moon; [if done] slowly, [it takes] two or three moons.[20]

Once the money-price has been fixed after examination and discussion, if a pearl or other such article is purchased, the price which must be paid for it is calculated by the chief and the Wei-no-chi who carried out the original transaction; [and] as to the quantity of the hemp-silk or other such article which must be given in exchange for it, goods are given in exchange according to [the price fixed by] the original hand-clasp—there is not the slightest deviation.[21]

In their method of calculation, they do not use a calculating-plate;[22] for calculating, they use only the two hands and two feet and the twenty digits on them; and they do not make the slightest mistake; [this is] very extraordinary.

[19] Another observer, Kung Chen, translates "accountant," and adds that the man in question was a broker; Kung Chen further notes that "they wrote out a contract in duplicate, and each [party] kept one [document]."

[20] Presumably the goods were unloaded, unless the Chinese left one or two ships behind; at any rate, on the seventh expedition the Chinese stayed only 4 days, from 10 to 14 December 1432, at Calicut.

[21] This instructive disquisition on administrative procedure illustrates the meticulous care taken to fix the rate of exchange in times prior to the advent of the Europeans.

[22] The abacus, a wooden frame in which are fixed a number of beads strung on parallel wires; used by the Chinese for all kinds of arithmetic calculations upon the decimal system; it came into use in late Sung times.

The king uses gold of sixty per cent [purity] to cast a coin for current use; it is named a *pa-nan*;[23] the diameter of the face of each coin is three *fen* eight *li* [in terms of] our official *ts'un*;[24] it has lines[25] on the face and on the reverse; [and] it weighs one *fen* on our official steelyard.[26] He also makes a coin of silver; it is named a *ta-erh*;[27] each coin weighs about three *li*;[28] [and] this coin is used for petty transactions. . . .

The people of the country also take the silk of the silk-worm, soften it by boiling, dye it in all colours, and weave it into kerchiefs with decorative stripes at intervals; the breadth is four or five *ch'ih*, and the length one *chang* two or three *ch'ih*;[29] [and] each length is sold for one hundred gold coins.[30]

As to the pepper: the inhabitants of the mountainous countryside have established gardens, and it is extensively cultivated. When the period of the tenth moon arrives, the pepper ripens; [and] it is collected, dried in the sun, and sold. Of course, big pepper-collectors come and collect it, and take it up to the official storehouse to be stored; if there is a buyer, an official gives permission for the sale; the duty is calculated according to the amount [of the purchase price] and is paid in to the authorities. Each one *po-ho* of pepper is sold for two hundred gold coins.[31]

The Che-ti mostly purchase all kinds of precious stones and pearls, and they manufacture coral beads and other such things.

Foreign ships from every place come there; and the king of the country also sends a chief and a writer and others to watch the sales; thereupon they collect the duty and pay it in to the authorities.

The wealthy people mostly cultivate coconut trees—sometimes a thousand trees, sometimes two thousand or three thousand—; this constitutes their property.

The coconut has ten different uses. The young tree has a syrup, very sweet, and good to drink; [and] it can be made into wine by fermentation, The old coconut has flesh, from which they express oil, and make sugar, and make a foodstuff for eating. From the fibre which envelops the outside [of the nut] they make ropes for ship-building. The shell of the coconut makes bowls and makes cups; it is also good for burning to

---

[23] Representing the sound *fanam*. The king was an independent sovereign minting his own coinage; but doubtless, as in 1443, he "lived in great fear" of Vijayanagar (Abdul Razzak).

[24] The diameter of the *fanam*, being 0.38 of the Chinese *ts'un* of 1.22 inches, equalled 0.46 of an English inch.

[25] Or "characters."

[26] The gold content weighed 3.45 grains or 0.00719 ounce troy.

[27] Representing the sound *tar* or *tare* (*tara*).

[28] If the silver was pure, the silver content weighed 0.00359 ounce troy.

[29] The equivalent of 4 *ch'ih* was 48.9 inches; 1 *chang* 2 *ch'ih* equaled 12 feet 2.9 inches.

[30] The gold content weighed 345.375 grains or 0.7195 ounce troy.

[31] The gold content of 200 *fanam* weighed 690.751 grains or 1.439 ounces troy.

ash for the delicate operation of inlaying[32] gold or silver. The trees are good for building houses, and the leaves are good for roofing houses.

For vegetables they have mustard plants, green ginger, turnips, caraway seeds, onions, garlic, bottle-gourds, egg-plants, cucumbers, and gourd-melons[33]—all these they have in [all] the four seasons [of the year]. They also have a kind of small gourd which is as large as [one's] finger, about two *ts'un*[34] long, and tastes like a green cucumber. Their onions have a purple skin; they resemble garlic; they have a large head and small leaves; [and] they are sold by the *chin*[35] weight.

The *mu-pieb-tzu*[36] tree is more than ten *chang* high; it forms a fruit which resembles a green persimmon and contains thirty or forty seeds; it falls of its own accord when ripe; [and] the bats, as large as hawks, all hang upside-down and rest on this tree.

They have both red and white rice, [but] barley and wheat are both absent; [and] their wheat-flour all comes from other places as merchandise for sale [here].

Fowls and ducks exist in profusion, [but] there are no geese. Their goats have tall legs and an ashen hue; they resemble donkey-foals. The water-buffaloes are not very large. Some of the yellow oxen weigh three or four hundred *chin*;[37] the people do not eat their flesh; [but] consume only the milk and cream. The people never eat rice without butter. Their oxen are cared for until they are old; [and] when they die, they are buried. The price of all kinds of sea-fish is very cheap. Deer and hares [from up] in the mountains are also for sale.

Many of the people rear peafowl. As to their other birds: they have crows, green hawks, egrets, and swallows; [but] of other kinds of birds besides these they have not a single one, great or small. The people of the country can also play and sing; they use the shell of a calabash to make a musical instrument, and copper wires to make the strings; and they play [this instrument] to accompany the singing of their foreign songs; the melodies are worth hearing.[38]

---

[32] *Hsiang*, "a box," used for *hsiang*, "side rooms," which in turn is used for *hsiang*, "to inlay."

[33] *Tung kua*, "eastern gourd," the same vegetable as *tung kua*, "winter gourd."

[34] That is, 2.4 inches.

[35] That is, 1.3 pounds avoirdupois.

[36] The tree is *Momordica cochinchinensis*. The editor is indebted to Dr. J. Needham, F.R.S., for the information that *Momordica* seeds were prescribed in the form of paste for abscesses, ulcers, and wounds, as well as in other ways for other affections. The equivalent of 10 *chang* was 102 feet.

[37] The equivalent of 300 *chin* was 394.6 pounds avoirdupois.

[38] Music was cultivated at the royal courts, and numbers of musicians were employed in the temples. Conti, in his account of Vijayanagar city, records solemn singing at religious festivals, and the celebration of weddings with "banquets, songs, trumpets, and instruments muche like unto ours." The instrument referred to by Ma Huan was probably the vina, a fretted instrument of the guitar kind, which was particularly favoured by Indian musicians.

As to the popular customs and the marriage- and funeral-rites, the So-li people and the Muslim people each follow the ritual forms of their own class, and these are different.

The king's throne does not descend to his son, but descends to his sister's son; descent is to the sister's son [because] they consider that the offspring of the women's body alone constitutes the legal family. If the king has no elder or younger sister, [the throne] descends to his younger brother; [and] if he has no younger brother, [the throne] is yielded up to some man of merit. Such is the succession from one generation to another.

3

Journal of the First Voyage of Vasco da Gama, 1498

In 1497 the Portuguese seaman Vasco da Gama left Portugal with a fleet of four ships, arriving in India ten months later. He benefited from the experience of Bartolomeu Dias, who ten years before had negotiated the rough waters of the South African Cape. But Dias had returned to Portugal. Da Gama continued up the African coast and sailed across the Indian Ocean to the port of Calicut, the center of a kingdom that encompassed much of the modern state of Kerala in southwest India. What seem to have been the motives of Portugal and da Gama in sailing to South Asia? How were the Portuguese intentions similar to, and different from, those of China earlier in the century? How would you compare the preparation and behavior of Chinese and Portuguese crews? How would you explain the differences between Chinese and Portuguese voyages?

THINKING HISTORICALLY

We do not know the identity of the author of this document. He was one of the officers or crewmen who sailed on this voyage, however, and many of their names are known to us. What indications do you have that they spanned a wide range of Portuguese society?

The fact that the author was a witness does not mean that he gets everything right. What does he miss? What might have caused him to be misled? Generally, primary sources get more things right than wrong. How do you know this is true for this selection? How do we determine where a primary source is reliable and where it is not?

Source: *A Journal of the First Voyage of Vasco da Gama, 1497–1499*, trans. and ed. E. G. Ravenstein (London: Hakluyt Society, 1898), 48–59, 60–63.

Calicut

[*Arrival.*][1] That night[2] [May 20] we anchored two leagues from the city of Calicut, and we did so because our pilot mistook *Capua*,[3] a town at that place, for Calicut. Still further there is another town called *Pandarani.*[4] We anchored about a league and a half from the shore. After we were at anchor, four boats (*almadias*) approached us from the land, who asked of what nation we were. We told them, and they then pointed out Calicut to us.

On the following day [May 21] these same boats came again alongside, when the captain-major[5] sent one of the convicts[6] to Calicut, and those with whom he went took him to two Moors from Tunis,[7] who could speak Castilian and Genoese. The first greeting that he received was in these words: "May the Devil take thee! What brought you hither?" They asked what he sought so far away from home, and he told them that we came in search of Christians and of spices. They said: "Why does not the King of Castile, the King of France, or the Signoria of Venice send thither?" He said that the King of Portugal would not consent to their doing so, and they said he did the right thing. After this conversation they took him to their lodgings and gave him wheaten bread and honey. When he had eaten he returned to the ships, accompanied by one of the Moors, who was no sooner on board, than he said these words: "A lucky venture, a lucky venture! Plenty of rubies, plenty of emeralds! You owe great thanks to God, for having brought you to a country holding such riches!" We were greatly astonished to hear his talk, for we never expected to hear our language spoken so far away from Portugal.

[*A description of Calicut.*] The city of Calicut is inhabited by Christians.[8] They are of tawny complexion. Some of them have big beards and long hair, whilst others clip their hair short or shave the head, merely allowing a tuft to remain on the crown as a sign that they are Christians.

---

[1] Brackets enclose editorial additions of translator, Ravenstein, unless otherwise indicated. [Ed.]

[2] Afternoon (*a tarde*), according to Glenn J. Ames, *Em Nome de Deus* (Leiden: Brill, 2009), 70. [Ed.]

[3] Kappatt, a village about 7 miles north of Calicut. [Ed.]

[4] About 14 miles north of Calicut. [Ed.]

[5] Da Gama. [Ed.]

[6] The crew included a number of "convict-exiles," men who had been convicted of a crime punishable by death who were pardoned by the king to sail as adventurers and live out their lives overseas. Da Gama wanted such people in his crew to create a permanent presence overseas. [Ed.]

[7] Likely Muslim exiles from Spain after the defeat of the last Muslim stronghold in Granada by Christians in 1492. [Ed.]

[8] There were Christians in southern India, but the population was overwhelmingly Hindu. [Ed.]

They also wear moustaches. They pierce the ears and wear much gold in them. They go naked down to the waist, covering their lower extremities with very fine cotton stuffs. But it is only the most respectable who do this, for the others manage as best they are able.

The women of this country, as a rule, are ugly and of small stature. They wear many jewels of gold round the neck, numerous bracelets on their arms, and rings set with precious stones on their toes. All these people are well-disposed and apparently of mild temper. At first sight they seem covetous and ignorant.

[*A messenger sent to the King.*] When we arrived at Calicut the king was fifteen leagues away. The captain-major sent two men to him with a message, informing him that an ambassador had arrived from the King of Portugal with letters, and that if he desired it he would take them to where the king then was.

The king presented the bearers of this message with much fine cloth. He sent word to the captain-major bidding him welcome, saying that he was about to proceed to Calicut. As a matter of fact, he started at once with a large retinue.

[*At Anchor at Pandarani, May* 27.] A pilot accompanied our two men, with orders to take us to a place called Pandarani, below the place [Capua] where we anchored at first. At this time we were actually in front of the city of Calicut. We were told that the anchorage at the place to which we were to go was good, whilst at the place we were then it was bad, with a stony bottom, which was quite true; and, moreover, that it was customary for the ships which came to this country to anchor there for the sake of safety. We ourselves did not feel comfortable, and the captain-major had no sooner received this royal message than he ordered the sails to be set, and we departed. We did not, however, anchor as near the shore as the king's pilot desired.

When we were at anchor, a message arrived informing the captain-major that the king was already in the city. At the same time the king sent a *bale*,[9] with other men of distinction, to Pandarani, to conduct the captain-major to where the king awaited him. This *bale* is like an *alcaide*,[10] and is always attended by two hundred men armed with swords and bucklers. As it was late when this message arrived, the captain-major deferred going.

[*Gama goes to Calicut.*] On the following morning, which was Monday, May 28th, the captain-major set out to speak to the king, and took with him thirteen men, of which I was one.[11] On landing, the captain-major was received by the *alcaide*, with whom were many men,

---

[9] Governor. [Ed.]

[10] Mayor. [Ed.]

[11] We know the names of about half of the thirteen, but not which of them is the author. [Ed.]

armed and unarmed. The reception was friendly, as if the people were pleased to see us, though at first appearances looked threatening, for they carried naked swords in their hands. A palanquin[12] was provided for the captain-major, such as is used by men of distinction in that country, as also by some of the merchants, who pay something to the king for this privilege. The captain-major entered the palanquin, which was carried by six men by turns. Attended by all these people we took the road of Calicut, and came first to another town, called Capua. The captain-major was there deposited at the house of a man of rank, whilst we others were provided with food, consisting of rice, with much butter, and excellent boiled fish. The captain-major did not wish to eat, and as we had done so, we embarked on a river close by, which flows between the sea and the mainland, close to the coast. The two boats in which we embarked were lashed together, so that we were not separated. There were numerous other boats, all crowded with people. As to those who were on the banks I say nothing; their number was infinite, and they had all come to see us. We went up that river for about a league, and saw many large ships drawn up high and dry on its banks, for there is no port here.

When we disembarked, the captain-major once more entered his palanquin. The road was crowded with a countless multitude anxious to see us. Even the women came out of their houses with children in their arms and followed us.

[*A Christian Church.*][13] When we arrived [at Calicut] they took us to a large church, and this is what we saw: —

The body of the church is as large as a monastery, all built of hewn stone and covered with tiles. At the main entrance rises a pillar of bronze as high as a mast, on the top of which was perched a bird, apparently a cock.[14] In addition to this, there was another pillar as high as a man, and very stout. In the center of the body of the church rose a chapel, all built of hewn stone, with a bronze door sufficiently wide for a man to pass, and stone steps leading up to it. Within this sanctuary stood a small image which they said represented Our Lady.[15] Along the walls, by the main entrance, hung seven small bells. In this church the captain-major said his prayers, and we with him.[16]

---

[12] An enclosed chair carried on poles front and rear. [Ed.]

[13] The translator, Ravenstein, who supplied this heading, added a note: "This 'church' was, of course, a pagoda or temple." [Ed.]

[14] Ravenstein (1898) believes the bird to be a Hindu war-god. Ames (2009) suggests it was an image of Garuda, the bird-god who carried Vishnu, the creator-god of the Hindu trinity. [Ed.]

[15] Possibly Mari, a local deity, protector from smallpox. [Ed.]

[16] Another source reports that at least one of the crew did not believe it was a Christian church. He is said to have knelt next to Vasco da Gama and said: "If this is the devil, I worship the True God" (Ames, 2009, 76). [Ed.]

We did not go within the chapel, for it is the custom that only certain servants of the church, called *quafees*,[17] should enter. These *quafees* wore some threads passing over the left shoulder and under the right arm, in the same manner as our deacons wear the stole. They threw holy water over us, and gave us some white earth,[18] which the Christians of this country are in the habit of putting on their foreheads, breasts, around the neck, and on the forearms. They threw holy water upon the captain-major and gave him some of the earth, which he gave in charge of someone, giving them to understand that he would put it on later.[19]

Many other saints were painted on the walls of the church, wearing crowns. They were painted variously, with teeth protruding an inch from the mouth, and four or five arms.

Below this church there was a large masonry tank, similar to many others which we had seen along the road.

[*Progress through the Town.*] After we had left that place, and had arrived at the entrance to the city [of Calicut] we were shown another church, where we saw things like those described above. Here the crowd grew so dense that progress along the street became next to impossible, and for this reason they put the captain-major into a house, and us with him.

The king sent a brother of the *bale*, who was a lord of this country, to accompany the captain-major, and he was attended by men beating drums, blowing *anafils* and bagpipes, and firing off matchlocks. In conducting the captain-major they showed us much respect, more than is shown in Spain to a king. The number of people was countless, for in addition to those who surrounded us, and among whom there were two thousand armed men, they crowded the roofs and houses.

[*The King's Palace.*] The further we advanced in the direction of the king's palace, the more did they increase in number. And when we arrived there, men of much distinction and great lords came out to meet the captain-major, and joined those who were already in attendance upon him. It was then an hour before sunset. When we reached the palace we passed through a gate into a courtyard of great size, and before we arrived at where the king was, we passed four doors, through which we had to force our way, giving many blows to the people. When, at last, we reached the door where the king was, there came forth from it a little old man, who holds a position resembling that of a bishop, and whose advice the king acts upon in all affairs of the church. This man embraced the captain-major when he entered the door. Several men were wounded at this door, and we only got in by the use of much force.

---

[17] Ames (2009) suggests that this term for Brahman priests was either the Arabic *quadi* (judge) or *kafir* (unbeliever). [Ed.]

[18] Possibly ash from burnt cow dung. [Ed.]

[19] Did da Gama's refusal to anoint himself with ash mean he questioned the legitimacy of ritual or church? [Ed.]

[*A Royal Audience, May 28.*] The king[20] was in a small court, reclining upon a couch covered with a cloth of green velvet, above which was a good mattress, and upon this again a sheet of cotton stuff, very white and fine, more so than any linen. The cushions were after the same fashion. In his left hand the king held a very large golden cup [spittoon], having a capacity of half an almude [8 pints]. At its mouth this cup was two palmas [16 inches] wide, and apparently it was massive. Into this cup the king threw the husks of a certain herb which is chewed by the people of this country because of its soothing effects, and which they call *atambor*.[21] On the right side of the king stood a basin of gold, so large that a man might just encircle it with his arms: this contained the herbs. There were likewise many silver jugs. The canopy above the couch was all gilt.

The captain, on entering, saluted in the manner of the country: by putting the hands together, then raising them towards Heaven, as is done by Christians when addressing God, and immediately afterwards opening them and shutting fists quickly. The king beckoned to the captain with his right hand to come nearer, but the captain did not approach him, for it is the custom of the country for no man to approach the king except only the servant who hands him the herbs, and when anyone addresses the king he holds his hand before the mouth, and remains at a distance. When the king beckoned to the captain he looked at us others, and ordered us to be seated on a stone bench near him, where he could see us. He ordered that water for our hands should be given us, as also some fruit, one kind of which resembled a melon, except that its outside was rough and the inside sweet, whilst another kind of fruit resembled a fig, and tasted very nice. There were men who prepared these fruits for them; and the king looked at them eating, and smiled; and talked to the servant who stood near him supplying him with the herbs referred to.

Then, throwing his eyes on the captain, who sat facing him, he invited him to address himself to the courtiers present, saying they were men of much distinction, that he could tell them whatever he desired to say, and they would repeat it to him (the king). The captain-major replied that he was the ambassador of the King of Portugal, and the bearer of a message which he could only deliver to him personally. The king said this was good, and immediately asked him to be conducted to a chamber. When the captain had entered, the king, too, rose and joined him, whilst we remained where we were. All this happened about sunset. An old man who was in the court took away the couch as soon as the king rose, but allowed the plate to remain. The king, when he joined

---

[20] Manivikraman Raja. [Ed.]
[21] Betel-nut. [Ed.]

the captain, threw himself upon another couch, covered with various stuffs embroidered in gold, and asked the captain what he wanted.

And the captain told him he was the ambassador of a King of Portugal, who was Lord of many countries and the possessor of great wealth of every description, exceeding that of any king of these parts; that for a period of sixty years his ancestors had annually sent out vessels to make discoveries in the direction of India, as they knew that there were Christian kings there like themselves. This, he said, was the reason which induced them to order this country to be discovered, not because they sought for gold or silver, for of this they had such abundance that they needed not what was to be found in this country. He further stated that the captains sent out traveled for a year or two, until their provisions were exhausted, and then returned to Portugal, without having succeeded in making the desired discovery. There reigned a king now whose name was Dom Manuel, who had ordered him to build three vessels, of which he had been appointed captain-major, and who had ordered him not to return to Portugal until he should have discovered this King of the Christians, on pain of having his head cut off. That two letters had been intrusted to him to be presented in case he succeeded in discovering him, and that he would do so on the ensuing day; and, finally, he had been instructed to say by word of mouth that he [the King of Portugal] desired to be his friend and brother.

In reply to this the king said that he was welcome; that, on his part, he held him as a friend and brother, and would send ambassadors with him to Portugal. This latter had been asked as a favor, the captain pretending that he would not dare to present himself before his king and master unless he was able to present, at the same time, some men of this country.

These and many other things passed between the two in this chamber, and as it was already late in the night, the king asked the captain with whom he desired to lodge, with Christians or with Moors? And the captain replied, neither with Christians nor with Moors, and begged as a favor that he be given a lodging by himself. The king said he would order it thus, upon which the captain took leave of the king and came to where the men were, that is, to a veranda lit up by a huge candlestick. By that time four hours of the night had already gone.[22] . . .

[*Presents for the King.*] On Tuesday, May 29, the captain-major got ready the following things to be sent to the king, viz., twelve pieces of *lambel*,[23] four scarlet hoods, six hats, four strings of coral, a case containing six wash-hand basins, a case of sugar, two casks of oil, and two of honey.[24] And as it is the custom not to send anything to the king

---

[22] Four hours after sunset, or about 10 P.M. [Ed.]

[23] Striped cloth. [Ed.]

[24] The ships had been loaded by Bartolomeu Dias (1451–1500), who used such goods effectively in trading with Africans. [Ed.]

without the knowledge of the Moor, his factor, and of the *bale*, the captain informed them of his intention. They came, and when they saw the present they laughed at it, saying that it was not a thing to offer to a king, that the poorest merchant from Mecca, or any other part of India, gave more, and that if he wanted to make a present it should be in gold, as the king would not accept such things. When the captain heard this he grew sad, and said that he had brought no gold, that, moreover, he was no merchant, but an ambassador; that he gave of that which he had, which was his own [private gift] and not the king's; that if the King of Portugal ordered him to return he would intrust him with far richer presents; and that if King Camolim[25] would not accept these things he would send them back to the ships. Upon this they declared that they would not forward his presents, nor consent to his forwarding them himself. When they had gone there came certain Moorish merchants, and they all depreciated the present which the captain desired to be sent to the king.

When the captain saw that they were determined not to forward his present, he said, that as they would not allow him to send his present to the palace he would go to speak to the king, and would then return to the ships. They approved of this, and told him that if he would wait a short time they would return and accompany him to the palace. And the captain waited all day, but they never came back. The captain was very wroth at being among so phlegmatic and unreliable a people, and intended, at first, to go to the palace without them. On further consideration, however, he thought it best to wait until the following day. The men diverted themselves, singing and dancing to the sound of trumpets, and enjoyed themselves much.

[*A Second Audience, May 30.*] On Wednesday morning the Moors returned, and took the captain to the palace, and others with him. The palace was crowded with armed men. Our captain was kept waiting with his conductors for fully four long hours, outside a door, which was only opened when the king sent word to admit him, attended by two men only, whom he might select. The captain-major said that he desired to have Fernao Martins with him, who could interpret, and his secretary. It seemed to him, as it did to us, that this separation portended no good.

When he had entered, the king said that he had expected him on Tuesday. The captain-major said that the long road had tired him, and that for this reason he had not come to see him. The king then said that he had told him that he came from a very rich kingdom, and yet had brought him nothing; that he had also told him that he was the bearer of

---

[25] Camorim (with a soft *c*) is a version of the king's title, more often written as Zamorin or Samorin, meaning ruler of the coasts or king of the seas. [Ed.]

a letter, which had not yet been delivered. To this the captain rejoined that he had brought nothing, because the object of his voyage was merely to make discoveries, but that when other ships came he would then see what they brought him; as to the letter, it was true that he had brought one, and would deliver it immediately.

The king then asked what it was he had come to discover: stones or men? If he came to discover men, as he said, why had he brought nothing? Moreover, he had been told that he carried with him the golden image of a Santa Maria. The captain-major said that the Santa Maria was not of gold, and that even if she were he would not part with her, as she had guided him across the ocean, and would guide him back to his own country. The king then asked for the letter. The captain said that he begged as a favor, that as the Moors wished him ill and might misinterpret him, a Christian able to speak Arabic should be sent for. The king said this was well, and at once sent for a young man, of small stature, whose name was Quaram. The captain-major then said that he had two letters, one written in his own language and the other in that of the Moors;[26] that he was able to read the former, and knew that it contained nothing but what would prove acceptable; but that as to the other he was unable to read it, and it might be good, or contain something that was erroneous. As the Christian was unable to *read* Moorish, four Moors took the letter and read it between them, after which they translated it to the king, who was well satisfied with its contents.

The king then asked what kind of merchandise was to be found in his country. The captain said there was much corn,[27] cloth, iron, bronze, and many other things. The king asked whether he had any merchandise with him. The captain-major replied that he had a little of each sort, as samples, and that if permitted to return to the ships he would order it to be landed, and that meantime four or five men would remain at the lodgings assigned them. The king said no! He might take all his people with him, securely moor his ships, land his merchandise, and sell it to the best advantage. Having taken leave of the king the captain-major returned to his lodgings, and we with him. As it was already late no attempt was made to depart that night.

---

[26] Arabic. [Ed.]

[27] Corn had already been transplanted from the Americas by this time, but the author more likely meant wheat (Ames, 2009, 83). [Ed.]

4

CHRISTOPHER COLUMBUS

Letter to King Ferdinand and Queen Isabella, 1493

Christopher Columbus sent this letter to his royal backers, King Ferdinand and Queen Isabella of Spain, on his return in March 1493 from his first voyage across the Atlantic. (See Map 15.3.)

An Italian sailor from Genoa, Columbus, in 1483–1484, tried to convince King John II of Portugal to underwrite his plan to sail across the western ocean to the spice-rich East Indies. Relying on a Florentine map that used Marco Polo's overstated distance from Venice to Japan across Asia and an understated estimate of the circumference of the globe, Columbus believed that Japan lay only 2,500 miles west of the Portuguese Azores. King John II rejected the proposal because he had more accurate estimates indicating that sailing around Africa was the shorter route, as the voyages of Bartolomeu Dias in 1488 and Vasco da Gama in 1497–1499 proved.

Less knowledgeable about navigation, the new Spanish monarchs, Ferdinand and Isabella, supported Columbus and financed his plan to sail west to Asia. In four voyages, Columbus touched a number of Caribbean islands and the coast of Central America, settled Spaniards on Hispaniola (Española), and began to create one of the largest empires in world history for Spain—all the while thinking he was near China and Japan, in the realm of the Great Khan whom Marco Polo had met and who had died hundreds of years earlier.

In what ways was the voyage of Columbus similar to that of da Gama? In what ways was it similar to that of Zheng He? In what ways was it different from both of these voyages? Taking the voyages of da Gama and Columbus together, what were the differences between Chinese and European expansion?

THINKING HISTORICALLY

Because this document comes from the period we are studying and is written by Columbus himself, it is a primary source. Primary sources have a great sense of immediacy and can often seem to transport us directly into the past. However, involvement when reading does not always lead to understanding, so it is important to

Source: "First Voyage of Columbus," in *The Four Voyages of Columbus*, ed. Cecil Jane (New York: Dover, 1988), 1–18.

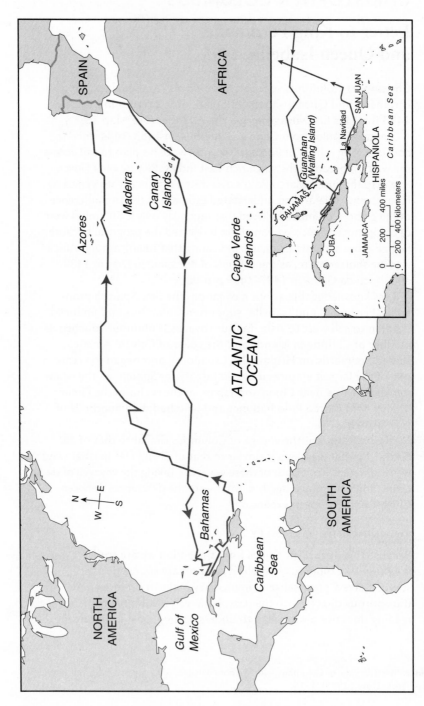

Map 15.3 Columbus's First Voyage, 1492–1493.

think critically about the source and the writer's intended audience as we read. First we must determine the source of the document. Where does it come from? Is it original? If not, is it a copy or a translation? Next, we must determine who wrote it, when it was written, and for what purpose. After answering these questions, we are able to read the document with a critical eye, which leads to greater understanding.

The original letter by Columbus has been lost. This selection is an English translation based on three different printed Spanish versions of the letter. So this text is a reconstruction, not an original, though it is believed to be quite close to the original.

The original letter was probably composed during a relaxed time on the return voyage before its date of February 15, 1493 — possibly as early as the middle of January — and sent to the Spanish monarchs from Lisbon in order to reach them by the time Columbus arrived in Barcelona.

What does Columbus want to impart to Ferdinand and Isabella? First and foremost, he wants them to know that he reached the Indies, that the voyage was a success. And so, the letter's opening sentence tells us something that Columbus certainly did not intend or know. We learn that on his return in 1493, Columbus thought he had been to the Indies when in fact he had not. (It is due to Columbus's confusion that we call the islands he visited the West Indies and Native Americans "Indians.")

Knowing what the author wants a reader to believe is useful information because it serves as a point of reference for other statements the author makes. The success of Columbus's voyage is a case in point. Columbus does not admit to the loss of one of his ships in his letter, nor does he explain fully why he had to build a fort at Navidad and leave some of his crew there, returning home without them. Clearly, Columbus had reason to worry that his voyage would be viewed as a failure. He had not found the gold mines he sought or the Asian cities described by Marco Polo. He thought he had discovered many spices, though only the chili peppers were new. Notice, as you read this letter, how Columbus presents his voyage in the best light.

Aside from what Columbus intends, what facts do you learn from the letter about Columbus, his first voyage, and his encounter with the New World? What seems to drive Columbus to do what he does? What is Columbus's attitude toward the "Indians"? What does Columbus's letter tell us about the society and culture of the Taino* — the people he met in the Caribbean?

* TY noh

Sir, As I know that you will be pleased at the great victory with which Our Lord has crowned my voyage, I write this to you, from which you will learn how in thirty-three days, I passed from the Canary Islands to the Indies with the fleet which the most illustrious king and queen, our sovereigns, gave to me. And there I found very many islands filled with people innumerable, and of them all I have taken possession for their highnesses, by proclamation made and with the royal standard unfurled, and no opposition was offered to me. To the first island which I found, I gave the name *San Salvador*, in remembrance of the Divine Majesty, Who has marvellously bestowed all this; the Indians call it "Guanahani."* To the second, I gave the name *Isla de Santa María de Concepción*; to the third, *Fernandina*; to the fourth, *Isabella*; to the fifth, *Isla Juana*, and so to each one I gave a new name.

When I reached Juana, I followed its coast to the westward, and I found it to be so extensive that I thought that it must be the mainland, the province of Catayo. And since there were neither towns nor villages on the seashore, but only small hamlets, with the people which I could not have speech, because they all fled immediately, I went forward on the same course, thinking that I should not fail to find great cities and towns. And, at the end of many leagues, seeing that there was no change and that the coast was bearing me northwards, which I wished to avoid, since winter was already beginning and I proposed to make from it to the south, and as moreover the wind was carrying me forward, I determined not to wait for a change in the weather and retraced my path as far as a certain harbour known to me. And from that point, I sent two men inland to learn if there were a king or great cities. They travelled three days' journey and found an infinity of small hamlets and people without number, but nothing of importance. For this reason, they returned.

I understood sufficiently from other Indians, whom I had already taken, that this land was nothing but an island. And therefore I followed its coast eastwards for one hundred and seven leagues to the point where it ended. And from that cape, I saw another island, distant eighteen leagues from the former, to the east, to which I at once gave the name "Española." And I went there and followed its northern coast, as I had in the case of Juana, to the eastward for one hundred and eighty-eight great leagues in a straight line. This island and all the others are very fertile to a limitless degree, and this island is extremely so. In it there are many harbours on the coast of the sea, beyond comparison with others which I know in Christendom, and many rivers, good and large, which is marvellous. Its lands are high, and there are in it very many sierras and very lofty mountains, beyond comparison with the island of Teneriffe. All are most beautiful, of a thousand shapes, and all are accessible and

* gwah nah HAH nee

filled with trees of a thousand kinds and tall, and they seem to touch the sky. And I am told that they never lose their foliage, as I can understand, for I saw them as green and as lovely as they are in Spain in May, and some of them were flowering, some bearing fruit, and some in another stage, according to their nature. And the nightingale was singing and other birds of a thousand kinds in the month of November there where I went. There are six or eight kinds of palm, which are a wonder to behold on account of their beautiful variety, but so are the other trees and fruits and plants. In it are marvellous pine groves, and there are very large tracts of cultivatable lands, and there is honey, and there are birds of many kinds and fruits in great diversity. In the interior are mines of metals, and the population is without number. Española is a marvel.

The sierras and mountains, the plains and arable lands and pastures, are so lovely and rich for planting and sowing, for breeding cattle of every kind, for building towns and villages. The harbours of the sea here are such as cannot be believed to exist unless they have been seen, and so with the rivers, many and great, and good waters, the majority of which contain gold. In the trees and fruits and plants, there is a great difference from those of Juana. In this island, there are many spices and great mines of gold and of other metals.

The people of this island, and of all the other islands which I have found and of which I have information, all go naked, men and women, as their mothers bore them, although some women cover a single place with the leaf of a plant or with a net of cotton which they make for the purpose. They have no iron or steel or weapons, nor are they fitted to use them, not because they are not well built men and of handsome stature, but because they are very marvellously timorous. They have no other arms than weapons made of canes, cut in seeding time, to the ends of which they fix a small sharpened stick. And they do not dare to make use of these, for many times it has happened that I have sent ashore two or three men to some town to have speech, and countless people have come out to them, and as soon as they have seen my men approaching they have fled, even a father not waiting for his son. And this, not because ill has been done to anyone; on the contrary, at every point where I have been and have been able to have speech, I have given to them of all that I had, such as cloth and many other things, without receiving anything for it; but so they are, incurably timid. It is true that, after they have been reassured and have lost their fear, they are so guileless and so generous with all they possess, that no one would believe it who has not seen it. They never refuse anything which they possess, if it be asked of them; on the contrary, they invite anyone to share it, and display as much love as if they would give their hearts, and whether the thing be of value or whether it be of small price, at once with whatever trifle of whatever kind it may be that is given to them, with that they are content. I forbade that they should be given things so worthless as fragments of broken crockery and scraps of broken glass, and ends of straps, although when they were able to get them, they fancied that they possessed the best jewel in the world. So it was found that a sailor for a strap received gold to the weight of two and a half *castellanos*, and others much more for other things which were worth much less. As for new *blancas*,[1] for them they would give everything which they had, although it might be two or three *castellanos'* weight of gold or an *arroba*[2] or two of spun cotton. . . . They took even the pieces of the broken hoops of the wine barrels and, like savages, gave what they had, so that it seemed to me to be wrong and I forbade it. And I gave a thousand handsome good things, which I had brought, in order that they might conceive affection, and more than that, might become Christians and be inclined to the love and service of their highnesses and of the whole Castilian nation, and strive to aid us and to give us of the things which they have in abundance and which are necessary to us. And they do not know any creed and are not idolaters; only they all believe that power and good are in the heavens, and they are very firmly convinced that I, with these ships and men, came from the heavens, and in this belief they everywhere received me, after they had overcome their fear. And this does not come because they are ignorant; on the contrary, they are of a very acute intelligence and are men who navigate all those seas, so that it is amazing how good an account they give of everything, but it is because they have never seen people clothed or ships of such a kind.

And as soon as I arrived in the Indies, in the first island which I found, I took by force some of them, in order that they might learn and give me information of that which there is in those parts, and so it was that they soon understood us, and we them, either by speech or signs, and they have been very serviceable. I still take them with me, and they are always assured that I come from Heaven, for all the intercourse which they have had with me; and they were the first to announce this wherever I went, and the others went running from house to house and to the neighbouring towns, with loud cries of, "Come! Come to see the people from Heaven!" So all, men and women alike, when their minds were set at rest concerning us, came, so that not one, great or small, remained behind, and all brought something to eat and drink, which they gave with extraordinary affection. In all the island, they have very many canoes, like rowing *fustas*,[3] some larger, some smaller, and some are larger than a *fusta* of eighteen benches. They are not so broad, because they are made of a single log of wood, but a *fusta* would not keep up with them in rowing, since their speed is a thing incredible. And in these they navigate among all those islands, which are innumerable,

---

[1] Spanish copper coins. [Ed.]

[2] A unit of weight (about 25 pounds) indicated by the @ symbol. [Ed.]

[3] Fast ships with oars and sails, probably of Arab origin. [Ed.]

and carry their goods. One of these canoes I have seen with seventy and eighty men in her, and each one with his oar.

In all these islands, I saw no great diversity in the appearance of the people or in their manners and language. On the contrary, they all understand one another, which is a very curious thing, on account of which I hope that their highnesses will determine upon their conversion to our holy faith, towards which they are very inclined.

I have already said how I have gone one hundred and seven leagues in a straight line from west to east along the seashore of the island Juana, and as a result of that voyage, I can say that this island is larger than England and Scotland together, for, beyond these one hundred and seven leagues, there remain to the westward two provinces to which I have not gone. One of these provinces they call "Avan," and there the people are born with tails; and these provinces cannot have a length of less than fifty or sixty leagues, as I could understand from those Indians whom I have and who know all the islands.

The other, Española, has a circumference greater than all Spain, from Colibre, by the sea-coast, to Fuenterabia in Vizcaya, since I voyaged along one side one hundred and eighty-eight great leagues in a straight line from west to east. It is a land to be desired and, seen, it is never to be left. And in it, although of all I have taken possession for their highnesses and all are more richly endowed than I know how, or am able, to say, and I hold them all for their highnesses, so that they may dispose of them as, and as absolutely as, of the kingdoms of Castile, in this Española, in the situation most convenient and in the best position for the mines of gold and for all intercourse as well with the mainland here as with that there, belonging to the Grand Khan, where will be great trade and gain, I have taken possession of a large town, to which I gave the name *Villa de Navidad*, and in it I have made fortifications and a fort, which now will by this time be entirely finished, and I have left in it sufficient men for such a purpose with arms and artillery and provisions for more than a year, and a *fusta*, and one, a master of all seacraft, to build others, and great friendship with the king of that land, so much so, that he was proud to call me, and to treat me as, a brother. And even if he were to change his attitude to one of hostility towards these men, he and his do not know what arms are and they go naked, as I have already said, and are the most timorous people that there are in the world, so that the men whom I have left there alone would suffice to destroy all that land, and the island is without danger for their persons, if they know how to govern themselves.

In all these islands, it seems to me that all men are content with one woman, and to their chief or king they give as many as twenty. It appears to me that the women work more than the men. And I have not been able to learn if they hold private property; what seemed to me to appear was that, in that which one had, all took a share, especially of eatable things.

In these islands I have so far found no human monstrosities, as many expected, but on the contrary the whole population is very well-formed, nor are they negros as in Guinea, but their hair is flowing, and they are not born where there is intense force in the rays of the sun; it is true that the sun has there great power, although it is distant from the equinoctial line twenty-six degrees. In these islands, where there are high mountains, the cold was severe this winter, but they endure it, being used to it and with the help of meats which they eat with many and extremely hot spices. As I have found no monsters, so I have had no report of any, except in an island "Quaris," the second at the coming into the Indies, which is inhabited by a people who are regarded in all the islands as very fierce and who eat human flesh. They have many canoes with which they range through all the islands of India and pillage and take as many as they can. They are no more malformed than the others, except that they have the custom of wearing their hair long like women, and they use bows and arrows of the same cane stems, with a small piece of wood at the end, owing to lack of iron which they do not possess. They are ferocious among these other people who are cowardly to an excessive degree, but I make no more account of them than of the rest. These are those who have intercourse with the women of "Matinino," which is the first island met on the way from Spain to the Indies, in which there is not a man. These women engage in no feminine occupation, but use bows and arrows of cane, like those already mentioned, and they arm and protect themselves with plates of copper, of which they have much.

In another island, which they assure me is larger than Española, the people have no hair. In it, there is gold incalculable, and from it and from the other islands, I bring with me Indians as evidence.

In conclusion, to speak only of that which has been accomplished on this voyage, which was so hasty, their highnesses can see that I will give them as much gold as they may need, if their highnesses will render me very slight assistance; moreover, spice and cotton, as much as their highnesses shall command; and mastic, as much as they shall order to be shipped and which, up to now, has been found only in Greece, in the island of Chios, and the Seignory sells it for what it pleases; and aloe wood, as much as they shall order to be shipped, and slaves, as many as they shall order to be shipped and who will be from the idolaters. And I believe that I have found rhubarb and cinnamon, and I shall find a thousand other things of value, which the people whom I have left there will have discovered, for I have not delayed at any point, so far as the wind allowed me to sail, except in the town of Navidad, in order to leave it secured and well established, and in truth, I should have done much more, if the ships had served me, as reason demanded.

This is enough . . . and the eternal God, our Lord, Who gives to all those who walk in His way triumph over things which appear to be impossible, and this was notably one; for, although men have talked or have written of these lands, all was conjectural, without suggestion of ocular evidence, but amounted only to this, that those who heard for the most part listened and judged it to be rather a fable than as having any vestige of truth. So that, since Our Redeemer has given this victory to our most illustrious king and queen, and to their renowned kingdoms, in so great a matter, for this all Christendom ought to feel delight and make great feasts and give solemn thanks to the Holy Trinity with many solemn prayers for the great exaltation which they shall have, in the turning of so many peoples to our holy faith, and afterwards for temporal benefits, for not only Spain but all Christians will have hence refreshment and gain.

This, in accordance with that which has been accomplished, thus briefly.

Done in the caravel,[4] off the Canary Islands, on the fifteenth of February, in the year one thousand four hundred and ninety-three.

At your orders.   El Almirante.

After having written this, and being in the sea of Castile, there came on me so great a south-south-west wind, that I was obliged to lighten ship. But I ran here to-day into this port of Lisbon, which was the greatest marvel in the world, whence I decided to write to their highnesses. In all the Indies, I have always found weather like May; where I went in thirty-three days and I had returned in twenty-eight, save for these storms which have detained me for fourteen days, beating about in this sea. Here all the sailors say that never has there been so bad a winter nor so many ships lost.

Done on the fourth day of March.

[4] Sailing ship, in this case the *Santa Maria*. [Ed.]

5

KIRKPATRICK SALE

The Conquest of Paradise, 1991

In this selection from his popular study of Columbus, Sale is concerned with Columbus's attitude toward nature in the New World. Sale regards Columbus as a symbol of European expansion. If Columbus is distinctly European, what is Sale saying about European expansion? How and what does Sale add to your understanding of the similarities and differences between Chinese and European expansion?

Source: Kirkpatrick Sale, *The Conquest of Paradise* (New York: Penguin, 1991), 92–104.

Was Columbus much different from Zheng He? Or were the areas and peoples they visited causes for different responses? Vasco da Gama visited the same areas as Zheng He. How similar, or different, was da Gama from Zheng He? If da Gama was a better symbol of European expansion, how different was the European experience from the Chinese?

THINKING HISTORICALLY

Clearly, this selection is a secondary source; Sale is a modern writer, not a fifteenth-century contemporary of Columbus. Still, you will not have to read very far into the selection to realize that Sale has a distinct point of view. Secondary sources, like primary ones, should be analyzed for bias and perspective, and the author's interpretation should be identified.

Sale is an environmentalist and a cultural critic. Do his beliefs and values hinder his understanding of Columbus, or do they inform and illuminate aspects of Columbus that might otherwise be missed? Does Sale help you recognize things you would not have seen on your own, or does he persuade you to see things that might not truly be there?

Notice how Sale uses primary sources in his text. He quotes from Columbus's journal and his letter to King Ferdinand and Queen Isabella. Do these quotes help you understand Columbus, or do they simply support Sale's argument? What do you think about Sale's use of the Spanish Colón* for Columbus? Does Sale "take possession" of Columbus by, in effect, "renaming" him for modern readers? Is the effect humanizing or debunking?

Notice how Sale sometimes calls attention to what the primary source did *not* say rather than what it did say. Is this a legitimate way to understand someone, or is Sale projecting a twentieth-century perspective on Columbus to make a point?

Toward the end of the selection, Sale extends his criticism beyond Columbus to include others. Who are the others? What is the effect of this larger criticism?

Admiral Colón spent a total of ninety-six days exploring the lands he encountered on the far side of the Ocean Sea—four rather small coralline islands in the Bahamian chain and two substantial coastlines of what he finally acknowledged were larger islands—every one of which he "took possession of" in the name of his Sovereigns.

The first he named San Salvador, no doubt as much in thanksgiving for its welcome presence after more than a month at sea as for the Son

* koh LOHN

of God whom it honored; the second he called Santa María de la Concepcíon, after the Virgin whose name his flagship bore; and the third and fourth he called Fernandina and Isabela, for his patrons, honoring Aragon before Castile for reasons never explained (possibly protocol, possibly in recognition of the chief sources of backing for the voyage). The first of the two large and very fertile islands he called Juana, which Fernando [Columbus's son] says was done in honor of Prince Juan, heir to the Castilian throne, but just as plausibly might have been done in recognition of Princess Juana, the unstable child who eventually carried on the line; the second he named la Ysla Española, the "Spanish Island," because it resembled (though he felt it surpassed in beauty) the lands of Castile.

It was not that the islands were in need of names, mind you, nor indeed that Colón was ignorant of the names that native peoples had already given them, for he frequently used those original names before endowing them with his own. Rather, the process of bestowing new names went along with "taking possession of" those parts of the world he deemed suitable for Spanish ownership, showing the royal banners, erecting various crosses, and pronouncing certain oaths and pledges. If this was presumption, it had an honored heritage: It was Adam who was charged by his Creator with the task of naming "every living creature," including the product of his own rib, in the course of establishing "dominion over" them.

Colón went on to assign no fewer than sixty-two other names on the geography of the islands—capes, points, mountains, ports—with a blithe assurance suggesting that in his (and Europe's) perception the act of name-giving was in some sense a talisman of conquest, a rite that changed raw neutral stretches of far-off earth into extensions of Europe. The process began slowly, even haltingly—he forgot to record, for example, until four days afterward that he named the landfall island San Salvador—but by the time he came to Española at the end he went on a naming spree, using more than two-thirds of all the titles he concocted on that one coastline. On certain days it became almost a frenzy: on December 6 he named six places, on the nineteenth six more, and on January 11 no fewer than ten—eight capes, a point, and a mountain. It is almost as if, as he sailed along the last of the islands, he was determined to leave his mark on it the only way he knew how, and thus to establish his authority—and by extension Spain's—even, as with baptism, to make it thus sanctified, and real, and official. . . .

This business of naming and "possessing" foreign islands was by no means casual. The Admiral took it very seriously, pointing out that "it was my wish to bypass no island without taking possession" (October 15) and that "in all regions [I] always left a cross standing" (November 16) as a mark of Christian dominance. There even seem to have been certain prescriptions for it (the instructions from the Sovereigns speak of "the administering of the oath and the performing of the rites prescribed in such cases"), and Rodrigo de Escobedo was sent along as secretary of the fleet explicitly to witness and record these events in detail.

But consider the implications of this act and the questions it raises again about what was in the Sovereigns' minds, what in Colón's. Why would the Admiral assume that these territories were in some way *un*possessed—even by those clearly inhabiting them—and thus available for Spain to claim? Why would he not think twice about the possibility that some considerable potentate—the Grand Khan of China, for example, whom he later acknowledged (November 6) "must be" the ruler of Española—might descend upon him at any moment with a greater military force than his three vessels commanded and punish him for his territorial presumption? Why would he make the ceremony of possession his very first act on shore, even before meeting the inhabitants or exploring the environs, or finding out if anybody there objected to being thus possessed—particularly if they actually owned the great treasures he hoped would be there? No European would have imagined that anyone—three small boatloads of Indians, say—could come up to a European shore or island and "take possession" of it, nor would a European imagine marching up to some part of North Africa or the Middle East and claiming sovereignty there with impunity. Why were these lands thought to be different?

Could there be any reason for the Admiral to assume he had reached "unclaimed" shores, new lands that lay far from the domains of any of the potentates of the East? Can that really have been in his mind—or can it all be explained as simple Eurocentrism, or Eurosuperiority, mixed with cupidity and naiveté? . . .

Once safely "possessed,"[1] San Salvador was open for inspection. Now the Admiral turned his attention for the first time to the "naked people" staring at him on the beach—he did not automatically give them a name, interestingly enough, and it would be another six days before he decided what he might call them—and tried to win their favor with his trinkets.

> They all go around as naked as their mothers bore them; and also the women, although I didn't see more than one really young girl. All that I saw were young people [*mancebos*], none of them more than 30 years old. They are very well built, with very handsome bodies and very good faces; their hair [is] coarse, almost like the silk of a horse's tail, and short. They wear their hair over their eyebrows, except for a little in the back that they wear long and never cut. Some of them paint themselves black (and they are the color of the Canary Islanders, neither black nor white), and some paint themselves white, and some red, and some with what they find. And some paint their faces, and some of them the whole body, and some the eyes only, and some of them only the nose.

It may fairly be called the birth of American anthropology.

---

[1] Given Spanish names. [Ed.]

A crude anthropology, of course, as superficial as Colón's descriptions always were when his interest was limited, but simple and straightforward enough, with none of the fable and fantasy that characterized many earlier (and even some later) accounts of new-found peoples. There was no pretense to objectivity, or any sense that these people might be representatives of a culture equal to, or in any way a model for, Europe's. Colón immediately presumed the inferiority of the natives, not merely because (a sure enough sign) they were naked, but because (his society could have no surer measure) they seemed so technologically backward. "It appeared to me that these people were very poor in everything," he wrote on that first day, and, worse still, "they have no iron." And they went on to prove their inferiority to the Admiral by being ignorant of even such a basic artifact of European life as a sword: "They bear no arms, nor are they acquainted with them," he wrote, "for I showed them swords and they grasped them by the blade and cut themselves through ignorance." Thus did European arms spill the first drops of native blood on the sands of the New World, accompanied not with a gasp of compassion but with a smirk of superiority.

Then, just six sentences further on, Colón clarified what this inferiority meant in his eyes:

> They ought to be good servants and of good intelligence [*ingenio*]. . . . I believe that they would easily be made Christians, because it seemed to me that they had no religion. Our Lord pleasing, I will carry off six of them at my departure to Your Highnesses, in order that they may learn to speak.

No clothes, no arms, no possessions, no iron, and now no religion—not even speech: hence they were fit to be servants, and captives. It may fairly be called the birth of American slavery.

Whether or not the idea of slavery was in Colón's mind all along is uncertain, although he did suggest he had had experience as a slave trader in Africa (November 12) and he certainly knew of Portuguese plantation slavery in the Madeiras and Spanish slavery of Guanches in the Canaries. But it seems to have taken shape early and grown ever firmer as the weeks went on and as he captured more and more of the helpless natives. At one point he even sent his crew ashore to kidnap "seven head of women, young ones and adults, and three small children"; the expression of such callousness led the Spanish historian Salvador de Madariaga to remark, "It would be difficult to find a starker utterance of utilitarian subjection of man by man than this passage [whose] form is no less devoid of human feeling than its substance."

To be sure, Colón knew nothing about these people he encountered and considered enslaving, and he was hardly trained to find out very much, even if he was moved to care. But they were in fact members of an extensive, populous, and successful people whom Europe, using its own peculiar taxonomy, subsequently called "Taino" (or "Taíno"), their own word for "good" or "noble," and their response when asked who they were. They were related distantly by both language and culture to the Arawak people of the South American mainland, but it is misleading (and needlessly imprecise) to call them Arawaks, as historians are wont to do, when the term "Taino" better establishes their ethnic and historical distinctiveness. They had migrated to the islands from the mainland at about the time of the birth of Christ, occupying the three large islands we now call the Greater Antilles and arriving at Guanahani (Colón's San Salvador) and the end of the Bahamian chain probably sometime around A.D. 900. There they displaced an earlier people, the Guanahacabibes (sometimes called Guanahatabeys), who by the time of the European discovery occupied only the western third of Cuba and possibly remote corners of Española; and there, probably in the early fifteenth century, they eventually confronted another people moving up the islands from the mainland, the Caribs, whose culture eventually occupied a dozen small islands of what are called the Lesser Antilles.

The Tainos were not nearly so backward as Colón assumed from their lack of dress. (It might be said that it was the Europeans, who generally kept clothed head to foot during the day despite temperatures regularly in the eighties, who were the more unsophisticated in garmenture—especially since the Tainos, as Colón later noted, also used their body paint to prevent sunburn.) Indeed, they had achieved a means of living in a balanced and fruitful harmony with their natural surroundings that any society might well have envied. They had, to begin with, a not unsophisticated technology that made exact use of their available resources, two parts of which were so impressive that they were picked up and adopted by the European invaders: *canoa* (canoes) that were carved and fire-burned from large silk-cotton trees, "all in one piece, and wonderfully made" (October 13), some of which were capable of carrying up to 150 passengers; and *hamaca* (hammocks) that were "like nets of cotton" (October 17) and may have been a staple item of trade with Indian tribes as far away as the Florida mainland. Their houses were not only spacious and clean—as the Europeans noted with surprise and appreciation, used as they were to the generally crowded and slovenly hovels and huts of south European peasantry—but more apropos, remarkably resistant to hurricanes; the circular walls were made of strong cane poles set deep and close together ("as close as the fingers of a hand," Colón noted), the conical roofs of branches and vines tightly interwoven on a frame of smaller poles and covered with heavy palm leaves. Their artifacts and jewelry, with the exception of a few gold trinkets and ornaments, were based largely on renewable materials, including bracelets and necklaces of coral, shells, bone, and stone, embroidered cotton belts, woven baskets, carved statues and chairs, wooden and shell utensils, and pottery of variously intricate decoration depending on period and place.

Perhaps the most sophisticated, and most carefully integrated, part of their technology was their agricultural system, extraordinarily productive and perfectly adapted to the conditions of the island environment. It was based primarily on fields of knee-high mounds, called *conucos*, planted with *yuca* (sometimes called manioc), *batata* (sweet potato), and various squashes and beans grown all together in multicrop harmony: The root crops were excellent in resisting erosion and producing minerals and potash, the leaf crops effective in providing shade and moisture, and the mound configurations largely resistant to erosion and flooding and adaptable to almost all topographic conditions including steep hillsides. Not only was the *conuco* system environmentally appropriate — "conuco agriculture seems to have provided an exceptionally ecologically well-balanced and protective form of land use," according to David Watts's recent and authoritative *West Indies* — but it was also highly productive, surpassing in yields anything known in Europe at the time, with labor that amounted to hardly more than two or three hours a week, and in continuous yearlong harvest. The pioneering American geographical scholar Carl Sauer calls Taino agriculture "productive as few parts of the world," giving the "highest returns of food in continuous supply by the simplest methods and modest labor," and adds, with a touch of regret, "The white man never fully appreciated the excellent combination of plants that were grown in conucos."

In their arts of government the Tainos seem to have achieved a parallel sort of harmony. Most villages were small (ten to fifteen families) and autonomous, although many apparently recognized loose allegiances with neighboring villages, and they were governed by a hereditary official called a *kaseke* (*cacique,** in the Spanish form), something of a cross between an arbiter and a prolocutor, supported by advisers and elders. So little a part did violence play in their system that they seem, remarkably, to have been a society without war (at least we know of no war music or signals or artifacts, and no evidence of intertribal combats) and even without overt conflict (Las Casas reports that no Spaniard ever saw two Tainos fighting). And here we come to what was obviously the Tainos' outstanding cultural achievement, a proficiency in the social arts that led those who first met them to comment unfailingly on their friendliness, their warmth, their openness, and above all — so striking to those of an acquisitive culture — their generosity.

"They are the best people in the world and above all the gentlest," Colón recorded in his *Journal* (December 16), and from first to last he was astonished at their kindness:

* kah SEEK

They became so much our friends that it was a marvel. . . . They traded and gave everything they had, with good will [October 12].

I sent the ship's boat ashore for water, and they very willingly showed my people where the water was, and they themselves carried the full barrels to the boat, and took great delight in pleasing us [October 16].

They are very gentle and without knowledge of what is evil; nor do they murder or steal [November 12].

Your Highnesses may believe that in all the world there can be no better or gentler people . . . for neither better people nor land can there be. . . . All the people show the most singular loving behavior and they speak pleasantly [December 24].

I assure Your Highnesses that I believe that in all the world there is no better people nor better country. They love their neighbors as themselves, and they have the sweetest talk in the world, and are gentle and always laughing [December 25].

Even if one allows for some exaggeration—Colón was clearly trying to convince Ferdinand and Isabella that his Indians could be easily conquered and converted, should that be the Sovereigns' wish—it is obvious that the Tainos exhibited a manner of social discourse that quite impressed the rough Europeans. But that was not high among the traits of "civilized" nations, as Colón and Europe understood it, and it counted for little in the Admiral's assessment of these people. However struck he was with such behavior, he would not have thought that it was the mark of a benign and harmonious society, or that from it another culture might learn. For him it was something like the wondrous behavior of children, the naive guilelessness of prelapsarian[2] creatures who knew no better how to bargain and chaffer and cheat than they did to dress themselves: "For a lacepoint they gave good pieces of gold the size of two fingers" (January 6), and "They even took pieces of the broken hoops of the wine casks and, like beasts [como besti], gave what they had" (Santangel Letter).[3] Like beasts; such innocence was not human.

It is to be regretted that the Admiral, unable to see past their nakedness, as it were, knew not the real virtues of the people he confronted. For the Tainos' lives were in many ways as idyllic as their surroundings, into which they fit with such skill and comfort. They were well fed and well housed, without poverty or serious disease. They enjoyed considerable leisure, given over to dancing, singing, ballgames, and sex, and expressed themselves artistically in basketry, woodworking, pottery, and

---

[2] Before the Fall. In other words, before the time, according to the Old Testament, when Adam and Eve sinned and were banished by God from the Garden of Eden. [Ed.]

[3] Santangel was the minister of Ferdinand and Isabella who received the letter. [Ed.]

jewelry. They lived in general harmony and peace, without greed or covetousness or theft. . . .

It is perhaps only natural that Colón should devote his initial attention to the handsome, naked, naive islanders, but it does seem peculiar that he pays almost no attention, especially in the early days, to the spectacular scenery around them. Here he was, in the middle of an old-growth tropical forest the likes of which he could not have imagined before, its trees reaching sixty or seventy feet into the sky, more varieties than he knew how to count much less name, exhibiting a lushness that stood in sharp contrast to the sparse and denuded lands he had known in the Mediterranean, hearing a melodious multiplicity of bird songs and parrot calls—why was it not an occasion of wonder, excitement, and the sheer joy at nature in its full, arrogant abundance? But there is not a word of that: He actually said nothing about the physical surroundings on the first day, aside from a single phrase about "very green trees" and "many streams," and on the second managed only that short sentence about a big island with a big lake and green trees. Indeed, for the whole two weeks of the first leg of his voyage through the Bahamas to Cuba, he devoted only a third of the lines of description to the phenomena around him. And there are some natural sights he seems not to have noticed at all: He did not mention (except in terms of navigation) the nighttime heavens, the sharp, glorious configurations of stars that he must have seen virtually every night of his journey, many for the first time.

Eventually Colón succumbed to the islands' natural charms as he sailed on—how could he not?—and began to wax warmly about how "these islands are very green and fertile and the air very sweet" (October 15), with "trees which were more beautiful to see than any other thing that has ever been seen" (October 17), and "so good and sweet a smell of flowers or trees from the land" (October 19). But his descriptions are curiously vapid and vague, the language opaque and lifeless:

> The other island, which is very big [October 15] . . . this island is very large [October 16] . . . these islands are very green and fertile [October 15] . . . this land is the best and most fertile [October 17] . . . in it many plants and trees . . . if the others are very beautiful, this is more so [October 19] . . . here are some great lagoons . . . big and little birds of all sorts . . . if the others already seen are very beautiful and green and fertile, this one is much more so [October 21] . . . full of very good harbors and deep rivers [October 28].

You begin to see the Admiral's problem: He cares little about the features of nature, at least the ones he doesn't use for sailing, and even when he admires them he has little experience in assessing them and less acquaintance with a vocabulary to describe them. To convey the lush density and stately grandeur of those tropical forests, for example, he had little more than the modifiers "green" and "very": "very green trees" (October 12), "trees very green" (October 13), "trees . . . so green and with leaves like those of Castile" (October 14), "very green and very big trees" (October 19), "large groves are very green" (October 21), "trees . . . beautiful and green" (October 28). And when he began to be aware of the diversity among those trees, he was still unable to make meaningful distinctions: "All the trees are as different from ours as day from night" (October 17), "trees of a thousand kinds" (October 21), "a thousand sorts of trees" (October 23), "trees . . . different from ours" (October 28), "trees of a thousand sorts" (November 14), "trees of a thousand kinds" (December 6).

Such was his ignorance—a failing he repeatedly bemoaned ("I don't recognize them, which gives me great grief," October 19)—that when he did stop to examine a species he often had no idea what he was looking at. "I saw many trees very different from ours," he wrote on October 16, "and many of them have branches of many kinds, and all on one trunk, and one twig is of one kind and another of another, and so different that it is the greatest wonder in the world how much diversity there is of one kind from the other. That is to say, one branch has leaves like a cane, and another like mastic, and thus on one tree five or six kinds, and all so different." There is no such tree in existence, much less "many of them," and never was: Why would anyone imagine, or so contrive, such a thing to be?

Colón's attempts to identify species were likewise frequently wrong-headed, usually imputing to them commercial worth that they did not have, as with the worthless "aloes" he loaded such quantities of. The "amaranth" he identified on October 28 and the "oaks" and "arbutus" of November 25 are species that do not grow in the Caribbean; the "mastic" he found on November 5 and loaded on board to sell in Spain was gumbo-limbo, commercially worthless. (On the other hand, one of the species of flora he deemed of no marketable interest— "weeds [*tizon*] in their hands to drink in the fragrant smoke" [November 6]—was tobacco.) Similarly, the "whales" he spotted on October 16 must have been simply large fish, the "geese" he saw on November 6 and again on December 22 were ducks, the "nightingales" that kept delighting him (November 6; December 7, 13) do not exist in the Americas, and the skulls of "cows" he identified on October 29 were probably not those of land animals but of manatees.

This all seems a little sad, revealing a man rather lost in a world that he cannot come to know, a man with a "geographic and naturalistic knowledge that doesn't turn out to be very deep or nearly complete," and "a limited imagination and a capacity for comparisons conditioned by a not very broad geographic culture," in the words of Gaetano Ferro, a Columbus scholar and professor of geography at the University of Genoa. One could not of course have expected that an adventurer and sailor of this era would also be a naturalist, or necessarily even have some genuine interest in or curiosity about the natural world, but it is a disappointment nonetheless that the Discoverer of the New World turns out to be quite so simple, quite so inexperienced, in the ways of discovering his environment.

Colón's limitations, I hasten to say, were not his alone; they were of his culture, and they would be found in the descriptions of many others — Vespucci, Cortés, Hawkins, Juet, Cartier, Champlain, Raleigh — in the century of discovery to follow. They are the source of what the distinguished English historian J. H. Elliott has called "the problem of description" faced by Europeans confronting the uniqueness of the New World: "So often the physical appearance of the New World is either totally ignored or else described in the flattest and most conventional phraseology. This off-hand treatment of nature contrasts strikingly with the many precise and acute descriptions of the native inhabitants. It is as if the American landscape is seen as no more than a backcloth against which the strange and perennially fascinating peoples of the New World are dutifully grouped." The reason, Elliott thinks, and this is telling, may be "a lack of interest among sixteenth-century Europeans, and especially those of the Mediterranean world, in landscape and in nature." This lack of interest was reflected in the lack of vocabulary, the lack of that facility common to nature-based peoples whose cultures are steeped in natural imagery. Oviedo, for example, setting out to write descriptions for his *Historia General* in the next century, continually threw his hands up in the air: "Of all the things I have seen," he said at one point, "this is the one which has most left me without hope of being able to describe it in words"; or at another, "It needs to be painted by the hand of a Berruguete or some other excellent painter like him, or by Leonardo da Vinci or Andrea Mantegna, famous painters whom I knew in Italy." Like Colón, visitor after visitor to the New World seemed mind-boggled and tongue-tied trying to convey the wonders before them, and about the only color they seem to have eyes for is green — and not very many shades of that, either. . . .

■ REFLECTIONS

It is difficult to ignore moral issues when considering explorations and explorers. The prefix *great* is used liberally, and words like *discovery* and *courage* readily fit when describing "firsts" and "unknowns." However, celebratory images, national myths, and heroic biographies inevitably breed skepticism. Sometimes the result is an opposite assessment. Kirkpatrick Sale charges Columbus with arrogance, ignorance, and insufficient curiosity. Chinese historians of the last twenty years have swung from ignoring to celebrating the voyages of Zheng He, and some more recently have criticized Zheng He for military suppression of those in the lands his fleet visited.

On the matter of preparation, the difference between the Chinese and European voyages is especially striking. Da Gama at least brought an Arabic interpreter, though the absence of valuable gifts undermined the success of the voyage. The floating Chinese scientific laboratories, traveling experts, sages, and interpreters contrast starkly with the lack of a single artist or naturalist on board Columbus's ships. But the inability to distinguish shades of green is not a moral failure. We might say that Columbus's voyage was premature, Zheng He's meticulously planned and prepared. Like the designers of a modern aircraft, the Chinese built in redundancies: separate compartments that could fill with water without sinking the ship, more rice and fresh water than they would need, experts to find plants that might cure diseases yet unknown. By contrast, Columbus seems like a loose cannon, unaware of where he was going or where he had been, capable of lighting a match inside a dark powder shed.

These were, and in many ways still are, the differences between Chinese and European (now Western) scientific innovation. No European king could organize an enterprise on the scale of Zhu Di, Zheng He's emperor. No Chinese emperor had reason to sanction an experimental voyage into the unknown. The domain of the emperor was the known world, of which he was the center. In the Europe of closely competing princes, a Columbus could hatch a personal scheme with minimal supervision and barely sufficient funding and the consequences could still be—indeed, were—momentous. (See Chapter 16.) Was such a system irresponsible? Today, as we begin to probe the heavens around us, even as we tamper with technologies that change the balance of natural forces on Earth, we might consider whether the Confucian scholars of six hundred years ago were on to something when they burned the ships and destroyed all the records of their age of great discovery.

Primary sources are not limited to artifacts, images, and old written records, however. In the recent phase of celebrating the memory of Zheng He, the Chinese claimed as their own a young woman from Kenya, Mwamaka Sharifu, who looked like some of the people Kristof saw in 1999. Chinese-African faces on the coast of East Africa are evidence of contact, but not of contact in 1421. Combined, however, with family stories, DNA tests, local histories, and archaeological finds, a single living primary source may become the basis for a new interpretation of a broader history. In the case of Mwamaka Sharifu, members of her family, and other residents of coastal Somalia and Kenya, the evidence has proved convincing.

16

Atlantic World Encounters

Europeans, Americans, and Africans,
1500–1850

■ HISTORICAL CONTEXT

European expansion in the Atlantic that began with Portuguese
voyages along the African coast in the 1440s and Columbus's discovery
of the Americas in 1492 created a new Atlantic zone of human contact
and communication that embraced four continents and one ocean.
Nothing prior—neither the Chinese contacts with Africa in the early
fifteenth century, nor the expansion of Islam throughout Eurasia in the
almost thousand years since the Prophet Muhammad's death in
632—had so thoroughly and so permanently changed the human and
ecological balance of the world.

Sub-Saharan Africa had already been integrated into the world of
Eurasia by 1450. African populations became more mixed as peoples
from the Niger River area migrated east and south throughout the continent during the fifteen hundred years before the arrival of the Portuguese. Muslims from North Africa and the Middle East aided or
established Muslim states and trading ports south of the Sahara in East
and West Africa after 1000. Cultural and technical innovations of the
Middle East, like the literacy that came with Islam, penetrated slowly,
and the spread of the many plants and animals of the Northern Hemisphere was slowed by the Sahara and equator. However, microbes
traveled swiftly and easily from Eurasia to Africa, creating a single
set of diseases and immunities for the peoples of the Afro-Eurasian
Old World.

The peoples of the Americas, having been isolated ecologically for
more than ten thousand years, were not so fortunate. The arrival of
Europeans and Africans in the Americas after 1492 had devastating
consequences for Native American populations. Old World diseases like

Map 16.1 The Atlantic Slave Trade.

smallpox were responsible for millions of Native American deaths—a tragedy of far greater scope than the casualties caused by wars. To work the mines and plantations of the New World, Europeans used Indian labor, but increasingly, especially for lowland plantations, they used African slaves (see Map 16.1). By 1850 the combination of Indian "die-off" and African and European migration resulted in vastly different populations in the Americas. On some Caribbean islands and in plantation areas like northeastern Brazil, Indian populations were entirely replaced by Africans. At the same time, European animals (for example, goats, cattle, horses) multiplied in the absence of natural predators.

The new Atlantic ecological system was not a uniform zone, however. Coastal regions in Western Europe and towns on the eastern seaboard of the Americas prospered, while American interiors and African populations in Africa stagnated or declined. The Atlantic Ocean became a vast lake that united port cities and plantations with sailing ships that carried African slaves to the Caribbean, Caribbean sugar and rum to North American and European industrial ports, and guns, pots, and liquor to the African "Slave Coast."

Thus, the Atlantic world was integrated with the Old World. Trade routes that began in Boston or Bahia, Brazil, stretched across Eurasia and around southern Africa into the Indian Ocean and the China Sea. Crops that had previously been known only to Native Americans—corn, potatoes, and tomatoes—fueled population explosions from Ireland to China and graced the tables of peasants and princes in between. What began as an effort by European merchants to import Asian spices directly became after 1650 (as European tastes for pepper and Asian spices moderated) a new global pantry of possibilities.

In this chapter, we will read selections that describe this new global dynamic. We will read of Europeans in the Americas and in West Africa and examine European depictions of natives from both North and South America. We will also explore some of the African and American responses to this European expansion. When studying these accounts and images, notice how individuals at the frontier of a new age understood and treated each other. Consider how these exchanges, so apparently fortuitous and transitory at the time, changed the face of the world.

■ THINKING HISTORICALLY

Comparing Primary Sources

By comparing and contrasting one thing with another, we learn more about each, and by examining related works in their proper context, we learn more about the whole of which they are part. In the first chapter we compared China and Europe or Chinese and European

expansion in the fifteenth century. In this chapter we look at the
Atlantic world, specifically at Europeans in Africa and the Americas.
We begin with three views of the Spanish conquest of Mexico—
separate accounts by the Spanish conquistadors, by the Mexicans, and
by a Dominican friar. The fourth selection juxtaposes two European
depictions of Native Americans.

The final five selections examine encounters between Europeans and
Africans and the development of the Atlantic slave trade. Did Europeans
treat Africans differently from the way they treated Native Americans? If
so, why? How were the African reactions to Europeans different from the
Native American reactions? What accounts for those differences?

1

BERNAL DÍAZ

The Conquest of New Spain, c. 1560

Bernal Díaz del Castillo was born in Spain in 1492, the year
Columbus sailed to America. After participating in two explorations
of the Mexican coast, Díaz joined the expedition of Hernán Cortés to
Mexico City in 1519. He wrote this history of the conquest much
later, when he was in his seventies; he died circa 1580, a municipal
official with a small estate in Guatemala.

The conquest of Mexico did not automatically follow from the first
Spanish settlements in Santo Domingo, Hispaniola, and then Cuba in
the West Indies. The Spanish crown had given permission for trade
and exploration, not colonization. But many Spaniards, from fortune-
seeking peasant-soldiers to minor nobility, were eager to conquer their
own lands and exploit the populations of dependent Indians.

Cortés, of minor noble descent, at the age of nineteen sailed to the
Indies, where he established a sizeable estate on the island of
Hispaniola. When he heard stories of Montezuma's gold, he was determined to find the fabled capital of the Aztec Empire, Tenochtitlán*
(modern Mexico City). He gathered more than five hundred amateur
soldiers, eleven ships, sixteen horses, and several pieces of artillery, then
sailed across the Caribbean and Gulf of Mexico and there began the
long march from the coast up to the high central plateau of Mexico.

* teh NOHCH teet LAHN

Source: Bernal Díaz, *The Conquest of New Spain*, trans. J. M. Cohen (Baltimore: Penguin
Books, 1963), 217–19, 221–25, 228–38, 241–43.

The Aztecs were new to central Mexico, arriving from the North American desert only about two hundred years before the Spanish, around 1325. By 1500 they had established dominion over almost all other city-states of Mexico, ruling an empire that stretched as far south as Guatemala and as far east as the Maya lands of the Yucatan Peninsula.

Aztec power relied on a combination of old and new religious ideas and a military system that conquered through terror. The older religious tradition that the Aztecs adopted from Toltec culture centered on Quetzalcoatl*—the feathered serpent, god of creation and brotherhood, whose nurturing forces continued in Aztec society in a system of universal education and in festivals dedicated to life, creativity, and procreation. But the Aztecs also worshiped Huitzilopochtli,[†] a warrior-god primed for death and sacrifice, who was given dominant status in the Aztec pantheon. Huitzilopochtli (rendered "Huichilobos"[‡] in this selection) was a force for building a powerful Aztec Empire. Drawing on the god's need for human sacrifice—a need not unknown among religions of central Mexico (or Christians)—Montezuma's predecessors built altars to Huitzilopochtli at Tenochtitlán, Cholula, and other sites. The war-god required a never-ending supply of human hearts, a need that prompted armies to ever-more remote sections of Central America in search of sacrificial victims and that created an endless supply of enemies of the Aztecs, among them, the Tlaxcalans.

With the help of his Indian captive and companion Doña Marina—called La Malinche[§] by some of the Indians (thus, Montezuma sometimes calls Cortés "Lord Malinche" in the selection)—Cortés was able to communicate with the Tlaxcalans and other Indians who were tired of Aztec domination. On his march toward Tenochtitlán, Cortés stopped to join forces with the Tlaxcalans, perhaps cementing the relationship and demonstrating his resolve through a brutal massacre of the people of Cholula, an Aztec ally and archenemy of the Tlaxcalans. By the time Cortés arrived at Tenochtitlán, Montezuma knew of the defeat of his allies at Cholula.

This selection from Bernal Díaz begins with the Spanish entry into Tenochtitlán. What impresses Díaz, and presumably other Spanish conquistadors, about the Mexican capital city? What parts of the city attract his attention the most? What conclusions does he draw about Mexican (or Aztec) civilization? Does he think Spanish civilization is equal, inferior, or superior to that of Mexico?

* keht zahl koh AH tuhl
[†] wheat zee loh po ACHT lee
[‡] wee chee LOH bohs
[§] lah mah LEEN cheh   A variation on "Marina." In contemporary Mexico a traitor is often called a "Malinchisto."

Díaz gives us a dramatic account of the meeting of Cortés and Montezuma. What do you think each is thinking and feeling? Do you see any signs of tension in their elaborate greetings? Why are both behaving so politely? What do they want from each other?

Notice how the initial hospitality turns tense. What causes this? Is either side more to blame for what happens next? Was conflict inevitable? Could the encounter have ended in some sort of peaceful resolution?

THINKING HISTORICALLY

Remember, we are going to compare Díaz's view with a Mexican view of these events. From your reading of Díaz, does he seem able to understand the Mexican point of view? Would you call him a sympathetic observer?

When Cortes saw, heard, and was told that the great Montezuma was approaching, he dismounted from his horse, and when he came near to Montezuma each bowed deeply to the other. Montezuma welcomed our Captain, and Cortes, speaking through Doña Marina, answered by wishing him very good health. Cortes, I think, offered Montezuma his right hand, but Montezuma refused it and extended his own. Then Cortes brought out a necklace which he had been holding. It was made of those elaborately worked and coloured glass beads called *margaritas*, . . . and was strung on a gold cord and dipped in musk to give it a good odour. This he hung round the great Montezuma's neck, and as he did so attempted to embrace him. But the great princes who stood round Montezuma grasped Cortes' arm to prevent him, for they considered this an indignity.

Then Cortes told Montezuma that it rejoiced his heart to have seen such a great prince, and that he took his coming in person to receive him and the repeated favours he had done him as a high honour. After this Montezuma made him another complimentary speech, and ordered two of his nephews who were supporting him, the lords of Texcoco and Coyoacan, to go with us and show us our quarters. Montezuma returned to the city with the other two kinsmen of his escort, the lords of Cuitlahuac and Tacuba; and all those grand companies of *Caciques*[1] and dignitaries who had come with him returned also in his train. . . .

On our arrival we entered the large court, where the great Montezuma was awaiting our Captain. Taking him by the hand, the prince led him

---

[1] kah SEEK Chiefs. [Ed.]

to his apartment in the hall where he was to lodge, which was very richly furnished in their manner. Montezuma had ready for him a very rich necklace, made of golden crabs, a marvellous piece of work, which he hung round Cortes' neck. His captains were greatly astonished at this sign of honour.

After this ceremony, for which Cortes thanked him through our interpreters, Montezuma said: "Malinche, you and your brothers are in your own house. Rest a while." He then returned to his palace, which was not far off.

We divided our lodgings by companies, and placed our artillery in a convenient spot. Then the order we were to keep was clearly explained to us, and we were warned to be very much on the alert, both the horsemen and the rest of us soldiers. We then ate a sumptuous dinner which they had prepared for us in their native style.

So, with luck on our side, we boldly entered the city of Tenochtitlán or Mexico on 8 November in the year of our Lord 1519.

The Stay in Mexico

. . . Montezuma had ordered his stewards to provide us with everything we needed for our way of living: maize, grindstones, women to make our bread, fowls, fruit, and plenty of fodder for the horses. He then took leave of us all with the greatest courtesy, and we accompanied him to the street. However, Cortes ordered us not to go far from our quarters for the present until we knew better what conduct to observe.

Next day Cortes decided to go to Montezuma's palace. But first he sent to know whether the prince was busy and to inform him of our coming. He took four captains with him: Pedro de Alvarado, Juan Velazquez de Leon, Diego de Ordaz, and Gonzalo de Sandoval, and five of us soldiers.

When Montezuma was informed of our coming, he advanced into the middle of the hall to receive us, closely surrounded by his nephews, for no other chiefs were allowed to enter his palace or communicate with him except upon important business. Cortes and Montezuma exchanged bows, and clasped hands. Then Montezuma led Cortes to his own dais, and setting him down on his right, called for more seats, on which he ordered us all to sit also.

Cortes began to make a speech through our interpreters, saying that we were all now rested, and that in coming to see and speak with such a great prince we had fulfilled the purpose of our voyage and the orders of our lord the King. The principal things he had come to say on behalf of our Lord God had already been communicated to Montezuma through his three ambassadors, on that occasion in the sandhills when he did us the favour of sending us the golden moon and sun. We had then told him that we were Christians and worshipped one God alone, named

Jesus Christ, who had suffered His passion and death to save us; and that what they worshipped as gods were not gods but devils, which were evil things, and if they were ugly to look at, their deeds were uglier. But he had proved to them how evil and ineffectual their gods were, as both the prince and his people would observe in the course of time, since, where we had put up crosses such as their ambassadors had seen, they had been too frightened to appear before them.

The favour he now begged of the great Montezuma was that he should listen to the words he now wished to speak. Then he very carefully expounded the creation of the world, how we are all brothers, the children of one mother and father called Adam and Eve; and how such a brother as our great Emperor, grieving for the perdition of so many souls as their idols were leading to hell, where they burnt in living flame, had sent us to tell him this, so that he might put a stop to it, and so that they might give up the worship of idols and make no more human sacrifices—for all men are brothers—and commit no more robbery or sodomy. He also promised that in the course of time the King would send some men who lead holy lives among us, much better than our own, to explain this more fully, for we had only come to give them warning. Therefore he begged Montezuma to do as he was asked.

As Montezuma seemed about to reply, Cortes broke off his speech, saying to those of us who were with him: "Since this is only the first attempt, we have now done our duty."

"My lord Malinche," Montezuma replied, "these arguments of yours have been familiar to me for some time. I understand what you said to my ambassadors on the sandhills about the three gods and the cross, also what you preached in the various towns through which you passed. We have given you no answer, since we have worshipped our own gods here from the beginning and know them to be good. No doubt yours are good also, but do not trouble to tell us any more about them at present. Regarding the creation of the world, we have held the same belief for many ages, and for this reason are certain that you are those who our ancestors predicted would come from the direction of the sunrise. As for your great King, I am in his debt and will give him of what I possess. For, as I have already said, two years ago I had news of the Captains who came in ships, by the road that you came, and said they were servants of this great king of yours. I should like to know if you are all the same people."

Cortes answered that we were all brothers and servants of the Emperor, and that they had come to discover a route and explore the seas and ports, so that when they knew them well we could follow, as we had done. Montezuma was referring to the expeditions of Francisco Hernandez de Cordoba and of Grijalva, the first voyages of discovery. He said that ever since that time he had wanted to invite some of these men to visit the cities of his kingdom, where he would receive them and do them honour, and that now his gods had fulfilled his desire, for we were in his house, which we might call our own. Here we might rest and enjoy ourselves, for we should receive good treatment. If on other occasions he had sent to forbid our entrance into his city, it was not of his own free will, but because his vassals were afraid. For they told him we shot out flashes of lightning, and killed many Indians with our horses, and that we were angry *Teules*,[2] and other such childish stories. But now that he had seen us, he knew that we were of flesh and blood and very intelligent, also very brave. Therefore he had a far greater esteem for us than these reports had given him, and would share with us what he had.

We all thanked him heartily for his . . . good will, and Montezuma replied with a laugh, because in his princely manner he spoke very gaily: "Malinche, I know that these people of Tlascala with whom you are so friendly have told you that I am a sort of god or *Teule*, and keep nothing in any of my houses that is not made of silver and gold and precious stones. But I know very well that you are too intelligent to believe this and will take it as a joke. See now, Malinche, my body is made of flesh and blood like yours, and my houses and palaces are of stone, wood, and plaster. It is true that I am a great king, and have inherited the riches of my ancestors, but the lies and nonsense you have heard of us are not true. You must take them as a joke, as I take the story of your thunders and lightnings."

Cortes answered also with a laugh that enemies always speak evil and tell lies about the people they hate, but he knew he could not hope to find a more magnificent prince in that land, and there was good reason why his fame should have reached our Emperor.

While this conversation was going on, Montezuma quietly sent one of his nephews, a great *Cacique*, to order his stewards to bring certain pieces of gold, which had apparently been set aside as a gift for Cortes, and ten loads of fine cloaks which he divided: the gold and cloaks between Cortes and the four captains, and for each of us soldiers two gold necklaces, each worth ten pesos, and two loads of cloaks. The gold that he then gave us was worth in all more than a thousand pesos, and he gave it all cheerfully, like a great and valiant prince.

As it was now past midday and he did not wish to be importunate, Cortes said to Montezuma: "My lord, the favours you do us increase, load by load, every day, and it is now the hour of your dinner." Montezuma answered that he thanked us for visiting him. We then took our leave with the greatest courtesy, and returned to our quarters, talking as we went of the prince's fine breeding and manners and deciding to show him the greatest respect in every way, and to remove our quilted caps in his presence, which we always did.

[2] Gods. [Ed.]

The great Montezuma was about forty years old, of good height, well proportioned, spare and slight, and not very dark, though of the usual Indian complexion. He did not wear his hair long but just over his ears, and he had a short black beard, well-shaped and thin. His face was rather long and cheerful, he had fine eyes, and in his appearance and manner could express geniality or, when necessary, a serious composure. He was very neat and clean, and took a bath every afternoon. He had many women as his mistresses, the daughters of chieftains, but two legitimate wives who were *Caciques* in their own right, and when he had intercourse with any of them it was so secret that only some of his servants knew of it. He was quite free from sodomy. The clothes he wore one day he did not wear again till three or four days later. He had a guard of two hundred chieftains lodged in rooms beside his own, only some of whom were permitted to speak to him. When they entered his presence they were compelled to take off their rich cloaks and put on others of little value. They had to be clean and walk barefoot, with their eyes downcast, for they were not allowed to look him in the face, and as they approached they had to make three obeisances, saying as they did so, "Lord, my lord, my great lord!" Then, when they had said what they had come to say, he would dismiss them with a few words. They did not turn their backs on him as they went out, but kept their faces towards him and their eyes downcast, only turning round when they had left the room. Another thing I noticed was that when other great chiefs came from distant lands about disputes or on business, they too had to take off their shoes and put on poor cloaks before entering Montezuma's apartments; and they were not allowed to enter the palace immediately but had to linger for a while near the door, since to enter hurriedly was considered disrespectful. . . .

Montezuma had two houses stocked with every sort of weapon; many of them were richly adorned with gold and precious stones. There were shields large and small, and a sort of broadsword, and two-handed swords set with flint blades that cut much better than our swords, and lances longer than ours, with five-foot blades consisting of many knives. Even when these are driven at a buckler or a shield they are not deflected. In fact they cut like razors, and the Indians can shave their heads with them. They had very good bows and arrows, and double and single-pointed javelins as well as their throwing-sticks and many slings and round stones shaped by hand, and another sort of shield that can be rolled up when they are not fighting, so that it does not get in the way, but which can be opened when they need it in battle and covers their bodies from head to foot. There was also a great deal of cotton armour richly worked on the outside with different coloured feathers, which they used as devices and distinguishing marks, and they had casques and helmets made of wood and bone which were also highly decorated with feathers on the outside. They had other arms of different kinds which I will not mention through fear of prolixity, and workmen skilled in the manufacture of such things, and stewards who were in charge of these arms. . . .

I have already described the manner of their sacrifices. They strike open the wretched Indian's chest with flint knives and hastily tear out the palpitating heart which, with the blood, they present to the idols in whose name they have performed the sacrifice. Then they cut off the arms, thighs, and head, eating the arms and thighs at their ceremonial banquets. The head they hang up on a beam, and the body of the sacrificed man is not eaten but given to the beasts of prey. They also had many vipers in this accursed house, and poisonous snakes which have something that sounds like a bell in their tails. These, which are the deadliest snakes of all, they kept in jars and great pottery vessels full of feathers, in which they laid their eggs and reared their young. They were fed on the bodies of sacrificed Indians and the flesh of the dogs that they bred. We know for certain, too, that when they drove us out of Mexico and killed over eight hundred and fifty of our soldiers, they fed those beasts and snakes on their bodies for many days, as I shall relate in due course. These snakes and wild beasts were dedicated to their fierce idols, and kept them company. As for the horrible noise when the lions and tigers roared, and the jackals and foxes howled, and the serpents hissed, it was so appalling that one seemed to be in hell. . . .

When our Captain and the Mercedarian friar realized that Montezuma would not allow us to set up a cross at Huichilobos' *cue*[3] or build a church there, it was decided that we should ask his stewards for masons so that we could put up a church in our own quarters. For every time we had said mass since entering the city of Mexico we had had to erect an altar on tables and dismantle it again.

The stewards promised to tell Montezuma of our wishes, and Cortes also sent our interpreters to ask him in person. Montezuma granted our request and ordered that we should be supplied with all the necessary material. We had our church finished in two days, and a cross erected in front of our lodgings, and mass was said there each day until the wine gave out. For as Cortes and some other captains and a friar had been ill during the Tlascalan campaign, there had been a run on the wine that we kept for mass. Still, though it was finished, we still went to church every day and prayed on our knees before the altar and images, firstly because it was our obligation as Christians and a good habit, and secondly so that Montezuma and all his captains should observe us and, seeing us worshipping on our knees before the cross—especially when we intoned the Ave Maria—might be inclined to imitate us.

It being our habit to examine and inquire into everything, when we were all assembled in our lodging and considering which was the best place for an altar, two of our men, one of whom was the carpenter

[3] The temple of the sun-god, who demanded human sacrifice. [Ed.]

Alonso Yañez, called attention to some marks on one of the walls which showed that there had once been a door, though it had been well plastered up and painted. Now as we had heard that Montezuma kept his father's treasure in this building, we immediately suspected that it must be in this room, which had been closed up only a few days before. Yañez made the suggestion to Juan Velazquez de Leon and Francisco de Lugo, both relatives of mine, to whom he had attached himself as a servant; and they mentioned the matter to Cortes. So the door was secretly opened, and Cortes went in first with certain captains. When they saw the quantity of golden objects—jewels and plates and ingots—which lay in that chamber they were quite transported. They did not know what to think of such riches. The news soon spread to the other captains and soldiers, and very secretly we all went in to see. The sight of all that wealth dumbfounded me. Being only a youth at the time and never having seen such riches before, I felt certain that there could not be a store like it in the whole world. We unanimously decided that we could not think of touching a particle of it, and that the stones should immediately be replaced in the doorway, which should be blocked again and cemented just as we had found it. We resolved also that not a word should be said about this until times changed, for fear Montezuma might hear of our discovery.

Let us leave this subject of the treasure and tell how four of our most valiant captains took Cortes aside in the church, with a dozen soldiers who were in his trust and confidence, myself among them, and asked him to consider the net or trap in which we were caught, to look at the great strength of the city and observe the causeways and bridges, and remember the warnings we had received in every town we had passed through that Huichilobos had counselled Montezuma to let us into the city and kill us there. We reminded him that the hearts of men are very fickle, especially among the Indians, and begged him not to trust the good will and affection that Montezuma was showing us, because from one hour to another it might change. If he should take it into his head to attack us, we said, the stoppage of our supplies of food and water, or the raising of any of the bridges, would render us helpless. Then, considering the vast army of warriors he possessed, we should be incapable of attacking or defending ourselves. And since all the houses stood in the water, how could our Tlascalan allies come in to help us? We asked him to think over all that we had said, for if we wanted to preserve our lives we must seize Montezuma immediately, without even a day's delay. We pointed out that all the gold Montezuma had given us, and all that we had seen in the treasury of his father Axayacatl, and all the food we ate was turning to poison in our bodies, for we could not sleep by night or day or take any rest while these thoughts were in our minds. If any of our soldiers gave him less drastic advice, we concluded, they would be senseless beasts charmed by the gold and incapable of looking death in the eye.

When he had heard our opinion, Cortes answered: "Do not imagine, gentlemen, that I am asleep or that I do not share your anxiety. You must have seen that I do. But what strength have we got for so bold a course as to take this great lord in his own palace, surrounded as he is by warriors and guards? What scheme or trick can we devise to prevent him from summoning his soldiers to attack us at once?"

Our captains (Juan Velazquez de Leon, Diego de Ordaz, Gonzalo de Sandoval, and Pedro de Alvarado) replied that Montezuma must be got out of his palace by smooth words and brought to our quarters. Once there, he must be told that he must remain as a prisoner, and that if he called out or made any disturbance he would pay for it with his life. If Cortes was unwilling to take this course at once, they begged him for permission to do it themselves. With two very dangerous alternatives before us, the better and more profitable thing, they said, would be to seize Montezuma rather than wait for him to attack us. Once he did so, what chance would we have? Some of us soldiers also remarked that Montezuma's stewards who brought us our food seemed to be growing insolent, and did not serve us as politely as they had at first. Two of our Tlascalan allies had, moreover, secretly observed to Jeronimo de Aguilar that for the last two days the Mexicans had appeared less well disposed to us. We spent a good hour discussing whether or not to take Montezuma prisoner, and how it should be done. But our final advice, that at all costs we should take him prisoner, was approved by our Captain, and we then left the matter till next day. All night we prayed God to direct events in the interests of His holy service. . . .

2

The Broken Spears: The Aztec Account of the Conquest of Mexico, c. 1540s

This Aztec account, one of several written by native priests and wise men of the encounter between the Spanish and the Indians of Mexico, was written some years after the events described. Spanish Christian monks helped a postconquest generation of Aztec Nahuatl* speakers translate the illustrated manuscripts of the conquest period. According to this account, how did Montezuma respond to Cortés?

*nah WAH tuhl

Source: *The Broken Spears: The Aztec Account of the Conquest of Mexico*, ed. Miguel Leon-Portilla (Boston: Beacon Press, 1990), 64–76.

Was Montezuma's attitude toward the Spanish shared by other Aztecs? How reliable is this account, do you think, in describing Montezuma's thoughts, motives, and behavior?

THINKING HISTORICALLY

How does the Aztec account of the conquest differ from that of the Spanish, written by Díaz? Is this difference merely a matter of perspective, or do the authors disagree about what happened? To the extent to which there are differences, how do you decide which account to believe and accept?

Speeches of Motecuhzoma and Cortes

When Motecuhzoma[1] had given necklaces to each one, Cortes asked him: "Are you Motecuhzoma? Are you the king? Is it true that you are the king Motecuhzoma?"

And the king said: "Yes, I am Motecuhzoma." Then he stood up to welcome Cortes; he came forward, bowed his head low and addressed him in these words: "Our lord, you are weary. The journey has tired you, but now you have arrived on the earth. You have come to your city, Mexico. You have come here to sit on your throne, to sit under its canopy.

"The kings who have gone before, your representatives, guarded it and preserved it for your coming. The kings Itzcoatl, Motecuhzoma the Elder, Axayacatl, Tizoc, and Ahuitzol ruled for you in the City of Mexico. The people were protected by their swords and sheltered by their shields.

"Do the kings know the destiny of those they left behind, their posterity? If only they are watching! If only they can see what I see!

"No, it is not a dream. I am not walking in my sleep. I am not seeing you in my dreams. . . . I have seen you at last! I have met you face to face! I was in agony for five days, for ten days, with my eyes fixed on the Region of the Mystery. And now you have come out of the clouds and mists to sit on your throne again.

"This was foretold by the kings who governed your city, and now it has taken place. You have come back to us; you have come down from the sky. Rest now, and take possession of your royal houses. Welcome to your land, my lords!"

When Motecuhzoma had finished, La Malinche translated his address into Spanish so that the Captain could understand it. Cortes replied in his strange and savage tongue, speaking first to La Malinche: "Tell

---

[1] Montezuma (earlier spelling). [Ed.]

Motecuhzoma that we are his friends. There is nothing to fear. We have wanted to see him for a long time, and now we have seen his face and heard his words. Tell him that we love him well and that our hearts are contented."

Then he said to Motecuhzoma: "We have come to your house in Mexico as friends. There is nothing to fear."

La Malinche translated this speech and the Spaniards grasped Motecuhzoma's hands and patted his back to show their affection for him.

Attitudes of the Spaniards and the Native Lords

The Spaniards examined everything they saw. They dismounted from their horses, and mounted them again, and dismounted again, so as not to miss anything of interest.

The chiefs who accompanied Motecuhzoma were: Cacama, king of Tezcoco; Tetlepanquetzaltzin, king of Tlacopan; Itzcuauhtzin the Tlacochcalcatl, lord of Tlatelolco; and Topantemoc, Motecuhzoma's treasurer in Tlatelolco. These four chiefs were standing in a file.

The other princes were: Atlixcatzin [chief who has taken captives];[2] Tepeoatzin, the Tlacochcalcatl; Quetzalaztatzin, the keeper of the chalk; Totomotzin; Hecateupatiltzin; and Cuappiatzin.

When Motecuhzoma was imprisoned, they all went into hiding. They ran away to hide and treacherously abandoned him!

The Spaniards Take Possession of the City

When the Spaniards entered the Royal House, they placed Motecuhzoma under guard and kept him under their vigilance. They also placed a guard over Itzcuauhtzin, but the other lords were permitted to depart.

Then the Spaniards fired one of their cannons, and this caused great confusion in the city. The people scattered in every direction; they fled without rhyme or reason; they ran off as if they were being pursued. It was as if they had eaten the mushrooms that confuse the mind, or had seen some dreadful apparition. They were all overcome by terror, as if their hearts had fainted. And when night fell, the panic spread through the city and their fears would not let them sleep.

In the morning the Spaniards told Motecuhzoma what they needed in the way of supplies: tortillas, fried chickens, hens' eggs, pure water, firewood, and charcoal. Also: large, clean cooking pots, water jars, pitchers, dishes, and other pottery. Motecuhzoma ordered that it be sent to them.

---

[2] Military title given to a warrior who had captured four enemies.

The chiefs who received this order were angry with the king and no longer revered or respected him. But they furnished the Spaniards with all the provisions they needed — food, beverages, and water, and fodder for the horses.

The Spaniards Reveal Their Greed

When the Spaniards were installed in the palace, they asked Motecuhzoma about the city's resources and reserves and about the warriors' ensigns and shields. They questioned him closely and then demanded gold.

Motecuhzoma guided them to it. They surrounded him and crowded close with their weapons. He walked in the center, while they formed a circle around him.

When they arrived at the treasure house called Teucalco, the riches of gold and feathers were brought out to them: ornaments made of quetzal feathers, richly worked shields, disks of gold, the necklaces of the idols, gold nose plugs, gold greaves,[3] and bracelets and crowns.

The Spaniards immediately stripped the feathers from the gold shields and ensigns. They gathered all the gold into a great mound and set fire to everything else, regardless of its value. Then they melted down the gold into ingots. As for the precious green stones, they took only the best of them; the rest were snatched up by the Tlaxcaltecas. The Spaniards searched through the whole treasure house, questioning and quarreling, and seized every object they thought was beautiful.

The Seizure of Motecuhzoma's Treasures

Next they went to Motecuhzoma's storehouse, in the place called Totocalco [Place of the Palace of the Birds],[4] where his personal treasures were kept. The Spaniards grinned like little beasts and patted each other with delight.

When they entered the hall of treasures, it was as if they had arrived in Paradise. They searched everywhere and coveted everything; they were slaves to their own greed. All of Motecuhzoma's possessions were brought out: fine bracelets, necklaces with large stones, ankle rings with little gold bells, the royal crowns, and all the royal finery — everything that belonged to the king and was reserved to him only. They seized these treasures as if they were their own, as if this plunder were merely a stroke of good luck. And when they had taken all the gold, they heaped up everything else in the middle of the patio.

[3] Leg armour. [Ed.]
[4] The zoological garden attached to the royal palaces.

La Malinche called the nobles together. She climbed up to the palace roof and cried: "Mexicanos, come forward! The Spaniards need your help! Bring them food and pure water. They are tired and hungry; they are almost fainting from exhaustion! Why do you not come forward? Are you angry with them?"

The Mexicans were too frightened to approach. They were crushed by terror and would not risk coming forward. They shied away as if the Spaniards were wild beasts, as if the hour were midnight on the blackest night of the year. Yet they did not abandon the Spaniards to hunger and thirst. They brought them whatever they needed, but shook with fear as they did so. They delivered the supplies to the Spaniards with trembling hands, then turned and hurried away.

The Preparations for the Fiesta

The Aztecs begged permission of their king to hold the fiesta of Huitzilopochtli.[5] The Spaniards wanted to see this fiesta to learn how it was celebrated. A delegation of the celebrants came to the palace where Motecuhzoma was a prisoner, and when their spokesman asked his permission, he granted it to them.

As soon as the delegation returned, the women began to grind seeds of the *chicalote*.[6] These women had fasted for a whole year. They ground the seeds in the patio of the temple.

The Spaniards came out of the palace together, dressed in armor and carrying their weapons with them. They stalked among the women and looked at them one by one; they stared into the faces of the women who were grinding seeds. After this cold inspection, they went back into the palace. It is said that they planned to kill the celebrants if the men entered the patio.

The Statue of Huitzilopochtli

On the evening before the fiesta of Toxcatl, the celebrants began to model a statue of Huitzilopochtli. They gave it such a human appearance that it seemed the body of a living man. Yet they made the statue with nothing but a paste made of the ground seeds of the chicalote, which they shaped over an armature of sticks.

When the statue was finished, they dressed it in rich feathers, and they painted crossbars over and under its eyes. They also clipped on its

---

[5] Aztec war-god. See Introduction to selections. [Ed.]
[6] Edible plants also used in medicines. [Ed.]

earrings of turquoise mosaic; these were in the shape of serpents, with gold rings hanging from them. Its nose plug, in the shape of an arrow, was made of gold and was inlaid with fine stones.

They placed the magic headdress of hummingbird feathers on its head. They also adorned it with an *anecuyotl*, which was a belt made of feathers, with a cone at the back. Then they hung around its neck an ornament of yellow parrot feathers, fringed like the locks of a young boy. Over this they put its nettle-leaf cape, which was painted black and decorated with five clusters of eagle feathers.

Next they wrapped it in its cloak, which was painted with skull and bones, and over this they fastened its vest. The vest was painted with dismembered human parts: skulls, ears, hearts, intestines, torsos, breasts, hands, and feet. They also put on its *maxtlatl*, or loincloth, which was decorated with images of dissevered limbs and fringed with amate paper. This *maxtlatl* was painted with vertical stripes of bright blue.

They fastened a red paper flag at its shoulder and placed on its head what looked like a sacrificial flint knife. This too was made of red paper; it seemed to have been steeped in blood.

The statue carried a *tehuehuelli*, a bamboo shield decorated with four clusters of fine eagle feathers. The pendant of this shield was blood-red, like the knife and the shoulder flag. The statue also carried four arrows.

Finally, they put the wristbands on its arms. These bands, made of coyote skin, were fringed with paper cut into little strips.

The Beginning of the Fiesta

Early the next morning, the statue's face was uncovered by those who had been chosen for that ceremony. They gathered in front of the idol in single file and offered it gifts of food, such as round seedcakes or perhaps human flesh. But they did not carry it up to its temple on top of the pyramid.

All the young warriors were eager for the fiesta to begin. They had sworn to dance and sing with all their hearts, so that the Spaniards would marvel at the beauty of the rituals.

The procession began, and the celebrants filed into the temple patio to dance the Dance of the Serpent. When they were all together in the patio, the songs and the dance began. Those who had fasted for twenty days and those who had fasted for a year were in command of the others; they kept the dancers in file with their pine wands. (If anyone wished to urinate, he did not stop dancing, but simply opened his clothing at the hips and separated his clusters of heron feathers.)

If anyone disobeyed the leaders or was not in his proper place they struck him on the hips and shoulders. Then they drove him out of the patio, beating him and shoving him from behind. They pushed him so hard that he sprawled to the ground, and they dragged him outside by the ears. No one dared to say a word about this punishment, for those who had fasted during the year were feared and venerated; they had earned the exclusive title "Brothers of Huitzilopochtli."

The great captains, the bravest warriors, danced at the head of the files to guide the others. The youths followed at a slight distance. Some of the youths wore their hair gathered into large locks, a sign that they had never taken any captives. Others carried their headdresses on their shoulders; they had taken captives, but only with help.

Then came the recruits, who were called "the young warriors." They had each captured an enemy or two. The others called to them: "Come, comrades, show us how brave you are! Dance with all your hearts!"

The Spaniards Attack the Celebrants

At this moment in the fiesta, when the dance was loveliest and when song was linked to song, the Spaniards were seized with an urge to kill the celebrants. They all ran forward, armed as if for battle. They closed the entrances and passageways, all the gates of the patio: the Eagle Gate in the lesser palace, the Gate of the Canestalk and the Gate of the Serpent of Mirrors. They posted guards so that no one could escape, and then rushed into the Sacred Patio to slaughter the celebrants. They came on foot, carrying their swords and their wooden or metal shields.

They ran in among the dancers, forcing their way to the place where the drums were played. They attacked the man who was drumming and cut off his arms. Then they cut off his head, and it rolled across the floor.

They attacked all the celebrants, stabbing them, spearing them, striking them with their swords. They attacked some of them from behind, and these fell instantly to the ground with their entrails hanging out. Others they beheaded: they cut off their heads, or split their heads to pieces.

They struck others in the shoulders, and their arms were torn from their bodies. They wounded some in the thigh and some in the calf.

They slashed others in the abdomen, and their entrails all spilled to the ground. Some attempted to run away, but their intestines dragged as they ran; they seemed to tangle their feet in their own entrails. No matter how they tried to save themselves, they could find no escape.

Some attempted to force their way out, but the Spaniards murdered them at the gates. Others climbed the walls, but they could not save themselves. Those who ran into the communal houses were safe there for a while; so were those who lay down among the victims and pretended to be dead. But if they stood up again, the Spaniards saw them and killed them.

The blood of the warriors flowed like water and gathered into pools. The pools widened, and the stench of blood and entrails filled the air. The Spaniards ran into the communal houses to kill those who were hiding. They ran everywhere and searched everywhere; they invaded every room, hunting and killing.

3

BARTOLOMÉ DE LAS CASAS

The Devastation of the Indies, 1555

Las Casas (1484–1566) emigrated with his father from Spain to the island of Hispaniola in 1502. Eight years later he became a priest, served as a missionary to the Taino of Cuba (1512), attempted to create a utopian society for the Indians of Venezuela, and became a Dominican friar in 1522. Repelled by his early experience among the conquistadors, Las Casas the priest and friar devoted his adult life to aiding the Indians in the Americas and defending their rights in the Spanish court. This selection is drawn from his brief history, *The Devastation of the Indies*, published in 1555. The work for this book and a larger volume, *In Defense of the Indians*, presented his case against Indian slavery in the great debate at the Spanish court at Valladolid in 1550. Along with his monumental *History of the Indies*, published after his death, the writings of Las Casas constituted such an indictment of Spanish colonialism that Protestant enemies were able to argue that Catholic slavery and exploitation of the "New World" was worse than their own, a dubious proposition that became known as "the Black Legend." What do you make of this account by Las Casas? Does he exaggerate, or is it likely that these events happened?

THINKING HISTORICALLY

Compare this account with the two previous selections. Do you think the Spanish treated the people of Hispaniola and Mexico differently? Do these three readings offer different interpretations of the role of Christianity in the Americas?

Source: Bartolomé de Las Casas, *The Devastation of the Indies: A Brief Account*, trans. Herma Briffault (Baltimore: Johns Hopkins University Press, 1992), 32–35, 40–41.

This [Hispaniola][1] was the first land in the New World to be destroyed and depopulated by the Christians, and here they began their subjection of the women and children, taking them away from the Indians to use them and ill use them, eating the food they provided with their sweat and toil. The Spaniards did not content themselves with what the Indians gave them of their own free will, according to their ability, which was always too little to satisfy enormous appetites, for a Christian eats and consumes in one day an amount of food that would suffice to feed three houses inhabited by ten Indians for one month. And they committed other acts of force and violence and oppression which made the Indians realize that these men had not come from Heaven. And some of the Indians concealed their foods while others concealed their wives and children and still others fled to the mountains to avoid the terrible transactions of the Christians.

And the Christians attacked them with buffets and beatings, until finally they laid hands on the nobles of the villages. Then they behaved with such temerity and shamelessness that the most powerful ruler of the islands had to see his own wife raped by a Christian officer.

From that time onward the Indians began to seek ways to throw the Christians out of their lands. They took up arms, but their weapons were very weak and of little service in offense and still less in defense. (Because of this, the wars of the Indians against each other are little more than games played by children.) And the Christians, with their horses and swords and pikes began to carry out massacres and strange cruelties against them. They attacked the towns and spared neither the children nor the aged nor pregnant women nor women in childbed, not only stabbing them and dismembering them but cutting them to pieces as if dealing with sheep in the slaughter house. They laid bets as to who, with one stroke of the sword, could split a man in two or could cut off his head or spill out his entrails with a single stroke of the pike. They took infants from their mothers' breasts, snatching them by the legs and pitching them headfirst against the crags or snatched them by the arms and threw them into the rivers, roaring with laughter and saying as the babies fell into the water, "Boil there, you offspring of the devil!" Other infants they put to the sword along with their mothers and anyone else who happened to be nearby. They made some low wide gallows on which the hanged victim's feet almost touched the ground, stringing up their victims in lots of thirteen, in memory of Our Redeemer and His twelve Apostles, then set burning wood at their feet and thus burned them alive. To others they attached straw or wrapped their whole bodies in straw and set them afire. With still others, all those they wanted to capture alive, they cut off their hands and hung them round the victim's neck, saying, "Go now, carry the message," meaning, Take the news to the Indians who have fled to the

---

[1] The island that today includes the Dominican Republic and Haiti. [Ed.]

mountains. They usually dealt with the chieftains and nobles in the following way: they made a grid of rods which they placed on forked sticks, then lashed the victims to the grid and lighted a smoldering fire underneath, so that little by little, as those captives screamed in despair and torment, their souls would leave them.

I once saw this, when there were four or five nobles lashed on grids and burning; I seem even to recall that there were two or three pairs of grids where others were burning, and because they uttered such loud screams that they disturbed the captain's sleep, he ordered them to be strangled. And the constable, who was worse than an executioner, did not want to obey that order (and I know the name of that constable and know his relatives in Seville), but instead put a stick over the victims' tongues, so they could not make a sound, and he stirred up the fire, but not too much, so that they roasted slowly, as he liked. I saw all these things I have described, and countless others.

And because all the people who could do so fled to the mountains to escape these inhuman, ruthless, and ferocious acts, the Spanish captains, enemies of the human race, pursued them with the fierce dogs they kept which attacked the Indians, tearing them to pieces and devouring them. And because on few and far between occasions, the Indians justifiably killed some Christians, the Spaniards made a rule among themselves that for every Christian slain by the Indians, they would slay a hundred Indians. . . .

Because the particulars that enter into these outrages are so numerous they could not be contained in the scope of much writing, for in truth I believe that in the great deal I have set down here I have not revealed the thousandth part of the sufferings endured by the Indians, I now want only to add that, in the matter of these unprovoked and destructive wars, and God is my witness, all these acts of wickedness I have described, as well as those I have omitted, were perpetrated against the Indians without cause, without any more cause than could give a community of good monks living together in a monastery. And still more strongly I affirm that until the multitude of people on this island of Hispaniola were killed and their lands devastated, they committed no sin against the Christians that would be punishable by man's laws, and as to those sins punishable by God's law, such as vengeful feelings against such powerful enemies as the Christians have been, those sins would be committed by the very few Indians who are hardhearted and impetuous. And I can say this from my great experience with them: their hardness and impetuosity would be that of children, of boys ten or twelve years old. I know by certain infallible signs that the wars waged by the Indians against the Christians have been justifiable wars and that all the wars waged by the Christians against the Indians have been unjust wars, more diabolical than any wars ever waged anywhere in the world. This I declare to be so of all the many wars they have waged against the peoples throughout the Indies.

After the wars and the killings had ended, when usually there survived only some boys, some women, and children, these survivors were distributed among the Christians to be slaves. The *repartimiento* or distribution was made according to the rank and importance of the Christian to whom the Indians were allocated, one of them being given thirty, another forty, still another, one or two hundred, and besides the rank of the Christian there was also to be considered in what favor he stood with the tyrant they called Governor. The pretext was that these allocated Indians were to be instructed in the articles of the Christian Faith. As if those Christians who were as a rule foolish and cruel and greedy and vicious could be caretakers of souls! And the care they took was to send the men to the mines to dig for gold, which is intolerable labor, and to send the women into the fields of the big ranches to hoe and till the land, work suitable for strong men. Nor to either the men or the women did they give any food except herbs and legumes, things of little substance. The milk in the breasts of the women with infants dried up and thus in a short while the infants perished.

4

European Views of Native Americans,
Sixteenth and Seventeenth Centuries

Las Casas's sympathetic view of the Indians was hardly one shared by the average Frenchman, Italian, or Scot. Indeed, many Europeans harbored fantastical and negative notions about the inhabitants of the "New World," envisioning them as wild and cannibalistic, savage and ruthless toward their enemies. Reinforcing this impression were images that circulated throughout Europe during the sixteenth and seventeenth centuries, such as this engraving from 1564, part of a series by Flemish engraver Theodore de Bry, based on paintings by an artist who had accompanied a French expedition to Florida a few decades earlier. Figure 16.1 shows the alleged cannibalistic practices by natives supposedly witnessed by the explorers. What is going on in this picture? It is likely that de Bry made adjustments to his engravings from the originals to please potential buyers. If so, what does this tell us about the expectations of European audiences about the Americas and their inhabitants?

Almost seventy-five years later, a very different set of no less remarkable images emerged from a Dutch colony in northeastern Brazil. Count Johan Maurits, the humanist governor general of the colony from 1636 to 1644, brought several artists and scientists with him to observe and record the region's flora and fauna as well as its

Figure 16.1   Cannibalism, engraving by Theodore de Bry.

Source: Scene of Cannibalism, from 'Brevis Narratio,' engraved by Theodore de Bry (1528–98) 1564 (coloured engraving), Le Moyne, Jacques (de Morgues) (1533–88) (after)/ Service Historique de la Marine, Vincennes, France/Giraudon/The Bridgeman Art Library.

inhabitants. Johan Maurits, who was fascinated by the local peoples and their cultures, commissioned from artist Albert Eckhout a number of still-lifes and group and individual portraits, including one showing a female Tapuya Indian (see Figure 16.2). According to Dutch accounts, the Tapuya were more warlike and less "civilized" than some of the other local peoples—for example, they sometimes consumed their dead instead of burying them. Aside from the body parts this woman carries in her hand and in her bag, what other signs of this warlike tendency do you see in Figure 16.2? Look closely at the many interesting details in this painting. What does the artist seem to be interested in showing?

THINKING HISTORICALLY

What are the differences in style and content between Figures 16.1 and 16.2, and how do you account for them? Which of the following factors do you think is most important in explaining their differences: chronology, agenda of the artist, the potential audience for the image, the

Figure 16.2 Tapuya Indian, by Albert Eckhout.
Source: The Granger Collection, New York.

setting in which they were produced? What might be the pitfalls for students of history in comparing these two images? How do you reconcile Las Casas's account in the previous source with the scene portrayed in Figure 16.1? Which source would you consider more reliable, and why? Which source would a sixteenth-century Spaniard have considered more reliable, and why? Consider how women are depicted in these works. What differences and similarities do you see? What might that tell us about European notions of women and gender in the New World?

NZINGA MBEMBA

Appeal to the King of Portugal, 1526

Although Europeans conquered the Americas beginning in the fifteenth century, they were unable to conquer the African continent until the nineteenth and twentieth centuries. Rivers that fell steeply to the sea, military defenses, and diseases like malaria proved insurmountable to Europeans before the age of the steamship, the machine gun, and antimalarial quinine. Before the last half of the nineteenth century, Europeans had to be content with alliances with African kings and rulers. The Portuguese had been the first to meet Africans in the towns and villages along the Atlantic coast, and they became the first European missionaries and trading partners.

Nzinga Mbemba, whose Christian name was Affonso, was king of the West African state of Congo (comprising what is today parts of Angola as well as the two Congo states) from about 1506 to 1543. He succeeded his father, King Nzinga, a Kuwu who, shortly after his first contact with the Portuguese in 1483, sent officials to Lisbon to learn European ways. In 1491 father and son were baptized, and Portuguese priests, merchants, artisans, and soldiers were provided with a coastal settlement.

What exactly is the complaint of the king of Congo? What seems to be the impact of Portuguese traders (called "factors") in the Congo? What does King Affonso want the king of Portugal to do?

THINKING HISTORICALLY

This selection offers an opportunity to compare European expansion in the Americas and Africa. Portuguese contact with Nzinga Mbemba of the Congo was roughly contemporaneous with Spanish colonialism in the Americas. What differences do you see between these two cases of early European expansion? Can you think of any reasons that Congo kings converted to Christianity whereas Mexican kings did not?

Compare the Europeans' treatment of Africans with their treatment of Native Americans. Why did Europeans enslave Africans and not, for the most part, American Indians?

Sir, Your Highness [of Portugal] should know how our Kingdom is being lost in so many ways that it is convenient to provide for the necessary remedy, since this is caused by the excessive freedom given by

Source: Basil Davidson, *The African Past* (Boston: Little, Brown, and Company, 1964), 191–94.

your factors and officials to the men and merchants who are allowed to come to this Kingdom to set up shops with goods and many things which have been prohibited by us, and which they spread throughout our Kingdoms and Domains in such an abundance that many of our vassals, whom we had in obedience, do not comply because they have the things in greater abundance than we ourselves; and it was with these things that we had them content and subjected under our vassalage and jurisdiction, so it is doing a great harm not only to the service of God, but to the security and peace of our Kingdoms and State as well.

And we cannot reckon how great the damage is, since the mentioned merchants are taking every day our natives, sons of the land and the sons of our noblemen and vassals and our relatives, because the thieves and men of bad conscience grab them wishing to have the things and wares of this Kingdom which they are ambitious of; they grab them and get them to be sold; and so great, Sir, is the corruption and licentiousness that our country is being completely depopulated, and Your Highness should not agree with this nor accept it as in your service. And to avoid it we need from those [your] Kingdoms no more than some priests and a few people to teach in schools, and no other goods except wine and flour for the holy sacrament. That is why we beg of Your Highness to help and assist us in this matter, commanding your factors that they should not send here either merchants or wares, because it is *our will that in these Kingdoms there should not be any trade of slaves nor outlet for them*.[1] Concerning what is referred above, again we beg of Your Highness to agree with it, since otherwise we cannot remedy such an obvious damage. Pray Our Lord in His mercy to have Your Highness under His guard and let you do for ever the things of His service. I kiss your hands many times.

> At our town of Congo, written on the sixth day of July.
> João Teixeira did it in 1526.
> The King. Dom Affonso.
> [On the back of this letter the following can be read:
> To the most powerful and excellent prince Dom João, King our Brother.]

Moreover, Sir, in our Kingdoms there is another great inconvenience which is of little service to God, and this is that many of our people [*naturaes*], keenly desirous as they are of the wares and things of your Kingdoms, which are brought here by your people, and in order to satisfy their voracious appetite, seize many of our people, freed and exempt men; and very often it happens that they kidnap even noblemen and the

---

[1] Emphasis in the original.

sons of noblemen, and our relatives, and take them to be sold to the white men who are in our Kingdoms; and for this purpose they have concealed them; and others are brought during the night so that they might not be recognized.

And as soon as they are taken by the white men they are immediately ironed and branded with fire, and when they are carried to be embarked, if they are caught by our guards' men the whites allege that they have bought them but they cannot say from whom, so that it is our duty to do justice and to restore to the freemen their freedom, but it cannot be done if your subjects feel offended, as they claim to be.

And to avoid such a great evil we passed a law so that any white man living in our Kingdoms and wanting to purchase goods in any way should first inform three of our noblemen and officials of our court whom we rely upon in this matter, and these are Dom Pedro Manipanza and Dom Manuel Manissaba, our chief usher, and Gonçalo Pires our chief freighter, who should investigate if the mentioned goods are captives or free men, and if cleared by them there will be no further doubt nor embargo for them to be taken and embarked. But if the white men do not comply with it they will lose the aforementioned goods. And if we do them this favor and concession it is for the part Your Highness has in it, since we know that it is in your service too that these goods are taken from our Kingdom, otherwise we should not consent to this. . . .

Sir, Your Highness has been kind enough to write to us saying that we should ask in our letters for anything we need, and that we shall be provided with everything, and as the peace and the health of our Kingdom depend on us, and as there are among us old folks and people who have lived for many days, it happens that we have continuously many and different diseases which put us very often in such a weakness that we reach almost the last extreme; and the same happens to our children, relatives, and natives owing to the lack in this country of physicians and surgeons who might know how to cure properly such diseases. And as we have got neither dispensaries nor drugs which might help us in this forlornness, many of those who had been already confirmed and instructed in the holy faith of Our Lord Jesus Christ perish and die; and the rest of the people in their majority cure themselves with herbs and breads and other ancient methods, so that they put all their faith in the mentioned herbs and ceremonies if they live, and believe that they are saved if they die; and this is not much in the service of God.

And to avoid such a great error and inconvenience, since it is from God in the first place and then from your Kingdoms and from Your Highness that all the goods and drugs and medicines have come to save us, we beg of you to be agreeable and kind enough to send us two physicians and two apothecaries and one surgeon, so that they may come with their drug-stores and all the necessary things to stay in our kingdoms, because we are in extreme need of them all and each of them. We shall do them all good and shall benefit them by all means, since they are sent by Your Highness, whom we thank for your work in their coming. We beg of Your Highness as a great favor to do this for us, because besides being good in itself it is in the service of God as we have said above.

6

CAPTAIN THOMAS PHILLIPS

Buying Slaves in 1693

Phillips, the captain of the English ship *Hannibal*, arrived at the African port of Ouidah (Whydah) in what is today Benin to purchase slaves for transport and sale in the West Indian islands of St. Thomas and Barbados. From this part of his journal, we can see that the Captain is well versed in the procedures for buying slaves on the African coast. What sorts of preparations has he made for the purchase? How does he go about making the purchase? What does this selection tell you about the African slave trade?

THINKING HISTORICALLY

The circumstances by which Europeans encountered Africans were clearly different from those by which they encountered Native Americans. What are these differences, and how do they account for differences in their attitudes toward Africans and Indians?

This day got our canoos and all things else ready, in order to go ashore to-morrow to purchase our slaves.

May the 21st. This morning I went ashore at Whidaw, accompany'd by my doctor and purser, Mr. Clay, the present captain of the *East India Merchant*, his doctor and purser, and about a dozen of our seamen for our guard, arm'd, in order here to reside till we could purchase 1300 negro slaves, which was the number we both wanted, to compleat 700 for the *Hannibal*, and 650 for the *East India Merchant*, according to our agreement in our charter-parties with the Royal African Company; in

Source: Capt. Thomas Phillips' Journal, in *Churchill's Collection of Voyages*, vol. 6, London, 1746. Reprinted in George Francis Dow, *Slave Ships and Slaving*, originally published by the Marine Research Society, Salem, MA, 1927. Reprinted by Dover Press, 2002, 58–64.

procuring which quantity of slaves we spent about nine weeks, during which time what observations my indisposition with convulsions in my head, &c. would permit me to make on this country, its trade, manners, &c. are as follows, viz. . . .

Our factory, built by Captain Wiburne, Sir John Wiburne's brother, stands low near the marshes, which renders it a very unhealthy place to live in; the white men the African Company send there, seldom returning to tell their tale; 'tis compass'd round with a mud wall, about six foot high, and on the south-side is the gate; within is a large yard, a mud thatch'd house, where the factor[1] lives, with the white men; also a store-house, a trunk for slaves, and a place where they bury their dead white men, call'd, very improperly, the hog-yard; there is also a good forge, and some other small houses: To the east are two small flankers of mud, with a few popguns and harquebusses,[2] which serve more to terrify the poor ignorant negroes than to do any execution. . . .

This factory, feared as 'tis, proved very beneficial to us, by housing our goods which came ashore late, and could not arrive at the king's town where I kept my warehouse, ere it was dark, when they would be very incident to be pilfer'd by the negro porters which carry them, at which they are most exquisite; for in the day-time they would steal the cowries,[3] altho' our white men that attended the goods from the marine watched them, they having instruments like wedges, made on purpose to force asunder the staves of the barrels, that contain'd the cowries, whereby the shells dropt out; and when any of our seamen that watch'd the goods came near such porters, they would take out their machine, and the staves would insensibly close again, so that no hole did appear, having always their wives and children running by them to carry off the plunder; which with all our threats and complaints made to the king, we could not prevent, tho' we often beat them cruelly, and piniar'd some, but it was all one, what was bred in the bone, &c. whatever we could do would not make them forbear.

The factory prov'd beneficial to us in another kind; for after we had procured a parcel of slaves, and sent them down to the sea-side to be carry'd off, it sometimes proved bad weather, and so great a sea, that the canoos could not come ashore to fetch them, so that they returned to the factory, where they were secured and provided for till good weather presented, and then were near to embrace the opportunity, we some-times shipping off a hundred of both sexes at a time.

We had our cook ashore, and eat as well as we could, provisions being plenty and cheap; but we soon lost our stomachs by sickness, most of my men having fevers, and myself such convulsions and aches in my

[1] Manager or agent. [Ed.]
[2] Firearms with a long barrel and a cord to ignite powder. [Ed.]
[3] Shells used as currency. [Ed.]

head, that I could hardly stand or go to the trunk without assistance, and there often fainted with the horrid stink of the negroes, it being an old house where all the slaves are kept together, and evacuate nature where they lie, so that no jakes[4] can stink worse; there being forced to sit three or four hours at a time, quite ruin'd my health, but there was no help.

When we were at the trunk, the king's slaves, if he had any, were the first offer'd to sale, which the cappasheirs[5] would be very urgent with us to buy, and would in a manner force us to it ere they would shew us any other, saying they were the Reys Cosa,[6] and we must not refuse them, tho' as I observed they were generally the worst slaves in the trunk, and we paid more for them than any others, which we could not remedy, it being one of his majesty's prerogatives. Then the cappasheirs each brought out his slaves according to his degree and quality, the greatest first, &c. and our surgeon examined them well in all kinds, to see that they were sound wind and limb, making them jump, stretch out their arms swiftly, looking in their mouths to judge of their age; for the cappasheirs are so cunning, that they shave them all close before we see them, so that let them be never so old we can see no grey hairs in their heads or beards; and then having liquor'd them well and sleeked with palm oil, 'tis no easy matter to know an old one from a middle-aged one, but by the teeths decay. But our greatest care of all is to buy none that are pox'd, lest they should infect the rest aboard; for tho' we separate the men and women aboard by partitions and bulk-heads, to prevent quarrels and wranglings among them, yet do what we can they will come together, and that distemper which they call the yaws, is very common here, and discovers itself by almost the same symptoms as the *Lues Venerea*[7] or clap does with us; therefore our surgeon is forc'd to examine the privities of both men and women with the nicest scrutiny, which is a great slavery, but what can't be omitted. When we had selected from the rest such as we liked, we agreed in what goods to pay for them, the prices being already stated before the king, how much of each sort of merchandize we were to give for a man, woman, and child, which gave us much ease, and saved abundance of disputes and wranglings, and gave the owner a note, signifying our agreement of the sorts of goods; upon delivery of which the next day he receiv'd them; then we mark'd the slaves we had bought in the breast, or shoulder, with a hot iron, having the letter of the ship's name on it, the place being before anointed with a little palm oil, which caused but little pain, the mark being usually well in four or five days, appearing very plain and white after.

When we had purchased to the number of 50 or 60, we would send them aboard, there being a cappasheir, intitled the captain of the slaves, whose care it was to secure them to the waterside, and see them all

[4] British slang for a latrine. [Ed.]
[5] Slave handlers appointed by the African king. [Ed.]
[6] The African king's special slaves. [Ed.]
[7] Venereal disease (STD). [Ed.]

off; and if in carrying to the marine any were lost, he was bound to make them good to us, the captain of the trunk being oblig'd to do the like, if any run away while under his care, for after we buy them we give him charge of them till the captain of the slaves comes to carry them away: There are two officers appointed by the king for this purpose, to each of which every ship pays the value of a slave in what goods they like best for their trouble, when they have done trading. . . .

There is likewise a captain of the sand, who is appointed to take care of the merchandise we have come ashore to trade with, that the negroes do not plunder them. . . .

When our slaves were come to the sea-side, our canoos were ready to carry them off to the longboat, if the sea permitted, and he convey'd them aboard ship, where the men were all put in irons, two and two shackl'd together, to prevent their mutiny, or swimming ashore.

The negroes are so wilful and loth to leave their own country, that they have often leap'd out of the canoos, boat and ship, into the sea, and kept under water till they were drowned, to avoid being taken up and saved by our boats, which pursued them; they having a more dreadful apprehension of Barbadoes than we can have of hell, tho' in reality they live much better there than in their own country; but home is home, &c. . . . We had about 12 negroes did wilfully drown themselves, and others starv'd themselves to death; for 'tis their belief that when they die they return home to their own country and friends again.

The best goods to purchase slaves here are cowries, the smaller the more esteemed; for they pay them all by tale, the smallest being as valuable as the biggest, but take them from us by measure or weight, of which about 100 pounds for a good man-slave. The next in demand are brass neptunes or basons, very large, thin, and flat; for after they have bought them they cut them in pieces to make anilias or bracelets, and collars for their arms, legs and necks. The other preferable goods are blue paper sletias, cambricks or lawns, caddy chints, broad ditto, coral, large, smooth, and of a deep red, rangoes large and red, iron bars, powder and brandy.[8]

With the above goods a ship cannot want slaves here, and may purchase them for about three pounds fifteen shillings a head, but near half the cargo value must be cowries or booges, and brass basons, to set off the other goods that we buy cheaper, as coral, rangoes, iron, &c. else they will not take them; for if a cappasheir sells five slaves, he will have two of them paid for in cowries, and one in brass, which are dear slaves; for a slave in cowries costs us above four pounds in England; whereas a slave in coral, rangoes, or iron, does not cost fifty shillings; but without

---

[8] Sletias were cloths, also called silesias, after their probable origin; cambricks were fine white linens from Cambray, Flanders; chints referred to chintz, an Indian cotton with brightly-colored design, usually flowers; broad referred to broad cloths; lawns were linens from Laorn, France; rangoes were beads. [Ed.]

the cowries and brass they will take none of the last goods, and but small quantities at best, especially, if they can discover that you have good store of cowries and brass aboard . . . therefore every man that comes here, ought to be very cautious in making his report to the king at first, of what sorts and quantities of goods he has, and be sure to say his cargo consists mostly in iron, coral, rangoes, chints, &c. so that he may dispose of those goods as soon as he can. . . .

7

J. B. ROMAIGNE

Journal of a Slave Ship Voyage, 1819

The French slave ship *Le Rodeur* sailed from the Guinea coast of Africa to the French Caribbean island of Guadeloupe in April, 1819. The ship carried twenty-two crewmen and a cargo of 160 African slaves. J. B. Romaigne, the twelve-year-old son of a Guadeloupe planter, was a passenger under the special care of the captain. This is his journal of the voyage, written for his mother. What happened on that voyage? How were the slaves treated? What does this account tell you about the transatlantic slave trade?

THINKING HISTORICALLY

Both this and the previous selection are taken from journals, or diaries. What unique characteristics and common elements of diaries should enhance their reliability for the historian? Is the journal of a twelve-year-old likely to be more or less reliable than that of a sea captain like Phillips? What aspects of this document make it seem more, or less, reliable to you?

I

"It is now just a week since we sailed; but, indeed, it is not my fault that I have not sooner sat down to write. The first two days I was sick, and the other five were so stormy that I could not sit at the table without holding. Even now we are rolling like a great porpoise yet I can sit very well and keep the pen steady. Since I am to send you what I do without

Source: Capt. Ernest H. Pentecost, RNR, "Introduction" to George Francis Dow, *Slave Ships and Slaving*, originally published by the Marine Research Society, Salem, MA, 1927. Reprinted by Dover Press, 2002, xxvii–xxxv.

copying it over again at the end of the voyage, I shall take what pains I can; but I hope, my dear mother, you will consider that my fingers are grown hard and tarry with hauling all day on the ropes, the Captain being determined, as he says, to make me a sailor. The Captain is very fond of me and is very good-tempered; he drinks a great deal of brandy; he is a fine, handsome man and I am sure I shall like him very much.

II

"I enquired of the Captain today, how long it would be before we should get to Guadaloupe; and he told me we had a great distance to go before we should steer that way at all. He asked how I should like to have a little black slave and I said very well; that I was to have plenty of them at Guadaloupe. He asked me what I could do with them. 'Feed them,' I said. 'That is right,' said the Captain; 'it will make them strong. But you will make them work won't you?' added he. 'Yes, to be sure,' said I. 'Then I can tell you you must flog them as well as feed them.' 'I will,' said I, 'it is what I intend, but I must not hurt them very much.' 'Of course not maim them,' returned he, 'for then they could not work; but if you do not make them feel to the marrow, you might as well throw them into the sea.'

III

"Since we have been at this place, Bonny Town in the Bonny river, on the coast of Africa, I have become more accustomed to the howling of these negroes. At first, it alarmed me, and I could not sleep. The Captain says that if they behave well they will be much better off at Guadaloupe; and I am sure, I wish the ignorant creatures would come quietly and have it over. Today, one of the blacks whom they were forcing into the hold, suddenly knocked down a sailor and attempted to leap overboard. He was caught, however, by the leg by another of the crew, and the sailor, rising up in a passion, hamstrung him with a cutlass. The Captain, seeing this, knocked the butcher flat upon the deck with a handspike. 'I will teach you to keep your temper,' said he, with an oath. 'He was the best slave in the lot.' I ran to the main chains and looked over; for they had dropped the black into the sea when they saw that he was useless. He continued to swim, even after he had sunk under water, for I saw the red track extending shoreward; but by and by, it stopped, widened, faded, and I saw it no more.

IV

"We are now fairly at sea again, and I am sure my dear Mother, I am heartily glad of it. The Captain is in the best temper in the world; he walks the deck, rubbing his hands and humming a tune. He says he has six dozen slaves on board, men, women and children, and all in prime marketable condition. I have not seen them, however, since we set sail. Their cries are so terrible that I do not like to go and look down into the hold. . . .

V

"Today, word was brought to the Captain, while we were at breakfast, that two of the slaves were dead, suffocated, as was supposed, by the closeness of the hold; and he immediately ordered the rest should be brought up, gang by gang, to the forecastle, to give them air. I ran up on deck to see them. They did not appear to me to be very unwell; but these blacks, who are not distinguished from one another by dress, are so much alike one can hardly tell.

"However, they had no sooner reached the ship's side, than first one, then another, then a third, sprang up on the gunwale, and darted into the sea, before the astonished sailors could tell what they were about. Many more made the attempt, but without success; they were all knocked flat to the deck, and the crew kept watch over them with handspikes and cutlasses till the Captain's pleasure should be known with regard to the revolt.

"The negroes, in the meantime, who had got off, continued dancing about among the waves, yelling with all their might, what seemed to me a song of triumph, in the burden of which they were joined by some of their companions on deck. Our ship speedily left the ignorant creatures behind; their voices came fainter and fainter upon the wind; the black head, first of one, then of another, disappeared; and then the sea was without a spot; and the air without a sound.

"When the Captain came up on deck, having finished his breakfast, and was told of the revolt, his face grew pale, and he gnashed his teeth. 'We must make an example,' said he, 'or our labour will be lost.' He then ordered the whole of the slaves in the ship to be tied together in gangs and placed upon the forecastle, and having selected six, who were known to have joined in the chorus of the revolters and might thus be considered as the ringleaders, he caused three of them to be shot, and the other three hanged, before the eyes of their comrades. . . .

VII

"The negroes, ever since the revolt, were confined closely to the lower hold and this brought on a disease called ophthalmia, which produced blindness. The sailors, who sling down the provisions from the upper hold, report that the disease is spreading frightfully and today, at dinner, the Captain and the surgeon held a conference on the subject. The surgeon declared that, from all he could learn, the cases were already so numerous as to be beyond his management; but the Captain insisted that every slave cured was worth his value and that it was better to lose a part than all. The disease, it seems, although generally fatal to the negro, is not always so. The patient is at first blind; but some escape, eventually, with the loss of one eye or a mere dimness of vision. The result of the conversation was, that the infected slaves were to be transferred to the upper hold and attended by the surgeon the same as if they were white men.

VIII

"All the slaves and some of the crew are blind. The Captain, the surgeon, and the mate are blind. There is hardly enough men left, out of our twenty-two, to work the ship. The Captain preserves what order he can and the surgeon still attempts to do his duty, but our situation is frightful.

IX

"All the crew are now blind but one man. The rest work under his orders like unconscious machines; the Captain standing by with a thick rope, which he sometimes applies, when led to any recreant by the man who can see. My own eyes begin to be affected; in a little while, I shall see nothing but death. I asked the Captain if he would not allow the blacks to come up on deck. He said it was of no use; that the crew, who were always on deck, were as blind as they; that if brought up, they would only drown themselves, whereas, if they remained where they were, there would, in all probability, be at least a portion of them salable, if we had ever the good fortune to reach Guadaloupe. . . .

X

"Mother, your son was blind for ten days, although now so well as to be able to write. I can tell you hardly anything of our history during that period. Each of us lived in a little dark world of his own, peopled by shadows and phantasms. . . .

"Then there came a storm. No hand was upon the helm, not a reef upon the sails. On we flew like a phantom ship of old, that cared not for wind or weather, our masts straining and cracking; . . . the furious sea one moment devouring us up, stem and stern, and the next casting us forth again, as if with loathing and disgust. . . . The wind, at last, died moaningly away, and we found ourselves rocking, without progressive motion, on the sullen deep. We at length heard a sound upon the waters, unlike that of the smooth swell which remained after the storm, and our hearts beat with a hope which was painful from its suddenness and intensity. We held our breath. The sound was continued; it was like the splashing of a heavy body in smooth water; and a simultaneous cry arose from every lip on deck and was echoed by the men in their hammocks below and by the slaves in the hold. . . .

"The Captain was the first to recover his self-possession, and our voices sank into silence when we heard him speak the approaching vessel with the usual challenge.

" 'Ship Ahoy! Ahoy! What ship?'

" 'The *Saint Leon* of Spain. Help us for God's sake!'

" 'We want help ourselves,' replied our Captain.

" 'We are dying of hunger and thirst. Send us on board some provisions and a few hands to work the ship and name your own terms.'

" 'We can give you food, but we are in want of hands. Come on board of us and we will exchange provisions with you for men,' answered our Captain.

" 'Dollars! dollars! We will pay you in money, a thousand fold; but we cannot send. We have negroes on board; they have infected us with ophthalmia, and we are all stone-blind.'

"At the announcement of this horrible coincidence, there was a silence among us, for some moments, like that of death. It was broken by a fit of laughter, in which I joined myself; and, before our awful merriment was over, we could hear, by the sound of the curses which the Spaniards shouted against us, that the *St. Leon* had drifted away.

"This vessel, in all probability, foundered at sea, as she never reached any port.

XI

"The man who preserved his sight the longest, recovered the soonest; and to his exertions alone, under the providence of God and the mercy of the blessed saints, is it owing that we are now within a few leagues of Guadaloupe, this twenty-first day of June 1819. I am myself almost well. The surgeon and eleven more are irrecoverably blind; the Captain has lost one eye; four others have met with the same calamity; and five are able to see, though dimly, with both. Among the slaves, thirty-nine are completely blind and the rest blind of one eye or their sight otherwise injured.

"This morning the Captain called all hands on deck, negroes and all. The shores of Guadaloupe were in sight. I thought he was going to return God thanks publicly for our miraculous escape.

"'Are you quite certain,' said the mate, 'that the cargo is insured?'

"'I am,' said the Captain. 'Every slave that is lost must be made good by the underwriters. Besides, would you have me turn my ship into a hospital for the support of blind negroes? They have cost us enough already. Do your duty.'

"The mate picked out thirty-nine negroes who were completely blind, and, with the assistance of the rest of the crew, tied a piece of ballast to the legs of each. The miserable wretches were then thrown into the sea."

8

Images of African-American Slavery, Eighteenth and Nineteenth Centuries

The visual record of slavery in the Americas is dominated by images rendered by members of the slave-owning societies; few images by slaves themselves exist. Nevertheless, much can be learned about the circumstances of slavery from the illustrations that do exist. Figure 16.3 shows a sale of slaves in Africa that was not atypical. Who are the slaves? Who is selling them? Who is buying them?

The work and living conditions of slaves varied among countries and slaveholders. Many slaves were put to work on large plantations to help with large-scale production, while others worked in smaller operations or as house servants and were sometimes hired out to work in other locations by their masters. A fortunate few were eventually granted their freedom after years of dedicated labor. Figure 16.4 depicts plantation work in Martinique in the early nineteenth century. Published in a traveler's account of the Americas, the text accompanying this image reads: "The slaves are called to work by the plantation bell at 6 in the morning, each person takes his hoe to the field under the supervision of overseers, either European or Creole; in a single line, they work in unison while chanting some African work song; the overseers occasionally use the whip to increase the work pace; at 11 the bell sounds, they take a meal, then resume their work until 6 in the evening." What does this image tell you that you might not have known about slavery?

Figure 16.3 Buying slaves in Africa, late 1700s or early 1800s.

Source: The Granger Collection, New York.

Figure 16.4 Plantation work, Martinique, 1826.

Source: *Voyage pittoresque dans les deux Amériques*, Albert and Shirley Small Special Collections Library, University of Virginia.

Figure 16.5   Slave market, Rio de Janeiro, Brazil, 1830s.
Source: Snark/Art Resource, NY.

Slaves were sold at auction both upon arrival from Africa and some-times when being sold by their owners. Figure 16.5 illustrates a slave auction in Brazil in the 1830s. Do slaves appear to be in high demand here? What does this image suggest to you about the cost and care of slaves in Brazil? Figure 16.6 offers a contrasting scene from a British newspaper of slaves awaiting sale in the United States. The article from the *Illustrated London News* reads: "The accompanying engraving repre-sents a gang of Negroes exhibited in the city of New Orleans, previous to an auction, from a sketch made on the spot by our artist. The men and women are well clothed, in their Sunday best — the men in blue cloth… with beaver hats; and the women in calico dresses, of more or less brilliancy, with silk bandana handkerchiefs bound round their heads. . . . they stand through a good part of the day, subject to the inspection of the purchasing or non-purchasing passing crowd. . . . An orderly silence is preserved as a general rule at these sales, although conversation does not seem to be altogether prohibited." What does this image suggest to you about slavery in New Orleans in 1861?

THINKING HISTORICALLY

These four images of African slavery in the Americas are selected out of thousands of paintings, engravings, and drawings, almost all done by Europeans who held varying attitudes toward slavery. Even if they accu-rately depict what the European artist saw at a particular moment in a

Figure 16.6 Slaves awaiting sale, New Orleans, 1861.

Source: A Slave-Pen at New Orleans—Before the Auction, from *Harper's Weekly*, 24th January 1863 (engraving) (b&w photo), American School (19th century)/Private Collection/The Bridgeman Art Library.

particular place, we should be careful to avoid making generalizations based on a single image. Nevertheless, often a primary source, written or visual, prompts new questions rather than answers to old ones. What questions occur to you when you view these images?

9

HARRIET JACOBS

Incidents in the Life of a Slave Girl, Written by Herself, 1861

Harriet Jacobs (1813–1897) was born a slave in North Carolina. In 1835, after the events described in this selection, she escaped her owner and managed to hide until fleeing to the North in 1842. Hers was one of the first accounts of slavery by a woman who had lived the

Source: Harriet Jacobs, *Incidents in the Life of a Slave Girl, Written by Herself* with Related Documents, ed. Jennifer Fleischner (Boston: Bedford/St. Martin's, 2010), 39–41, 52–53, 55–61.

experience. The book was published under the pseudonym of Linda Brent in 1861, the first year of the Civil War. Popular among Northern abolitionists, it was greeted as a major work of literature in England. What does her story tell you about slavery in the United States?

THINKING HISTORICALLY

This is the only one of our selections on slavery that was written by a former slave. It is also the only one written by a woman. How do these factors shape the narrative? In what ways do they make her account more or less reliable?

III. The Slaves' New Year's Day

Dr. Flint owned a fine residence in town, several farms, and about fifty slaves, besides hiring a number by the year.

Hiring-day at the south takes place on the 1st of January. On the 2d, the slaves are expected to go to their new masters. On a farm, they work until the corn and cotton are laid. They then have two holidays. Some masters give them a good dinner under the trees. This over, they work until Christmas eve. If no heavy charges are meantime brought against them, they are given four or five holidays, whichever the master or over-seer may think proper. Then comes New Year's eve; and they gather together their little alls, or more properly speaking, their little nothings, and wait anxiously for the dawning of day. At the appointed hour the grounds are thronged with men, women, and children, waiting, like criminals, to hear their doom pronounced. The slave is sure to know who is the most humane, or cruel master, within forty miles of him.

It is easy to find out, on that day, who clothes and feeds his slaves well; for he is surrounded by a crowd, begging, "Please, massa, hire me this year. I will work *very* hard, massa."

If a slave is unwilling to go with his new master, he is whipped, or locked up in jail, until he consents to go, and promises not to run away during the year. Should he chance to change his mind, thinking it justifiable to violate an extorted promise, woe unto him if he is caught! The whip is used till the blood flows at his feet; and his stiffened limbs are put in chains, to be dragged in the field for days and days!

If he lives until the next year, perhaps the same man will hire him again, without even giving him an opportunity of going to the hiring-ground. After those for hire are disposed of, those for sale are called up.

O, you happy free women, contrast *your* New Year's day with that of the poor bond-woman! With you it is a pleasant season, and the light of the day is blessed. Friendly wishes meet you every where, and gifts are showered upon you. Even hearts that have been estranged from you soften at this season, and lips that have been silent echo back, "I wish you a happy New Year." Children bring their little offerings, and raise their rosy lips for a caress. They are your own, and no hand but that of death can take them from you.

But to the slave mother New Year's day comes laden with peculiar sorrows. She sits on her cold cabin floor, watching the children who may all be torn from her the next morning; and often does she wish that she and they might die before the day dawns. She may be an ignorant creature, degraded by the system that has brutalized her from childhood; but she has a mother's instincts, and is capable of feeling a mother's agonies.

On one of these sale days, I saw a mother lead seven children to the auction-block. She knew that *some* of them would be taken from her; but they took *all*. The children were sold to a slave-trader, and their mother was bought by a man in her own town. Before night her children were all far away. She begged the trader to tell her where he intended to take them; this he refused to do: How *could* he, when he knew he would sell them, one by one, wherever he could command the highest price? I met that mother in the street, and her wild, haggard face lives to-day in my mind. She wrung her hands in anguish, and exclaimed, "Gone! All gone! Why *don't* God kill me?" I had no words wherewith to comfort her. Instances of this kind are of daily, yea, of hourly occurrence.

Slaveholders have a method, peculiar to their institution, of getting rid of *old* slaves, whose lives have been worn out in their service. I knew an old woman, who for seventy years faithfully served her master. She had become almost helpless, from hard labor and disease. Her owners moved to Alabama, and the old black woman was left to be sold to any body who would give twenty dollars for her. . . .

V. The Trials of Girlhood

During the first years of my service in Dr. Flint's family, I was accustomed to share some indulgences with the children of my mistress. Though this seemed to me no more than right, I was grateful for it, and tried to merit the kindness by the faithful discharge of my duties. But I now entered on my fifteenth year—a sad epoch in the life of a slave girl. My master began to whisper foul words in my ear. Young as I was, I could not remain ignorant of their import. I tried to treat them with indifference or contempt. The master's age, my extreme youth, and the fear that his conduct would be reported to my grandmother, made him bear this treatment for many months. He was a crafty man, and resorted to many means to accomplish his purposes. Sometimes he had stormy, terrific ways, that made his victims tremble; sometimes he assumed a gentleness that he thought must surely subdue. Of the two, I preferred his stormy moods, although they left me trembling. He tried his utmost to corrupt the pure principles my grandmother had instilled. He peopled my young mind with unclean images, such as only a vile monster could think of. I turned from him with disgust and hatred. But he was my master. I was compelled to live under the same roof with him—where I saw a man forty years my senior daily violating the most sacred commandments of nature. He told me I was his property; that I must be subject to his will in all things. My soul revolted against the mean tyranny. But where could I turn for protection? . . .

I longed for some one to confide in. I would have given the world to have laid my head on my grandmother's faithful bosom, and told her all my troubles. But Dr. Flint swore he would kill me, if I was not as silent as the grave.

VI. The Jealous Mistress

. . . Mrs. Flint possessed the key to her husband's character before I was born. She might have used this knowledge to counsel and to screen the young and the innocent among her slaves; but for them she had no sympathy. They were the objects of her constant suspicion and malevolence. She watched her husband with unceasing vigilance; but he was well practised in means to evade it. . . .

I had entered my sixteenth year, and every day it became more apparent that my presence was intolerable to Mrs. Flint. Angry words frequently passed between her and her husband. He had never punished me himself, and he would not allow any body else to punish me. In that respect, she was never satisfied; but, in her angry moods, no terms were too vile for her to bestow upon me. Yet I, whom she detested so bitterly, had far more pity for her than he had, whose duty it was to make her life happy. I never wronged her, or wished to wrong her, and one word of kindness from her would have brought me to her feet.

After repeated quarrels between the doctor and his wife, he announced his intention to take his youngest daughter, then four years old, to sleep in his apartment. It was necessary that a servant should sleep in the same room, to be on hand if the child stirred. I was selected for that office, and informed for what purpose that arrangement had been made. By managing to keep within sight of people, as much as possible, during the day time, I had hitherto succeeded in eluding my master, though a razor was often held to my throat to force me to change this line of policy. At night I slept by the side of my great aunt, where I felt safe. He was too prudent to come into her room. She was an old woman, and had been in the family many years. Moreover, as a married man, and a professional man, he deemed it necessary to save appearances in some degree. But he resolved to remove the obstacle in the way of his scheme; and he thought he had planned it so that he should evade suspicion. He was well aware how much I prized my refuge by the side of my old aunt, and he determined to dispossess me of it. The first night the doctor had the little child in his room alone. The next morning, I was ordered to take my station as nurse the following night. A kind Providence interposed in my favor. During the day Mrs. Flint heard of this new arrangement, and a storm followed. I rejoiced to hear it rage.

After a while my mistress sent for me to come to her room. Her first question was, "Did you know you were to sleep in the doctor's room?"

"Yes, ma'am."

"Who told you?"

"My master."

"Will you answer truly all the questions I ask?"

"Yes, ma'am."

"Tell me, then, as you hope to be forgiven, are you innocent of what I have accused you?"

"I am."

She handed me a Bible, and said, "Lay your hand on your heart, kiss this holy book, and swear before God that you tell me the truth."

I took the oath she required, and I did it with a clear conscience.

"You have taken God's holy word to testify your innocence," said she. "If you have deceived me, beware! Now take this stool, sit down, look me directly in the face, and tell me all that has passed between your master and you."

I did as she ordered. As I went on with my account her color changed frequently, she wept, and sometimes groaned. She spoke in tones so sad, that I was touched by her grief. The tears came to my eyes; but I was soon convinced that her emotions arose from anger and wounded pride. She felt that her marriage vows were desecrated, her dignity insulted; but she had no compassion for the poor victim of her husband's perfidy. She pitied herself as a martyr; but she was incapable of feeling for the condition of shame and misery in which her unfortunate, helpless slave was placed.

Yet perhaps she had some touch of feeling for me; for when the conference was ended, she spoke kindly, and promised to protect me. I should have been much comforted by this assurance if I could have had confidence in it; but my experiences in slavery had filled me with distrust. She was not a very refined woman, and had not much control over her passions. I was an object of her jealousy, and, consequently, of her hatred; and I knew I could not expect kindness or confidence from her under the circumstances in which I was placed. I could not blame her. Slaveholders' wives feel as other women would under similar circumstances. The fire of her temper kindled from small sparks, and now the flame became so intense that the doctor was obliged to give up his intended arrangement.

I knew I had ignited the torch, and I expected to suffer for it afterwards; but I felt too thankful to my mistress for the timely aid she rendered me to care much about that. She now took me to sleep in a room adjoining her own. There I was an object of her especial care, though not of her especial comfort, for she spent many a sleepless night to watch over me. . . .

. . . I pitied Mrs. Flint. She was a second wife, many years the junior of her husband; and the hoary-headed miscreant was enough to try the patience of a wiser and better woman. She was completely foiled, and knew not how to proceed. She would gladly have had me flogged for my supposed false oath; but, as I have already stated, the doctor never allowed any one to whip me. The old sinner was politic. The application of the lash might have led to remarks that would have exposed him in the eyes of his children and grandchildren. How often did I rejoice that I lived in a town where all the inhabitants knew each other! If had been on a remote plantation, or lost among the multitude of a crowded city, I should not be a living woman at this day.

The secrets of slavery are concealed like those of the Inquisition. My master was, to my knowledge, the father of eleven slaves. But did the mothers dare to tell who was the father of their children? Did the other slaves dare to allude to it, except in whispers among themselves? No, indeed! They knew too well the terrible consequences. . . .

Reader, I draw no imaginary pictures of southern homes. I am telling you the plain truth. Yet when victims make their escape from this wild beast of Slavery, northerners consent to act the part of bloodhounds, and hunt the poor fugitive back into his den, "full of dead men's bones, and all uncleanness."[1] Nay, more, they are not only willing, but proud, to give their daughters in marriage to slave-holders. . . . The young wife soon learns that the husband in whose hands she has placed her happiness pays no regard to his marriage vows. Children of every shade of complexion play with her own fair babies, and too well she knows that they are born unto him of his own household. . . .

Southern women often marry a man knowing that he is the father of many little slaves. They do not trouble themselves about it. They regard such children as property, as marketable as the pigs on the plantation; and it is seldom that they do not make them aware of this by passing them into the slave-trader's hands as soon as possible, and thus getting them out of their sight.

---

[1] Biblical reference to Matthew 23:27. [Ed.]

■ REFLECTIONS

This chapter asks you to compare European encounters with Native Americans and Africans. Why did Europeans enslave Africans and not, for the most part, American Indians? Because so many Africans were brought to the Americas to work on plantations, this topic is especially compelling.

Initially, of course, Indians *were* enslaved. Recall the letter of Columbus (Chapter 15, selection 4). Part of the reason this enslavement did not continue was the high mortality of Native Americans exposed to smallpox and other Old World diseases. In addition, Native Americans who survived the bacterial onslaught had the "local knowledge" and support needed to escape from slavery.

Above and beyond this were the humanitarian objections of Spanish priests like Bartolomeo de Las Casas and the concerns of the Spanish monarchy that slavery would increase the power of the conquistadors at the expense of the Crown. In 1542 the enslavement of Indians was out-lawed in Spanish dominions of the New World. Clearly, these "New Laws" were not always obeyed by Spaniards in the Americas or by the Portuguese subjects of the unified Spanish-Portuguese crown between 1580 and 1640. Still, the different legal positions of Africans and Indians in the minds of Europeans require further explanation.

Some scholars have suggested that the difference in treatment lies in the differing needs of the main European powers involved in the encounter. The anthropologist Marvin Harris makes the argument this way:

> The most plausible explanation of the New Laws [of 1542] is that they represented the intersection of the interests of three power groups: the Church, the Crown, and the colonists. All three of these interests sought to maximize their respective control over the aboriginal populations. Outright enslavement of the Indians was the method preferred by the colonists. But neither the Crown nor the Church could permit this to happen without surrendering their own vested and potential interests in the greatest resource of the New World—its manpower.[1]

Why then did Europeans permit and even encourage the enslave-ment of Africans? In this matter all three power groups stood to gain. Africans who remained in Africa were of no use to anybody, since effective military and political domination of that continent by Europeans was not achieved until the middle of the nineteenth century. To make use of African manpower, Africans had to be removed from their homelands. The only way to accomplish this was

[1] Marvin Harris, *Patterns of Race in the Americas* (New York: W. W. Norton, 1964), 17.

to buy them as slaves from dealers on the coast. For both the Crown and the church, it was better to have Africans under the control of the New World colonists than to leave Africans under the control of Africans.

But of course the Atlantic world slave trade was just one of the lasting outcomes of Atlantic world encounters. Toward the end of his dramatic account of the Spanish conquest of Mexico (selection 1), Bernal Díaz describes a grizzly discovery made by the victorious conquistadors:

> I solemnly swear that all the houses and stockades in the lake were full of heads and corpses. I do not know how to describe it but it was the same in the streets and courts of Tlatelolco. We could not walk without treading on the bodies and heads of dead Indians. (Díaz, 1963, 405)

After two years of continual and heavy warfare, the fortunes of the Spanish turned in their favor and they seized a ravaged city where, according to Bernal Díaz, "the stench was so bad, no one could endure it." Díaz assumed that the Mexicans had been starved and denied fresh water, but we now know that at least part of the cause was the spread of smallpox, a disease that the Spanish carried from the Old World and for which the Native Americans had no immunities. Because of thousands of years of contact, Africans shared many of the same immunities as Europeans, but Native Americans, having inhabited a separate biological realm for over ten thousand years, were completely vulnerable to the new diseases and perished in droves.

Ultimately, slavery came to an end, even if in some cases—the work of Italians on Brazilian sugar plantations, Chinese rail workers, or free African day laborers—it was hard to see a difference in working conditions. In any case, the long-term impact of the "Columbian exchange" was more ecological than economic. The potatoes of South America and the corn of Mexico fed more families in Afro-Eurasia than had ever existed in the Americas. Conversely, the flora and fauna of the Americas were transformed through the introduction of the grasses, trees, fruits, grains, horses, cattle, pigs, and chickens that had nourished the ancestors of the conquistadors.

17

State and Religion

Asian, Islamic, and Christian States, 1500–1800

■ HISTORICAL CONTEXT

The relationship between state and religion is a matter of concern and debate almost everywhere in the modern world. In the United States, the issue of the separation of church and state engenders conflicts about the legality of abortion, prayer in the schools, government vouchers for religious schools, and the public display of religious symbols like the Ten Commandments, Nativity scenes, and Chanukah menorahs. Governments in countries as diverse as France and Turkey have recently debated the wearing of headscarves and the display of religious symbols in public schools and other public spaces.

Few states in the world today are dedicated to a single religion as are Saudi Arabia, Israel, and the Vatican. Yet even such places where religious devotion is extreme allow citizenship, residence, and rights in some measure for people of other religions. A few other states have official religions: Brazil is officially Roman Catholic, as was Italy until 1984; Iran is officially Muslim. But, with some notable exceptions, these types of designations often have little effect on what people believe or how they behave.

Although the role of religion in public life and the relationship between church and state are important current issues, from the long-term historical view, the state has become more important in peoples' lives while religion has become less influential. In the period before 1500, with the notable exception of China, many religious organizations were more important than political entities. But, in much of the world, the story of the last five hundred years has been the replacement of religious authority by that of the state. With the increased power of the state, secularism has become more pervasive, often triggering revivals of religious fundamentalism in reaction.

In this chapter, we look at religion and the state in various parts of the world two to five hundred years ago to see how different things were, but also to locate the roots of present church-state conflicts. We look first at China, where state formation began over two thousand years ago and official Confucianism supported the authority of the emperor. Japan, by contrast, emerged from feudalism to state formation after 1600. Both East Asian societies struggled with the claims of Buddhists, Christians, Muslims, and popular religious sects. Next we look at India, conquered by the Muslim Mughals after 1500, many of whom were remarkably tolerant of Hindus and Hinduism. Similarly, the Ottoman Empire protected a wide range of minority religions despite its Muslim majority. We conclude with the West (Europe and colonial America) to understand how Christian states struggled with some of the challenges posed by religion. Ultimately, we will be looking for the roots of religious toleration.

Kings and political leaders are almost all more comfortable with some kind of orthodoxy (conventional belief and practice) than with heterodoxy (dissident or heretical belief and practice). But one person's orthodox belief is another's heterodoxy. Most Islamic states, for instance, see Iran's Shi'ism as heterodox, but Shi'ism has been the orthodox norm for most Iranians for centuries. Orthodoxy frequently undermines religious toleration. In modern society, we often see toleration as a product of secularism. In fact, the history of church and state suggests something very different.

■ THINKING HISTORICALLY

Appreciating Context

Normally a quote taken "out of context" refers to a quote separated out from other words, which, if included, would qualify or change the meaning. For instance if you quoted Martin Luther as saying "A Christian is a perfectly free lord of all, subject to none"[1] in order to establish the Protestant Reformer as a proponent of individual freedom, but you failed to quote Luther's next sentence, which is "A Christian is a perfectly dutiful servant of all, subject to all," then you would be guilty of taking the first quote out of context. You would have misconstrued Luther's meaning and failed to understand his complexity.

That is the simple meaning of context: the surrounding words of a quotation that must be included to grasp its full meaning. Context can mean much more than that, however. It can mean not only words, but actions too, that are not only adjacent, but close enough to be relevant.

[1] Martin Luther, "The Freedom of a Christian" (1520), in *Luther-Selected Political Writings*, ed. J.M. Porter (Philadelphia: Fortress Press, 1974), 25.

Context helps us understand any words or event. Your mother shouts at you with uncharacteristic anger for a simple thing like not taking out the garbage. You might try to put it in context by recalling she's had a bad day. For her, the context might be that you have been negligent about other responsibilities. There can be many different contextual explanations. The job of an historian is to discover the context or contexts that increase the meaning of something. Was a strongly antiwar letter written just after a devastating battle? Did a religious conversion occur in a mass revival, or after a near-death experience?

As we examine the following primary sources, we will see that sometimes an important context is apparent in the document and sometimes it is not. When it is not, we will have to look beyond the source.

1

JONATHAN SPENCE

Emperor Kangxi on Religion, 1661–1722

Kangxi[1] was emperor of China from 1661 to 1722. A descendant of conquering Manchu warriors, Kangxi overcame the last resistance of the previous Ming dynasty and, during his reign, which was the longest of any Chinese emperor, brought the Qing (or Manchu) dynasty to its greatest size and strength. In this selection, the modern historian Jonathan Spence presents the emperor in his own voice, drawn from innumerable primary sources and often the emperor's own words. How would you describe Kangxi's attitude toward religion? What do you think he would say if asked about the proper relationship between religion and the state? What characteristics of Chinese society might explain these ideas?

THINKING HISTORICALLY

Kangxi's reflections on religion and the state developed not in a vacuum, but in the context of the recent arrival of Roman Catholic Christians in China, especially Jesuit missionaries. China encountered Nestorian Christians from Syria as early as the seventh century (see document 7.3), but they assimilated into Chinese culture and practically disappeared before the Mongols came in the thirteenth century (some Mongols, incidentally, with their Nestorian Christian wives). After the Mongols, the Ming dynasty banned Christians in China,

[1] Cong SHE   Spelled K'ang Hsi in older Wade-Giles system of Romanization.

Source: Jonathan D. Spence, *Emperor of China: Self-Portrait of K'ang-Hsi* (New York: Vintage Books, 1975), 80–85.

while allowing Jews and Muslims to remain. So Kangxi was ruling at a pivotal moment when the new Jesuit order was attempting to convert the Chinese to Christianity. Matteo Ricci, the founder of the Jesuit mission to China, taught fellow Jesuits to impress the emperor with clocks and scientific instruments and offers to share their knowledge, while at the same time demonstrating humility toward traditional Chinese Confucianism. They learned Chinese, wore Chinese clothing, and accepted Confucianism as a moral code rather than a competing religion. As you read the selection, note Kangxi's references to Christians. How are his concerns about Christians different from concerns about followers of other religions? How might Christians pose a greater or different threat to Kangxi? How much of Kangxi's attitude toward religion seems based on his encounter with Christians? How different do you think it would be if the Christians never arrived?

Every country must have some spirits that it reveres. This is true for our dynasty, as for Mongols or Mohammedans, Miao or Lolo, or other foreigners. Just as everyone fears something, some snakes but not toads, some toads but not snakes; and as all countries have different pronunciations and different alphabets. But in this Catholic religion, the Society of Peter quarrels with the Jesuits, Bouvet[2] quarrels with Mariani, and among the Jesuits the Portuguese want only their own nationals in their church while the French want only French in theirs. This violates the principles of religion. Such dissension cannot be inspired by the Lord of Heaven but by the Devil, who, I have heard the Westerners say, leads men to do evil since he can't do otherwise. . . .

Since I discovered on the Southern Tour of 1703 that there were missionaries wandering at will over China, I had grown cautious and determined to control them more tightly: to bunch them in the larger cities and in groups that included men from several different countries, to catalogue their names and residences, and to permit no new establishments without my express permission. For with so many Westerners coming to China it has been hard to distinguish the real missionaries from other white men pretending to be missionaries. As I clarified it for de Tournon[3]: "Hereafter we will permit residence in China to all those who come from the West

---

[2] Joachim Bouvet (1656–1730) was a French Jesuit who taught Kangxi astronomy and mathematics and, according to the emperor, understood Chinese better than other Westerners. As a leading "Figurist," Bouvet believed that all of Christianity could be found in the ancient Chinese religious text, the *I Ching*. This idea was criticized by other missionaries who thought it understated the importance of the Bible. [Ed.]

[3] Charles-Thomas Maillard de Tournon (1668–1710) was a papal legate to China to control missionaries and end the acceptance of some Chinese phrases and Confucian rites by Chinese Christians; this led to his imprisonment by Kangxi. [Ed.]

and will not return there. Residence permission will not be granted to those who come one year expecting to go home the next—because such people are like those who stand outside the main gate and discuss what people are doing inside the house. Besides these meddlers there are also those out for profit, greedy traders, who should not be allowed to live here." After the arguments with de Tournon and Maigrot[4] I made all missionaries who wanted to stay on in China sign a certificate, stating that they would remain here for life and follow Ricci on the Rites.[5] Forty or fifty who refused were exiled to Canton; de Tournon was sent to Macao, his secretary, Appiani, we kept in prison in Peking.

Despite these sterner restrictions, the Westerners continued to cause me anxiety. Our ships were being sold overseas; reports came of ironwood for keel blocks being shipped out of Kwangtung; Luzon and Batavia became havens for Chinese outlaws; and the Dutch were strong in the Southern Seas. I ordered a general inquiry among residents of Peking who had once lived on the coast, and called a conference of the coastal governors-general. "I fear that some time in the future China is going to get into difficulties with these various Western countries," I said. "That is my prediction." Similarly I had warned earlier that China must be strong to forestall a possible threat from Russia. General Ch'en Mao insisted even more strongly on the dangers from Holland and France, Spain and England, and of missionaries and merchants conniving together. I did not agree with him that we should disarm all their ships, but I did agree to reiterate the 1669 edict that banned Westerners from preaching in the provinces.

Three of the Peking Jesuits—Suares, Parrenin, and Mourao—came to protest: "We learn that the Boards have pronounced a strict sentence and the Christian religion is proscribed."

I reassured them: "No. The sentence is not strict, and the Christian religion is not proscribed. Only Westerners without the certificate are forbidden to preach. This prohibition does not affect those who have the certificate."

"This distinction as made by the Emperor is not clearly expressed in the sentence."

"It is clearly expressed. I have read the sentence with care. If you were hoping that those without certificates might be permitted to preach your laws, then that hope is no longer possible."

"But at the beginning of the sentence the 1669 edict is cited."

[4] Charles Maigrot (1652–1730) was administrator of Christian missions in China after 1684. In 1692 Kangxi issued an Edict of Toleration that formally allowed Chinese to become Christians. The following year Maigrot condemned the rites honoring Confucius and rituals associated with ancestor worship. [Ed.]

[5] Refers to the position of Matteo Ricci (1552–1610), a founder of the Jesuit mission to China, and later of Joachim Bouvet that the rites of Confucius were moral and civic rather than religious and that therefore they could be practiced by Chinese Christians. [Ed.]

"That is true, but the point of it is to prevent those without certificates from preaching."

"We are just afraid that the provincial officials will treat us all alike, and that they will not permit even those of us who have certificates to preach the holy law."

"If that occurs, those who have certificates have only to produce them. The officials will see that permission to preach your laws is granted. You can preach the law, and it's up to the Chinese to listen—if they so choose. As for those without a certificate, let them come here, and I will give them one." (I smiled during these last words.) "Anyway, even those with the certificate are only being permitted to preach for a time. Later on we'll see what decision to take in their case."

"But if they cause trouble to those with certificates, we will come to the Emperor for help."

"Take care to inform me if such is the case."

"There is one thing that causes us particular anguish—namely, that the Boards treat us as rebels."

"Don't worry about that. It's just a conventional formula that the Boards use."

"As soon as this edict is published, the officials will search out the missionaries and Christians and stir up trouble."

"As far as this searching out goes, it's essential. When I sent Li Ping-chung to Canton I gave him an order for the Governor-General, telling him to search out and to assemble in one place all those without certificates. And I've just given similar orders to Governor-General Yang Lin on his return to Canton, and am awaiting his reply."

The Westerners in China were only as drops of rain in the immensity of the ocean, said de Tournon in our audience, and I had to laugh. Yet some of their words were no different from the wild or improper teachings of Buddhists and Taoists, and why should they be treated differently? One of my censors wrote that the Western god fashioned a man with a human soul from the blood of a virgin, Mary; and they claimed that Jesus was born in the reign of Han Ai-ti [reigned 6 B.C.–A.D. 1], that he was killed on a cross for man's sins, and that they had meetings in which slaves and masters, men and women, mixed together and drank some holy substance. I had asked Verbiest[6] why God had not forgiven his son without making him die, but though he had tried to answer I had not understood him. Also, though in China there had been a flood at about the same time as that reported for Noah, those on the Chinese plains had been drowned, while those who escaped to the mountains were saved. And I told Fontaney[7] that I would gladly witness some of the miracles they talked about, but none was forthcoming.

[6] Ferdinand Verbiest (1623–1688), Flemish Jesuit missionary in China; mathematician and astronomer. [Ed.]

[7] Baptist de Fontenay (1643–1710), missionary, mathematician, and astronomer. [Ed.]

In the past, both Buddhists and Taoists had been made to fill out certificates, and the superiors in the various temples have to register their monks—they are not allowed to chant or beg for alms or set out their sacred images in the streets of Peking, and may not act as exorcists for patients suffering from seizures without getting official permission. Certainly there are more Buddhists and Taoists—the census of 1667 listed 140,193 monks divided among 79,622 temples of various sizes—but there were many Christians also. When I asked Verbiest for exact figures in 1688 he said there were 15,758 Christians just in Peking. Even though I realized it was quite impractical to close down temples, and order people to return to secular life, there was no harm in following the principle of "preparing for trouble before trouble comes." So I strictly banned all the sects[8] such as the "non-action," "white lotus," "incense smelling," "origin of the dragon," and "all-submerging Yang," and stiffened the penalties for all officials who failed to report heterodox teachers in their localities. Also I banned the so-called "incense associations," where men and women mixed together and sold erotic works and special medicines; I ordered the printing blocks of certain mystical and magical books burned; and I continued to enforce the prohibitions against the private ownership of forbidden books—though I allowed exceptions for those working at home in astronomy and mathematics.

[8] These were Daoist and Buddhist sects. [Ed.]

2

Japanese Edicts Regulating Religion, 1645 and 1665

The history of the state in Japan was very different from that of China. Between 1200 and 1600 Japan went through a period in which the state was eclipsed by aristocratic, warrior, and religious groups. When the Tokugawa Shogunate reasserted the authority of a central state in 1600, the memory of monk-soldiers and numerous independent armies called for a series of measures directed at controlling religious institutions and other independent powers. In one measure, all farmers were forbidden to have swords. Another regulated all religious temples. Between 1633 and 1639 the Tokugawa government took the further step of closing the country to all foreign religions, a move directed mainly at the influence previously enjoyed by Portuguese Catholic missionaries.

Source: Yosaburo Takekoshi, *The Economic Aspects of the History of the Civilization of Japan* (New York: Macmillan, 1930), 2:88–89. Reprinted in *Japan: A Documentary History*, ed. David J. Lu (Armonk, NY: M. E. Sharpe, 2005), 1:224–25.

The first of the two documents in this selection is a vow by which Japanese Christians renounced their faith in 1645. The second document is a government edict regulating temples, mainly Buddhist, in 1665. What do these documents tell you about the relationship between the state and religion in Tokugawa Japan?

THINKING HISTORICALLY

The first document, from 1645, in which a group of Japanese swear they are renouncing Christianity is full of contradictions that cry out for contextual explanation. The Japanese history of Christianity was similar to the Chinese. Whether or not there was a Nestorian Christian presence by 500 C.E. as some argue, Roman Catholic Christianity came to Japan with the first Jesuits, including Francis Xavier in 1549. At the end of the sixteenth century and the beginning of the seventeenth century, Christians were persecuted and the church was banned. In response some Japanese Christians went underground, disguising their religion with the appearance of a return to Japanese culture, including Buddha-like images of Jesus and Mary. They were called *Kakure Kirishitans* ("hidden Christians"). What are the contradictions in this document that suggest these people had been or continued to be hidden Christians? What parts of the document suggest a false renunciation? What might account for the difference in the last paragraph?

The second Japanese document was written in the time of the Chinese Emperor Kangxi. How might Kangxi's meditations on religion provide a context that might also help us understand this document?

Renouncing the Kirishitan[1] Faith, 1645

Vow of Namban (Southern Barbarians): We have been Kirishitans for many years. But the more we learn of the Kirishitan doctrines the greater becomes our conviction that they are evil. In the first place, we who received instructions from the padre regarding the future life were threatened with excommunication which would keep us away from association with the rest of humanity in all things in the present world, and would cast us into hell in the next world. We were also taught that, unless a person committing a sin confesses it to the padre and secures his pardon, he shall not be saved in the world beyond. In that way the people were led into believing in the padres. All that was for the purpose of taking the lands of others.

When we learned of it, we "shifted" from Kirishitan and became adherents of Hokkekyō[2] while our wives became adherents of Ikkōshō.[3]

---

[1] Christian. [Ed.]
[2] Buddhist sect based on the Lotus Sutra sermon of the Buddha. [Ed.]
[3] Pure Land Buddhism. [Ed.]

We hereby present a statement in writing to you, worshipful Magistrate, as a testimony.

Hereafter we shall not harbor any thought of the Kirishitan in our heart. Should we entertain any thought of it at all, we shall be punished by Deus Paternus (God the Father), Jesus (His Son), Spirito Santo (the Holy Ghost), as well as by Santa Maria (St. Mary), various angels, and saints.

The grace of God will be lost altogether. Like Judas Iscariot, we shall be without hope, and shall be mere objects of ridicule to the people. We shall never rise. The foregoing is our Kirishitan vow.

Japanese Pledge: We have no thought of the Kirishitan in our hearts. We have certainly "shifted" our faith. If any falsehood be noted in our declaration now or in the future, we shall be subject to divine punishment by Bonten, Taishaku, the four deva kings, the great or little gods in all the sixty or more provinces of Japan, especially the Mishima Daimyōjin, the representatives of the god of Izu and Hakone, Hachiman Daibosatsu, Temman Daijizai Tenjin, especially our own family gods, Suwa Daimyōjin, the village people, and our relatives. This is to certify to the foregoing.

The second year of Shōhō [1645]
Endorsement.

Regulations for Buddhist Temples, 1665

1. The doctrines and rituals established for different sects must not be mixed and disarranged. If there is anyone who does not behave in accordance with this injunction, an appropriate measure must be taken expeditiously.

2. No one who does not understand the basic doctrines or rituals of a given sect is permitted to become the chief priest of a temple. Addendum: If a new rite is established, it must not preach strange doctrines.

3. The regulations which govern relationships between the main temple and branch temples must not be violated. However, even the main temple cannot take measures against branch temples in an unreasonable manner.

4. Parishioners of the temples can choose to which temple they wish to belong and make contributions. Therefore priests must not compete against one another for parishioners.

5. Priests are enjoined from engaging in activities unbecoming of priests, such as forming groups or planning to fight one another.

6. If there is anyone who has violated the law of the land, and that fact is communicated to a temple, it must turn him away without question.

7. When making repairs to a temple or a monastery, do not make them ostentatiously. Addendum: Temples must be kept clean without fail.

8. The estate belonging to a temple is not subject to sale, nor can it be mortgaged.

9. Do not allow anyone who has expressed a desire to become a disciple but is not of good lineage to enter the priesthood freely. If there is a particular candidate who has an improper and questionable background, the judgment of the domanial lord or magistrate of his domicile must be sought and then act accordingly.

The above articles must be strictly observed by all the sects. . . .

Fifth year of Kanbun [1665], seventh month, 11th day.

3

BADA'UNI
Akbar and Religion, 1595

At the same time the Chinese and Japanese were confronting Christian missionaries, the descendants of Muslim Turkic and Mongol peoples of Central Asia were conquering the Hindu kingdoms of northern India. Babur (1483–1530), the first of these Mughal rulers, swept into India from Afghanistan in 1525. Successive Mughal emperors enlarged the empire, so that by the time of Akbar (r. 1556–1605) it included all of northern India. Like his contemporaries Philip II of Spain (r. 1556–1598) and Elizabeth of England (r. 1558–1603), Akbar created an elaborate and enduring administrative bureaucracy. But unlike Philip and Elizabeth, who waged religious wars against each other and forcibly converted their domestic subjects and newly conquered peoples, Akbar reached out to his Hindu subjects in ways that would have astonished his European contemporaries. In fact, he angered many of his own Muslim advisors, including Bada'uni, the author of the following memoir. What bothered Bada'uni about Akbar? What does this selection tell you about Akbar's rule? What factors might have motivated his toleration of heterodoxy?

Source: 'Abdul Qadir Bada'uni, *Muntakhab ut-Tawarikh*, trans. G. S. A. Ranking and W. H. Lowe (Calcutta: Asiatic Society of Bengal, 1895–1925), 2:200–201, 255–61 *passim*, 324. Edited and reprinted in *Sources of Indian Tradition*, ed. Ainslie T. Embree (New York: Columbia University Press, 1988), 465–68.

THINKING HISTORICALLY

We know from other sources that Akbar made special efforts to include Hindus in his administration. About a third of his governing bureaucracy was Hindu, and he gave Hindu-governed territories a large degree of self-rule, allowing them to retain their own law and courts. Various taxes normally paid by non-Muslims were abolished. Among Akbar's five thousand wives, many were Hindus including his favorite, the mother of his successor, Jahangir (r. 1605–1628).

Akbar's policy of toleration continued under his son and grandson, Jahangir and Shah Jahan (r. 1628–1658), but was largely reversed by his great grandson, Aurangzeb (r. 1658–1707). How does this understanding of a particular past provide context?

Context can also help us understand our distance from the past. Our contemporary mind-set can blind us to those differences. To give a small example, Bada'uni writes in this selection of people who behaved "like Jews and Egyptians for hatred of each other." The modern reader may take this as a reference to the modern conflict between Jews and Muslims, especially that between Israel and Egypt: an idea that reinforces the conviction that Jews and Muslims are eternal enemies. But Bada'uni is not thinking of Egypt as Muslim, even though it was Muslim in the seventeenth century and had been for a thousand years. If he had, there would be no reason to single out Egypt, then under Ottoman rule, since so many other states were Muslim and contained Jews. Bada'uni had to be referring to the biblical account of Moses in Pharoah's Egypt, pre-Muslim by two thousand years. Consequently, rather than suggest Muslim antipathy to Jews, Bada'uni's reference shows us how Muslims were familiar with the Hebrew Bible, and how they understood Judaism and the Bible as part of their Muslim heritage.

Modern ideas might distort the meaning not only of a minor reference like the above, but the meaning, impact, or uniqueness of the entire text. For instance, most of us in modern society believe in toleration and religious freedom. But did Bada'uni? How is Bada'uni's attitude toward his subject different from ours? How might that difference lead us to misunderstand what Bada'uni is trying to convey? What is the value of keeping Bada'uni's ideas in mind alongside Akbar's?

In the year nine hundred and eighty-three [1605] the buildings of the 'Ibādatkhāna[1] were completed. The cause was this. For many years previously the emperor had gained in succession remarkable and decisive victories. The empire had grown in extent from day to day; everything

[1] Hall of Religious Discussions. [Ed.]

turned out well, and no opponent was left in the whole world. His Majesty had thus leisure to come into nearer contact with ascetics and the disciples of his reverence [the late] Mucīn, and passed much of his time in discussing the word of God and the word of the Prophet. Questions of Sufism,[2] scientific discussions, inquiries into philosophy and law, were the order of the day.

And later that day the emperor came to Fatehpur. There he used to spend much time in the Hall of Worship in the company of learned men and shaikhs and especially on Friday nights, when he would sit up there the whole night continually occupied in discussing questions of religion, whether fundamental or collateral. The learned men used to draw the sword of the tongue on the battlefield of mutual contradiction and op-position, and the antagonism of the sects reached such a pitch that they would call one another fools and heretics. The controversies used to pass beyond the differences of Sunni, and Shī'a, of Hanafī and Shā fi'ī, of lawyer and divine, and they would attack the very bases of belief. And Makhdūm-ul-Mulk wrote a treatise to the effect that Shaikh 'Abd-al-Nabī had unjustly killed Khizr Khān Sarwānī, who had been suspected of blaspheming the Prophet [peace be upon him!], and Mīr Habsh, who had been suspected of being a Shī'a, and saying that it was not right to repeat the prayers after him, because he was undutiful toward his father, and was himself afflicted with hemorrhoids. Shaikh 'Abd-al-Nabī re-plied to him that he was a fool and a heretic. Then the mullās [Muslim theologians] became divided into two parties, and one party took one side and one the other, and became very [much like] Jews and Egyptians for hatred of each other. And persons of novel and whimsical opinions, in accordance with their pernicious ideas and vain doubts, coming out of ambush, decked the false in the garb of the true, and wrong in the dress of right, and cast the emperor, who was possessed of an excellent disposition, and was an earnest searcher after truth, but very ignorant and a mere tyro,[3] and used to the company of infidels and base persons, into perplexity, till doubt was heaped upon doubt, and he lost all definite aim, and the straight wall of the clear law and of firm religion was bro-ken down, so that after five or six years not a trace of Islam was left in him: and everything was turned topsy-turvy. . . .

And samanas [Hindu or Buddhist ascetics] and brāhmans (who as far as the matter of private interviews is concerned gained the advantage over everyone in attaining the honor of interviews with His Majesty, and in associating with him, and were in every way superior in reputation to all learned and trained men for their treatises on morals, and on physical and religious sciences, and in religious ecstasies, and stages of spiritual

[2] Mystical, poetic Islamic tradition. [Ed.]
[3] Beginner. [Ed.]

progress and human perfections) brought forward proofs, based on reason and traditional testimony, for the truth of their own, and the fallacy of our religion, and inculcated their doctrine with such firmness and assurance, that they affirmed mere imaginations as though they were self-evident facts, the truth of which the doubts of the sceptic could no more shake "Than the mountains crumble, and the heavens be cleft!" And the Resurrection, and Judgment, and other details and traditions, of which the Prophet was the repository, he laid all aside. And he made his courtiers continually listen to those revilings and attacks against our pure and easy, bright and holy faith. . . .

Some time before this a brāhman, named Puruk'hotam, who had written a commentary on the Book, *Increase of Wisdom* (Khirad-afzā), had had private interviews with him, and he had asked him to invent particular Sanskrit names for all things in existence. And at one time a brāhman, named Debi, who was one of the interpreters of the *Mahābhā rata*,[4] was pulled up the wall of the castle sitting on a bedstead till he arrived near a balcony, which the emperor had made his bedchamber. Whilst thus suspended he instructed His Majesty in the secrets and legends of Hinduism, in the manner of worshiping idols, the fire, the sun and stars, and of revering the chief gods of these unbelievers, such as Brahma, Mahadev [Shiva], Bishn [Vishnu], Kishn [Krishna], Ram, and Mahama (whose existence as sons of the human race is a supposition, but whose nonexistence is a certainty, though in their idle belief they look on some of them as gods, and some as angels). His Majesty, on hearing further how much the people of the country prized their institutions, began to look upon them with affection. . . .

Sometimes again it was Shaikh Tā j ud-dīn whom he sent for. This shaikh was son of Shaikh Zakarīya of Ajodhan. . . . He had been a pupil of Rashīd Shaikh Zamān of Panipat, author of a commentary on the *Paths* (*Lawā'ih*), and of other excellent works, was most excellent in Sufism, and in the knowledge of theology second only to Shaikh Ibn 'Arabī and had written a comprehensive commentary on the *Joy of the Souls* (*Nuzhat ul-Arwāh*). Like the preceding he was drawn up the wall of the castle in a blanket, and His Majesty listened the whole night to his Sufic obscenities and follies. The shaikh, since he did not in any great degree feel himself bound by the injunctions of the law, introduced arguments concerning the unity of existence, such as idle Sufis discuss, and which eventually lead to license and open heresy. . . .

Learned monks also from Europe, who are called *Padre*, and have an infallible head, called *Papa*,[5] who is able to change religious ordinances as he may deem advisable for the moment, and to whose authority kings must submit, brought the Gospel, and advanced proofs for the

---

[4] Classical Indian epic; source of Hinduism. See Volume 1, selection 5 in Chapter 3. [Ed.]
[5] The Roman Catholic pope. [Ed.]

Trinity. His Majesty firmly believed in the truth of the Christian religion, and wishing to spread the doctrines of Jesus, ordered Prince Murād to take a few lessons in Christianity under good auspices, and charged Abū'l Fazl to translate the Gospel. . . .

Fire worshipers also came from Nousarīin Gujarat, proclaimed the religion of Zardusht [Zarathustra] as the true one, and declared reverence to fire to be superior to every other kind of worship. They also attracted the emperor's regard, and taught him the peculiar terms, the ordinances, the rites and ceremonies of the Kaianians [a pre-Muslim Persian dynasty]. At last he ordered that the sacred fire should be made over to the charge of Abū'l Fazl, and that after the manner of the kings of Persia, in whose temples blazed perpetual fires, he should take care it was never extinguished night or day, for that it is one of the signs of God, and one light from His lights. . . .

His Majesty also called some of the yogis, and gave them at night private interviews, inquiring into abstract truths; their articles of faith; their occupation; the influence of pensiveness; their several practices and usages; the power of being absent from the body; or into alchemy, physiognomy, and the power of omnipresence of the soul.

4

MARTIN LUTHER

Sermon on Religion and the State, 1528–1540

Martin Luther (1483–1546), the iconic father of the Protestant Reformation, was a Catholic monk, priest, and then professor of theology in Germany when in 1517 he challenged the papacy, first on the issue of the church selling indulgences that were said to speed a soul to heaven and then, increasingly, over issues of corruption and church power. Luther believed that the church had gone astray, becoming materialistic and out of touch with its original mission. He sought a return to the origins of Christianity, quoting Paul on the need for faith alone. He translated the Bible from Latin into German so that anyone could understand their religion, without the intervention of priests, pope, or all of the trappings of what he viewed as a bloated church. According to Luther, every believer was a priest, and

Source: Martin Luther, *The Sermons of Martin Luther*, vol. 5 (Grand Rapids, MI: Baker Book House, 1983), 294–306.

therefore priests could marry. The Catholic hierarchy, ceremony, even most of the sacraments were unnecessary. After an effort to defend his beliefs, Luther was summoned by the Church to recant. He refused and in 1521 was excommunicated from the Catholic Church. By then he had fled capture by the Catholic Holy Roman Emperor and the Roman papacy, receiving the protection of the German princes, splitting Roman Christianity into Catholicism and Protestantism and creating a new church and doctrine, Lutheranism, with a German national identity.

Luther's writings, including the German Bible, theological treatises, weekly hymns and sermons, periodic tracts, thoughts, and musings, fill over sixty volumes. This selection comes from one of his sermons. Luther began by quoting Matthew 22:15–22, the best known Christian statement about the relationship between the state and religion. What is that position? Would you call it a belief in the separation of church and state? How would you compare it to Akbar's position on church and state?

THINKING HISTORICALLY

In this sermon, Luther tries to define the relationship between church and state in a way that he believes is most true to the account of Matthew and, therefore, most true for his time. But his time was different from that of Matthew, with two different political contexts. How was the relationship of Luther to the state different from that of Jesus as described in the sermon? Which of the two was more dependent on state support? What evidence do you see in Luther's sermon that would suggest greater trust in the state than Jesus expressed?

Another context is suggested at the very end of this selection. Luther refers to the peasant revolt of 1523–1524, when peasants rebelled against their landlords, feudal obligations, and even the German princes. Some believed that Luther's ideas of individual justification by faith and the freedom of a Christian fomented the rebellion. Why might the revolt and accusations make Luther more inclined to frame the question of church and state the way he did here?

Sermon for 23rd Sunday after Trinity: Matthew 22:15–22

Then the Pharisees went out and laid plans to trap him in his words. They sent their disciples to him along with the Herodians. "Teacher," they said, "we know that you are a man of integrity and that you teach the way of God in accordance with the truth. You aren't swayed by others, because you pay no attention to who they are. Tell us then, what is your opinion? Is it right to pay the imperial tax to Caesar or not?"

But Jesus, knowing their evil intent, said, "You hypocrites, why are you trying to trap me? Show me the coin used for paying the tax." They brought him a denarius, and he asked them, "Whose image is this? And whose inscription?"

"Caesar's," they replied.

Then he said to them, "So give back to Caesar what is Caesar's, and to God what is God's."

When they heard this, they were amazed. So they left him and went away.

"Give back to Caesar what is Caesar's, and to God what is God's."

Although the Pharisees did not deserve it, the Lord teaches them the right way. And with these words he also confirms the worldly sword or government. They had hoped he would condemn it and speak against it; he does not do it, however, but praises earthly government and commands to render unto it what is due to it. It is therefore his desire that there should be magistrates, princes and masters, whom we are to obey, be they what they may and what they list; neither should we ask whether they possess and exercise government and authority justly or unjustly. We should only pay heed to that power and authority which is good, for it is ordered and instituted by God, Rom. 13, 1: You are not allowed to upbraid the government, when at times you are oppressed by princes and tyrants, who abuse the power they have from God: some day they will surely have to answer for it. The abuse of a thing does not make it bad, if it was good in itself. A golden chain is good, and it is not made worse by being worn around a whore's neck; or if someone were to destroy one of my eyes with it, should I therefore blame the chain? Truly nay.

Thus one must also bear the authority of the ruler. If he abuses it, I am not therefore to bear him a grudge, nor take revenge of and punish him with my hands. One must obey him solely for God's sake, for he stands in God's stead. Let them impose taxes as intolerable as they may: one must obey them and, suffer everything patiently, for God's sake. Whether they do right or not, that will be taken care of in due time. If therefore your possessions, aye, your life and whatsoever you have, be taken from you by those in power, then you are to say: I give it to you willingly, I acknowledge you as my masters, gladly will I be obedient to you. Whether you use the power given to you by God well or ill, that is your affair.

But what if they would take the Gospel from us or forbid us to preach it? Then you are to say: The Gospel and Word of God, I will not give up to you. This is not within your power, for your rule is a temporal rule, over worldly matters; but the Gospel is a spiritual, heavenly treasure, and therefore your authority does not extend over the Gospel and God's Word. We recognize the emperor as a master of temporal affairs, not of God's Word; this we shall not suffer to be torn from us, for it is the power of God, Rom. 1, 16, against which not even the gates of hell shall prevail.

Therefore, the Lord beautifully summarizes these two things, and in one saying distinguishes them from each other: "Render unto Caesar the things that are Caesar's, and unto God the things that are God's." This honor is due to God, that we are to hold him as a true, almighty and wise God, and attribute to him all the good things that can be named. And even if I do not render him this honor, he still keeps it; nothing is added to or subtracted from it. But in me he is true, almighty and wise, if I consider him as such, and believe him to be such as he proclaims himself. To the emperor, however, and to all in power, are due reverence, taxes, revenue and obedience. God will have the heart; body and possessions are the government's, which is to rule over them in God's stead. This St. Paul says to the Romans in round and clear words, Rom. 13, 1–7: "Let every soul be in subjection to the higher powers: for there is no power but of God; and the powers that be are ordained of God. Therefore he that resisteth the power, withstandeth the ordinance of God: and they that withstand shall receive to themselves judgment. For rulers are not a terror to the good work, but to the evil. And wouldest thou have no fear of the power? do that which is good, and thou shalt have praise from the same: for he is a minister of God to thee for good. But if thou do that which is evil, be afraid; for he beareth not the sword in vain: for he is a minister of God, an avenger for wrath to him that doeth evil. Wherefore ye must needs be in subjection, not only because of the wrath, but also for conscience' sake. Hence for this cause ye pay tribute also, for they are ministers of God's service, attending continually upon this very thing. Render to all their dues: tribute to whom tribute is due; custom to whom custom; fear to whom fear; honor to whom honor."

And for this reason also has government been ordained by God, that it may uphold general peace, which thing alone cannot be paid for by all the money in the world. We just noticed a few things in the uprising of the peasant, what damage, misery and woe are caused by rebellion and the breaking of peace. God grant that things do not go further and that we experience no more. Enough is said on this Gospel. Of temporal government we have written a special booklet. Whoever desires to read it may do so. There he will find more on this subject.

5

BENJAMIN J. KAPLAN

European Faiths and States, 2007

In Europe the state emerged as a major force after 1500. But the rise of the European state was accompanied by a cultural revolution. That revolution was the creation of self-conscious faith-based communities, spurred by the Protestant Reformation and the Catholic response. In this selection, Benjamin J. Kaplan, a modern historian, shows the novelty and intolerance of this combination of confessional community and state power. Why was this combination so volatile? Did it make European society and European governments more intolerant than were other societies like China, Japan, or India? How were these changes in Europe similar to, and different from, those in the other societies during the same period?

THINKING HISTORICALLY

If we were reading Benjamin Kaplan as a primary source, we might ask about the context of someone writing in the first decade of the present century (notice publication was 2007) about religious intolerance. But we are reading Kaplan as a secondary source. So instead, let us consider how he provides context that helps us understand sources from the period he discusses. How does he help you understand Martin Luther? In what ways does his work change your view of Luther? Does he put Luther in a different context?

No religion is static, and over its two millennia of existence the Roman Catholic Church has transformed itself several times. The so-called Investiture Controversy[1] of the eleventh century precipitated one such transformation; in the 1960s, Vatican II[2] decreed another. So too in the sixteenth century, partly in response to the Protestant challenge, partly driven by internal impulses for renewal and reform, the Catholic Church initiated sweeping changes in everything from ecclesiastic administration and the training of priests to liturgy and forms of private devotion.

---

[1] A struggle in Europe in the eleventh and twelfth centuries over whether kings or the pope had authority to appoint church officials. [Ed.]

[2] An important series of changes under Pope John XXIII said to modernize the Catholic Church (1962–1965). [Ed.]

Source: Benjamin J. Kaplan, *Divided by Faith: Religious Conflict and the Practice of Toleration in Early Modern Europe* (Cambridge: Harvard University Press, 2007), 28–32, 100–03.

Conventionally, the drive to enact these changes is referred to as either the Counter-Reformation or the Catholic Reformation, the first term emphasizing its reactive quality, the second its self-generation. Both terms, however, obscure a crucial fact: that changes in Catholicism resembled in some respects the reforms instituted by Protestants. That is, for all the differences and points of contention that bitterly divided them, in some respects the churches of early modern Europe were developing in parallel to one another. Christianity was changing, irrespective of church. The new type of Christianity that resulted from this process is known as "confessional." Its emergence, also called the "rise of confessionalism" or the "formation of confessions," can be charted beginning in the sixteenth century and continuing through the seventeenth.

To dispel any confusion, it must be explained that the term *confession* and its derivatives do not refer in this context to the Catholic sacrament of penance. Rather they refer to a type of document, the "confession of faith," a declaration of the fundamental doctrines held by a church. Perhaps the most famous was the Augsburg Confession of 1530, which came to define Lutheran orthodoxy. All early modern churches issued such documents, which embodied three of the most basic trends then in Christianity: the internalization of church teaching, the drawing of sharp dichotomies, and the quest for "holy uniformity." Each fueled intolerance.

The timing and modalities of these trends varied greatly by church and by region, and in Ireland they had hardly affected the vast majority of peasants (who remained loyal to Catholicism) by the 1660s. According to Englishman Jeremy Taylor, the Irish peasantry could "give no account of their religion what it is: only they believe as their priest bids them and go to mass which they understand not, and reckon their beads to tell the number and the tale of their prayers, and abstain from eggs and flesh in Lent, and visit St. Patrick's well, and leave pins and ribbons, yarn or thread in their holy wells, and pray to God, S. Mary and S. Patrick, S. Columbanus and S. Bridget, and desire to be buried with S. Francis cord about them, and to fast on Saturdays in honour of our Lady."[3]

Granted that Taylor was a hostile outsider, his description not only matches what we know about seventeeth-century Ireland, it captures a state of affairs that was quite the norm across Europe prior to the Reformation. For medieval Christians, religion was as much a set of ritual practices as a set of beliefs. It entailed feasting and fasting on prescribed days; attending mass; reciting prayers in a language (Latin) they scarcely understood; making pilgrimages to holy places, where they offered sacrifices to wonder-working saints; and a wide array of other "works."

---

[3] Keith Thomas, *Religion and the Decline of Magic* (New York, 1971), pp. 76–77.

These had merit, according to theologians, only if performed in a devout frame of mind. In practice, though, priests and laity attributed to them an efficacy as reliable as transubstantiation, the miracle of the mass whereby wafer and wine became Christ's body and blood. The more frequently they were performed, it was said, the more divine grace they conveyed and the better your chances of going to heaven. Many religious acts, in any event, were directed less toward attaining salvation after death than toward escaping misfortune in life. Making the sign of the cross, wearing an amulet containing the words from the Gospel of John, parading images of saints through parish streets: such acts were believed to ward off evil, offering protection from disease, accident, war, and famine.

In medieval Europe, ordinary laypeople knew little church doctrine. They received no formal religious instruction, and their pastors rarely preached. Like Taylor's peasants, they could establish their orthodoxy simply by declaring they "believe as their priest bids them." Such ignorance did not matter greatly in a world where everyone was by default Catholic. It did after Europe split into competing "confessions," each propounding a rival truth. As each church began to define its identity in terms of its unique teachings, doctrine took on an unprecedented importance, and the expectation, echoed in Taylor's disdain, began to build that church members know what their church taught and how it differed from other churches. For Protestants, this expectation was built into the very definition of their religion, which taught that salvation is "by faith alone." All the Protestant churches accepted it as their mission to teach Christians what they needed to believe to be saved. At the same time, a more general dynamic operated: the very existence of alternatives created pressure for Christians to be better informed and more self-conscious in their commitments. Catholic reformers too began to demand that ordinary church members internalize the teachings of their church. Religion itself thus came increasingly to mean belief in a particular creed, and a life lived in accordance with it.

It was easy for churches to enunciate such dramatically raised standards. Implementing them required decades, in some regions as much as two centuries, of strenuous effort. The churches had to undertake massive pedagogic campaigns, which they conducted via preaching, education, printed propaganda, church discipline, and revamped rituals. In all these areas Protestant reformers broke new ground. They made the sermon the centerpiece of Protestant worship. They required that children receive elementary religious instruction, either at school or through special catechism[4] classes. They released torrents of printed propaganda and encouraged ordinary Christians to read scripture. They established new institutions and procedures to supervise parish life. . . .

---

[4] Indoctrination; memorizing doctrine. [Ed.]

Facing many of the same challenges as Protestant reformers, Catholic reformers had no qualms about adopting the former's pedagogic methods (and vice versa). The Jesuits in particular engaged in a range of activities that show striking parallels to those of their enemies. They became renowned preachers, wrote catechisms (that of Peter Canisius was the most popular in Catholic Europe), and founded hundreds of new schools, mostly at the secondary and college level. Using the *Spiritual Exercises* written by their founder, Ignatius of Loyola, they taught people how to examine their own consciences and achieve pious goals through a remarkable self-discipline. As confessors, chaplains, and organizers of a new type of club, the Marian sodality, they encouraged frequent confession and Communion. This disciplinary routine encouraged the internalization of norms even as it provided an external mechanism for enforcing them. . . .

Just as the welfare of towns and villages depended on God's favor, Europeans believed, so did that of countries. . . . In 1663, when Ottoman armies launched an offensive into central Europe, prayers went up across the Continent. One pietist preacher warned his Dutch congregation that the Turks would conquer all unless lax, indifferent Christians put into practice the teachings they mouthed. Two decades later the Turks attacked again, this time reaching the walls of Vienna. At this critical juncture, Pope Innocent XI marshaled an international alliance to relieve the imperial capital. Protestant as well as Catholic princes of Germany sent troops to fight alongside Poles and Austrians. After the combined Christian army broke the Turks' siege, Innocent organized a "Holy League" whose forces drove the Turks once and for all back to the Balkans. This crusade was the last hurrah for the medieval concept of a united Christendom led by pope and emperor.

By then, two developments had made the concept almost completely anachronistic. One we have already examined: the division of Christendom into competing confessions. The other was the emergence of political units resembling modern nation-states. Particularism[5] did not disappear, either as a set of power relationships or as a mentality. Increasingly, though, Europe's rulers asserted an impersonal authority that can be called sovereignty, rather than (or, perhaps better, in addition to) the personal suzerainty[6] of the feudal Middle Ages. They codified laws, issued regulations, raised taxes, formalized institutions, and mobilized networks of officials, casting in this way a tighter net of control over society. One must not exaggerate the control rulers achieved, for early modern governments never had the tools of law enforcement modern ones take for granted. More than is often realized, their

[5] Local, personal, and decentralized politics, as in medieval feudalism. [Ed.]
[6] Dependence. [Ed.]

authority depended on the consent of the governed. Nevertheless, by the late seventeenth century some princes had achieved what at the time was called "absolute" authority: they could wage war, issue laws, and impose taxes without the approval of representative institutions, or with sure knowledge of their rubber stamp. "Absolutism" vested all sovereign power in a single individual, but even in polities that remained fragmented, like those of the Dutch and Swiss, there developed "a more encompassing, more systematic, and more literate articulation of power and authority."[7] The development took as many forms as there were forms of polity, but across Europe it was clear: the state grew stronger as an institution and more cohesive as a political community.

The fusion of these two developments, confessionalism and state formation, was explosive. The fictional Irishman Dooley, creation of modern humorist Finley Peter Dunne, once observed: "Rellijon is a quare thing. Be itself it's all right. But sprinkle a little pollyticks into it an' dinnymit is bran flour compared with it. Alone it prepares a man f'r a better life. Combined with polyticks it hurries him to it."[8] The observation has a special ring of truth in the mouth of an Irishman, for in modern Ireland, religious and political causes—Protestantism and Union with Britain, Catholicism and Irish Nationalism—have become inseparable. In the sixteenth century, religion and politics combined similarly across Europe. Religious enemies, their hatreds fanned by confessional ideology, became political enemies, and vice versa, as people at odds with one another for social or political reasons tended to choose opposing sides religiously as well. In this way, Europe's religious divisions not only created new conflicts, they threw ideological fuel on the fires of existing ones. Competitions for power, wealth, or land became cosmic struggles between the forces of God and Satan. Inversely, the bonds of a common confession brought people together in equally powerful ways. When they cut across social or political lines, they could make friends of strangers or even former enemies. On every level, from the local to the international, co-religionists felt an impulse to make common cause with one another.

To Europe's rulers, then, the rise of confessionalism held out both perils and promises. A difference in religion could alienate their subjects from them and undermine their authority. As the French Wars of Religion demonstrated, to the horror of contemporaries, it could set citizen against fellow citizen and tear states apart in civil war. A shared religion, on the other hand, could bolster rulers' authority, binding their subjects

[7] So characterized by Randolph C. Head in "Fragmented Dominion, Fragmented Churches: The Institutionalization of the *Landfrieden* in the Thurgau, 1531–1610," *Archiv fur Reformationsgeschichte* 96 (205): 119.

[8] Leonard W. Levy, *The Establishment Clause: Religion and the First Amendment* (New York, 1986), ix.

to them and to one another more firmly. Given these starkly contrasting possibilities, it is no wonder rulers tried to impose religious uniformity on their territories. Their personal piety impelled many to do the same. Since the thirteenth century, the Catholic Church had asked them to swear they would "strive in good faith and to the best of their ability to exterminate in the territories subject to their jurisdiction all heretics pointed out by the Church."[9] The division of Western Christendom gave them compelling new reasons to do so.

In its wake, Europe's rulers tried to make their personal choice of faith official for their state. Most succeeded, though, as we shall see, not all. Either way, the resulting confessional allegiance eventually became a defining aspect of political identity. Whether or not it initially had wide support, the allegiance was institutionalized and sank popular roots. In some essential and irreversible way, England became a Protestant country, Poland a Catholic one, Sweden Lutheran, the Dutch Republic Calvinist, and so forth. This fusion of religious and political identity, piety and patriotism, was (after confessionalism and the communal quest for holiness) the third great cause of religious intolerance in early modern Europe. Forged in the course of Europe's religious wars, it led both rulers and ordinary people to equate orthodoxy with loyalty and religious dissent with sedition. It gave national politics and even foreign affairs the power to spark waves of religious riots as well as official persecution.

[9] Robert I. Moore, *The Formation of a Persecuting Society: Power and Deviance in Western Europe, 950–1250* (Oxford, 1987), 7.

6

Remonstrance of the Inhabitants of the Town of Flushing to Governor Stuyvesant, December 27, 1657

A guiding principle in Europe after 1555 was that the religion of the prince would be the religion of the people. Thus, religious freedom meant moving somewhere else. Many did, including the Pilgrims, Puritans, Catholics, and later, Quakers, Baptists, and Methodists who came to the Americas. But those who sought religious freedom for themselves rarely sought it for others. In New England, it took the voice of Roger Williams (1603–1683), a religious fundamentalist in a colony

Source: http://www.queensbp.org/remonstrance/index.html.

of more establishment Protestantism, to demand the separation of church and state. The principle of religious freedom originated to protect the conscience of a minority against the state, though Williams retained the principle in his own colony of Providence, which became Rhode Island.

The colony of New Netherland (comprising settlements in today's New York, New Jersey, Delaware, and Connecticut), with its capital, New Amsterdam, on the southern tip of Manhattan, was founded by the Dutch. Less to save souls than to make money, the colony was to be a center of trade, very much like its parent, the Netherlands. The Netherlands enshrined freedom of religion from its origins in 1579, declaring "no one shall be persecuted or investigated because of his religion." In 1625 the same principle was to hold in the Dutch West India Company colony. To a great extent freedom of conscience did prevail. The first Jews in North America were welcomed in New Amsterdam in 1654, refugees from a New Holland, Brazil, recently conquered by Portugal.

Nevertheless, the official religion of New Netherland was the Dutch Reformed Church and Peter Stuyvesant, the Dutch General Director of the colony from 1647 to 1664, drew the line at Quakers, who he thought to be particularly troublesome. In 1657 Stuyvesant made it a crime for anyone in the colony to harbor Quakers. Citizens of Flushing (now Queens) directed the following response to Stuyvesant. What did they declare? What reasons did they give? What was the significance of their action?

THINKING HISTORICALLY

Sometimes, knowing the context of a document enhances its impact. To the modern ear, the sentiments expressed in the Flushing Remonstrance are admirable, but quite familiar. In the modern context, it might not seem like such a courageous act. But in the context of the time, the stakes were quite high. Earlier in1657 Stuyvesant had publicly tortured a Quaker preacher. The signers could certainly expect retribution. In fact, many of the signers were imprisoned or exiled. By scanning the names of the signers, you cannot tell that none of them were Quakers, but you can tell something of their nationality and social standing (at least as indicated by education). Were they all the same nationality: Was it Dutch or English? Were they powerful legal adversaries of the Governor General or ordinary men? How do these contexts make their statement more impressive?

Right Honourable [Governor Stuyvesant]
You have been pleased to send unto us a certain prohibition or command that we should not receive or entertain any of those people called

Quakers because they are supposed to be, by some, seducers of the people. For our part we cannot condemn them in this case, neither can we stretch out our hands against them, for out of Christ God is a consuming fire, and it is a fearful thing to fall into the hands of the living God.

Wee desire therefore in this case not to judge least we be judged, neither to condemn least we be condemned, but rather let every man stand or fall to his own Master. Wee are bounde by the law to do good unto all men, especially to those of the household of faith. And though for the present we seem to be unsensible for the law and the Law giver, yet when death and the Law assault us, if wee have our advocate to seeke, who shall plead for us in this case of conscience betwixt God and our own souls; the powers of this world can neither attach us, neither excuse us, for if God justifye who can condemn and if God condemn there is none can justifye.

And for those jealousies and suspicions which some have of them, that they are destructive unto Magistracy and Ministerye, that cannot bee, for the Magistrate hath his sword in his hand and the Minister hath the sword in his hand, as witnesse those two great examples, which all Magistrates and Ministers are to follow, Moses and Christ, whom God raised up maintained and defended against all enemies both of flesh and spirit; and therefore that of God will stand, and that which is of man will come to nothing. And as the Lord hath taught Moses or the civil power to give an outward liberty in the state, by the law written in his heart designed for the good of all, and can truly judge who is good, who is evil, who is true and who is false, and can pass definitive sentence of life or death against that man which arises up against the fundamental law of the States General; soe he hath made his ministers a savor of life unto life and a savor of death unto death.

The law of love, peace and liberty in the states extending to Jews, Turks and Egyptians, as they are considered sons of Adam, which is the glory of the outward state of Holland, soe love, peace and liberty, extending to all in Christ Jesus, condemns hatred, war and bondage. And because our Saviour sayeth it is impossible but that offences will come, but woe unto him by whom they cometh, our desire is not to offend one of his little ones, in whatsoever form, name or title hee appears in, whether Presbyterian, Independent, Baptist or Quaker, but shall be glad to see anything of God in any of them, desiring to doe unto all men as we desire all men should doe unto us, which is the true law both of Church and State; for our Saviour sayeth this is the law and the prophets.

Therefore if any of these said persons come in love unto us, we cannot in conscience lay violent hands upon them, but give them free egresse and regresse unto our Town, and houses, as God shall persuade our consciences, for we are bounde by the law of God and man to doe good unto all men and evil to noe man. And this is according to the patent and charter of our Towne, given unto us in the name of the States General, which we are not willing to infringe, and violate, but shall houlde to our patent and shall remaine, your humble subjects, the inhabitants of Vlishing.

Written this 27th of December in the year 1657, by mee.

Edward Hart, Clericus

Additional Signers

Tobias Feake

The marke of William Noble

William Thorne, Seignior

The marke of William Thorne, Jr.

Edward Tarne

John Store

Nathaniel Hefferd

Benjamin Hubbard

The marke of William Pidgion

The marke of George Clere

Elias Doughtie

Antonie Feild

Richard Stocton

Edward Griffine

John Townesend

Nathaniell Tue

Nicholas Blackford

The marke of Micah Tue

The marke of Philip Ud

Robert Field, senior

Robert Field, junior

Nich Colas Parsell

Michael Milner

Henry Townsend

George Wright

John Foard

Henry Semtell

Edward Hart

John Mastine

Edward Farrington

■ REFLECTIONS

Religious hospitals, school choice, abortion, the public display of religious symbols—what is the proper relationship of government and religion? The North American colonies of the seventeenth century evolved a principle of the separation of church and state, largely out of religious, not secular motives. It was an idea that had recent roots in Europe, originating in the formation of the Dutch Republic in 1579, but its roots ran deep in Christianity. Christians in the Middle Ages talked about the two swords of power (clerical and secular), St Augustine wrote about the two cities (of God and man) and Jesus distinguished between the responsibilities to God and Caesar. In the sixteenth century, Luther reaffirmed this distinction, but he gave German princes far greater authority over religious matters than most Christians would allow today.

Luther, John Calvin, Henry VIII, and most early Protestants were vigorous proponents of state religions, the legislation of Christian morality, and the censorship and proscription of contrary beliefs and behavior. Benjamin Kaplan shows how both the Protestant Reformation and the similar Catholic Counter-Reformation created robustly intolerant religious communities. New kings and parliaments put religious doctrines into the service of national states as if they were badges of identity or flags to be saluted.

It is a modern conceit that tolerance must have gradually increased since the "dark ages." Kaplan shows us how intolerance increased in Europe with the rise of confessional faiths and the state. A similar transition occurred in India from Akbar to Aurangzeb. In both cases, the religious fundamentalists made government less tolerant of diversity or heterodoxy. The religious leaders who suffered most under the Mughals were not Hindus, but reformers who attempted to unite Hinduism and Islam under a new monotheism, the Sikhs. As often happens, the reformers closest to home smelled the foulest.

Neither the Chinese nor Japanese traditions held religious orthodoxies. But both required proper observance of certain social and political proprieties. Strong governments, as in most of Chinese history, turned principles like Confucian filial piety into virtual religions but they had the force of law and made little appeal to conscience or individual choice. Daoism and Buddhism appealed to the inner lives of Chinese and Japanese devotees, but normally posed no conflict to state power. Only in periods of unrest, feudalism, or the breakdown of the state did Buddhist or Daoist priests and monks exercise political power. Even then, however, they did not challenge the state as much as they filled the vacuum left by its disappearance. In both Japan and Europe, the post-feudal age was one in which the state's rise depended, in part, on the reclamation and monopolization of powers previously exercised by religious institutions.

Many pasts, but increasingly one present. As cultural differences meld with the force of rockets and the speed of the Internet, one might well ask what separate histories matter to a common present. Increasingly principles of toleration are enshrined by international organizations in declarations of human rights and the proceedings of international tribunals. Whether we see the roots of modern principles of tolerance in Confucian secularism, Christian separation of church and state, or Muslim cosmopolitanism, we live in a world where intolerance is widely condemned and legitimately prosecuted.

And yet, fanaticism and intolerance have not disappeared. Religious fundamentalists of various stripes declare their missions to take over governments, convert populations, and bring about the rule of God. History has shown that tolerance need not be secular. Indeed even the aggressively secular regimes of the twentieth and twenty-first centuries have demonstrated and continue to demonstrate a capacity for brutal persecution of dissidents, religious and otherwise.

18

Women, Marriage, and Family
China and Europe, 1550–1700

■ HISTORICAL CONTEXT

The family is the oldest and most important social institution. For those who marry, marriage can be one of the most important passages in one's life. Yet up until the last few decades these subjects rarely registered as important topics in world history. There were at least three reasons for this: One was the tendency to think of history as the story of public events only—the actions of political officials, governments, and their representatives—instead of the private and domestic sphere. The second was the assumption that the private or domestic sphere had no history, that it had always been the same. As the documents in this chapter will show, nothing could be further from the truth. The third is that most history was written by men until about forty years ago.

Since the urban revolution five thousand years ago, most societies have been patriarchal. The laws, social codes, and dominant ideas have enshrined the power and prestige of men over women, husbands over wives, fathers over children, gods over goddesses, even brothers over sisters. Double standards for adultery, inheritance laws that favor sons, and laws that deny women property or political rights all attest to the power of patriarchal culture and norms. Almost everywhere patriarchies have limited women to the domestic sphere while granting men public and political power.

To better focus our investigation, we will concentrate on two of the important patriarchal civilizations of the Early Modern period: China and Europe. We will study a variety of sources from each, including laws, diaries, and fiction. Our goal will be to notice and characterize customs and ideas about marriage and family life in these two civilizations.

■ THINKING HISTORICALLY

Making Comparisons

We learn by making comparisons. Every new piece of knowledge we acquire leads to a comparison with what we already know. For example, we arrive in a new town and we are struck by something that we have not seen before. The town has odd street lamps, flowerpots on the sidewalks, or lots of trucks on the street. We start to formulate a theory about the differences between what we observe in the new town and what we already know about our old town. We think we're on to something, but our theory falls apart when we make more observations by staying in the new town another day, or traveling on to the next town, or going halfway across the world. As we gain more experience and make more observations, our original theory explaining an observed difference is supplanted by a much more complex theory about *types* of towns.

History is very much like travel. We learn by comparison, one step at a time, and the journey is never ending. On this trip we begin in China and then move on to Europe. We begin with primary sources and then conclude with a secondary source that will allow us to draw upon our previous readings to make increasingly informed and complex comparisons. Welcome aboard. Next stop, China.

1

Family Instructions for the Miu Lineage, Late Sixteenth Century

Chinese families in Ming times (1368–1644) often organized themselves into groups by male lineage. These groups often shared common land, built ancestral halls, published genealogies, honored their common ancestors, and ensured the success and well-being of future generations. To accomplish the last of these, lineage groups frequently compiled lists of family rules or instructions. This particular example, from the various lines of the Miu family of the Guangdong province in the south, shows how extensive these instructions could be. What values did these family instructions encourage? What activities did the Miu lineage regulate? What kind of families, and what kind of individuals, were these rules intended to produce? How would these rules have had a different impact on women and men?

Source: "Family Instructions for the Miu Lineage, Late Sixteenth Century," trans. Clara Yu, in *Chinese Civilization: A Sourcebook*, 2nd ed., ed. Patricia Ebrey (New York: Free Press, 1993), 238–40, 241–43.

THINKING HISTORICALLY

It is difficult to read this selection without thinking of one's own family and of families in one's own society. How many of the Miu lineage's concerns are concerns of families you know? Family instructions and lineage organizations are not common features of modern American society, even among Chinese Americans who may have a sense of their lineage and family identity. What institutions in modern American society regulate the activities addressed by these family instructions? Or are these activities left for self-regulation or no regulation at all? From reading this document, what do you think are some of the differences between Ming-era Chinese families and modern American families?

Work Hard at One of the Principal Occupations

1. To be filial to one's parents, to be loving to one's brothers, to be diligent and frugal—these are the first tenets of a person of good character. They must be thoroughly understood and faithfully carried out.

One's conscience should be followed like a strict teacher and insight should be sought through introspection. One should study the words and deeds of the ancients to find out their ultimate meanings. One should always remember the principles followed by the ancients, and should not become overwhelmed by current customs. For if one gives in to cruelty, pride, or extravagance, all virtues will be undermined, and nothing will be achieved.

Parents have special responsibilities. *The Book of Changes*[1] says: "The members of a family have strict sovereigns." The "sovereigns" are the parents. Their position in a family is one of unique authority, and they should utilize their authority to dictate matters to maintain order, and to inspire respect, so that the members of the family will all be obedient. If the parents are lenient and indulgent, there will be many troubles which in turn will give rise to even more troubles. Who is to blame for all this? The elders in a family must demand discipline of themselves, following all rules and regulations to the letter, so that the younger members emulate their good behavior and exhort each other to abide by the teachings of the ancient sages. Only in this way can the family hope to last for generations. If, however, the elders of a family should find it difficult to abide by these regulations, the virtuous youngsters of the family should help them along. Because the purpose of my work is to make such work easier, I am not afraid of giving many small details. . . .

2. Those youngsters who have taken Confucian scholarship as their hereditary occupation should be sincere and hard-working, and try to

[1] The *I Ching*, a Chinese classic. [Ed.]

achieve learning naturally while studying under a teacher. Confucianism is the only thing to follow if they wish to bring glory to their family. Those who know how to keep what they have but do not study are as useless as puppets made of clay or wood. Those who study, even if they do not succeed in the examinations, can hope to become teachers or to gain personal benefit. However, there are people who study not for learning's sake, but as a vulgar means of gaining profit. These people are better off doing nothing.

Youngsters who are incapable of concentrating on studying should devote themselves to farming; they should personally grasp the ploughs and eat the fruit of their own labor. In this way they will be able to support their families. If they fold their hands and do nothing, they will soon have to worry about hunger and cold. If, however, they realize that their forefathers also worked hard and that farming is a difficult way of life, they will not be inferior to anyone. In earlier dynasties, officials were all selected because they were filial sons, loving brothers, and diligent farmers. This was to set an example for all people to devote themselves to their professions, and to ensure that the officials were familiar with the hardships of the common people, thereby preventing them from exploiting the commoners for their own profit.

3. Farmers should personally attend to the inspection, measurement, and management of the fields, noting the soil as well as the terrain. The early harvest as well as the grain taxes and the labor service obligations should be carefully calculated. Anyone who indulges in indolence and entrusts these matters to others will not be able to distinguish one kind of crop from another and will certainly be cheated by others. I do not believe such a person could escape bankruptcy.

4. The usual occupations of the people are farming and commerce. If one tries by every possible means to make a great profit from these occupations, it usually leads to loss of capital. Therefore it is more profitable to put one's energy into farming the land; only when the fields are too far away to be tilled by oneself should they be leased to others. One should solicit advice from old farmers as to one's own capacity in farming.

Those who do not follow the usual occupations of farming or business should be taught a skill. Being an artisan is a good way of life and will also shelter a person from hunger and cold. All in all, it is important to remember that one should work hard when young, for when youth expires one can no longer achieve anything. Many people learn this lesson only after it is too late. We should guard against this mistake.

5. Fish can be raised in ponds by supplying them with grass and manure. Vegetables need water. In empty plots one can plant fruit trees such as the pear, persimmon, peach, prune, and plum, and also beans, wheat, hemp, peas, potatoes, and melons. When harvested, these vegetables and fruits can sustain life. During their growth, one should give

them constant care, nourishing them and weeding them. In this way, no labor is wasted and no fertile land is left uncultivated. On the contrary, to purchase everything needed for the morning and evening meals means the members of the family will merely sit and eat. Is this the way things should be?

6. Housewives should take full charge of the kitchen. They should make sure that the store of firewood is sufficient, so that even if it rains several days in succession, they will not be forced to use silver or rice to pay for firewood, thereby impoverishing the family. Housewives should also closely calculate the daily grocery expenses, and make sure there is no undue extravagance. Those who simply sit and wait to be fed only are treating themselves like pigs and dogs, but also are leading their whole households to ruin. . . .

Exercise Restraint

1. Our young people should know their place and observe correct manners. They are not permitted to gamble, to fight, to engage in lawsuits, or to deal in salt[2] privately. Such unlawful acts will only lead to their own downfall.

2. If land or property is not obtained by righteous means, descendants will not be able to enjoy it. When the ancients invented characters, they put gold next to two spears to mean "money," indicating that the danger of plunder or robbery is associated with it. If money is not accumulated by good means, it will disperse like overflowing water; how could it be put to any good? The result is misfortune for oneself as well as for one's posterity. This is the meaning of the saying: "The way of Heaven detests fullness, and only the humble gain." Therefore, accumulation of great wealth inevitably leads to great loss. How true are the words of Laozi![3]

A person's fortune and rank are predestined. One can only do one's best according to propriety and one's own ability; the rest is up to Heaven. If one is easily contented, then a diet of vegetables and soups provides a lifetime of joy. If one does not know one's limitations and tries to accumulate wealth by immoral and dishonest means, how can one avoid disaster? To be able to support oneself through life and not leave one's sons and grandsons in hunger and cold is enough; why should one toil so much?

3. Pride is a dangerous trait. Those who pride themselves on wealth, rank, or learning are inviting evil consequences. Even if one's accomplishments

---

[2] Get involved in the salt trade, a state monopoly. Salt was used as a preservative for fish, meat, and other foods. [Ed.]

[3] Lao Tzu, legendary Chinese philosopher and author of the *Dao de Jing*, the Daoist classic. [Ed.]

are indeed unique, there is no need to press them on anyone else. "The way of Heaven detests fullness, and only the humble gain." I have seen the truth of this saying many times.

4. Taking concubines in order to beget heirs should be a last resort, for the sons of the legal wife and the sons of the concubine are never of one mind, causing innumerable conflicts between half brothers. If the parents are in the least partial, problems will multiply, creating misfortune in later generations. Since families have been ruined because of this, it should not be taken lightly.

5. Just as diseases are caused by what goes into one's mouth, misfortunes are caused by what comes out of one's mouth. Those who are immoderate in eating and unrestrained in speaking have no one else to blame for their own ruin.

6. Most men lack resolve and listen to what their women say. As a result, blood relatives become estranged and competitiveness, suspicion, and distance arise between them. Therefore, when a wife first comes into a family, it should be made clear to her that such things are prohibited. "Start teaching one's son when he is a baby; start teaching one's daughter-in-law when she first arrives." That is to say, preventive measures should be taken early.

7. "A family's fortune can be foretold from whether its members are early risers" is a maxim of our ancient sages. Everyone, male and female, should rise before dawn and should not go to bed until after the first drum. Never should they indulge themselves in a false sense of security and leisure, for such behavior will eventually lead them to poverty.

8. Young family members who deliberately violate family regulations should be taken to the family temple, have their offenses reported to the ancestors, and be severely punished. They should then be taught to improve themselves. Those who do not accept punishment or persist in their wrongdoings will bring harm to themselves.

9. As a preventive measure against the unpredictable, the gates should be closed at dusk, and no one should be allowed to go out. Even when there are visitors, dinner parties should end early, so that there will be no need for lighting lamps and candles. On very hot or very cold days, one should be especially considerate of the kitchen servants.

10. For generations this family had dwelt in the country, and everyone has had a set profession; therefore, our descendants should not be allowed to change their place of residence. After living in the city for three years, a person forgets everything about farming; after ten years, he does not even know his lineage. Extravagance and leisure transform people, and it is hard for anyone to remain unaffected. I once remarked that the only legitimate excuse to live in a city temporarily is to flee from bandits.

11. The inner and outer rooms, halls, doorways, and furniture should be swept and dusted every morning at dawn. Dirty doorways and courtyards and haphazardly placed furniture are sure signs of a

declining family. Therefore, a schedule should be followed for cleaning them, with no excuses allowed.

12. Those in charge of cooking and kitchen work should make sure that breakfast is served before nine o'clock in the morning and dinner before five o'clock in the afternoon. Every evening the iron wok and other utensils should be washed and put away, so that the next morning, after rising at dawn, one can expect tea and breakfast to be prepared immediately and served on time. In the kitchen no lamps are allowed in the morning or at night. This is not only to save the expense, but also to avoid harmful contamination of food. Although this is a small matter, it has a great effect on health. Furthermore, since all members of the family have their regular work to do, letting them toil all day without giving them meals at regular hours is no way to provide comfort and relief for them. If these rules are deliberately violated, the person in charge will be punished as an example to the rest.

13. On the tenth and twenty-fifth days of every month, all the members of this branch, from the honored aged members to the youngsters, should gather at dusk for a meeting. Each will give an account of what he has learned, by either calling attention to examples of good and evil, or encouraging diligence, or expounding his obligations, or pointing out tasks to be completed. Each member will take turns presenting his own opinions and listening attentively to others. He should examine himself in the matters being discussed and make efforts to improve himself. The purpose of these meetings is to encourage one another in virtue and to correct each other's mistakes.

The members of the family will take turns being the chairman of these meetings, according to schedule. If someone is unable to chair a meeting on a certain day, he should ask the next person in line to take his place. The chairman should provide tea, but never wine. The meetings may be canceled on days of ancestor worship, parties, or other such occasions, or if the weather is severe. Those who are absent from these meetings for no reason are only doing themselves harm.

There are no set rules for where the meeting should be held, but the place should be convenient for group discussions. The time of the meeting should always be early evening, for this is when people have free time. As a general precaution the meeting should never last until late at night.

14. Women from lower-class families who stop at our houses tend to gossip, create conflicts, peek into the kitchens, or induce our women to believe in prayer and fortune-telling, thereby cheating them out of their money and possessions. Consequently, one should question these women often and punish those who come for no reason, so as to put a stop to the traffic.

15. Blood relatives are as close as the branches of a tree, yet their relationships can still be differentiated according to importance and

priority: Parents should be considered before brothers, and brothers should be considered before wives and children. Each person should fulfill his own duties and share with others profit and loss, joy and sorrow, life and death. In this way, the family will get along well and be blessed by Heaven. Should family members fight over property or end up treating each other like enemies, then when death or misfortune strikes they will be of even less use than strangers. If our ancestors have consciousness, they will not tolerate these unprincipled descendants who are but animals in man's clothing. Heaven responds to human vices with punishments as surely as an echo follows a sound. I hope my sons and grandsons take my words seriously.

16. To get along with patrilineal relatives, fellow villages, and relatives through marriage, one should be gentle in speech and mild in manners. When one is opposed by others, one may remonstrate with them; but when others fall short because of their limitations, one should be tolerant. If one's youngsters or servants get into fights with others, one should look into oneself to find the blame. It is better to be wronged than to wrong others. Those who take affront and become enraged, who conceal their own shortcomings and seek to defeat others, are courting immediate misfortune. Even if the other party is unbearably unreasonable, one should contemplate the fact that the ancient sages had to endure much more. If one remains tolerant and forgiving, one will be able to curb the other party's violence.

2

PU SONGLING

The Lady Knight-Errant, 1679

Born into a poor landlord-merchant family in Qing China, Pu Songling (1640–1715) succeeded in passing a low-level civil service exam but not the higher level exam until he was seventy-one. He spent most of his life tutoring and gathering stories for *Strange Stories from a Chinese Studio*, a collection of supernatural tales that made him famous. The following tale from this collection is a story of a courtship but not a marriage, and it is a story of a woman who is more than she seems.

What core values does this story celebrate?

Source: P'u Sung-ling, "The Lady Knight-Errant," ed. & trans. Lorraine S. Y. Lieu, Ma Yau-Woon, and Joseph S. M. Lau, *Traditional Chinese Stories: Themes and Variations* (New York: Columbia University Press, 1978), 77–81.

THINKING HISTORICALLY

All cultures tell stories related to courtship or marriage. How is the world described here similar to, and different from, that of the previous selection? In what ways is this "boy meets girl story" similar to those of your own culture? In what ways is it different? How might a North American version of this go? How would the moral of the story be different?

There was once a young man by the name of Ku, born of a poor family in Chin-ling.[1] He was talented and skilled in a variety of arts and crafts. However, since he could not bear to leave his aging mother, he made a simple living by selling calligraphy and paintings. He was single even at the age of twenty-five.

Opposite to where he lived was an empty house. One day, an old woman and a young girl came by to rent the place, but since there was no man in their family, Ku did not feel that it was appropriate for him to make a courtesy call.

One day when he returned home he saw the young girl coming out of his mother's room. She was about eighteen or nineteen, and of rare beauty and gracefulness. She made no attempt to hide when she saw Ku. There was an air of awe-inspiring composure about her. Ku went inside and questioned his mother. Mrs. Ku said, "That is the girl across the street. She came to borrow my scissors and ruler. She told me that only her mother lived with her. She doesn't seem to come from a poor family. When I asked why she isn't married, she said that she has to take care of her aged mother. I shall pay her mother a visit tomorrow, and sound her out. If they don't ask for too much, perhaps you can take care of her mother for her."

The next day, she went over to the young girl's house. She found the mother hard of hearing, and when she looked around the house, there did not seem to be enough food there for the following day. She asked the old woman how they managed to get by, and the latter replied that they depended solely on the young girl's needlework. Finally, Mrs. Ku brought up the question of a possible marriage between the two families. The old woman seemed agreeable and turned around to seek the opinion of her daughter. Though the girl did not say anything, she was apparently not too happy about it. So Mrs. Ku returned home.

Later, as she thought about the girl's reaction, she said to her son, "Do you think we've been turned down because we're too poor?

___
[1] Nanking, China. [Ed.]

What a strange girl! So quiet and so straight-faced. Just as the saying goes, 'As beautiful as the peach and pear blossoms, but cold as the frost and snow.'" Mother and son exchanged their views on the matter for a good while and then ended their discussion with a sigh.

One day, Ku was at his studio when a young man came to buy paintings. He looked handsome enough, but his manner was rather frivolous. Ku asked where he came from, and the young man replied that he came from the neighboring village. From then on, he came over every two or three days, and became fairly close to Ku. Later, they started to tease and joke with each other; and when Ku embraced the young man, he made no more than a show of refusing. Thus they carried on a secretive relationship which was to become more intimate by the day.

One day, as the girl happened to pass by, the young man gazed at her for a while and asked Ku who she was. Ku told him what he knew about her and the young man said, "What a beautiful and fearsome girl she is!"

Later, when Ku went inside, his mother said, "The young girl just came over to borrow some rice. She said that they haven't eaten for one whole day. This girl is devoted to her mother; what a pity that she should be in such circumstances. We should try to help her."

Ku agreed with what his mother said, and carried a peck of rice over to the girl's house, conveying his mother's goodwill. The girl accepted the rice but did not say a word of thanks to him.

After that, she often went over to Ku's house, helping with his mother's sewing and other needlework. She took care of all the household chores like a housewife. So Ku held her in even higher esteem. Whenever he had some delicacies, he would bring a portion over to her mother. The girl never thanked him. Once, when Ku's mother got an abscess on her private parts which caused her to cry out day and night in pain, the girl frequently stayed by her bedside, looking after her, washing the wound, and applying medicine to it three or four times a day. Mrs. Ku felt uneasy, but the girl did not seem to mind the task at all. Ku's mother sighed and said to her, "Ah, where can I find a daughter-in-law such as you to see me through the end of my days?" As she said that, her voice was choked with tears.

"Your son is devoted to you," the girl comforted her, "so you're much better off than my mother, who has only a helpless girl to look after her."

"But surely even a devoted son can't do bedside chores like these! Anyhow, I'm old and could die any day. What I'm worried about is an heir for the family."

As she spoke, Ku came in. Mrs. Ku wept and said, "I'm grateful for all that this young lady has done for us. Don't you forget to repay her kindness."

Ku bowed deeply, but the girl said, "You were kind to my mother and I didn't thank you, so why should you thank me now?"

Ku's respect and love for her grew deeper; yet she remained just as cold and aloof to him as before.

One day, Ku had his gaze fixed on the girl as she walked out the door. Suddenly she turned around and smiled bewitchingly at Ku. Ku was overjoyed and followed her to her house. When he flirted with her, she did not rebuke him, so they went to bed happily and made love. Afterward, she cautioned Ku, "I hope you understand that this is a one-time thing." Ku returned home without saying anything.

The next day, he approached the girl again, but she flatly refused him and left. However, she went to Ku's place as frequently as before and met him quite often; but she did not give him the slightest encouragement. Any effort on his part to exchange pleasantries with her was met with unyielding sternness.

One day, when they had a moment to themselves, she abruptly asked Ku, "Who is that young man you were talking to the other day?" Ku told her and she said, "He has taken liberties with me several times. Seeing that you're quite close to him. I didn't want to mention it earlier. But please tell him this time: if he doesn't mend his ways, he won't live to see another day."

Ku relayed her message to the young man when he came in the evening, adding, "You must be careful. Don't offend her again!"

"If she's so chaste," the young man said, "how come the two of you are on such good terms?" Ku protested his innocence, but the young man retorted, "If there is nothing between the two of you, then why would she tell you improper things like these?" Ku could not answer, whereupon the young man said, "Well, tell her this for me, too. Tell her, don't be so self-righteous and try to put up such a chaste appearance; otherwise, I shall certainly spread this whole thing far and wide!"

Ku was extremely angry and his face showed it, so the young man left.

One night, when Ku was sitting alone at home, the girl came in unexpectedly and greeted him with a smile. "It seems that our love hasn't ended yet."

Ku was overwhelmed with joy and held the girl tightly in his arms. Suddenly they heard footsteps and both jumped up. The door was pushed open and the young man walked in. Startled, Ku asked him, "What are you doing here?"

The young man laughed. "I've come to watch the show of some virtuous and chaste people!" Then he looked at the girl and said, "You can't blame anyone now, can you?"

The girl scowled and flushed with anger. Without a word, she pulled up her topcoat and took out a shiny foot-long dagger from a leather bag, the sight of which frightened the young man so much that he immediately took to his heels. The girl gave chase, but there was no one in sight outside. She flung the dagger into the air; it rose with a loud twang and was as bright as a rainbow. Then something fell to the ground with a loud thud. Ku hurried to look at it by candlelight. It was a white fox with a severed head. Ku was terrified.

"This is your Boy Charmer!" the girl told him. "I've spared him time and again, only he didn't seem to care enough for his life."

As she was replacing the dagger in the leather bag, Ku pulled her toward the house, but she said, "I don't feel like it anymore. Your Boy Charmer has spoiled the game. Wait until tomorrow night." And she left immediately without looking back.

The next evening, the girl came as promised and they spent the night together. When Ku asked her about her magic, she said, "This is something you shouldn't know about. Also, keep what you saw last night to yourself; otherwise it will bring you only trouble."

Ku then brought up the subject of marriage again, and in reply she said, "I sleep with you in the same bed, and I do all the housework here; what am I if not a wife to you? Since we live like husband and wife already, why talk about marriage?"

"Is it because I'm poor?"

"If you're poor, I'm not any better off. It's only because I feel for you in your poverty that I'm here with you tonight."

Before she left, she reminded Ku again, "Meetings such as this can't be repeated too often. If I can come, I will; but if I cannot, it's no use forcing me."

Afterward, whenever they ran into each other and Ku wanted to talk privately with her, she avoided him. Yet she kept doing all the housework and needlework in Ku's house, as before.

Several months later, the girl's mother died. Ku exhausted all his resources to help the girl bury her. From then on, the girl lived alone. Ku thought that he could take advantage of the situation, so one day he climbed over the wall and called to her from outside the window. When there was no answer, he looked through the doorway and found the house empty. He suspected that the girl had gone out to meet someone else. He returned at night but again the girl was not there. He left his jade pendant by the window and departed.

The next day, they met in his mother's room. When Ku came out, the girl followed him out and said, "You seem to have doubts about me, am I right? Everyone has his own secrets that can't be shared with others. How can I make you believe me? Anyway, there is something urgent which I must discuss with you right now." Ku asked her what it was, and she said, "I'm already eight months pregnant and I'm afraid that the child might come any time. Since I have no legitimate position in your family, I can only give you a child; I can't raise it for you. You can tell your mother secretly to look for a wet nurse, under the pretext that she herself wants to adopt a child. Don't tell anyone that the child is mine."

Ku agreed and relayed her wish to his mother. She smiled and said, "What a strange girl! She refused to marry you and yet she has no qualms at carrying on an affair with you!"

She carried out the girl's plan happily and waited for her delivery.

More than a month had passed, and when the girl failed to show up for several days in a row, Mrs. Ku became suspicious and went over to have a look. The door was tightly shut and all was quiet inside. She knocked for a long time before the girl came out, with her hair all disheveled and her face soiled. She opened the door for Ku's mother and closed it immediately. Inside her room, Mrs. Ku found a baby crying on the bed. The old woman was surprised and asked, "When was he born?"

"Three days ago," she replied.

Mrs. Ku unwrapped the baby and found it to be a chubby boy with a wide forehead. Overjoyed, she said, "You have given me a grandson, but what is a single girl like you going to do all alone in the world?"

"This is my secret, and I'm afraid I can't explain it to you," the girl replied. "You can carry the baby home at night when there is no one around."

The old lady returned and told her son, and both of them were puzzled. They went over and took the baby home at night.

Several nights later, the girl suddenly came over around midnight, carrying a leather bag in her hand. She smiled and said, "I've accomplished my goal. It's time for me to say good-bye."

Ku immediately pressed her for a reason, to which she answered, "I've always remembered your kindness in helping me to support my mother. I once told you that our bedding together was a one-time affair because one should not repay one's debt in bed. But since you're so poor and could not afford to get married, I tried to give you an heir. I was hoping to bear you a boy by taking you just once, but unfortunately my period came as usual afterward so I had to break my rules and do it again. Now that I have repaid your kindness, my wish is fulfilled and I have no regrets."

"What is inside that bag?"

"The head of my enemy."

Ku picked it up and looked inside. He saw a bearded head, all smashed and smeared with blood. Though frightened out of his wits, he managed to get the story from the girl, who finally took him into her confidence. "I've never mentioned it to you before because I was afraid that you might let the secret out inadvertently. Now that my work is finished, I can tell you about it freely. I'm originally from Chekiang Province. My father was a prefect. He was falsely charged and killed by his enemy, and our house was confiscated. I took my mother away and we lived quiet for three whole years under concealed identities. The reason why I waited so long before avenging my father was that my mother was still alive. And after my mother died, I was held up by my pregnancy.

Remember the night you came by and I was out? Well, I went out to better acquaint myself with the ways in and out of the enemy's house. I didn't want to take chances." As she was leaving, she said these parting words to Ku: "Please take good care of my son. You yourself will not be blessed with long life, but this son of yours can bring fame and great honor to your family. Since it's so late, I don't want to wake your mother. Good-bye!"

Grief-stricken, Ku was about to ask her where she was going when, quick as a lightning flash, the girl disappeared. Ku sighed and stood there petrified for a long time.

He told his mother everything the next morning, but they could do no more than express their sorrow and admiration for her.

Three years later, just as was predicted by the girl, Ku died a premature death. His son later became a *chin-shih*[2] at the age of eighteen, and he took care of his grandmother throughout her old age.

[2] The highest academic degree. [Ed.]

3

Qing Law Code on Marriage, 1644–1810

The Chinese law code of the Qing dynasty was essentially the same as the preceding Ming dynasty. The entire code covered no more than about 600 pages. Implementation was left up to judges who seemed to have based decisions more on the facts of the case than legal precedent. This selection contains sections from the code on the subject of marriage. Keep in mind that these are only selections from the code, so the absence of an issue does not mean that the code did not cover it.

Try to determine the reasons for these laws. What purpose did each of these serve? What do these laws tell you about Qing China?

THINKING HISTORICALLY

How would you compare this document with the previous two selections? Which of these laws are similar to those in your own society? Which are not? For those that are not similar, does your society have a different way of solving the problem or is the issue not a problem?

Source: Ta Tsing leu lee, *Being the Fundamental Laws, and a Selection from the Supplementary Statutes, of the Penal Code of China,* trans. George Thomas Staunton (London: T. Cadell & W. Davies, 1810), 107–08, 110–12, 116–18, 120. Spelling modernized.

Section 101

Marriages: How Regulated

When a marriage is intended to be contracted, it shall be, in the first instance reciprocally explained to, and clearly understood by, the families interested, whether the parties who design to marry are or are not, diseased, infirm, aged, or under age; and whether they are the children of their parents by blood, or only by adoption; if either of the contracting families then object, the proceedings shall be carried no further; if they still approve, they shall then in conjunction with the negotiators of the marriage, if such there be, draw up the marriage-articles.

If, after the woman is thus regularly affianced by the recognition of the marriage-articles, or by a personal interview and agreement between the families, the family of the intended bride should repent having entered into the contract, and refuse to execute it, the person amongst them who had authority to give her away shall be punished with 50 blows, and the marriage shall be completed agreeably to the original contract. — Although the marriage-articles should not have been drawn up in writing, the acceptance of the marriage-presents shall be sufficient evidence of the agreement between the parties. . . .

Section 102

Lending Wives or Daughters on Hire

Whoever lends any one of his wives, to be hired as a temporary wife, shall be punished with 80 blows, — whoever lends his daughter in like manner, shall be punished with 60 blows; the wife or daughter in such cases, shall not be held responsible.

Whoever, falsely representing any of his wives as his sister, gives her away in marriage, shall receive 100 blows, and the wife consenting thereto, shall be punished with 80 blows.

Those who knowingly receive in marriage the wives, or hire for a limited time the wives or daughters of others, shall participate equally in the aforesaid punishment, and the parties thus unlawfully connected, shall be separated; the daughter shall be returned to her parents, and the wife to the family to which she originally belonged; the pecuniary confederation in each case shall be forfeited to government. Those who ignorantly receive such persons in marriage, contrary to the laws, shall be excused, and recover the amount of the marriage-presents.

Section 103

Regard to Rank and Priority among Wives

Whoever degrades his first or principal wife to the condition of an inferior wife or concubine, shall be punished with 100 blows. Whoever, during the life-time of his first wife, raises an inferior wife to the rank and condition of a first wife, shall be punished with 90 blows, and in both the cases, each of the several wives shall be replaced in the rank to which she was originally entitled upon her marriage.

Whoever, having a first wife living, enters into marriage with another female as a first wife, shall likewise be punished with 90 blows; and the marriage being considered null and void, the parties shall be separated, and the woman returned to her parents.

Section 105

Marriage During the Legal Period of Mourning

If any man or woman enters into an equal marriage during the legal period of mourning for a deceased parent, or any widow enters into a second and equal marriage within the legal period of mourning for her deceased husband, the offending party shall be punished with 100 blows.

If it is not an equal match, that is to say, if a man takes an inferior wife from a subordinate rank, or a woman connects herself in marriage as one of the inferior wives of her husband, the punishment attending a breach of this law shall be less by two degrees.

If a widow who, during the life of her husband, had received honorary rank from the Emperor, ever marries again, she shall suffer punishment as above described, and moreover lose her rank, as well as be separated from her second husband. . . .

Section 110

Marriage of Officers of Government into Families Subject to Their Jurisdiction

If any officer belonging to the government of a city of the first, second, or third order, marries, while in office, the wife or daughter of any inhabitant of the country under his jurisdiction, he shall be punished with 80 blows.

If any officer of government marries the wife or daughter of any person having an interest in the legal proceedings at the same time under his investigation, he shall be punished with 100 blows, and the member of the family of the bride, who gave her away, shall be equally punishable. The woman, whether previously married or not, shall be restored to her parents, and the marriage-present forfeited in every case to government.

If the officer of government accomplishes the marriage by the force or influence of his authority, his punishment shall be increased two degrees, and the family of the female, being in such a case exempt from responsibility, she shall, if previously single, be restored to her parents; and if previously married, to her former husband; the marriage-present shall, not in either case be forfeited. . . .

Section 113

Marriage with Female Musicians and Comedians

If any officer or clerk of government, either in the civil or military department, marries, as his first or other wife, a female musician or comedian, he shall be punished with 60 blows, and the marriage being null and void, the female shall be sent back to her parents and rendered incapable of returning to her profession. The marriage-present shall be forfeited to government.

If the son or grand-son, being the heir of any officer of government having hereditary rank, commits this offence; he shall suffer the same punishment, and whenever he succeeds to the inheritance, his parental honours shall descend to him under a reduction of one degree.

Section 116

Law of Divorce

If a husband repudiates his first wife, without her having broken the matrimonial connection by the crime of adultery, or otherwise; and without her having furnished him with any of the seven justifying causes of divorce, he shall in every such case be punished with 80 blows. Moreover, although one of the seven justifying causes of divorce should be chargeable upon the wife, namely, (1) barrenness; (2) lasciviousness;. (3) disregard of her husband's parents; (4) talkativeness; (5) thievish propensities; (6) envious and suspicious temper; and, lastly, (7) inveterate infirmity; yet, if any of the three reasons against a divorce should exist, namely, (1) the wife's having mourned three years for her husband's parents; (2) the family's having become rich after having been poor previous to, and at the time of, marriage; and, (3) the wife's having no parents living to receive her back again; in these cases, none of the seven aforementioned causes will justify a divorce, and the husband who puts away his wife upon such grounds, shall suffer punishment two degrees less than that last stated, and be obliged to receive her again.

If the wife shall have broken the matrimonial connection by an act of adultery, or by any other act, which by law not only authorizes but requires that the parties should be separated, the husband shall receive a punishment of 80 blows, if he retains her.

When the husband and wife do not agree, and both parties are desirous of separation, the law limiting the right of divorce shall not be enforced to prevent it. . . .

4

ANNA BIJNS

"Unyoked Is Best! Happy the Woman without a Man," 1567

Anna Bijns* (1494–1575) was a Flemish nun and poet who lived in Antwerp, taught in a Catholic school in that city, wrote biting criticism of Martin Luther and the Protestant Reformation, and in her many works helped shape the Dutch language. The impact of Luther, and Protestantism more generally, on the lives of women has been the subject of much debate. Luther opposed nunneries and monasticism, believing that it was the natural duty of all women to marry and bear children. At the same time, he encouraged a level of reciprocal love and respect in marriage that was less emphasized in Catholicism. The Protestant translations of the Bible from Latin also opened a pathway for individuals, including educated women, to participate in the religious life, though not as nuns. Whether or not the sentiments of this poem are more Catholic than Protestant, are they more European than Chinese? Why or why not?

THINKING HISTORICALLY

No one should imagine that the ideas conveyed in this poem were typical or representative of European thought in the sixteenth century. This was obviously an extreme view that ran counter to traditional and commonly accepted ideas. Note how some phrases of the

* bynz

Source: Anna Bijns, "Unyoked Is Best," trans. Kristiaan P. G. Aercke, in *Women and Writers of the Renaissance and Reformation*, ed. Katharina M. Wilson (Athens: The University of Georgia Press, 1987), 382–83.

poem convey the recognition that most people will disagree with the sentiments being expressed.

When we are comparing documents from different cultures, we must always try to understand how representative they are of the views of the larger population. The Miu family document (selection 1) expresses the views of a single family, but lineage regulations were common in sixteenth-century China, and their ubiquity reflected an even greater consensus on the importance of the family. Anna Bijns's poem is a personal view that expresses a minority opinion. But in what sense is this a European, rather than Chinese, minority view? Do you think Anna Bijns's view might appeal to more people today than it did in the sixteenth century? If so, why?

How good to be a woman, how much better to be a man!
Maidens and wenches, remember the lesson you're about to hear.
Don't hurtle yourself into marriage far too soon.
The saying goes: "Where's your spouse? Where's your honor?"
But one who earns her board and clothes
Shouldn't scurry to suffer a man's rod.
So much for my advice, because I suspect—
Nay, see it sadly proven day by day—
'T happens all the time!
However rich in goods a girl might be,
Her marriage ring will shackle her for life.
If however she stays single
With purity and spotlessness foremost,
Then she is lord as well as lady, Fantastic, not?
Though wedlock I do not decry:
Unyoked is best! Happy the woman without a man.

Fine girls turning into loathly hags—
'Tis true! Poor sluts! Poor tramps! Cruel marriage!
Which makes me deaf to wedding bells.
Huh! First they marry the guy, luckless dears,
Thinking their love just too hot to cool.
Well, they're sorry and sad within a single year.
Wedlock's burden is far too heavy.
They know best whom it harnessed.
So often is a wife distressed, afraid.
When after troubles hither and thither he goes
In search of dice and liquor, night and day,
She'll curse herself for that initial "yes."
So, beware ere you begin.
Just listen, don't get yourself into it.
Unyoked is best! Happy the woman without a man.

A man oft comes home all drunk and pissed
Just when his wife had worked her fingers to the bone
(So many chores to keep a decent house!),
But if she wants to get in a word or two,
She gets to taste his fist—no more.
And that besotted keg she is supposed to obey?
Why, yelling and scolding is all she gets,
Such are his ways—and hapless his victim.
And if the nymphs of Venus he chooses to frequent,
What hearty welcome will await him home.
Maidens, young ladies: learn from another's doom,
Ere you, too, end up in fetters and chains,
Please don't argue with me on this,
No matter who contradicts, I stick to it:
Unyoked is best! Happy the woman without a man.

A single lady has a single income,
But likewise, isn't bothered by another's whims.
And I think: that freedom is worth a lot.
Who'll scoff at her, regardless what she does,
And though every penny she makes herself,
Just think of how much less she spends!
An independent lady is an extraordinary prize—
All right, of a man's boon she is deprived,
But she's lord and lady of her very own hearth.
To do one's business and no explaining sure is lots of fun!
Go to bed when she list,[1] rise when she list, all as she will,
And no one to comment! Grab tight your independence then.
Freedom is such a blessed thing.
To all girls: though the right Guy might come along:
Unyoked is best! Happy the woman without a man.

Regardless of the fortune a woman might bring,
Many men consider her a slave, that's all.
Don't let a honeyed tongue catch you off guard,
Refrain from gulping it all down. Let them rave,
For, I guess, decent men resemble white ravens.
Abandon the airy castles they will build for you.
Once their tongue has limed[2] a bird:
Bye bye love—and love just flies away.
To women marriage comes to mean betrayal
And the condemnation to a very awful fate.

[1] Wants. [Ed.]
[2] Caught. [Ed.]

All her own is spent, her lord impossible to bear.
It's *peine forte et dure*[3] instead of fun and games.
Oft it was the money, and not the man
Which goaded so many into their fate.
Unyoked is best! Happy the woman without a man.

[3] Long and forceful punishment; a form of torture whereby the victim was slowly crushed by heaping rocks on a board laid over his or her body. [Ed.]

5

The Autobiography of Mrs. Alice Thornton, 1645–1657

Alice Thornton (1626–1706/7) had a comfortable childhood in Ireland where her father was Lord Deputy, the king's representative. After her father's death in 1640, family circumstances declined, but despite the eruption of the English Civil War and the family's loyalty to the deposed King Charles and the Church of England, they managed an upper-middle-class standard of living in England.

Our selections from Alice Thornton's autobiography are drawn from events that occurred between 1645 and 1657. What happened in 1645 that might have influenced her idea of marriage? How did she feel about marriage when the idea was proposed in 1651? How would you characterize her married life?

THINKING HISTORICALLY

How were the author's family circumstances different from those of a woman born into the Miu lineage? How would you compare the author's relationship with her mother to that of the characters to their mothers in Pu Songling's story? What differences between European and Chinese marriage is revealed in this account?

The Death of My Sister Danby, Sept. 30, 1645

About this year, my dear and only sister, the Lady Danby, drew near her time for delivery of her sixteenth child. Ten whereof had been baptized, the other six were stillborn, when she was above half gone with them,

Source: *The Autobiography of Mrs. Alice Thornton, of East Norton, Co., York* (London: The Surtees Society, 1875), 49–50, 75–77, 81–88, 91, 94–95. For ease of reading the spelling has been modernized in some instances. [Ed.]

she having miscarried of them all upon frights by fire in her chamber, falls, and such like accidents happening. . . .

She had been very ill long time before her delivery, and much altered in the heat of her body, being feverish. After exceeding sore travail she was delivered of a goodly son about August 3rd, by one dame Sworre. This boy was named Francis, after another of that name, a sweet child that died that summer of the smallpox. This child came double into the world, with such extremity that she was exceedingly tormented with pains, so that she was deprived of the benefit of sleep for fourteen days, except a few frightful slumbers; neither could she eat anything for her nourishment as usual. Yet still did she spend her time in discourse of goodness excellently pious, godly, and religious, instructing her children and servants, and preparing her soul for her dear Redeemer, as it was her saying she should not be long from Him. . . .

The Marriage of Alice Wandesforde, December 15, 1651

After many troubles and afflictions under which it pleased God to exercise my mother and self in since the death of my father, she was desirous to see me comfortably settled in the estate of marriage, in which she hoped to receive some satisfaction, finding age and weakness to seize more each year, which added a spur to her desires for the future well-being of her children, according to every one of their capacities. As to myself, I was exceedingly satisfied in that happy and free condition, wherein I enjoyed my time with delight abundantly in the service of my God, and the obedience I owed to such an excellent parent, in whose enjoyment I accounted my days spent with great content and comfort; the only fears which possessed me was least I should be deprived of that great blessing I had in her life. Nor could I, without much reluctance, draw my thoughts to the change of my single life, knowing too much of the cares of this world sufficiently without the addition of such incident to the married estate. As to the fortune left by my father, it was fair, and more then competent, so that I needed not fear (by God's blessing) to have been troublesome to my friends, but to be rather in a condition to assist them if need had required. . . .

Nevertheless, such was my dear mother's affection to the family for it's preservation, that she harkened to the proposal made for Mr. Thornton's marriage, albeit therein she disobliged some persons of very good worth and quality which had solicited her earnestly in my behalf, and such as were of large and considerable estates of her neighbors about her. And, after the first and second view betwixt us, she closed so far with him that she was willing he should proceed in his suit, and that cordially, if I should see cause to accept. For my own particular, I was not hasty to change my free estate without much consideration, both as to my present and future, the first inclining me rather to continue so still, wherein none could be more satisfied. The second would contract much more trouble, twisted inseparably with those comforts God gave in that estate. Yet might I be hopeful to serve God in those duties incumbent on a wife, a mother, a mistress, and governess in a family. And if it pleased God so to dispose of me in marriage, making me a more public instrument of good to those several relations, I thought it rather duty in me to accept my friends' desires for a joint benefit, then my own single retired content, so that Almighty God might receive the glory of my change, and I more capacitated to serve Him in this generation, in what He thus called me unto. Therefore it highly concerned me to enter into this greatest change of my life with abundance of fear and caution, not lightly, nor unadvisedly, nor, as I may take my God to witness that knows the secrets of hearts, I did it not to fulfill the lusts of the flesh, but in chastity and singleness of heart, as marrying in the Lord. And to that end that I might have a blessing upon me, in all my undertakings, I powered out my petitions before the God of my life to direct, strengthen, lead, and counsel me what to do in this concern, which so much tended to my future comfort or discomfort. . . . After which petitions to my God, I was the more inclined to accept of this proposition of my friends' finding; also that the gentleman seemed to be a very godly, sober, and discreet person, free from all manner of vice, and of a good conversation. . . .

Alice Wandesforde, the daughter of Christopher Wandesford, Esq., late Lord Deputy of Ireland, was married to William Thornton, esquire, of Easte Newton, at my mother's house in Hipswell, by Mr. Siddall, December the 15th, 1651. Mr. Siddall made a most pious and profitable exhortation to us, showing our duties, and teaching us the fear of the Lord in this our new estate of life, with many zealous prayers for us. My dear and honored mother gave me in marriage, in the presence of my own brother John Wandesforde; my uncle Norton, my uncle Darley (Francis), my cousin Dodsworth of Wattlosse, George Lightfoote, and Dafeny, Robert Webster, Martha Richison, Ralfe Ianson, Robert Loftus the elder. . . .

A Deliverance from Death That Day on Which I Was Married, December 15th, 1651

That very day on which I was married, having been in health and strength for many years before, I fell suddenly so ill and sick after two o'clock in the afternoon that I thought, and all that saw me did believe, it would have been my last night, being surprised with a violent pain in my head and stomach, causing a great vomiting and sickness at my heart, which lasted eight hours before I had any intermission; but, blessed be the Lord our God, the Father of mercies, Which had compassion on me, and by the means that was used I was strengthened wonderfully beyond expectation, being pretty well about ten o'clock at night. My dear husband, with my mother, was exceeding tender over me, which was a great comfort to my spirits. What the cause of this fit was I could not conjecture, save that I might have brought it upon me by cold taken the night before, when I sat up late in preparing for the next day, and washing my feet at that time of the year, which my mother did believe was the cause of that dangerous fit the next day. But, however it was, or from what cause it proceeded, I received a great mercy in my preservation from God, and shall ever acknowledge the same in humble gratitude for His infinite loving kindness forever. I looked upon this first business of my new condition to be a little discouragement, although God was able to turn all things for the best and to my good, that I might not build too much hopes of happiness in things of this world, nor in the comforts of a loving husband, whom God had given me, but set my desires more upon the love of my Lord and God.

Meditations upon My Deliverance of My First Child, and of the Great Sickness Followed for Three-Quarters of a Year; August 6, 1652, Lasted til May 12, 1653

About seven weeks after I married it pleased God to give me the blessing of conception. The first quarter I was exceeding sickly in breeding, till I was with quick childe; after which I was very strong and healthy, I bless God, only much hotter than formerly, as is usual in such cases from a natural cause, insomuch that my nose bled much when I was about half gone, by reason of the increase of heat. Mr. Thornton had a desire that I should visit his friends, in which I freely joined, his mother living about fifty miles from Hipswell, and all at Newton and Buttercrambe. In my passage thither I sweat exceedingly, and was much inclining to be feverish, wanting not eight weeks of my time, so that Dr. Wittie said that I should go near to fall into a fever, or some desperate sickness, if I did not cool my blood, by taking some away, and if I had stayed but two days longer, I had followed his advice. In his return home from Newton, his own estate, I was carried over Hambleton towards Sir William Askough's house, where I passed down on foot a very high wall betwixt Hudhill and Whitsoncliffe, which is above a mile steep down, and indeed so bad that I could not scarce tread the narrow steps, which was exceeding bad for me in that condition, and sore to endure, the way so straight and none to lead me but my maid [Susan Gosling], which could scarce make shift to get down herself, all our company being gone down before. Each step did very much strain me, being so big with child, nor could I have got down if I had not then been in my full strength and nimble on foot. But, I bless God, I got down safe at last, though much tired, and hot and weary, finding myself not well, but troubled with pains after my walk. Mr. Thornton would not have brought me that way if he had known it so dangerous, and I was a stranger in that place; but he was advised by some to go that way before we came down the hill. This was the first occasion which brought me a great deal of misery, and killed my sweet infant in my womb. . . . The doctor came post the next day, when he found me very weak, and durst not let me blood that night, but gave me cordials, etc., till the next day, and if I got but one hour's rest that night, he would do it the morning following. That night the two doctors had a dispute about the letting me bleed. Mr. Mahum was against it, and Dr. Wittie for it; but I soon decided that dispute, and told them, if they would save my life, I must bleed. So the next day I had six or seven ounces taken which was turned very bad by my sickness, but I found a change immediately in my sight, which was exceeding dim before, and then I see as well as ever clearly, and my strength began a little to return; these things I relate that I may set forth the mercy of my ever gracious God, Who had blessed the means in such manner. Who can sufficiently extol His Majesty for His boundless mercies to me His weak creature, for from that time I was better, and he had hopes of my life. The doctor stayed with me seven days during my sickness; my poor infant within me was greatly forced with violent motions perpetually, till it grew so weak that it had left stirring, and about the 27th of August I found myself in great pains as it were the colic, after which I began to be in travail, and about the next day at night I was delivered of a goodly daughter, who lived not so long as that we could get a minister to baptize it, though we presently sent for one. This my sweet babe and first child departed this life half an hour after its birth, being received, I hope, into the arms of Him that gave it. She was buried that night, being Friday, the 27th of August, 1652, at Easby church. The effects of this fever remained by several distempers successively, first, after the miscarriage I fell into a most terrible shaking ague, lasting one quarter of a year, by fits each day twice, in much violence, so that the sweat was great with faintings, being thereby weakened till I could not stand or go. The hair on my head came off, my nails of my fingers and toes came off, my teeth did shake, and ready to come out and grew black. After the ague left me, upon a medicine of London treacle, I fell into the jaundice, which vexed me very hardly one full quarter and a half more. I finding Dr. Wittie's judgment true, that it would prove a chronic distemper; but blessed be the Lord, upon great and many means used and all remedies, I was at length cured of all distempers and weaknesses, which, from its beginning, had lasted three-quarters of a year full out. Thus had I a sad entertainment and beginning of my change of life, the comforts thereof being turned into much discomforts and weaknesses, but still I was upheld by an Almighty Power, therefore will I praise the Lord my God. Amen. . . .

Upon the Birth of My Second Child and Daughter, Born at Hipswell on the 3rd of January in the Year 1654

Alice Thornton, my second child, was born at Hipswell near Richmond in Yorkshire the 3rd day of January, 1654, baptized the 5th of the same. Witnesses, my mother the Lady Wandesforde, my uncle Mr. Major Norton, and my cousin Yorke his daughter, at Hipswell, by Mr. Michell Siddall, minister then of Caterick.

It was the pleasure of God to give me but a week time after my daughter Alice her birth, and she had many preservations from death in the first year, being one night delivered from being overlaid by her nurse, who laid in my dear mother's chamber a good while. One night my mother was writing pretty late, and she heard my dear child make a groaning troublesomely, and stepping immediately to nurse's bedside she saw the nurse fallen asleep, with her breast in the child's mouth, and lying over the child; at which she, being affrighted, pulled the nurse suddenly off from her, and so preserved my dear child from being smothered. . . .

Elizabeth Thornton's Death, the 5th of September, 1656

It pleased God to take from me my dear child Betty, which had been long in the rickets and consumption, gotten at first by an ague, and much gone in the rickets, which I conceived was caused by ill milk at two nurses. And notwithstanding all the means I used, and had her with Naly at St. Mungno's Well for it, she grew weaker, and at the last, in a most desperate cough that destroyed her lungs, she died. . . .

Elizabeth Thornton, my third child, died the 5th of September, 1656, betwixt the hours of five and six in the morning. Her age was one year six months and twenty-one days. Was buried the same day at Catterick by Mr. Siddall.

Meditations on the Deliverance of My First Son and Fifth Child at Hipswell the 10th of December, 1657

It pleased God, in much mercy, to restore me to strength to go to my full time, my labor beginning three days; but upon the Wednesday, the ninth of December, I fell into exceeding sharp travail in great extremity, so that the midwife did believe I should be delivered soon. But lo! it fell out contrary, for the child stayed in the birth, and came cross with his feet first, and in this condition continued till Thursday morning between two and three o'clock, at which time I was upon the rack in bearing my child with such exquisite torment, as if each lime were divided from other, for the space of two hours; when at length, being speechless and breathless, I was, by the infinite providence of God, in great mercy delivered. But I having had such sore travail in danger of my life so long, and the child coming into the world with his feet first, caused the child to be almost strangled in the birth, only living about half an hour, so died before we could get a minister to baptize him, although he was sent for.

6

Diary of the Countess de Rochefort, 1689

The Countess de Rochefort was an aristocrat in the court of Louis XIV. She lived on an estate in Avignon in the south of France. A good deal of the time, her husband[1] was away on military campaigns. To do so in 1689 he needed most of the family's available cash for expenses, leaving the countess to manage the estate under financial pressure. These selections from her diary for 1689 give us an idea of the daily life of a woman of the aristocracy who still is quite busy.

How does she spend her days? How dependent or independent does she seem? Does this source tell you anything about the lives of aristocratic women in Europe? If so, what?

THINKING HISTORICALLY

In both China and Europe, aristocrats lived very different lives from the middle classes. How different was the world of the countess from that of Alice Thornton? In what ways might the author's life have been different from a noble's wife in China? What would account for those differences?

25 May, 1689. I wrote to M. Carretier, my attorney at the Court of Toulouse, to ask for news. . . . I wrote to M. Penaut, my attorney at

[1] Comte de Rochefort (1630–1712), younger son of Louis de Rohan, duc de Montbazon.

Source: Julia O'Faolain and Lauro Martines, eds., *Not in God's Image: Women in History from the Greeks to the Victorians* (New York: Harper & Row, 1973), 234–37. From *Une Grande Dame dans son ménage au temps de Louis XIV, D'apres le journal de la comtesse de Rochefort* (1689).

Montpellier, to proceed with our suit against the community of Beaucaire. The same day I wrote also to M. Belot, attorney at the Court of Toloze, for news of M. Brocardy's case.

M. Odoacre, the community's arbiter arrived today. He and the royal attorney began discussing things after dinner. It does not look to me as though we can hope for an amicable settlement. . . . Today I also went to Mormont to look at the woods. I found that far too much had been cut, but what is left is growing back very well. The part that is for sale is worth more than 40 écus, for the wood is thicker there. . . .

1 June. I ordered that on all our lands prayers be offered for M. de Rochefort until he returns.

The butcher from Roche paid me 34 livres, 10 sols of what he owes me, plus 71 pounds of mutton at 2 sols and 4 deniers per pound, and 15 pounds of beef at 18 deniers. Adding it all up, he has paid off 43 livres, 10 sols of his debt. . . .

Toward evening, being at Bégude, I inspected my crops and found them very fine. However, the tenant tells me that if he had sowed earlier the wheat would be finer and more plentiful. I decided therefore to let him follow his own judgment as to when he should sow. He also told me that the ditches need scouring, and I admitted that they did.

I got the carders in today to work on a hundredweight of washed wool from which I aim to make 8 cannes [1 canne = between 2 and 3 meters] of crépon, 14 of light wool, 13 of floss serge, and 30 of caddis.

3 June. I forgot to note that on the first of the month I had work started on one of the two mill stones at the Rochefort mill. It was very urgent because the wheat was coming out unground. I am giving the mason his food while he works on it.

10 June. M. Jean Artaud came to see me to offer to lease the small farm house at Beaujeu. . . .

13 June. We began reeling the silk today. . . . Nine pounds of cocoons produced fifteen ounces of fine silk.

14 June. I got up early to supervise the storing of the casks in the cellar. I had the vats made and the small cellars got ready for the fair. I'm having a large wooden vat made for pressing the grapes. . . .

A small pewter carafe I had made has been delivered. I have also had dishes and two dozen plates remade. All my pewter has been reworked and I have had it marked as well.

I sent 4 lbs. of soap to Pernes, where I'm having thread bleached. . . .

The same day I sent to M. Patron, the trimmer, to ask how much braid would be needed for my livery. He said I would need 80 cannes [160 meters] of the wide and 30 [60 meters] of the narrow and that to make that much would take 10 lbs. of heavy silk and 8 lbs. of fine floss silk. . . . I sent 2 cannes of red caddis to T. to make the footmen's jackets. . . .

Catin came from Rochefort today where she had been supervising the carders. She brought 100 chickens which were left of those I had bought; adding the 28 I had here, that makes 128. I have over 40 hens as well, one cock and 10 turkeys. . . .

15 June. I ordered the guard at Rochefort to sell my wine. He sold two casks to the butcher and is keeping the third one for the harvest.

I have arranged to have the Gazette sent and held for me twice a week at Tarascon.

20 June. I got up early and heard Mass, then went to see my meadow at Maubuisson. I have had all the wines in my cellar tasted; they were pronounced to be excellent. There are 22 casks altogether. I have decided to keep three and sell the rest.

I spent the rest of the day cutting out and having underclothes made up for my children.

21 June. I got up early as usual to write to M. de Rochefort and to M. Sicard. After Mass, I had the attics prepared for the new wheat; what's left of the old will be ground into flour for the servants. Next I gave orders to have my old skirts cut up to make dresses for my son, the chevalier.

M. Treven de Villeneuve came to see me to tell me that . . . he was obliged to ask me for money owed for two pensions, which amounts to 733 livres, 6 sols, 8 deniers. I answered that it was not too good a time to ask me for money, that M. de Rochefort had taken all I had to pay for his campaign and that I even had letters from the government dispensing me from paying any money out before his return. . . .

27 June. I got up early to prepare for the bleeding I am to have done on my ankle because of the bad headaches I have been suffering for some time. . . .

5 July . . . the Sisters of Mercy wrote from Avignon asking for their pension and back payments. I wrote asking them to wait until the harvest, when I would pay them; otherwise I would use my *lettres d'Etat* to stop their suit.

6 July . . . I spent the rest of the day making an inventory of the furniture, beds, chairs and so forth to make sure that nothing gets damaged during the fair.

I had good news from M. de Rochefort.

12 July. I spent the morning having beds made up in the rooms that are to be let during the fair.

I wrote to my attorney. . . .

I went down to the cellar and tasted my wines. I had the three best casks marked; they will be kept for Monsieur, and three others for the commonalty.

27 July. I spent the day doing my accounts. . . .

17 September. I sent M. Trevenin the rest of what I owed him. . . . The tenant at Jonquieres says . . . the owner of a neighboring farmhouse has been encroaching on our land. This will have to be looked into at once. . . .

26 September. M. de Rochefort came home. . . .

30 May, 1690. From November 10 until February I was so depressed with melancholy at the bad state in which I saw my business that I was neither eating nor sleeping; . . . melancholy is good for neither the body nor the soul. . . . Now I'm partly over it. . . . I am getting back to work. . . . God has remedied my affairs when I was least expecting it. With His grace, I hope to get things into shape in a few years. But the house will have to be carefully run; I must economize all I can or else in a bad year it is impossible to make ends meet. And then we must deprive ourselves of a lot so as to be able to help the poor. . . .

7

Court Case on Marriage in High Court of Aix, 1689

At the same time as the Countess of Rochefort was managing her estate in Avignon without the help of her husband, Joseph Cabassol and his wife, Anne Geniere, were called to the High Court of Aix, France, 42 miles away. The couple's marriage was being challenged by some of the members of Cabassol's family. Who were these people? What was the reason for the suit? What was the reasoning of the court? What does this case tell you about social class and marriage in France at this time?

THINKING HISTORICALLY

Compare this document to the Qing law code (document 3). How do you think judges in Qing China might have handled a case like this? To what extent were the Chinese interests in this sort of case similar to, and different from, those of Louis XIV's France? How is our U.S. law similar or different?

Case tried before the High Court of Aix in 1689. Joseph Cabassol . . . was the eldest of the seven children of a lawyer at the High Court of Aix. . . . [After his parent's death he succeeded to his inheritance. Then some years later] he fell in love with the woman Anne Geniere, a widow [who] had been brought before the Provost of Marseille because of her

Source: Julia O'Faolain and Lauro Martines, eds., *Not in God's Image: Women in History from the Greeks to the Victorians* (New York: Harper & Row, 1973), 222–24.

scandalous life. Convicted of prostitution and pimping, she had been sentenced by the judge to three years' banishment. . . . This sentence was confirmed, after appeal, by a decision of the High Court of Aix in 1683.

On 19 April 1688, Joseph Cabassol and Anne Geniere appeared before the bishop of Avignon, told him they were inhabitants of that town, that they wanted to get married, and that there was no canonical impediment. In proof of this, they brought three witnesses . . . and asked to be dispensed from publishing banns [request granted]. . . . They were married the following day . . . and returned to Aix on the following fourth of May. . . .

On the fourteenth of that same month of May, Joseph Cabassol's family, hearing of his marriage, his uncle, two brothers, and a sister put in a petition to have it annulled.

In Joseph Cabassol's defense, it was said that an adult of thirty years of age is free according to all the laws of God and man to choose his own wife. . . . Joseph Cabassol said that neither his uncle nor his brothers and sister were entitled to attack his marriage.

Monsieur de Saint-Martin, Director of Public Prosecutions . . . admitted that the consent of brothers and uncles is not necessary in the case of the marriage of an adult. . . .

One could not, however, conclude that such persons are never entitled to oppose the marriage of an adult. . . . The grounds for attacking this marriage were essentially two: that it was celebrated without publishing the banns and that it was not celebrated by the parties' own parish priest. . . . It was claimed that Anne Geniere had rented two furnished rooms, paying for three years rent in advance, in the town of Avignon. But we can state right away that this pretended domicile is not of the sort required by the holy decretals and the statutes . . . [which demand] that one should have lived a year or the best part of a year in a parish before one becomes really a parishioner. But the defendants had lived neither a year nor anything like it in Avignon when they got married there. . . . And so they did not satisfy the first condition. . . . If it were enough to change house for a while in order to establish domicile in order to get married, then the forethought of the Council of Trent would be illusory and that of the Royal Statute would be useless. One could make a parish priest for oneself according to one's needs, and where then could parents turn to get their authority respected? . . . Would this not be authorizing the worst license and covering it with a specious veil of marriage? . . . In order to determine whether the plaintiffs are entitled to petition for the invalidation of the marriage we must decide whether . . . the defendants' marriage is prejudicial to their honor. . . . If Anne Geniere had no other faults but those of her low rank and fortune, we would find the plaintiffs too fastidious. . . . But this is a woman who, over and above the inequality. . . . has led a scandalous life. She has been stigmatized by a sentence which is a perpetual monument to her infamy. . . . If a man who wastes his patrimony can be declared incapable of managing his affairs, does it not seem that since Cabassol is wasting his honor, and managing his true interests so badly, we should listen to the voice of his relatives? . . . When the vapors with which mad passion have confused his mind withdraw . . . he will approve what he condemns today. . . .

For these reasons we believe that the petition to invalidate the marriage should be allowed . . . and that the defendants be condemned to give alms to the amount of ten pounds each to the hospitals of this town and forbidden to frequent each other, yet that they be allowed the recourse of taking any steps they think fit toward lodging an appeal in an ecclesiastical court. . . . Judgment given in conformity with these conclusions on the 14th March, 1689.

8

MARY JO MAYNES AND ANN WALTNER

Women and Marriage in Europe and China, 2001

This article is the product of a rich collaboration between historians of China and Europe who show us how a study of women and marriage is anything but peripheral to a study of these areas. What is their thesis about European and Chinese marriage patterns? What do marriage patterns tell us about a society? How do the other readings in this chapter support or challenge their thesis?

THINKING HISTORICALLY

The authors begin by comparing the role of religion, the state, and the family in setting marriage patterns in both China and Europe. Did Christianity allow European women more independence than Confucianism allowed women in China? In which society was the patriarchal family more powerful, and what was the relative impact of patriarchy on women in both societies? How did the age and rate at which people married in each society compare? What was the importance of Chinese concubinage and Christian ideals of chastity?

Source: Mary Jo Maynes and Ann Waltner, "Childhood, Youth, and the Female Life Cycle: Women's Life-Cycle Transitions in a World-Historical Perspective: Comparing Marriage in China and Europe," *Journal of Women's History* 12, no. 4 (Winter 2001): 11–19.

The authors' questions about marriage in Europe and China lead finally to a consideration of one of the most frequently asked comparative questions: Why did Europe industrialize before China? Do the different European and Chinese marriage patterns answer this question? What other comparative questions would we have to ask to arrive at a full answer?

Comparing Marriage Cross-Culturally

. . . Beginning in the late 1500s, women in northern Italy began to appeal to legal courts run by the Catholic Church when they got into disputes with their families over arranged marriages. Within the early modern Italy family system the father held a great deal of authority over his children and it was usual for the parents to determine when and whom sons and daughters married. Women and children held little power in comparison with adult men. But the Catholic Church's insistence that both parties enter into the marriage willingly gave some women an out—namely, an appeal to the Church court, claiming that the marriage their family wanted was being forced upon them without their consent. Surprisingly, these young women often won their cases against their fathers. In early modern China, by way of contrast, state, religion, and family were bound together under the veil of Confucianism. Paternal authority echoed and reinforced the political and the moral order. Religious institutions could rarely be called upon to intervene in family disputes. Therefore, young women (or young men, for that matter) had no clearly established institutional recourse in situations of unwanted marriage. So, despite the fact that paternal power was very strong in both early modern Italy and early modern China, specific institutional differences put young women at the moment of marriage in somewhat different positions.

We began with the presumption that however different the institution of "marriage" was in Italy and China, it nevertheless offered enough similarities that it made sense to speak comparatively about a category called "marriage." Parallels in the two cultures between the institution of marriage and the moment in the woman's life course that it represented make comparison useful. Nevertheless, this particular comparison also isolates some of the variable features of marriage systems that are especially significant in addressing gender relations in a world-historical context. In China, the rules of family formation and family governance were generally enforced within the bounds of each extended family group. State and religious influences were felt only indirectly through family leaders as mediators or enforcers of state and religious law. Throughout Europe, beginning in the Middle Ages, the institution of marriage was altered first by the effort of the Catholic Church to wrest some control over marriage from the family by defining it as a sacrament, and then eventually by the struggle between churches and state authorities to regulate families.

This contest among church, state, and family authorities over marriage decisions turns out to have been a particular feature of European history that had consequences for many aspects of social life. A focus on the moment of marriage presents special opportunities for understanding connections between the operation of gender relations in everyday life and in the realm of broader political developments. Marriage is a familial institution, of course, but, to varying degrees, political authorities also have a stake in it because of its implications for property transfer, reproduction, religion, and morality—in short, significant aspects of the social order. In this essay, we compare one dimension of marriage—its timing in a woman's life cycle—in two contexts, Europe and China. We argue that variations in marriage timing have world-historical implications. We examine how a woman's status and situation shifted at marriage and then suggest some implications of comparative differences in the timing and circumstances of this change of status.

The Moment of Marriage in European History

One striking peculiarity of Central and Western European history between 1600 and 1850 was the relatively late age at first marriage for men and women compared with other regions of the world. The so-called "Western European marriage pattern" was marked by relatively late marriage—that is, relative to other regions of the world where some form of marriage usually occurred around the time of puberty. In much of Europe, in contrast, men did not typically marry until their late twenties and women their mid-twenties. This practice of relatively late marriage was closely connected with the custom of delaying marriage until the couple commanded sufficient resources to raise a family. For artisans this traditionally meant having a shop and master status. For merchants it entailed saving capital to begin a business. In the case of peasant couples, this meant having a house and land and basic farming equipment. It was the responsibility of the family and the community to oversee courtship, betrothal, and marriage to assure that these conditions were met. This phenomenon was also rooted in the common practice of neolocality—the expectation that a bride and groom would set up their own household at or soon after marriage. This "delayed" marriage has attracted the attention of European historical demographers. The delay of marriage meant, quite significantly, that most European women did not begin to have children until their twenties. But this marriage pattern also has significance in other realms as well. In particular, young people of both sexes experienced a relatively long hiatus between puberty and marriage.

Unmarried European youth played a distinctive role in economic, social, cultural, and political life through such institutions as guilds, village youth groups, and universities. For the most part, historians' attention to European youth has centered on young men. Major works on the history of youth in Europe, like theories of adolescent development, tend to center on the male experience as normative. Only when gender differences in youth are recognized and the history of young women is written will the broad historical significance of the European marriage pattern become clear. Contrast between European demographic history and that of other world regions suggests a comparative pattern of particular significance for girls: Delayed marriage and childbearing meant that teenage girls were available for employment outside the familial household (either natal or marital) to a degree uncommon elsewhere. Household divisions of labor according to age and gender created constant demand for servants on larger farms; typically, unmarried youth who could be hired in from neighboring farms as servants filled this role. A period of service in a farm household, as an apprentice, or as a domestic servant in an urban household characterized male and female European youth in the life-cycle phase preceding marriage. Historians have noted but never fully explored the role young women played in European economic development, and in particular their role in the early industrial labor force.

Late marriage had gender-specific cultural ramifications as well. Whereas it was considered normal and even appropriate for teenage men to be initiated into heterosexual intercourse at brothels, in most regions of Europe, young women were expected to remain chaste until marriage. Delay of marriage heightened anxiety over unmarried women's sexuality, especially the dangers to which young women were increasingly exposed as the locus of their labor shifted from home and village to factory and city. Premarital or extramarital sexuality was uncommon, and was rigorously policed especially in the period following the religious upheavals of the Reformation in the sixteenth century. In rural areas, church and community, in addition to the family, exerted control over sexuality. Moreover, the unmarried male youth cohort of many village communities often served, in effect, as "morals police," enforcing local customs. These young men regulated courtship rituals, organized dances that young people went to, and oversaw the formation of couples. Sometimes, judging and public shaming by the youth group was the fate of couples who were mismatched by age or wealth or who violated sexual taboos. Some customs, at least symbolically, punished young men from far away who married local women, removing them from the marriage pool. Often, such a bridegroom had to pay for drinks in each village that the bridal couple passed through as they moved from the bride's parish church to their new abode—the longer the distance, the more expensive his bill.

Once married, a couple would usually begin having children imme- diately. Demographic evidence suggests that for most of Central and Western Europe there was virtually no practice of contraception among lower classes prior to the middle of the nineteenth century. Women had babies about every two years (more or less frequently according to re- gion and depending on such local customs as breast-feeding length and intercourse taboos). Even though completed family sizes could be large by modern standards, the number of children most women bore was still less than if they had married in their teens. And prevailing high mor- tality rates further reduced the number of children who survived to adulthood.

The Moment of Marriage in Chinese History

The Chinese marriage system was traditionally characterized by early age at marriage, nearly universal marriage for women, virilocal resi- dence (a newly married couple resided with the groom's parents), concu- binage for elite men, and norms that discouraged widow remarriage. From the sixteenth through twentieth centuries, Chinese men and women married much younger on average than did their European counterparts—late teens or early twenties for women and a bit later for men. A bride typically moved to her husband's family home, which was often in a different village from her own. The moment of marriage not only meant that a girl would leave her parents but that she would also leave her network of kin and friends, all that was familiar. Families chose marriage partners, and a matchmaker negotiated the arrangements. Nothing resembling courtship existed; the bride and groom would often first meet on their wedding day.

Because a newly married Chinese couple would typically reside in an already-existing household, it was not necessary for an artisan to be- come established, a merchant to accumulate capital, or a peasant to own a farm before marrying. Newly married couples participated in ongoing domestic and economic enterprises that already supported the groom's family. New households were eventually established by a process of household division, which typically happened at the death of the father rather than the moment of marriage (although it could happen at other points in the family cycle as well).

Daughters were groomed from birth for marriage. They were taught skills appropriate to their social class or the social class into which their parents aspired to marry them. (In the ideal Chinese mar- riage, the groom was in fact supposed to be of slightly higher social status than the bride.) The feet of upper-class girls (and some who were not upper class) were bound, since Chinese men found this erotic. Bound feet also symbolically, if not actually, restricted upper-class women's movement. Thus bound feet simultaneously enhanced the sexual desirability of upper-class women and served to contain their sexuality within domestic bounds.

Virtually all Chinese girls became brides, though not all of them married as principal wives. (This contrasts with the European pattern where a substantial minority of women in most regions never married.) Upper-class men might take one or more concubines in addition to a principal wife. The relationship between a man and his concubine was recognized legally and ritually, and children born of these unions were legitimate. A wife had very secure status: divorce was almost nonexistent. A concubine's status, in contrast, was much more tenuous. She could be expelled at the whim of her "husband"; her only real protection was community sentiment. Although only a small percentage of Chinese marriages (no more than 5 percent) involved concubines, the practice remained an important structural feature of the Chinese marriage system until the twentieth century. Concubinage also provides a partial explanation of why, despite the fact that marriage was nearly universal for women, a substantial proportion of men (perhaps as high as 10 percent) never married. Also contributing to this apparent anomaly was the practice of sex-selective infanticide, a common practice that discriminated against girl babies and, ultimately, reduced the number of potential brides.

Once married, Chinese couples began to have children almost immediately, generally spacing births at longer intervals than did European couples. The reasons for this are not yet completely understood, although infanticide, extended breast-feeding, and the fairly large number of days on which sexual intercourse was forbidden all seem to have played a role in lowering Chinese family size.

Early marriage in China meant that the category of "youth," which has been so significant for European social and economic history, has no precise counterpart in Chinese history. Young Chinese women labored, to be sure, but the location of their work was domestic—either in the household of their father or husband. Female servants existed in China, but their servitude was normally of longer duration than the life-cycle servitude common in Europe. The domestic location of young women's labor in the Chinese context also had implications for the particular ways in which Chinese industries were organized, as we suggest below.

Patterns of Marriage in Europe and China

To sum up, then, there are differences of both timing of and residency before and after marriage that are particularly germane to the comparative history of young women. As demographic historians James Z. Lee and Wang Feng also have argued, "in China, females have always married universally and early . . . in contrast to female marriage in Western Europe, which occurred late or not at all." Whereas, in the nineteenth century, all but 20 percent of young Chinese women were married by age twenty, among European populations, between 60 and 80 percent of young women remained single at this age. In traditional China, only 1 or 2 percent of women remained unmarried at age thirty, whereas between 15 and 25 percent of thirty-year-old Western European women were still single. (For men, the differences though in the same direction are far less stark.) As for residence, in the Western European neolocal pattern, norms and practices in many regions resulted in a pattern whereby newly married couples moved into a separate household at marriage; but concomitant with this was their delaying marriage until they could afford a new household. In China, newly married couples generally resided in the groom's father's household. In Western Europe, the majority of postpubescent young men and many young women left home in their teenage years for a period of employment. In the early modern era, such employment was often as a servant or apprentice in either a craft or a farm household, but, over time, that employment was increasingly likely to be in a nondomestic work setting, such as a factory, store, or other urban enterprise. "Youth" was a distinctive phase in the life course of young men and increasingly of young women in Europe, although there were important gender distinctions. Such a period of postpubescent semiautonomy from parental households did not exist for Chinese youth, especially not for young women in traditional China. Young men more typically remained in their father's household and young women moved at marriage in their late teens from their own father's household to that of their husband's father.

Comparing the Moment of Marriage: Implications and Cautions

We would now like to discuss some of the world-historical implications of this important (if crude) comparison in the marriage systems of China and Western Europe. There are obviously many possible realms for investigation. For example, these patterns imply differences in young women's education, intergenerational relationships among women (especially between mothers and daughters and mothers-in-law and daughters-in-law), and household power relations. Here, we restrict our discussion to two areas of undoubted world-historical significance, namely economic development, on the one hand, and sexuality and reproduction, on the other.

The question of why the Industrial Revolution, or, alternatively, the emergence of industrial capitalism, occurred first in Europe, has been and remains salient for both European and world historians. R. Bin Wong explores this question in his innovative comparative study of economic development in Europe and China. Wong argues that there were rough parallels in the dynamics linking demographic expansion and economic growth in China and Europe until the nineteenth century. Both economies were expanding on the basis of growth of rural industrial enterprises in which peasant families supplemented agricultural work and income with part-time industrial production. What the Chinese case demonstrates, Wong argues, is that this so-called protoindustrial form of development may be viewed as an alternative route to industrialization rather than merely a precursor of factory production. Indeed, Charles Tilly has suggested that a prescient contemporary observer of the European economy in 1750 would likely have predicted such a future—that is "a countryside with a growing proletariat working in both agriculture and manufacturing."

While Wong's study is devoted to comparative examination of the economic roots and implications of varying paths to industrial development, he also connects economic and demographic growth. In particular, Wong mentions the link between marriage and economic opportunity: "in both China and Europe, rural industry supported lower age at marriage and higher proportions of ever married than would have been plausible in its absence. This does not mean that ages at marriage dropped in Europe when rural industry appeared, but the possibility was present. For China, the development of rural industry may not have lowered ages at marriage or raised proportions married as much as it allowed previous practices of relatively low ages at marriage and high proportions of women ever married to continue." What Wong does not explore is the way in which these "previous practices" that connected the low age at marriage with both virilocality and a relatively high commitment to the domestic containment of daughters and wives also had implications for patterns of economic development. In a comparative account of why Chinese industrial development relied heavily on domestic production, the fact that the young female labor force in China was to an extent far greater than that of Europe both married and "tied" to the male-headed household needs to be part of the story. This pattern of female marriage and residency held implications for entrepreneurial choice that helped to determine the different paths toward industrialization in Europe and China. World-historical comparison, taking into account aspects of gender relations and marriage and kinship systems, highlights their possible significance for economic development, a significance that has not been given proper attention by economic historians. Indeed, it is arguable that the family and marital status of the young women who played so significant a role in the workforce (especially those employed in the textile industry, which was key to early industrial development in both Europe and China) were major factors in the varying paths to development followed in China and Europe in the centuries of protoindustrial growth and industrialization.

A second set of implications concerns sexuality and reproduction. Again, we are aided by another recent study, which, in a fashion parallel to Wong's, uses Chinese historical evidence to call into question generalizations about historical development based on a European model. In their book on Chinese demographic history, Lee and Wang argue against the hegemonic Malthusian (mis)understandings according to which the family and population history to China has been seen as an example of a society's failure to curb population growth by any means other than recurrent disaster (by "positive" rather than "preventive" checks in Malthusian terms). They note the important difference in marriage systems that we have just described, but they dispute conclusions too often drawn from the Chinese historical pattern concerning overpopulation. Instead, according to Lee and Wang "persistently high nuptiality . . . did not inflate Chinese fertility, because of . . . the low level of fertility within marriage."

This second example points to another important realm for which the age at which women marry has great consequences. But the findings reported by Lee and Wang also caution scholars against leaping to comparative conclusions about one society on the basis of models established in another, even while their claims still suggest the value of comparison. We should not presume that since Chinese women were married universally and young, they therefore had more children or devoted a greater proportion of their time and energy to childbearing and child rearing than did their later married counterparts in Europe. Although the evidence is far from definitive, it nevertheless indicates that total marital fertility may have been somewhat lower in China than in Europe until the late nineteenth or early twentieth centuries. The factors in China that produced this pattern included relatively high rates of infanticide, especially of female infants, as well as different beliefs and practices about child care and sexuality. For example, babies were apparently breast-fed longer in China than in Europe (a pattern in turn related to the domestic location of women's work), which would have both increased infants' chances of survival and also lengthened the intervals between births.[1] In the realm of sexuality, pertinent factors include both prescriptions for men against overly frequent intercourse, and coresidence with a parental generation whose vigilance included policing young couples' sexual behavior.

These two examples are meant to suggest how looking at women's life cycles comparatively both enhances our understanding of the implications of varying patterns for women's history and also suggests the very broad ramifications, indeed world-historical significance, of different ways of institutionalizing the female life cycle.

---

[1] Breastfeeding temporarily lowers female fertility. [Ed.]

■ REFLECTIONS

Women's history has entered the mainstream during the last few decades. An older view, still pervasive in the academic world forty years ago, assumed that women's history was adequately covered by general history, which was largely the story of the exploits of men. Political, military, and diplomatic history took precedence over historical fields seen as less resolutely masculine, such as social and cultural history.

Today, women's history not only stands independently in college and university curriculums but has also helped open doors to a wide range of new fields in social history—gender, family, childhood, sexuality, domesticity, and health, to name but a few. These new research fields have contributed significantly to issues of general history, as the authors of the last reading show. In fact, the growth and development of new fields of research and teaching in social and cultural history have had the effect of relegating the study of presidents, wars, and treaties to the periphery of the profession. A recent meeting of the American Historical Association, where historians came together to talk about their work, had more sessions on women, gender, and sexuality than on politics, diplomacy, military, war, World War I, World War II, and the American Civil War combined.

Some more traditional historians complain that this is a fad, and that sooner or later the profession will get back to the more "important" topics. But others respond that it is hard to think of anything more important than the history of half of humanity. This debate leads to questions about the importance of particular individuals in history. Who had a greater impact, for instance, thirtieth U.S. president Calvin Coolidge (1872–1933) or Marie Curie (1867–1934), who won the Nobel Prize for isolating radium for therapeutic purposes?

What role do individuals play on the historical canvas anyway? A president or Nobel laureate works according to social norms, available resources, supporting institutions, and the work of hundreds or thousands of others, living and dead. Forty years ago, historians put greater stress on institutions, movements, and perceived forces than they do today. In recent years, historians have looked for the "agency" of individuals and groups, perhaps in an effort to see how people can have an impact on their world. The power of slavery and the impact of imperialism have been balanced with the tales of slave revolts, the stories of successful collaborators, adapters, and resisters, and the voices of slaves and indigenous and colonized peoples. We see this in the study of women's history as well.

We began this chapter with the observation that we live in a patriarchy. Even if we are dismantling it in the twenty-first century, it was a powerful force between 1500 and 1800: a historical force, not natural, but a product of the urban revolution, perhaps, beginning about five thousand years ago. It is useful to understand its causes, describe its workings, and relate its history. But does doing so only hamper our capacity for change? Does it ignore the stories of women who have made a difference? Conversely, are women empowered, humanity enriched, by knowing how individual women were able to work within the system, secure their needs, engage, negotiate, compromise? Do the stories of a Pu Songling or the poems of an Anna Bijns inspire us? Or do they misrepresent the past and, by consequence, delude us?

Perhaps there are no easy answers to those questions, but our exercise in comparison might come in handy. The rich and varied detail of the human past should warn us against absolute declarations. We may emphasize patriarchy or emphasize women's power, but we would be foolish to deny either. In consequence, it may be most useful to ask more specific questions and to compare. Can women own property here? Is there more restriction on women's movement in this society or that? Only then can we begin to understand why here and not there, why then and not now. And only then can we use our understanding of the past to improve the present.

19

The Scientific Revolution

Europe, the Ottoman Empire, China, Japan, and the Americas, 1600–1800

■ HISTORICAL CONTEXT

Modern life is unthinkable apart from science. We surround ourselves with its products, from cars and computers to telephones and televisions; we are dependent on its institutions — hospitals, universities, and research laboratories; and we have internalized the methods and procedures of science in every aspect of our daily lives, from balancing checkbooks to counting calories. Even on social and humanitarian questions, the scientific method has become almost the exclusive model of knowledge in modern society.

We can trace the scientific focus of modern society to what is often called the "scientific revolution" of the seventeenth century. The seventeenth-century scientific revolution was a European phenomenon, marked by the work of such notables as Nicolas Copernicus (1473–1543) in Poland, Galileo Galilei (1564–1642) in Tuscany, and Isaac Newton (1642–1727) in England. But it was also a global event, prompted initially by Europe's new knowledge from Asia, Africa, and the Americas, and ultimately spread as a universal method for understanding and manipulating the world.

What was the scientific revolution? How revolutionary was it? How similar, or different, was European science from that practiced elsewhere in the world? And how much did the European revolution affect scientific traditions elsewhere? These are some of the issues we will study in this chapter.

■ THINKING HISTORICALLY

Distinguishing Change from Revolution

The world is always changing; it always has been changing. Sometimes, however, the change seems so formidable, extensive, important, or quick that we use the term *revolution*. In fact, we will use the term in this and the next two chapters. In this chapter we will examine what historians call the scientific revolution. The next chapter will deal with political revolutions and the chapter following with the industrial revolution. In each of these cases there are some historians who object that the changes were not really revolutionary, that they were more gradual or limited. Thus, we ask the question, how do we distinguish between mere change and revolutionary change?

In this chapter you will be asked, how revolutionary were the changes that are often called the scientific revolution? The point, however, is not to get your vote, pro or con, but to get you to think about how you might answer such a question. Do we, for instance, compare "the before" with "the after" and then somehow divide by the time it took to get from one to the other? Do we look at what people said at the time about how things were changing? Are we gauging speed of change or extent of change? What makes things change at different speeds? What constitutes a revolution?

1

JACK GOLDSTONE

Why Europe? 2009

This selection is drawn from a book by a modern historian who asks one of the enduring questions of modern history: Why was it that people in Europe pioneered the breakthroughs in modern scientific thought in the seventeenth century that led to an industrial revolution? This is a particularly intriguing question when you realize, as Goldstone points out, that between 1000 and 1500 China, India, and the Muslim world made far greater strides in science than Europe. What were the obstacles to advancement in scientific thought in most societies before 1500? What happened in Europe between 1500 and 1650 to change the way people thought about

Source: Jack Goldstone, *Why Europe? The Rise of the West in World History 1500–1850* (New York: McGraw-Hill, 2009), 144–53.

nature, and how did that thinking change? How did rationalism and empiricism change European science after 1650? How does a combination of rationalism and empiricism produce better science than either separately or than the other two sources of authority: tradition and religion?

THINKING HISTORICALLY

Goldstone does not use the term *scientific revolution* in this selection, but he discusses a number of changes in European society, politics, and beliefs that might be called revolutionary. What are these changes? What would make them revolutionary changes? Is it a matter of how fast they occurred, how widespread they were, what impact they had, or how unusual or uniquely European they were? Which of these measures makes them more revolutionary?

One must ask, given the glorious achievements of Islamic and other scientific traditions that were sustained over many centuries: Why did they not develop the same kind of advances leading to industrialization as did the modern European sciences?

Varieties of World Science and Different Approaches to Understanding Nature

Approaches to natural science varied across time and across different civilizations. Some traditions, such as that of China, made enormous advances in herbal medicine but remained weak in basic anatomy. Other traditions, like that of the Mayan Indians of Central America, were extremely accurate in observational astronomy but very weak in physics and chemistry.

Nonetheless, most premodern scientific traditions shared several common elements. First, their scientific understanding of nature was generally embedded in the framework for understanding the universe laid out in their society's major religious or philosophical traditions. Although there was potential for great conflict if scientific studies of nature should contradict elements of religion, this was usually avoided by making the religious views dominant, so that scientific findings would have to be reconciled with or subordinated to religious beliefs. This does *not* mean that religions were opposed to science—quite the opposite! Most political and religious leaders sponsored both scientific and religious studies, believing that each supported the other. Many distinguished Confucian scholars, Islamic judges, and Catholic priests were also outstanding mathematicians and scientists. For the most part, detailed observations of nature, including accurate measurements of planetary motions and natural phenomena, were considered valuable as privileged knowledge to political and religious elites or socially useful for improving architecture, farming, and medicine.

However, science generally remained intermingled with religious and philosophical beliefs, and any inconsistencies were generally resolved in favor of preserving the established religion. This meant that truly novel work risked being suppressed by political and religious authorities, especially during periods of religious conservatism or state enforcement of orthodox religious views.

Second, most premodern sciences maintained a separation between mathematics and natural philosophy (the study of nature). Mathematics was considered useful for exploring the properties of numbers (arithmetic) and relationships in space (geometry). It was also useful for a host of practical problems, such as surveying; compiling tables of planetary positions in the skies for navigation, calendars, and astrology; and accounting. But most premodern scientific traditions—including those of the ancient Greeks, medieval Europeans, Arabs, and the Chinese—held that mathematics was *not* useful for studying the basic constitution of the universe. This was the main subject matter of natural philosophy (the study of the natural world) and theology (the study of religious issues, including the relationship of humans and the natural world to the creator).

If one wanted to know the nature of God or the soul, or the relations between humankind and God, or the purpose of animals, or the nature of the stuff that composed the world—plants, stones, fire, air, liquids, gases, crystals—well, these were problems for reasoning based on experience and logic, not on mathematical equations. The task of philosophy was to comprehend the essential nature of things and their relationships. Measurement was a practical matter, useful but best left to surveyors, craftspeople, moneylenders, and other practical folks.

Thus the Chinese and Indian traditions believed in a basic hidden force of nature—*qi* in China and *prana* in India—that animated and infused the world. For Chinese scientists, the world was always changing, and these changes formed complex cycles and flows of opposing forces that operated to maintain an overall harmony. Thus despite their enormous skill and use of detailed mathematics and observation in areas from canals and irrigation works to astronomy and clocks, it never occurred to orthodox Chinese scientists to regard the universe as a mechanical clockwork or to apply mathematical equations to understand why natural processes occurred. What mattered was understanding signs of the ever-shifting flows of *qi* between opposing conditions—*yin* and *yang*—to avoid excesses and to maintain the harmony of the whole.

The Greeks too, since the time of Aristotle, similarly maintained a separation of mathematics from natural philosophy. Aristotle's philosophy of nature, which by the Middle Ages had become the dominant natural philosophy in Europe, analyzed nature by identifying the basic elements that composed all things. For Aristotle, there were four basic elements—earth, fire, air, and water—which were defined in terms of how they behaved. Things made of earth are solid and naturally tend to fall to the center of the universe, which is why the solid earth beneath us consists of a sphere, and all solid things fall toward it. Fire naturally rises, so things infused with fire rise. Air is transparent and moves across the surface of the Earth as winds; water flows and moves in currents and puddles and fills the seas and oceans. Since the Moon and Sun and stars and planets neither move up nor down but remain in the heavens, moving in circles in the skies, they must be composed of yet another, distinct element that was perfect and unchanging, which the Greeks called the "aether."

The way these principles were discovered and proved was through logic and argument based on experience, not through mathematics. Although mathematical forms and principles could help identify and measure relationships in nature, the true "essence" of reality was set by philosophy. For example, even though the planets actually move at varying speeds in elliptical orbits around the Sun, for over 1,000 years Islamic and European astronomers sought to describe their orbits solely in terms of combinations of uniform and circular motions, because Aristotle's natural philosophy had decreed that this was the only way that heavenly bodies could move.

In the Middle Ages, European scholars continued to treat mathematics as mainly a practical field, while focusing their attention on logic and argument as the keys to advancing knowledge. Although medieval scholars in Europe did make significant advances in the study of motion and absorbed much of the critical commentary on Greek science and philosophy from the Islamic world, they did not reject or replace the major tenets of classical Greek science or their own religious theology. Rather, much of the effort of European thought in the Middle Ages consisted of efforts to reconcile and synthesize the writings of the Greek authors on science and politics with the precepts of the Christian Bible and other religious texts, culminating in the work of St. Thomas Aquinas.

The Islamic scientific tradition went further than any other in using experiments and mathematical reasoning to challenge the arguments of Ptolemy, Galen, and others of the ancient Greeks, creating new advances in medicine, chemistry, physics, and astronomy. Yet within Islam, the discussion of the fundamental relationships and characteristics of nature was separated into the teachings of the Islamic sciences, based on classical religious texts, and the teachings of the foreign sciences, including all the works of Greek and Indian authors. After the writings of the philosophical critic Al-Ghazali in the eleventh century, who championed the value of the Islamic sciences on truly fundamental issues, this division was generally maintained, and even the most remarkable advances and findings with regard to revisions of Greek learning were not permitted to challenge the fundamental views of the universe as expressed in Islamic religious works.

Thus in all the major scientific traditions, whereas precise measurement and sophisticated mathematics were widely used, mathematical reasoning was not used to challenge the fundamental understanding of nature that was expressed in natural philosophy and religious thought.

Third, in most places, the dominant assumptions and traditions of science were so distinctive and so well established that they could hardly be shaken even by encounters with different notions and ideas. These scientific traditions tended to grow incrementally, with each successive generation modifying yet building on the works of their predecessors, so that over time a rich and longstanding tradition of scientific methods and findings grew up, intertwined with an established religious tradition. These structures of thought tended to resist wholesale change or replacement and to marginalize heterodox or conflicting views.

Thus by 1500, there were many different varieties of science in the world, each with their own strengths and distinctive characteristics. Most had developed precise observations of the Earth and heavens and had systematized a great number and variety of discoveries about nature. Most had developed a classification of essential relationships or characteristics of natural things. Most were linked in some fashion to one of the great axial age religions and over many centuries had worked to accumulate knowledge while building frameworks that were compatible with those religions. And in the next century or two, most scientific traditions would be driven to greater subordination to classical and religious orthodoxy by rulers who were responding to the political and social conflicts that struck over almost all of Europe and Asia.

How then was it possible that any culture could develop . . . technical innovations, based on new instruments and mathematical natural science . . . ? To understand this, we have to grasp the unusual events and discoveries that led to unexpected changes in Europe's approach to science.

Europe's Unusual Trajectory: From Embracing to Escaping Its Classical Tradition, 1500–1650

The study of ancient schools of thought was given a new direction by the realization, by the early 1500s, that the Spanish voyages to the west had discovered not just an alternate route to India, but in fact a whole new continent, a "New World" unknown to ancient geographers and scientists. Navigators came to realize that practically all of Greek geography was badly mistaken. Also in the early 1500s, the research of the Belgian anatomist Andreas Vesalius (who was building on the prior work of Arab scholars) demonstrated to Europeans that Galen's knowledge of human anatomy was, in many respects, inaccurate or deficient because it was based on deductions from animal dissections rather than on empirical study of human cadavers. Vesalius showed that many of Galen's (and Aristotle's) statements about the heart, the liver, the blood vessels, and the skeleton were wrong.

Then in 1543, Copernicus published his new methods for calculating the movements of the planets based on a solar system with a moving Earth circling the Sun. Although some supporters, trying to avoid conflict with the church, argued that his work should only be taken as a new method of predicting planetary positions, Copernicus argued quite forcefully that the structure and dynamics of the solar system made more sense, logically and aesthetically, if the Earth and all other planets revolved around the Sun. If so, then the system of Ptolemy and Aristotle, with the Earth as the center of all motion, was in error.

In 1573, the Danish astronomer Tycho Brahe published his account of the supernova that had suddenly appeared near the constellation of Cassiopeia in 1572. This was a phenomenon that had never been recorded in European astronomy. Indeed, since the time of Aristotle, it was assumed that the skies were unchanging and constant in their perfection. Comets and meteors were known, of course, but they were considered weather phenomena, like lightning that occurred close to the Earth rather than in the celestial heavens. But the supernova was not a comet or meteorite, because it showed no motion: It was a new body that behaved like a fixed star—something that was, according to Aristotle's philosophy, impossible.

Five years later, Brahe showed by careful observation of the movements of the great comet of 1577 that this comet must be farther away from the Earth than the Moon and thus was moving through the celestial heavens, not the atmosphere, striking yet another blow against Aristotle's cosmic system. Supernovae that can be observed from Earth by the naked eye are rare, but as chance would have it, in 1604, yet another supernova made its appearance, thus showing conclusively that the heavens were not unchanging after all.

By the late 1500s and early 1600s, therefore, the wisdom of Aristotle, Galen, and Ptolemy, which had been accepted for over 1,000 years, was coming under widespread attack. European scholars sought out new observations and new instruments for studying nature that could help determine who was correct, or incorrect, in their description of nature and the universe.

In 1609, Galileo used the new spyglass or telescope—invented by Dutch lens-grinders and then improved by Galileo himself—to observe the heavens. Looking at the Moon through a telescope rather than only the unaided eye, Galileo saw what looked like giant mountains and craters on the surface, which through the telescope looked positively Earthlike! Jupiter was found to have its own moons circling it, implying that the Earth could not be the center of all celestial motions. In every direction were previously unknown stars, and even the Milky Way was revealed to consist of thousands of tiny stars. Though many critics at first dismissed the views through the telescope as false magic, enough people acquired their own telescopes and confirmed Galileo's discoveries that they were widely accepted. People came to realize that the universe in which they lived was nothing like that described by the ancient Greek authorities.

Copernicus was not the first astronomer to suggest that the Earth revolved on its axis and moved around the Sun, instead of being the fixed center of the universe; a few ancient Greek and Islamic astronomers had also suggested that this was possible. However, until telescopic observations of the moons of Jupiter demonstrated the fact of motion around a body other than the Earth, there was no evidence on which to base a successful overthrow of Aristotle's views. It was only after 1600, with so many new observations that contradicted the ancient Greeks' knowledge—of geography, of anatomy, and of astronomy—piling up in all directions, that it became possible, even imperative, to adopt alternatives to Aristotle in particular and to Greek science and philosophy as a whole.

From 1600 to 1638, a series of books presenting new knowledge or proclaiming the need for a "new science" made a compelling case that the knowledge of the ancients was seriously flawed.

> 1600: William Gilbert, *On the Magnet*
> 1620: Francis Bacon, *The New Organon, or True Directions Concerning the Interpretation of Nature*
> 1620: Johannes Kepler, *The New Astronomy*
> 1626: Francis Bacon, *The New Atlantis*
> 1628: William Harvey, *On the Motion of the Heart and Blood*
> 1638: Galileo, *Discourses on Two New Sciences*

Gilbert argued that compass needles pointed north because the whole earth acted as a giant magnet. Francis Bacon argued that Aristotle's mainly deductive logic (collected under the title *Organon*—which means "instrument or tool") could not be trusted as a guide to understanding nature; instead Bacon argued for the use of inductive logic, based on a program of experiment and observation, as a superior method for discovering knowledge of the world. Kepler showed that the planets actually traveled in elliptical orbits around the sun, not in circles. And William Harvey showed that, contrary to Galen's teachings, the supposedly separate veins and arteries were in fact one system through which the blood was circulated by the beating of the heart.

By the mid-1600s, therefore, European philosophers and scientists found themselves in a world where the authority of ancient texts was clearly no longer a secure foundation for knowledge. Other major civilizations did not suffer such blows. For the Chinese, Indians, and Muslims—accustomed to operating in a vast intercontinental trade sphere from China to Europe and generally seeing themselves at the center of all that mattered—the discovery of new, lightly peopled lands far to the west made little difference. But for Europeans—who had long seen themselves on the literal edge of the civilized world with all that mattered lying to the east—the discovery of new and wholly unknown lands to the west changed their fundamental position in the world.

Similarly, Chinese and Indian astronomers had observed supernovae before (accurately recording observations of the heavens for thousands of years) and had long ago developed philosophies of nature that were built around ideas of continuous change as the normal course of things in the universe. Unlike the Greeks and Europeans, they had no rigid notions of perfect and unchanging heavens, separate from the Earth, that would cause their classical traditions to be fundamentally challenged by new observations of comets and stars.

Moreover, just when Europeans started their impassioned debates over these new observations and put forth their alternative ideas, the Ottoman, Mughal, and Chinese Empires were focused on internal concerns, seeking to recover from internal rebellions by closing off outside influences and strengthening traditional orthodox beliefs.

Thus the Europeans, more than any other major civilization, suddenly found that the classical tradition that they had sought to embrace now had to be escaped if they were going to understand the true nature of their world and their universe. This led Europeans to undertake a search for new systems of philosophy and new ways of studying and describing nature.

Searching for New Directions in European Science: Cartesian Reasoning and British Empiricism, 1650–1750

Prior to 1650, all major civilizations drew on four basic sources to justify knowledge and authority (which were generally closely connected). These were

1. Tradition—knowledge that was revered for its age and long use
2. Religion or revelation—knowledge that was based on sacred texts or the sayings of prophets, saints, and other spiritual leaders
3. Reason—knowledge that was obtained from logical demonstration, either in arithmetic and geometry or by deductive reasoning from basic premises

4. Repeated observation and experience—knowledge that was
    confirmed by widely shared and repeated observations and
    everyday experience, such as that day follows night, the sun
    rises in the east, objects fall, heat rises. This also includes various
    agricultural and manufacturing techniques that were proven
    in use.

We have noted that in Europe by the early 1600s new discoveries,
observations, and concepts about the Earth and the universe had already
started to chip away at tradition and religious belief as guides to knowledge about the natural world. In addition, the seventeenth century was
a period of sharp religious schism and conflict in Europe, capped by the
Thirty Years' War (1618–1648). During these years Catholics, Lutherans,
Calvinists, and other sects all claimed to be correcting the errors of
others' interpretation of Christian faith, and various religious groups
rebelled and embroiled Europe in massive civil and international wars.
The lack of accepted religious authority and of any way to choose
between competing claims seemed to offer nothing but the prospect of
endless conflict.

The same problems, as we have noted, led Asian empires to promote
a return to their traditional orthodox beliefs to suppress these conflicts.
Some European states tried to do the same thing. In Spain and Italy and
part of Germany and Poland, the counter-Reformation led to the suppression of heresies and unorthodox views and enforcement of traditional Catholic beliefs. These states banned books that threatened
Catholic orthodoxy and sought to curtail the actions of "dangerous"
authors, such as Giordano Bruno and Galileo (Bruno was burned at the
stake for his heresies; Galileo, more prudent and better connected, was
allowed to live under house arrest). France and the Netherlands, though
less severe, and Britain through 1640, also tried to restore uniform state
religions and force dissenters underground or into exile. However, in a
few states—including Britain after 1689, Denmark, and Prussia—
religious tolerance remained, and throughout western Europe, there
was a checkerboard of different states following different varieties of
religion—Catholic, Calvinist, Lutheran. Throughout Europe, the result
of the rise and spread of Protestantism in the sixteenth and seventeenth
centuries was that the authority of the Catholic Church—and of the
philosophical and scientific work that was closely associated with the
church's teachings—was seriously weakened. This provided an additional
reason for philosophers to struggle to find a new basis for more certain
knowledge.

European thinkers therefore turned away from the first and second
major sources of knowledge and authority—tradition and religion—to
seek new systems of knowledge. After 1650, two major directions were
proposed to deal with this dilemma—rationalism and empiricism.

One way to set aside traditional and revelation-based assumptions was to try to get down to bedrock conclusions by reasoning purely from logic. The critical figure leading this approach was the French philosopher and mathematician René Descartes, who resolved to begin by doubting everything—the teaching of the ancients, the teachings of the church, and even his own experience. He extended his doubt until only one thing remained certain—the fact of his own doubt! This fact could then be the basis for logical deductions. After all, if Descartes could not escape the fact of his own doubt, he—as a doubting, thinking entity—must exist! This conclusion was rendered in his famous statement "I think, therefore I am."

Descartes continued this argument further. If he doubted, he could not be perfect. But if he was aware of his imperfection, this could only be because a perfect entity existed, thus there must be a perfect being, or God. And because we can only conceive of God as perfect, and hence perfectly logical, the universe constructed by God must also follow perfect logic. Descartes further argued that we can only logically perceive space if something is there, extending through space (empty space, Descartes argued, was a logical contradiction). What must fill space, then, are invisible particles whose motions and interactions must cause all that we see.

In this fashion, Descartes built up a logically consistent model of a mechanical universe in which all phenomena are to be explained by the movements and collisions of moving particles. This led Descartes to numerous valuable insights, such as the notion that we see things because invisible particles of light move from the objects we see to strike our eyes. But it also led him to deduce things that we now know are simply not true, such as the idea that the planets travel around the Sun because they are caught up in vortexes or whirlpools of swirling invisible particles.

This Cartesian rationalism provided a very attractive alternative to Aristotelian philosophy, which was now in disrepute. It seemed to have the power of purely logical demonstration behind its ideas. Also, because all phenomena were reduced to the motions of particles, it held the promise of applying mathematical principles—already worked out by Galileo for many kinds of particle motion—to all of nature. Finally, it allowed one to explain almost anything by coming up with some characteristics of particles. For example, one could suggest that spicy or sweet flavors were the respective results of sharp or smooth particles hitting the tongue or that different colors of light were produced by particles of light spinning at different speeds.

However, Cartesian rationalism also had its defects. In putting reason above experience, Cartesians disdained experiments. This limited what could be learned or discovered and often led to significant errors. Descartes' assumptions led him to misjudge the way bodies acted in collisions and turned his followers away from studying the properties of vacuums (since empty space could not exist, they must be tricks or errors by experimenters). Descartes also flatly ruled out the possibility of forces acting directly across space between objects, such as gravity. For all of its virtues, Cartesian rationalism therefore saddled its followers with a variety of errors and false explanations of the mechanics of motion in nature.

The motion of the Earth, the weight of the atmosphere, and the properties of vacuums were all discoveries whose proof rested on the use of scientific instruments (telescopes, barometers, vacuum pumps) to capture information not ordinarily available to the senses. The use of such instruments was a prime feature of the Baconian plan of developing scientific knowledge by experiments.

The experimental program reached its most systematic organization in the work of the Royal Society of London, led by Robert Boyle and later by Isaac Newton. The Royal Society based its research on experiments with scientific instruments and apparatus publicly performed at meetings of the society, and accounts of those experiments were widely published. The Royal Society used air pumps, telescopes, microscopes, electrostatic generators, prisms, lenses, and a variety of other tools to carry out its investigations. Indeed, the society came to rely on specially trained craftspeople to supply the growing demand for scientific instruments for its members.

The fame of the Royal Society in Britain skyrocketed with the achievements of Isaac Newton. Newton was the first to demonstrate that both motion on the Earth—whether the movement of falling apples, cannonballs, or the tides—and the motions of the planets through the heavens could *all* be explained by the action of a universal force of gravity. This force acted to attract objects to each other with a strength that increased with their mass but decreased with the inverse square of the distance between them. Newton's theory of gravity made it possible, for the first time, to explain the precise path and speed that the planets followed through the skies, as well as the movement of the Moon and the tides.

Newton also discovered the correct laws of mechanical force—that force was needed for all changes in the direction or speed of motion of an object, in proportion to the mass of the object and the magnitude of the change. Newton's laws of force made it possible to easily figure out the amount of work provided by, for example, a volume of falling water based on the height that it fell, or the amount of work it would take to raise a certain weight a desired distance. Newton further discovered the key principle of optics: that white light was composed of a number of different colors of light, each of which bent slightly differently when moving through water or a glass lens, thus creating rainbows in the sky and color patterns in prisms and lenses. . . .

2

Images of Anatomy, Fourteenth and Sixteenth Centuries

Andreas Vesalius (1514–1564), like generations of physicians before him, learned anatomy from the writings of Galen (129–216 C.E.), a Greek-born Roman. Because of Galen's authority, and subsequent Christian and Muslim strictures against conducting dissections, very little was learned about human anatomy for the next thousand years. Only gradually after 1200 were dissections performed again, and yet most physicians still read Galen while surgeons (formerly barbers) did the cutting. Vesalius himself began as a defender of Galen, until he moved from his native Belgium to teach at the University of Padua in Italy in 1537. There he was able to secure enough cadavers of executed criminals to perform multiple dissections and discover that Galen (who had only been able to dissect animals) had been wrong about elements of human anatomy. A facile artist himself, Vesalius engaged leading Italian draftsmen for the publication of his findings in *De humani corporis fabrica* (On the Structure of the Human Body), published in 1543.

Two images from the fourteenth century (Figures 19.1 and 19.2) are followed by two images from the *Fabrica*, one showing muscles (Figure 19.3) and another showing bones of the human skeleton (Figure 19.4). How would you describe the differences between the drawings in the *Fabrica* and those of the fourteenth century?

THINKING HISTORICALLY

The actual mistakes that Vesalius found in Galen might seem relatively trivial. For instance, Vesalius realized that the human jaw was one bone, not two as Galen claimed after dissecting monkeys. He also saw that the sternum (which protects the chest) is three bones instead of seven and that, also contrary to Galen, the fibula and tibia of the human leg were longer than the arm. In this regard we might think of his work as evolutionary rather than revolutionary. Yet when we compare the images of the fourteenth century with those of Vesalius, barely more than a hundred years later, the differences strike us as revolutionary. Why do you think that is? Was this a revolution? If so, in what?

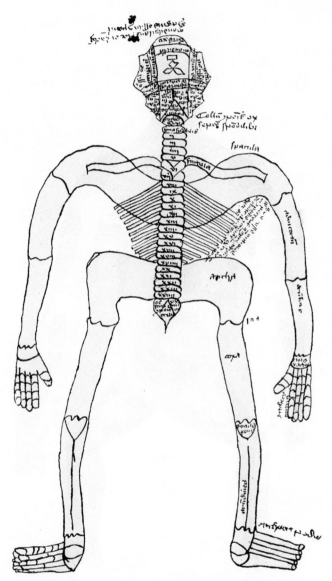

Figure 19.1   Skeleton drawing, from the Latin Munich MS Codex, fourteenth century.

Source: Wellcome Library, London.

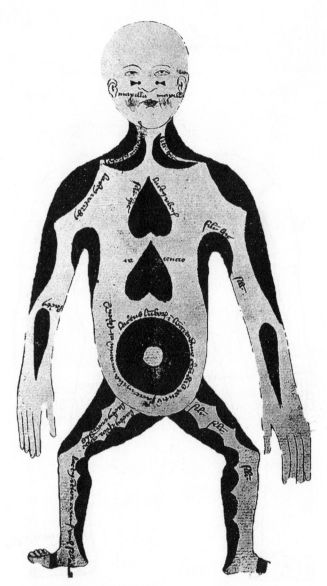

Figure 19.2   Muscular system of a man, from the Rudnitz Five-Figure Series, 1399.

Source: Wellcome Library, London.

Figure 19.3 Woodcut of muscles, from Vesalius, *De humani corporis fabrica*, 1543.

Source: The Granger Collection, New York.

Figure 19.4 Woodcut of a skeleton, from Vesalius, *De humani corporis fabrica,*1543.

Source: The Granger Collection, New York.

3

ISAAC NEWTON

The Mathematical Principles of Natural Philosophy, 1687

Isaac Newton (1643–1727) was probably the most influential scientist in world history. His range was breathtaking, covering optics, astronomy, mathematics, and physics. He invented calculus, discovered the relationship between light and color, and devised laws of motion and gravity that provided the framework of modern science for the next two hundred years. *The Mathematical Principles of Natural Philosophy* (1687) was his most influential work. We include here only the four "Rules of Reasoning in Philosophy."[1] Try to put each one in your own words. Why do you think he called them general rules of reasoning rather than specific rules for science?

In the first selection, Jack Goldstone underlined the importance of the European method of applying mathematics to the study of nature and the British empirical or experimental method of creating knowledge. How do these passages in Newton's writing emphasize both of these approaches?

THINKING HISTORICALLY

When we look at *The Mathematical Principles of Natural Philosophy,* or the *Principia,* as it is called in abbreviated Latin form, and once we cut through the seventeenth-century language, we come upon ideas that seem fairly obvious to us today. That they were not obvious then is a measure of how revolutionary they were. Try to imagine what people believed before Newton established these principles. For example, before Newton established the law of gravity, people did not believe that objects flew around at will; so what exactly is new here? Give examples of thinking that ignores these rules of reasoning.

Rule I
We are to admit no more causes of natural things, than such as are both true and sufficient to explain their appearances.

To this purpose the philosophers say, that Nature does nothing in vain, and more is in vain, when less will serve; for Nature is pleased with simplicity, and affects not the pomp of superfluous causes.

[1] As they were revised in a later edition (1726).

Source: Isaac Newton, *The Mathematical Principles of Natural Philosophy,* trans. A. Motte (London, 1729). Available on the American Libraries website at http://www.archive.org /details/newtonspmathema00newtrich (accessed October 25, 2009).

Rule II

Therefore to the same natural effects we must, as far as possible, assign the same causes.

As to respiration in a man, and in a beast; the descent of stones in Europe and in America; the light of our culinary fire and of the sun; the reflection of light in the earth, and in the planets.

Rule III

The qualities of bodies, which admit neither intension nor remission of degrees,[2] and which are found to belong to all bodies within reach of our experiments, are to be esteemed the universal qualities of all bodies whatsoever.

For since the qualities of bodies are only known to us by experiments, we are to hold for universal, all such as universally agree with experiments; and such as are not liable to diminution, can never be quite taken away. We are certainly not to relinquish the evidence of experiments for the sake of dreams and vain fictions of our own devising; nor are we to recede from the analogy of Nature, which is wont to be simple, and always consonant to itself. We no other way know the extension of bodies, than by our senses, nor do these reach it in all bodies; but because we perceive extension in all that are sensible, therefore we ascribe it universally to all others, also. That abundance of bodies are hard we learn by experience. And because the hardness of the whole arises from the hardness of the parts, we therefore justly infer the hardness of the undivided particles not only of the bodies we feel but of all others. That all bodies are impenetrable we gather not from reason, but from sensation. The bodies which we handle we find impenetrable and thence conclude impenetrability to be a universal property of all bodies whatsoever. That all bodies are moveable, and endowed with certain powers (which we call the forces of inertia) of persevering in their motion or in their rest, we only infer from the like properties observed in the bodies which we have seen. The extension, hardness, impenetrability, mobility, and force of inertia of the whole result from the extension, hardness, impenetrability, mobility, and forces of inertia of the parts: and thence we conclude that the least particles of all bodies to be also all extended, and hard, and impenetrable, and moveable, and endowed with their proper forces of inertia. And this is the foundation of

---

[2] Qualities of bodies that do not get larger or smaller, harder or softer, etc. Refers to permanent qualities of bodies: their extension, hardness, movability. The point is that we can assume these qualities are universal, and that they will be found in similar bodies, even those that are in the heavens (and therefore not measurable). [Ed.]

all philosophy. Moreover, that the divided but contiguous particles of bodies may be separated from one another, is a matter of observation; and, in the particles that remain undivided, our minds are able to distinguish yet lesser parts, as is mathematically demonstrated. But whether the parts so distinguished, and not yet divided, may, by the powers of nature, be actually divided and separated from one another, we cannot certainly determine. Yet had we the proof of but one experiment, that any undivided particle, in breaking a hard and solid body, suffered a division, we might by virtue of this rule, conclude, that the undivided as well as the divided particles, may be divided and actually separated into infinity.

Lastly, if it universally appears, by experiments and astronomical observations, that all bodies about the earth, gravitate toward the earth; and that in proportion to the quantity of matter which they severally contain; that the moon likewise, according to the quantity of its matter, gravitates toward the earth; that on the other hand our sea gravitates toward the moon; and all the planets mutually one toward another; and the comets in like manner towards the sun; we must, in consequence of this rule, universally allow, that all bodies whatsoever are endowed with a principle of mutual gravitation. For the argument from the appearances concludes with more force for the universal gravitation of all bodies, than for their impenetrability, of which among those in the celestial regions, we have no experiments, nor any manner of observation. Not that I affirm gravity to be essential to all bodies. By their inherent force I mean nothing but their force of` inertia. This is immutable. Their gravity is diminished as they recede from the earth.

Rule IV

In experimental philosophy we are to look upon propositions collected by general induction[3] from phenomena as accurately or very nearly true, notwithstanding any contrary hypotheses that may be imagined, till such time as other phenomena occur, by which they may either be made more accurate, or liable to exceptions.

This rule we must follow to ensure that the argument of induction may not be evaded by hypotheses.

---

[3] Induction is reasoning from the specific to the general: deriving a general principle from specific examples or instances. For example: This, that, and the other frog are gray, so frogs must be gray. [Ed.]

4

BONNIE S. ANDERSON AND
JUDITH P. ZINSSER

Women and Science, 1988

This selection from a history of European women shows how some
women, especially the better educated, could participate in the scientific
revolution of the seventeenth and eighteenth centuries. But Anderson
and Zinsser also demonstrate how much of the scientific revolution endowed male prejudices with false scientific respectability. What factors
seem to have enabled women to participate in the scientific revolution?
In what ways was the scientific revolution a new bondage for women?

THINKING HISTORICALLY

What do the authors mean when they say that for women "there was
no Scientific Revolution"? In what ways were women's lives different
after the scientific revolution? In what ways were they the same? Were
the differences caused by the scientific revolution?

Women Scientists

In the same way that women responded to and participated in
Humanism,[1] so they were drawn to the intellectual movement known
as the Scientific Revolution. The excitement of the new discoveries of
the seventeenth and eighteenth centuries, in particular, inspired a few
gifted women scientists to formulate their own theories about the natural world, to perform their own experiments, and to publish their findings. In contrast to those educated strictly and formally according to
Humanist precepts, these women had little formal training, and chose
for themselves what they read and studied. Rather than encouraging
them, their families at best left them to their excitement with the
wonders of the "Scientific Revolution"; at worst, parents criticized
their daughters' absorption in such inappropriate, inelegant, and
unfeminine endeavors.

All across Europe from the sixteenth to the eighteenth centuries
these women found fascination in the natural sciences. They corresponded and studied with the male scientists of their day. They observed,

---

[1] A faith in the capacities of humans that reached religious dimensions in the sixteenth
century. Renaissance humanism valued reason, classical culture and literature, and civic
engagement. [Ed.]

Source: Bonnie S. Anderson and Judith P. Zinsser, *A History of Their Own: Women in Europe
from Prehistory to the Present* (New York: Harper & Row, 1988) 2:87–89, 96–99.

and they formulated practical applications from their new knowledge of botany, horticulture, and chemistry. The Countess of Chinchon, wife of the Viceroy to Peru, brought quinine bark to Spain from Latin America because it had cured her malaria. Some noblewomen, like the German Anna of Saxony (1532–1582), found medical uses for the plants they studied. The most gifted of these early naturalists is remembered not as a scientist but as an artist. Maria Sibylla Merian (1647–1717) learned drawing and probably acquired her interest in plants and insects from her stepfather, a Flemish still-life artist. As a little girl she went with him into the fields to collect specimens. Though she married, bore two daughters, and ran a household, between 1679 and her death in 1717 she also managed to complete and have published six collections of engravings of European flowers and insects. These were more than artist's renderings. For example, her study of caterpillars was unique for the day. Unlike the still life done by her contemporaries, the drawings show the insect at every stage of development as observed from the specimens that she collected and nursed to maturity. She explained:

> From my youth I have been interested in insects, first I started with silkworms in my native Frankfurt-am-Main. After that . . . I started to collect all the caterpillars I could find to observe their changes.

Merian's enthusiasm, patience, and skill brought her to the attention of the director of the Amsterdam Botanical Gardens and other male collectors. When her daughter married and moved to the Dutch colony of Surinam, their support was important when she wanted to raise the money for a new scientific project. In 1699, at the age of fifty-two, Maria Sibylla Merian set off on what became a two-year expedition into the interior of South America. She collected, made notations and sketches. Only yellow fever finally forced her to return to Amsterdam in 1701. The resulting book of sixty engravings established her contemporary reputation as a naturalist.

Mathematics, astronomy, and studies of the universe also interested these self-taught women scientists. In 1566 in Paris Marie de Coste Blanche published *The Nature of the Sun and Earth*. Margaret Cavendish (1617–1673), the seventeenth-century Duchess of Newcastle, though haphazard in her approach to science, produced fourteen books on everything from natural history to atomic physics.

Even more exceptional in the eighteenth century was the French noblewoman and courtier, Emilie du Châtelet (1706–1749). She gained admission to the discussions of the foremost mathematicians and scientists of Paris, earned a reputation as a physicist and as an interpreter of the theories of Leibnitz and Newton. Emilie du Châtelet showed unusual intellectual abilities even as a child. By the age of ten she had read Cicero, studied mathematics and metaphysics. At twelve she could speak English, Italian, Spanish, and German and translated Greek and Latin texts like

Aristotle and Virgil. Presentation at court and life as a courtier changed none of her scientific interests and hardly modified her studious habits. She seemed to need no sleep, read incredibly fast, and was said to appear in public with ink stains on her fingers from her notetaking and writing. When she took up the study of Descartes, her father complained to her uncle: "I argued with her in vain; she would not understand that no great lord will marry a woman who is seen reading every day." Her mother despaired of a proper future for such a daughter who "flaunts her mind, and frightens away the suitors her other excesses have not driven off." It was her lover and lifelong friend, the Duke de Richelieu, who encouraged her to continue and to formalize her studies by hiring professors in mathematics and physics from the Sorbonne to tutor her. In 1733 she stormed her way into the Café Gradot, the Parisian coffee-house where the scientists, mathematicians, and philosophers regularly met. Barred because she was a woman, she simply had a suit of men's clothes made for herself and reappeared, her long legs now in breeches and hose, to the delight of cheering colleagues and the consternation of the management. . . .

Châtelet made her reputation as a scientist with her three-volume work on the German mathematician and philosopher Leibnitz, *The Institutions of Physics*, published in 1740. Contemporaries also knew of her work from her translation of Newton's *Principles of Mathematics*, her book on algebra, and her collaboration with Voltaire on his treatise about Newton.

From the fifteenth to the eighteenth centuries privileged women participated in the new intellectual movements. Like the men of their class, they became humanist scholars, naturalists, and scientists. Unfortunately, many of these women found themselves in conflict with their families and their society. A life devoted to scholarship conflicted with the roles that women, however learned, were still expected to fulfill.

Science Affirms Tradition

In the sixteenth and seventeenth centuries Europe's learned men questioned, altered, and dismissed some of the most hallowed precepts of Europe's inherited wisdom. The intellectual upheaval of the Scientific Revolution caused them to examine and describe anew the nature of the universe and its forces, the nature of the human body and its functions. Men used telescopes and rejected the traditional insistence on the smooth surface of the moon. Galileo, Leibnitz, and Newton studied and charted the movement of the planets, discovered gravity and the true relationship between the earth and the sun. Fallopio dissected the human body, Harvey discovered the circulation of the blood, and Leeuwenhoek found spermatozoa with his microscope.

For women, however, there was no Scientific Revolution. When men studied female anatomy, when they spoke of female physiology, of women's reproductive organs, of the female role in procreation, they ceased to be scientific. They suspended reason and did not accept the evidence of their senses. Tradition, prejudice, and imagination, not scientific observation, governed their conclusions about women. The writings of the classical authors like Aristotle and Galen continued to carry the same authority as they had when first written, long after they had been discarded in other areas. Men spoke in the name of the new "science" but mouthed words and phrases from the old misogyny. In the name of "science" they gave a supposed physiological basis to the traditional views of women's nature, function, and role. Science affirmed what men had always known, what custom, law, and religion had postulated and justified. With the authority of their "objective," "rational" inquiry they restated ancient premises and arrived at the same traditional conclusions: the innate superiority of the male and the justifiable subordination of the female.

In the face of such certainty, the challenges of women like Lucrezia Marinella and María de Zayas had little effect. As Marie de Gournay, the French essayist, had discovered at the beginning of the seventeenth century, those engaged in the scientific study of humanity viewed the female as if she were of a different species—less than human, at best; nature's mistake, fit only to "play the fool and serve [the male]."

The standard medical reference work, *Gynaecea,* reprinted throughout the last decades of the sixteenth century, included the old authorities like Aristotle and Galen, and thus the old premises about women's innate physical inferiority. A seventeenth-century examination for a doctor in Paris asked the rhetorical question "Is woman an imperfect work of nature?" All of the Aristotelian ideals about the different "humors" of the female and male survived in the popular press even after they had been rejected by the medical elite. The colder and moister humors of the female meant that women had a passive nature and thus took longer to develop in the womb. Once grown to maturity, they were better able to withstand the pain of childbirth.

Even without reference to the humors, medical and scientific texts supported the limited domestic role for women. Malebranche, a French seventeenth-century philosopher, noted that the delicate fibers of the woman's brain made her overly sensitive to all that came to it; thus she could not deal with ideas or form abstractions. Her body and mind were so relatively weak that she must stay within the protective confines of the home to be safe.

No amount of anatomical dissection dispelled old bits of misinformation or changed the old misconceptions about women's reproductive organs. Illustrations continued to show the uterus shaped like a flask with two horns, and guides for midwives gave the principal role in labor to the fetus. As in Greek and Roman medical texts these new "scientific" works assumed that women's bodies dictated their principal function, procreation. Yet even this role was devalued. All of the evidence of dissection and deductive reasoning reaffirmed the superiority of the male's role in reproduction. Men discovered the spermatazoon, but not the ovum. They believed that semen was the single active agent. Much as Aristotle had done almost two millennia earlier, seventeenth-century scientific study hypothesized that the female supplied the "matter," while the life and essence of the embryo came from the sperm alone.

These denigrating and erroneous conclusions were reaffirmed by the work of the seventeenth-century English scientist William Harvey. Having discovered the circulation of the blood, Harvey turned his considerable talents to the study of human reproduction and published his conclusions in 1651. He dissected female deer at all stages of their cycle, when pregnant and when not. He studied chickens and roosters. With all of this dissection and all of this observation he hypothesized an explanation for procreation and a rhapsody to male semen far more extreme than anything Aristotle had reasoned. The woman, like the hen with her unfertilized egg, supplies the matter, the man gives it form and life. The semen, he explained, had almost magical power to "elaborate, concoct"; it was "vivifying" . . . endowed with force and spirit and generative influence," coming as it did from "vessels so elaborate, and endowed with such vital energy." So powerful was this fluid that it did not even have to reach the woman's uterus or remain in the vagina. Rather he believed it gave off a "fecundating power," leaving the woman's body to play a passive, or secondary, role. Simple contact with this magical elixir of life worked like lightning, or—drawing on another set of his experiments—"in the same way as iron touched by the magnet is endowed with its powers and can attract other iron to it." The woman was but the receiver and the receptacle.

Anatomy and physiology confirmed the innate inferiority of woman and her limited reproductive function. They also proved as "scientific truth" all of the traditional negative images of the female nature. A sixteenth-century Italian anatomist accepted Galen's view and believed the ovaries to be internal testicles. He explained their strange placement so "as to keep her from perceiving and ascertaining her sufficient perfection," and to humble her "continual desire to dominate." An early-seventeenth-century French book on childbirth instructed the midwife to tie the umbilical cord far from the body to assure a long penis and a well-spoken young man for a male child and close to the body to give the female a straighter form and to ensure that she would talk less.

No one questioned the equally ancient and traditional connection between physiology and nature: the role of the uterus in determining a woman's behavior. The organ's potential influence confirmed the female's irrationality and her need to accept a subordinate role to the male. The sixteenth-century Italian anatomist Fallopio repeated Aristotle's idea that the womb lusted for the male in its desire to procreate. The French sixteenth-century doctor and writer Rabelais took Plato's view of the womb as insatiable, like an animal out of control when denied sexual intercourse, the cause of that singularly female ailment, "hysteria." Other sixteenth- and seventeenth-century writers on women and their health adopted all of the most misogynistic explanations of the traditional Greek and Roman authorities. No menstruation meant a diseased womb, an organ suffocating in a kind of female excrement. Only intercourse with a man could prevent or cure the condition. Left untreated the uterus would put pressure on other organs, cause convulsions, or drive the woman crazy. Thus, the male remained the key agent in the woman's life. She was innately inferior, potentially irrational, and lost to ill-health and madness without his timely intervention.

So much changed from the fifteenth to the eighteenth centuries in the ways in which women and men perceived their world, its institutions and attitudes. The Renaissance offered the exhilaration of a society in which the individual could be freed from traditional limitations. In the spirit of Humanistic and scientific inquiry men questioned and reformulated assumptions about the mind's capabilities and the description of the natural universe. New methods of reasoning and discourse, of observation and experimentation, evolved and led to the reorientation of the natural universe and more accurate descriptions of the physical world, including man's own body. Yet when it came to questions and assumptions about women's function and role and to descriptions of her nature and her body, no new answers were formulated. Instead, inspired by the intellectual excitement of the times and the increasing confidence in their own perceptions of the spiritual and material world, men argued even more strongly from traditional premises, embellishing and revitalizing the ancient beliefs. Instead of breaking with tradition, descriptions of the female accumulated traditions: the classical, the religious, the literary, the customary, and the legal—all stated afresh in the secular language of the new age. Instead of being freed, women were ringed with yet more binding and seemingly incontrovertible versions of the traditional attitudes about their inferior nature, their proper function and role, and their subordinate relationship to men.

With the advent of printing, men were able to disseminate these negative conclusions about women as they never could before. From the sixteenth century on the printing presses brought the new tracts, pamphlets, treatises, broadsides, and engravings to increasing numbers of Europeans: pictures of the sperm as a tiny, fully formed infant; works by scholars and jurists explaining the female's "natural" physical and legal incapacity; romances and ballads telling of unchaste damsels and vengeful wives set to plague man.

Although these misogynistic attitudes about women flourished and spread, the defense of women had also begun. In her *Book of the City of Ladies* Christine de Pizan, the fifteenth-century writer, asks why no one had spoken on their behalf before, why the "accusations and slanders" had gone uncontradicted for so long? Her allegorical mentor, "Rectitude," replies, "Let me tell you that in the long run, everything comes to a head at the right time."

The world of the courts had widened the perimeters of women's expectations and given some women increased opportunities. However, for the vast majority of women, still not conscious of their disadvantaged and subordinate status, changes in material circumstances had a far greater impact. From the seventeenth to the twentieth centuries more women were able to live the life restricted in previous ages to the few. In Europe's salons and parlors they found increased comfort, greater security, and new ways to value their traditional roles and functions. For these women, "the right time"—the moment for questioning and rejecting the ancient premises of European society—lay in the future.

5

LADY MARY WORTLEY MONTAGUE

Letter on Turkish Smallpox Inoculation, 1717

Lady Mary Wortley Montague, an English aristocrat, came down with smallpox in 1715. She survived, but was badly scarred by the rash that accompanied the often-fatal disease. Her younger brother died from smallpox, one of the tens of thousands who succumbed in epidemics across Europe and around the world in the eighteenth and nineteenth centuries. Two years after her recovery Montague traveled to Istanbul with her husband, who was the British ambassador to the Ottoman Empire. There, she witnessed a new approach to warding off smallpox infections, as she described in the following letter to a friend in England. What process does Montague describe in her letter? What was her response to the events she witnessed in Turkey?

Source: *Letters of Lady Mary Wortley Montague, written during her travels in Europe, Asia, and Africa, to which are added poems by the same author* (Bordeaux: J. Pinard, 1805). The UCLA Louis M. Darling Biomedical Library, History and Special Collections Division. Also available from Gutenberg E-Books at Lady Mary Wortley Montague, Her Life and Letters (1689–1762). Author: Lewis Melville. Release Date: January 4, 2004 [EBook #10590].

THINKING HISTORICALLY

This letter provides a clear example of how scientific observation can change the material world in which we live. After observing the Turkish smallpox inoculation, Montague had her son and daughter inoculated. In fact, she became an advocate for smallpox inoculation in England and played an important role in persuading the English medical profession to support the innovative procedure. Montague paved the way for a safer vaccine, developed by Edward Jenner in 1796, that would eventually eradicate the disease from the planet.

Despite her admirable efforts, it was difficult to convince Europeans to embrace smallpox inoculation, which had been practiced in Asia for centuries. Even though the effectiveness of this technology came to be recognized in England during Montague's lifetime, the French and other Europeans, according to Voltaire, thought that the English were "fools and madmen" for experimenting with inoculation. What does this suggest about the nature of scientific discovery? Besides lack of knowledge, what other obstacles need to be overcome? What does this resistance say about how revolutionary the "scientific revolution" was?

To Mrs. S. C., Adrianople, April 1, O.S.

A Propos of distempers, I am going to tell you a thing, that will make you wish yourself here. The small pox, so fatal, and so general amongst us, is here entirely harmless, by the invention of ingrafting, which is the term they give it. There is a set of old women, who make it their business to perform the operation, every autumn, in the month of September, when the great heat is abated. People send to one another to know if any of their family has a mind to have the small-pox; they make parties for this purpose, and when they are met (commonly fifteen or sixteen together) the old woman comes with a nut-shell full of the matter of the best sort of small pox, and asks what vein you please to have opened. She immediately rips open that you offer to her, with a large needle (which gives you no more pain than a common scratch), and puts into the vein as much matter as can lie upon the head of her needle, and after that, binds up the little wound with a hollow bit of shell, and in this manner opens four or five veins. The Grecians have commonly the superstition of opening one in the middle of the forehead, one in each arm, and one in the breast, to mark the sign of the cross; but this has a very ill effect, all these wounds leaving little scars, and is not done by those that are not superstitious, who choose to have them in the legs, or that part of the arm that is concealed. The children or young patients play together all the rest of the day, and are in perfect health to the eighth.

Then the fever begins to seize them, and they keep their beds two days, very seldom three. They have very rarely above twenty or thirty in their faces, which never mark, and in eight days time they are as well as before their illness. Where they are wounded, there remains running sores during the distemper, which I don't doubt is a great relief to it. Every year thousands undergo this operation, and the French ambassador says pleasantly that they take the small-pox here by way of diversion, as they take the waters in other countries. There is no example of any one that has died in it, and you may believe I am well satisfied of the safety of this experiment, since I intend to try it on my dear little son. I am patriot enough to take pains to bring this useful invention into fashion in England, and I should not fail to write to some of our doctors very particularly about it, if I knew any one of them that I thought had virtue enough to destroy such a considerable branch of their revenue, for the good of mankind. But that distemper is too beneficial to them, not to expose to all their resentment the hardy wight[1] that should undertake to put an end to it. Perhaps if I live to return, I may, however have the courage to war with them. Upon this occasion, admire the heroism in the heart of

Your friend, etc. etc.

[1] Creature. [Ed.]

6

LYNDA NORENE SHAFFER

China, Technology, and Change, 1986–1987

In this essay an important contemporary world historian asks us to compare the revolutionary consequences of scientific and technological changes that occurred in China and Europe before the seventeenth century. What is Shaffer's argument? In what ways was the European scientific revolution different from the changes in China she describes here?

THINKING HISTORICALLY

What exactly was the impact of printing, the compass, and gunpowder in Europe? What was the "before" and "after" for each of these innovations? What, according to Shaffer, was the situation in China before and after each of these innovations? Were these innovations as revolutionary in China as they were in Europe?

Source: Lynda Norene Shaffer, "China, Technology, and Change," *World History Bulletin* 4, no. 1 (Fall/Winter 1986–1987): 1–6.

Francis Bacon (1561–1626), an early advocate of the empirical method, upon which the scientific revolution was based, attributed Western Europe's early modern take-off to three things in particular: printing, the compass, and gunpowder. Bacon had no idea where these things had come from, but historians now know that all three were invented in China. Since, unlike Europe, China did not take off onto a path leading from the scientific to the Industrial Revolution, some historians are now asking why these inventions were so revolutionary in Western Europe and, apparently, so unrevolutionary in China.

In fact, the question has been posed by none other than Joseph Needham, the foremost English-language scholar of Chinese science and technology. It is only because of Needham's work that the Western academic community has become aware that until Europe's take-off, China was the unrivaled world leader in technological development. That is why it is so disturbing that Needham himself has posed this apparent puzzle. The English-speaking academic world relies upon him and repeats him; soon this question and the vision of China that it implies will become dogma. Traditional China will take on supersociety qualities — able to contain the power of printing, to rein in the potential of the compass, even to muffle the blast of gunpowder.

The impact of these inventions on Western Europe is well known. Printing not only eliminated much of the opportunity for human copying errors, it also encouraged the production of more copies of old books and an increasing number of new books. As written material became both cheaper and more easily available, intellectual activity increased. Printing would eventually be held responsible, at least in part, for the spread of classical humanism and other ideas from the Renaissance. It is also said to have stimulated the Protestant Reformation, which urged a return to the Bible as the primary religious authority.

The introduction of gunpowder in Europe made castles and other medieval fortifications obsolete (since it could be used to blow holes in their walls) and thus helped to liberate Western Europe from feudal aristocratic power. As an aid to navigation the compass facilitated the Portuguese- and Spanish-sponsored voyages that led to Atlantic Europe's sole possession of the Western Hemisphere, as well as the Portuguese circumnavigation of Africa, which opened up the first all-sea route from Western Europe to the long-established ports of East Africa and Asia.

Needham's question can thus be understood to mean, Why didn't China use gunpowder to destroy feudal walls? Why didn't China use the compass to cross the Pacific and discover America, or to find an all-sea route to Western Europe? Why didn't China undergo a Renaissance or Reformation? The implication is that even though China possessed these technologies, it did not change much. Essentially Needham's question is asking, What was wrong with China?

Actually, there was nothing wrong with China. China was changed fundamentally by these inventions. But in order to see the changes, one must abandon the search for peculiarly European events in Chinese history, and look instead at China itself before and after these breakthroughs.

To begin, one should note that China possessed all three of these technologies by the latter part of the Tang dynasty (618–906) — between four and six hundred years before they appeared in Europe. And it was during just that time, from about 850, when the Tang dynasty began to falter, until 960, when the Song dynasty (960–1279) was established, that China underwent fundamental changes in all spheres. In fact, historians are now beginning to use the term *revolution* when referring to technological and commercial changes that culminated in the Song dynasty, in the same way that they refer to the changes in eighteenth- and nineteenth-century England as the Industrial Revolution. And the word might well be applied to other sorts of changes in China during this period.

For example, the Tang dynasty elite was aristocratic, but that of the Song was not. No one has ever considered whether the invention of gunpowder contributed to the demise of China's aristocrats, which occurred between 750 and 960, shortly after its invention. Gunpowder may, indeed, have been a factor although it is unlikely that its importance lay in blowing up feudal walls. Tang China enjoyed such internal peace that its aristocratic lineages did not engage in castle-building of the sort typical in Europe. Thus, China did not have many feudal fortifications to blow up.

The only wall of significance in this respect was the Great Wall, which was designed to keep steppe nomads from invading China. In fact, gunpowder may have played a role in blowing holes in this wall, for the Chinese could not monopolize the terrible new weapon, and their nomadic enemies to the north soon learned to use it against them. The Song dynasty ultimately fell to the Mongols, the most formidable force ever to emerge from the Eurasian steppe. Gunpowder may have had a profound effect on China — exposing a united empire to foreign invasion and terrible devastation — but an effect quite opposite to the one it had on Western Europe.

On the other hand, the impact of printing on China was in some ways very similar to its later impact on Europe. For example, printing contributed to a rebirth of classical (that is, preceding the third century A.D.) Confucian learning, helping to revive a fundamentally humanistic outlook that had been pushed aside for several centuries.

After the fall of the Han dynasty (206 B.C.–A.D. 220), Confucianism had lost much of its credibility as a world view, and it eventually lost its central place in the scholarly world. It was replaced by Buddhism, which had come from India. Buddhists believed that much human pain and confusion resulted from the pursuit of illusory pleasures and dubious ambitions: Enlightenment and, ultimately, salvation would come from a progressive disengagement from the real world, which they also believed to be illusory. This point of view dominated Chinese intellectual life until the ninth century. Thus the academic and intellectual comeback of classical Confucianism was in essence a return to a more optimistic literature that affirmed the world as humans had made it.

The resurgence of Confucianism within the scholarly community was due to many factors, but printing was certainly one of the most important. Although it was invented by Buddhist monks in China, and at first benefited Buddhism, by the middle of the tenth century, printers were turning out innumerable copies of the classical Confucian corpus. This return of scholars to classical learning was part of a more general movement that shared not only its humanistic features with the later Western European Renaissance, but certain artistic trends as well.

Furthermore, the Protestant Reformation in Western Europe was in some ways reminiscent of the emergence and eventual triumph of Neo-Confucian philosophy. Although the roots of Neo-Confucianism can be found in the ninth century, the man who created what would become its most orthodox synthesis was Zhu Xi (Chu Hsi, 1130–1200). Neo-Confucianism was significantly different from classical Confucianism, for it had undergone an intellectual (and political) confrontation with Buddhism and had emerged profoundly changed. It is of the utmost importance to understand that not only was Neo-Confucianism new, it was also heresy, even during Zhu Xi's lifetime. It did not triumph until the thirteenth century, and it was not until 1313 (when Mongol conquerors ruled China) that Zhu Xi's commentaries on the classics became the single authoritative text against which all academic opinion was judged.

In the same way that Protestantism emerged out of a confrontation with the Roman Catholic establishment and asserted the individual Christian's autonomy, Neo-Confucianism emerged as a critique of Buddhist ideas that had taken hold in China, and it asserted an individual moral capacity totally unrelated to the ascetic practices and prayers of the Buddhist priesthood. In the twelfth century Neo-Confucianists lifted the work of Mencius (Meng Zi, 370–290 B.C.) out of obscurity and assigned it a place in the corpus second only to that of the *Analects of Confucius*. Many facets of Mencius appealed to the Neo-Confucianists, but one of the most important was his argument that humans by nature are fundamentally good. Within the context of the Song dynasty, this was an assertion that morality could be pursued through an engagement in human affairs, and that the Buddhist monks' withdrawal from life's mainstream did not bestow upon them any special virtue.

The importance of these philosophical developments notwithstanding, printing probably had its greatest impact on the Chinese political system. The origin of the civil service examination system in China can be traced back to the Han dynasty, but in the Song dynasty government-administered examinations became the most important route to political power in China. For almost a thousand years (except the early period of Mongol rule), China was governed by men who had come to power simply because they had done exceedingly well in examinations on the Neo-Confucian canon. At any one time thousands of students were studying for the exams, and thousands of inexpensive books were required. Without printing such a system would not have been possible.

The development of this alternative to aristocratic rule was one of the most radical changes in world history. Since the examinations were ultimately open to 98 percent of all males (actors were one of the few groups excluded), it was the most democratic system in the world prior to the development of representative democracy and popular suffrage in Western Europe in the eighteenth and nineteenth centuries. (There were some small-scale systems, such as the classical Greek city-states, which might be considered more democratic, but nothing comparable in size to Song China or even the modern nation-states of Europe.)

Finally we come to the compass. Suffice it to say that during the Song dynasty, China developed the world's largest and most technologically sophisticated merchant marine and navy. By the fifteenth century its ships were sailing from the north Pacific to the east coast of Africa. They could have made the arduous journey around the tip of Africa and on into Portuguese ports; however, they had no reason to do so. Although the Western European economy was prospering, it offered nothing that China could not acquire much closer to home at much less cost. In particular, wool, Western Europe's most important export, could easily be obtained along China's northern frontier.

Certainly, the Portuguese and the Spanish did not make their unprecedented voyages out of idle curiosity. They were trying to go to the Spice Islands, in what is now Indonesia, in order to acquire the most valuable commercial items of the time. In the fifteenth century these islands were the world's sole suppliers of the fine spices, such as cloves, nutmeg, and mace, as well as a source for the more generally available pepper. It was this spice market that lured Columbus westward from Spain and drew Vasco Da Gama around Africa and across the Indian Ocean.

After the invention of the compass, China also wanted to go to the Spice Islands and, in fact, did go, regularly—but Chinese ships did not have to go around the world to get there. The Atlantic nations of Western Europe, on the other hand, had to buy spices from Venice (which controlled the Mediterranean trade routes) or from other Italian city-states;

or they had to find a new way to the Spice Islands. It was necessity that mothered those revolutionary routes that ultimately changed the world.

Gunpowder, printing, the compass—clearly these three inventions changed China as much as they changed Europe. And it should come as no surprise that changes wrought in China between the eighth and tenth centuries were different from changes wrought in Western Europe between the thirteenth and fifteenth centuries. It would, of course, be unfair and ahistorical to imply that something was wrong with Western Europe because the technologies appeared there later. It is equally unfair to ask why the Chinese did not accidentally bump into the Western Hemisphere while sailing east across the Pacific to find the wool markets of Spain.

7

SUGITA GEMPAKU

A Dutch Anatomy Lesson in Japan, 1771

Sugita Gempaku* (1733–1817) was a Japanese physician who, as he tells us here in his memoir, suddenly discovered the value of Western medical science when he chanced to witness a dissection shortly after he obtained a Dutch anatomy book.

What was it that Sugita Gempaku learned on that day in 1771? What were the differences between the treatments of anatomy in the Chinese *Book of Medicine* and the Dutch medical book? What accounts for these differences?

THINKING HISTORICALLY

How might the Dutch book have changed the way the author practiced medicine? How did it change his knowledge of the human body? How did it change the relevance of his knowledge of the human body to the medicine he practiced? How revolutionary was the new knowledge for Sugita Gempaku?

---

* SOO gee tah gehm PAH koo

Source: Sugita Gempaku, *Ranto Kotohajime* (The Beginning of Dutch Studies in the East), in *Japan: A Documentary History*, ed. David J. Lu (Armonk, NY: M. E. Sharpe, 2005), 1:264–66. Iwanami Shoten, *Nihon Koten Bunka Taikei* (Major Compilation of Japanese Classics) (Tokyo: Iwanami Shoten, 1969), 95:487–93.

Whenever I met Hiraga Gennai (1729–1779), we talked to each other on this matter: "As we have learned, the Dutch method of scholarly investigation through field work and surveys is truly amazing. If we can directly understand books written by them, we will benefit greatly. However, it is pitiful that there has been no one who has set his mind on working in this field. Can we somehow blaze this trail? It is impossible to do it in Edo. Perhaps it is best if we ask translators in Nagasaki to make some translations. If one book can be completely translated, there will be an immeasurable benefit to the country." Every time we spoke in this manner, we deplored the impossibility of imple-menting our desires. However, we did not vainly lament the matter for long.

Somehow, miraculously I obtained a book on anatomy written in that country. It may well be that Dutch studies in this country began when I thought of comparing the illustrations in the book with real things. It was a strange and even miraculous happening that I was able to obtain that book in that particular spring of 1771. Then at the night of the third day of the third month, I received a letter from a man by the name of Tokuno Bambei, who was in the service of the then Town Commissioner, Magaribuchi Kai-no-kami. Tokuno stated in his letter that "A post-mortem examination of the body of a condemned criminal by a resident physician will be held tomorrow at Senjukotsukahara. You are welcome to witness it if you so desire." At one time my colleague by the name of Kosugi Genteki had an occasion to witness a post-mortem dissection of a body when he studied under Dr. Yamawaki Tōyō of Kyoto. After seeing the dissection firsthand, Kosugi remarked that what was said by the people of old was false and simply could not be trusted. "The people of old spoke of nine internal organs, and nowadays, people divide them into five viscera and six internal organs. That [perpetuates] inaccuracy," Kosugi once said. Around that time (1759) Dr. Tōyō published a book entitled *Zōshi* (*On Internal Organs*). Having read that book, I had hoped that some day I could witness a dissection. When I also acquired a Dutch book on anatomy, I wanted above all to compare the two to find out which one accurately described the truth. I rejoiced at this unusually fortunate circumstance, and my mind could not entertain any other thought. However, a thought occurred to me that I should not monopolize this good fortune, and decided to share it with those of my colleagues who were diligent in the pursuit of their medicine. . . . Among those I invited was one [Maeno] Ryōtaku (1723–1803). . . .

The next day, when we arrived at the location . . . Ryōtaku reached under his kimono to produce a Dutch book and showed it to us. "This is a Dutch book of anatomy called *Tabulae Anatomicae*. I bought this a few years ago when I went to Nagasaki, and kept it." As I examined it, it was the same book I had and was of the same edition. We held each other's

hands and exclaimed: "What a coincidence!" Ryōtaku continued by saying: "When I went to Nagasaki, I learned and heard," and opened his
book. "These are called *long* in Dutch, they are lungs," he taught us. "This
is *hart*, or the heart. When it says *maag* it is the stomach, and when it says
milt it is the spleen." However, they did not look like the heart given in the
Chinese medical books, and none of us were sure until we could actually
see the dissection.

Thereafter we went together to the place which was especially set for
us to observe the dissection in Kotsukahara. . . . The regular man who
performed the chore of dissection was ill, and his grandfather, who was
ninety years of age, came in his place. He was a healthy old man. He had
experienced many dissections since his youth, and boasted that he dissected
a number of bodies. Those dissections were performed in those days by
men of the *eta*[1] class. . . . That day, the old butcher pointed to this and that
organ. After the heart, liver, gall bladder, and stomach were identified, he
pointed to other parts for which there were no names. "I don't know their
names. But I have dissected quite a few bodies from my youthful days.
Inside of everyone's abdomen there were these parts and those parts."
Later, after consulting the anatomy chart, it became clear to me that I saw
an arterial tube, a vein, and the suprarenal gland. The old butcher again
said, "Every time I had a dissection, I pointed out to those physicians many
of these parts, but not a single one of them questioned 'what was this?' or
'what was that?'" We compared the body as dissected against the charts
both Ryōtaku and I had, and could not find a single variance from
the charts. The Chinese *Book of Medicine* (*Yi Jing*) says that the lungs are
like the eight petals of the lotus flower, with three petals hanging in front,
three in back, and two petals forming like two ears and that the liver has
three petals to the left and four petals to the right. There were no such
divisions, and the positions and shapes of intestines and gastric organs
were all different from those taught by the old theories. The official physicians, Dr. Okada Yōsen and Dr. Fujimoto Rissen, have witnessed dissection
seven or eight times. Whenever they witnessed the dissection, they found
that the old theories contradicted reality. Each time they were perplexed
and could not resolve their doubts. Every time they wrote down what they
thought was strange. They wrote in their books. "The more we think of it,
there must be fundamental differences in the bodies of Chinese and of the
eastern barbarians [i.e., Japanese]." I could see why they wrote this way.

---

[1] The *eta* were an untouchable caste in Japan, defined by their restriction to certain
occupations associated with death: tanning or working with hides, cremating the dead,
butchering meat, and, thus, doing autopsies. They could not be physicians. The term is derogatory. Their descendants today are called Burakumin. [Ed.]

That day, after the dissection was over, we decided that we also should examine the shape of the skeletons left exposed on the execution ground. We collected the bones, and examined a number of them. Again, we were struck by the fact that they all differed from the old theories while conforming to the Dutch charts.

The three of us, Ryōtaku, [Nakagawa] Junan (1739–1786), and I went home together. On the way home we spoke to each other and felt the same way. "How marvelous was our actual experience today. It is a shame that we were ignorant of these things until now. As physicians who serve their masters through medicine, we performed our duties in complete ignorance of the true form of the human body. How disgraceful it is. Somehow, through this experience, let us investigate further the truth about the human body. If we practice medicine with this knowledge behind us, we can make contributions for people under heaven and on this earth." Ryōtaku spoke to us. "Indeed, I agree with you wholeheartedly." Then I spoke to my two companions. "Somehow if we can translate anew this book called *Tabulae Anatomicae*, we can get a clear notion of the human body inside out. It will have great benefit in the treatment of our patients. Let us do our best to read it and understand it without the help of translators." Ryōtaku responded: "I have been wanting to read Dutch books for some time, but there has been no friend who would share my ambitions. I have spent days lamenting it. If both of you wish, I have been in Nagasaki before and have retained some Dutch. Let us use it as a beginning to tackle the book together." After hearing it, I answered, "This is simply wonderful. If we are to join our efforts, I shall also resolve to do my very best." . . .

The next day, we assembled at the house of Ryōtaku and recalled the happenings of the previous day. When we faced that *Tabulae Anatomicae*, we felt as if we were setting sail on a great ocean in a ship without oars or a rudder. With the magnitude of the work before us, we were dumbfounded by our own ignorance. However, Ryōtaku had been thinking of this for some time, and he had been in Nagasaki. He knew some Dutch through studying and hearing, and knew some sentence patterns and words. He was also ten years older than I, and we decided to make him head of our group and our teacher. At that time I did not know the twenty-five letters of the Dutch alphabet. I decided to study the language with firm determination, but I had to acquaint myself with letters and words gradually.

BENJAMIN FRANKLIN

Letter on a Balloon Experiment in 1783

Benjamin Franklin (1706–1790) was the preeminent statesman, diplomat, and spokesman for the British colonies that became the United States during his long lifetime. Trained as a candle maker and printer, he became a journalist, publisher, merchant, homespun philosopher, and inveterate inventor. He invented the lightning rod, the Franklin stove, bifocals, and the medical catheter, among other things. His inventions sprang from a gift of immense curiosity and an exhaustive reading in the science of his day.

Franklin, sometimes called "the first American," represented the fledging Republic in France during the Revolution, ensuring French participation against the British. In 1783 he signed the second Treaty of Paris, by which the British recognized the independence of the United States. Franklin was the only founding father to sign the Declaration of Independence (1776), the Treaty of Paris (1783), and the Constitution of the United States (1789). Throughout his life Franklin furthered his interest in scientific experiment and invention. In December of 1783, he wrote to a friend in England about a recent invention that he had witnessed in Paris: an early experiment in air travel in a balloon. What did Franklin see, and what did it mean to him?

THINKING HISTORICALLY

What evidence do you see in this letter that the scientific revolution was a genuinely revolutionary change? What was revolutionary about it? What evidence do you see that the people of the time thought they were living in a revolutionary age? How would you compare their attitudes with those of people today toward modern technological innovations?

To Sir Joseph Banks[1]

Passy, Dec. 1, 1783.

Dear Sir:—

In mine of yesterday I promised to give you an account of Messrs. Charles & Robert's experiment, which was to have been made this day,

---

[1] Banks (1743–1820) was a leading British botanist and naturalist. He sailed to the South Pacific with Captain James Cook and served as president of the Royal Society, trustee of the British Museum, and advisor to George III, whom he encouraged to fund numerous scientific expeditions. (He was also an early British recipient of a smallpox vaccination, in 1760.) [Ed.]

Source: Nathan G. Goodman, ed., *The Ingenious Dr. Franklin, Selected Scientific Letters of Benjamin Franklin* (Philadelphia: University of Pennsylvania Press, 1931), 99–102.

and at which I intended to be present. Being a little indisposed, and the air cool, and the ground damp, I declined going into the garden of the Tuileries, where the balloon was placed, not knowing how long I might be obliged to wait there before it was ready to depart, and chose to stay in my carriage near the statue of Louis XV, from whence I could well see it rise, and have an extensive view of the region of air through which, as the wind sat, it was likely to pass. The morning was foggy, but about one o'clock the air became tolerably clear, to the great satisfaction of the spectators, who were infinite, notice having been given of the intended experiment several days before in the papers, so that all Paris was out, either about the Tuileries, on the quays and bridges, in the fields, the streets, at the windows, or on the tops of houses, besides the inhabitants of all the towns and villages of the environs. Never before was a philosophical experiment so magnificently attended. Some guns were fired to give notice that the departure of the balloon was near, and a small one was discharged, which went to an amazing height, there being but little wind to make it deviate from its perpendicular course, and at length the sight of it was lost. Means were used, I am told, to prevent the great balloon's rising so high as might endanger its bursting. Several bags of sand were taken on board before the cord that held it down was cut, and the whole weight being then too much to be lifted, such a quantity was discharged as to permit its rising slowly. Thus it would sooner arrive at that region where it would be in equilibrio with the surrounding air, and by discharging more sand afterwards, it might go higher if desired. Between one and two o'clock, all eyes were gratified with seeing it rise majestically from among the trees, and ascend gradually above the buildings, a most beautiful spectacle. When it was about two hundred feet high, the brave adventurers held out and waved a little white pennant, on both sides [of] their car, to salute the spectators, who returned loud claps of applause. The wind was very little, so that the object though moving to the northward, continued long in view; and it was a great while before the admiring people began to disperse. The persons embarked were Mr. Charles, professor of experimental philosophy, and a zealous promoter of that science; and one of the Messieurs Robert, the very ingenious constructors of the machine. When it arrived at its height, which I suppose might be three or four hundred toises,[2] it appeared to have only horizontal motion. I had a pocket-glass, with which I followed it, till I lost sight first of the men, then of the car, and when I last saw the balloon, it appeared no bigger than a walnut. I write this at seven in the evening. What became of them is not yet known here. I hope they descended by daylight, so as to see and avoid falling among trees or on houses, and that the experiment was completed without any mischievous accident, which the novelty of it and the want of experience might

---

[2] twaz   A height rod equal to 1.949 meters (or about 2 yards). [Ed.]

well occasion. I am the more anxious for the event, because I am not well informed of the means provided for letting themselves down, and the loss of these very ingenious men would not only be a discouragement to the progress of the art, but be a sensible loss to science and society.

I shall inclose one of the tickets of admission, on which the globe was represented, as originally intended, but is altered by the pen to show its real state when it went off. When the tickets were engraved the car was to have been hung to the neck of the globe, as represented by a little drawing I have made in the corner.

I suppose it may have been an apprehension of danger in straining too much the balloon or tearing the silk, that induced the constructors to throw a net over it, fixed to a hoop which went round its middle, and to hang the car to that hoop.

Tuesday morning, December 2d.—I am relieved from my anxiety by hearing that the adventurers descended well near L'Isle Adam before sunset. This place is near seven leagues from Paris. Had the wind blown fresh they might have gone much farther.

If I receive any further particulars of importance, I shall communicate them hereafter.

With great esteem, I am, dear sir, your most obedient and most humble servant,

FRANKLIN

P.S. *Tuesday evening.*—Since writing the above I have received the printed paper and the manuscript containing some particulars of the experiment, which I enclose. I hear further that the travellers had perfect command of their carriage, descending as they pleased by letting some of the inflammable air escape, and rising again by discharging some sand; that they descended over a field so low as to talk with the labourers in passing, and mounted again to pass a hill. The little balloon falling at Vincennes shows that mounting higher it met with a current of air in a contrary direction, an observation that may be of use to future aerial voyagers.

■ REFLECTIONS

Was there a scientific revolution in the seventeenth and eighteenth centuries? By most measures we would have to say "yes." There were new polished-glass instruments with which to observe and measure; books, theories, diagrams, debates, and discoveries emerged at a dizzying pace. Age-old authorities—Aristotle, Ptolemy, even the Bible—were called into question. The wisdom of the ages was interrogated for evidence and forced to submit to tests by experiment.

There was a revolution in the way Europeans looked at their surroundings. In the words of Shakespeare, the great English dramatist, the world became a stage, a spectacle apart that could be viewed and analyzed by objective observers. Nature no longer displayed its forces as omens or metaphors. The rainbow was no longer a sign of hope, the comet a harbinger of divine disapproval. Heavenly events might be explained in the same way as were events on Earth. Newton's rules underline the simplicity of assumptions that nature is uniform and not unnecessarily complex. We can assume that the fire in the fireplace has the same qualities as the fire of the sun, that unchanging qualities of hardness, mobility, or gravity would apply to objects too distant to measure as they do to those within our grasp. Nature follows laws that humans can derive by experiment and induction.

Goldstone reminds us that many of the scientific developments in Europe sprang from foreign innovations, and in some fields Europe was not as advanced as other societies. Lady Mary Montague provides a dramatic example of that fact. Yet the scientific revolution's unique combination of observation and generalization, experimentation and mathematics, induction and deduction established a body of knowledge and a method for research that proved lasting and irreversible.

Why was it that China, so scientifically and technologically adept during the Sung dynasty, pictured hearts and lungs as flower petals in the late-Ming and early-Qing seventeenth century? Was it that Chinese science lost momentum or changed direction? Or does such a question, as Lynda Shaffer warns, judge China unfairly by Western standards? Do the petal hearts reflect a different set of interests rather than a failure of Chinese science?

Chinese scientists excelled in acupuncture, massage, and herbal medicine, while European scientists excelled in surgery. It turned out that the inner workings of the human body were better revealed in surgical dissection than in muscle manipulation or pharmacology. And, as Sugita Gempaku reminds us, the Europeans not only cut and removed, but they also named what they found and tried to understand how it worked. Perhaps the major difference between science in Europe and that in India, China, and Japan in the seventeenth century was one of perspective: Europeans were beginning to imagine the human body as a machine and asking how it worked. In some respects, the metaphor of man as a machine proved more fruitful than organic metaphors of humans as plants or animals.

Asking probing questions and testing the answers also changed our understanding of the heavens. If mathematical calculations indicated that a star would appear at a particular spot in the heavens and it did not, Galileo might just as soon have questioned the observation as the math. From the seventeenth century on, scientists would check one or the other on the assumption that observation and mathematics could be brought together to understand the same event, that they would have to be in agreement, and that such agreement could lead to laws that could then be tested and proved or disproved.

It is this method of inquiry, not the discoveries, that was new. For the scientific method that emerged during this period constituted a systematic means of inquiry based on agreed-upon rules of hypothesis, experimentation, theory testing, law, and dissemination. This scientific inquiry was a social process in two important ways: First, any scientific discovery had to be reproducible and recognized by other scientists to gain credence. Second, a community of scientists was needed to question, dismiss, or validate the work of its members.

Europe in the seventeenth century saw the proliferation of numerous scientific associations, academies, institutes, and public experiments. These numerous organizations testified not only to a growing interest in science but also to a continuing public conversation. Science in Europe thus became a matter of public concern, a popular endeavor. Compare the masses of Parisians Ben Franklin described who turned out to view the balloon experiment with the few physicians gathered around Sugita Gempaku who could learn from the expertise of outcast butchers.

Ultimately, then, the difference between European science and that of India or China in the seventeenth century may have had more to do with society than with culture. The development of modern scientific methods relied on the numerous debates and discussions of a self-conscious class of gentlemen scientists in a Europe where news traveled quickly and ideas could be translated and tested with confidence across numerous borders. To what extent does science everywhere today demonstrate the hallmarks of the seventeenth-century scientific revolution?

20

Enlightenment and Revolution

Europe, the Americas, and India, 1650–1850

■ HISTORICAL CONTEXT

Much of the modern world puts its faith in science, reason, and democracy. The seventeenth-century scientific revolution established reason as the key to understanding nature. During the eighteenth century, philosophy, social organization, and government all came under the critical light of reason. Historians call this movement the "Enlightenment," and its consequences were revolutionary. Most — though, as we shall see, not all — people believed that reason would eventually lead to freedom. Freedom of thought, religion, and association, and political liberties and representative governments were hailed as hallmarks of the Age of Enlightenment.

For some, enlightened society meant a more controlled rather than a more democratic society. Philosophers like Immanuel Kant and Jean Jacques Rousseau wanted people to become free but thought most people were incapable of achieving such a state. Rulers who were called "enlightened despots" believed that the application of reason to society would make people happier, but not necessarily freer.

Ultimately, however, the Enlightenment's faith in reason led to calls for political revolution as well as for schemes of order. In England in the seventeenth century, in America and France at the end of the eighteenth century, and in Latin America shortly thereafter, revolutionary governments were created according to rational principles of liberty and equality that dispatched monarchs and enshrined the rule of the people. In this chapter we will concentrate on the heritage of the Enlightenment, examining competing tendencies toward order and revolution, stability and liberty, equality and freedom. We will also compare the American and the French Revolutions, and these with the later revolutions in Latin America. Finally, we will extend our understanding of the global nature of the Enlightenment by looking at similar developments in India.

Map 20.1 Latin American Independence, 1804–1830.

■ THINKING HISTORICALLY

Close Reading and Interpretation of Texts

At the core of the Enlightenment was a trust in reasoned discussion, a belief that people could understand each other, even if they were not in agreement. Such understanding demanded clear and concise communication in a world where the masses were often swayed by fiery sermons and flamboyant rhetoric. But the Enlightenment also put its faith in the written word and a literate public. Ideas were debated face-to-face in the salons and coffeehouses of Europe and its colonies, but it was through letters, diaries, the new world of newspapers, and the burgeoning spread of printed books that the people of the Enlightenment learned what they and their neighbors thought.

It is appropriate, then, for us to read the selections in this chapter—most primary sources—in the spirit in which they were written. We will pay special attention to the words and language that the authors use and will attempt to understand exactly what they meant, even why they chose the words they did. Such explication is a twofold process; we must understand the words first and foremost; then we must strive to understand the words in their proper context, as they were intended by the author. To achieve our first goal, we will paraphrase, a difficult task because the eighteenth-century writing style differs greatly from our own: Sentences are longer and arguments are often complex. Vocabularies were broad during this period, and we may encounter words that are used in ways unknown to us and out of usage today. As to our latter goal, we must try to make the vocabulary and perspective of the authors our own. Grappling with what makes the least sense to us and trying to understand why it was said is the challenge.

1

DAVID HUME
On Miracles, 1748

The European Enlightenment of the eighteenth century was the expression of a new class of intellectuals, independent of the clergy but allied with the rising middle class. Their favorite words were *reason, nature,* and *progress.* They applied the systematic doubt of René Descartes (1596–1650) and the reasoning method of the scientific revolution to human affairs, including religion and politics. With caustic wit and good humor, they asked new questions and popularized new points of view that would eventually revolutionize Western politics and culture. While the French *philosophes* and Voltaire (1694–1778) may be the best known, the Scottish philosopher David Hume (1711–1776) may have been the most brilliant. What does Hume argue in this selection? Does he prove his point to your satisfaction? How does he use reason and nature to make his case? Is reason incompatible with religion?

THINKING HISTORICALLY

The first step in understanding what Hume means in this essay must come from a careful reading — a sentence-by-sentence exploration. Try to paraphrase each sentence, putting it into your own words. For example, you might paraphrase the first sentence like this: "I've found a way to disprove superstition; this method should be useful as long as superstition exists, which may be forever." Notice the content of such words as *just* and *check.* What does Hume mean by these words and by *prodigies?*

Source: *The Philosophical Works of David Hume* (Edinburgh: A. Black and W. Tait, 1826).

The second sentence is a concise definition of the scientific method. How would you paraphrase it? The second and third sentences summarize the method Hume has discovered to counter superstition. What is the meaning of the third sentence?

In the rest of the essay, Hume offers four proofs, or reasons, why miracles do not exist. How would you paraphrase each of these? Do you find these more or less convincing than his more general opening and closing arguments? What does Hume mean by *miracles*?

I flatter myself that I have discovered an argument . . . , which, if just, will, with the wise and learned, be an everlasting check to all kinds of superstitious delusion, and consequently will be useful as long as the world endures; for so long, I presume, will the accounts of miracles and prodigies be found in all history, sacred and profane. . . .

A wise man proportions his belief to the evidence. . . .

A miracle is a violation of the laws of nature; and as a firm and unalterable experience has established these laws, the proof against a miracle, from the very nature of the fact, is as entire as any argument from experience can possibly be imagined. . . . Nothing is esteemed a miracle, if it ever happens in the common course of nature. It is no miracle that a man, seemingly in good health, should die on a sudden; because such a kind of death, though more unusual than any other, has yet been frequently observed to happen. But it is a miracle that a dead man should come to life; because that has never been observed in any age or country. There must, therefore, be an uniform experience against every miraculous event, otherwise the event would not merit that appellation. And as an uniform experience amounts to a proof, there is here a direct and full *proof*, from the nature of the fact, against the existence of any miracle. . . .

(Further) there is not to be found, in all history, any miracle attested by a sufficient number of men, of such unquestioned good sense, education, and learning, as to secure us against all delusion in themselves; of such undoubted integrity, as to place them beyond all suspicion of any design to deceive others; of such credit and reputation in the eyes of mankind, as to have a great deal to lose in case of their being detected in any falsehood. . . .

Secondly, We may observe in human nature a principle which, if strictly examined, will be found to diminish extremely the assurance, which we might, from human testimony, have in any kind of prodigy. . . . The passion of *surprise* and *wonder*, arising from miracles, being an agreeable emotion, gives a sensible tendency towards the belief of those events from which it is derived. . . .

With what greediness are the miraculous accounts of travellers received, their descriptions of sea and land monsters, their relations of wonderful adventures, strange men, and uncouth manners? But if the spirit of religion join itself to the love of wonder, there is an end of common sense; and human testimony, in these circumstances, loses all pretensions to authority. A religionist may be an enthusiast, and imagine he sees what has no reality: He may know his narrative to be false, and yet persevere in it, with the best intentions in the world, for the sake of promoting so holy a cause: Or even where this delusion has not place, vanity, excited by so strong a temptation, operates on him more powerfully than on the rest of mankind in any other circumstances; and self-interest with equal force. . . .

The many instances of forged miracles and prophecies and supernatural events, which, in all ages, have either been detected by contrary evidence, or which detect themselves by their absurdity, prove sufficiently the strong propensity of mankind to the extraordinary and marvellous, and ought reasonably to beget a suspicion against all relations of this kind.[1] . . .

Thirdly, It forms a strong presumption against all supernatural and miraculous relations, that they are observed chiefly to abound among ignorant and barbarous nations; or if a civilized people has ever given admission to any of them, that people will be found to have received them from ignorant and barbarous ancestors, who transmitted them with that inviolable sanction and authority which always attend received opinions. . . .

I may add, as a *fourth* reason, which diminishes the authority of prodigies, that there is no testimony for any, even those which have not been expressly detected, that is not opposed by any infinite number of witnesses; so that not only the miracle destroys the credit of testimony, but the testimony destroys itself. To make this the better understood, let us consider, that in matters of religion, whatever is different is contrary; and that it is impossible the religions of ancient Rome, of Turkey, of Siam, and of China, should all of them be established on any solid foundation. Every miracle, therefore, pretended to have been wrought in any of these religions (and all of them abound in miracles), as its direct scope is to establish the particular system to which it is attributed; so has it the same force, though more indirectly, to overthrow every other system. In destroying a rival system, it likewise destroys the credit of those miracles on which that system was established, so that all the prodigies of different religions are to be regarded as contrary facts, and the evidences of these prodigies, whether weak or strong, as opposite to each other. . . .

Upon the whole, then, it appears, that no testimony for any kind of miracle has ever amounted to a probability, much less to a proof; and that, even supposing it amounted to proof, it would be opposed by another proof, derived from the very nature of the fact which it would endeavour to establish. It is experience only which gives authority to human testimony; and it is the same experience which assures us of the

---

[1] Accounts of miracles. [Ed.]

laws of nature. When, therefore, these two kinds of experience are contrary, we have nothing to do but to subtract the one from the other, and embrace an opinion either on one side or the other, with that assurance which arises from the remainder. But according to the principle here explained, this subtraction with regard to all popular religions amounts to an entire annihilation; and therefore we may establish it as a maxim, that no human testimony can have such force as to prove a miracle, and make it a just foundation for any such system of religion.

2

JEAN JACQUES ROUSSEAU
The Social Contract, 1762

Jean Jacques Rousseau (1712–1778) was one of the leading thinkers of the Enlightenment, whose ideas were as central as those of Diderot (with whom he studied and quarreled), Voltaire (next to whom he is buried in the Pantheon), and Hume (who sheltered him in England toward the end of his life). Rousseau's indifference to formal religion both reflected and influenced French Enlightenment thought, and his political ideas affected the radicals of the French Revolution, though he died eleven years before its outbreak. In both his native Geneva and France, where he spent most of his life, Rousseau's work was often banned. In fact, most of his work was not published until after his death.

The Social Contract, Or Principles of Political Right (1762) challenged the monarchy and called for a government of the people, a force Rousseau saw not in individuals or the competing classes of a society of unequals, but in a "general will" that was greater than any institution or the sum of the people. Which ideas expressed here would be a threat to the French monarchy or establishment? Why would Rousseau's writing appeal to people who wanted to overthrow the regime?

THINKING HISTORICALLY

The power of Enlightenment thought was its radical willingness to ask, and try to answer, fundamental questions. What are some of the fundamental questions this selection grapples with? What does Rousseau mean by such phrases as the "state of nature," the "social compact," and the "general will"?

Source: Jean Jacques Rousseau, *The Social Contract, Or Principles of Political Right,* trans. G. D. H. Cole. Rendered into HTML and text by Jon Roland of the Constitution Society. Available at www. constitution.org/jjr/socon.htm.

Book I

I mean to inquire if, in the civil order,[1] there can be any sure and legitimate rule of administration, men being taken as they are and laws as they might be. In this inquiry I shall endeavor always to unite what right sanctions with what is prescribed by interest, in order that justice and utility may in no case be divided.

I enter upon my task without proving the importance of the subject. I shall be asked if I am a prince or a legislator, to write on politics. I answer that I am neither, and that is why I do so. If I were a prince or a legislator, I should not waste time in saying what wants doing; I should do it, or hold my peace.

As I was born a citizen of a free State, and a member of the Sovereign,[2] I feel that, however feeble the influence my voice can have on public affairs, the right of voting on them makes it my duty to study them: and I am happy, when I reflect upon governments, to find my inquiries always furnish me with new reasons for loving that of my own country.

1. Subject of the First Book

Man is born free; and everywhere he is in chains. One thinks himself the master of others, and still remains a greater slave than they. How did this change come about? I do not know. What can make it legitimate? That question I think I can answer.

If I took into account only force, and the effects derived from it, I should say: "As long as a people is compelled to obey, and obeys, it does well; as soon as it can shake off the yoke, and shakes it off, it does still better; for, regaining its liberty by the same right as took it away, either it is justified in resuming it, or there was no justification for those who took it away." But the social order is a sacred right which is the basis of all other rights. Nevertheless, this right does not come from nature, and must therefore be founded on conventions. . . .

4. Slavery

Since no man has a natural authority over his fellow, and force creates no right, we must conclude that conventions[3] form the basis of all legitimate authority among men. . . .

So, from whatever aspect we regard the question, the right of slavery is null and void, not only as being illegitimate, but also because it is

---

[1] Civil order: opposed to the state of nature; civic society, the world of citizens. [Ed.]

[2] The ultimate authority, which Rousseau says should be the General Will. [Ed.]

[3] Agreements, compacts. [Ed.]

absurd and meaningless. The words *slave* and *right* contradict each other, and are mutually exclusive. It will always be equally foolish for a man to say to a man or to a people: "I make with you a convention wholly at your expense and wholly to my advantage; I shall keep it as long as I like, and you will keep it as long as I like."

6. The Social Compact

I suppose men to have reached the point at which the obstacles in the way of their preservation in the state of nature[4] show their power of resistance to be greater than the resources at the disposal of each individual for his maintenance in that state. That primitive condition can then subsist no longer; and the human race would perish unless it changed its manner of existence.

But, as men cannot engender new forces, but only unite and direct existing ones, they have no other means of preserving themselves than the formation, by aggregation, of a sum of forces great enough to overcome the resistance. These they have to bring into play by means of a single motive power, and cause to act in concert.

This sum of forces can arise only where several persons come together: but, as the force and liberty of each man are the chief instruments of his self-preservation, how can he pledge them without harming his own interests, and neglecting the care he owes to himself? This difficulty, in its bearing on my present subject, may be stated in the following terms:

"*The problem is to find a form of association which will defend and protect with the whole common force the person and goods of each associate, and in which each, while uniting himself with all, may still obey himself alone, and remain as free as before.*" This is the fundamental problem of which the *Social Contract* provides the solution. . . .

. . . [F]or, in the first place, as each gives himself absolutely, the conditions are the same for all; and, this being so, no one has any interest in making them burdensome to others. Moreover, the alienation being without reserve,[5] the union is as perfect as it can be, and no associate has anything more to demand: for, if the individuals retained certain rights, as there would be no common superior to decide between them and the public, each, being on one point his own judge, would ask to be so on all; the state of nature would thus continue, and the association would necessarily become inoperative or tyrannical.

Finally, each man, in giving himself to all, gives himself to nobody; and as there is no associate over whom he does not acquire the same right as he yields others over himself, he gains an equivalent for everything he loses, and an increase of force for the preservation of what he has.

---

[4] A hypothetical or primitive existence before government; a frequent starting point in Enlightenment thinking about government. [Ed.]

[5] Each gives his freedom to the whole freely and completely. [Ed.]

If then we discard from the social compact what is not of its essence, we shall find that it reduces itself to the following terms:

"Each of us puts his person and all his power in common under the supreme direction of the general will, and, in our corporate capacity, we receive each member as an indivisible part of the whole."

3

The American Declaration of Independence, 1776

If anyone had taken a poll of Americans in the thirteen colonies as late as 1775, independence would not have won a majority vote anywhere. Massachusetts might have come close, perhaps, but nowhere in the land was there a definitive urge to separate from the British Empire. Still, three thousand miles was a long way for news, views, appointees, and petitions to travel, and tensions between the colonies and Britain had been growing.

Of course, each side looked at the cost of colonial administration differently. The British believed that they had carried a large part of the costs of migration, administration of trade, and control of the sea, while the colonists resented the humiliation resulting from their lack of political representation and the often inept royal officials and punitive legislation imposed on them from afar by the Parliament and the king.

By the spring of 1775, events were rapidly pushing the colonies toward independence. In April, British troops engaged colonial forces at Lexington and Concord, instigating a land war that was to last until 1781. In the midst of other urgent business, most notably raising an army, the Continental Congress asked a committee that included Thomas Jefferson, Benjamin Franklin, and John Adams to compose a statement outlining these and other reasons for separation from Britain. Jefferson wrote the first draft, the bulk of which became the final version accepted by the Continental Congress on July 4, 1776.

The Declaration of Independence was preeminently a document of the Enlightenment. Its principal author, Thomas Jefferson, exemplified the Enlightenment intellectual. Conversant in European literature, law, and political thought, he made significant contributions to

Source: *A Documentary History of the United States*, ed. Richard D. Heffner (New York: Penguin Books, 1991), 15–18.

eighteenth-century knowledge in natural science and architecture. Benjamin Franklin and other delegates to the Congress in Philadelphia were similarly accomplished.

It is no wonder, then, that the Declaration and the establishment of an independent United States of America should strike the world as the realization of the Enlightenment's basic tenets. That a wholly new country could be created by people with intelligence and foresight, according to principles of reason, and to realize human liberty, was heady stuff.

What were the goals of the authors of this document? In what ways was the Declaration a call for democracy? In what ways was it not?

THINKING HISTORICALLY

Before interpreting any document, we must read it carefully and put it into context—that is, determine the what, where, and why. Some of this information may be available in the text itself. For instance, to whom is the Declaration addressed? What is the reason given for writing it?

The urgency and immediate purpose of the Declaration of Independence separate it from the more theoretical *Social Contract* by Rousseau. But the age of Enlightenment enshrined similar concerns, and therefore similar ideas and language. What words or phrases are similar in both documents? How is their meaning similar or different?

Consider also the disparity between the lofty sentiments of liberty and independence and the existence of slavery in the Americas. How is Rousseau's treatment of slavery different from Jefferson's? How is it possible that Jefferson and some of the signers of the Declaration could own slaves while declaring it "self-evident that all men are created equal"? To whom did this statement apply?

In Congress, July 4, 1776, the Unanimous Declaration of the Thirteen United States of America

When in the course of human events, it becomes necessary for one people to dissolve the political bands which have connected them with another, and to assume among the powers of the earth, the separate and equal station to which the Laws of Nature and of Nature's God entitle them, a decent respect to the opinions of mankind requires that they should declare the causes which impel them to the separation.

We hold these truths to be self-evident, that all men are created equal, that they are endowed by their Creator with certain unalienable rights, that among these are life, liberty, and the pursuit of happiness. That to secure these rights, governments are instituted among men, deriving their just powers from the consent of the governed. That whenever any form of government becomes destructive of these ends, it is the right of the people to alter or to abolish it, and to institute new government, laying its foundation on such principles and organizing its powers in such form, as to them shall seem most likely to effect their safety and happiness. Prudence, indeed, will dictate that governments long established should not be changed for light and transient causes; and accordingly all experience hath shown, that mankind are more disposed to suffer, while evils are sufferable, than to right themselves by abolishing the forms to which they are accustomed. But when a long train of abuses and usurpations, pursuing invariably the same object evinces a design to reduce them under absolute despotism, it is their right, it is their duty, to throw off such government, and to provide new guards for their future security. Such has been the patient sufferance of these Colonies; and such is now the necessity which constrains them to alter their former systems of government. The history of the present King of Great Britain is a history of repeated injuries and usurpations, all having in direct object the establishment of an absolute tyranny over these States. To prove this, let facts be submitted to a candid world.

He has refused his assent to laws, the most wholesome and necessary for the public good.

He has forbidden his Governors to pass laws of immediate and pressing importance, unless suspended in their operation till his assent should be obtained; and when so suspended, he has utterly neglected to attend to them.

He has refused to pass other laws for the accommodation of large districts of people, unless those people would relinquish the right of representation in the Legislature, a right inestimable to them and formidable to tyrants only.

He has called together legislative bodies at places unusual, uncomfortable, and distant from the depository of their public records, for the sole purpose of fatiguing them into compliance with his measures.

He has dissolved representative houses repeatedly, for opposing with manly firmness his invasions on the rights of the people.

He has refused for a long time, after such dissolutions, to cause others to be elected; whereby the legislative powers, incapable of annihilation, have returned to the people at large for their exercise; the State remaining in the meantime exposed to all the dangers of invasion from without and convulsions within.

He has endeavoured to prevent the population of these states; for that purpose obstructing the laws of naturalization of foreigners; refusing to pass others to encourage their migration hither, and raising the conditions of new appropriations of lands.

He has obstructed the administration of justice, by refusing his assent to laws for establishing judiciary powers.

He has made judges dependent on his will alone, for the tenure of their offices, and the amount and payment of their salaries.

He has erected a multitude of new offices, and sent hither swarms of officers to harass our people, and eat out their substance.

He has kept among us, in times of peace, standing armies without the consent of our legislatures.

He has affected to render the military independent of and superior to the civil power.

He has combined with others to subject us to a jurisdiction foreign to our constitution, and unacknowledged by our laws; giving his assent to their acts of pretended legislation:

For quartering large bodies of armed troops among us:

For protecting them, by a mock trial, from punishment for any murders which they should commit on the inhabitants of these States:

For cutting off our trade with all parts of the world:

For imposing taxes on us without our consent:

For depriving us in many cases, of the benefits of trial by jury:

For transporting us beyond seas to be tried for pretended offences:

For abolishing the free system of English laws in a neighbouring Province, establishing therein an arbitrary government, and enlarging its boundaries so as to render it at once an example and fit instrument for introducing the same absolute rule into these Colonies:

For taking away our Charters, abolishing our most valuable laws, and altering fundamentally the forms of our governments:

For suspending our own Legislatures, and declaring themselves invested with power to legislate for us in all cases whatsoever.

He has abdicated government here, by declaring us out of his protection and waging war against us.

He has plundered our seas, ravaged our coasts, burnt our towns, and destroyed the lives of our people.

He is at this time transporting large armies of foreign mercenaries to complete the works of death, desolation, and tyranny, already begun with circumstances of cruelty and perfidy scarcely paralleled in the most barbarous ages, and totally unworthy the head of a civilized nation.

He has constrained our fellow citizens taken captive on the high seas to bear arms against their country, to become the executioners of their friends and brethren, or to fall themselves by their hands.

He has excited domestic insurrections amongst us, and has endeavoured to bring on the inhabitants of our frontiers, the merciless Indian savages, whose known rule of warfare, is an undistinguished destruction of all ages, sexes, and conditions.

In every state of these oppressions we have petitioned for redress in the most humble terms: our repeated petitions have been answered only by repeated injury. A prince whose character is thus marked by every act which may define a tyrant is unfit to be the ruler of a free people.

Nor have we been wanting in attention to our British brethren. We have warned them from time to time of attempts by their legislature to extend an unwarrantable jurisdiction over us. We have reminded them of the circumstances of our emigration and settlement here. We have appealed to their native justice and magnanimity, and we have conjured them by the ties of our common kindred to disavow these usurpations, which would inevitably interrupt our connections and correspondence. They too have been deaf to the voice of justice and of consanguinity. We must, therefore, acquiesce in the necessity, which denounces our separation, and hold them, as we hold the rest of mankind, enemies in war, in peace friends.

We, therefore, the Representatives of the United States of America, in General Congress assembled, appealing to the Supreme Judge of the world for the rectitude of our intentions, do, in the name, and by authority of the good people of these Colonies, solemnly publish and declare, That these United Colonies are, and of right ought to be Free and Independent States; that they are absolved from all allegiance to the British Crown, and that all political connection between them and the State of Great Britain, is and ought to be totally dissolved; and that as Free and Independent States, they have full power to levy war, conclude peace, contract alliances, establish commerce, and to do all other acts and things which Independent States may of right do. And for the support of this declaration, with a firm reliance on the protection of Divine Province, we mutually pledge to each other our lives, our fortunes, and our sacred honor.

4

ABIGAIL ADAMS AND JOHN ADAMS
Remember the Ladies, 1776

As a delegate to the Second Continental Congress, future American president John Adams was in Philadelphia in the spring of 1776, collaborating on writing the Declaration of Independence. In the meantime his wife, Abigail, assumed the role of the head of the household, caring for their children and managing the family farm in Braintree,

Source: Letters from Abigail Adams to John Adams, 31 March–5 April 1776, John Adams to Abigail Adams, 14 April 1776, Abigail Adams to John Adams, 7–9 May 1776 [electronic editions]. *Adams Family Papers: An Electronic Archive* (Boston: Massachusetts Historical Society, 2002), http://www.masshist.org/digitaladams/.

Massachusetts. Their relationship had always been characterized by robust intellectual debate, and John even referred to his wife as "Sister Delegate." In their famous correspondence during this period, Abigail urged her husband to "remember the ladies" as he and his fellow revolutionaries constructed the basis for the new American government. What did she mean by this? How did her husband respond? What did she think of his response?

THINKING HISTORICALLY

Enlightenment thinkers often employed grand abstractions like "all men are created equal" for both their rational simplicity and their dramatic revolutionary claim. As a consequence, such abstractions were often more sweeping in their implications than even the revolutionaries of the era intended. For example, John and Abigail Adams, both of whom opposed slavery, did not intend for "all men" to include blacks, either enslaved or free. But men like Adams might not have seriously considered how women would respond to the proclamation of universal equality. What in Adams's response to his wife reveals that he did not intend to extend universal equality to women? Does his response somehow undermine the Declaration of Independence?

Letter from Abigail Adams to John Adams, 31 March–5 April 1776

. . . I long to hear that you have declared an independency—and by the way in the new Code of Laws which I suppose it will be necessary for you to make I desire you would Remember the Ladies, and be more generous and favourable to them than your ancestors. Do not put such unlimited power into the hands of the Husbands. Remember all Men would be tyrants if they could. If perticuliar care and attention is not paid to the Ladies we are determined to foment a Rebellion, and will not hold ourselves bound by any Laws in which we have no voice, or Representation.

That your Sex is Naturally Tyrannical is a Truth so thoroughly established as to admit of no dispute, but such of you as wish to be happy willingly give up the harsh title of Master for the more tender and endearing one of Friend. Why then, not put it out of the power of the vicious and the Lawless to use us with cruelty and indignity [with impunity]. Men of Sense in all Ages abhor those customs which treat us only as the vassals of your Sex. Regard us then as Beings placed by providence under your protection and in imitation of the Supreme Being make use of the power only for our happiness.

Letter from John Adams to Abigail Adams, 14 April 1776

... As to Declarations of Independency, be patient. Read our Privateering Laws, and our Commercial Laws. What signifies a Word.

As to your extraordinary Code of Laws, I cannot but laugh. We have been told that our Struggle has loosened the bands of Government every where. That Children and Apprentices were disobedient—that schools and Colleges were grown turbulent—that Indians slighted their Guardians and Negroes grew insolent to their Masters.

But your Letter was the first Intimation that another Tribe more numerous and powerfull than all the rest were grown discontented.—This is rather too coarse a Compliment but you are so saucy, I wont blot it out.

Depend upon it, We know better than to repeal our Masculine systems. Altho they are in full Force, you know they are little more than Theory. We dare not exert our Power in its full Latitude. We are obliged to go fair, and softly, and in Practice you know We are the subjects. We have only the Name of Masters, and rather than give up this, which would compleatly subject Us to the Despotism of the Peticoat, I hope General Washington, and all our brave Heroes would fight. I am sure every good Politician would plot, as long as he would against Despotism, Empire, Monarchy, Aristocracy, Oligarchy, or Ochlocracy. ...

Letter from Abigail Adams to John Adams, 7–9 May 1776

... I can not say that I think you very generous to the Ladies, for whilst you are proclaiming peace and good will to Men, Emancipating all Nations, you insist upon retaining an absolute power over Wives. But you must remember that Arbitary power is like most other things which are very hard, very liable to be broken—and notwithstanding all your wise Laws and Maxims we have it in our power not only to free ourselves but to subdue our Masters, and without violence throw both your natural and legal authority at our feet. ...

5

The French Declaration of the Rights of Man and Citizen, 1789

The founding of the Republic of the United States of America provided a model for other peoples chafing under oppressive rule to emulate. Not surprisingly then, when the French movement to end political injustices turned to revolution in 1789 and the revolutionaries convened at the National Assembly, the Marquis de Lafayette (1757–1834), hero of the American Revolution, proposed a Declaration of the Rights of Man and Citizen. Lafayette had the American Declaration in mind, and he had the assistance of Thomas Jefferson, present in Paris as the first United States ambassador to France.

While the resulting document appealed to the French revolutionaries, the French were not able to start afresh as the Americans had done. In 1789 Louis XVI was still king of France: He could not be made to leave by a turn of phrase. Nor were men created equal in France in 1789. Those born into the nobility led lives different from those born into the Third Estate (the 99 percent of the population who were not nobility or clergy), and they had different legal rights as well. This disparity was precisely what the revolutionaries and the Declaration sought to change. Inevitably, though, such change would prove to be a more violent and revolutionary proposition than it had been in the American colonies.

In what ways did the Declaration of the Rights of Man and Citizen resemble the American Declaration of Independence? In what ways was it different? Which was more democratic?

THINKING HISTORICALLY

Compare the language of the Declaration of the Rights of Man and Citizen with that of Rousseau and that of Jefferson. In what ways does it borrow from each? Like both prior documents, the French Declaration is full of abstract, universal principles. But notice how such abstractions can claim our consent by their rationality without informing us as to how they will be implemented. What is meant by the first right, for instance? What does it mean to say that men are "born free"? Why is it necessary to distinguish between "born" and "remain"? What is meant by the phrase "general usefulness"? Do statements like these increase people's liberties, or are they intentionally vague so they can be interpreted at will?

The slogan of the French Revolution was "Liberty, Equality, Fraternity." Which of the rights in the French Declaration emphasize liberty, which equality? Can these two goals be opposed to each other? Explain how.

Source: *A Documentary History of the French Revolution*, ed. John Hall Stewart (London: Macmillan, 1979), 113–15.

The representatives of the French people, organized in National Assembly, considering that ignorance, forgetfulness, or contempt of the rights of man are the sole causes of public misfortunes and of the corruption of governments, have resolved to set forth in a solemn declaration the natural, inalienable, and sacred rights of man, in order that such declaration, continually before all members of the social body, may be a perpetual reminder of their rights and duties; in order that the acts of the legislative power and those of the executive power may constantly be compared with the aim of every political institution and may accordingly be more respected; in order that the demands of the citizens, founded henceforth upon simple and incontestable principles, may always be directed towards the maintenance of the Constitution and the welfare of all.

Accordingly, the National Assembly recognizes and proclaims, in the presence and under the auspices of the Supreme Being, the following rights of man and citizen.

1. Men are born and remain free and equal in rights; social distinctions may be based only upon general usefulness.

2. The aim of every political association is the preservation of the natural and inalienable rights of man; these rights are liberty, property, security, and resistance to oppression.

3. The source of all sovereignty resides essentially in the nation; no group, no individual may exercise authority not emanating expressly therefrom.

4. Liberty consists of the power to do whatever is not injurious to others; thus the enjoyment of the natural rights of every man has for its limits only those that assure other members of society the enjoyment of those same rights; such limits may be determined only by law.

5. The law has the right to forbid only actions which are injurious to society. Whatever is not forbidden by law may not be prevented, and no one may be constrained to do what it does not prescribe.

6. Law is the expression of the general will; all citizens have the right to concur personally, or through their representatives, in its formation; it must be the same for all, whether it protects or punishes. All citizens, being equal before it, are equally admissible to all public offices, positions, and employments, according to their capacity, and without other distinction than that of virtues and talents.

7. No man may be accused, arrested, or detained except in the cases determined by law, and according to the forms prescribed thereby. Whoever solicit, expedite, or execute arbitrary orders, or have them executed, must be punished; but every citizen summoned or apprehended in pursuance of the law must obey immediately; he renders himself culpable by resistance.

8. The law is to establish only penalties that are absolutely and obviously necessary; and no one may be punished except by virtue of a law established and promulgated prior to the offence and legally applied.

9. Since every man is presumed innocent until declared guilty, if arrest be deemed indispensable, all unnecessary severity for securing the person of the accused must be severely repressed by law.

10. No one is to be disquieted because of his opinions, even religious, provided their manifestation does not disturb the public order established by law.

11. Free communication of ideas and opinions is one of the most precious of the rights of man. Consequently, every citizen may speak, write, and print freely, subject to responsibility for the abuse of such liberty in the cases determined by law.

12. The guarantee of the rights of man and citizen necessitates a public force; therefore, is instituted for the advantage of all and not for the particular benefit of those to whom it is entrusted.

13. For the maintenance of the public force and for the expenses of administration a common tax is indispensable; it must be assessed equally on all citizens in proportion to their means.

14. Citizens have the right to ascertain, by themselves or through their representatives, the necessity of the public tax, to consent to it freely, to supervise its use, and to determine its quota, assessment, payment, and duration.

15. Society has the right to require of every public agent an accounting of his administration.

16. Every society in which the guarantee of rights is not assured or the separation of powers not determined has no constitution at all.

17. Since property is a sacred and inviolate right, no one may be deprived thereof unless a legally established public necessity obviously requires it, and upon condition of a just and previous indemnity.

6

OLYMPE DE GOUGES

French Declaration of Rights for Women, 1791

Olympe de Gouges (1748–1793) was a French playwright whose writings became increasingly political as the French Revolution progressed after 1789. When the revolutionary government of the National Assembly passed a new constitution in 1791 with the Declaration of the Rights of Man and Citizen of 1789 as the preamble, and still did not give women the vote, de Gouges wrote the following document.

Source: http://fr.wikisource.org/wiki/D%C3%A9claration_des_droits_de_la_femme_et_de_la_citoyenne. Translated from the French by the editor.

What was Olympe de Gouges's argument? What specific rights for women was she seeking?

THINKING HISTORICALLY

Compare this document with the Declaration of the Rights of Man and Citizen. What are the similarities and differences? What is the purpose of the similarities? What is the significance of the differences?

Mankind, are you capable of being just? It is a woman who asks the question; you will not deprive her of that right at least. Tell me? Who has given you the soverign empire to oppress my sex? Your strength? Your talents? Observe the creator in his wisdom; survey nature in all its grandeur, with which you seem to want to be in harmony, and give me, if you dare, an example of this tryanical empire.

Go back to animals. Consult the elements, study plants, finally glance at all the modifications of organic matter; and surrender to the evidence as I offer you the means; search, probe, and distinguish, if you can, the sexes in the administration of nature. Everywhere you will find them mingled, everywhere they cooperate in the harmonious unity of this immortal masterpiece.

Man alone has raised his exception to a principle. Bizarre, blind, bloated with science and degenerated, in a century of enlightenment and wisdom, in the crassest ignorance, he wants to command as a despot a sex which has received all intellectual faculties; he pretends to be revolutionary, and claims his rights to equality, in order to say nothing more about it.

Preamble

Mothers, daughters, sisters, representatives of the nation, demand to be constituted a national assembly. Considering that ignorance, forgetfulness or contempt of the rights of women are the only causes of public misfortunes and government corruption, they resolve to expose in a solemn declaration, the natural, inalienable, and sacred rights of women, so that this declaration, being constantly before the public, reminds them constantly of their rights and their duties, so that the authoritative acts of men and women are always comparable to the goals of every political institution, and deserving of respect, so that citizens' demands, from now on based on simple and incontestable principles, will always support the constitution, good morals, and the happiness of all.

Consequently, the sex that is as superior in beauty as in the courage of maternity recognizes and declares, in the presence and under the auspices of the Supreme Being, the following Rights of Woman as Citizen.

I. Woman is born free and remains equal to man in rights. Social distinctions may be founded only on general usefulness.

II. The aim of every political association is the preservation of the natural and inalienable rights of Women and Men: these are the rights to liberty, property, security, and especially the resistance to oppression.

III. The source of all sovereignty resides essentially in the Nation, which is the meeting of women and men: no body, no individual, may exercise authority not emanating expressly therefrom.

IV. Liberty and Justice consist of restoring the rights of others; since the exercise of the rights of women has no limits other than those imposed by perpetual male tyranny, these limits must be made to conform to natural law and reason.

V. Laws of nature and reason forbid all acts harmful to society; everything which is not prohibited by these wise and divine laws cannot be prevented, and no one can be constrained to do what they do not prescribe.

VI. Law is be the expression of the general will; all citizens, male and female, have the right to concur personally or through their representatives in its formation; it must be the same for all; all citizens being equal before it, are equally admissable to all public offices, positions, and employments, according to their capacity and without other distinction than that of virtues and talents. . . .

X. No one is to be disquieted because of his opinions; woman has the right to mount the scaffold; she must equally have the right to mount the rostrum, provided that her demonstrations do not disturb the legally established public order.

XI. The free communication of thoughts and opinions is one of the most precious rights of woman, since that liberty assures recognition of children by their fathers. Any female citizen thus may say freely, I am the mother of a child which belongs to you, without being forced by a barbarous prejudice to hide the truth; subject to responsibility for the abuse of this liberty in cases determined by law. . . .

XIII. For the maintenance of the public force and the expenses of administration, the contributions of woman and man are equal; she shares all the duties and all the painful tasks; therefore, she must have the same share in the distribution of positions, employment, offices, honors, and jobs. . . .

XVI. Every society in which the guarantee of rights is not assured or the separation of powers not determined has no constitution at all; the constitution is void if the majority of individuals comprising the nation have not cooperated in drafting it.

XVII. Property belongs to both sexes whether united or separate; for each it is an inviolable and sacred right; no one may be deprived thereof unless a legally established public necessity obviously requires it, and upon condition of a just and previous indemnity.

7

TOUSSAINT L'OUVERTURE
Letter to the Directory, 1797

When the French revolutionaries proclaimed the Declaration of the Rights of Man and Citizen in 1789, the French colony of Saint-Domingue[1] (now Haiti) contained a half million African slaves, most of whom worked on the sugar plantations that made France one of the richest countries in the world. Thus, the French were confronted with the difficult problem of reconciling their enlightened principles with the extremely profitable, but fundamentally unequal, institution of slavery.

French revolutionaries remained locked in debate about this issue when in 1791, the slaves of Saint-Domingue organized a revolt that culminated in establishing Haiti's national independence twelve years later. François Dominique Toussaint L'Ouverture,* a self-educated Haitian slave, led the revolt and the subsequent battles against the French planter class and French armies, as well as the Spanish forces of neighboring Santo Domingo — the eastern side of the island now known as the Dominican Republic — and the antirevolutionary forces of Britain, all of whom vied for control of the island at the end of the eighteenth century.

---

* too SAN   loo vehr TUR
[1] san doh MANG   *Santo Domingo* was the Spanish name for the eastern half of Hispaniola (now the Dominican Republic). *Saint-Domingue* was the French name for the western half of the island, now Haiti. *San Domingo*, which is used in the text, is a nineteenth-century abbreviation for *Saint-Domingue*. To further complicate matters, both the Spanish and French sometimes used their term for the whole island of Hispaniola. Spain controlled the entire island until 1697, when the Spanish recognized French control of the west.

Source: Toussaint L'Ouverture, "Letter to the Directory, November 5, 1797," in *The Black Jacobins*, ed. C. L. R. James (New York: Vintage Books, 1989), 195–97.

At first Toussaint enjoyed the support of the revolutionary govern-ment in Paris; in the Decree of 16 Pluviôse[2] (1794) the National Convention abolished slavery in the colonies. But after 1795 the revo-lution turned on itself, and Toussaint feared that the new conserva-tive government, called the Directory, might send troops to restore slavery on the island.

In 1797 he wrote the Directory the letter that follows. Notice how Toussaint negotiated a difficult situation. How did he try to reassure the government of his allegiance to France? At the same time, how did he attempt to convince the Directory that a return to slavery was unthinkable?

THINKING HISTORICALLY

Notice how Toussaint defines different groups of people. What does he mean, for instance, by "the proprietors of San Domingo" as opposed to "the people of San Domingo"? What does he mean by "the colonists" and "our common enemies"? How does the use of these terms aid his cause?

... The impolitic and incendiary discourse of Vaublanc[3] has not affected the blacks nearly so much as their certainty of the projects which the proprietors of San Domingo are planning: insidious declarations should not have any effect in the eyes of wise legislators who have decreed lib-erty for the nations. But the attempts on that liberty which the colonists propose are all the more to be feared because it is with the veil of patri-otism that they cover their detestable plans. We know that they seek to impose some of them on you by illusory and specious promises, in order to see renewed in this colony its former scenes of horror. Already perfidi-ous emissaries have stepped in among us to ferment the destructive leaven prepared by the hands of liberticides. But they will not succeed. I swear it by all that liberty holds most sacred. My attachment to France, my knowledge of the blacks, make it my duty not to leave you ignorant either of the crimes which they meditate or the oath that we renew, to bury ourselves under the ruins of a country revived by liberty rather than suffer the return of slavery.

It is for you, Citizens Directors, to turn from over our heads the storm which the eternal enemies of our liberty are preparing in the shades

---

[2] PLOO vee ohs   Rainy; the name of the second winter month according to the revolu-tionary calendar.

[3] Vincent-Marie Viénot, Count of Vaublanc (1756–1845). Born into an aristocratic family in San Domingo, he was a French royalist politician. In Paris in September 1797, he gave a speech intended to impeach republican Directors and trigger a royalist coup. [Ed.]

of silence. It is for you to enlighten the legislature, it is for you to prevent the enemies of the present system from spreading themselves on our unfortunate shores to sully it with new crimes. Do not allow our brothers, our friends, to be sacrificed to men who wish to reign over the ruins of the human species. But no, your wisdom will enable you to avoid the dangerous snares which our common enemies hold out for you. . . .

I send you with this letter a declaration which will acquaint you with the unity that exists between the proprietors of San Domingo who are in France, those in the United States, and those who serve under the English banner. You will see there a resolution, unequivocal and carefully constructed, for the restoration of slavery; you will see there that their determination to succeed has led them to envelop themselves in the mantle of liberty in order to strike it more deadly blows. You will see that they are counting heavily on my complacency in lending myself to their perfidious views by my fear for my children. It is not astonishing that these men who sacrifice their country to their interests are unable to conceive how many sacrifices a true love of country can support in a better father than they, since I unhesitatingly base the happiness of my children on that of my country, which they and they alone wish to destroy.

I shall never hesitate between the safety of San Domingo and my personal happiness; but I have nothing to fear. It is to the solicitude of the French Government that I have confided my children. . . . I would tremble with horror if it was into the hands of the colonists that I had sent them as hostages; but even if it were so, let them know that in punishing them for the fidelity of their father, they would only add one degree more to their barbarism, without any hope of ever making me fail in my duty. . . . Blind as they are! They cannot see how this odious conduct on their part can become the signal of new disasters and irreparable misfortunes, and that far from making them regain what in their eyes liberty for all has made them lose, they expose themselves to a total ruin and the colony to its inevitable destruction. Do they think that men who have been able to enjoy the blessing of liberty will calmly see it snatched away? They supported their chains only so long as they did not know any condition of life more happy than that of slavery. But to-day when they have left it, if they had a thousand lives they would sacrifice them all rather than be forced into slavery again. But no, the same hand which has broken our chains will not enslave us anew. France will not revoke her principles, she will not withdraw from us the greatest of her benefits. She will protect us against all our enemies; she will not permit her sublime morality to be perverted, those principles which do her most honour to be destroyed, her most beautiful achievement to be degraded, and her Decree of 16 Pluviôse which so honours humanity to be revoked. *But if, to re-establish slavery in San Domingo, this was done, then I declare to you it would be to attempt the impossible: we have known how to face dangers to obtain our liberty, we shall know how to brave death to maintain it.*

This, Citizens Directors, is the morale of the people of San Domingo, those are the principles that they transmit to you by me.

My own you know. It is sufficient to renew, my hand in yours, the oath that I have made, to cease to live before gratitude dies in my heart, before I cease to be faithful to France and to my duty, before the god of liberty is profaned and sullied by the liberticides, before they can snatch from my hands that sword, those arms, which France confided to me for the defence of its rights and those of humanity, for the triumph of liberty and equality.

8

DIPESH CHAKRABARTY

Compassion and the Enlightenment, 2000

In this essay, a modern historian argues that the Enlightenment was not confined to Europe and was more profound than is often thought. Here Chakrabarty demonstrates an Indian Enlightenment in the northeastern region of Bengal. He further reveals the profound way in which the Enlightenment changed not only peoples' ideas but also their feelings, signaling the beginning of the modern self. What does he mean by "the modern self"? What, according to the author, is the role of reason and compassion in creating the modern self? How did the Enlightenment change human feelings?

Compare the ideas noted in this essay of the Bengali Indian authors, Rammohun Roy and Iswarchandra Vidyasagar, with the ideas of European Enlightenment thinkers that you have read in this chapter. How is Roy's compassion for women similar to, or different from, that of Abigail Adams and Olympe de Gouges? How is it like the compassion of Toussaint?

THINKING HISTORICALLY

Chakrabarty underscores the use of some key Enlightenment concepts by these Bengali authors. What does he mean by "compassion in general"? What are the connections, according to Chakrabarty, among such concepts as suffering, compassion, reason, natural sentiments, universality, and custom?

Source: Dipesh Chakrabarty, *Provincializing Europe: Postcolonial Thought and Historical Difference*, Princeton Studies in Culture/Power/History (Princeton: Princeton University Press, 2000), 119–24.

The capacity to notice and document suffering (even if it be one's own suffering) from the position of a generalized and necessarily disembodied observer is what marks the beginnings of the modern self. This self has to be generalizable in principle; in other words, it should be such that it signifies a position available for occupation by anybody with proper training. If it were said, for instance, that only a particular type of person—such as a Budhha or a Christ—was capable of noticing suffering and of being moved by it, one would not be talking of a generalized subject position. To be a Budhha or Christ is not within the reach of everybody through simple education and training. So the capacity for sympathy must be seen as a potential inherent in the nature of man in general and not in the uniqueness of a particular person. Such a "natural theory of sentiments," as we shall see, was indeed argued by Enlightenment philosophers such as David Hume and Adam Smith.

A critical distinction also has to be made between the act of displaying suffering and that of observing or facing the sufferer. To display suffering in order to elicit sympathy and assistance is a very old—and perhaps universal and still current—practice. The deformed beggars of medieval Europe or of contemporary Indian or U.S. cities are subjects of suffering, but they are not disembodied subjects. The sufferer here is an embodied self, which is always a particular self, grounded in this or that body. Nor would the sympathy felt for only a particular sufferer (such as a kin or a friend) be "modern" in my sense. The person who is not an immediate sufferer but who has the capacity to become a secondary sufferer through sympathy for a generalized picture of suffering, and who documents this suffering in the interest of eventual social intervention—such a person occupies the position of the modern subject. In other words, the moment of the modern observation of suffering is a certain moment of self-recognition on the part of an abstract, general human being. It is as though a person who is able to see in himself or herself the general human also recognizes the same figure in the particular sufferer, so that the moment of recognition is a moment when the general human splits into the two mutually recognizing and mutually constitutive figures of the sufferer and the observer of suffering. It was argued, however, in the early part of the nineteenth century that this could not happen without the aid of reason, for habit and custom— unopposed by reason—could blunt the natural human capacity for sympathy. Reason, that is, education in rational argumentation, was seen as a critical factor in helping to realize in the modern person this capacity for seeing the general.

Something like such a natural theory of sentiments was argued, in effect, by the two most important nineteenth-century Bengali social reformers who exerted themselves on questions concerning the plight of widows: Rammohun Roy (1772/4–1833) and Iswarchandra Vidyasagar (1820–1901). Roy was instrumental in the passing of the act that made *sati* illegal in 1829, and Vidyasagar successfully agitated for widows to have the legal right to remarry, a right enshrined in the Act for the Remarriage of Hindu Widows, 1856. These legal interventions also allow us to make a further distinction between suffering as viewed by religions such as Buddhism and suffering as a subject of modern social thought. In religious thought, suffering is existential. It shadows man in his life. In social thought, however, suffering is not an existential category. It is specific and hence open to secular interventions.

Rammohun Roy's well-known tract entitled *Brief Remarks Regarding Modern Encroachments on the Ancient Right of Females*, was one of the first written arguments in modern India in favor of women's right to property. This document on property rights also discusses the place of sentiments such as cruelty, distress, wounding feelings, misery, and so on, in human relations. Both strands—rights and sentiments—were intertwined in Roy's argument connecting the question of property with the issue of sentiments, and both saw suffering as an historical and eradicable problem in society:

> In short a widow, according to the [current] exposition of the law, can receive nothing . . . [unless her husband dies] leaving two or more sons, and all of them survive and be inclined to allot a share to their mother. . . . The consequence is, that a woman who is looked upon as the sole mistress of a family one day, on the next becomes dependent on her sons, and subject to the slights of her daughters-in-law. . . . Cruel sons often wound the feelings of their dependent mothers. . . . Step-mothers, who are often numerous on account of polygamy, are still more shamefully neglected in general by their step-sons, and sometimes dreadfully treated by their sisters-in-law. . . . [The] restraints on female inheritance encourage, in a great degree, polygamy, a frequent source of the greatest misery in native families.[1]

There are two interesting features of this document that make it the work of a modern observer of suffering. First, in observing this cruelty to widows and women, Roy put himself in the transcendental position of the modern subject. This becomes clear if we look closely at the following sentence of his text: "How distressing it must be to the female community and to those who interest themselves in their behalf, to

---

[1] Rammohun Roy, "Brief Remarks Regarding Modern Encroachments on the Ancient Rights of Females," in Ajitkumar Ghosh, ed., *Rammohan rachanabali* (Calcutta: Haraf Prakashani, 1973), pp. 496–497.

observe daily that several daughters in a rich family can prefer no claim to any portion of the property . . . left by their deceased father . . . ; while they . . . are exposed to be given in marriage to individuals who already have several wives and have no means of maintaining them."[2] Roy presents himself here both as a subject experiencing affect—"distress"—as well as a representative subject, one who "interests [himself] in their [women's] behalf." The capacity for sympathy is what unites the representative person with those who are represented; they share the same "distress." The second clause in the sentence refers to a new type of representation: people who took an interest in women's condition on behalf of women. But who were these women? They were not particular, specific women marked by their belonging to particular families or particular networks of kinship. Women here are a collective subject; the expression "female community" connotes a general community. It is this "general community" that shares the distress of a Rammohun Roy, the observer who observes on behalf of this collective community. And therefore the feeling of "distress" that Rammohun Roy speaks of refers to a new kind of compassion, something one could feel for suffering beyond one's immediate family. Compassion in general, we could call it.

But from where would such compassion or sympathy spring? What made it possible for a Rammohun or Vidyasagar to feel this "compassion in general" that most members of their community (presumably) did not yet feel? How would society train itself to make this compassion a part of the comportment of every person, so that compassion became a generally present sentiment in society? It is on this point that both Rammohun and Vidyasagar gave an answer remarkable for its affiliation to the European Enlightenment. Reason, they argued in effect, was what could release the flow of the compassion that was naturally present in all human beings, for only reason could dispel the blindness induced by custom and habit. Reasonable human beings would see suffering and that would put to work the natural human capacity for sympathy, compassion, and pity.

Rammohun raised the question of compassion in a pointed manner in his 1819 answer to Kashinath Tarkabagish's polemical tract *Bidhayak nishedhak shombad* directed against his own position on *sati*. "What is a matter of regret," he said, "is that the fact of witnessing with your own eyes women who have thus suffered much sadness and domination, does not arouse even a small amount of compassion in you so that the forcible burning [of widows] may be stopped."[3] Why was this so? Why did the act of seeing not result in sympathy? Rammohun's answer is clearly given in his 1818 tract

---

[2] Ibid., pp. 496–497, 500–501.
[3] "Prabartak o nibartaker dvitiyo shombad," in *Rammohun rachanabali*, p. 203.

called *Views on Burning Widows Alive*, which targeted the advocates of the practice. Here Rammohun refers to the forcible way in which widows were "fastened" to the funeral pyre in the course of the performance of *sati*, and directly raises the question of mercy or compassion (*daya*): "you are unmercifully resolved to commit the sin of female murder." His opponent, the "advocate" of *sati*, replies: "You have repeatedly asserted that from want of feeling we promote female destruction. This is incorrect. For it is declared in our Veda and codes of law, that mercy is the root of virtue, and from our practice of hospitality, &c., our compassionate dispositions are well known."[4]

Rammohun's response to this introduces an argument for which he presents no scriptural authority and which went largely unanswered in the debates of the time. This is the argument about "habits of insensibility." Much like the Enlightenment thinkers of Europe, and perhaps influenced by them, Rammohun argued that it was because the practice of *sati* had become a custom—a matter of blind repetition—that people were prevented from experiencing sympathy even when they watched somebody being forced to become a *sati*. The natural connection between their vision and feelings of pity was blocked by habit. If this habit could be corrected or removed, the sheer act of seeing a woman being forced to die would evoke compassion. Roy said:

> That in other cases you show charitable dispositions is acknowledged. But by witnessing from your youth the voluntary burning of women amongst your elder relatives, your neighbours and the inhabitants of the surrounding villages, and by observing the indifference at the time when the women are writhing under the torture of the flames, habits of insensibility are produced. For the same reason, when men or women are suffering the pains of death, you feel for them no sense of compassion, like worshippers of female deities who, witnessing from their infancy the slaughter of kids and buffaloes, feel no compassion for them in the time of their suffering death.[5]

We encounter the same argument about the relationship between sight and compassion in the writings of Iswarchandra Vidyasagar, the

---

[4] *Rammohan rachanabali*, p. 575. This is Rammohun's own translation of his 1818 text "sahamaran bishaye prabartak o nibartaker shombad," ibid., p. 175.

[5] Ibid. Distinguishing between "custom" and "reason," Hume equated the former with "habit." David Hume, *Enquiries Concerning Human Understanding and Concerning the Principles of Morals* (1777), introduction by L. A. Sigby-Bigge (Oxford: Clarendon Press, 1990), p. 43. In his *Treatise,* he argues that it is "custom or repetition" that can convert "pain into pleasure." See idem, *A Treatise of Human Nature* (1739–1740), edited by L. A. Selby-Bigge, revised by P. H. Nidditch (Oxford: Clarendon, 1978), p. 422.

Bengali reformer responsible for the act that in 1856 permitted Hindu widows to remarry. Vidyasagar's fundamental reasoning as to the solution of widows' problems had some critical differences from the position of Rammohun Roy but like the latter, he too argued that it was custom and habit that stymied the otherwise natural relationship between the sight and compassion:[6]

> People of India! . . . Habit has so darkened and overwhelmed your intellect and good sense that it is hard for the juice of compassion to flow in the ever-dry hearts of yours even when you see the plight of hapless widows. . . . Let no woman be born in a country where men have no compassion, no feelings of duty and justice, no sense of good and bad, no consideration, where only the preservation of custom is the main and supreme religion—let the ill-fated women not take birth in such a country.
>
> Women! I cannot tell what sins [of past lives] cause you to be born in India![7]

Both Rammohun and Vidyasagar thus espoused a natural theory of compassion, the idea that compassion was a sentiment universally present in something called "human nature," however blocked its expression might be in a particular situation. This recalls Adam Smith, explaining his theory of sympathy: "How selfish soever man may be supposed, there are some principles in his nature which interest him in the fortune of others. . . . Of this kind is pity or compassion, the emotion we feel for the misery of others."[8] Hume also defined "pity" as a general sentiment, as "a concern for . . . the misery of others, without any friendship . . . to occasion this concern," and connected it to the general human capacity for sympathy. He wrote: "No quality of human nature is more remarkable . . . than that propensity we have to sympathize with others."[9] It is only on the basis of this kind of an understanding that Roy and Vidyasagar assigned to reason a critical role in fighting the effects of custom. Reason did not produce the sentiment of compassion; it simply helped in letting sentiments take their natural course by removing the obstacle of mindless custom. Needless to say, the underlying vision of the human being was truly a universal one.

---

[6] Vidyasagar's intellectual positions are discussed with insight and critical sympathy in Asok Sen, *Iswarchandra Vidyasagar and His Elusive Milestones* (Calcutta: Ridhhi, 1975).

[7] I have followed and modified the translation provided in Isvarchandra Vidyasagar, *Marriage of Hindu Widows*, edited by Arabindo Poddar (Calcutta, 1976), pp. 107–108.

[8] Adam Smith, *The Theory of Moral Sentiments*, edited by D. D. Raphael and A. L. Macfie (Indianapolis: Liberty Fund, 1984), p. 9. See also p. 22. Raphael and Macfie explain (p. 14n) that Smith's theories were in part a refutation of Hobbes's and Mandeville's contention that all sentiments arose from self-love.

[9] Hume, *Treatise*, pp. 316, 369.

■ REFLECTIONS

The Enlightenment and its political legacies — secular order and revolutionary republicanism — were European in origin but global in impact. In this chapter, we have touched on just a few of the crosscurrents of what some historians call an "Atlantic Revolution." A tide of revolutionary fervor swept through France, the United States, and Latin America, found sympathy in Russia in 1825, and echoed in the Muslim heartland, resulting in secular, modernizing regimes in Turkey and Egypt in the next century. Chakrabarty helps us ask if there may have been independent roots of reasoned compassion in India as well.

The political appeal of the Enlightenment, of rationally ordered society, and of democratic government continues. Some elements of this eighteenth-century revolution — the rule of law; regular, popular elections of representatives; the separation of church and state, of government and politics, and of civil and military authority — are widely recognized ideals and emerging global realities. Like science, the principles of the Enlightenment are universal in their claims and often seem universal in their appeal. Nothing is simpler, more rational, or easier to follow than a call to reason, law, liberty, justice, or equality. And yet every society has evolved its own guidelines under different circumstances, often with lasting results. France had its king and still has a relatively centralized state. The United States began with slavery and still suffers from racism. South American states became free of Europe only to dominate Native Americans, and they continue to do so. None of the enlightened or revolutionary societies of the eighteenth century extended the "rights of man" to women. One democratic society had a king, another a House of Lords, another a national church. Are these different adaptations of the Enlightenment ideal? Or are these examples of incomplete revolution, cases of special interests allowing their governments to fall short of principle?

The debate continues today as more societies seek to realize responsive, representative government and the rule of law while oftentimes respecting conflicting traditions. Muslim countries and Israel struggle with the competing demands of secular law and religion, citizenship and communalism. Former communist countries adopt market economies and struggle with traditions of collective support and the appeal of individual liberty.

Perhaps these are conflicts within the Enlightenment tradition itself. How is it possible to have both liberty and equality? How can we claim inalienable rights on the basis of a secular, scientific creed? How does a faith in human reason lead to revolution? And how can ideas of order or justice avoid the consequences of history and human nature?

The great revolutionary declarations of the Enlightenment embarrass the modern skeptic with their naïve faith in natural laws, their universal prescriptions to cure all ills, and their hypocritical avoidance of slaves, women, and the colonized. The selections by Toussaint L'Ouverture and Abigail Adams, however, remind us that Enlightenment universalism was based not only on cool reason and calculation and the blind arrogance of the powerful. At least some of the great Enlightenment thinkers based their global prescription on the *felt* needs, even the sufferings, of others. For Toussaint, Adams, Olympe de Gouges, and Rammohun Roy, the recognition of human commonality began with a reasoned capacity for empathy that the Enlightenment may have bequeathed to the modern world, even shaping modern sensibility.

21

Capitalism and the Industrial Revolution

Europe and the World, 1750–1900

■ HISTORICAL CONTEXT

Two principal forces have shaped the modern world: capitalism and the industrial revolution. As influential as the transformations discussed in Chapters 19 and 20 (the rise of science and the democratic revolution), these two forces are sometimes considered to be one and the same, because the industrial revolution occurred first in capitalist countries such as England, Belgium, and the United States. In fact, the rise of capitalism preceded the industrial revolution by centuries.

Capitalism denotes a particular economic organization of a society, whereas *industrial revolution* refers to a particular transformation of technology. Specifically, in capitalism market forces (supply and demand) set money prices that determine how goods are distributed. Before 1500, most economic behavior was regulated by family, religion, tradition, and political authority rather than by markets. Increasingly after 1500 in Europe, feudal dues were converted into money rents, periodic fairs became institutionalized, banks were established, modern bookkeeping procedures were developed, and older systems of inherited economic status were loosened. After 1800, new populations of urban workers had to work for money to buy food and shelter; after 1850 in urban areas even clothing was usually purchased in the new "department stores." By 1900, the market had become the operating metaphor of society: One sold oneself; everything had its price. Viewed positively, a capitalist society is one in which buyers and sellers, who together compose the market, make most decisions about the production and distribution of resources. Viewed less favorably, it is the capitalists— those who own the "capital" (resources, stores, factories, and money)—who make the decisions about production and distribution.

The industrial revolution made mass production possible with the use of power-driven machines. Mills driven by waterwheels existed in ancient times, but the construction of identical, replaceable machinery—the machine production of machines—revolutionized industry and enabled the coordination of production on a vast scale, occurring first in England's cotton textile mills at the end of the eighteenth century. The market for such textiles was capitalist, though the demand for many early mass-produced goods, such as muskets and uniforms, was government-driven.

The origins of capitalism are hotly debated among historians. Because the world's first cities, five thousand years ago, created markets, merchants, money, and private ownership of capital, some historians refer to an ancient capitalism. In this text, *capitalism* refers to those societies whose markets, merchants, money, and private ownership became central to the way society operated. As such, ancient Mesopotamia, Rome, and Sung dynasty China, which had extensive markets and paper money a thousand years ago, were not among the first capitalist societies. Smaller societies in which commercial interests and merchant classes took hold to direct political and economic matters were the capitalist forerunners. Venice, Florence, Holland, and England, the mercantile states of the fifteenth to seventeenth centuries, exemplify *commercial capitalism* or mercantile capitalism. Thus, the shift to industrial capitalism was more than a change in scale; it was also a transition from a trade-based economy to a manufacturing-based economy, a difference that meant an enormous increase in productivity, profits, and prosperity.

■ THINKING HISTORICALLY

Distinguishing Historical Processes

When two distinct historical processes occur simultaneously and in mutually reinforcing ways, like the spread of agriculture and languages—or capitalism and industrialization—we might confuse one process of change with the other. This confusion makes it difficult to see exactly what causes what. Here you will be encouraged to distinguish between the latter two historical processes. As you read these selections, keep in mind that capitalism is an economic system that spreads markets, commerce, and the interests of private capital; the industrial revolution was a transformation in technology. How did these two very different processes coincide in the nineteenth century? In what ways were they moving toward different ends, causing different effects, or benefiting different interests?

1

ARNOLD PACEY

Asia and the Industrial Revolution, 1990

Here a modern historian of technology demonstrates how Indian and East Asian manufacturing techniques were assimilated by Europeans, particularly by the English successors of the Mughal Empire, providing a boost to the industrial revolution in Britain. In what ways was Indian technology considered superior prior to the industrial revolution? How did European products gain greater markets than those of India?

THINKING HISTORICALLY

Notice how the author distinguishes between capitalism and the industrial revolution. Was India more industrially advanced than capitalistic? Did the British conquest of India benefit more from capitalism, industry, or something else?

Deindustrialization

During the eighteenth century, India participated in the European industrial revolution through the influence of its textile trade, and through the investments in shipping made by Indian bankers and merchants. Developments in textiles and shipbuilding constituted a significant industrial movement, but it would be wrong to suggest that India was on the verge of its own industrial revolution. There was no steam engine in India, no coal mines, and few machines. . . . [E]xpanding industries were mostly in coastal areas. Much of the interior was in economic decline, with irrigation works damaged and neglected as a result of the breakup of the Mughal Empire and the disruption of war. Though political weakness in the empire had been evident since 1707, and a Persian army heavily defeated Mughal forces at Delhi in 1739, it was the British who most fully took advantage of the collapse of the empire. Between 1757 and 1803, they took control of most of India except the Northwest. The result was that the East India Company now administered major sectors of the economy, and quickly reduced the role of the big Indian bankers by changes in taxes and methods of collecting them.

Meanwhile, India's markets in Europe were being eroded by competition from machine-spun yarns and printed calicoes made in Lancashire, and high customs duties were directed against Indian imports into

Source: Arnold Pacey, *Technology in World Civilization* (Cambridge: MIT Press, 1990), 128–35.

Britain. Restrictions were also placed on the use of Indian-built ships for voyages to England. From 1812, there were extra duties on any imports they delivered, and that must be one factor in the decline in shipbuilding. A few Indian ships continued to make the voyage to Britain, however, and there was one in Liverpool Docks in 1839 when Herman Melville arrived from America. It was the *Irrawaddy* from Bombay and Melville commented: "Forty years ago, these merchantmen were nearly the largest in the world; and they still exceed the generality." They were "wholly built by the native shipwrights of India, who . . . surpassed the European artisans." . . .

Attitudes to India changed markedly after the subcontinent had fallen into British hands. Before this, travellers found much to admire in technologies ranging from agriculture to metallurgy. After 1803, however, the arrogance of conquest was reinforced by the rapid development of British industry. This meant that Indian techniques which a few years earlier seemed remarkable could now be equalled at much lower cost by British factories. India was then made to appear rather primitive, and the idea grew that its proper role was to provide raw materials for western industry, including raw cotton and indigo dye, and to function as a market for British goods. This policy was reflected in 1813 by a relaxation of the East India Company's monopoly of trade so that other British companies could now bring in manufactured goods freely for sale in India. Thus the textile industry, iron production, and shipbuilding were all eroded by cheap imports from Britain, and by handicaps placed on Indian merchants.

By 1830, the situation had become so bad that even some of the British in India began to protest. One exclaimed, "We have destroyed the manufactures of India," pleading that there should be some protection for silk weaving, "the last of the expiring manufactures of India." Another observer was alarmed by a "commercial revolution" which produced "so much present suffering to numerous classes in India."

The question that remains is the speculative one of what might have happened if a strong Mughal government had survived. Fernand Braudel argues that although there was no lack of "capitalism" in India, the economy was not moving in the direction of home-grown industrialization. The historian of technology inevitably notes the lack of development of machines, even though there had been some increase in the use of water-wheels during the eighteenth century both in the iron industry and at gunpowder mills. However, it is impossible not to be struck by the achievements of the shipbuilding industry, which produced skilled carpenters and a model of large-scale organizations. It also trained up draughtsmen and people with mechanical interests. It is striking that one of the Wadia shipbuilders installed gas lighting in his home in 1834 and built a small foundry in which he made parts for steam engines. Given an independent and more prosperous India, it is difficult not to believe that a response to British industrialization might well have taken the form of a spread of skill and innovation from the shipyards into other industries.

As it was, such developments were delayed until the 1850s and later, when the first mechanized cotton mill opened. It is significant that some of the entrepreneurs who backed the development of this industry were from the same Parsi families as had built ships in Bombay and invested in overseas trade in the eighteenth century.

Guns and Rails: Asia, Britain, and America

Britain's "conquest" of India cannot be attributed to superior armaments. Indian armies were also well equipped. More significant was the prior breakdown of Mughal government and the collaboration of many Indians. Some victories were also the result of good discipline and bold strategy, especially when Arthur Wellesley, the future Duke of Wellington, was in command. Wellesley's contribution also illustrates the distinctive western approach to the organizational aspect of technology. Indian armies might have had good armament, but because their guns were made in a great variety of different sizes, precise weapons drill was impossible and the supply of shot to the battlefield was unnecessarily complicated. By contrast, Wellesley's forces standardized on just three sizes of field gun, and the commander himself paid close attention to the design of gun carriages and to the bullocks which hauled them, so that his artillery could move as fast as his infantry, and without delays due to wheel breakages.

Significantly, the one major criticism regularly made of Indian artillery concerned the poor design of gun carriages. Many, particularly before 1760, were little better than four-wheeled trolleys. But the guns themselves were often of excellent design and workmanship. Whilst some were imported and others were made with the assistance of foreign craftworkers, there was many a brass cannon and mortar of Indian design, as well as heavy muskets for camel-mounted troops. Captured field guns were often taken over for use by the British, and after capturing ninety guns in one crucial battle, Wellesley wrote that seventy were "the finest brass ordnance I have ever seen." They were probably made in northern India, perhaps at the great Mughal arsenal at Agra.

Whilst Indians had been making guns from brass since the sixteenth century, Europeans could at first only produce this alloy in relatively small quantities because they had no technique for smelting zinc. By the eighteenth century, however, brass was being produced in large quantities in Europe, and brass cannon were being cast at Woolwich Arsenal near London. Several European countries were importing metallic zinc from China for this purpose. However, from 1743 there was a smelter near Bristol in England producing zinc, using coke[1] as fuel, and zinc smelters were also developed in Germany. At the end of the century, Britain's imports of zinc from the Far East were only about forty tons per year. Nevertheless, a British party which visited China in 1797 took particular note of zinc smelting methods. These were similar to the process used in India, which involved vaporizing the metal and then condensing it. There is a suspicion that the Bristol smelting works of 1743 was based on Indian practice, although the possibility of independent invention cannot be excluded.

A much clearer example of the transfer of technology from India occurred when British armies on the subcontinent encountered rockets, a type of weapon of which they had no previous experience. The basic technology had come from the Ottoman Turks or from Syria before 1500, although the Chinese had invented rockets even earlier. In the 1790s, some Indian armies included very large infantry units equipped with rockets. French mercenaries in Mysore had learned to make them, and the British Ordnance Office was enquiring for somebody with expertise on the subject. In response, William Congreve, whose father was head of the laboratory at Woolwich Arsenal, undertook to design a rocket on Indian lines. After a successful demonstration, about two hundred of his rockets were used by the British in an attack on Boulogne in 1806. Fired from over a kilometre away, they set fire to the town. After this success, rockets were adopted quite widely by European armies, though some commanders, notably the Duke of Wellington, frowned on such imprecise weapons, and they tended to drop out of use later in the century. What happened next, however, was typical of the whole British relationship with India. William Congreve set up a factory to manufacture the weapons in 1817, and part of its output was exported to India to equip rocket troops operating there under British command.

Yet another aspect of Asian technology in which eighteenth-century Europeans were interested was the design of farm implements. Reports on seed drills and ploughs were sent to the British Board of Agriculture from India in 1795. A century earlier the Dutch had found much of interest in ploughs and winnowing machines of a Chinese type which they saw in Java. Then a Swedish party visiting Guangzhou (Canton) took a winnowing machine back home with them. Indeed, several of these machines were imported into different parts of Europe, and similar devices for cleaning threshed grain were soon being made there. The

---

[1] Fuel from soft coal. [Ed.]

inventor of one of them, Jonas Norberg, admitted that he got "the initial idea" from three machines "brought here from China," but had to create a new type because the Chinese machines "do not suit our kinds of grain." Similarly, the Dutch saw that the Chinese plough did not suit their type of soil, but it stimulated them to produce new designs with curved metal mould-boards in contrast to the less efficient flat wooden boards used in Europe hitherto.

In most of these cases, and especially with zinc smelting, rockets, and winnowing machines, we have clear evidence of Europeans studying Asian technology in detail. With rockets and winnowers, though perhaps not with zinc, there was an element of imitation in the European inventions which followed. In other instances, however, the more usual course of technological dialogue between Europe and Asia was that European innovation was challenged by the quality or scale of Asian output, but took a different direction, as we have seen in many aspects of the textile industry. Sometimes, the dialogue was even more limited, and served mainly to give confidence in a technique that was already known. Such was the case with occasional references to China in the writings of engineers designing suspension bridges in Britain. The Chinese had a reputation for bridge construction, and before 1700 Peter the Great had asked for bridge-builders to be sent from China to work in Russia. Later, several books published in Europe described a variety of Chinese bridges, notably a long-span suspension bridge made with iron chains.

Among those who developed the suspension bridge in the West were James Finley in America, beginning in 1801, and Samuel Brown and Thomas Telford in Britain. About 1814, Brown devised a flat, wrought-iron chain link which Telford later used to form the main structural chains in his suspension bridges. But beyond borrowing this specific technique, what Telford needed was evidence that the suspension principle was applicable to the problem he was then tackling. Finley's two longest bridges had spanned seventy-four and ninety-three metres, over the Merrimac and Schuylkill Rivers in the eastern United States. Telford was aiming to span almost twice the larger distance with his 176-metre Menai Bridge. Experiments at a Shropshire ironworks gave confidence in the strength of the chains. But Telford may have looked for reassurance even further afield. One of his notebooks contains the reminder, "Examine Chinese bridges." It is clear from the wording which follows that he had seen a recent booklet advocating a "bridge of chains," partly based on a Chinese example, to cross the Firth of Forth in Scotland.

2

ADAM SMITH

The Wealth of Nations, 1776

An Inquiry into the Nature and Causes of the Wealth of Nations might justly be called the bible of free-market capitalism. Written in 1776 in the context of the British (and European) debate over the proper role of government in the economy, Smith's work takes aim at *mercantilism,* or government supervision of the economy. Mercantilists believed that national economies required government assistance and direction to prosper.

Smith argues that free trade will produce greater wealth than mercantilist trade and that free markets allocate resources more efficiently than the government. His notion of *laissez-faire* (literally "let do") capitalism assumes neither that capitalists are virtuous nor that governments should absent themselves entirely from the economy. However, Smith does believe that the greed of capitalists generally negates itself and produces results that are advantageous to, but unimagined by, the individual. "It is not from the benevolence of the butcher, the brewer, or the baker, that we expect our dinner," Smith writes, "but from their regard of their own interest. We address ourselves not to their humanity, but to their self-love, and never talk to them of our own necessities, but of their advantage."[1] Each person seeks to maximize his or her own gain, thereby creating an efficient market in which the cost of goods is instantly adjusted to exploit changes in supply and demand, while the market provides what is needed at the price people are willing to pay "as if by an invisible hand."

According to Smith, what is the relationship between money and industry, and which is more important? What would Smith say to a farmer or manufacturer who wanted to institute tariffs or quotas to limit the number of cheaper imports entering the country and to minimize competition? What would he say to a government official who wanted to protect an important domestic industry? What would he say to a worker who complained about low wages or boring work? What would Smith think about a "postindustrial" or "service" economy in which few workers actually make products? What would he think of a prosperous country that imported more than it exported?

THINKING HISTORICALLY

The Wealth of Nations was written in defense of free capitalism at a moment when the industrial revolution was just beginning. Some elements

[1] Book I, chapter 2.

Source: Adam Smith, *An Inquiry into the Nature and Causes of the Wealth of Nations* (Indianapolis: Liberty Fund, 1981, a reprint of the Oxford University Press edition of 1976), 1:13–15, 31, 47, 73–74, 449–50, 455–57.

of Smith's writing suggest a preindustrial world, as in the quotation about the butcher, brewer, and baker mentioned earlier. Still, Smith was aware how new industrial methods were transforming age-old labor relations and manufacturing processes. In some respects, Smith recognized that capitalism could create wealth, not just redistribute it, because he appreciated the potential of industrial technology.

As you read this selection, note when Smith is discussing capitalism, the economic system, and the power of the new industrial technology. In his discussion of the division of labor, what relationship does Smith see between the development of a capitalistic market and the rise of industrial technology? To what extent could the benefits that Smith attributes to a free market be attributed to the new system of industrial production?

Book I
Of the Causes of Improvement in the Productive Powers of Labour, and of the Order According to Which Its Produce Is Naturally Distributed among the Different Ranks of the People

Chapter 1: Of the Division of Labour

The greatest improvement in the productive powers of labour, and the greater part of the skill, dexterity, and judgment with which it is anywhere directed, or applied, seem to have been the effects of the division of labour.

The effects of the division of labour, in the general business of society, will be more easily understood by considering in what manner it operates in some particular manufactures. . . .

To take an example, therefore, from a very trifling manufacture; but one in which the division of labour has been very often taken notice of, the trade of the pin-maker; a workman not educated to this business (which the division of labour has rendered a distinct trade), nor acquainted with the use of the machinery employed in it (to the invention of which the same division of labour has probably given occasion), could scarce, perhaps, with his utmost industry, make one pin in a day, and certainly could not make twenty. But in the way in which this business is now carried on, not only the whole work is a peculiar trade, but it is divided into a number of branches, of which the greater part are likewise peculiar trades. One man draws out the wire, another straights it, a third cuts it, a fourth points it, a fifth grinds it at the top for receiving the head; to make the head requires two or three distinct operations; to put it on is a peculiar business, to whiten the pins is another; it is even a trade by itself to put them into the paper; and the important business of making a pin is, in this manner, divided into about eighteen distinct operations, which, in some manufactories, are all performed by distinct hands, though in others the same man will sometimes perform two or three of them. I have seen a small manufactory of this kind where ten men only were employed, and where some of them consequently performed two or three distinct operations. But though they were very poor, and therefore but indifferently accommodated with the necessary machinery, they could, when they exerted themselves, make among them about twelve pounds of pins in a day. There are in a pound upwards of four thousand pins of a middling size. Those ten persons, therefore, could make among them upwards of forty-eight thousand pins in a day. Each person, therefore, making a tenth part of forty-eight thousand pins, might be considered as making four thousand eight hundred pins in a day. But if they had all wrought separately and independently, and without any of them having been educated to this peculiar business, they certainly could not each of them have made twenty, perhaps not one pin in a day; that is, certainly, not the two hundred and fortieth, perhaps not the four thousand eight hundredth part of what they are at present capable of performing, in consequence of a proper division and combination of their different operations.

In every other art and manufacture, the effects of the division of labour are similar to what they are in this very trifling one; though, in many of them, the labour can neither be so much subdivided, nor reduced to so great a simplicity of operation. . . .

Chapter 3: That the Division of Labour Is Limited by the Extent of the Market

As it is the power of exchanging that gives occasion to the division of labour, so the extent of this division must always be limited by the extent of that power, or, in other words, by the extent of the market. When the market is very small, no person can have any encouragement to dedicate himself entirely to one employment, for want of the power to exchange all that surplus part of the produce of his own labour, which is over and above his own consumption, for such parts of the produce of other men's labour as he has occasion for.

There are some sorts of industry, even of the lowest kind, which can be carried on nowhere but in a great town. A porter, for example, can find employment and subsistence in no other place. A village is by much too narrow a sphere for him. . . .

Chapter 5: Of the Real and Nominal Price of Commodities, or Their Price in Labour, and Their Price in Money

Every man is rich or poor according to the degree in which he can afford to enjoy the necessaries, conveniences, and amusements of human life. But after the division of labour has once thoroughly taken place, it is but a very small part of these with which a man's own labour can supply him. The far greater part of them he must derive from the labour of other people, and he must be rich or poor according to the quantity of that labour which he can command, or which he can afford to purchase. The value of any commodity, therefore, to the person who possesses it, and who means not to use or consume it himself, but to exchange it for other commodities, is equal to the quantity of labour which it enables him to purchase or command. Labour, therefore, is the real measure of the exchangeable value of all commodities. . . .

Chapter 7: Of the Natural and Market Price of Commodities

. . . When the quantity of any commodity which is brought to market falls short of the effectual demand, all those who are willing to pay the whole value of the rent, wages, and profit, which must be paid in order to bring it thither, cannot be supplied with the quantity which they want. Rather than want[2] it altogether, some of them will be willing to give more. A competition will immediately begin among them, and the market price will rise more or less above the natural price, according as either the greatness of the deficiency, or the wealth and wanton luxury of the competitors, happen to animate more or less the eagerness of the competition. Among competitors of equal wealth and luxury the same deficiency will generally occasion a more or less eager competition, according as the acquisition of the commodity happens to be of more or less importance to them. Hence the exorbitant price of the necessaries of life during the blockade of a town or in a famine.

When the quantity brought to market exceeds the effectual demand, it cannot be all sold to those who are willing to pay the whole value of the rent, wages, and profit, which must be paid in order to bring it thither. Some part must be sold to those who are willing to pay less, and the low price which they give for it must reduce the price of the whole. The market price will sink more or less below the natural price, according as the greatness of the excess increases more or less the competition of the sellers, or according as it happens to be more or less important to them to get immediately rid of the commodity. The same excess in the importation of perishables will occasion a much greater competition than in that of durable commodities; in the importation of oranges, for example, than in that of old iron.

When the quantity brought to market is just sufficient to supply the effectual demand, and no more, the market price naturally comes to be either exactly, or as nearly as can be judged of, the same with the natural price. The whole quantity upon hand can be disposed of for this price,

---

[2] Be without it. [Ed.]

and cannot be disposed of for more. The competition of the different dealers obliges them all to accept of this price, but does not oblige them to accept of less.

The quantity of every commodity brought to market naturally suits itself to the effectual demand. It is the interest of all those who employ their land, labour, or stock, in bringing any commodity to market, that the quantity never should exceed the effectual demand; and it is the interest of all other people that it never should fall short of that demand.

Book IV
Of Systems of Political Economy

Chapter 1: Of the Principle of the Commercial or Mercantile System

. . . I thought it necessary, though at the hazard of being tedious, to examine at full length this popular notion that wealth consists in money, or in gold and silver. Money in common language, as I have already observed, frequently signifies wealth, and this ambiguity of expression has rendered this popular notion so familiar to us that even they who are convinced of its absurdity are very apt to forget their own principles, and in the course of their reasonings to take it for granted as a certain and undeniable truth. Some of the best English writers upon commerce set out with observing that the wealth of a country consists, not in its gold and silver only, but in its lands, houses, and consumable goods of all different kinds. In the course of their reasonings, however, the lands, houses, and consumable goods seem to slip out of their memory, and the strain of their argument frequently supposes that all wealth consists in gold and silver, and that to multiply those metals is the great object of national industry and commerce. . . .

Chapter 2: Of Restraints upon the Importation from Foreign Countries of Such Goods as Can Be Produced at Home

. . . The produce of industry is what it adds to the subject or materials upon which it is employed. In proportion as the value of this produce is great or small, so will likewise be the profits of the employer. But it is only for the sake of profit that any man employs a capital in the support of industry; and he will always, therefore, endeavour to employ it in the support of that industry of which the produce is likely to be of the greatest value, or to exchange for the greatest quantity either of money or of other goods.

But the annual revenue of every society is always precisely equal to the exchangeable value of the whole annual produce of its industry, or rather is precisely the same thing with that exchangeable value. As every individual, therefore, endeavours as much as he can both to employ his capital in the support of domestic industry, and so to direct that industry that its produce may be of the greatest value; every individual necessarily labours to render the annual revenue of the society as great as he can. He generally, indeed, neither intends to promote the public interest, nor knows how much he is promoting it. By preferring the support of domestic to that of foreign industry, he intends only his own security; and by directing that industry in such a manner as its produce may be of the greatest value, he intends only his own gain, and he is in this, as in many other cases, led by an invisible hand to promote an end which was no part of his intention. Nor is it always the worse for the society that it was no part of it. By pursuing his own interest he frequently promotes that of the society more effectually than when he really intends to promote it. I have never known much good done by those who affected to trade for the public good. It is an affectation, indeed, not very common among merchants, and very few words need be employed in dissuading them from it.

What is the species of domestic industry which his capital can employ, and of which the produce is likely to be of the greatest value, every individual, it is evident, can, in his local situation, judge much better than any statesman or lawgiver can do for him. The statesman who should attempt to direct private people in what manner they ought to employ their capitals would not only load himself with a most unnecessary attention, but assume an authority which could safely be trusted, not only to no single person, but to no council or senate whatever, and which would nowhere be so dangerous as in the hands of a man who had folly and presumption enough to fancy himself fit to exercise it.

To give the monopoly of the home market to the produce of domestic industry, in any particular art or manufacture, is in some measure to direct private people in what manner they ought to employ their capitals, and must, in almost all cases, be either a useless or a hurtful regulation. If the produce of domestic can be brought there as cheap as that of foreign industry, the regulation is evidently useless. If it cannot, it must generally be hurtful. It is the maxim of every prudent master of a family never to attempt to make at home what it will cost him more to make than to buy. The tailor does not attempt to make his own shoes, but buys them of the shoemaker. The shoemaker does not attempt to make his own clothes, but employs a tailor. The farmer attempts to make neither the one nor the other, but employs those different artificers. All of them find it for their interest to employ their whole industry in a way in which they have some advantage over their neighbours, and to purchase with a part of its produce, or what is the same thing, with the price of a part of it, whatever else they have occasion for.

What is prudence in the conduct of every private family can scarce be folly in that of a great kingdom. If a foreign country can supply us with a commodity cheaper than we ourselves can make it, better buy it of them with some part of the produce of our own industry employed in a way in which we have some advantage. The general industry of the country, being always in proportion to the capital which employs it, will not thereby be diminished, no more than that of the abovementioned artificers; but only left to find out the way in which it can be employed with the greatest advantage. It is certainly not employed to the greatest advantage when it is thus directed towards an object which it can buy cheaper than it can make. . . .

3

The Sadler Report of the House of Commons, 1832

Although, for many factory owners, children were among the ideal workers in the factories of the industrial revolution, increasingly their exploitation became a concern of the British Parliament. One important parliamentary investigation, chaired by Michael Sadler, took volumes of testimony from child workers and older people who had worked as children in the mines and factories. The following is a sample of that testimony: an interview with a former child worker named Matthew Crabtree who had worked in a textile factory. The Sadler Commission report led to child-labor reform in the Factory Act of 1833.

What seem to be the causes of Crabtree's distress? How could it have been alleviated? If the owner were asked why he didn't pay more, shorten the workday, provide more time for meals, or provide medical assistance when it was needed, how do you think he would have responded? Do you think Crabtree would have been in favor of reduced hours if it meant reduced wages?

THINKING HISTORICALLY

To what extent are the problems faced by Crabtree the inevitable results of machine production? To what extent are his problems caused by capitalism? How might the owner of this factory have addressed these issues?

Source: From *The Sadler Report: Report from the Committee on the Bill to Regulate the Labour of Children in the Mills and Factories of the United Kingdom* (London: The House of Commons, Parliamentary Papers, 1831–1832), 15:95–97.

Friday, 18 May 1832—Michael Thomas Sadler, Esquire, in the Chair

Mr. Matthew Crabtree, *called in; and Examined.*

What age are you?—Twenty-two.

What is your occupation?—A blanket manufacturer.

Have you ever been employed in a factory?—Yes.

At what age did you first go to work in one?—Eight.

How long did you continue in that occupation?—Four years.

Will you state the hours of labour at the period when you first went to the factory, in ordinary times?—From 6 in the morning to 8 at night.

Fourteen hours?—Yes.

With what intervals for refreshment and rest?—An hour at noon.

Then you had no resting time allowed in which to take your breakfast, or what is in Yorkshire called your "drinking"?—No.

When trade was brisk what were your hours?—From 5 in the morning to 9 in the evening.

Sixteen hours?—Yes.

With what intervals at dinner[1]?—An hour.

How far did you live from the mill?—About two miles.

Was there any time allowed for you to get your breakfast in the mill?—No.

Did you take it before you left your home?—Generally.

During those long hours of labour could you be punctual; how did you awake?—I seldom did awake spontaneously; I was most generally awoke or lifted out of bed, sometimes asleep, by my parents.

Were you always in time?—No.

What was the consequence if you had been too late?—I was most commonly beaten.

Severely?—Very severely, I thought.

In whose factory was this?—Messrs. Hague & Cook's, of Dewsbury.

Will you state the effect that those long hours had upon the state of your health and feelings?—I was, when working those long hours, commonly very much fatigued at night, when I left my work; so much so that I sometimes should have slept as I walked if I had not stumbled and started awake again; and so sick often that I could not eat, and what I did eat I vomited.

Did this labour destroy your appetite?—It did.

In what situation were you in that mill?—I was a piecener.

Will you state to this Committee whether pieening is a very laborious employment for children, or not?—It is a very laborious employment. Pieceners are continually running to and fro, and on their feet the whole day.

[1] The main meal, in the afternoon. Not the evening supper. [Ed.]

The duty of the piecener is to take the cardings from one part of the machinery, and to place them on another?—Yes.

So that the labour is not only continual, but it is unabated to the last?—It is unabated to the last.

Do you not think, from your own experience, that the speed of the machinery is so calculated as to demand the utmost exertions of a child supposing the hours were moderate?—It is as much as they could do at the best; they are always upon the stretch, and it is commonly very difficult to keep up with their work.

State the condition of the children toward the latter part of the day, who have thus to keep up with the machinery.—It is as much as they can do when they are not very much fatigued to keep up with their work, and toward the close of the day, when they come to be more fatigued, they cannot keep up with it very well, and the consequence is that they are beaten to spur them on.

Were you beaten under those circumstances?—Yes.

Frequently?—Very frequently.

And principally at the latter end of the day?—Yes.

And is it your belief that if you had not been so beaten, you should not have got through the work?—I should not if I had not been kept up to it by some means.

Does beating then principally occur at the latter end of the day, when the children are exceedingly fatigued?—It does at the latter end of the day, and in the morning sometimes, when they are very drowsy, and have not got rid of the fatigue of the day before.

What were you beaten with principally?—A strap.

Anything else?—Yes, a stick sometimes; and there is a kind of roller which runs on the top of the machine called a billy, perhaps two or three yards in length, and perhaps an inch and a half, or more in diameter; the circumference would be four or five inches; I cannot speak exactly.

Were you beaten with that instrument?—Yes.

Have you yourself been beaten, and have you seen other children struck severely with that roller?—I have been struck very severely with it myself, so much so as to knock me down, and I have seen other children have their heads broken with it.

You think that it is a general practice to beat the children with the roller?—It is.

You do not think then that you were worse treated than other children in the mill?—No, I was not, perhaps not so bad as some were.

In those mills is chastisement towards the latter part of the day going on perpetually?—Perpetually.

So that you can hardly be in a mill without hearing constant crying?—Never an hour, I believe.

Do you think that if the overlooker were naturally a humane person it would be still found necessary for him to beat the children, in order to keep up their attention and vigilance at the termination of those extraordinary days of labour? — Yes, the machine turns off a regular quantity of cardings, and of course they must keep as regularly to their work the whole of the day; they must keep with the machine, and therefore however humane the slubber may be, as he must keep up with the machine or be found fault with, he spurs the children to keep up also by various means but that which he commonly resorts to is to strap them when they become drowsy.

At the time when you were beaten for not keeping up with your work, were you anxious to have done it if you possibly could? — Yes; the dread of being beaten if we could not keep up with our work was a sufficient impulse to keep us to it if we could.

When you got home at night after this labour, did you feel much fatigued? — Very much so.

Had you any time to be with your parents, and to receive instruction from them? — No.

What did you do? — All that we did when we got home was to get the little bit of supper that was provided for us and go to bed immediately. If the supper had not been ready directly, we should have gone to sleep while it was preparing.

Did you not, as a child, feel it a very grievous hardship to be roused so soon in the morning? — I did.

Were the rest of the children similarly circumstanced? — Yes, all of them; but they were not all of them so far from their work as I was.

And if you had been too late you were under the apprehension of being cruelly beaten? — I generally was beaten when I happened to be too late; and when I got up in the morning the apprehension of that was so great, that I used to run, and cry all the way as I went to the mill.

That was the way by which your punctual attendance was secured? — Yes.

And you do not think it could have been secured by any other means? — No.

Then it is your impression from what you have seen, and from your own experience, that those long hours of labour have the effect of rendering young persons who are subject to them exceedingly unhappy? — Yes.

You have already said it had a considerable effect upon your health? — Yes.

Do you conceive that it diminished your growth? — I did not pay much attention to that; but I have been examined by some persons who said they thought I was rather stunted, and that I should have been taller if I had not worked at the mill.

What were your wages at that time? — Three shillings (per week).

And how much a day had you for overwork when you were worked so exceedingly long? — A halfpenny a day.

Did you frequently forfeit that if you were not always there to a moment? — Yes; I most frequently forfeited what was allowed for those long hours.

You took your food to the mill; was it in your mill, as is the case in cotton mills, much spoiled by being laid aside? — It was very frequently covered by flues from the wool; and in that case they had to be blown off with the mouth, and picked off with the fingers before it could be eaten.

So that not giving you a little leisure for eating your food, but obliging you to take it at the mill, spoiled your food when you did get it? — Yes, very commonly.

And that at the same time that this over-labour injured your appetite? — Yes.

Could you eat when you got home? — Not always.

What is the effect of this piecening upon the hands? — It makes them bleed; the skin is completely rubbed off, and in that case they bleed in perhaps a dozen parts.

The prominent parts of the hand? — Yes, all the prominent parts of the hand are rubbed down till they bleed; every day they are rubbed in that way.

All the time you continue at work? — All the time we are working. The hands never can be hardened in that work, for the grease keeps them soft in the first instance, and long and continual rubbing is always wearing them down, so that if they were hard they would be sure to bleed.

It is attended with much pain? — Very much.

Do they allow you to make use of the back of the hand? — No; the work cannot be so well done with the back of the hand, or I should have made use of that.

4

KARL MARX AND FRIEDRICH ENGELS

The Communist Manifesto, 1848

The Communist Manifesto was written in 1848 in the midst of European upheaval, a time when capitalist industrialization had spread from England to France and Germany. Marx and Engels were Germans who studied and worked in France and England. In the *Manifesto*, they

Source: Karl Marx and Friedrich Engels, *The Communist Manifesto* (1888; Boston: Bedford/ St. Martin's, 1999), 65–72.

imagine a revolution that will transform all of Europe. What do they see as the inevitable causes of this revolution? How, according to their analysis, is the crisis of "modern" society different from previous crises? Were Marx and Engels correct?

THINKING HISTORICALLY

Notice how Marx and Engels describe the notions of capitalism and industrialization without using those words. The term *capitalism* developed later from Marx's classic *Das Kapital* (1859), but the term *bourgeoisie*,* as Engels notes in this selection, stands for the capitalist class. For Marx and Engels, the industrial revolution (another later phrase) is the product of a particular stage of capitalist development. Thus, if Marx and Engels were asked whether capitalism or industry was the principal force that created the modern world, what would their answer be?

   The Communist Manifesto is widely known as the classic critique of capitalism, but a careful reading reveals a list of achievements of capitalist or "bourgeois civilization." What are these achievements? Did Marx and Engels consider them to be achievements? How could Marx and Engels both praise and criticize capitalism?

Bourgeois and Proletarians[1]

The history of all hitherto existing society is the history of class struggles.

   Freeman and slave, patrician and plebeian, lord and serf, guild-master and journeyman, in a word, oppressor and oppressed, stood in constant opposition to one another, carried on an uninterrupted, now hidden, now open fight, a fight that each time ended, either in a revolutionary reconstitution of society at large, or in the common ruin of the contending classes.

   In the earlier epochs of history, we find almost everywhere a complicated arrangement of society into various orders, a manifold gradation of social rank. In ancient Rome we have patricians, knights, plebeians, slaves; in the Middle Ages, feudal lords, vassals, guildmasters, journeymen, apprentices, serfs; in almost all of these classes, again, subordinate gradations.

---

* bohr zhwah ZEE

[1] In French *bourgeois* means a town-dweller. *Proletarian* comes from the Latin *proletarius*, which meant a person whose sole wealth was his offspring (*proles*). [Ed.] [Note by Engels] By "bourgeoisie" is meant the class of modern capitalists, owners of the means of social production and employers of wage labor; by "proletariat," the class of modern wage-laborers who, having no means of production of their own, are reduced to selling their labor power in order to live.

The modern bourgeois society that has sprouted from the ruins of feudal society, has not done away with class antagonisms. It has but established new classes, new conditions of oppression, new forms of struggle in place of the old ones.

Our epoch, the epoch of the bourgeoisie, possesses, however, this distinctive feature: It has simplified the class antagonisms. Society as a whole is more and more splitting up into the two great hostile camps, into two great classes directly facing each other—bourgeoisie and proletariat.

From the serfs of the Middle Ages sprang the chartered burghers of the earliest towns. From these burgesses the first elements of the bourgeoisie were developed.

The discovery of America, the rounding of the Cape, opened up fresh ground for the rising bourgeoisie. The East-Indian and Chinese markets, the colonization of America, trade with the colonies, the increase in the means of exchange and in commodities generally, gave to commerce, to navigation, to industry, an impulse never before known, and thereby, to the revolutionary element in the tottering feudal society, a rapid development.

The feudal system of industry, in which industrial production was monopolized by closed guilds, now no longer sufficed for the growing wants of the new markets. The manufacturing system took its place. The guildmasters were pushed aside by the manufacturing middle class; division of labor between the different corporate guilds vanished in the face of division of labor in each single workshop.

Meantime the markets kept ever growing, the demand ever rising. Even manufacture[2] no longer sufficed. Thereupon, steam and machinery revolutionized industrial production. The place of manufacture was taken by the giant, modern industry, the place of the industrial middle class, by industrial millionaires—the leaders of whole industrial armies, the modern bourgeois.

Modern industry has established the world market, for which the discovery of America paved the way. This market has given an immense development to commerce, to navigation, to communication by land. This development has, in its turn, reacted on the extension of industry; and in proportion as industry, commerce, navigation, railways extended, in the same proportion the bourgeoisie developed, increased its capital, and pushed into the background every class handed down from the Middle Ages.

We see, therefore, how the modern bourgeoisie is itself the product of a long course of development, of a series of revolutions in the modes of production and of exchange.

---

[2] By *manufacture* Marx meant the system of production that succeeded the guild system but that still relied mainly on direct human labor for power. He distinguished it from modern industry, which arose when machinery driven by water and steam was introduced. [Ed.]

Each step in the development of the bourgeoisie was accompanied by a corresponding political advance of that class. An oppressed class under the sway of the feudal nobility, it became an armed and self-governing association in the medieval commune; here independent urban republic (as in Italy and Germany), there taxable "third estate" of the monarchy (as in France); afterwards, in the period of manufacture proper, serving either the semifeudal or the absolute monarchy as a counterpoise against the nobility, and, in fact, cornerstone of the great monarchies in general—the bourgeoisie has at last, since the establishment of modern industry and of the world market, conquered for itself, in the modern representative state, exclusive political sway. The executive of the modern state is but a committee for managing the common affairs of the whole bourgeoisie.

The bourgeoisie has played a most revolutionary role in history.

The bourgeoisie, wherever it has got the upper hand, has put an end to all feudal, patriarchal, idyllic relations. It has pitilessly torn asunder the motley feudal ties that bound man to his "natural superiors," and has left no other bond between man and man than naked self-interest, than callous "cash payment." It has drowned the most heavenly ecstasies of religious fervor, of chivalrous enthusiasm, of philistine sentimentalism, in the icy water of egotistical calculation. It has resolved personal worth into exchange value, and in place of the numberless indefensible chartered freedoms, has set up that single, unconscionable freedom—Free Trade. In one word, for exploitation, veiled by religious and political illusions, it has substituted naked, shameless, direct, brutal exploitation.

The bourgeoisie has stripped of its halo every occupation hitherto honored and looked up to with reverent awe. It has converted the physician, the lawyer, the priest, the poet, the man of science, into its paid wage-laborers.

The bourgeoisie has torn away from the family its sentimental veil, and has reduced the family relation to a mere money relation.

The bourgeoisie has disclosed how it came to pass that the brutal display of vigor in the Middle Ages, which reactionaries so much admire, found its fitting complement in the most slothful indolence. It has been the first to show what man's activity can bring about. It has accomplished wonders far surpassing Egyptian pyramids, Roman aqueducts, and Gothic cathedrals; it has conducted expeditions that put in the shade all former migrations of nations and crusades.

The bourgeoisie cannot exist without constantly revolutionizing the instruments of production, and thereby the relations of production, and with them the whole relations of society. Conservation of the old modes of production in unaltered form, was, on the contrary, the first condition of existence for all earlier industrial classes. Constant revolutionizing of production, uninterrupted disturbance of all social conditions, everlasting uncertainty and agitation distinguished the bourgeois epoch from all earlier ones. All fixed, fast-frozen relations, with their train of ancient and venerable prejudices and opinions, are swept away, all new-formed ones become antiquated before they can ossify. All that is solid melts into air, all that is holy is profaned, and man is at last compelled to face with sober senses his real conditions of life and his relations with his kind.

The need of a constantly expanding market for its products chases the bourgeoisie over the whole surface of the globe. It must nestle everywhere, settle everywhere, establish connections everywhere.

The bourgeoisie has through its exploitation of the world market given a cosmopolitan character to production and consumption in every country. To the great chagrin of reactionaries, it has drawn from under the feet of industry the national ground on which it stood. All old-established national industries have been destroyed or are daily being destroyed. They are dislodged by new industries, whose introduction becomes a life and death question for all civilized nations, by industries that no longer work up indigenous raw material, but raw material drawn from the remotest zones; industries whose products are consumed, not only at home, but in every quarter of the globe. In place of the old wants, satisfied by the production of the country, we find new wants, requiring for their satisfaction the products of distant lands and climes. In place of the old local and national seclusion and self-sufficiency, we have intercourse in every direction, universal interdependence of nations. And as in material, so also in intellectual production. The intellectual creations of individual nations become common property. National one-sidedness and narrow-mindedness become more and more impossible, and from the numerous national and local literatures there arises a world literature.

The bourgeoisie, by the rapid improvement of all instruments of production, by the immensely facilitated means of communication, draws all nations, even the most barbarian, into civilization. The cheap prices of its commodities are the heavy artillery with which it batters down all Chinese walls, with which it forces the barbarians' intensely obstinate hatred for foreigners to capitulate. It compels all nations, on pain of extinction, to adopt the bourgeois mode of production; it compels them to introduce what it calls civilization into their midst, i.e., to become bourgeois themselves. In a word, it creates a world after its own image.

The bourgeoisie has subjected the country to the rule of the towns. It has created enormous cities, has greatly increased the urban population as compared with the rural, and has thus rescued a considerable part of the population from the idiocy of rural life. Just as it has made the country dependent on the towns, so it has made barbarian and semi-barbarian countries dependent on the civilized ones, nations of peasants on nations of bourgeois, the East on the West.

More and more the bourgeoisie keeps doing away with the scattered state of the population, of the means of production, and of property. It has agglomerated population, centralized means of production, and has concentrated property in a few hands. The necessary consequence of this was political centralization. Independent, or but loosely connected provinces, with separate interests, laws, governments and systems of taxation, became lumped together into one nation, with one government, one code of laws, one national class interest, one frontier and one customs tariff.

The bourgeoisie, during its rule of scarce one hundred years, has created more massive and more colossal productive forces than have all preceding generations together. Subjection of nature's forces to man, machinery, application of chemistry to industry and agriculture, steam-navigation, railways, electric telegraphs, clearing of whole continents for cultivation, canalization of rivers, whole populations conjured out of the ground—what earlier century had even a presentiment that such productive forces slumbered in the lap of social labor?

We see then that the means of production and of exchange, which served as the foundation for the growth of the bourgeoisie, were generated in feudal society. At a certain stage in the development of these means of production and of exchange, the conditions under which feudal society produced and exchanged, the feudal organization of agriculture and manufacturing industry, in a word, the feudal relations of property became no longer compatible with the already developed productive forces; they became so many fetters. They had to be burst asunder; they were burst asunder.

Into their place stepped free competition, accompanied by a social and political constitution adapted to it, and by the economic and political sway of the bourgeois class.

A similar movement is going on before our own eyes. Modern bourgeois society with its relations of production, of exchange and of property, a society that has conjured up such gigantic means of production and exchange, is like the sorcerer who is no longer able to control the powers of the nether world whom he has called up by his spells. For many a decade past the history of industry and commerce is but the history of the revolt of modern productive forces against modern conditions of production, against the property relations that are the conditions for the existence of the bourgeoisie and of its rule. It is enough to mention the commercial crises that by their periodical return put the existence of the entire bourgeoisie society on trial, each time more threateningly. In these crises a great part not only of the existing products, but also of the previously created productive forces, are periodically destroyed. In these crises there breaks out an epidemic that, in all earlier epochs, would have seemed an absurdity—the epidemic of overproduction. Society suddenly finds itself put back into a state of momentary barbarism; it appears as if a famine, a universal war of devastation had cut off the supply of every means of subsistence; industry and commerce seem to be destroyed. And why? Because there is too much civilization, too much means of subsistence, too much industry, too much commerce. The productive forces at the disposal of society no longer tend to further the development of the conditions of bourgeois property; on the contrary, they have become too powerful for these conditions, by which they are fettered, and no sooner do they overcome these fetters than they bring disorder into the whole of bourgeois society, endanger the existence of bourgeois property. The conditions of bourgeois society are too narrow to comprise the wealth created by them. And how does the bourgeoisie get over these crises? On the one hand by enforced destruction of a mass of productive forces; on the other, by the conquest of new markets, and by the more thorough exploitation of the old ones. That is to say, by paving the way for more extensive and more destructive crises, and by diminishing the means whereby crises are prevented.

The weapons with which the bourgeoisie felled feudalism to the ground are now turned against the bourgeoisie itself.

But not only has the bourgeoisie forged the weapons that bring death to itself; it has also called into existence the men who are to wield those weapons—the modern working class—the proletarians.

In proportion as the bourgeoisie, i.e., capital, is developed, in the same proportion is the proletariat, the modern working class, developed—a class of labourers, who live only so long as they find work, and who find work only so long as their labour increases capital. These labourers, who must sell themselves piece-meal, are a commodity, like every other article of commerce, and are consequently exposed to all the vicissitudes of competition, to all the fluctuations of the market.

Owing to the extensive use of machinery and to division of labour, the work of the proletarians has lost all individual character, and consequently, all charm for the workman. He becomes an appendage of the machine, and it is only the most simple, most monotonous, and most easily acquired knack, that is required of him. Hence, the cost of production of a workman is restricted, almost entirely, to the means of subsistence that he requires for his maintenance, and for the propagation of his race. But the price of a commodity, and therefore also of labour, is equal to its cost of production. In proportion therefore, as the repulsiveness of the work increases, the wage decreases. Nay more, in proportion as the use of machinery and division of labour increases, in the same proportion the burden of toil also increases, whether by prolongation of the working hours, by increase of the work exacted in a given time or by increased speed of the machinery, etc.

Modern industry has converted the little workshop of the patriarchal master into the great factory of the industrial capitalist. Masses of labourers, crowded into the factory, are organised like soldiers.

As privates of the industrial army they are placed under the command of a perfect hierarchy of officers and sergeants. Not only are they slaves of the bourgeois class, and of the bourgeois State; they are daily and hourly enslaved by the machine, by the over-looker, and, above all, by the individual bourgeois manufacturer himself. The more openly this despotism proclaims gain to be its end and aim, the more petty, the more hateful and the more embittering it is.

The less the skill and exertion of strength implied in manual labour, in other words, the more modern industry becomes developed, the more is the labour of men superseded by that of women. Differences of age and sex have no longer any distinctive social validity for the working class. All are instruments of labour, more or less expensive to use, according to their age and sex.

No sooner is the exploitation of the labourer by the manufacturer, so far, at an end, that he receives his wages in cash, than he is set upon by the other portions of the bourgeoisie, the landlord, the shopkeeper, the pawnbroker, etc.

The lower strata of the middle class—the small tradespeople, shopkeepers, retired tradesmen generally, the handicraftsmen and peasants—all these sink gradually into the proletariat, partly because their diminutive capital does not suffice for the scale on which Modern Industry is carried on, and is swamped in the competition with the large capitalists, partly because their specialized skill is rendered worthless by the new methods of production. Thus the proletariat is recruited from all classes of the population.

5

PETER N. STEARNS

The Industrial Revolution outside the West, 1993

Stearns, a modern historian, discusses the export of industrial machinery and techniques outside the West (Europe and North America) in the nineteenth century. Again and again, he finds that initial attempts at industrialization—in Russia, India, Egypt, and South America—led to increased production of export crops and resources but failed to stimulate true industrial revolutions. Consequently, as producers of raw materials, these countries became more deeply dependent on

Source: Peter N. Stearns, *The Industrial Revolution in World History* (Boulder, CO: Westview Press, 1993), 71–79.

Western markets for their products, while at the same time importing from the West more valuable manufactured products like machinery. What common reasons can you find for these failures?

THINKING HISTORICALLY

Did nineteenth-century efforts to ignite industrial revolutions outside the West fail because these societies neglected to develop capitalism, or did they fail because their local needs were subordinated to those of Western capitalists? Explain.

Before the 1870s no industrial revolution occurred outside Western society. The spread of industrialization within western Europe, while by no means automatic, followed from a host of shared economic, cultural, and political features. The quick ascension of the United States was somewhat more surprising—the area was not European and had been far less developed economically during the eighteenth century. Nevertheless, extensive commercial experience in the northern states and the close mercantile and cultural ties with Britain gave the new nation advantages for its rapid imitation of the British lead. Abundant natural resources and extensive investments from Europe kept the process going, joining the United States to the wider dynamic of industrialization in the nineteenth-century West.

Elsewhere, conditions did not permit an industrial revolution, an issue that must be explored in dealing with the international context for this first phase of the world's industrial experience. Yet the West's industrial revolution did have substantial impact. It led to a number of pilot projects whereby initial machinery and factories were established under Western guidance. More important, it led to new Western demands on the world's economies that instigated significant change without industrialization; indeed, these demands in several cases made industrialization more difficult.

Pilot Projects

Russia's contact with the West's industrial revolution before the 1870s offers an important case study that explains why many societies could not follow the lead of nations like France or the United States in imitating Britain. Yet Russia did introduce some new equipment for economic and military-political reasons, and these initiatives did generate change—they were not mere window dressing.

More than most societies not directly part of Western civilization, Russia had special advantages in reacting to the West's industrial lead and special motivation for paying attention to this lead. Russia had been part of Europe's diplomatic network since about 1700. It saw itself as one of Europe's great powers, a participant in international conferences and military alliances. The country also had close cultural ties with western Europe, sharing in artistic styles and scientific developments—though Russian leadership had stepped back from cultural alignment because of the shock of the French Revolution in 1789 and subsequent political disorders in the West. Russian aristocrats and intellectuals routinely visited western Europe. Finally, Russia had prior experience in imitating Western technology and manufacturing: importation of Western metallurgy and shipbuilding had formed a major part of Peter the Great's reform program in the early eighteenth century.

Contacts of this sort explain why Russia began to receive an industrial outreach from the West within a few decades of the advent of the industrial revolution. British textile machinery was imported beginning in 1843. Ernst Knoop, a German immigrant to Britain who had clerked in a Manchester cotton factory, set himself up as export agent to the Russians. He also sponsored British workers who installed the machinery in Russia and told any Russian entrepreneur brash enough to ask not simply for British models but for alterations or adaptations: "That is not your affair; in England they know better than you." Despite the snobbism, a number of Russian entrepreneurs set up small factories to produce cotton, aware that even in Russia's small urban market they could make a substantial profit by underselling traditional manufactured cloth. Other factories were established directly by Britons.

Europeans and Americans were particularly active in responding to calls by the tsar's government for assistance in establishing railway and steamship lines. The first steamship appeared in Russia in 1815, and by 1820 a regular service ran on the Volga River. The first public railroad, joining St. Petersburg to the imperial residence in the suburbs, opened in 1837. In 1851 the first major line connected St. Petersburg and Moscow, along a remarkably straight route desired by Tsar Nicholas I himself. American engineers were brought in, again by the government, to set up a railroad industry so that Russians could build their own locomotives and cars. George Whistler, the father of the painter James McNeill Whistler (and thus husband of Whistler's mother), played an important role in the effort. He and some American workers helped train Russians in the needed crafts, frequently complaining about their slovenly habits but appreciating their willingness to learn.

Russian imports of machinery increased rapidly; they were over thirty times as great in 1860 as they had been in 1825. While in 1851 the nation manufactured only about half as many machines as it imported, by 1860 the equation was reversed, and the number of machine-building factories had quintupled (from nineteen to ninety-nine). The new cotton industry surged forward with most production organized in factories using wage labor.

These were important changes. They revealed that some Russians were alert to the business advantages of Western methods and that some Westerners saw the great profits to be made by setting up shop in a huge but largely agricultural country. The role of the government was vital: The tsars used tax money to offer substantial premiums to Western entrepreneurs, who liked the adventure of dealing with the Russians but liked their superior profit margins even more.

But Russia did not then industrialize. Modern industrial operations did not sufficiently dent established economic practices. The nation remained overwhelmingly agricultural. High percentage increases in manufacturing proceeded from such a low base that they had little general impact. Several structural barriers impeded a genuine industrial revolution. Russia's cities had never boasted a manufacturing tradition; there were few artisans skilled even in preindustrial methods. Only by the 1860s and 1870s had cities grown enough for an artisan core to take shape—in printing, for example—and even then large numbers of foreigners (particularly Germans) had to be imported. Even more serious was the system of serfdom that kept most Russians bound to agricultural estates. While some free laborers could be found, most rural Russians could not legally leave their land, and their obligation to devote extensive work service to their lords' estates reduced their incentive even for agricultural production. Peter the Great had managed to adapt serfdom to a preindustrial metallurgical industry by allowing landlords to sell villages and the labor therein for expansion of ironworks. But this mongrel system was not suitable for change on a grander scale, which is precisely what the industrial revolution entailed.

Furthermore, the West's industrial revolution, while it provided tangible examples for Russia to imitate, also produced pressures to develop more traditional sectors in lieu of structural change. The West's growing cities and rising prosperity claimed rising levels of Russian timber, hemp, tallow, and, increasingly, grain. These were export goods that could be produced without new technology and without altering the existing labor system. Indeed, many landlords boosted the work-service obligations of the serfs in order to generate more grain production for sale to the West. The obvious temptation was to lock in an older economy—to respond to new opportunity by incremental changes within the traditional system and to maintain serfdom and the rural preponderance rather than to risk fundamental internal transformation.

The proof of Russia's lag showed in foreign trade. It rose but rather modestly, posting a threefold increase between 1800 and 1860. Exports of raw materials approximately paid for the imports of some machinery, factory-made goods from abroad, and a substantial volume of luxury products for the aristocracy. And the regions that participated most in the growing trade were not the tiny industrial enclaves (in St. Petersburg, Moscow, and the iron-rich Urals) but the wheat-growing areas of southern Russia where even industrial pilot projects had yet to surface. Russian manufacturing exported nothing at all to the West, though it did find a few customers in Turkey, central Asia, and China.

The proof of Russia's lag showed even more dramatically in Russia's new military disadvantage. Peter the Great's main goal had been to keep Russian military production near enough to Western levels to remain competitive, with the huge Russian population added into the equation. This strategy now failed, for the West's industrial revolution changed the rules of the game. A war in 1854 pitting Russia against Britain and France led to Russia's defeat in its own backyard. The British and French objected to new Russian territorial gains (won at the expense of Turkey's Ottoman Empire) that brought Russia greater access to the Black Sea. The battleground was the Crimea. Yet British and French steamships connected their armies more reliably with supplies and reinforcements from home than did Russia's ground transportation system with its few railroads and mere three thousand miles of first-class roads. And British and French industry could pour out more and higher-quality uniforms, guns, and munitions than traditional Russian manufacturing could hope to match. The Russians lost the Crimean War, surrendering their gains and swallowing their pride in 1856. Patchwork change had clearly proved insufficient to match the military, much less the economic, power the industrial revolution had generated in the West.

After a brief interlude, the Russians digested the implications of their defeat and launched a period of basic structural reforms. The linchpin was the abolition of serfdom in 1861. Peasants were not entirely freed, and rural discontent persisted, but many workers could now leave the land; the basis for a wage labor force was established. Other reforms focused on improving basic education and health, and while change in these areas was slow, it too set the basis for a genuine commitment to industrialization. A real industrial revolution lay in the future, however. By the 1870s Russia's contact with industrialization had deepened its economic gap vis-à-vis the West but had yielded a few interesting experiments with new methods and a growing realization of the need for further change.

Societies elsewhere in the world—those more removed from traditional ties to the West or more severely disadvantaged in the ties that did exist—saw even more tentative industrial pilot projects during the West's industrialization period. The Middle East and India tried some industrial imitation early on but largely failed—though not without generating some important economic change. Latin America also launched some revealingly limited technological change. Only eastern Asia and sub-Saharan Africa were largely untouched by any explicit industrial imitations until the late 1860s or beyond; they were too distant from European culture to venture a response so quickly.

Prior links with the West formed the key variable, as Russia's experience abundantly demonstrated. Societies that had some familiarity with Western merchants and some preindustrial awareness of the West's steady commercial gains mounted some early experiments in industrialization. Whether they benefited as a result compared with areas that did nothing before the late nineteenth century might be debated.

One industrial initiative in India developed around Calcutta, where British colonial rule had centered since the East India Company founded the city in 1690. A Hindu Brahman family, the Tagores, established close ties with many British administrators. Without becoming British, they sponsored a number of efforts to revivify India, including new colleges and research centers. Dwarkanath Tagore controlled tax collection in part of Bengal, and early in the nineteenth century he used part of his profit to found a bank. He also bought up a variety of commercial landholdings and traditional manufacturing operations. In 1834 he joined with British capitalists to establish a diversified company that boasted holdings in mines (including the first Indian coal mine), sugar refineries, and some new textile factories; the equipment was imported from Britain. Tagore's dominant idea was a British-Indian economic and cultural collaboration that would revitalize his country. He enjoyed a high reputation in Europe and for a short time made a success of his economic initiatives. Tagore died on a trip abroad, and his financial empire declined soon after.

This first taste of Indian industrialization was significant, but it brought few immediate results. The big news in India, even as Tagore launched his companies, was the rapid decline of traditional textiles under the bombardment of British factory competition; millions of Indian villagers were thrown out of work. Furthermore, relations between Britain and the Indian elite worsened after the mid-1830s as British officials sought a more active economic role and became more intolerant of Indian culture. One British official, admitting no knowledge of Indian scholarship, wrote that "all the historical information" and science available in Sanskrit was "less valuable than what may be found in the most paltry abridgements used at preparatory schools in England." With these attitudes, the kind of collaboration that might have aided Indian appropriation of British industry became impossible.

The next step in India's contact with the industrial revolution did not occur until the 1850s when the colonial government began to build a significant railroad network. The first passenger line opened in 1853. Some officials feared that Hindus might object to traveling on such smoke-filled monsters, but trains proved very popular and there ensued a period of rapid economic and social change. The principal result, however, was not industrial development but further extension of commercial agriculture (production of cotton and other goods for export) and intensification of British sales to India's interior. Coal mining did expand, but manufacturing continued to shrink. There was no hint of an industrial revolution in India.

Imitation in the Middle East was somewhat more elaborate, in part because most of this region, including parts of North Africa, retained independence from European colonialism. Muslims had long disdained Western culture and Christianity, and Muslim leaders, including the rulers of the great Ottoman Empire, had been very slow to recognize the West's growing dynamism after the fifteenth century. Some Western medicine was imported, but technology was ignored. Only in the eighteenth century did this attitude begin, haltingly, to change. The Ottoman government imported a printing press from Europe and began discussing Western-style technical training, primarily in relationship to the military.

In 1798 a French force briefly seized Egypt, providing a vivid symbol of Europe's growing technical superiority. Later an Ottoman governor, Muhammed Ali, seized Egypt from the imperial government and pursued an ambitious agenda of expansionism and modernization. Muhammed Ali sponsored many changes in Egyptian society in imitation of Western patterns, including a new tax system and new kinds of schooling. He also destroyed the traditional Egyptian elite. The government encouraged agricultural production by sponsoring major irrigation projects and began to import elements of the industrial revolution from the West in the 1830s. English machinery and technicians were brought in to build textile factories, sugar refineries, paper mills, and weapons shops. Muhammed Ali clearly contemplated a sweeping reform program in which industrialization would play a central role in making Egypt a powerhouse in the Middle East and an equal to the European powers. Many of his plans worked well, but the industrialization effort failed. Egyptian factories could not in the main compete with European imports, and the initial experiments either failed or stagnated. More durable changes involved the encouragement to the production of cash crops like sugar and cotton, which the government required in order to earn tax revenues to support its armies and its industrial imports. Growing concentration on cash crops also enriched a new group of Egyptian landlords and merchants. But the shift actually formalized Egypt's dependent position in the world economy, as European businesses and governments increasingly interfered with the internal economy. The Egyptian reaction to the West's industrial revolution, even more than the Russian response, was to generate massive economic redefinition without industrialization, a strategy that locked peasants into landlord control and made a manufacturing transformation at best a remote prospect.

Spurred by the West's example and by Muhammed Ali, the Ottoman government itself set up some factories after 1839, importing equipment from Europe to manufacture textiles, paper, and guns. Coal and iron mining were encouraged. The government established a postal system in 1834, a telegraph system in 1855, and steamships and the beginning of railway construction from 1866 onward. These changes increased the role of European traders and investors in the Ottoman economy and produced no overall industrial revolution. Again, the clearest result of improved transport and communication was a growing emphasis on the export of cash crops and minerals to pay for necessary manufactured imports from Europe. An industrial example had been set, and, as in Egypt, a growing though still tiny minority of Middle Easterners gained some factory experience, but no fundamental transformation occurred. . . .

Developments of preliminary industrial trappings — a few factories, a few railroads — nowhere outside Europe converted whole economies to an industrialization process until late in the nineteenth century, though they provided some relevant experience on which later (mainly after 1870) and more intensive efforts could build. A few workers became factory hands and experienced some of the same upheaval as their Western counterparts in terms of new routines and pressures on work pace. Many sought to limit their factory experience, leaving for other work or for the countryside after a short time; transience was a problem for much the same reasons as in the West: the clash with traditional work and leisure values. Some technical and business expertise also developed. Governments took the lead in most attempts to imitate the West, which was another portent for the future; with some exceptions, local merchant groups had neither the capital nor the motivation to undertake such ambitious and uncertain projects. By the 1850s a number of governments were clearly beginning to realize that some policy response to the industrial revolution was absolutely essential, lest Western influence become still more overwhelming. On balance, however, the principal results of very limited imitation tended to heighten the economic imbalance with western Europe, a disparity that made it easier to focus on nonindustrial exports. This too was a heritage for the future. . . .

6

MARY ANTIN
The Promised Land, 1894/1912

The industrial revolution moved huge capital fortunes and millions of laborers across continents and oceans to places where they could be combined to further new and ever larger capitalist and industrial ventures. Not everyone, however, became a major capitalist or industrial worker. Some like Mary Antin's father played barely supporting roles in the new infrastructure.

Source: Mary Antin, *The Promised Land* (Houghton Mifflin, 1912; Penguin Classics, 1997), 146–49, 153–57.

Mary Antin (1881–1949) grew up in a Jewish family in Polotzk, Russia (now in Bellarus). In 1891 her father sailed to America, three years later calling the rest of the family (Mary, her siblings, and their mother) to join him in Boston. This selection from Antin's memoir contains part of her account of that first year in the United States, initially in Boston and then nearby in Crescent Beach and Chelsea. How did the lives of the Antins change from Polotzk to their first year in the United States? How did they view that change? What connection do you see between immigration and nationalism?

THINKING HISTORICALLY

This selection has numerous references to the material world, capitalism, and the products of the industrial revolution. What are these references? In what ways were their lives in the United States more or less material, capitalist, or industrial than they were in Polotzk?

In our days of affluence in Russia we had been accustomed to upholstered parlors, embroidered linen, silver spoons and candlesticks, goblets of gold, kitchen shelves shining with copper and brass. We had featherbeds heaped halfway to the ceiling; we had clothes presses dusky with velvet and silk and fine woollen. The three small rooms into which my father now ushered us, up one flight of stairs, contained only the necessary beds, with lean mattresses; a few wooden chairs; a table or two; a mysterious iron structure, which later turned out to be a stove; a couple of unornamental kerosene lamps; and a scanty array of cooking-utensils and crockery. And yet we were all impressed with our new home and its furniture. It was not only because we had just passed through our seven lean years, cooking in earthen vessels, eating black bread on holidays and wearing cotton; it was chiefly because these wooden chairs and tin pans were American chairs and pans that they shone glorious in our eyes. And if there was anything lacking for comfort or decoration we expected it to be presently supplied—at least, we children did. Perhaps my mother alone, of us newcomers, appreciated the shabbiness of the little apartment, and realized that for her there was as yet no laying down of the burden of poverty.

Our initiation into American ways began with the first step on the new soil. My father found occasion to instruct or correct us even on the way from the pier to Wall Street, which journey we made crowded together in a rickety cab. He told us not to lean out of the windows, not to point, and explained the word "greenhorn." We did not want to be "greenhorns," and gave the strictest attention to my father's instructions. I do not know when my parents found opportunity to review together the history of Polotzk in the three years past, for we children had no patience with the subject; my mother's narrative was constantly interrupted by irrelevant questions, interjections, and explanations.

The first meal was an object lesson of much variety. My father produced several kinds of food, ready to eat, without any cooking, from little tin cans that had printing all over them. He attempted to introduce us to a queer, slippery kind of fruit, which he called "banana," but had to give it up for the time being. After the meal, he had better luck with a curious piece of furniture on runners, which he called "rocking-chair." There were five of us newcomers, and we found five different ways of getting into the American machine of perpetual motion, and as many ways of getting out of it. One born and bred to the use of a rocking-chair cannot imagine how ludicrous people can make themselves when attempting to use it for the first time. We laughed immoderately over our various experiments with the novelty, which was a wholesome way of letting off steam after the unusual excitement of the day.

In our flat we did not think of such a thing as storing the coal in the bathtub. There was no bathtub. So in the evening of the first day my father conducted us to the public baths. As we moved along in a little procession, I was delighted with the illumination of the streets. So many lamps, and they burned until morning, my father said, and so people did not need to carry lanterns. In America, then, everything was free, as we had heard in Russia. Light was free; the streets were as bright as a synagogue on a holy day. Music was free; we had been serenaded, to our gaping delight, by a brass band of many pieces, soon after our installation on Union Place.

Education was free. That subject my father had written about repeatedly, as comprising his chief hope for us children, the essence of American opportunity, the treasure that no thief could touch, not even misfortune or poverty. It was the one thing that he was able to promise us when he sent for us; surer, safer than bread or shelter. On our second day I was thrilled with the realization of what this freedom of education meant. A little girl from across the alley came and offered to conduct us to school. My father was out, but we five between us had a few words of English by this time. We knew the word school. We understood. This child, who had never seen us till yesterday, who could not pronounce our names, who was not much better dressed than we, was able to offer us the freedom of the schools of Boston! No application made, no questions asked, no examinations, rulings, exclusions; no machinations, no fees. The doors stood open for every one of us. The smallest child could show us the way.

This incident impressed me more than anything I had heard in advance of the freedom of education in America. It was a concrete proof—almost the thing itself. One had to experience it to understand it.

It was a great disappointment to be told by my father that we were not to enter upon our school career at once. It was too near the end of the term, he said, and we were going to move to Crescent Beach in a week or so. We had to wait until the opening of the schools in September. What a loss of precious time—from May till September!

Not that the time was really lost. Even the interval on Union Place was crowded with lessons and experiences. We had to visit the stores and be dressed from head to foot in American clothing; we had to learn the mysteries of the iron stove, the washboard, and the speaking-tube; we had to learn to trade with the fruit peddler through the window, and not to be afraid of the policeman; and, above all, we had to learn English. . . .

I am forgetting the more serious business which had brought us to Crescent Beach. While we children disported ourselves like mermaids and mermen in the surf, our respective fathers dispensed cold lemonade, hot peanuts, and pink popcorn, and piled up our respective fortunes, nickel by nickel, penny by penny. I was very proud of my connection with the public life of the beach. I admired greatly our shining soda fountain, the rows of sparkling glasses, the pyramids of oranges, the sausage chains, the neat white counter, and the bright array of tin spoons. It seemed to me that none of the other refreshment stands on the beach—there were a few—were half so attractive as ours. I thought my father looked very well in a long white apron and shirt sleeves. He dished out ice cream with enthusiasm, so I supposed he was getting rich. It never occurred to me to compare his present occupation with the position for which he had been originally destined; or if I thought about it, I was just as well content, for by this time I had by heart my father's saying, "America is not Polotzk." All occupations were respectable, all men were equal, in America.

If I admired the soda fountain and the sausage chains, I almost worshipped the partner, Mr. Wilner. I was content to stand for an hour at a time watching him make potato chips. In his cook's cap and apron, with a ladle in his hand and a smile on his face, he moved about with the greatest agility, whisking his raw materials out of nowhere, dipping into his bubbling kettle with a flourish, and bringing forth the finished product with a caper. Such potato chips were not to be had anywhere else on Crescent Beach. Thin as tissue paper, crisp as dry snow, and salt as the sea—such thirst-producing, lemonade-selling, nickel-bringing potato chips only Mr. Wilner could make. On holidays, when dozens of family parties came out by every train from town, he could hardly keep up with the demand for his potato chips. And with a waiting crowd around him our partner was at his best. He was as voluble as he was skilful, and as witty as he was voluble; at least so I guessed from the laughter that frequently drowned his voice. I could not understand his jokes, but if I could get near enough to watch his lips and his smile and his merry eyes, I was happy. That any one could talk so fast, and in English, was marvel enough, but that this prodigy should belong to *our* establishment was a fact to thrill me. I had never seen anything like Mr. Wilner, except a wedding jester; but then he spoke common Yiddish. So proud was I of the talent and good taste displayed at our stand that if my father beckoned to me in the crowd and sent me on an errand, I hoped the people noticed that I, too, was connected with the establishment.

And all this splendor and glory and distinction came to a sudden end. There was some trouble about a license—some fee or fine—there was a storm in the night that damaged the soda fountain and other fixtures—there was talk and consultation between the houses of Antin and Wilner—and the promising partnership was dissolved. No more would the merry partner gather the crowd on the beach; no more would the twelve young Wilners gambol like mermen and mermaids in the surf. And the less numerous tribe of Antin must also say farewell to the jolly seaside life, for men in such humble business as my father's carry their families, along with their other earthly goods, wherever they go, after the manner of the gypsies. We had driven a feeble stake into the sand. The jealous Atlantic, in conspiracy with the Sunday law, had torn it out. We must seek our luck elsewhere.

In Polotzk we had supposed that "America" was practically synonymous with "Boston." When we landed in Boston, the horizon was pushed back, and we annexed Crescent Beach. And now, espying other lands of promise, we took possession of the province of Chelsea, in the name of our necessity.

In Chelsea, as in Boston, we made our stand in the wrong end of the town. Arlington Street was inhabited by poor Jews, poor Negroes, and a sprinkling of poor Irish. The side streets leading from it were occupied by more poor Jews and Negroes. It was a proper locality for a man without capital to do business. My father rented a tenement with a store in the basement. He put in a few barrels of flour and of sugar, a few boxes of crackers, a few gallons of kerosene, an assortment of soap of the "save the coupon" brands; in the cellar, a few barrels of potatoes, and a pyramid of kindling-wood; in the showcase, an alluring display of penny candy. He put out his sign, with a gilt-lettered warning of "Strictly Cash," and proceeded to give credit indiscriminately. That was the regular way to do business on Arlington Street. My father, in his three years' apprenticeship, had learned the tricks of many trades. He knew when and how to "bluff." The legend of "Strictly Cash" was a protection against notoriously irresponsible customers; while none of the "good" customers, who had a record for paying regularly on Saturday, hesitated to enter the store with empty purses.

If my father knew the tricks of the trade, my mother could be counted on to throw all her talent and tact into the business. Of course she had no English yet, but as she could perform the acts of weighing, measuring, and mental computation of fractions mechanically, she was able to give her whole attention to the dark mysteries of the language, as intercourse with her customers gave her opportunity. In this she made such rapid progress that she soon lost all sense of disadvantage, and conducted herself behind the counter very much as if she were back in her old store in Polotzk. It was far more cosey than Polotzk — at least, so it seemed to me; for behind the store was the kitchen, where, in the intervals of slack trade, she did her cooking and washing. Arlington Street customers were used to waiting while the storekeeper salted the soup or rescued a loaf from the oven.

Once more Fortune favored my family with a thin little smile, and my father, in reply to a friendly inquiry, would say, "One makes a living," with a shrug of the shoulders that added "but nothing to boast of." It was characteristic of my attitude toward bread-and-butter matters that this contented me, and I felt free to devote myself to the conquest of my new world. Looking back to those critical first years, I see myself always behaving like a child let loose in a garden to play and dig and chase the butterflies. Occasionally, indeed, I was stung by the wasp of family trouble; but I knew a healing ointment — my faith in America. My father had come to America to make a living. America, which was free and fair and kind, must presently yield him what he sought. I had come to America to see a new world, and I followed my own ends with the utmost assiduity, only, as I ran out to explore, I would look back to see if my house were in order behind me — if my family still kept its head above water.

In after years, when I passed as an American among Americans, if I was suddenly made aware of the past that lay forgotten, — if a letter from Russia, or a paragraph in the newspaper, or a conversation overheard in the street-car, suddenly reminded me of what I might have been, — I thought it miracle enough that I, Mashke, the granddaughter of Raphael the Russian, born to a humble destiny, should be at home in an American metropolis, be free to fashion my own life, and should dream my dreams in English phrases. But in the beginning my admiration was spent on more concrete embodiments of the splendors of America; such as fine houses, gay shops, electric engines and apparatus, public buildings, illuminations, and parades. My early letters to my Russian friends were filled with boastful descriptions of these glories of my new country. No native citizen of Chelsea took such pride and delight in its institutions as I did. It required no fife and drum corps, no Fourth of July procession, to set me tingling with patriotism. Even the common agents and instruments of municipal life, such as the letter carrier and the fire engine, I regarded with a measure of respect. I know what I thought of people who said that Chelsea was a very small, dull, unaspiring town, with no discernible excuse for a separate name or existence.

The apex of my civic pride and personal contentment was reached on the bright September morning when I entered the public school. That day I must always remember, even if I live to be so old that I cannot tell my name. To most people their first day at school is a memorable occasion. In my case the importance of the day was a hundred times magnified, on account of the years I had waited, the road I had come, and the conscious ambitions I entertained.

I am wearily aware that I am speaking in extreme figures, in superlatives. I wish I knew some other way to render the mental life of the immigrant child of reasoning age. I may have been ever so much an exception in acuteness of observation, powers of comparison, and abnormal self-consciousness; none the less were my thoughts and conduct typical of the attitude of the intelligent immigrant child toward American institutions. And what the child thinks and feels is a reflection of the hopes, desires, and purposes of the parents who brought him overseas, no matter how precocious and independent the child may be. Your immigrant inspectors will tell you what poverty the foreigner brings in his baggage, what want in his pockets. Let the overgrown boy of twelve, reverently drawing his letters in the baby class, testify to the noble dreams and high ideals that may be hidden beneath the greasy caftan of the immigrant. Speaking for the Jews, at least, I know I am safe in inviting such an investigation.

7

Italians in Two Worlds: An Immigrant's Letters from Argentina, 1901

One of the distinctive features of the capitalist industrial revolution was the globalization of capital and labor. The capital for the British industrial revolution, beginning toward the end of the eighteenth century, filtered in from the treasures of the Indies — East and West — and owed much to the labor of slaves and legally free workers who were shipped from one end of the world to the other. By the

Source: *One Family, Two Worlds: An Italian Family's Correspondence across the Atlantic*, ed. Samuel L. Baily and Franco Ramella, trans. John Lenaghan (New Brunswick: Rutgers University Press, 1988), 34–42.

second half of the nineteenth century, the owners of farms, factories, mines, and railroads called for many more laborers.

Millions of these workers came from Italy alone. From 1860 to 1885, most traveled from northern Italy to South America, mainly Argentina. Between 1890 and 1915, Italian immigration to Argentina continued, but even more came from southern Italy to the United States. By the beginning of the twentieth century, New York City and Buenos Aires each had larger Italian populations than many Italian cities.

This selection contains the first few letters sent back home by one of those Italian immigrants, Oreste Sola, who arrived in Buenos Aires in 1901 from northern Italy. What do these letters tell you about this immigrant's expectations? What sort of work did he do? How did he manage to navigate his new world? What were his challenges? How would you describe his strengths? Based on the few hints of events in Italy, how was his life in Argentina different from what it would have likely been in Italy?

THINKING HISTORICALLY

What signs do you see in these letters of industrialization in Argentina? What signs do you see of a capitalist economic system? How is the life of Oreste shaped by the needs of capitalists? How is it shaped by a capitalist economic system? How is his life shaped by industrialization?

Letter 1

Buenos Ayres, 17 August 1901

Dearest parents,

I have been here since the 5th of this month; I am in the best of health as are my two companions. As soon as we got here, we went to the address of Godfather Zocco, who then introduced us to several people from Valdengo who have been in America for some years and all are doing well more or less. The language here is Castilian, quite similar to Spanish, but you don't hear anyone speaking it. Wherever you go, whether in the hotel or at work, everyone speaks either Piedmontese or Italian, even those from other countries, and the Argentines themselves speak Italian.[1]

---

[1] He does not speak or understand Spanish and therefore does not realize that Spanish and Castilian are the same thing. Although 25 percent of the total population and an even higher percentage of the adult population of Buenos Aires was Italian-born, and therefore the Italian language was indeed spoken in many places, Oreste obviously exaggerates when he claims that everyone speaks it.

This city is very beautiful. There is an enormous amount of luxury. All the streets—they call them *calle* [sic] here—are paved either with hard wood or in cement as smooth as marble, even too smooth since the horses, tram horses as well as carriage horses, which run here, keep slipping constantly. It is not unusual to see twenty or more of them fall in one day. . . .

The piazza Victoria (Plaza de Mayo) is also beautiful, where all around on two sides there are only banks. They are of all nations: English, French, Italian, Spanish, North American, etc., etc. On another side is the government building where the president of the Argentine Republic resides. He is Italian, Rocca by name, the third Italian president in a row who sits on the Argentine throne.[2] There is also the railway station of the south, which is something colossal. With workshops, offices, and the station itself it will cover one million square meters. Now they are at work on a government building for the Congress (Parliament). The architect was an Italian, as is the chief contractor, who is supervising all the work. It is a job which in the end will cost more than 700 million lire. It will occupy an area of a block which is 10,000 square meters and will be surrounded by a square, which, along with the building, will constitute an area of about 100,000 square meters. This work will be better than the first [the railway station], but perhaps I shall not be able to see it finished.

All of this is inside the city, but if you should go outside for a few hours, it's worse than a desert. You only find houses made solely out of mortar, with only a ground floor and a door you have to enter on all fours. Outside you don't see a plant; everything is desert. The plains stretch as far as the eye can see; it takes hours on the train before you come to the mountains. There are a few tracts of land, sort of green, where they may let a few horses loose to graze. Here they let the animals go out no matter what the weather might be. Here you can't find a rock, though you pay its weight in gold for it. All the ground is black like manure, thick and muddy. When it doesn't rain, it gets hard, and if you try to dig, it shoots out as if it were rock.

The food here is pretty good, but it doesn't have much flavor. This is true for all Argentina.

All the guys here are jolly as crazy men. In the evening when we get together before going to bed we split our sides laughing. They would all like to go back to Italy, but they don't ever budge. Perhaps I will do

---

[2] Oreste is in error here. The president to whom he refers, Julio Roca, was Argentine not Italian. The preceding president, José Uriburu, also was not Italian. However, Carlos Pelligrini, president from 1890 to 1892, was the son of a French-Italian father from Savoy.

the same. Here we eat, drink, and laugh and enjoy ourselves; we are in America. . . .

Take one last loving kiss and hug
from your always loving son,
Oreste

Letter 2

Mendoza, 18 September 1901

Dearest parents,

I am still in good spirits and happy that I am in America. I am now at Mendoza instead of Buenos Ayres. I didn't like Buenos Ayres too much because you don't get good wine there; and then every day the temperature changes twenty times, and I was always chilly. Otherwise it was fine.

One day I got the idea, knowing that Secondino's brother-in-law and sister were in Mendoza. Since the boss advanced me the money for the trip,[3] I made up my mind to come here, where you see nothing but hills and mountains in the distance, like at home. You drink very well here; the wine costs half what it does in Buenos Ayres and is pure and delicious. I am living here with Carlo and his wife and a man by the name of Luigi Ferraro from Chiavazza, who has been here for seven years traveling around in America. There are few people here from Biella, but there is no shortage of Italians. I still haven't learned a word of Castilian because, everywhere you go, they speak Italian or Piedmontese.

I am better off here than in Buenos Ayres. I am only sorry to be so far from my friends—they didn't want to come—and from Godfather and the rest.

This city is ugly; it never rains even though it is close to the mountains. I have written a friend to send me the address of my schoolmate Berretta, and I might just go and see him in Peru; it takes four days or more on the train. From Buenos Ayres to Mendoza takes two nights and a day on the railroad without ever changing trains or getting off. The longest stop is a half hour. In the entire journey you don't see a plant. [There are] two or three rivers about 400 meters wide. They are all in the plain, so calm that you can't tell which way the water is going, and yet they flow on in an imperceptible way.

---

[3] The government of the province of Mendoza and many individual employers made a major effort to attract European immigrants during the two decades preceding World War I. It was not unusual for an employer to advance money to pay for the trip from Buenos Aires to Mendoza.

Throughout the journey one meets only horses, cows, and goats, none of which have stables. On the rail line you don't see a house for three hours or more, and everything is like that. . . .

Everyone, Carlo, Cichina, and Luigi, give their regards to you. Tell Secondino to come and see America, to drink and eat and travel.

Time is pressing since I have to work every evening until ten. I work at home after work.

You should write me at:

El Taller del Ferro Carril G.O.A.
Mendoza

Goodbye everybody. Kisses to Abele and Narcisa. Tell Abele to study hard and to learn to work. Send him to the technical schools; I imagine he has been promoted. Goodbye, Mom and Dad. Be in good spirits as I am.

Yours always,
Orestes

Letter 3

Mendoza, 13 November 1901

Dearest Father, Mother, brother, and sister,

This morning Secondino arrived as you had already indicated he would in your letter of 14 October. He had a very good trip, and he made everyone happy to see him healthy and cheerful—as we are, Carlo, Cichina, and Luigi. He gave me the trousers which you gave him to bring me and the letter written by Dad and Narcisa.

I have been here in Mendoza for about three months, and I am happy that Secondino is here now too. But I don't plan to stay fixed here. I would like to go to Peru with Berretta or to Cuba, where dear Cousin Edvino is staying, since I know that those who are there are doing well now. It wouldn't be bad here except you aren't sure about employment or about anything, especially for the type of work I do. So you can't even be sure of staying in one place. Before leaving I am waiting to get the address of Berretta.

I thought that I could send something, instead I had to make some purchases. Be patient. I think of our family conditions too often to be able to think of anything else. Excuse me if I have been slow in writing. It's because I hoped to get a particular job, and I wanted to let you know. I was waiting for the decision of the company. The job went to another, also Italian, with whom nobody could compete. But let's leave the subject of work because here there are so many professions and so many trades that you can't say what you are doing. Today it's this and tomorrow it's that. I tried to go into the construction business for myself, but it didn't work out. So much effort and expense. Now I am doing something else, and I shall change again soon.

My friends as well as Godfather are still in Buenos Aires. They are fine and want to be remembered to you. I receive news (from Buenos Aires) almost every week.

Pardon me, dear parents, brother, and sister, if I am sometimes slow in writing. It is not that I forget, quite the contrary. Only please don't reproach me the way Narcisa does because, if you knew how painful these reproaches are to us here, especially when they come from the family, you would not believe it. I shall try to write more often.

Narcisa asks me for postcards, Abele for stamps. I cannot satisfy anyone since they don't sell illustrated postcards here even though there would be many beautiful things [to show], like, for example, the ruins of Mendoza of 1860 caused by the earthquake, which often happens here six or seven times a year.[4] If it is a special earthquake, you seem to be in a boat, rocking like at sea. But if it gets a bit strong, you have to lie down so as not to fall. Some attribute it to the various volcanoes, mostly extinct however, which are in the mountains here. Others say it is because of the huge storms of the Pacific meeting the winds that come from the Atlantic. However, no one can verify it.

From what I make out from Dad's letter, he says that he was planning to send me some clothes when I get established here. Excuse me, dear parents, your sacrifices are already excessive. Now it is my job to pay them back at least in part, and I shall do everything possible to that end. But excuse me, I am old enough now to earn my bread. I beg you not to be offended about this. If later I shall be in a position to, I shall send you money and everything. But for now, first of all, I have clothes to wear. I have already purchased here two suits and four pairs of trousers. So don't be upset then. Rather, I repeat, as soon as I am able, I'll see that you get something. Now I cannot; it has gone badly for me before I got started. When I shall again be the way I was in the beginning—but I don't know when because here [in] America [things] can change from one day to the next—you will have some repayment.

I have received your newspapers and bulletins, letters and all, because the telegraph and postal service here is something very precise. I was very pleased to get them. I read also in the bulletin of the professional school that they are asking for the address of members who are living outside the country. If I should send it and then, before publication, I should move, I would be in the same situation I was before. Also they want you to indicate the kind of work you are doing for publication in the bulletin because it will be, I believe, an issue with all the graduates of the professional school, and I can't tell them that. I change from one day to

---

[4] The earthquake to which he refers occurred on March 20, 1861. It destroyed the entire city of Mendoza and killed much of its population.

the next. At that moment I was a draftsman second grade in the workshop of the Trans Andes railway. It is a direct railway to Chile now under construction. But I am not doing it anymore because the section that the four of us were assigned to work on has been finished.

Now I am working as a smith and various things for the Great Western Railway of Argentina. But since they don't pay me as I want and I have to be first a blacksmith, then work as a planer, then at the lathe, I don't like it. At the first other job that comes along, I'm off. When I find something better, I don't want to work as a laborer for low wages anymore. . . .

Your most loving son and
brother,
Oreste Sola

Letter 4

Mendoza, 25 November 1901

Dearest ones,

A few days before this letter you will have received another written on the day of Secondino's arrival; a few days later he received some newspapers which indicated that you were on strike.[5] I understand that in this season such a big strike will be very distressing. I, however, right now absolutely cannot, for the moment, help you in any way. If I had been able to get that damned construction job, I assure you I would have "hit the jackpot." From one day to the next another bit of bad luck could come my way; but everything is in doubt, there is then no certainty nor prospect.

Now they are coming here every day on the emigration train, about 600 persons a week. They are then sent out of the city in great numbers; but many remain, and we are beginning to see some unemployment but only in a small way. It's just that working in such conditions you only earn a bare living and with difficulty at that. If I have bad luck, I'm not staying here any longer. I want to go to Cuba with Boffa and the rest since Berretta doesn't answer. Nothing is certain however. The ideas come in crowds, but the execution is just miserable. Still I am not losing heart ever. I have been through a good period at first, then an excellent one, and now I am in a third one that is very tough. But I'll get back on my feet. We are in America.

Be patient then. I too am aware that Mom is working at night, that you are working on Sundays, etc. — things that don't happen here. Here

---

[5] Oreste is referring to the major strike at the Biella textile factory in which [his parents] Luigi and Margherita worked. The strike, which ended in defeat for the workers, was provoked when the owners increased the work load without increasing salaries.

in every profession and everywhere you work nine hours a day and only 'til noon on Saturday. You don't work on Sunday nor after midday meal on Saturday, and you get more respect. When you ask for some improvement in pay, the owners don't say that they will show up with a rifle and fire at the first one who makes trouble, as the famous Giovanni Rivetti used to say.[6] Here, if they don't want to give it to you, they look into it, they review it; but generally they give it to you, and all this without unions or anything. They are capitalists who are more aware; that's all there is to it.

Think always of your loving son who is in America, always in good spirits, even when things are going badly for him.

Oreste Sola

Secondino, like me, is always in good spirits, and we are always together. He sends you his warmest greetings and so does Carlo's family. Secondino would like you to say hello to his wife if it is not too much trouble.

[6] Giovanni Rivetti was one of the owners of the Biella textile factory in which Luigi and Margherita worked. Given the size and importance of the factory, Rivetti's conduct greatly influenced that of the other owners in the entire area.

■ REFLECTIONS

> It was because of certain traits in private capitalism that the machine—which was a neutral agent—has often seemed, and in fact has sometimes been, a malicious element in society, careless of human life, indifferent to human interests. The machine has suffered for the sins of capitalism; contrariwise, capitalism has often taken credit for the virtues of the machine.[1]

Our chapter turns the above proposition by writer Lewis Mumford into a series of questions: What has been the impact of capitalism? Is the machine only neutral, or does it have its own effects? How can we distinguish between the economic and the technological chains of cause and effect?

Capitalism and industrialization are difficult concepts to distinguish. Adam Smith illustrated the power of the market and the division of labor by imagining their impact not on a shop or trading firm but on a pin factory, an early industrial enterprise. Karl Marx summarized the achievements of the capitalist age by enumerating "wonders far surpassing Egyptian pyramids," which included chemical industries, steam navigation, railroads, and electric telegraphs. Neither Smith nor

[1] Lewis Mumford, *Technics and Civilization* (New York: Harcourt Brace, 1963), 27.

Marx used the terms *capitalism* or *industrial revolution,* although such variants as *capitalist* and *industrial* were already in circulation. Modern historians fought over their meaning and relevance as explanations of change through most of the last century. To understand the great transformation into modernity, some emphasized the expansion of market capitalism; others emphasized the power of the machine. The rise of state-capitalist and communist industrial societies politicized the debate, but even after the fall of communism, the historical questions remained. Peter Stearns looks for the forces that spread or retarded industrialization. The letters of Oreste Sola support the argument of some historians of Latin America that the continent was modernized more by trade and capital than by industrialization.

After 1900 the industrial revolution spread throughout the world, but its pace was not always revolutionary. Even today some societies are still largely rural, with a majority of workers engaged in subsistence farming or small-scale manufacturing by hand. But over the long course of history people have always tried to replace human labor with machines and increase the production of machine-made goods. In some cases, the transformation has been dramatic. Malaysia, once a languid land of tropical tea and rubber plantations, sprouted enough microchip and electronics factories after 1950 to account for 60 percent of its exports by the year 2000. By the 1990s an already highly industrialized country like Japan could produce luxury cars in factories that needed only a handful of humans to monitor the work of computer-driven robots. Despite occasional announcements of the arrival of a "postindustrial" society, the pressure to mechanize continues unabated in the twenty-first century.

The fate of capitalism in the twentieth century was more varied. The second wave of industrial revolutions—beginning with Germany after 1850 and Japan after 1880—was directed by governments as much as capitalists. Socialist parties won large support in industrial countries in the first half of the twentieth century, creating welfare states in some after World War II. In Russia after 1917, the Communist Party pioneered a model of state-controlled industrialization that attracted imitators from China to Chile and funded anticapitalist movements throughout the world.

The Cold War (1947–1991) between the United States and the Soviet Union, though largely a power struggle between two superpowers, was widely seen as an ideological contest between capitalism and socialism. Thus the demise of the Soviet Union and its Communist Party in 1991 was heralded as the victory of capitalism over socialism. As Russia, China, and other previously communist states embraced market economies, socialism was declared dead.

But could proclaiming the death of socialism be as premature as heralding the end of industrial society? *The Communist Manifesto* of 1848 long predates the Russian Revolution of 1917. Karl Marx died in

1883. Socialists like Rosa Luxembourg criticized Lenin and the Russian communists for misinterpreting Marxism in their impatience to transform Russian society. Socialists, even Marxists, continue to write, advise, and govern today, often urging restraints on the spread of global capital markets and the threat of unregulated capitalism for the global environment. Rarely are they willing to relinquish the advantages of industrial technology; rather, they seek to release the "virtues of the machine."

22

Colonized and Colonizers

Europeans in Africa and Asia, 1850–1930

■ HISTORICAL CONTEXT

The first stage of European colonialism, beginning with Columbus, was a period in which Europeans—led by the Spanish and Portuguese—settled in the Western Hemisphere and created plantations with African labor. From 1492 to 1776, European settlement in Asia was limited to a few coastal port cities where merchants and missionaries operated. The second stage—the years between 1776, when Britain lost most of its American colonies, and 1880, when the European scramble for African territory began—has sometimes been called a period of *free-trade imperialism*. This term refers to the desire by European countries in general and by Britain in particular to expand their zones of free trade. It also refers to a widespread opposition to the expense of colonization, a conviction held especially among the British, who garnered all of the advantages of political empire without the costs of occupation and outright ownership.

The British used to quip that their second global empire was created in the nineteenth century "in a fit of absentmindedness." But colonial policy in Britain and the rest of Europe was more planned and continuous than that comment might suggest. British control of India (including Burma) increased throughout the nineteenth century, as did British control of South Africa, Australia, the Pacific, and parts of the Americas. At the same time, France, having lost most of India to the British, began building an empire that included parts of North Africa, Southeast Asia, and the Pacific.

Thus, a third stage of colonialism, beginning in the mid-nineteenth century, reached a fever pitch with the partition of Africa after 1880. The period between 1888 and 1914 spawned renewed settlement and massive population transfers, with most European migrants settling in the older colonies of the Americas (as well as in South Africa and Australia), where indigenous populations had been reduced. Even where settlement remained light, however, Europeans took political control of large areas of the Earth's surface (see Map 22.1).

■ THINKING HISTORICALLY

Using Literature in History

This chapter also explores how literature can be used in the quest to better understand history. We examine a number of fictional accounts of colonialism, some written by the colonizers, others by the colonized or their descendants, in addition to a critical study of a historical novel and a poem. How do these pieces of literature add to, or detract from, a historical understanding of colonialism? We explore this question because the European colonial experience produced a rich, evocative literature, which, used carefully, can offer a wide range of detail and insight about the period and colonialism.

Historical novels are particularly tricky. The structure of a novel bears certain similarities to history—a description of a place, proper names and biographies, descriptions of human interactions, an accounting of change, and a story. There are also structural differences in a novel—a lot of dialogue, greater attention to physical appearance and character, and a more prominent narrative. These fictional elements are often unattainable for historians. Dialogue, a person's actual words, especially thoughts, are often absent from the historical sources. A good novelist creates these elements based on historical research and familiarity with the time and place. Such details provide a great sense of verisimilitude (resemblance to reality). We feel as if we are there, a feeling that further reinforces our sense of the novel's truth. But in this regard we are captives of the novelist, caught in the web of his or her imagination. In good hands we may see what would otherwise be invisible. In bad hands, we may vividly see what was never there.

A good novel, like a good history, shows us something we did not know, something unexpected, even surprising. But the problem is that we are most easily seduced by what is most familiar to us. Thus, in the hands of the uninformed, we are most likely to believe we have seen the historical truth when we have only projected our own world onto the past. How successfully do the authors of these fictional pieces show you something about the past that is likely true?

Map 22.1 European Colonialism in Africa and Asia, 1880–1914.

GEORGE ORWELL

Burmese Days, 1934

George Orwell, the pen name of Eric Arthur Blair (1903–1950), is best known for such novels as *Animal Farm* (1945) and *Nineteen Eighty-Four* (1949), from which the term *Orwellian* has come to define totalitarianism. *Burmese Days* (1934) was Orwell's first novel, based on his experience in the British police in Burma from 1922 to 1927.

This selection from the novel captures the life of the British colonial class in a remote "upcountry" town in Burma in the 1920s, a hundred years after British conquest and settlement had begun and fifty years after all of Burma had been integrated into the British Indian empire.

The central character is Flory, the only Englishman at all sympathetic to the Burmese. Though he has befriended the Indian physician, Dr. Veraswami, Flory is too weak to propose him as the first "native" member of the club. The other main characters are Westfield, district superintendent of police; Ellis, local company manager and the most racist of the group; Lackersteen, local manager of a timber company who is usually drunk; Maxwell, a forest officer; and Macgregor, deputy commissioner and secretary of the club.

Why does the club loom so large in the lives of these Englishmen? If they complain so much, why are they in Burma? How do you account for the virulent racism of these men? Why does Ellis "correct" the butler's English? What does this story suggest about women in the colonial world?

THINKING HISTORICALLY

Orwell knew Burma quite well. He was born in India in 1903, and his father worked in the Opium Department of the Indian Civil Service. After attending school at Eton in England, Orwell spent five years as a member of the Indian Imperial Police in Burma. Orwell's mother had grown up in Burma, and his grandmother continued to live there in the 1920s. In his various postings, Orwell no doubt spent time in British social clubs like the one that serves as the setting for this chapter. Orwell, therefore, had a broad knowledge of Burma on which to base his story. Is there any way to determine what Orwell invented and what he merely described in this account?

Orwell was politically engaged throughout his life. Would political ideas make him better or worse as a historian or novelist? How so?

Source: George Orwell, *Burmese Days* (1934; reprint, San Diego: Harcourt Brace, 1962), 17–27.

Flory's house was at the top of the maidan,[1] close to the edge of the jungle. From the gate the maidan sloped sharply down, scorched and khaki-coloured, with half a dozen dazzling white bungalows scattered round it. All quaked, shivered in the hot air. There was an English cemetery within a white wall half-way down the hill, and nearby a tiny tin-roofed church. Beyond that was the European Club, and when one looked at the Club — a dumpy one-storey wooden building — one looked at the real centre of the town. In any town in India the European Club is the spiritual citadel, the real seat of the British power, the Nirvana for which native officials and millionaires pine in vain. It was doubly so in this case, for it was the proud boast of Kyauktada Club that, almost alone of Clubs in Burma, it had never admitted an Oriental[2] to membership. Beyond the Club, the Irrawaddy flowed huge and ochreous, glittering like diamonds in the patches that caught the sun; and beyond the river stretched great wastes of paddy fields, ending at the horizon in a range of blackish hills.

The native town, and the courts and the jail, were over to the right, mostly hidden in green groves of peepul trees. The spire of the pagoda rose from the trees like a slender spear tipped with gold. Kyauktada[3] was a fairly typical Upper Burma town, that had not changed greatly between the days of Marco Polo and 1910, and might have slept in the Middle Ages for a century more if it had not proved a convenient spot for a railway terminus. In 1910 the Government[4] made it the headquarters of a district and a seat of Progress — interpretable as a block of law courts, with their army of fat but ravenous pleaders, a hospital, a school, and one of those huge, durable jails which the English have built everywhere between Gibraltar and Hong Kong. The population was about four thousand, including a couple of hundred Indians, a few score Chinese and seven Europeans. There were also two Eurasians named Mr. Francis and Mr. Samuel, the sons of an American Baptist missionary and a Roman Catholic missionary respectively. The town contained no curiosities of any kind, except an Indian fakir[5] who had lived for twenty years in a tree near the bazaar, drawing his food up in a basket every morning.

---

[1] Parade-ground. [Ed.]

[2] The term *Oriental* included all Asians or people of the "East" as opposed to Occidentals or Westerners, as in Rudyard Kipling's *Barrack-room Ballads*: "East is East and West is West, and never the twain [two] shall meet" (1892). But in this case, Orwell means Indians and Burmese as well as the few Chinese. [Ed.]

[3] Fictional name for Katha or Kathar, a town on the Irrawaddy (or Ayeyarwady) River and the railroad, in northern Burma, where Orwell lived from 1926–1927. [Ed.]

[4] The British government eliminated the Burmese monarchy, exiling the king to India, and abolished the traditional role of the Buddhist monks, imposing instead the kind of bureaucracy they used to rule India. [Ed.]

[5] Originally a term for a Muslim Sufi mystic, here used to mean any ascetic, Hindu or Muslim, or even a beggar. [Ed.]

Flory yawned as he came out of the gate. He had been half drunk the night before, and the glare made him feel liverish. "Bloody, bloody hole!" he thought, looking down the hill. And, no one except the dog being near, he began to sing aloud, "Bloody, bloody, bloody, oh, how thou art bloody" to the tune of "Holy, holy, holy, oh how Thou art holy," as he walked down the hot red road, switching at the dried-up grasses with his stick. It was nearly nine o'clock and the sun was fiercer every minute. The heat throbbed down on one's head with a steady, rhythmic thumping, like blows from an enormous bolster. Flory stopped at the Club gate, wondering whether to go in or to go farther down the road and see Dr. Veraswami. Then he remembered that it was "English mail day" and the newspapers would have arrived. He went in, past the big tennis screen, which was overgrown by a creeper with starlike mauve flowers.

In the borders beside the path swathes of English flowers, phlox and larkspur, hollyhock and petunia, not yet slain by the sun, rioted in vast size and richness. The petunias were huge, like trees almost. There was no lawn, but instead a shrubbery of native trees and bushes—gold mohur trees like vast umbrellas of blood-red bloom, frangipanis with creamy, stalkless flowers, purple bougainvillea, scarlet hibiscus, and the pink, Chinese rose, bilious-green crotons, feathery fronds of tamarind. The clash of colours hurt one's eyes in the glare. A nearly naked *mali*,[6] watering-can in hand, was moving in the jungle of flowers like some large nectar-sucking bird.

On the Club steps a sandy-haired Englishman, with a prickly mous-tache, pale grey eyes too far apart, and abnormally thin calves to his legs, was standing with his hands in the pockets of his shorts. This was Mr. Westfield, the District Superintendent of Police. With a very bored air he was rocking himself backwards and forwards on his heels and pouting his upper lip so that his moustache tickled his nose. He greeted Flory with a slight sideways movement of his head. His way of speaking was clipped and soldierly, missing out every word that well could be missed out. Nearly everything he said was intended for a joke, but the tone of his voice was hollow and melancholy.

"Hullo, Flory me lad. Bloody awful morning, what?"

"We must expect it at this time of year, I suppose," Flory said. He had turned himself a little sideways, so that his birthmarked cheek was away from Westfield.

"Yes, dammit. Couple of months of this coming. Last year we didn't have a spot of rain till June. Look at that bloody sky, not a cloud in it. Like one of those damned great blue enamel saucepans. God! What'd you give to be in Piccadilly now, eh?"

"Have the English papers come?"

[6] Gardener. [Ed.]

"Yes. Dear old *Punch, Pink'un,* and *Vie Parisienne.* Makes you home-sick to read 'em, what? Let's come in and have a drink before the ice all goes. Old Lackersteen's been fairly bathing in it. Half pickled already."

They went in, Westfield remarking in his gloomy voice, "Lead on, Macduff." Inside, the Club was a teak-walled place smelling of earthoil, and consisting of only four rooms, one of which contained a forlorn "library" of five hundred mildewed novels, and another an old and mangy billiard-table—this, however, seldom used, for during most of the year hordes of flying beetles came buzzing round the lamps and lit-tered themselves over the cloth. There were also a card-room and a "lounge" which looked towards the river, over a wide veranda; but at this time of day all the verandas were curtained with green bamboo chicks. The lounge was an unhomelike room, with coco-nut matting on the floor, and wicker chairs and tables which were littered with shiny illustrated papers. For ornament there were a number of "Bonzo" pictures,[7] and the dusty skulls of sambhur.[8] A punkah,[9] lazily flapping, shook dust into the tepid air.

There were three men in the room. Under the punkah a florid, fine-looking, slightly bloated man of forty was sprawling across the table with his head in his hands, groaning in pain. This was Mr. Lackersteen, the local manager of a timber firm. He had been badly drunk the night before, and he was suffering for it. Ellis, local manager of yet another company, was standing before the notice board studying some notice with a look of bitter concentration. He was a tiny wiry-haired fellow with a pale, sharp-featured face and restless movements. Maxwell, the acting Divisional Forest Officer, was lying in one of the long chairs read-ing the *Field,* and invisible except for two large-boned legs and thick downy forearms.

"Look at this naughty old man," said Westfield, taking Mr. Lackersteen half affectionately by the shoulders and shaking him. "Example to the young, what? There, but for the grace of God and all that. Gives you an idea what you'll be like at forty."

Mr. Lackersteen gave a groan which sounded like "brandy."

"Poor old chap," said Westfield; "regular martyr to booze, eh? Look at it oozing out of his pores. Reminds me of the old colonel who used to sleep without a mosquito net. They asked his servant why and the ser-vant said: 'At night, master too drunk to notice mosquitoes; in the morn-ing, mosquitoes too drunk to notice master.' Look at him—boozed last night and then asking for more. Got a little niece coming to stay with him, too. Due tonight, isn't she, Lackersteen?"

[7] Bulldog puppy cartoons created by G. E. Studdy in the 1920s for magazines like *Punch.* [Ed.]

[8] Large South Asian deer, like elk. [Ed.]

[9] Large cloth panel fan hanging from the ceiling, usually pulled by a rope to move the air. [Ed.]

"Oh, leave that drunken sot alone," said Ellis without turning round. He had a spiteful cockney voice. Mr. Lackersteen groaned again, "—the niece! Get me some brandy, for Christ's sake."

"Good education for the niece, eh? Seeing uncle under the table seven times a week.—Hey, butler! Bringing brandy for Lackersteen master!"

The butler, a dark, stout Dravidian[10] with liquid, yellow-irised eyes like those of a dog, brought the brandy on a brass tray. Flory and Westfield ordered gin. Mr. Lackersteen swallowed a few spoonfuls of brandy and sat back in his chair, groaning in a more resigned way. He had a beefy, ingenuous face, with a toothbrush moustache. He was really a very simple-minded man, with no ambitions beyond having what he called "a good time." His wife governed him by the only possible method, namely, by never letting him out of her sight for more than an hour or two. Only once, a year after they were married, she had left him for a fortnight, and had returned unexpectedly a day before her time, to find Mr. Lackersteen, drunk, supported on either side by a naked Burmese girl, while a third up-ended a whisky bottle into his mouth. Since then she had watched him, as he used to complain, "like a cat over a bloody mousehole." However, he managed to enjoy quite a number of "good times," though they were usually rather hurried ones.

"My Christ, what a head I've got on me this morning," he said. "Call that butler again, Westfield. I've got to have another brandy before my missus gets here. She says she's going to cut my booze down to four pegs a day when our niece gets here. God rot them both!" he added gloomily.

"Stop playing the fool, all of you, and listen to this," said Ellis sourly. He had a queer wounding way of speaking, hardly ever opening his mouth without insulting somebody. He deliberately exaggerated his cockney accent, because of the sardonic tone it gave to his words. "Have you seen this notice of old Macgregor's? A little nosegay for everyone. Maxwell, wake up and listen!"

Maxwell lowered the *Field*. He was a fresh-coloured blond youth of not more than twenty-five or six—very young for the post he held. With his heavy limbs and thick white eyelashes he reminded one of a carthorse colt. Ellis nipped the notice from the board with a neat, spiteful little movement and began reading it aloud. It had been posted by Mr. Macgregor, who, besides being Deputy Commissioner, was secretary of the Club.

"Just listen to this. 'It has been suggested that as there are as yet no Oriental members of this club, and as it is now usual to admit officials of gazetted rank, whether native or European, to membership of most European Clubs, we should consider the question of following this practice in Kyauktada. The matter will be open for discussion at the next

---

[10] Dated racial term used to refer to darker-skinned inhabitants of southern India. [Ed.]

general meeting. On the one hand it may be pointed out' — oh, well, no need to wade through the rest of it. He can't even write out a notice without an attack of literary diarrhoea. Anyway, the point's this. He's asking us to break all our rules and take a dear little nigger-boy into this Club. *Dear* Dr. Veraswami, for instance. Dr. Very-slimy, I call him. That *would* be a treat, wouldn't it? Little pot-bellied niggers breathing garlic in your face over the bridge-table. Christ, to think of it! We've got to hang together and put our foot down on this at once. What do you say, Westfield? Flory?"

Westfield shrugged his thin shoulders philosophically. He had sat down at the table and lighted a black, stinking Burma cheroot.

"Got to put up with it, I suppose," he said. "B_____s of natives are getting into all the Clubs nowadays. Even the Pegu Club, I'm told. Way this country's going, you know. We're about the last Club in Burma to hold out against 'em."

"We are; and what's more, we're damn well going to go on holding out. I'll die in the ditch before I'll see a nigger in here." Ellis had produced a stump of pencil. With the curious air of spite that some men can put into their tiniest action, he re-pinned the notice on the board and pencilled a tiny, neat "B. F." against Mr. Macgregor's signature — "There, that's what I think of his idea. I'll tell him so when he comes down. What do *you* say, Flory?"

Flory had not spoken all this time. Though by nature anything but a silent man, he seldom found much to say in Club conversations. He had sat down at the table and was reading G. K. Chesterton's article in the *London News*, at the same time caressing [his dog] Flo's head with his left hand. Ellis, however, was one of those people who constantly nag others to echo their own opinions. He repeated his question, and Flory looked up, and their eyes met. The skin round Ellis's nose suddenly turned so pale that it was almost grey. In him it was a sign of anger. Without any prelude he burst into a stream of abuse that would have been startling, if the others had not been used to hearing something like it every morning.

"My God, I should have thought in a case like this, when it's a question of keeping those black, stinking swine out of the only place where we can enjoy ourselves, you'd have the decency to back me up. Even if that pot-bellied, greasy little sod of a nigger doctor *is* your best pal. *I* don't care if you choose to pal up with the scum of the bazaar. If it pleases you to go to Veraswami's house and drink whisky with all his nigger pals, that's your look-out. Do what you like outside the Club. But, by God, it's a different matter when you talk of bringing niggers in here. I suppose you'd like little Veraswami for a Club member, eh? Chipping into our conversation and pawing everyone with his sweaty hands and breathing his filthy garlic breath in our faces. By God, he'd go out with my boot behind him if ever I saw his black snout inside that door. Greasy, pot-bellied little————!" etc.

This went on for several minutes. It was curiously impressive, because it was so completely sincere. Ellis really did hate Orientals—hated them with a bitter, restless loathing as of something evil or unclean. Living and working, as the assistant of a timber firm must, in perpetual contact with the Burmese, he had never grown used to the sight of a black face. Any hint of friendly feeling towards an Oriental seemed to him a horrible perversity. He was an intelligent man and an able servant of his firm, but he was one of those Englishmen—common, unfortunately—who should never be allowed to set foot in the East.

Flory sat nursing Flo's head in his lap, unable to meet Ellis's eyes. At the best of times his birthmark made it difficult for him to look people straight in the face. And when he made ready to speak, he could feel his voice trembling—for it had a way of trembling when it should have been firm; his features, too, sometimes twitched uncontrollably.

"Steady on," he said at last, sullenly and rather feebly. "Steady on. There's no need to get so excited. *I* never suggested having any native members in here."

"Oh, didn't you? We all know bloody well you'd like to, though. Why else do you go to that oily little babu's house every morning, then? Sitting down at table with him as though he was a white man, and drinking out of glasses his filthy black lips have slobbered over—it makes me spew to think of it."

"Sit down, old chap, sit down," Westfield said. "Forget it. Have a drink on it. Not worth while quarrelling. Too hot."

"My God," said Ellis a little more calmly, taking a pace or two up and down, "my God, I don't understand you chaps. I simply don't. Here's that old fool Macgregor wanting to bring a nigger into this Club for no reason whatever, and you all sit down under it without a word. Good God, what are we supposed to be doing in this country? If we aren't going to rule, why the devil don't we clear out? Here we are, supposed to be governing a set of damn black swine who've been slaves since the beginning of history, and instead of ruling them in the only way they understand, we go and treat them as equals. And all you silly b———s take it for granted. There's Flory, makes his best pal of a black babu who calls himself a doctor because he's done two years at an Indian so-called university. And you, Westfield, proud as Punch of your knock-kneed, bribe-taking cowards of policemen. And there's Maxwell, spends his time running after Eurasian tarts. Yes, you do, Maxwell; I heard about your goings-on in Mandalay with some smelly little bitch called Molly Pereira. I supposed you'd have gone and married her if they hadn't transferred you up here? You all seem to *like* the dirty black brutes. Christ, I don't know what's come over us all. I really don't."

"Come on, have another drink," said Westfield. "Hey, butler! Spot of beer before the ice goes, eh? Beer, butler!"

The butler brought some bottles of Munich beer. Ellis presently sat down at the table with the others, and he nursed one of the cool bottles between his small hands. His forehead was sweating. He was sulky, but not in a rage any longer. At all times he was spiteful and perverse, but his violent fits of rage were soon over, and were never apologised for. Quarrels were a regular part of the routine of Club life. Mr. Lackersteen was feeling better and was studying the illustrations in *La Vie Parisienne*. It was after nine now, and the room, scented with the acrid smoke of Westfield's cheroot, was stifling hot. Everyone's shirt stuck to his back with the first sweat of the day. The invisible *chokra*[11] who pulled the punkah rope outside was falling asleep in the glare.

"Butler!" yelled Ellis, and as the butler appeared, "go and wake that bloody *chokra* up!"

"Yes, master."

"And butler!"

"Yes, master?"

"How much ice have we got left?"

"'Bout twenty pounds, master. Will only last to-day, I think. I find it very difficult to keep ice cool now."

"Don't talk like that, damn you—'I find it very difficult!' Have you swallowed a dictionary? 'Please, master, can't keeping ice cool'—that's how you ought to talk. We shall have to sack this fellow if he gets to talk English too well. I can't stick servants who talk English. D'you hear, butler?"

"Yes, master," said the butler, and retired.

"God! No ice till Monday," Westfield said. "You going back to the jungle, Flory?"

"Yes. I ought to be there now. I only came in because of the English mail."

"Go on tour myself, I think. Knock up a spot of Travelling Allowance. I can't stick my bloody office at this time of year. Sitting there under the damned punkah, signing one chit after another. Paperchewing. God, how I wish the war was on again!"

"I'm going out the day after to-morrow," Ellis said. "Isn't that damned padre coming to hold his service this Sunday? I'll take care not to be in for that, anyway. Bloody knee-drill."

"Next Sunday," said Westfield. "Promised to be in for it myself. So's Macgregor. Bit hard on the poor devil of a padre, I must say. Only gets here once in six weeks. Might as well get up a congregation when he does come."

"Oh, hell! I'd snivel psalms to oblige the padre, but I can't stick the way these damned native Christians come shoving into our church. A

---

[11] Person who pulls the punkah rope that moves a large panel to let in a breeze. [Ed.]

pack of Madrassi servants and Karen[12] school-teachers. And then those two yellow-bellies, Francis and Samuel—they call themselves Christians too. Last time the padre was here they had the nerve to come up and sit on the front pews with the white men. Someone ought to speak to the padre about that. What bloody fools we were ever to let those missionaries loose in this country! Teaching bazaar sweepers they're as good as we are. 'Please, sir, me Christian same like master.' Damned cheek."

[12] An ethnic minority group in Burma. [Ed.]

2

JOSEPH CONRAD
Heart of Darkness, 1899

Although his native tongue was Polish (and French his second language), Joseph Conrad (1857–1924) became one of the leading English novelists of the era of British imperialism. Drawing on his experience as a mariner and ship captain, he secured a post as an officer on river steamboats on the Congo River in 1890. Nine years later he published *Heart of Darkness*, a novel that has introduced generations since to Africa, the Congo, the era of colonialism, and European ideas of "the other."

In this selection from the novel, Conrad's narrator, Marlow, tells of his voyage up the Congo to meet the enigmatic European Kurtz, who has secured prodigious amounts of ivory for his Belgian employer but (we learn at the end of the novel) has lost his mind in the process.

What impression does *Heart of Darkness* give of Africa and Africans? What does it suggest were the motives or intentions of European explorers and traders in Africa? What feeling does this selection convey about European colonization of Africa?

THINKING HISTORICALLY

Like many novels, *Heart of Darkness* is based on the actual experiences of the author. Despite the basis in fact, however, it is very different from historical writing. Imagine Conrad writing a history of the events described in this selection. How would it be different? Would one account be truer, or merely reveal different truths?

Source: Joseph Conrad, *Heart of Darkness*, A Norton Critical Edition (New York: Norton, 1988), 35–39. Originally published by *Blackwood's Magazine* (London, 1899, 1902).

Going up that river was like travelling back to the earliest beginnings of the world, when vegetation rioted on the earth and the big trees were kings. An empty stream, a great silence, an impenetrable forest. The air was warm, thick, heavy, sluggish. There was no joy in the brilliance of sunshine. The long stretches of the waterway ran on, deserted, into the gloom of overshadowed distances. On silvery sandbanks hippos and alligators sunned themselves side by side. The broadening waters flowed through a mob of wooded islands. You lost your way on that river as you would in a desert and butted all day long against shoals trying to find the channel till you thought yourself bewitched and cut off for ever from everything you had known once—somewhere—far away—in another existence perhaps. There were moments when one's past came back to one, as it will sometimes when you have not a moment to spare to yourself; but it came in the shape of an unrestful and noisy dream remembered with wonder amongst the overwhelming realities of this strange world of plants and water and silence. And this stillness of life did not in the least resemble a peace. It was the stillness of an implacable force brooding over an inscrutable intention. It looked at you with a vengeful aspect. I got used to it afterwards. I did not see it any more. I had no time. I had to keep guessing at the channel; I had to discern, mostly by inspiration, the signs of hidden banks; I watched for sunken stones; I was learning to clap my teeth smartly before my heart flew out when I shaved by a fluke some infernal sly old snag that would have ripped the life out of the tin-pot steamboat and drowned all the pilgrims; I had to keep a look-out for the signs of dead wood we could cut up in the night for next day's steaming. When you have to attend to things of that sort, to the mere incidents of the surface, the reality—the reality I tell you—fades. The inner truth is hidden—luckily, luckily. But I felt it all the same; I felt often its mysterious stillness watching me at my monkey tricks. . . .

I managed not to sink that steamboat on my first trip. It's a wonder to me yet. Imagine a blindfolded man set to drive a van over a bad road. I sweated and shivered over that business considerably, I can tell you. After all, for a seaman, to scrape the bottom of the thing that's supposed to float all the time under his care is the unpardonable sin. No one may know of it, but you never forget the thump—eh? A blow on the very heart. You remember it, you dream of it, you wake up at night and think of it—years after—and go hot and cold all over. I don't pretend to say that steamboat floated all the time. More than once she had to wade for a bit, with twenty cannibals splashing around and pushing. We had enlisted some of these chaps on the way for a crew. Fine fellows—cannibals— in their place. They were men one could work with, and I am grateful to them. And, after all, they did not eat each other before my face: they had brought along a provision of hippo-meat which went rotten and made the mystery of the wilderness stink in my nostrils. Phoo! I can sniff it now. I had the Manager on board and three or four pilgrims with their staves—all complete. Sometimes we came upon a station close by the bank clinging to the skirts of the unknown, and the white men rushing out of a tumbledown hovel with great gestures of joy and surprise and welcome seemed very strange, had the appearance of being held there captive by a spell. The word "ivory" would ring in the air for a while—and on we went again into the silence, along empty reaches, round the still bends, between the high walls of our winding way, reverberating in hollow claps the ponderous beat of the stern-wheel. Trees, trees, millions of trees, massive, immense, running up high, and at their foot, hugging the bank against the stream, crept the little begrimed steamboat like a sluggish beetle crawling on the floor of a lofty portico. It made you feel very small, very lost, and yet it was not altogether depressing, that feeling. After all, if you were small, the grimy beetle crawled on—which was just what you wanted it to do. Where the pilgrims imagined it crawled to I don't know. To some place where they expected to get something, I bet! For me it crawled towards Kurtz—exclusively; but when the steam-pipes started leaking we crawled very slow. The reaches opened before us and closed behind, as if the forest had stepped leisurely across the water to bar the way for our return. We penetrated deeper and deeper into the heart of darkness. It was very quiet there. At night sometimes the roll of drums behind the curtain of trees would run up the river and remain sustained faintly, as if hovering in the air high over our heads till the first break of day. Whether it meant war, peace, or prayer we could not tell. The dawns were heralded by the descent of a chill stillness. The woodcutters slept, their fires burned low, the snapping of a twig would make you start. We were wanderers on a prehistoric earth, on an earth that wore the aspect of an unknown planet. We could have fancied ourselves the first of men taking possession of an accursed inheritance, to be subdued at the cost of profound anguish and of excessive toil. But suddenly as we struggled round a bend there would be a glimpse of rush walls, of peaked grass-roofs, a burst of yells, a whirl of black limbs, a mass of hands clapping, of feet stamping, of bodies swaying, of eyes rolling under the droop of heavy and motionless foliage. The steamer toiled along slowly on the edge of a black and incomprehensible frenzy. The prehistoric man was cursing us, praying to us, welcoming us—who could tell? We were cut off from the comprehension of our surroundings; we glided past like phantoms, wondering and secretly appalled, as sane men would be before an enthusiastic outbreak in a madhouse. We could not understand because we were too far and could not remember because we were travelling in the night of first ages, of those ages that are gone, leaving hardly a sign—and no memories.

The earth seemed unearthly. We are accustomed to look upon the shackled form of a conquered monster, but there—there you could look at a thing monstrous and free. It was unearthly and the men were.... No they were not inhuman. Well, you know that was the worst of it—this suspicion of their not being inhuman. It would come slowly to one. They howled and leaped and spun and made horrid faces, but what thrilled you was just the thought of their humanity—like yours—the thought of your remote kinship with this wild and passionate uproar. Ugly. Yes, it was ugly enough, but if you were man enough you would admit to yourself that there was in you just the faintest trace of a re- sponse to the terrible frankness of that noise, a dim suspicion of there being a meaning in it which you—you so remote from the night of first ages—could comprehend. And why not? The mind of man is capable of anything—because everything is in it, all the past as well as all the fu- ture. What was there after all? Joy, fear, sorrow, devotion, valour, rage—who can tell?—but truth—truth stripped of its cloak of time. Let the fool gape and shudder—the man knows and can look on with- out a wink. But he must at least be as much of a man as these on the shore. He must meet that truth with his own true stuff—with his own inborn strength. Principles? Principles won't do. Acquisitions, clothes, pretty rags—rags that would fly off at the first good shake. No. You want a deliberate belief. An appeal to me in this fiendish row—is there? Very well. I hear, I admit, but I have a voice too, and for good or evil mine is the speech that cannot be silenced. Of course, a fool, what with sheer fright and fine sentiments, is always safe. Who's that grunting? You wonder I didn't go ashore for a howl and a dance? Well, no—I didn't. Fine sentiments, you say? Fine sentiments be hanged! I had no time. I had to mess about with whitelead and strips of woollen blanket helping to put bandages on those leaky steam-pipes—tell you. I had to watch the steering and circumvent those snags and get the tin-pot along by hook or by crook. There was surface-truth enough in these things to save a wiser man. And between whiles I had to look after the savage who was fireman. He was an improved specimen; he could fire up a vertical boiler. He was there below me and, upon my word, to look at him was as edifying as seeing a dog in a parody of breeches and a feather hat walking on his hind legs. A few months of training had done for that really fine chap. He squinted at the steam-gauge and at the water-gauge with an evident effort of intrepidity—and he had filed teeth too, the poor devil, and the wool of his pate shaved into queer patterns, and three ornamental scars on each of his cheeks. He ought to have been clapping his hands and stamping his feet on the bank, instead of which he was hard at work, a thrall to strange witchcraft, full of improving knowledge. He was useful because he had been instructed; and what he knew was this—that should the water in that transparent thing disap- pear the evil spirit inside the boiler would get angry through the greatness of his thirst and take a terrible vengeance. So he sweated and fired up and watched the glass fearfully (with an impromptu charm, made of rags, tied to his arm and a piece of polished bone as big as a watch stuck flatways through his lower lip) while the wooded banks slipped past us slowly, the shore noise was left behind, the interminable miles of silence—and we crept on, towards Kurtz.

3

CHINUA ACHEBE

An Image of Africa: Racism in Conrad's *Heart of Darkness*, 1975

Chinua Achebe* is modern Africa's most read novelist. His *Things Fall Apart,* about the impact of European missionaries in his native Nigeria at the end of the nineteenth century, is a classic that is as widely read as *Heart of Darkness.* In this selection, which first took form as an address to an American college audience in 1975, Achebe tackles *Heart of Darkness.* What is his argument? Are you persuaded?

THINKING HISTORICALLY

Achebe is a novelist criticizing another novelist for distorting history. Could any of Achebe's criticisms be directed at Orwell? What are the responsibilities of a novelist to historical accuracy? How does a critique of literature like this add to our understanding of the past?

Heart of Darkness projects the image of Africa as "the other world," the antithesis of Europe and therefore of civilization, a place where man's vaunted intelligence and refinement are finally mocked by triumphant bestiality. The book opens on the River Thames, tranquil, resting, peacefully "at the decline of day after ages of good service done to the

---

* chih NOO ah ah CHEH bay

Source: Chinua Achebe, "An Image of Africa: Racism in Conrad's *Heart of Darkness*," an emended version (1987) of the second Chancellor's Lecture at the University of Massachusetts, Amherst, February 18, 1975; later published in the *Massachusetts Review* 18 (1977): 782–94. Reprinted in *Heart of Darkness*, A Norton Critical Edition (New York: Norton, 1988), 252–54, 257–60.

race that peopled its banks." But the actual story will take place on the River Congo, the very antithesis of the Thames. The River Congo is quite decidedly not a River Emeritus. It has rendered no service and enjoys no old-age pension. We are told that "Going up that river was like travelling back to the earliest beginnings of the world."

Is Conrad saying then that these two rivers are very different, one good, the other bad? Yes, but that is not the real point. It is not the differentness that worries Conrad but the lurking hint of kinship, of common ancestry. For the Thames too "has been one of the dark places of the earth." It conquered its darkness, of course, and is now in daylight and at peace. But if it were to visit its primordial relative, the Congo, it would run the terrible risk of hearing grotesque echoes of its own forgotten darkness, and falling victim to an avenging recrudescence of the mindless frenzy of the first beginnings.

These suggestive echoes comprise Conrad's famed evocation of the African atmosphere in *Heart of Darkness*. In the final consideration his method amounts to no more than a steady, ponderous, fake-ritualistic repetition of two antithetical sentences, one about silence and the other about frenzy. We can inspect samples of this on pages 36 and 37[1] of the present edition: a) *It was the stillness of an implacable force brooding over an inscrutable intention* and b) *The steamer toiled along slowly on the edge of a black and incomprehensible frenzy.* Of course there is a judicious change of adjective from time to time, so that instead of *inscrutable*, for example, you might have *unspeakable*, even plain *mysterious*, etc., etc.

The eagle-eyed English critic F. R. Leavis drew attention long ago to Conrad's "adjectival insistence upon inexpressible and incomprehensible mystery." That insistence must not be dismissed lightly, as many Conrad critics have tended to do, as a mere stylistic flaw; for it raises serious questions of artistic good faith. When a writer while pretending to record scenes, incidents, and their impact is in reality engaged in inducing hypnotic stupor in his readers through a bombardment of emotive words and other forms of trickery much more has to be at stake than stylistic felicity. Generally normal readers are well armed to detect and resist such underhand activity. But Conrad chose his subject well—one which was guaranteed not to put him in conflict with the psychological pre-disposition of his readers or raise the need for him to contend with their resistance. He chose the role of purveyor of comforting myths.

The most interesting and revealing passages in *Heart of Darkness* are, however, about people. I must crave the indulgence of my reader to quote almost a whole page from about the middle of the story when

[1] See pp. 858 and 859. [Ed.]

representatives of Europe in a steamer going down the Congo encounter the denizens of Africa.

> We were wanderers on a prehistoric earth, on an earth that wore the aspect of an unknown planet. We could have fancied ourselves the first of men taking possession of an accursed inheritance, to be subdued at the cost of profound anguish and of excessive toil. But suddenly as we struggled round a bend there would be a glimpse of rush walls, of peaked grass-roofs, a burst of yells, a whirl of black limbs, a mass of hands clapping, of feet stamping, of bodies sway-ing, of eyes rolling under the droop of heavy and motionless foliage. The steamer toiled along slowly on the edge of a black and incom-prehensible frenzy. The prehistoric man was cursing us, praying to us, welcoming us—who could tell? We were cut off from the com-prehension of our surroundings; we glided past like phantoms, wondering and secretly appalled, as sane men would be before an enthusiastic outbreak in a madhouse. We could not understand be-cause we were too far and could not remember, because we were travelling in the night of first ages, of those ages that are gone, leav-ing hardly a sign—and no memories.

> The earth seemed unearthly. We are accustomed to look upon the shackled form of a conquered monster, but there—there you could look at a thing monstrous and free. It was unearthly and the men were. . . . No they were not inhuman. Well, you know that was the worst of it—this suspicion of their not being inhuman. It would come slowly to one. They howled and leaped and spun and made horrid faces, but what thrilled you was just the thought of their hu-manity—like yours—the thought of your remote kinship with this wild and passionate uproar. Ugly. Yes, it was ugly enough, but if you were man enough you would admit to yourself that there was in you just the faintest trace of a response to the terrible frankness of that noise, a dim suspicion of there being a meaning in it which you—you so remote from the night of first ages—could comprehend.

Herein lies the meaning of *Heart of Darkness* and the fascination it holds over the Western mind: "What thrilled you was just the thought of their humanity—like yours. . . . Ugly."

Having shown us Africa in the mass, Conrad then zeros in, half a page later, on a specific example, giving us one of his rare descriptions of an African who is not just limbs or rolling eyes:

> And between whiles I had to look after the savage who was fire-man. He was an improved specimen; he could fire up a vertical boiler. He was there below me and, upon my word, to look at him was as edifying as seeing a dog in a parody of breeches and a feather hat walking on his hind legs. A few months of training had done for

that really fine chap. He squinted at the steam-gauge and at the water-gauge with an evident effort of intrepidity—and he had filed his teeth too, the poor devil, and the wool of his pate shaved into queer patterns, and three ornamental scars on each of his cheeks. He ought to have been clapping his hands and stamping his feet on the bank, instead of which he was hard at work, a thrall to strange witchcraft, full of improving knowledge.

As everybody knows, Conrad is a romantic on the side. He might not exactly admire savages clapping their hands and stamping their feet but they have at least the merit of being in their place, unlike this dog in a parody of breeches. For Conrad things being in their place is of the utmost importance.

"Fine fellows—cannibals—in their place," he tells us pointedly. Tragedy begins when things leave their accustomed place, like Europe leaving its safe stronghold between the policeman and the baker to take a peep into the heart of darkness. . . .

The point of my observations should be quite clear by now, namely that Joseph Conrad was a thoroughgoing racist. That this simple truth is glossed over in criticisms of his work is due to the fact that white racism against Africa is such a normal way of thinking that its manifestations go completely unremarked. Students of *Heart of Darkness* will often tell you that Conrad is concerned not so much with Africa as with the deterioration of one European mind caused by solitude and sickness. They will point out to you that Conrad is, if anything, less charitable to the Europeans in the story than he is to the natives, that the point of the story is to ridicule Europe's civilizing mission in Africa. A Conrad student informed me in Scotland that Africa is merely a setting for the disintegration of the mind of Mr. Kurtz.

Which is partly the point. Africa as setting and backdrop which eliminates the African as human factor. Africa as a metaphysical battlefield devoid of all recognizable humanity, into which the wandering European enters at his peril. Can nobody see the preposterous and perverse arrogance in thus reducing Africa to the role of props for the break-up of one petty European mind? But that is not even the point. The real question is the dehumanization of Africa and Africans which this age-long attitude has fostered and continues to foster in the world. And the question is whether a novel which celebrates this dehumanization, which depersonalizes a portion of the human race, can be called a great work of art. My answer is: No, it cannot. I do not doubt Conrad's great talents. Even *Heart of Darkness* has its memorably good passages and moments:

> The reaches opened before us and closed behind, as if the forest had stepped leisurely across the water to bar the way for our return.

Its exploration of the minds of the European characters is often pene-
trating and full of insight. But all that has been more than fully discussed
in the last fifty years. His obvious racism has, however, not been addressed. And it is high time it was!

Conrad was born in 1857, the very year in which the first Anglican
missionaries were arriving among my own people in Nigeria. It was certainly not his fault that he lived his life at a time when the reputation of
the black man was at a particularly low level. But even after due allowances have been made for all the influences of contemporary prejudice on
his sensibility there remains still in Conrad's attitude a residue of antipathy to black people which his peculiar psychology alone can explain. His
own account of his first encounter with a black man is very revealing:

> A certain enormous buck nigger encountered in Haiti fixed my con-
> ception of blind, furious, unreasoning rage, as manifested in the
> human animal to the end of my days. Of the nigger I used to dream
> for years afterwards.

Certainly Conrad had a problem with niggers. His inordinate love of
that word itself should be of interest to psychoanalysts. Sometimes his
fixation on blackness is equally interesting as when he gives us this brief
description:

> A black figure stood up, strode on long black legs, waving long
> black arms. . .

As though we might expect a black figure striding along on black
legs to wave white arms! But so unrelenting is Conrad's obsession. . . .

Whatever Conrad's problems were, you might say he is now safely
dead. Quite true. Unfortunately his heart of darkness plagues us still.
Which is why an offensive and deplorable book can be described by a
serious scholar as "among the half dozen greatest short novels in the
English language." And why it is today perhaps the most commonly
prescribed novel in twentieth-century literature courses in English
Departments of American universities.

There are two probable grounds on which what I have said so far
may be contested. The first is that it is no concern of fiction to please
people about whom it is written. I will go along with that. But I am not
talking about pleasing people. I am talking about a book which parades
in the most vulgar fashion prejudices and insults from which a section of
mankind has suffered untold agonies and atrocities in the past and continues to do so in many ways and many places today. I am talking about
a story in which the very humanity of black people is called in question.

Secondly, I may be challenged on the grounds of actuality. Conrad,
after all, did sail down the Congo in 1890 when my own father was still
a babe in arms. How could I stand up more than fifty years after his

death and purport to contradict him? My answer is that as a sensible man I will not accept just any traveller's tales solely on the grounds that I have not made the journey myself. I will not trust the evidence even of a man's very eyes when I suspect them to be as jaundiced as Conrad's. And we also happen to know that Conrad was, in the words of his biographer, Bernard C. Meyer, "notoriously inaccurate in the rendering of his own history."

But more important by far is the abundant testimony about Conrad's savages which we could gather if we were so inclined from other sources and which might lead us to think that these people must have had other occupations besides merging into the evil forest or materializing out of it simply to plague Marlow and his dispirited band. For as it happened, soon after Conrad had written his book an event of far greater consequence was taking place in the art world of Europe. This is how Frank Willett, a British art historian, describes it:

> Gaugin had gone to Tahiti, the most extravagant individual act of turning to a non-European culture in the decades immediately before and after 1900, when European artists were avid for new artistic experiences, but it was only about 1904–5 that African art began to make its distinctive impact. One piece is still identifiable; it is a mask that had been given to Maurice Vlaminck in 1905. He records that Derain was "speechless" and "stunned" when he saw it, bought it from Vlaminck and in turn showed it to Picasso and Matisse, who were also greatly affected by it. Ambroise Vollard then borrowed it and had it cast in bronze. . . . The revolution of twentieth century art was under way!

The mask in question was made by other savages living just north of Conrad's River Congo. They have a name too: the Fang people, and are without a doubt among the world's greatest masters of the sculptured form. The event Frank Willett is referring to marked the beginning of cubism and the infusion of new life into European art, which had run completely out of strength.

The point of all this is to suggest that Conrad's picture of the peoples of the Congo seems grossly inadequate even at the height of their subjection to the ravages of King Leopold's International Association for the Civilization of Central Africa.[2]

---

[2] King Leopold II of Belgium established the International Association for the Exploration and Civilization of Central Africa in 1876, with himself as president. The expeditions of the association, particularly those of the explorer Henry Stanley (1880–1884), led to the claim by the association of sovereignty over the Congo basin. The territory of what was then known as the International African Association was reorganized by Leopold as the Congo Free State in 1885. [Ed.]

CHINUA ACHEBE
Things Fall Apart, 1958

In this selection from his novel, *Things Fall Apart*, Chinua Achebe imagines the arrival and impact of some of the first Anglican missionaries among the Ibo people of Nigeria — his own ances- tors — after 1857. Missionaries were among the earliest European colonialists. The first missionaries went to the Americas with the Spanish conquistadors in the decades after Columbus. But long after the conquistadors were replaced by professional soldiers, administrators, policemen, mining engineers, company agents, and other representatives of a more bureaucratic and industrial age, the missionaries continued to seek out souls to save beyond the frontiers of colonial settlement. What, according to Achebe, were the princi- pal obstacles faced by the missionaries? What elements in Christian- ity attracted some Africans? What elements repelled others? Judging from this selection, how would you characterize the overall impact of Christianity in Africa?

THINKING HISTORICALLY

Unlike Orwell and Conrad, Achebe is not describing historical events he witnessed, since he is writing about a period before he was born. And yet, he has a firsthand experience of Ibo culture. How does that experience make his fiction different from that of Conrad and Orwell? What does Achebe's fiction add to a historical understand- ing of missionaries in Africa? How would you compare Achebe with Conrad?

The arrival of the missionaries had caused a considerable stir in the vil- lage of Mbanta. There were six of them and one was a white man. Every man and woman came out to see the white man. Stories about these strange men had grown since one of them had been killed in Abame and his iron horse tied to the sacred silk-cotton tree. And so everybody came to see the white man. It was the time of the year when everybody was at home. The harvest was over.

When they had all gathered, the white man began to speak to them. He spoke through an interpreter who was an Ibo man, though his dialect was different and harsh to the ears of Mbanta. Many people laughed at his dialect and the way he used words strangely. Instead of saying

Source: Chinua Achebe, *Things Fall Apart* (Oxford: Heinemann, 1958), 101–09.

"myself" he always said "my buttocks." But he was a man of commanding presence and the clansmen listened to him. He said he was one of
them, as they could see from his colour and his language. The other four
black men were also their brothers, although one of them did not speak
Ibo. The white man was also their brother because they were all sons of
God. And he told them about this new God, the Creator of all the world
and all the men and women. He told them that they worshipped false
gods, gods of wood and stone. A deep murmur went through the crowd
when he said this. He told them that the true God lived on high and that
all men when they died went before Him for judgment. Evil men and all
the heathen who in their blindness bowed to wood and stone were
thrown into a fire that burned like palm-oil. But good men who worshipped the true God lived for ever in His happy kingdom. "We have
been sent by this great God to ask you to leave your wicked ways and
false gods and turn to Him so that you may be saved when you die," he
said.

"Your buttocks understand our language," said someone lightheart-
edly and the crowd laughed.

"What did he say?" the white man asked his interpreter. But before
he could answer, another man asked a question: "Where is the white
man's horse?" he asked. The Ibo evangelists consulted among themselves and decided that the man probably meant bicycle. They told the
white man and he smiled benevolently.

"Tell them," he said, "that I shall bring many iron horses when we
have settled down among them. Some of them will even ride the iron
horse themselves." This was interpreted to them but very few of them
heard. They were talking excitedly among themselves because the white
man had said he was going to live among them. They had not thought
about that.

At this point an old man said he had a question. "Which is this god
of yours," he asked, "the goddess of the earth, the god of the sky, Amadiora of the thunderbolt, or what?"

The interpreter spoke to the white man and he immediately gave his
answer. "All the gods you have named are not gods at all. They are gods
of deceit who tell you to kill your fellows and destroy innocent children.
There is only one true God and He has the earth, the sky, you and me,
and all of us."

"If we leave our gods and follow your god," asked another man,
"who will protect us from the anger of our neglected gods and
ancestors?"

"Your gods are not alive and cannot do you any harm," replied the
white man. "They are pieces of wood and stone."

When this was interpreted to the men of Mbanta they broke into
derisive laughter. These men must be mad, they said to themselves. How

else could they say that Ani and Amadiora were harmless? And Idemili and Ogwugwu too? And some of them began to go away.

Then the missionaries burst into song. It was one of those gay and rollicking tunes of evangelism which had the power of plucking at silent and dusty chords in the heart of an Ibo man. The interpreter explained each verse to the audience, some of whom now stood enthralled. It was a story of brothers who lived in darkness and in fear, ignorant of the love of God. It told of one sheep out on the hills, away from the gates of God and from the tender shepherd's care.

After the singing the interpreter spoke about the Son of God whose name was Jesu Kristi. Okonkwo, who only stayed in the hope that it might come to chasing the men out of the village or whipping them, now said:

"You told us with your own mouth that there was only one god. Now you talk about his son. He must have a wife, then." The crowd agreed.

"I did not say He had a wife," said the interpreter, somewhat lamely.

"Your buttocks said he had a son," said the joker. "So he must have a wife and all of them must have buttocks."

The missionary ignored him and went on to talk about the Holy Trinity. At the end of it Okonkwo was fully convinced that the man was mad. He shrugged his shoulders and went away to tap his afternoon palm-wine.

But there was a young lad who had been captivated. His name was Nwoye, Okonkwo's first son. It was not the mad logic of the Trinity that captivated him. He did not understand it. It was the poetry of the new religion, something felt in the marrow. The hymn about brothers who sat in darkness and in fear seemed to answer a vague and persistent question that haunted his young soul—the question of the twins crying in the bush and the question of Ikemefuna who was killed. He felt a relief within as the hymn poured into his parched soul. The words of the hymn were like the drops of frozen rain melting on the dry plate of the panting earth. Nwoye's callow mind was greatly puzzled.

The missionaries spent their first four or five nights in the market-place, and went into the village in the morning to preach the gospel. They asked who the king of the village was, but the villagers told them that there was no king. "We have men of high title and the chief priests and the elders," they said.

It was not very easy getting the men of high title and the elders together after the excitement of the first day. But the missionaries persevered, and in the end they were received by the rulers of Mbanta. They asked for a plot of land to build their church.

Every clan and village had its "evil forest." In it were buried all those who died of the really evil diseases, like leprosy and smallpox. It was also the dumping ground for the potent fetishes of great medicine-men when they died. An "evil forest" was, therefore, alive with sinister forces and powers of darkness. It was such a forest that the rules of Mbanta gave to the missionaries. They did not really want them in their clan, and so they made them that offer which nobody in his right senses would accept.

"They want a piece of land to build their shrine," said Uchendu to his peers when they consulted among themselves. "We shall give them a piece of land." He paused, and there was a murmur of surprise and disagreement. "Let us give them a portion of the Evil Forest. They boast about victory over death. Let us give them a real battlefield in which to show their victory." They laughed and agreed, and sent for the missionaries, whom they had asked to leave them for a while so that they might "whisper together." They offered them as much of the Evil Forest as they cared to take. And to their greatest amazement the missionaries thanked them and burst into song.

"They do not understand," said some of the elders. "But they will understand when they go to their plot of land tomorrow morning." And they dispersed.

The next morning the crazy men actually began to clear a part of the forest and to build their house. The inhabitants of Mbanta expected them all to be dead within four days. The first day passed and the second and third and fourth, and none of them died. Everyone was puzzled. And then it became known that the white man's fetish had unbelievable power. It was said that he wore glasses on his eyes so that he could see and talk to evil spirits. Not long after, he won his first three converts.

Although Nwoye had been attracted to the new faith from the very first day, he kept it secret. He dared not go too near the missionaries for fear of his father. But whenever they came to preach in the open market-place or the village playground, Nwoye was there. And he was already beginning to know some of the simple stories they told.

"We have now built a church," said Mr Kiaga, the interpreter, who was now in charge of the infant congregation. The white man had gone back to Umuofia, where he built his headquarters and from where he paid regular visits to Mr Kiaga's congregation at Mbanta.

"We have now built a church," said Mr Kiaga, "and we want you all to come in every seventh day to worship the true God."

On the following Sunday, Nwoye passed and re-passed the little red-earth and thatch building without summoning enough courage to enter. He heard the voice of singing and although it came from a handful of men it was loud and confident. Their church stood on a circular clearing that looked like the open mouth of the Evil Forest. Was it waiting to snap its teeth together? After passing and re-passing by the church, Nwoye returned home.

It was well known among the people of Mbanta that their gods and ancestors were sometimes long-suffering and would deliberately allow a man to go on defying them. But even in such cases they set their limit at seven market weeks or twenty-eight days. Beyond that limit no man was suffered to go. And so excitement mounted in the village as the seventh week approached since the impudent missionaries built their church in the Evil Forest. The villagers were so certain about the doom that awaited these men that one or two converts thought it wise to suspend their allegiance to the new faith.

At last the day came by which all the missionaries should have died. But they were still alive, building a new red-earth and thatch house for their teacher, Mr Kiaga. That week they won a handful more converts. And for the first time they had a woman. Her name was Nneka, the wife of Amadi, who was a prosperous farmer. She was very heavy with child.

Nneka had had four previous pregnancies and childbirths. But each time she had borne twins, and they had been immediately thrown away. Her husband and his family were already becoming highly critical of such a woman and were not unduly perturbed when they found she had fled to join the Christians. It was a good riddance.

One morning Okonkwo's cousin, Amikwu, was passing by the church on his way from the neighbouring village, when he saw Nwoye among the Christians. He was greatly surprised, and when he got home he went straight to Okonkwo's hut and told him what he had seen. The women began to talk excitedly, but Okonkwo sat unmoved.

It was late afternoon before Nwoye returned. He went into the *obi* and saluted his father, but he did not answer. Nwoye turned round to walk into the inner compound when his father, suddenly overcome with fury, sprang to his feet and gripped him by the neck.

"Where have you been?" he stammered.

Nwoye struggled to free himself from the choking grip.

"Answer me," roared Okonkwo, "before I kill you!" He seized a heavy stick that lay on the dwarf wall and hit him two or three savage blows.

"Answer me!" he roared again. Nwoye stood looking at him and did not say a word. The women were screaming outside, afraid to go in.

"Leave that boy at once!" said a voice in the outer compound. It was Okonkwo's uncle Uchendu. "Are you mad?"

Okonkwo did not answer. But he left hold of Nwoye, who walked away and never returned.

He went back to the church and told Mr Kiaga that he had decided to go to Umuofia, where the white missionary had set up a school to teach young Christians to read and write.

Mr Kiaga's joy was very great. "Blessed is he who forsakes his father and his mother for my sake," he intoned. "Those that hear my words are my father and my mother."

Nwoye did not fully understand. But he was happy to leave his father. He would return later to his mother and his brothers and sisters and convert them to the new faith.

As Okonkwo sat in his hut that night, gazing into a log fire, he thought over the matter. A sudden fury rose within him and he felt a strong desire to take up his matchet, go to the church, and wipe out the entire vile and miscreant gang. But on further thought he told himself that Nwoye was not worth fighting for. Why, he cried in his heart, should he, Okonkwo, of all people, be cursed with such a son? He saw clearly in it the finger of his personal god or *chi*. For how else could he explain his great misfortune and exile and now his despicable son's behaviour? Now that he had time to think of it, his son's crime stood out in its stark enormity. To abandon the gods of one's father and go about with a lot of effeminate men clucking like old hens was the very depth of abomination. Suppose when he died all his male children decided to follow Nwoye's steps and abandon their ancestors? Okonkwo felt a cold shudder run through him at the terrible prospect, like the prospect of annihilation. He saw himself and his father crowding round their ancestral shrine waiting in vain for worship and sacrifice and finding nothing but ashes of bygone days, and his children the while praying to the white man's god. If such a thing were ever to happen, he, Okonkwo, would wipe them off the face of the earth.

Okonkwo was popularly called the "Roaring Flame." As he looked into the log fire he recalled the name. He was a flaming fire. How then could he have begotten a son like Nwoye, degenerate and effeminate? Perhaps he was not his son. No! He could not be. His wife had played him false. He would teach her! But Nwoye resembled his grandfather, Unoka, who was Okonkwo's father. He pushed the thought out of his mind. He, Okonkwo, was called a flaming fire. How could he have begotten a woman for a son? At Nwoye's age Okonkwo had already become famous throughout Umuofia for his wrestling and his fearlessness.

He sighed heavily, and as if in sympathy the smouldering log also sighed. And immediately Okonkwo's eyes were opened and he saw the whole matter clearly. Living fire begets cold, impotent ash. He sighed again, deeply.

5

FRANCIS BEBEY

King Albert, 1981

Francis Bebey (1929–2001) was an African writer, artist, and musician from Cameroon. In this novel, he carries the reader to a village called Effidi in the twilight of European imperialism after World War II

Source: Francis Bebey, *King Albert*, trans. Joyce A. Hutchinson (Westport, CT: Lawrence Hill & Co., 1981), 109–18.

but before the late 1950s and early 1960s, when Cameroon and other former colonies became independent states. In this brief selection from the novel, the young Bikounou, whom everyone calls Vespasian because he rides a Vespa Motor Scooter, has returned to Effidi to speak with Chief Ndengué. What is his message? What do his message and his manner of delivery tell you about the chief, the village, and the larger world of which it is a part at this time?

THINKING HISTORICALLY

The dialogue between Bikounou and the chief tells a story about how parts of Africa changed in the period leading up to independence. What are these changes? Where and how did they occur? In a few paragraphs, write a brief history that summarizes these changes. How is your history different from the section in the novel?

The next day, a Sunday, Bikounou went to see Chief Ndengué while the other villagers were at Mass.

"I have come to thank you for the welcome which you permitted the people of Effidi to extend to us, myself and my friend Féfé."

"My son, I permitted nothing. The village spoke for itself. As you could see yourself, nobody bears you any grudge. On the contrary, everybody is very fond of you. But, as a matter of interest, where is your friend Féfé?"

"I wanted to see you alone, Chief Ndengué, to talk to you while the others are not around."

"And what is so important that you need this secrecy?"

"You are the Chief of us all, and you have a right to hear the news first. The others will hear it later if they don't know it already."

"Bikounou, I think I have understood. You are going to get married. That's good, my son, but you know our procedure."

"I'm in a good position to know, Chief Ndengué. But that is not the news I have for you."

"Ah? What do you mean?"

"I mean I want to talk to you about something quite different from my marriage. Besides, as you have just reminded yourself, would you expect me to think of marriage again without consulting all the elders of our community? One should not make the same mistakes more than once in one's life."

"I see, my son. I see that your experience has widened, and you know, I am absolutely delighted. Now I know that you have come back to live among us as we live ourselves, following the laws laid down by our tradition, and not the examples given by people who are not our own people, whether their skin is black or white."

"Chief Ndengué, may all my links with our community be severed if I am not determined to follow the advice of my elders, which is dictated by the experience of generations and generations who lived before our own generation came into the world."

"You speak well, my son."

"But please, let me tell you what brings me here this morning."

"I am listening."

"Now, Chief Ndengué, there is going to be an election."

"What?"

"I am saying there is going to be an election."

"My son, please explain: what does that mean?"

"It means that the whites are going to ask us to choose a person to represent us."

"A person to represent us? But, my son, why do we have to choose someone to represent us? Am I not, myself, the man whom tradition has placed at the head of our community to represent everybody? Am I not the Chief of this community, the person to whom you turn to obtain this or that? The person who says yes, or maybe no, according to whether he sees in his answer some means of benefiting the whole community? Tell me, my son, what is this story you've brought back from the town?"

"Chief Ndengué, I knew you wouldn't understand me straightaway. You are the Chief of our community. You will remain our Chief until the day—when—until the time when—"

"Until my death, my son. Do not be afraid to say so. We are all destined to live for a period and then to die. You know, man is like a flower. He smiles at life as it smiles at the sunlight. Then at the end of his life he closes his eyes just as it droops its head and wilts. There is nothing to be afraid of, Bikounou. I should be lying if I told you that Chief Ndengué would never die. In any case, you would't believe me."

"I am saying, Chief Ndengué, that you will remain at the head of our community until the day when you are no longer with us. So it's not a question of choosing someone to replace you among us."

"Then what is it about?"

"I will explain. You know that our country is governed by the whites?"

"I know, I know. But what have they done now, these whites?"

"Nothing, except that they now realize the need to let us govern our country ourselves."

"What? What country are you talking about, my son?"

"This one, where we live, the country which takes in Effidi, Zaabat, Nkool, Palmtree Village, and even Ngala, as well as other towns."

"My son, what you have just told me is perhaps important, but you can't make me believe that Effidi, Nkool, Zaabat, Palmtree Village, and even Ngala are part of one and the same country and that they will let themselves be governed by one man, one single great Chief! For if you tell me that I shall remain at the head of the community of Effidi, then another chief will be needed to be responsible for governing the whole country, isn't that so?"

"Chief Ndengué, for a long time the whites have occupied our country and governed it in their own way. We, the educated men, have told them that we've had enough and that we wish to govern ourselves, since we are now capable of doing so."

"And the whites agreed?"

"Yes, they have agreed. . . . yes. . . . that is to say that— "

"My son, tell me the exact truth."

"That is to say that they don't believe we are capable of governing ourselves all alone."

"That is exactly what I think, too."

"But, Chief Ndengué, don't take their side! They think we can't govern ourselves alone, but *we* want to prove the opposite. We want to show them that we can live without them and govern ourselves."

"And so?"

"So they have decided to put us to the test."

"By doing what?"

"Precisely, by organizing elections. That's what I wanted— "

"Bikounou, you're mixing everything up—the country, the whites, ourselves, elections. How do you expect me to understand anything in all that?"

"Let me explain it to you, Chief Ndengué. The whites have a way of governing a country which is different from ours. With us, there is a Chief—that's to say, somebody like you—to govern the whole community. But *they* put several people at the head of the country. It is those people who make decisions for the good of the whole country because they have been chosen by the whole country to represent them. It is this new way of governing the country that the whites wish to teach us, and that is why there is going to be an election."

"Now it's becoming clearer," said Chief Ndengué.

He remained plunged in thought for several minutes, during which Bikounou realized that he should say nothing.

"Now, it's becoming clearer," he added. "If I understand correctly, each community like ours will have to choose someone to represent it— "

"In an assembly which will therefore represent the whole country," Bikounou continued.

"Yes, yes, I see."

He thought for a few more moments, then suggested:

"Naturally, if Effidi is asked to choose, I don't see who our brothers will elect to represent them other than myself, do you?"

A logical argument on the part of a village chief incapable of under-standing the evolution of a whole of the society of which his community is a part, and only a small part, when all's said and done. Bikounou would not have replied immediately if the Chief had not insisted:

"That is how things will turn out, isn't it?"

"Chief, when you talk about elections, you must not say in advance which man or woman is going to win."

"Which man or woman? What do you mean? Are the women also invited to stand for election? And to represent whom? The men?"

"Chief Ndengué, you must not get carried away. There may well not be a woman presumptuous enough to stand as a candidate in the elec-tion. But in the new system that the whites wish to teach us, the women have the right to stand, just like the men."

"What, what are you saying? Is that the kind of thing they wish to introduce here, and for what purpose?"

"Chief Ndengué, times change. Even in this village, which lives in closer proximity to the town than others on account of the road passing through it, people are not sufficiently informed about the evolution of the country."

"Our country is here!" Chief Ndengué shouted. "If you young people and those others educated by the whites wish to sell it, that's different. But, my son, I warn you that there are still enough people at Effidi to op-pose such an idea should it ever cross your mind one day. The evolution of the country . . . the evolution of what country? Do you think you know better than old Ndengué what is our country and what it means?"

"Chief Ndengué," said Bikounou, trying to appease him, "you are right. Our country exists inasmuch as you exist as our Chief. All that is built on the tradition of our ancestors."

"Then why have you come back to the village to tell me what other people want, people who have nothing to do with what our ancestors wished this country to be? Why do you all obey these foreigners?"

"Chief Ndengué, you must not give way to sudden anger and refuse to hear the other reasons which bring me here. I can understand your wish to exclude women from any competition concerning the govern-ment of the country. The women are in the village to bear children for their husbands and perpetuate the community with boys and girls who will follow traditional ways. I accept it myself, and I shall oppose any person who might seek to give to women the opportunity, the slightest opportunity, of interfering in men's affairs, such as, for example, the government of our society. But, you know, times change. In any case, they have changed a lot since, at the wish of our ancestors, you yourself became our Chief. You have to admit that, these days, you need the sup-port of the whites to make everybody obey you."

"You're lying! You're lying, Bikounou, you're lying! What had the whites to do with your return to the village? Was it not because you felt the ancestral power commanding you to return to your own people that you came back? And this ancestral power, who else but me represents it here?"

"It's true. It's true that what I said was not quite fair. It is not the whites who order all the members of the community to come to you to settle their differences, or to organize tactics about a possible marriage, or to talk about future sowings or the distribution of the harvest to come. But today there is nevertheless something changed about a village chief like yourself. I'm thinking particularly of the allowance paid you by the government."

"Allowance! Look at it! I am compensated because I have the unpleasant task of raising taxes among my people, and you dare call that an allowance? My son, you are too young for me to tell you all I think. But don't force me to believe that you have adopted the mentality of the foreigners who come and make us work for them, in our own country, and afterwards boast that they are doing it for our own good! For, tell me, what happens to all these taxes that I collect each year? Who uses the money that I am responsible for collecting? And after that, you come and defend your bosses and remind me that I am paid by them."

Bikounou wondered what answer he could possibly give to all that. He had come with the firm intention of being submissive, and you, too, must have noticed how diplomatic he was being in order not to shock Chief Ndengué. That is understandable, for it must be realized that, however innocent he might seem, on this Sunday morning when the other inhabitants of Effidi had gone to sing Mass in Latin—too bad for Father Bonsot if he hears about it—the Vespasian had the difficult job of explaining to the old chief that his period of glory and prestige based on tradition was over, and worse still, that new leaders would take his place, chosen with no reference to the law of bygone days. The young man knew what this would mean for this old man accustomed to considering as his personal property what some people would pompously call "power." He therefore decided to introduce into the conversation as much subtlety as was desirable or indeed necessary to lead Chief Ndengué gradually to accept the very principle of an election during which the people of Effidi would be free to choose him or to elect some other candidate.

"If I mentioned an allowance, Chief Ndengué, you must forgive me. You know the village people are not always aware what an unpleasant task the Administration expects you to carry out, and we have all come more or less to believe that you are paid for doing it. I confess that I personally should know something about it, since I work in a government office. In any case, I was joking when I said that, but I'm already at fault for joking with my elder. You must forgive me, Chief Ndengué. I came to see you as an obedient son comes to see his father and not to presume to make you angry."

"Now you're talking sense, my son. So, you inform me there is going to be an election. But tell me, if *I* am not elected, then who will be?"

"I have no idea, Chief Ndengué. What matters now is to know who else at Effidi might intend to stand at this election when you consider all the qualities and the knowledge a person needs to have to represent our community successfully."

"What do you mean?"

"Well, how can I explain it? It must first be understood that the elected representative will have to go to Ngala."

"Each village will have to send someone to Ngala?"

"That is where all the representatives will meet to discuss the measures to be taken concerning the country."

"Then I shall have to go to Ngala?"

"If you are elected by our community, yes."

"That's true. It's true that the community, according to your system, could very well decide that it didn't want me to represent them at Ngala. In any case, I must tell you from the start that, if things really turn out as you have just explained, I am not interested in your story of an election. I have no intention of going to sit at the side of the road every morning and wait for a truck to be kind enough to stop and take me to the town."

Bikounou gave an almost imperceptible sigh of relief. But Chief Ndengué was a crafty old man, who missed no detail of the attitude of those speaking with him. He noticed the suppressed satisfaction of the young man.

"What's the matter? Did I say something unpleasant?"

"No, Chief Ndengué, it's not that. I was in fact wondering whether you realized how difficult it would be for you to make frequent visits to the town if you were elected to represent Effidi."

"I realize it perfectly well. I also realize that in future—if your system works as you have said—it will be someone else who will go to the town to bring back orders to be passed on to the community. Yes, my son, I understand what you were saying just now: times change."

The pathos of these last words was perfectly clear to Bikounou. Nevertheless, he kept his poise, trying to allay the old man's fears:

"Oh, Chief Ndengué, don't take it like that. It's possible that someone else will go to the town to represent our community in the assembly which will meet there, but not to bring back orders, as long as you remain our Chief."

"My son, you are trying to calm me down, but since you began talking to me, I have a feeling that there is to be a change much greater than that suffered by our fathers when the whites arrived."

"There can't be any change more important for our country than when the whites arrived."

"You mean it's a continuation of the same change?"

"Yes and no, Chief Ndengué. Yes, because if the whites had not come, we should perhaps never have felt the need to prove that we are capable of governing ourselves. As a result, there would have been no need to talk of elections. But, on the other hand, we now have to choose from among us people to whom we shall entrust the conduct of our affairs."

"And you believe that, my son? You believe that one day the whites will leave us to manage our own affairs?"

"That is what the younger generation is asking them more and more urgently. They will simply be forced to leave us alone one day."

"Forced? Forced? Who can force them to do anything? These people who manufacture guns and arms who would kill us all if we refused to obey them, who can force them?"

"Chief Ndengué, these people are doubtless very intelligent. They manufacture guns, arms, motor cars, airplanes, the good Lord gives them all they desire. But they overlooked one thing."

"What thing, my son?"

"They overlooked that they shouldn't have taught us to read and write."

"I don't understand what you mean by that."

"You see, by teaching us to read, they gave us the key to their own knowledge, and there we discovered that they spoke of liberty, equality and fraternity."

"So?"

"So they are obliged to give us liberty, equality and fraternity. That's what we're asking for, Chief Ndengué."

"And that is really why there is going to be an election?"

"Actually, this election will not give us liberty, but the assembly which will be established will pave the way for the independence of the whole country."

"My son, I tell you that our country is Effidi!" the Chief growled again.

"You are right, Chief Ndengué, but I tell you that times change. And since times began to change, our country has grown bigger."

"You mean that those savages of Palmtree Village are going to send a representative to the town just like us?"

"They will have the right to do so."

"Like us? With no difference?"

"Like us. But they may be obliged to choose a representative elsewhere than among themselves."

"Why?"

"Well, Chief, because the fact that the elected representative can get to the town fairly often won't be the end of the matter. The representative will also have to be someone educated, someone who understands politics and who—"

"What? What did you say?"

"Politics."

"And poli—, poli—. This thing, what is it?"

"To be exact, it is politics that the representatives will be engaged in when they meet."

"So they won't be speaking?"

"Yes, they will, Chief Ndengué. They will probably speak a great deal. That's what politics is all about. They talk, they talk, they talk. And then they say, good, we will build a road to Nkool, or to Palmtree Village."

Chief Ndengué burst out laughing, and at once, a shaft of sunlight coming through a little hole in the wall and falling on the beaten earth floor in a small luminous circle also began to laugh, with all the particles of fine colored dust dancing in the rainbow that penetrated the half-light. Bikounou wondered what on earth he had said or done that was so amusing.

"My son," said Chief Ndengué at last, "don't be surprised to hear me laugh like this. The fact is that for some time I had been worrying for no reason and it's only now that I've realized my error."

"I don't understand," the Vespasian confessed.

"I will explain," replied the Chief, reverting to his normal serious manner. "This is why I am laughing. Since you began talking to me about your elections, I had become convinced that you were preparing to see someone else take my place at the head of our community, with the help, obviously, of your friends, the white Administrators. And now I see that I was stupid to imagine that. For if the poli—, poli—Oh, what did you say just now the representatives would do in the town?"

"Politics."

"Yes, that's it. If poli—, poli—. If whatever it is consists of talking and saying you're going to build a road, then it will have no effect on Effidi, seeing that we already have our road. Is that not true, my son?"

The serious tone showed that the man wished to be reassured.

"That is to say—I mean, Chief Ndengué—yes, you are right, partly," the Vespasian replied, in a somewhat embarrassed tone. "But I spoke of building a road just as an example. In fact, politics means doing lots and lots of other things."

"Ah?"

"Yes, yes, and that's why I was telling you that we must elect representatives who understand these things. And as I cannot see in Palmtree Village anybody who can claim to understand them, then I think those people will be obliged to choose a representative from outside their own community."

"How shameful for them!"

"I suppose, in fact, that they will not be very proud when they have to come to Effidi to ask if we can provide somebody to represent them in the assembly in the town."

"And if they come, my son, you who understand these things, tell me: what answer do we give these idiots?"

"I don't yet exactly know how these things will work out. But I think we shall be obliged to represent them because, in any case, there will not be a separate representative from each village."

"This business of yours is complicated, my son. I hope that you at least will be able to understand it, so that we don't make a laughing-stock of ourselves in the eyes of our neighbors. You know that they will seize on the slightest opportunity — "

"I'll take care of it, Chief."

The conversation went on into details until the time when the other villagers returned from Mass. It was the Chief's job to announce the news of the coming election, as it had been given him by Bikounou. He did this solemnly, during an evening meeting. The news was received and commented upon in almost as many ways as there were men present at the meeting, for the people of Effidi, outstandingly intelligent, at least in their own opinion, were keen to show that they had understood what they had just been told, and that they would be perfectly capable of play-ing the new game which was being wished on them by the town. Natu-rally, many chests swelled with pride at the idea that, once again, the neighboring villagers would remain in the background of the regional scene, since their sons were unable to compete with those of Effidi.

6

RUDYARD KIPLING

The White Man's Burden, 1899

This poem, written by Rudyard Kipling (1865–1936), is often pre-sented as the epitome of colonialist sentiment, though some readers see in it a critical, satirical attitude toward colonialism. Do you find the poem to be for or against colonialism? Can it be both?

THINKING HISTORICALLY

"The White Man's Burden" is a phrase normally associated with European colonialism in Africa. In fact, however, Kipling wrote the poem in response to the annexation of the Philippines by the United States. How does this historical context change the meaning of the poem for you?

Source: Rudyard Kipling, "The White Man's Burden," *McClure's Magazine* 12, no. 4 (February 1899): 290–91.

Neither fiction nor fact, a poem conveys emotions. How does this poem help us understand something about the feelings of people like Kipling? How would you describe that feeling?

Take up the White Man's burden—
Send forth the best ye breed—
Go, bind your sons to exile
To serve your captives' need;
To wait, in heavy harness,
On fluttered folk and wild—
Your new-caught sullen peoples,
Half devil and half child.

Take up the White Man's burden—
In patience to abide,
To veil the threat of terror
And check the show of pride;
By open speech and simple,
An hundred times made plain,
To seek another's profit
And work another's gain.

Take up the White Man's burden—
The savage wars of peace—
Fill full the mouth of Famine,
And bid the sickness cease;
And when your goal is nearest
(The end for others sought)
Watch sloth and heathen folly
Bring all your hope to nought.

Take up the White Man's burden—
No iron rule of kings,
But toil of serf and sweeper—
The tale of common things.
The ports ye shall not enter,
The roads ye shall not tread,
Go, make them with your living
And mark them with your dead.

Take up the White Man's burden,
And reap his own reward—
The blame of those ye better

The hate of those ye guard—
The cry of hosts ye humour
(Ah, slowly!) toward the light:—
"Why brought ye us from bondage,
Our loved Egyptian night?"

Take up the White Man's burden—
Ye dare not stoop to less—
Nor call too loud on Freedom
To cloke your weariness.
By all ye will or whisper,
By all ye leave or do,
The silent sullen peoples
Shall weigh your God and you.

Take up the White Man's burden!
Have done with childish days—
The lightly-proffered laurel,
The easy ungrudged praise:
Comes now, to search your manhood
Through all the thankless years,
Cold, edged with dear-bought wisdom,
The judgment of your peers.

■ REFLECTIONS

Many of the selections within this chapter as well as its title point to
the dual character of colonial society. There are the colonized and the
colonizers, the "natives" and the Europeans, and, as racial categories
hardened in the second half of the nineteenth century, the blacks and
the whites. Colonialism centered on the construction of an accepted inequality. The dominant Europeans invested enormous energy in keeping the double standards, dual pay schedules, and separate rules and
residential areas—the two castes.

One problem with maintaining a neat division between the colonized and the colonizers is that the Europeans were massively outnum-
bered by the indigenous people. Thus, the colonizers needed a vast
class of middle-status people to staff the army, police, and bureaucracy.
These people might be educated in Paris or London, raised in European
culture, and encouraged to develop a sense of pride in their similarity
to the Europeans ("me Christian, same like master") and their differences from the other "natives." Often, like the Indian Dr. Veraswami,
they were chosen for their ethnic or religious differences from the rest
of the colonized population.

In short, colonialism created a whole class of people who were neither fully colonized nor colonizers. They were in between. To the extent that the colonial enterprise was an extension of European social class differences, these in-between people could be British as well as "native." Orwell's Flory is only one of the characters in *Burmese Days* caught between two worlds. One of the most notorious of this class of Europeans "gone native" is the Mr. Kurtz that Conrad's crew will meet upriver. Achebe's point that Africa becomes a setting for the breakup of a European mind might be generalized to apply to the European perception of the colonial experience. It is certainly one of the dominant themes of the European colonial novel. Even the great ones often center on the real or imagined rape, ravishing, or corruption of the European by the seething foreign unknown. This attitude also helps us understand how Kipling could be both anti-imperialist and racist. Imperialism could seem like a thankless act to those who tried to carry civilization to "sullen peoples, half devil and half child."

All the novels and poetry excerpted in this chapter are well worth reading in their entirety, and many other excellent colonial novels can be chosen from this period as well as from the 1930s and 1940s. E. M. Forster's *A Passage to India* and Paul Scott's *The Raj Quartet* stand out as fictional introductions to British colonialism in India. (Both have also received excellent adaptations to film, the latter as the series for television called *The Jewel in the Crown*.) In addition to Chinua Achebe, Amos Tutuola and Wole Soyinka have written extensively on Nigeria. Besides Francis Bebey, Ferdinand Oyono and Mongo Beti address French colonialism in Cameroon. On South Africa, the work of Alan Payton, Andre Brink, J. M. Coetzee, Peter Abrams, and James McClure, among many others, stands out.

The advantage of becoming engrossed in a novel is that we feel part of the story and have a sense that we are learning something firsthand. Of course, we are reading a work of fiction, not gaining firsthand experience or reading an accurate historical account of events. A well-made film poses an even greater problem. Its visual and aural impact imparts a psychological reality that becomes part of our experience. If it is about a subject of which we know little, the film quickly becomes our "knowledge" of the subject, and this knowledge may be incomplete or inaccurate.

On the other hand, a well-written novel or film can whet our appetite and inspire us to learn more. Choose and read a novel about colonialism or some other historical subject. Then read a biography of the author or research his or her background to determine how much the author knew about the subject. Next, read a historical account of the subject. How much attention does the historian give to the novelist's subject? How does the novel add depth to the historical account? How does the historical account place the novel in perspective? Finally, how does the author's background place the novel in historical context?

23

Westernization and Nationalism

Japan, India, and the West, 1820–1939

■ HISTORICAL CONTEXT

By the second half of the nineteenth century, the West (meaning Europe and North America) had industrialized, created more representative governments and open societies than the world had known before, and demonstrated the power of its science, technology, and military might by colonizing much of the rest of the world. For those who looked on from outside, the West was a force to be reckoned with.

Some of those observers knew the impact of the West firsthand. The Japanese had experienced Western traders and missionaries since 1543 but had controlled their numbers and influence. The Act of Seclusion in 1636 limited European contact in Japan to a small colony of Dutch traders for the next two hundred years. Not until the appearance of Commodore Perry's steam fleet in 1853 did a new policy toward the West seem necessary.

India had experienced Western colonization and trade since the early 1600s, losing coastal trading cities to various European powers until the English consolidated their hold in the eighteenth century. By 1880 all but a few princely states had come under the rule of the British Indian Empire.

We have then, in these two examples, different degrees of Western influence and penetration. Nevertheless, both of these societies were forced to confront the power of the West. In both cases, the effort to become independent of the West meant considering what might be imitated or borrowed. Broadly speaking, this meant some degree of Westernization.

How did the people of Japan and India answer the challenge of the West? What motivated some to seek to Westernize? What led others to reject Westernization entirely? And what role did nationalism play in the struggle over Westernization?

Nationalism had been a potent force in Europe since the French Revolution, with its national draft army, National Assembly, nationalization of church lands, national flag, national anthem, and celebration of French citizenship. Napoleon's armies inadvertently spread national consciousness among his enemies. Poets and politicians from Vienna to Madrid sought to create and establish the elements of their own national cultures and nation states. European colonization ignited the same spark of national identity in Asia and Africa. Nationalism was itself a Western movement, but nationalism could be built from any indigenous or traditional culture. Extreme Westernizers might be willing to dispense with traditional ways entirely. Extreme anti-Westernizers could invoke nationalism alone. But most thoughtful subjects of Western influence between the mid-nineteenth and mid-twentieth centuries recognized the need to draw on old strengths while borrowing what worked. How did the authors of these selections face the challenge?

■ THINKING HISTORICALLY

Appreciating Contradictions

The process of Westernization, like the experience of conquest and colonization that often preceded it, was fraught with conflict and led to frequent contradictions. Often, the struggle for national independence meant the borrowing of Western practices and ideologies, both Marxist and liberal. Indeed, the idea of national self-determination was a product of the French and American revolutions, as we have seen. Even the words and languages employed in the debate reflected Western origins, as English or French was often the only common language of educated colonized peoples. Therefore, it is not surprising that contradictory behavior and ambivalent relationships were endemic in the postcolonial world, just as they had been under colonialism. These contradictions usually manifested themselves in an individual's cultural identity. How do colonized persons adopt Western ways, embrace traditional culture, and not feel as though their identity has been divided between the two? Such individuals may not fit entirely into either world and so may be torn between who they were and who they have become. The somewhat anguished experiences of these colonized people are difficult to understand. We typically want to accept one view or another, to praise or to blame. But as we have learned, the history of peoples and nations is rarely that clear. In examining some of the fundamental contradictions in the history of Westernization, we might better understand how people were variously affected.

The historical thinking skill one learns in reading documents from people torn between different ideals is the appreciation of contradictions. This operates on a number of levels. We learn that people can hold two contradictory ideas in their minds at the same time; and, in consequence, we learn to do it ourselves. This prevents us from jumping to conclusions or oversimplifying the historical process. In addition, we learn how the struggle over contradictory goals, whether internalized or expressed in group conflict, moves history forward.

1

THEODORE VON LAUE

The World Revolution of Westernization, 1987

Western colonialism, according to von Laue, a modern historian, brought about a "world revolution of Westernization," the victory of Western culture that accompanied Western political domination. What, according to von Laue, are these Western ideas that spread throughout the world during the nineteenth century? Did these ideas spread peacefully or were they forced on non-Western peoples? What groups of people were most attracted to Western ideas? Why did some non-Western people prefer Western culture to their own?

Does von Laue believe that this "world revolution" was a good thing? Does he believe it is over? What, according to von Laue, must still be done?

THINKING HISTORICALLY

Von Laue is particularly interested in the plight of what he calls the "Westernized non-Western intelligentsia." Who are these people? What is their problem? What does von Laue mean when he says that "as a result of their Westernization they became anti-Western nationalists"? How could Westernization make people anti-Western?

Throughout this selection, von Laue discusses paradoxical or ironic behavior. He writes of people learning lessons that were not

Source: Theodore von Laue, *The World Revolution of Westernization* (New York: Oxford University Press, 1987), 27–34.

formally taught and of psychological conflicts or love-hate attitudes. At one point he generalizes this phenomenon of seemingly contradictory behavior by quoting an eighteenth-century maxim that states, "To do just the opposite is also a form of imitation." Is von Laue describing some paradoxical aspect of human nature, or are these conflicts a particular product of colonialism?

While the world revolution of Westernization created a political world order radically above the horizons of all past human experience, it also unhinged, in the revolutionary manner sensed by Lord Lytton,[1] the depths of non-Western societies constituting the bulk of humanity. As he had said, "The application of the most refined principles of European government and some of the most artificial institutions of European society to a . . . vast population in whose history, habits, and traditions they have had no previous existence" was a risky enterprise, perhaps more than he had anticipated.

Examining the history of colonial expansion, one can discern a rough but generally applicable pattern for the revolutionary subversion of non-Western societies. Subversion began at the apex, with the defeat, humiliation, or even overthrow of traditional rulers. The key guarantee of law, order, and security from external interference was thus removed. With it went the continuity of tradition, whether of governance or of all other social institutions down to the subtle customs regulating the individual psyche. Thus ended not only political but also cultural self-determination. Henceforth, the initiatives shaping collective existence came from without, "mysterious formulas of a foreign and more or less uncongenial system" not only of administration but also of every aspect of life.

Once the authority of the ruler (who often was the semi-divine intermediary between Heaven and Earth) was subverted, the Western attack on the other props of society intensified. Missionaries, their security guaranteed by Western arms, discredited the local gods and their guardians, weakening the spiritual foundations of society. At the same time, colonial administrators interfered directly in indigenous affairs by suppressing hallowed practices repulsive to them, including human sacrifice, slavery, and physical cruelty in its many forms. Meanwhile, Western businessmen and their local agents redirected the channels of trade and economic life, making local producers and consumers dependent on a world market beyond their comprehension and control. In a thousand ways the colonial administration and its allies, though not necessarily in agreement with each other, introduced a new set of rewards and punishments, of prestige and authority. The changeover was obvious even in

---

[1] British viceroy of India from 1876 to 1880.

the externals of dress. Africans became ashamed of their nudity, women covered their breasts; Chinese men cut off their queues and adopted Western clothes. The boldest even tried to become like Westerners "in taste, in opinion, in morals, and intellect."

The pathways of subversion here outlined indicate the general pattern and the directions which it followed over time. Its speed depended on Western policy and the resilience of local society. Things seemingly fell apart quickly in the case of the most vulnerable small-scale societies of Africa and much more slowly in India or China, if at all in Japan. Often the colonial administration itself, under the policy of "indirect rule," slowed the Western impact for fear of causing cultural chaos and making trouble for itself. In all cases, tradition (however subverted) persisted in a thousand forms, merely retreating from the external world into the subliminally conditioned responses of the human psyche, its last refuge. It is still lurking in the promptings of "soul" today.

And did things really fall apart? The world revolution of Westernization prevailed by the arts of both war and peace. Certain aspects of Western power possessed an intrinsic appeal which, even by indigenous judgment, enhanced life. New crops often brought ampler food; European rule often secured peace. Through their command of the seas and of worldwide trade Europeans and Americans opened access to survival and opportunity in foreign lands to countless millions of people in China and India. Or take even the persuasion of raw power: Once convinced of the superiority of European weapons, who would not crave possession of them too? And more generally, being associated with European power also carried weight; it patently held the keys to the future. More directly perhaps, doing business with Westerners promised profit. If they played it right, compradors would get rich.

More subtly, certain categories of the local population eagerly took to foreign ways. Missionaries sheltered outcasts: slaves held for sacrifice, girls to be sold into prostitution or abandoned, or married women feeling abused and oppressed. The struggle for sexual equality is still raging in our midst, yet by comparison even Victorian England offered hope to women in Africa or East Asia. Regarding Japan, Fukuzawa[2] related the story of a highborn dowager lady who "had had some unhappy trials in earlier days." She was told of "the most remarkable of all the Western customs . . . the relations between men and women," where "men and women had equal rights, and monogamy was the strict rule in any class of people. . . ." It was, Fukuzawa reported, "as if her eyes were suddenly opened to something new. . . ." As a messenger of women's rights he certainly had Japanese women, "especially the ladies of the higher society," on his side. In China liberated women rushed to unbind their feet.

---

[2] See selection 2 on page 893. [Ed.]

In addition, the Westerners introduced hospitals and medicines that relieved pain and saved lives, a fact not unappreciated. Besides, whose greed was not aroused by the plethora of Western goods, all fancier than local products: stronger liquor, gaudier textiles, faster transport? Simple minds soon preferred Western goods merely because they were Western. Given the comparative helplessness of local society, was it surprising that everything Western tended to be judged superior?

The Westerners with their sense of mission also introduced their education. It was perhaps not enough, according to anti-Western nationalists suspicious of European desires, to keep the natives down, yet it offered access to Western skills at some sacrifice on the part of teachers willing to forgo the easier life in their own culture. Privileged non-Westerners even attended schools and universities in the West. Thus, as part of the general pattern of Westernization, a new category of cultural half-breeds was created, the Westernized non-Western intelligentsia. It differed somewhat according to cultural origins, but shared a common predicament. Product of one culture, educated in another, it was caught in invidious comparison. As [philosopher] Thomas Hobbes observed "Man, whose Joy consisteth in comparing himselfe with other men, can relish nothing but what is eminent." Riveted to Western preeminence, this intelligentsia struggled for purpose, identity, and recognition in the treacherous no-man's-land in between—and most furiously in lands where skin color added to its disabilities. Talented and industrious, these intellectuals threw themselves heroically into the study of Western society and thought so alien to their own.

Along the way they soon acquired a taste for the dominant ideals of the West, foremost the liberal plea for equality, freedom, and self-determination and the socialists' cry of social justice for all exploited and oppressed peoples and classes. They were delighted by the bitter self-criticism they discovered among Westerners—Western society produced many doubters, especially among its fringes in central and eastern Europe. At the same time, non-Western intellectuals quickly perceived the pride that lurked behind Western humanitarianism. They might be treated as equals in London or Paris, but "east of Aden" on the Indian circuit or anywhere in the colonies, they were "natives"—natives hypersensitive to the hypocrisy behind the Western mission of exporting high ideals without the congenital ingredient of equality. Thus they learned the lessons of power not formally taught by their masters. They needed power—state power—not only to carry the Western vision into practice on their own but also to make equality real.

Inevitably, the non-Western intellectuals turned their lessons to their own use. The ideals of freedom and self-determination justified giving free rein not only to the promptings of their own minds and souls, but also to protests over the humiliation of their countries and cultures. As a result of their Westernization they became anti-Western nationalists, outwardly curtailing, in themselves and their compatriots, the abject imitation of the West. Yet, as an 18th-century German wag had said, "To do just the opposite is also a form of imitation." Anti-Western self-assertion was a form of Westernization copying the cultural self-assertion of the West. Moreover, limiting western influence in fact undercut any chance of matching Western power (and the issue of power was never far from their minds). Thus anti-Western intellectuals were caught in a love-hate attitude toward the West, anti-Western purveyors of further Westernization.

Take Mohandas Gandhi,[3] perhaps the greatest among the Westernized non-Western intellectuals. Born into a prominent tradition-oriented Hindu family and of a lively, ambitious mind, he broke with Hindu taboo and studied English law in London, fashionably dressed and accepted in the best society, though by preference consorting with vegetarians and students of Eastern religion. After his return he confessed that "next to India, [he] would rather live in London than in any other place in the world." From 1892 to 1914, however, he lived in South Africa, using his legal training for defending the local Indian community against white discrimination. There he put together from Indian and Western sources a philosophy as well as a practice of nonviolent resistance, strengthening the self-confidence and civil status of his clients. . . .

One of Gandhi's precursors, Narendranath Datta, better known as Swami Vivekananda, had gone even further. At a lecture in Madras he exhorted his audience: "This is the great ideal before us, and everyone must be ready for it—the conquest of the whole world by India—nothing less than that. . . . Up India and conquer the world with your spirituality." Western globalized nationalism, obviously, was working its way around the world, escalating political ambition and cultural messianism to novel intensity. . . .

. . . [T]he run of Westernized non-Western intellectuals led awkward lives—"in a free state," as [Indian novelist] V. S. Naipaul has put it—forever in search of roots, and certitude; inwardly split, part backward, part Western, camouflaging their imitation of the West by gestures of rejection; forever aspiring to build lofty halfway houses that bridged the disparate cultural universes, often in all-embracing designs, never admitting the fissures and cracks in their lives and opinions; and always covering up their unease with a compensating presumption of moral superiority based on the recognition that the promptings of heart and soul are superior to the dictates of reason. Knowing their own traditions and at least some of the essentials of the West, they sensed that they had a more elevated grasp of human reality; the future belonged to them rather than to the "decadent" West. Out of that existential misery of "heightened consciousness" (as [Russian novelist] Dostoyevsky

[3] See selection 6 on page 909. [Ed.]

called it) have come some of the most seminal contributions to the intellectual and political developments of the 20th century, including the anti-Western counterrevolutions.

. . . Let it be said first that the relations between the colonized and the colonizer are exceedingly subtle and complex, subject to keen controversy among all observers, all of them partisans, all of them now judging not by indigenous but by Westernized standards. Western ideals and practices have shaped and intensified the protests of Westernized non-Western intellectuals taking full advantage of the opportunities offered by Western society. Their protests, incidentally, were hardly ever turned against past inhumanities committed by their own kind (because traditionally they were not considered as such).

Next, having already surveyed the not inconsiderable side benefits of Western domination, let us ask: Did the Westerners in their expansion behave toward the non-Westerners worse than they behaved toward themselves? While they never treated their colonial subjects as equals, they never killed as many people in all their colonial campaigns as they did in their own wars at home (the brutality of Europe's cultural evolution has been carefully rinsed out of all current historical accounts). And in their peaceful intercourse with non-Westerners we find the whole range of emotions common in Western society. It was darkness at heart on one extreme and saintliness on the other, and every mix in between, with the balance perhaps tending toward darkness. As one colonial officer in East Africa confided to his diary: "It is but a small percentage of white men whose characters do not in one way or another undergo a subtle process of deteriorization when they are compelled to live for any length of time among savage races and under conditions as exist in tropical climates." The colonial district commissioner, isolated among people whose ways sharply contradicted his own upbringing, often suffering from tropical sickness, and scared at heart, found himself perhaps in a worse dilemma than the Westernized non-Western intellectuals. Some of them, no doubt, were unscrupulous opportunists seeking escape from the trammels of civic conformity at home; they turned domineering sadists in the colonies. On the other hand, missionaries often sacrificed their lives, generally among uncomprehending local folk. It was perhaps a credit to the Westerners that the victims of imperialism found considerable sympathy in their own midst. The evils stood out while the good intentions were taken for granted.

Yet—to take a longer view—even compassionate Western observers generally overlook the fact that among all the gifts of the West the two most crucial boons were missing: cultural equality as the basis for political equality and reasonable harmony in the body politic. The world revolution of Westernization perpetuated inequality and ruinous cultural subversion while at the same time improving the material conditions of life. More people survived, forever subject to the agonies of inequality and disorientation resulting from enforced change originating beyond their ken. Collectively and individually, they straddled the border between West and non-West, on the one side enjoying the benefits of Western culture, on the other feeling exploited as victims of imperialism. Indigenous populations always remained backward and dependent, unable to match the resources and skills of a fast-advancing West.

What we should weigh, then, in any assessment of Western colonial expansion before World War I is perhaps not only the actions, good or evil, of the colonial powers, but also the long-run consequences thereafter. The victims of Western colonialism do not include only the casualties of colonial wars but also the far greater multitudes killed or brutalized in the civil commotions in the emerging modern nation-states. Whatever the mitigating circumstances, the anti-Western fury has its justifications indeed.

2

FUKUZAWA YUKICHI

Good-bye Asia, 1885

Fukuzawa* Yukichi (1835–1901) was one of the most important Japanese Westernizers during Japan's late-nineteenth-century rush to catch up with the West. The son of a lower samurai (military) family, his pursuit of Western knowledge took him to a Dutch school in Osaka, where he studied everything from the Dutch language to chemistry, physics, and anatomy, and to Yedo, where he studied English. Due to his privileged background and Western schooling, he was naturally included in the first Japanese mission to the United States in 1860 as well as in the first diplomatic mission to Europe in 1862. After he returned to Japan, he spent many years teaching and writing the books that would make him famous. The best known of these was Seiyo Jijo (Things Western), which in 1866 introduced Japanese readers to the daily life and typical institutions of Western society. According to Fukuzawa Yukichi, the main obstacle that prevented Japanese society from catching up with the West was a long heritage of Chinese Confucianism, which stifled educational independence.

In the years after the Meiji Restoration of 1868, in which feudalism was abolished and power was restored to the emperor, Fukuzawa

* foo koo ZAH wah

Source: Fukuzawa Yukichi, "Datsu-a Ron" ("On Saying Good-bye to Asia"), in *Japan: A Documentary History*, ed. David J. Lu (Armonk, NY: M. E. Sharpe, 1997), 2:351–53. From Takeuchi Yoshimi, ed., *Azia Shugi (Asianism) Gendai Nihon Shisō Taikei (Great Compilation of Modern Japanese Thought)* (Tokyo: Chikuma Shobō, 1963), 8:38–40.

Yukichi became the most popular spokesman for the Westernizing policies of the new government. In this essay, "Good-bye Asia," written in 1885, he describes the spread of Western civilization in Japan. Why does he believe that it is both inevitable and desirable? What do you make of his attitude toward Chinese and Korean civilizations?

THINKING HISTORICALLY

Fukuzawa Yukichi is an unapologetic Westernizer. How does his attitude resemble that of a religious convert? Despite his lack of doubt about the advantages of Western ways, however, he does not criticize Japanese culture. He shows how a Westernizer could at the same time be nationalistic. In what ways is his attitude also nationalistic?

Transportation has become so convenient these days that once the wind of Western civilization blows to the East, every blade of grass and every tree in the East follow what the Western wind brings. Ancient Westerners and present-day Westerners are from the same stock and are not much different from one another. The ancient ones moved slowly, but their contemporary counterparts move vivaciously at a fast pace. This is possible because present-day Westerners take advantage of the means of transportation available to them. For those of us who live in the Orient, unless we want to prevent the coming of Western civilization with a firm resolve, it is best that we cast our lot with them. If one observes carefully what is going on in today's world, one knows the futility of trying to prevent the onslaught of Western civilization. Why not float with them in the same ocean of civilization, sail the same waves, and enjoy the fruits and endeavors of civilization?

The movement of a civilization is like the spread of measles. Measles in Tokyo start in Nagasaki and come eastward with the spring thaw. We may hate the spread of this communicable disease, but is there any effective way of preventing it? I can prove that it is not possible. In a communicable disease, people receive only damages. In a civilization, damages may accompany benefits, but benefits always far outweigh them, and their force cannot be stopped. This being the case, there is no point in trying to prevent their spread. A wise man encourages the spread and allows our people to get used to its ways.

The opening to the modern civilization of the West began in the reign of Kaei (1848–58).[1] Our people began to discover its utility and

---

[1] Refers to the Kaei era of the emperor Kōmei (r. 1846–1867). The emperor opposed Western influences but was forced to allow Dutch vaccination in 1849, admit Commodore Perry's U.S. fleet in 1853, permit coaling rights to U.S. ships in 1854, and accept the Treaty of Amity and Commerce in 1859. [Ed.]

gradually and yet actively moved toward its acceptance. However, there was an old-fashioned and bloated government that stood in the way of progress. It was a problem impossible to solve. If the government were allowed to continue, the new civilization could not enter. The modern civilization and Japan's old conventions were mutually exclusive. If we were to discard our old conventions, that government also had to be abolished. We could have prevented the entry of this civilization, but it would have meant loss of our national independence. The struggles taking place in the world civilization were such that they would not allow an Eastern island nation to slumber in isolation. At that point, dedicated men (*shijin*) recognized the principle of "the country is more important than the government," relied on the dignity of the Imperial Household, and toppled the old government to establish a new one.[2] With this, public and the private sectors alike, everyone in our country accepted the modern Western civilization. Not only were we able to cast aside Japan's old conventions, but we also succeeded in creating a new axle toward progress in Asia. Our basic assumptions could be summarized in two words: "Good-bye Asia (*Datsu-a*)."

Japan is located in the eastern extremities of Asia, but the spirit of her people have already moved away from the old conventions of Asia to the Western civilization. Unfortunately for Japan, there are two neighboring countries. One is called China and another Korea. These two peoples, like the Japanese people, have been nurtured by Asiatic political thoughts and mores. It may be that we are different races of people, or it may be due to the differences in our heredity or education; significant differences mark the three peoples. The Chinese and Koreans are more like each other and together they do not show as much similarity to the Japanese. These two peoples do not know how to progress either personally or as a nation. In this day and age with transportation becoming so convenient, they cannot be blind to the manifestations of Western civilization. But they say that what is seen or heard cannot influence the disposition of their minds. Their love affairs with ancient ways and old customs remain as strong as they were centuries ago. In this new and vibrant theater of civilization when we speak of education, they only refer back to Confucianism. As for school education, they can only cite [Chinese philosopher Mencius's] precepts of humanity, righteousness, decorum, and knowledge. While professing their abhorrence to ostentation, in reality they show their ignorance of truth and principles. As for their morality, one only has to observe their unspeakable acts of cruelty

---

[2] The Meiji Restoration (1868). Meiji was a son of Kōmei (who died of smallpox in 1867). Meiji restored the power of the emperor over the Tokugawa Shogunate, a feudal council that had ruled since 1603. Meiji eagerly sought contacts with the West so that Japan would not fall behind. [Ed.]

and shamelessness. Yet they remain arrogant and show no sign of self-examination.

In my view, these two countries cannot survive as independent nations with the onslaught of Western civilization to the East.[3] Their concerned citizens might yet find a way to engage in a massive reform, on the scale of our Meiji Restoration, and they could change their governments and bring about a renewal of spirit among their peoples. If that could happen they would indeed be fortunate. However, it is more likely that would never happen, and within a few short years they will be wiped out from the world with their lands divided among the civilized nations. Why is this so? Simply at a time when the spread of civilization and enlightenment (*bummei kaika*) has a force akin to that of measles, China and Korea violate the natural law of its spread. They forcibly try to avoid it by shutting off air from their rooms. Without air, they suffocate to death. It is said that neighbors must extend helping hands to one another because their relations are inseparable. Today's China and Korea have not done a thing for Japan. From the perspectives of civilized Westerners, they may see what is happening in China and Korea and judge Japan accordingly, because of the three countries' geographical proximity. The governments of China and Korea still retain their autocratic manners and do not abide by the rule of law. Westerners may consider Japan likewise a lawless society. Natives of China and Korea are deep in their hocus pocus of nonscientific behavior. Western scholars may think that Japan still remains a country dedicated to the *yin* and *yang* and five elements.[4] Chinese are meanspirited and shameless, and the chivalry of the Japanese people is lost to the Westerners. Koreans punish their convicts in an atrocious manner, and that is imputed to the Japanese as heartless people. There are many more examples I can cite. It is not different from the case of a righteous man living in a neighborhood of a town known for foolishness, lawlessness, atrocity, and heartlessness. His action is so rare that it is always buried under the ugliness of his neighbors' activities. When these incidents are multiplied, that can affect our normal conduct of diplomatic affairs. How unfortunate it is for Japan.

What must we do today? We do not have time to wait for the enlightenment of our neighbors so that we can work together toward the development of Asia. It is better for us to leave the ranks of Asian nations and cast our lot with civilized nations of the West. As for the way

---

[3] By 1885 China had been "opened" by Western powers in two opium wars (1839–1842, 1856–1860). Korea had been invaded by France (1866) and the United States (1871). Its isolation ended in 1885 by treaty with the United States. [Ed.]

[4] *Yin* and *yang* is a traditional Chinese duality (cold/hot, passive/active, female/male) illustrated by a circle divided by an "s" to show unity within duality. The five elements suggest another traditional, prescientific idea that everything is made of five basic ingredients. [Ed.]

of dealing with China and Korea, no special treatment is necessary just because they happen to be our neighbors. We simply follow the manner of the Westerners in knowing how to treat them. Any person who cherishes a bad friend cannot escape his bad notoriety. We simply erase from our minds our bad friends in Asia.

3

Images from Japan: Views of Westernization, Late Nineteenth Century

This selection consists of two prints by Japanese artists from the Meiji period of Westernization. The first print, Figure 23.1 is called *Monkey Show Dressing Room* (1879), by Honda Kinkachiro. What is this print's message? What is the artist's attitude toward Westernization?

The second piece, Figure 23.2, *The Exotic White Man*, shows a child born to a Western man and a Japanese woman. What is the artist's message? Does the artist favor such unions? What does the artist think of Westerners?

Figure 23.1   Monkey Show Dressing Room.

Source: Honda Kinkachiro, *Monkey Show Dressing Room*, in Julia Meech-Pekarik, *The World of the Meiji Print* (New York: John Weatherhill, 1986).

Figure 23.2   The Exotic White Man.

Source: Japanese color print, late 19th c., Dutch private collection, in C. A. Burland, *The Exotic White Man* (New York: McGraw-Hill, 1969), fig. 38. Werner Forman/Art Resource, NY.

THINKING HISTORICALLY

Compare the attitudes of these artists with that of Fukuzawa Yukichi. Prints, like cartoons, are a shorthand that must capture an easily recognizable trait. What, evidently, were the widely understood Japanese images of the West? Where do you think these stereotypes of the West came from? Do you see any signs in these prints of ambivalence on the part of the artist?

4

KAKUZO OKAKURA

The Ideals of the East, 1904

Kakuzo Okakura (1862–1913) was a Japanese scholar who was responsible for the development and preservation of the arts in Japan. In addition to creating important art schools and journals, he was the director of the Imperial Art School in Tokyo. In 1890 he founded the first Japanese art academy. In later life he worked and lectured in England and the United States, serving as the director of the Chinese and Japanese department at Harvard and, after 1910, as Curator of the Museum of Fine Arts in Boston. He is best known for *The Book of Tea*, which introduced the ritual beauty of the Japanese tea service to a Western audience. He also wrote for a Western audience *The Awakening of Japan* and *The Ideals of the East*, from which this selection is taken.

What are the "ideals of the East" that Okakura celebrates? What are the features of the West that he wants Japan to avoid?

THINKING HISTORICALLY

In Okakura the contradictions abound. He was a cosmopolitan world traveler, living in Europe, the United States, China, and India, as well as Japan. Yet, at the Imperial Art School in Tokyo, he offered no courses in Western Art. He spent his last years in Boston, developing the Asian art collection of an American museum. He wrote all of his major books in English, albeit to extol Asian, especially Japanese, art to the wider world. He was a modern urbanite who sought strength of identity in blood and the past.

How does he use the then popular Western idea of "race" in this selection? How does he negotiate the conflict between Japanese nationalism and a broader Pan-Asian identity? How does he combine love of monarchy with ideas of democracy? How does he reconcile tradition and individualism?

The Range of Ideals

Asia is one. The Himalayas divide, only to accentuate, two mighty civilisations, the Chinese with its communism of Confucius, and the Indian with its individualism of the Vedas. But not even the snowy

---

Source: Kakuzo Okakura, *Ideals of the East: The Spirit of Japanese Art* (Mineola, NY: Dover Publications, Inc., 2005), 1–4, 103–06.

barriers can interrupt for one moment that broad expanse of love for the Ultimate and Universal, which is the common thought-inheritance of every Asiatic race, enabling them to produce all the great religions of the world, and distinguishing them from those maritime peoples of the Mediterranean and the Baltic, who love to dwell on the Particular, and to search out the means, not the end, of life. . . .

For if Asia be one, it is also true that the Asiatic races form a single mighty web. We forget, in an age of classification, that types are after all but shining points of distinctness in an ocean of approximations, false gods deliberately set up to be worshipped, for the sake of mental convenience, but having no more ultimate or mutually exclusive validity than the separate existence of two interchangeable sciences. . . .

Buddhism—that great ocean of idealism, in which merge all the river-systems of Eastern Asiatic thought—is not coloured only with the pure water of the Ganges, for the Tartaric nations[1] that joined it made their genius also tributary, bringing new symbolism, new organisation, new powers of devotion, to add to the treasures of the Faith.

It has been, however, the great privilege of Japan to realise this unity-in-complexity with a special clearness. The Indo-Tartaric blood of this race was in itself a heritage which qualified it to imbibe from the two sources, and so mirror the whole of Asiatic consciousness. The unique blessing of unbroken sovereignty, the proud self-reliance of an unconquered race, and the insular isolation which protected ancestral ideas and instincts at the cost of expansion, made Japan the real repository of the trust of Asiatic thought and culture. Dynastic upheavals, the inroads of Tartar horsemen, the carnage and devastation of infuriated mobs—all these things, sweeping over her again and again, have left to China no landmarks, save her literature and her ruins, to recall the glory of the Tang emperors or the refinement of Sung society. . . .

It is in Japan alone that the historic wealth of Asiatic culture can be consecutively studied through its treasured specimens. The Imperial collection, the Shinto[2] temples, and the opened dolmens, reveal the subtle curves of Hang[3] workmanship. The temples of Nara[4] are rich in representations of Tang culture, and of that Indian art, then in its splendour, which so much influenced the creations of this classic period—natural heirlooms of a nation which has preserved the music, pronunciation, ceremony, and costumes, not to speak of the religious rites and philosophy, of so remarkable an age, intact.

---

[1] He means Central Asian Turks and Mongols. [Ed.]
[2] Traditional Japanese religion. [Ed.]
[3] Han, i.e., classical Chinese. [Ed.]
[4] City in Japan, capital 710–784 (the Nara Period). [Ed.]

The treasure-stores of the daimyos,[5] again, abound in works of art and manuscripts belonging to the Sung and Mongol dynasties, and as in China itself the former were lost during the Mongol conquest, and the latter in the age of the reactionary Ming, this fact animates some Chinese scholars of the present day to seek in Japan the fountain-head of their own ancient knowledge.

Thus Japan is a museum of Asiatic civilisation; and yet more than a museum, because the singular genius of the race leads it to dwell on all phases of the ideals of the past, in that spirit of living Advaitism[6] which welcomes the new without losing the old. The Shinto still adheres to his pre-Buddhistic rites of ancestor-worship; and the Buddhists themselves cling to each various school of religious development which has come in its natural order to enrich the soil.

The Yamato poetry,[7] and Bugaku music,[8] which reflect the Tang ideal under the régime of the Fujiwara aristocracy,[9] are a source of inspiration and delight to the present day, like the sombre Zennism[10] and No-dances,[11] which were the product of Sung illumination. It is this tenacity that keeps Japan true to the Asiatic soul even while it raises her to the rank of a modern power.

The history of Japanese art becomes thus the history of Asiatic ideals—the beach where each successive wave of Eastern thought has left its sand-ripple as it beat against the national consciousness. Yet I linger with dismay on the threshold of an attempt to make an intelligible summary of those art-ideals. For art, like the diamond net of Indra,[12] reflects the whole chain in every link. It exists at no period in any final mould. It is always a growth, defying the dissecting knife of the chronologist. To discourse on a particular phase of its development means to deal with infinite causes and effects throughout its past and present. Art with us, as elsewhere, is the expression of the highest and noblest of our national culture, so that, in order to understand it, we must pass in review the various phases of Confucian philosophy; the different ideals which the Buddhist mind has from time to time revealed; those mighty political cycles which have one after another unfurled the banner of nationality; the reflection in patriotic thought of the lights of poetry and the shadows of heroic characters; and the echoes, alike of the wailing of a multitude, and of the mad-seeming merriment of the laughter of a race. . . .

---

[5] Warlords of feudal Japan. [Ed.]

[6] Indian philosophy of wholeness and immediacy. [Ed.]

[7] Earliest Japanese poetry, seventh–tenth centuries; also period of Tang dynasty in China. [Ed.]

[8] Ceremonial dance music of elite of same period. [Ed.]

[9] Ruling clan in Heian period (794–1185). [Ed.]

[10] Japanese Zen Buddhism. [Ed.]

[11] Highly stylized Japanese dance theater. [Ed.]

[12] Indian god. [Ed.]

The Vista

The simple life of Asia need fear no shaming from that sharp contrast with Europe in which steam and electricity have placed it to-day. The old world of trade, the world of the craftsman and the pedlar, of the village market and the saints'-day fair, where little boats row up and down great rivers laden with the produce of the country, where every palace has some court in which the travelling merchant may display his stuffs and jewels for beautiful screened women to see and buy, is not yet quite dead. And, however its form may change, only at a great loss can Asia permit its spirit to die, since the whole of that industrial and decorative art which is the heirloom of ages has been in its keeping, and she must lose with it not only the beauty of things, but the joy of the worker, his individuality of vision, and the whole age-long humanising of her labour. For to clothe oneself in the web of one's own weaving is to house oneself in one's own house, to create for the spirit its own sphere.

Asia knows, it is true, nothing of the fierce joys of a time-devouring locomotion, but she has still the far deeper travel-culture of the pilgrimage and the wandering monk. For the Indian ascetic, begging his bread of village housewives, or seated at evenfall beneath some tree, chatting and smoking with the peasant of the district, is the real traveller. To him a countryside does not consist of its natural features alone. It is a nexus of habits and associations. Of human elements and traditions, suffused with the tenderness and friendship of one who has shared, if only for a moment, the joys and sorrows of its personal drama. The Japanese peasant-traveller, again, goes from no place of interest on his wanderings without leaving his *hokku* or short sonnet, an art-form within reach of the simplest.

Through such modes of experience is cultivated the Eastern conception of individuality as the ripe and living knowledge, the harmonised thought and feeling of staunch yet gentle manhood. Through such modes of interchange is maintained the Eastern notion of human intercourse, not the printed index, as the true means of culture.

The chain of antitheses might be indefinitely lengthened. But the glory of Asia is something more positive than these. It lies in that vibration of peace that beats in every heart; that harmony that brings together emperor and peasant; that sublime intuition of oneness which commands all sympathy, all courtesy, to be its fruits, making Takakura, Emperor of Japan, remove his sleeping-robes on a winter night, because the frost lay cold on the hearths of his poor; or Taiso, of Tang, forego food, because his people were feeling the pinch of famine. It lies in the dream of renunciation that pictures the Boddhi-Sattva[13] as

---

[13] Buddhist Boddisattva: saint; model of compassion. [Ed.]

refraining from Nirvana till the last atom of dust in the universe shall have passed in before to bliss. It lies in that worship of Freedom which casts around poverty the halo of greatness, imposes his stern simplicity of apparel on the Indian prince, and sets up in China a throne whose imperial occupant — alone amongst the great secular rulers of the world — never wears a sword.

These things are the secret energy of the thought, the science, the poetry, and the art of Asia. Torn from their tradition, India, made barren of that religious life which is the essence of her nationality, would become a worshipper of the mean, the false, and the new; China, hurled upon the problems of a material instead of a moral civilisation, would writhe in the death-agony of that ancient dignity and ethics which long ago made the word of her merchants like the legal bond of the West, the name of her peasants a synonym for prosperity; and Japan, the Fatherland of the race of Ama,[14] would betray the completeness of her undoing in the tarnishing of the purity of the spiritual mirror, the bemeaning of the sword-soul from steel to lead. The task of Asia to-day, then, becomes that of protecting and restoring Asiatic modes. But to do this she must herself first recognise and develop consciousness of those modes. For the shadows of the past are the promise of the future. No tree can be greater than the power that is in the seed. Life lies ever in the return to self. How many of the Evangels have uttered this truth! "Know thyself," was the greatest mystery spoken by the Delphic Oracle. "All in thyself," said the quiet voice of Confucius. And more striking still is the Indian story that carries the same message to its hearers. For once it happened, say the Buddhists, that, the Master having gathered his disciples round him, there shone forth before them suddenly — blasting the sight of all save Vajrapani, the completely-learned — a terrible figure, the figure of Siva, the Great God. Then Vajrapani, his companions being blinded, turned to the Master and said, "Tell me why, searching amongst all the stars and gods, equal in number to the sands of the Ganges, I have nowhere seen this glorious form. Who is he?" And the Buddha said, "He is thyself!" and Vajrapani, it is told, immediately attained the highest.

It was some small degree of this self-recognition that re-made Japan, and enabled her to weather the storm under which so much of the Oriental world went down. And it must be a renewal of the same self-consciousness that shall build up Asia again into her ancient steadfastness and strength. The very times are bewildered by the manifoldness of the possibilities opening out before them. Even Japan cannot, in the tangled skein of the Meiji period,[15] find that single thread which will give

[14] Japanese divers. [Ed.]
[15] 1868–1912. [Ed.]

her the clue to her own future. Her past has been clear and continuous as a mala, a rosary, of crystals. From the early days of the Asuka period,[16] when the national destiny was first bestowed, as the receiver and concentrator, by her Yamato genius, of Indian ideals and Chinese ethics; through the succeeding preliminary phases of Nara and Heian, to the revelation of her vast powers in the unmeasured devotion of her Fujiwara period, in her heroic reaction of Kamakura,[17] culminating in the stern enthusiasm and lofty abstinence of that Ashikaga[18] knighthood who sought with so austere a passion after death—through all these phases the evolution of the nation is clear and unconfused, like that of a single personality. Even through Toyotomi,[19] and Tokugawa,[20] it is clear that after the fashion of the East we are ending a rhythm of activity with the lull of the democratising of the great ideals. The populace and the lower classes, notwithstanding their seeming quiescence and commonplaceness, are making their own the consecration of the Samurai, the sadness of the poet, the divine self-sacrifice of the saint are becoming liberated, in fact, into their national inheritance.

But to-day the great mass of Western thought perplexes us. The mirror of Yamato is clouded, as we say. With the Revolution, Japan, it is true, returns upon her past, seeking there for the new vitality she needs. Like all genuine restorations, it is a reaction with a difference. For that self-dedication of art to nature which the Ashikaga inaugurated has become now a consecration to the race, to man himself. We know instinctively that in our history lies the secret of our future, and we grope with a blind intensity to find the clue. But if the thought be true, if there be indeed any spring of renewal hidden in our past, we must admit that it needs at this moment some mighty reinforcement, for the scorching drought of modern vulgarity is parching the throat of life and art.

We await the flashing sword of the lightning which shall cleave the darkness. For the terrible hush must be broken, and the raindrops of a new vigour must refresh the earth before new flowers can spring up to cover it with their bloom. But it must be from Asia herself, along the ancient roadways of the race, that the great voice shall be heard.

Victory from within, or a mighty death without.

---

[16] 552–645. [Ed.]

[17] 1185–1333. [Ed.]

[18] 1336–1573, Feudal period. [Ed.]

[19] Toyotomi Hideyoshi (1537–1598). A feudal lord who ended feudalism. [Ed.]

[20] Tokugawa Ieyasu (1543–1616). Founder and first shogun of the Tokugawa Shogunate (1603–1868). [Ed.]

5

RAMMOHUN ROY

Letter on Indian Education, 1823

India's Westernization was less voluntary than Japan's. While Japan successfully limited European colonialism to a few seaports in the seventeenth century and was not forced to deal with the West again until after Commodore Perry's steam-age arrival in 1853, India became increasingly colonized by England throughout the eighteenth and nineteenth centuries. Because of India's long history as a British colony, aspects of Westernization there were deeper and more complex, the most obvious being use of the English language.

A colonial and foreign tongue, English had the advantage of uniting a country with dozens of regional languages (some of which were also imposed by foreign conquerors), while at the same time providing access to universities and a body of knowledge and literature as advanced as any in the world. English instruction — rather than ancient Sanskrit or Hindi or another Indian regional language — was championed by Britons who thought it would make Indians loyal and by Indians who thought it would unite them as a nation. The Indian use of English had its detractors, too: Britons who thought it dangerous or unseemly, and Britons and Indians who thought it patronizing and demeaning.

The debate over teaching English or Indian languages was part of a larger debate about the relative value of Western and Indian culture. Increasingly, toward the end of the nineteenth century as science took center stage in English culture, Indians found themselves torn between the claim of science and the appeal of traditional Indian religious knowledge.

Rammohun Roy (1772–1833) was an Indian social and religious reformer, as well as one of the earliest proponents of English education. Roy was an accomplished linguist who knew Latin, Greek, Hebrew, Arabic, Persian, and ancient Indian Sanskrit as well as his native Bengali. Yet when the British proposed to build a new Sanskrit school in Calcutta, Roy fired off the following letter to the British prime minister. Why did Roy object to a school that taught Sanskrit, the sacred language of ancient Hindu culture? What were his reasons for preferring English education for Indians?

Source: Rammohun Roy, Letter on Indian Education, in H. Sharp, ed., *Selections from Educational Records, Part I, 1781–1839* (Calcutta: Superintendent Government Printing, 1920; reprint, Delhi: National Archives of India, 1965), 98–101.

THINKING HISTORICALLY

To effectively communicate his ideas on Indian education, Roy had to strike a delicate balance in expressing deference to the British government while asserting enough authority to be taken seriously. How did he accomplish this dual task? How did he suggest that he knew more about the issue than his superiors in the English government, without seeming arrogant or ungrateful? How does his letter show that he was an Indian who benefited from an English education but did not pose a threat to British rule? What does his letter reveal about the inherent tensions in colonial India, within individuals and the society as a whole?

To His Excellency the Right Hon'ble William Pitt, Lord Amherst
My Lord,

Humbly reluctant as the natives of India are to obtrude upon the notice of Government the sentiments they entertain on any public measure there are circumstances when silence would be carrying this respectful feeling to culpable excess. The present Rulers of India, coming from a distance of many thousand miles to govern a people whose language, literature, manners, customs, and ideas are almost entirely new and strange to them, cannot easily become so intimately acquainted with their real circumstances, as the natives of the country are themselves. We should therefore be guilty of a gross dereliction of duty to ourselves, and afford our Rulers just ground of complaint at our apathy, did we omit on occasions of importance like the present to supply them with such accurate information as might enable them to devise and adopt measures calculated to be beneficial to the country, and thus second by our local knowledge and experience their declared benevolent intentions for its improvement.

The establishment of a new Sanskrit School in Calcutta evinces the laudable desire of Government to improve the Natives of India by Education, a blessing for which they must ever be grateful; and every well wisher of the human race must be desirous that the efforts made to promote it should be guided by the most enlightened principles, so that the stream of intelligence may flow into the most useful channels.

When this Seminary of learning was proposed, we understood that the Government in England had ordered a considerable sum of money to be annually devoted to the instruction of its Indian Subjects. We were filled with sanguine hopes that this sum would be laid out in employing European Gentlemen of talents and education to instruct the natives of India in Mathematics, Natural Philosophy, Chemistry, Anatomy and other useful Sciences, which the Nations of Europe have carried to a degree of perfection that has raised them above the inhabitants of other parts of the world.

While we looked forward with pleasing hope to the dawn of knowledge thus promised to the rising generation, our hearts were filled with mingled feelings of delight and gratitude; we already offered up thanks to Providence for inspiring the most generous and enlightened of the Nations of the West with the glorious ambitions of planting in Asia the Arts and Sciences of modern Europe.

We now find that the Government are establishing a Sanskrit school under Hindu Pundits to impart such knowledge as is already current in India. This Seminary (similar in character to those which existed in Europe before the time of Lord Bacon[1]) can only be expected to load the minds of youth with grammatical niceties and metaphysical distinctions of little or no practicable use to the possessors or to society. The pupils will there acquire what was known two thousand years ago, with the addition of vain and empty subtilties [sic] since produced by speculative men, such as is already commonly taught in all parts of India.

The Sanskrit language, so difficult that almost a life time is necessary for its perfect acquisition, is well known to have been for ages a lamentable check on the diffusion of knowledge; and the learning concealed under this almost impervious veil is far from sufficient to reward the labour of acquiring it. But if it were thought necessary to perpetuate this language for the sake of the portion of the valuable information it contains, this might be much more easily accomplished by other means than the establishment of a new Sanskrit College; for there have been always and are now numerous professors of Sanskrit in the different parts of the country, engaged in teaching this language as well as the other branches of literature which are to be the object of the new Seminary. Therefore their more diligent cultivation, if desirable, would be effectually promoted by holding out premiums and granting certain allowances to those most eminent Professors, who have already undertaken on their own account to teach them, and would by such rewards be stimulated to still greater exertions.

From these considerations, as the sum set apart for the instruction of the Natives of India was intended by the Government in England, for the improvement of its Indian subjects, I beg leave to state, with due deference to your Lordship's exalted situation, that if the plan now adopted be followed, it will completely defeat the object proposed; since no improvement can be expected from inducing young men to consume a dozen of years of the most valuable period of their lives in acquiring the niceties of the Byakurun or Sanskrit Grammar. For

---

[1] Francis Bacon (1561–1626), English philosopher often credited with developing the scientific method. [Ed.]

instance, in learning to discuss such points as the following: *Khad* signifying to eat, *khaduti,* he or she or it eats. Query, whether does the word *khaduti,* taken as a whole, convey the meaning *he, she,* or *it eats,* or are separate parts of this meaning conveyed by distinct portions of the word? As if in the English language it were asked, how much meaning is there in the *eat,* how much in the *s*? and is the whole meaning of the word conveyed by those two portions of it distinctly, or by them taken jointly?

Neither can much improvement arise from such speculations as the following, which are the themes suggested by the Vedanta: In what manner is the soul absorbed into the deity? What relation does it bear to the divine essence? Nor will youths be fitted to be better members of society by the Vedantic doctrines, which teach them to believe that all visible things have no real existence; that as father, brother, etc., have no actual entirety, they consequently deserve no real affection, and therefore the sooner we escape from them and leave the world the better. Again, no essential benefit can be derived by the student of the Meemangsa from knowing what it is that makes the killer of a goat sinless on pronouncing certain passages of the Vedas, and what is the real nature and operative influence of passages of the Veda, etc.

Again the student of the Nyaya Shastra cannot be said to have improved his mind after he has learned from it into how many ideal classes the objects in the Universe are divided, and what speculative relation the soul bears to the body, the body to the soul, the eye to the ear, etc.

In order to enable your Lordship to appreciate the utility of encouraging such imaginary learning as above characterised, I beg your Lordship will be pleased to compare the state of science and literature in Europe before the time of Lord Bacon, with the progress of knowledge made since he wrote.

If it had been intended to keep the British nation in ignorance of real knowledge the Baconian philosophy would not have been allowed to displace the system of the schoolmen, which was the best calculated to perpetuate ignorance. In the same manner the [Sanskrit] system of education would be the best calculated to keep this country in darkness, if such had been the policy of the British Legislature. But as the improvement of the native population is the object of the Government, it will consequently promote a more liberal and enlightened system of instruction, embracing mathematics, natural philosophy, chemistry and anatomy, with other useful sciences which may be accomplished with the sum proposed by employing a few gentlemen of talents and learning educated in Europe, and providing a college furnished with the necessary books, instruments, and other apparatus.

In representing this subject to your Lordship I conceive myself discharging a solemn duty which I owe to my countrymen and also to that enlightened Sovereign and Legislature which have extended their benevolent cares to this distant land actuated by a desire to improve its inhabitants and I therefore humbly trust you will excuse the liberty I have taken in thus expressing my sentiments to your Lordship.

I have, etc.,

Rammohun Roy
Calcutta;
The 11th December 1823

6

MOHANDAS K. GANDHI
Hind Swaraj, 1921

Mohandas K. Gandhi (1869–1948), the father of Indian independence, combined the education of an English lawyer with the temperament of an Indian ascetic to lead a national resistance movement against the British. In the century that followed British-supported reforms to the Indian education system (in the early nineteenth century), British rule had become far more pervasive and increasingly hostile toward Indian culture. Unlike Indian educational reformers, who had embraced Western culture as a means to uplift Indians, Gandhi became extremely critical of Western culture as he witnessed the havoc British rule wreaked on his country.

Gandhi began to develop his ideas of *Hind Swaraj*,* or Indian Home Rule, in 1909 while he sailed from England to South Africa, where he served as a lawyer for fellow Indians. An early version of this essay, published then, was reissued in its present form in 1921, two years after he returned to his birthplace, India, and again in 1938, in the last years of struggle against British rule.

After Gandhi's introduction, the essay takes the form of questions and answers. The questions are posed by a presumed "reader" of Gandhi's pamphlet. As "editor," Gandhi explains what he means. How does Gandhi compare life in Europe and India? What does he think of the possibility of Hindus and Muslims living together? What

---

* hihnd swah RAHJ

Source: M. K. Gandhi, *Hind Swaraj* (Ahmedabad, India: Navajivan, 1938), 31–33, 44–45, 58–59, 69–71.

does he mean by passive resistance or soul-force (Satyagraha)? Why does he think it is preferable to violence, or body-force? Gandhi was assassinated by a Hindu extremist in 1948 before he had a chance to shape the new nation. What kind of India would Gandhi have tried to create had he lived? Compare Gandhi's response to the West with that of Rammohan Roy in the previous selection. In what respects is his attitude like his contemporary, Kakuzo Okakura?

THINKING HISTORICALLY

Some historians have argued that Gandhi's contradictory roles—Hindu philosopher espousing secular nationalism and anti-modernist revolutionary—were ultimately unbridgeable. Notice how Gandhi makes a lawyer's case for traditional Indian values. How does he combine both religious and secular goals for India? How does he combine Hindu religious ideas with respect for Muslims? Were Gandhi's contradictions a fatal flaw, or could they have been his strength?

Civilization

READER   Now you will have to explain what you mean by civilization.

EDITOR   Let us first consider what state of things is described by the word "civilization." Its true test lies in the fact that people living in it make bodily welfare the object of life. We will take some examples. The people of Europe today live in better-built houses than they did a hundred years ago. This is considered an emblem of civilization, and this is also a matter to promote bodily happiness. Formerly, they wore skins, and used spears as their weapons. Now, they wear long trousers, and, for embellishing their bodies, they wear a variety of clothing, and, instead of spears, they carry with them revolvers containing five or more chambers. If people of a certain country, who have hitherto not been in the habit of wearing much clothing, boots, etc., adopt European clothing, they are supposed to have become civilized out of savagery. Formerly, in Europe, people ploughed their lands mainly by manual labour. Now, one man can plough a vast tract by means of steam engines and can thus amass great wealth. This is called a sign of civilization. Formerly, only a few men wrote valuable books. Now, anybody writes and prints anything he likes and poisons people's minds. Formerly, men travelled in waggons. Now, they fly through the air in trains at the rate of four hundred and more miles per day. This is considered the height of civilization. It has been stated that, as men progress, they shall be able to travel in airship and reach any part of the world in a few hours. Men will not need the use of their hands and feet. They will press a button, and they will have their clothing at their side. They will press another button, and they will have their newspaper. A third, and motor-car will be in waiting for them. They will have a variety of delicately dished up food. Everything will be done by machinery. Formerly, when people wanted to fight with one another, they measured between them their bodily strength; now it is possible to take away thousands of lives by one man working behind a gun from a hill. This is civilization. Formerly, men worked in the open air only as much as they liked. Now thousands of workmen meet together and for the sake of maintenance work in factories or mines. Their condition is worse than that of beasts. They are obliged to work, at the risk of their lives, at most dangerous occupations, for the sake of millionaires. Formerly, men were made slaves under physical compulsion. Now they are enslaved by temptation of money and of the luxuries that money can buy. There are now diseases of which people never dreamt before, and an army of doctors is engaged in finding out their cures, and so hospitals have increased. This is a test of civilization. Formerly, special messengers were required and much expense was incurred in order to send letters; today, anyone can abuse his fellow by means of a letter for one penny. True, at the same cost, one can send one's thanks also. Formerly, people had two or three meals consisting of home-made bread and vegetables; now, they require something to eat every two hours so that they have hardly leisure for anything else. What more need I say? . . . Even a child can understand that in all I have described above there can be no inducement to morality.

The Hindus and the Mahomedans

READER Has the introduction to Mahomedanism [Islam] not unmade the nation?

EDITOR India cannot cease to be one nation because people belonging to different religions live in it. The introduction of foreigners does not necessarily destroy the nation; they merge in it. A country is one nation only when such a condition obtains in it. That country must have a faculty for assimilation. India has ever been such a country. In reality there are as many religions as there are individuals; but those who are conscious of the spirit of nationality do not interfere with one another's religion. If they do, they are not fit to be considered a nation. If the Hindus believe that India should be peopled only by Hindus, they are living in dreamland. The Hindus, the Mahomedans, the Parsis and the Christians who have made India their country are fellow-countrymen, and they will have to live in unity, if only for their own interest. In no part of the world are one nationality and one religion synonymous terms; nor has it ever been so in India.

READER But what about the inborn enmity between Hindus and Mahomedans?

EDITOR That phrase has been invented by our mutual enemy. When the Hindus and Mahomedans fought against one another, they certainly spoke in that strain. They have long since ceased to fight. How, then, can there be any inborn enmity? Pray remember this too, that we did not cease to fight only after British occupation. The Hindus flourished under Moslem sovereigns and Moslems under the Hindu. Each party recognized that mutual fighting was suicidal, and that neither party would abandon its religion by force of arms. Both parties, therefore, decided to live in peace. With the English advent quarrels recommenced. . . .

How Can India Become Free?

READER If Indian civilization is, as you say, the best of all, how do you account for India's slavery?

EDITOR This civilization is unquestionably the best, but it is to be observed that all civilizations have been on their trial. That civilization which is permanent outlives it. Because the sons of India were found wanting, its civilization has been placed in jeopardy. But its strength is to be seen in its ability to survive the shock. Moreover, the whole of India is not touched. Those alone who have been affected by Western civilization have become enslaved. We measure the universe by our own miserable foot-rule. When we are slaves, we think that the whole universe is enslaved. Because we are in an abject condition, we think that the whole of India is in that condition. As a matter of fact, it is not so, yet it is as well to impute our slavery to the whole of India. But if we bear in mind the above fact, we can see that if we become free, India is free. And in this thought you have a definition of Swaraj. It is Swaraj when we learn to rule ourselves. It is, therefore, in the palm of our hands. Do not consider this Swaraj to be like a dream. There is no idea of sitting still. The Swaraj that I wish to picture is such that, after we have once realized it, we shall endeavour to the end of our life-time to persuade others to do likewise. But such Swaraj has to be experienced, by each one for himself. One drowning man will never save another. Slaves ourselves, it would be a mere pretension to think of freeing others. Now you will have seen that it is not necessary for us to have as our goal the expulsion of the English. If the English become Indianized, we can accommodate them. If they wish to remain in India along with their civilization, there is no room for them. It lies with us to bring about such a state of things. . . .

Passive Resistance

READER   Is there any historical evidence as to the success of what you have called soul-force or truth-force? No instance seems to have happened of any nation having risen through soul-force. I still think that the evil-doers will not cease doing evil without physical punishment.

EDITOR   The [Hindu] poet Tulsidas [1532–1623] has said: "Of religion, pity, or love, is the root, as egotism of the body. Therefore, we should not abandon pity so long as we are alive." This appears to me to be a scientific truth. We have evidence of its working at every step. The universe would disappear without the existence of that force. . . .

   The fact that there are so many men still alive in the world shows that it is based not on the force of arms but on the force of truth or love. Therefore, the greatest and most unimpeachable evidence of the success of this force is to be found in the fact that, in spite of the wars of the world, it still lives on.

   Thousands, indeed tens of thousands, depend for their existence on a very active working of this force. Little quarrels of millions of families in their daily lives disappear before the exercise of this force. Hundreds of nations live in peace. History does not and cannot take note of this fact. History is really a record of every interruption of the even working of the force of love or of the soul. Two brothers quarrel; one of them repents and re-awakens the love that was lying dormant in him; the two again begin to live in peace; nobody takes note of this. But if the two brothers, through the intervention of solicitors or some other reason take up arms or go to law — which is another form of the exhibition of brute force, — their doings would be immediately noticed in the press, they would be the talk of their neighbours and would probably go down to history. And what is true of families and communities is true of nations. There is no reason to believe that there is one law for families and another for nations. History, then, is a record of an interruption of the course of nature. Soul-force, being natural, is not noted in history.

READER   According to what you say, it is plain that instances of this kind of passive resistance are not to be found in history. It is necessary to understand this passive resistance more fully. It will be better, therefore, if you enlarge upon it.

EDITOR   Passive resistance is a method of securing rights by personal suffering; it is the reverse of resistance by arms. When I refuse to do a thing that is repugnant to my conscience, I use soul-force. For instance, the Government of the day has passed a law which is applicable to me. I do not like it. If by using violence I force the Government to repeal the law, I am employing what may be termed body-force. If I do not obey the law and accept the penalty for its breach, I use soul-force. It involves sacrifice of self.

7

JAWAHARLAL NEHRU

Gandhi, 1936

Mohandas K. Gandhi and Jawaharlal Nehru* were the two most important leaders of India's national independence movement. In 1936 Nehru published his autobiography, excerpted here, in which he had much to say about the importance of Gandhi in his life. Though they worked together and Nehru was Gandhi's choice as the first Indian prime minister, they expressed in their personalities and ideas two very different Indias. How would you describe these two Indias? Was it Gandhi's or Nehru's vision of the future that was realized? Who do you think was a better guide for India? Why?

THINKING HISTORICALLY

Think of Gandhi and Nehru as the two sides of the Indian struggle for independence. Did India benefit from having both of these sides represented? What would have happened if there had been only Gandhi's view or only Nehru's?

How was the debate in India about the influence of the West different from the debate in Japan?

I imagine that Gandhiji[1] is not so vague about the objective as he sometimes appears to be. He is passionately desirous of going in a certain direction, but this is wholly at variance with modern ideas and conditions, and he has so far been unable to fit the two, or to chalk out all the

---

* jah wah HAHR lahl　NAY roo
[1] Term of endearment for Gandhi. [Ed.]

Source: Jawaharlal Nehru, *An Autobiography* (New Delhi: Allied Publishers, 1942–1962), 510–11.

intermediate steps leading to his goal. Hence the appearance of vagueness and avoidance of clarity. But his general inclination has been clear enough for a quarter of a century, ever since he started formulating his philosophy in South Africa. I do not know if those early writings still represent his views. I doubt if they do so in their entirety, but they do help us to understand the background of his thought.

"India's salvation consists," he wrote in 1909, "in unlearning what she has learned during the last fifty years. The railways, telegraphs, hospitals, lawyers, doctors, and suchlike have all to go; and the so-called upper classes have to learn consciously, religiously, and deliberately the simple peasant life, knowing it to be a life giving true happiness." And again: "Every time I get into a railway car or use a motor bus I know that I am doing violence to my sense of what is right"; "to attempt to reform the world by means of highly artificial and speedy locomotion is to attempt the impossible."

All this seems to me utterly wrong and harmful doctrine, and impossible of achievement. Behind it lies Gandhiji's love and praise of poverty and suffering and the ascetic life. For him progress and civilization consist not in the multiplication of wants, of higher standards of living, "but in the deliberate and voluntary restriction of wants, which promotes real happiness and contentment, and increases the capacity for service." If these premises are once accepted, it becomes easy to follow the rest of Gandhiji's thought and to have a better understanding of his activities. But most of us do not accept those premises, and yet we complain later on when we find that his activities are not to our liking.

Personally I dislike the praise of poverty and suffering. I do not think they are at all desirable, and they ought to be abolished. Nor do I appreciate the ascetic life as a social ideal, though it may suit individuals. I understand and appreciate simplicity, equality, self-control; but not the mortification of the flesh. Just as an athlete requires to train his body, I believe that the mind and habits have also to be trained and brought under control. It would be absurd to expect that a person who is given to too much self-indulgence can endure much suffering or show unusual self-control or behave like a hero when the crisis comes. To be in good moral condition requires at least as much training as to be in good physical condition. But that certainly does not mean asceticism or self-mortification.

Nor do I appreciate in the least the idealization of the "simple peasant life." I have almost a horror of it, and instead of submitting to it myself I want to drag out even the peasantry from it, not to urbanization, but to the spread of urban cultural facilities to rural areas. Far from his life's giving me true happiness, it would be almost as bad as imprisonment for me. What is there in "The Man with the Hoe" to idealize over? Crushed and exploited for innumerable generations, he is only little removed from the animals who keep him company.

Who made him dead to rapture and despair,
A thing that grieves not and that never hopes,
Stolid and stunned, a brother to the ox?[2]

This desire to get away from the mind of man to primitive conditions where mind does not count, seems to me quite incomprehensible. The very thing that is the glory and triumph of man is decried and discouraged, and a physical environment which will oppress the mind and prevent its growth is considered desirable. Present-day civilization is full of evils, but it is also full of good; and it has the capacity in it to rid itself of those evils. To destroy it root and branch is to remove that capacity from it and revert to a dull, sunless, and miserable existence. But even if that were desirable it is an impossible undertaking. We cannot stop the river of change or cut ourselves adrift from it, and psychologically we who have eaten of the apple of Eden cannot forget that taste and go back to primitiveness.

[2] From poem by Edwin Markam, "The Man with the Hoe" (1899), which was a response to the painting of the same title by Jean Millet. [Ed.]

■ REFLECTIONS

We have looked at the conflict between Westernization and nationalism through windows on Japan and India. For the Japanese, the borrowing of Western institutions and ideas provided an escape from colonization. By the time India gained political independence in 1947, it had become partially Westernized by three hundred years of colonialism. Yet in both countries there were those who resisted Western ways, those who embraced them, and others still who developed ambivalent feelings toward the West.

This last response — often accepting the contradictions: treasuring the traditional while trying the new — may have been the most difficult, but ultimately the most useful. It must have been far easier to cast off everything Asian, as Fukuzawa Yukichi urged, or make fun of any contact with the West as monkeying around or frightful miscegenation, as the Japanese cartoons suggested. Japan may have made the most successful non-Western transition to industrial modernity because it steered a path between Fukuzawa Yukichi's prescription for wholesale cultural capitulation and the cartoonists' blanket rejection of anything new and foreign.

India, with older indigenous traditions than Japan but also a longer period confronting the influence of Western culture, approached independence in 1947 with a political elite trained in English law, liberal and Marxist political parties, a literate English-speaking middle class, and a long-suppressed hunger for economic freedom and material well-being. Gandhi feared violence, anticolonial in 1909 and anti-Muslim in 1947, more than the repressions of the old society. While he sought a new social cohesion in traditional religious spiritualism, Nehru hoped to forge a new solidarity along the Western industrial socialist model.

Some may find the nationalist vision of Okakura more unsettling. Certainly his celebration of Asian art was long overdue. Though Japanese art, especially, was well known to a Western elite of artists and collectors (Gaughin for one made it his own), most Westerners ignorantly dismissed it. It is interesting that even today many college courses in art history ignore Asian art, relegating it at best to a separate course. In introducing Asian art to the West, Okakura began a Herculean task, still not fully accomplished. But Okakura's nationalism had a sharp edge that cut aggressively in the next generation. In his eagerness to embrace a deep Asian past as his own, he adopted for Japan centuries of oppressive Asian dynasties including the Mongols, in the process turning cultural heritage into racial inheritance. The idea of race, initially a Western pseudo-science to rationalize dominion, would be turned against the West with consequences as devastating as those experienced in Europe and the United States in the 1930s and 1940s. That is not to blame Okakura for later Japanese nationalism. He merely participated in a kind of nationalism that turned lethal.

Nationalism could always turn inward or outward. Even when it turned outward, it did not have to denigrate "the other." The idea that the nation consisted of those who lived on the same soil and the idea that each nation had its own individual attributes were beliefs of what historians have come to call "liberal nationalism," the nationalist movement that prevailed especially in the first half of the nineteenth century. The antagonistic idea that national identity was in the blood, and that, therefore, not only are some nations better than others, but their superiority is in their genes, were beliefs of the "ethnic nationalism" that developed along with racism at the end of the century. A belief that nations were based on blood would help spawn two world wars.

24

World War I and Its Consequences

Europe and the World, 1914–1929

■ HISTORICAL CONTEXT

The Europe that so many non-European intellectuals sought to imitate or reject between 1880 and 1920 came very close to self-destructing between 1914 and 1918, and bringing many of the world's peoples from Asia, Africa, and the Americas down with it. The orgy of bloodletting, then known as the "Great War," put seventy million men in uniform, of whom ten million were killed and twenty million were wounded. Most of the soldiers were Western European, though Russia contributed more soldiers than France or Germany, while Japan enlisted as many as the Austro-Hungarian Empire that began the war. Enlisted men also came from the United States, Canada, Australia, New Zealand, South Africa, and the colonies: India, French West Africa, and German East Africa, among others. The majority of soldiers were killed in Europe, especially along the German Western Front—four hundred miles of trenches that spanned from Switzerland to the English Channel, across northeastern France. But battles were also fought along the borders of German, French, and English colonies in Africa, and there were high Australian casualties on the coast of Gallipoli in Ottoman Turkey.

The selections in this chapter focus on the lives and deaths of the soldiers, as well as the efforts of some of their political leaders to redefine the world around them. We examine the experiences of soldiers and how the war changed the lives of those who survived its devastating toll. We compare the accounts of those who fought on both sides of the great divide. Germany and the Austro-Hungarian Empire, joined by the Ottoman Empire, formed an alliance called the Central Powers (see Map 24.1). In opposition, England, France, and Russia,

918

Map 24.1 Allied Powers and Central Powers in World War I.

the Allied Powers, were later joined by Italy, Greece, Japan, and the United States. We compare views across the generational divide as well as from the trenches and government offices.

■ THINKING HISTORICALLY

Understanding Causes and Consequences

From 1914 to 1920, the greatest divide was the war itself. It marked the end of one era and the beginning of another. Few events have left the participants with such a profound sense of fundamental change. And so our study of the war is an appropriate place to ask two of the universal questions of major historical change: What caused it? What were the consequences?

The *causes* are those events or forces that came before; the *consequences* are the results, what the war itself prompted to occur. Thus, causes and consequences are part of the same continuum. Still, we must remember that not everything that happened before the war was a cause of the war. Similarly, not everything that happened afterward was a result of the war.

In this chapter we explore specific ideas about cause and consequence. Our goal is not to compile a definitive list of either but, rather, to explore some of the ways that historians and thoughtful readers can make sense of the past.

1

DAVID FROMKIN

Europe's Last Summer, 2004

The author, a modern lawyer and historian, has written extensively on the Middle East as it was shaped by the First World War. In his book *Europe's Last Summer*, subtitled "Who Started the Great War in 1914?," he argues that Germany most wanted the war. In this selection from that work, he discusses three of the background causes of the war: imperialism, social-class conflicts, and nationalism. According to Fromkin, how did the clash of empires become more severe in the last decade or so of the nineteenth century? How did domestic social conflicts increase the chances of war? How did nationalism undermine the European peace?

Source: David Fromkin, *Europe's Last Summer* (New York: Vintage Books, 2005), 17–27.

THINKING HISTORICALLY

While the development of imperialism, social-class conflicts, and nationalism are often counted as background causes of World War I, there is little agreement among historians as to which of the three is the most important. What factors would you weigh or what questions would you ask to make such a determination? Secondly, historians might argue that there were other background causes. Even in this brief selection, Fromkin touches on other changes in Europe that might be considered background causes. What are these? How important are they?

Empires Clash

At the start of the twentieth century Europe was at the peak of human accomplishment. In industry, technology, and science it had advanced beyond all previous societies. In wealth, knowledge, and power it exceeded any civilization that ever had existed.

Europe is almost the smallest of the continents: 3 or 4 million square miles in extent, depending on how you define its eastern frontiers. By contrast, the largest continent, Asia, has 17 million square miles. Indeed, some geographers viewed Europe as a mere peninsula of Asia.

Yet, by the beginning of the 1900s, the Great Powers of Europe—a mere handful of countries—had come to rule most of the earth. Between them, Austria-Hungary, France, Germany, Great Britain, Italy, and Russia dominated Europe, Africa, Asia, the Pacific, and even substantial parts of the Western Hemisphere. Of what little remained, much belonged to less powerful European states: Belgium, Holland, Portugal, and Spain. When all of its empires were added together, Europe spanned the globe.

But the European empires were of greatly unequal size and strength, an imbalance that led to instability; and as they were rivals, their leaders were continuously matching them against one another in their minds, trying to guess who would defeat whom in case of war and with whom, therefore, it would be best to ally. Military prowess was seen as a supreme value in an age that mistakenly believed Charles Darwin's survival of the fittest to refer to the most murderous rather than (as we now understand it) to the best adapted.

The British Empire was the wealthiest, most powerful, and largest of the Great Powers. It controlled over a quarter of the land surface and a quarter of the population of the globe, and its navy dominated the world ocean that occupies more than 70 percent of the planet. Germany, a newly created confederation led by militarist Prussia, commanded the most powerful land army. Russia, the world's largest country, a backward giant that sprawled across two continents, remained an enigma;

enfeebled by a war it lost to Japan in 1904–05, and by the revolution of 1905, it turned itself around by industrializing and arming with financial backing from France. France, despite exploiting a large empire, no longer was a match for Germany and therefore backed Russia as a counterweight to Teutonic power. The Dual Monarchy of Austria-Hungary ruled a variety of nationalities who were restless and often in conflict. Italy, a new state, as a latecomer aspiring to take its place among the powers, hungered to be treated as an equal.

It was commonly believed at the time that the road to wealth and greatness for European powers was through the acquisition of more colonies. The problem was that the Great Powers already controlled so much of the world that there was little left for others to take. Repeatedly, in going forward, the European powers ran up against one another. Time and again, war threatened, and only skilled diplomacy and self-restraint enabled them to pull back from the brink. The decades before 1914 were punctuated by crises, almost any one of which might have led to war.

It was no accident that some of the more conspicuous of these crises resulted from moves by Germany. It was because Germany's emperor—the Kaiser, or Caesar—in changing his Chancellor in 1890 also changed his government's policy. Otto von Bismarck, the iron-willed leader who had created Germany in 1870–71, was skeptical of imperialism.[1] Far from believing that overseas colonies bring additional wealth and power, he apparently viewed them as a drain on both. In order to distract France from thoughts of recovering territories in Europe that Germany had seized—in Alsace-Lorraine—Bismarck encouraged and supported France in seeking new acquisitions in North Africa and Asia. As such a policy would bring France into frequent collisions with imperial England and Russia, thus dividing Germany's potential rivals, it suited all of Bismarck's purposes.

Post-Bismarck Germany coveted the overseas territories that the Iron Chancellor had regarded as mere fool's gold. It positioned itself to take part in the coming partition of China. But the rulers in Berlin had come to the game too late. Germany no longer could win an empire on a scale proportioned to its position as the greatest military power in Europe. There was not world enough. No more continents were there for the taking: no more Africas, no more Americas. Nonetheless—heedlessly—Wilhelmine Germany displayed an interest in overseas land.

As France moved deeper into Morocco at the beginning of the twentieth century to round out its North African empire, Germany, instead of offering encouragement and support, as Bismarck would have done, stepped in to oppose. These German moves misfired and sparked two of the more high-profile international crises of those years:

---

[1] For reasons not entirely clear, Bismarck briefly departed from this policy in the early 1880s, when Germany acquired a small number of colonies.

the Morocco crises of 1905–06 and of 1911. To the German government these maneuvers may have been mere probes, but they caused genuine alarm in Europe.

In retrospect, it is clear the problem was that Germany's post-1890 hunger for empire could no longer be satisfied except by taking overseas territories away from the other European countries. This was not something likely to be accomplished by peaceful means. Could Germany therefore content itself with remaining the leading military and industrial power on the Continent but with African and Asian empires smaller than those of England or France? Germans themselves disagreed, of course, about what the answer to that question ought to be, and the climate of opinion was changing. Germany in 1914 was the only country on the Continent with more industrial than farm workers, and the growing strength of its socialist and working-class masses suggested that the nation might be compelled to focus its attention on solving problems at home rather than on adventures abroad. Alternatively, it suggested that Germany's leaders would have to pursue an aggressive foreign policy in order to distract attention from problems at home that remained unsolved.

Classes Struggle

Nor was Germany alone in being divided against itself. Europe before the war was in the grip of social and economic upheavals that were reshaping its structure and its politics. The Industrial Revolution that had begun in eighteenth-century France and England continued, at an accelerated pace, to effect radical changes in those two countries, as well as in Germany, and was making similar changes in others. Agrarian Europe, in part still feudal, and smokestack Europe, bringing modernity, lived literally at the same time but figuratively centuries apart. Some still were living as though in the fourteenth century, with their pack animals and their slow, almost unchanging village rhythms, while others inhabited the crowded, sprawling cities of the twentieth century, driven by the newly invented internal combustion machine and informed by the telegraph.

At the same time, the growth of an urban factory-working population in the Industrial Revolution brought conflict between that population and factory owners over wages and working conditions. It also pitted both workers and manufacturers, on the one hand, who could expand their exports only in a free-trade world, against farmers, who needed protection, and the cash-poor landed gentry on the other. Class became a line of division and loyalty — the chief line according to many. Domestic strife threatened all the countries of Western Europe.

In Britain, the Labour party was formed to speak for a working class no longer content to be represented by the Liberal party, which sympathized with wage-earners but spoke as the voice of the professional classes and even some of the well-born. On the Continent, labor also turned to socialism, with growing success at the polls: in the German elections of 1912, the Social Democrats emerged as the largest single party in the Reichstag. It should have been some consolation to German and British conservatives that workers in their countries usually expressed their socialism peacefully by voting rather than (as Syndicalists did in France, Spain, and Italy) by strikes, riots, and terrorist attacks. But governments, in these times of frequent war crises, worried that their peoples might not support them if war broke out. The issue had another side to it: foreign adventures could distract from class and social conflict and bring the people instead to rally around the flag. Which would it be? Would class and social clashes divide, or would international conflicts unite?

Nations Quarrel

To socialist internationalism, the rival was nationalism, a passion that increasingly was taking priority over all else in the minds and hearts of Europeans as the nineteenth century departed and the twentieth arrived. Even Britain contracted the fever. Ireland—or at any rate its Roman Catholic majority—agitated violently for autonomy or independence, and clashed with the Protestants of Ulster who prepared to take up arms to defend the union with Great Britain.

Edwardian England already was a surprisingly violent country, torn by such issues as industrial wages and working conditions and also by the cause of woman suffrage. It was rocked, too, by a constitutional crisis that was also a class crisis. The crisis focused on two interrelated issues: the budget, and the power of the hereditary House of Lords to veto legislation enacted by the popularly elected House of Commons. Between them these conflicts eroded the sense of national solidarity.

Now that the country also was polarized on the question of home rule for Ireland, large sections of the army and of the Unionist-Conservative party seemed prepared to defy law and government in order to hold on to the union with Ireland. The precedent set by the United States in 1861 was troubling. Would there be a British civil war?

On the continent of Europe the flames of nationalism threatened to burn down even structures that had endured for centuries. Hapsburg-ruled Austria, a holdover from the Middle Ages that until recently had been headed by the so-called Holy Roman Empire, remained, as it had been in the nineteenth century, the principal enemy of European nationalism. The two great new nations of Germany and Italy had been carved out of domains that the Hapsburgs once had dominated. At universities, coffeehouses, and in the dimly lit hiding places of secret societies and terrorists, in the Balkans and Central Europe in the early years of the twentieth century, plans were being hatched by ethnic groups that aspired to achieve something similar. The nationalists were in contact with one another and with nihilists, anarchists, socialists, and others who lived and conspired in the obscurity of the political underground. It was there that Serbs, Croats, Czechs, and others plotted to disrupt and destroy the Austrian Empire.

The Hapsburgs were a dynasty that over the course of a thousand years had come to rule a motley collection of territories and peoples—a multinational empire that held no prospect of ever becoming a homogeneous national state. Centered in German-speaking Vienna, Austria-Hungary encompassed a variety of languages, ethnic groups, and climates. Its 50 million people comprised perhaps eleven or so nations or parts thereof. Many of its lands originally had been dowries that had come with marriage to territorial heiresses: whatever else you might say about them, the Hapsburg family wedded well. At its height in the sixteenth century, when it included Spain and much of the New World, the Hapsburg family holdings comprised the largest empire in the world. Hapsburg roots went back to Christmas Day 800, when Charlemagne the Frank was crowned emperor of the Roman Empire in the West by the pope. As Holy Roman Emperor, a post to which a Hapsburg was almost always elected from the fifteenth century until it was abolished in the early nineteenth century, the Hapsburgs dominated Central Europe, including its many German- and Italian-speaking political entities. In the aftermath of the 1848 revolutions, they lost their Italian possessions to the newly unified Italy, and they were excluded from Prussian-organized, newly unified Germany in 1870–71. Once the leader of Europe's Germans and Italians, the Hapsburg emperor was left as the odd man out.

Left alone with a German core—of Austria's 28 million inhabitants, only 10 million were German—and a restive empire of Central European and Balkan peoples, mostly Slavs, the Hapsburg ruler Franz Joseph found himself presiding over a political entity that arguably was not viable. The solution that he found in 1867 was a compact between Austria and a Hungary that was ruled by its Magyar minority, in which Franz Joseph served both as emperor of Austria and king of Hungary. The Dual Monarchy, as it was called, was a state in which Austria and Hungary each had its own parliament and its own Prime Minister, but there was only one foreign minister, one war minister, one finance minister—and, of course, only one monarch of both the Austrian empire and the Hungarian kingdom. The peoples who ruled were the minority Germans of Austria and the Magyar minority in Hungary. What they attempted to rule, in the words of one Hapsburg statesman, was "eight nations, seventeen countries, twenty parliamentary groups, twenty-seven parties"—and a spectrum of peoples and religions.

Europe was rapidly becoming a continent of nation-states. As it entered the twentieth century, a chief weakness of Austria-Hungary was that it was on what looked to be the wrong side of history. But what was threatening to bring it down was a force that was not entirely progressive either; nationalism had its atavistic aspects.

Whether considered to be a political philosophy or its contrary, a type of mass delirium, nationalism was ambivalent. It was the democratic belief that each nation had the right to become independent and to rule itself. But it also was the illiberal insistence that nonmembers of the nation should assimilate, be denied civic rights, be expelled, or even be killed. Nationalism was hating some as an expression of loving others. To add to the murkiness, there was no agreement on what constitutes a nationality. The 1911 edition of the *Encyclopaedia Britannica* calls it a "vague term" and remarked that "a 'nationality'. . . represents a common feeling and an organized claim rather than distinct attributes which can be comprised in a strict definition." So there was no general agreement on which groups were nations and which were not. It was one more issue for Europe to fight about. Some thought—some still think—that it was the main thing that Europe had to fight about.

In the absence of scientific measurement of public opinion through polls, historians are unable to tell us with any certainty what the people of Europe thought or felt in the pre-1914 age. This leaves a gap in our knowledge. It is not so great a gap as it would be today, for a century ago the public played little role in the formation of foreign policy. But public opinion was of some significance, in that decision-makers presumably did take it into account—to the extent that they knew what it was.

Evidence suggests that the most widespread feeling in Europe at the time was xenophobia: a great deal of hostility toward one another. The ethnic groups of the Balkans provided a conspicuous example of mutual hatred, but countries far more advanced exhibited such tendencies too.

England is a case in point. It had been in conflict or at war with France on and off since the eleventh century—in other words, for about a thousand years. Anti-French feeling remained high well into the twentieth century. Even during the First World War, in which the two countries were allies, British and French officers schemed and maneuvered against one another to take control of the postwar Arab Middle East.

Britain came into collision with Russia much later than it did with France, but once they did clash it was all across the board. The two countries opposed each other on one point after another, economically, politically, militarily, and ideologically, until Britons grew to object to Russians not merely for what they did but for who they were. The story is recounted at length in a classic: *The Genesis of Russophobia in Great Britain* by John Howes Gleason.

Germany came into existence as a state only in 1871, and seemed to be a possible ally—the idea was discussed at the highest levels more than once—

but the British became suspicious of Germany and then antagonistic. This was for a variety of reasons, thoroughly discussed in Paul Kennedy's definitive account, *The Rise of the Anglo-German Antagonism.*

So the British, though they believed themselves to be open-minded, detested the peoples of the next three ranking Great Powers: the French, the Russians, and the Germans.

The questions that European statesmen attempted to resolve at the dawn of the twentieth century therefore were being faced against a background of peoples who harbored hostile, sometimes warlike, sentiments.

The rise of independent mass-circulation newspapers in the nineteenth century in such European countries as England and France brought to bear upon decision-making yet another powerful influence impossible to calculate precisely. Appealing to popular fears and prejudices in order to win circulation, the press seems to have exacerbated hatred and divisions among Europeans. Of the anti-German British press and the anti-British German press, the German emperor wrote to the King of England in 1901: "The Press is awful on both sides."

2

ERICH MARIA REMARQUE
All Quiet on the Western Front, 1929

All Quiet on the Western Front, one of the most famous war novels ever written, follows the daily routines of the German army on the "Western Front," the long line of trenches that stretched across northern France from Switzerland to the English Channel for most of the war between 1914 and 1918. Born in Germany, Erich Maria Remarque (1898–1970) served on the Western Front during the war until he was wounded. In this selection from the beginning of the novel, the narrator recalls how his teacher, Kantorek, induced him and his friends to enlist. Now one of them, Franz Kemmerich, has been seriously wounded and the group of friends visit him. What does this selection suggest about the types of people recruited to serve in the army? How do they experience the war, and how does it change them? Do you imagine these German soldiers behaved very differently from French or English soldiers?

Source: Erich Maria Remarque, *All Quiet on the Western Front*, trans. A. W. Wheen (New York: Fawcett Books, 1929), 1–18.

THINKING HISTORICALLY

Remarque's novel is not intended as an explanation of the causes of war, but this excerpt sheds light on what caused men to support the war and enlist. How might you use material from this novel, assuming that it is based on fact, to propose at least one cause of World War I?

In this brief selection, the author also suggests something about the consequences of the war. What are the war's likely outcomes projected here?

Kantorek had been our schoolmaster, a stern little man in a grey tail-coat, with a face like a shrew mouse. He was about the same size as Corporal Himmelstoss, the "terror of Klosterberg." It is very queer that the unhappiness of the world is so often brought on by small men. They are so much more energetic and uncompromising than the big fellows. I have always taken good care to keep out of sections with small company commanders. They are mostly confounded little martinets.

During drill-time Kantorek gave us long lectures until the whole of our class went, under his shepherding, to the District Commandant and volunteered. I can see him now, as he used to glare at us through his spectacles and say in a moving voice: "Won't you join up, Comrades?"

These teachers always carry their feelings ready in their waistcoat pockets, and trot them out by the hour. But we didn't think of that then.

There was, indeed, one of us who hesitated and did not want to fall into line. That was Joseph Behm, a plump, homely fellow. But he did allow himself to be persuaded, otherwise he would have been ostracized. And perhaps more of us thought as he did, but no one could very well stand out, because at that time even one's parents were ready with the word "coward"; no one had the vaguest idea what we were in for. The wisest were just the poor and simple people. They knew the war to be a misfortune, whereas those who were better off, and should have been able to see more clearly what the consequences would be, were beside themselves with joy.

Katczinsky said that was a result of their upbringing. It made them stupid. And what Kat said, he had thought about.

Strange to say, Behm was one of the first to fall. He got hit in the eye during an attack, and we left him lying for dead. We couldn't bring him with us, because we had to come back helter-skelter. In the afternoon suddenly we heard him call, and saw him crawling about in No Man's Land. He had only been knocked unconscious. Because he could not see, and was mad with pain, he failed to keep under cover, and so was shot down before anyone could go and fetch him in.

Naturally we couldn't blame Kantorek for this. Where would the world be if one brought every man to book? There were thousands of

Kantoreks, all of whom were convinced that they were acting for the best—in a way that cost them nothing.

And that is why they let us down so badly.

For us lads of eighteen they ought to have been mediators and guides to the world of maturity, the world of work, of duty, of culture, of progress—to the future. We often made fun of them and played jokes on them, but in our hearts we trusted them. The idea of authority, which they represented, was associated in our minds with a greater insight and a more humane wisdom. But the first death we saw shattered this belief. We had to recognize that our generation was more to be trusted than theirs. They surpassed us only in phrases and in cleverness. The first bombardment showed us our mistake, and under it the world as they had taught it to us broke in pieces.

While they continued to write and talk, we saw the wounded and dying. While they taught that duty to one's country is the greatest thing, we already knew that death-throes are stronger. But for all that we were no mutineers, no deserters, no cowards—they were very free with all these expressions. We loved our country as much as they; we went courageously into every action; but also we distinguished the false from true, we had suddenly learned to see. And we saw that there was nothing of their world left. We were all at once terribly alone; and alone we must see it through.

Before going over to see Kemmerich we pack up his things: He will need them on the way back.

In the dressing station there is great activity: It reeks as ever of carbolic, pus, and sweat. We are accustomed to a good deal in the billets, but this makes us feel faint. We ask for Kemmerich. He lies in a large room and receives us with feeble expressions of joy and helpless agitation. While he was unconscious someone had stolen his watch.

Müller shakes his head: "I always told you that nobody should carry as good a watch as that."

Müller is rather crude and tactless, otherwise he would hold his tongue, for anybody can see that Kemmerich will never come out of this place again. Whether he finds his watch or not will make no difference, at the most one will only be able to send it to his people.

"How goes it, Franz?" asks Kropp.

Kemmerich's head sinks.

"Not so bad . . . but I have such a damned pain in my foot."

We look at his bed covering. His leg lies under a wire basket. The bed covering arches over it. I kick Müller on the shin, for he is just about to tell Kemmerich what the orderlies told us outside: that Kemmerich has lost his foot. The leg is amputated. He looks ghastly, yellow and wan. In his face there are already the strained lines that we know so well, we have seen them now hundreds of times. They are not so much lines as marks. Under the skin the life no longer pulses, it has already pressed out the boundaries of the body. Death is working through from within. It already has command in the eyes. Here lies our comrade, Kemmerich, who a little while ago was roasting horse flesh with us and squatting in the shellholes. He it is still and yet it is not he any longer. His features have become uncertain and faint, like a photographic plate from which two pictures have been taken. Even his voice sounds like ashes.

I think of the time when we went away. His mother, a good plump matron, brought him to the station. She wept continually, her face was bloated and swollen. Kemmerich felt embarrassed, for she was the least composed of all; she simply dissolved into fat and water. Then she caught sight of me and took hold of my arm again and again, and implored me to look after Franz out there. Indeed he did have a face like a child, and such frail bones that after four weeks' pack-carrying he already had flat feet. But how can a man look after anyone in the field!

"Now you will soon be going home," says Kropp. "You would have had to wait at least three or four months for your leave."

Kemmerich nods. I cannot bear to look at his hands, they are like wax. Under the nails is the dirt of the trenches, it shows through blue-black like poison. It strikes me that these nails will continue to grow like lean fantastic cellar-plants long after Kemmerich breathes no more. I see the picture before me. They twist themselves into corkscrews and grow and grow, and with them the hair on the decaying skull, just like grass in a good soil, just like grass, how can it be possible———

Müller leans over. "We have brought your things, Franz."

Kemmerich signs with his hands. "Put them under the bed."

Müller does so. Kemmerich starts on again about the watch. How can one calm him without making him suspicious?

Müller reappears with a pair of airman's boots. They are fine English boots of soft, yellow leather which reach to the knees and lace up all the way—they are things to be coveted.

Müller is delighted at the sight of them. He matches their soles against his own clumsy boots and says: "Will you be taking them with you then, Franz?"

We all three have the same thought; even if he should get better, he would be able to use only one—they are no use to him. But as things are now it is a pity that they should stay here; the orderlies will of course grab them as soon as he is dead.

"Won't you leave them with us?" Müller repeats.

Kemmerich doesn't want to. They are his most prized possessions.

"Well, we could exchange," suggests Müller again. "Out here one can make some use of them." Still Kemmerich is not to be moved.

I tread on Müller's foot; reluctantly he puts the fine boots back again under the bed.

We talk a little more and then take our leave.

"Cheerio, Franz."

I promise him to come back in the morning. Müller talks of doing so, too. He is thinking of the lace-up boots and means to be on the spot.

Kemmerich groans. He is feverish. We get hold of an orderly outside and ask him to give Kemmerich a dose of morphia.

He refuses. "If we were to give morphia to everyone we would have to have tubs full————"

"You only attend to officers properly," says Kropp viciously.

I hastily intervene and give him a cigarette. He takes it.

"Are you usually allowed to give it, then?" I ask him.

He is annoyed. "If you don't think so, then why do you ask?"

I press a few more cigarettes into his hand. "Do us the favour————"

"Well, all right," he says.

Kropp goes in with him. He doesn't trust him and wants to see. We wait outside.

Müller returns to the subject of the boots. "They would fit me perfectly. In these boots I get blister after blister. Do you think he will last till tomorrow after drill? If he passes out in the night, we know where the boots————"

Kropp returns. "Do you think————?" he asks.

"Done for," said Müller emphatically.

We go back to the huts. I think of the letter that I must write tomorrow to Kemmerich's mother. I am freezing. I could do with a tot of rum. Müller pulls up some grass and chews it. Suddenly little Kropp throws his cigarette away, stamps on it savagely, and looking around him with a broken and distracted face, stammers "Damned shit, the damned shit!"

We walk on for a long time. Kropp has calmed himself; we understand, he saw red; out there every man gets like that sometime.

"What has Kantorek written to you?" Müller asks him.

He laughs. "We are the Iron Youth."

We all three smile bitterly, Kropp rails: He is glad that he can speak.

Yes, that's the way they think, these hundred thousand Kantoreks! Iron Youth! Youth! We are none of us more than twenty years old. But young? Youth? That is long ago. We are old folk.

World War I Propaganda Posters, 1915–1918

Posters were the communication medium of the First World War. In an age when governments had still not taught most people how to read but increasingly needed their consent or compliance, images often spoke louder than words, but those images had to be *persuasive*.

The American poster from 1917 and the German poster from 1915–1916 (Figures 24.1 and 24.3) implore men to enlist in the army; the Italian poster from 1917 (Figure 24.2) encourages people

Figure 24.1 Recruiting Poster for U.S. Army, 1917.
Source: Library of Congress.

Figure 24.2 Italian Poster for National War Loan, 1917.
Source: Snark/Art Resource, NY.

to buy war bonds. What do you think accounts for the similar graphic style used in these three posters? How effective do you think they were, and why?

Another strategy for promoting loyalty, patriotism, and support for a war that was lasting far longer than anyone had anticipated was to demonize or ridicule the enemy. What feelings does the

Figure 24.3 Recruiting Poster for German Army, 1915–1916.
Source: Library of Congress.

U.S. anti-German poster from 1917–1918 (Figure 24.4) attempt to provoke in viewers, and how does the scene shown achieve this?

Women contributed to the war in various ways. Figure 24.5 asks German women to contribute their gold. Figure 24.6 urges women in London to come to work in the munitions industry. What images of women do these posters portray? Finally, Figure 24.7 asks Americans to support Armenian refugees from the Ottoman Empire in newly proclaimed independent Armenia and Syria. What response is the image of woman and child supposed to evoke?

THINKING HISTORICALLY

When war broke out overseas in 1914, President Woodrow Wilson declared it a European matter that had nothing to do with the United

Figure 24.4   Propaganda Poster, United States, 1917–1918.

States, and most Americans agreed. Indeed, the United States did not join the war and throw its crucial weight behind the Allied Powers until April 1917. What role do you think propaganda such as Figure 24.4 played in swaying public opinion? This and the other posters illustrate both sides' efforts to promote and sustain the cause of war. What do they tell you about the causes of the war? What do they tell you about the consequences?

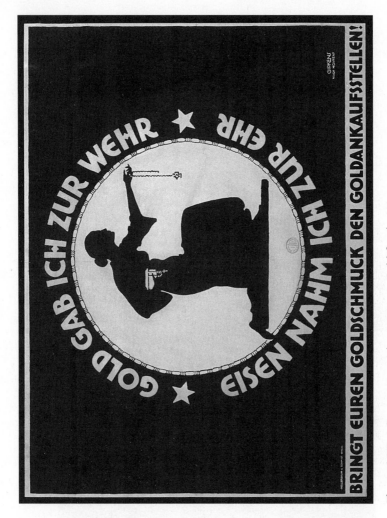

Figure 24.5   German Appeal to Women: Gold for the War.
Source: Library of Congress.

Figure 24.6   English Appeal to Women: Munitions Work.

Source: World War Poster Collection (MSS36), University of Minnesota Libraries, Archives and Special Collections, Minneapolis, MN.

Figure 24.7 "Your Bit Saves a Life."

4

WILFRED OWEN

Dulce et Decorum Est, 1917

Wilfred Owen (1893–1918) enlisted in the British Army in 1915, was wounded in 1917, and was hospitalized, released, and sent back to the front, where he died on November 4, 1918, one week before the end of the war. In this poem, he describes a poison gas attack. Like the machine gun and the airplane, gas was a common element of the new mechanized mass warfare. Owen describes how physically debilitating the effects of gas were. Why was gas such an effective and deadly weapon? How, according to Owen, had the nature of war changed?

THINKING HISTORICALLY

The concluding phrase, which means "Sweet and proper it is to die for one's country," was a Latin declaration of patriotic duty that English students repeated as a lesson, not only in Latin classes but, more important, in their political education as subjects of the British Empire. How does Owen portray this lesson as a cause of the war? What does he imagine to be the consequences of fighting a war with such patriotic slogans in mind? How does Owen's attitude toward patriotism compare with that of Remarque?

Dulce et Decorum Est

Bent double, like old beggars under sacks,
Knock-kneed, coughing like hags, we cursed through sludge,
Till on the haunting flares we turned our backs
And towards our distant rest began the trudge.
Men marched asleep. Many had lost their boots
But limped on, blood-shod. All went lame; all blind;
Drunk with fatigue; deaf even to the hoots
Of tired, outstripped Five-Nines[1] that dropped behind.

Gas! GAS! Quick, boys!—An ecstasy of fumbling,
Fitting the clumsy helmets just in time;
But someone still was yelling out and stumbling,
And flound'ring like a man in fire or lime. . . .

---

[1] German artillery shells. [Ed.]

Source: Wilfred Owen, *Poems*, ed. Siegfried Sassoon (London: Chatto and Windus, 1920).

Dim, through the misty panes and thick green light,
As under a green sea, I saw him drowning.

In all my dreams, before my helpless sight,
He plunges at me, guttering, choking, drowning.

If in some smothering dreams you too could pace
Behind the wagon that we flung him in,
And watch the white eyes writhing in his face,
His hanging face, like a devil's sick of sin;
If you could hear, at every jolt, the blood
Come gargling from the froth-corrupted lungs,
Obscene as cancer, bitter as the cud
Of vile, incurable sores on innocent tongues,
My friend, you would not tell with such high zest,
To children ardent for some desperate glory.
The old Lie: Dulce et decorum est
Pro patria mori.

5

Memories of Senegalese Soldiers, 1914–1918/1981–1999

Not only did the roots of the First World War lie in competing imperial claims, but some of the fighting took place along imperial divides of colonies as well. Africans in French and English colonies were mobilized to fight Africans in neighboring German colonies, and vice versa. In addition, many Africans were mobilized to fight in Europe, especially after European troops suffered heavy losses along the Western Front. Over 140,000 West Africans were re-cruited into the French Army between 1914 and 1918 to serve in Europe. Some 45,000 never returned. Senegal mobilized more than other colonies: 29,000, probably more than one-third of the men of military age.

Source: Joe Lunn, *Memoirs of the Maelstrom: A Senegalese Oral History of the First World War* (Portsmouth, NH: Heinemann, 1999), 40, 42, 78–79, 97–98, 102–3, 110, 137, 165–66, 172–73, 174, 108–9, 190, 230, 232–33. Headings added, individual names and footnotes deleted.

The historian Joe Lunn interviewed eighty-five of these Senegalese veterans for his book *Memoirs of the Maelstrom: A Senegalese Oral History of the First World War*, from which these selections are drawn. What do these various Senegalese voices tell you about the African experience in the First World War? How was their experience of the war different from that of European soldiers? How were Senegalese soldiers recruited, and why did they enlist? What were their expectations?

THINKING HISTORICALLY

These memories provide greater insight into the consequences than the causes of World War I. How did the war change the lives of those African troops who survived? How did it change the way the Senegalese and French thought of themselves and each other?

[Recruitment]

Many of the young men fled from the village [when the *chef de canton* came to take soldiers]. [But] they used to arrest their fathers [if] they [did not] come back. [And] often their mothers used to say to their sons [when they returned from the countryside for food]: "You know that your name has been written [down by the *che de canton*] and [yet] you ran away. And now your father has been arrested and he will be taken [to] prison. So go and enter the army." And often they used to go and enter the army [so that] their fathers [would be] released.

In each family they only took one young man, never two. And my father decided that I should go and enter the army instead of my elder brother. Because, he told me: "If I die, your elder brother could care for the family, but you are too young for that." That's why he sent me into the army. I was not happy to go, [but] because I was very close to my father . . . I felt obliged to.

I was in Bamako [on leave] when Blaise Diagne and Galandou Diouf[1] came to recruit soldiers. [And my friend and I] attended the meeting he called for recruitment. [And] Blaise Diagne's propaganda [at] this meeting [was very effective]. Because, before he came, he had made the son of the

---

[1] Blaise Diagne (1872–1934), from Senegal, became in 1914 the first black African elected to the French national parliament where he fought for and won the right of urban Senegalese to be citizens and soldiers. He was appointed by French prime minister George Clemenceau to head the recruitment drive in French West Africa during the war. Galandou Diouf (1875–1941), the first black African elected (in 1909) to the Senegalese assembly, was Diagne's assistant. They argued that military service was a vehicle to full and equal citizenship for Africans. [Ed.]

chef de quartier in Bamako a lieutenant. [So] almost all the town was there, because the chief had called everybody, and there were a lot, a lot, a lot of people! The fact that Blaise Diagne had made his son a lieutenant was a very important thing for him personally, because . . . for the Bambara becoming an officer in the army was a very great honor. [And Diagne came] with many, many people—August Brunet [the lieutenant governor of Haut-Sénégal et Niger] and [other] French administrators. [And] he was [accompanied by] some Bambara soldiers too. But they were not simple soldiers; all of them had *"grades."*[2] [And after speeches by Galandou Diouf, the *chef de quartier*, and his son, Diagne spoke.] [And although] I have forgotten almost all his speech, I remember that he told them that he was sent by the President of the Republic of France who needed [more] soldiers to go on fighting. And after [he finished], he introduced the son of the *chef de quartier* to [all] the other parents that were at the meeting. [And he told them:] "I want some other soldiers to enter the army, so perhaps they too can become lieutenants." So as soon as he said that, everybody gave him the name of his son. And the secretary was writing down their names. [And] that's why he succeeded with his recruitment mission [among the Bambara]—[because] everybody was expecting his son to become an officer one day.

[Becoming Soldiers]

We all joined the same army—the French army. . . . So we did not think about our [previous] way of living, our behavior, our [former] kingdoms. We were bound to follow the French regulations and their way of thinking about all these things. [And although] little arguments sometimes [occurred] between soldiers from the same country, [the status of a man's family] wasn't stressed. . . . There wasn't any [social] differentiation [with regard to slaves] because we were following another system—another [way of] life—which was the French one.

[Departures]

We [sailed from Dakar] on a boat called *l'Afrique* on May 9, 1916. There was a French officer with us—[a lieutenant called Oeuvre]—[who] was a very very bad man. We spent [the first] three days [being allowed to go on deck] in the boat . . . and we had a good journey. [But] when we arrived at a place called "the Gulf" [Golfe de Gascogne] . . . this French officer said that all the soldiers had to go downstairs—deep inside the ship. And he put [a guard] at the door [to prevent] any of us

[2] Ranks. [Ed.]

from going out. . . . And we [were confined for] the [next] six days in the bottom [of the boat near] the keel. [And] we suffered a lot in the bottom of the ship because there was no air. From time to time they opened the [portholes] to let some air [in, but] after that they closed them [again]. And even during meals, we were eating in the bottom of the ship. And it was very hot [there] and it was very tight.

[In France]

When we went [to the camps in France,] Diagne joined us [there] to see about our conditions. Whenever you had problems, he came and solved them. Sometimes the food was bad or insufficient, for example. [So] when Diagne came, if we said the food was not good, he called the officers together and asked [them] why. He said, "I brought soldiers to fight for you and to help you. And I don't see why you treat them like this!" So he would tear off the ranks [of insignia] of the officers and put them on the table.

We felt very proud after the attack because the French had tried many times to retake the fort, but finally, we [were the ones] that took it. . . . And when we were leaving the fort, our officers told us not to wash our uniforms even though they were very dirty and covered with mud. But we were told: "Don't wash your uniforms. Cross the country as you are so that everyone who meets you will know that you made the attack on Fort Douaumont." And we took the train [and traveled] for three days between Douaumont and St. Raphäel. And in every town we crossed, the French were clapping their hands and shouting: "*Vive les tirailleurs sénégalais!*" . . . And afterwards, whenever we were walking in the country—everywhere we used to go—if we told people that we made the attack on Fort Douaumont, the French were looking at us with much admiration.

One day I was in the [mess hall] in the camp [where] we used to eat. And often after eating, we used to drink coffee in cups. But before drinking it, we used to make "cheers" with the other soldiers. So on this day, I took my cup and I wanted to make "cheers" with a French soldier who was sitting next to me. So I made the "cheers," [but] the soldier said to me, "don't touch my cup, you are too dirty!" And [this made] me very angry. [So] I punched him and we began to fight. And when they went to get the captain, the captain told me that I was right, and he told the French soldier that he would be punished. But afterwards, I became very friendly with this same soldier.

I had a very good [French] friend—his name was Perout—[and we] were in the same unit. . . . I was his only African friend, [but] we spent a

lot of time together. [And] I often went to his house [when on leave].
He invited me [there] for lunch, or dinner, and sometimes I spent the
night. . . . And when his [family] came to visit him, they kissed me before
they kissed him—his father, his mother, and his sisters.

"*Marraine de guerre*" . . . was the term used by the soldiers to say "my
girlfriend"; instead of saying "my girlfriend," they said "my *marraine de
guerre.*" [And] the African soldiers in France had their *marraines de guerre*
too. They were not prostitutes. They were girls of good families who saw
us and knew that we were [far from] our countries. [And they realized] we
needed some affection and some money . . . to buy cigarettes with, to go
to the movies, and so on.

   [And we met them] on the street or in cafés. A French girl saw you
and felt very pleased by [your appearance]. And she said to you that she
wanted to take you to her house to present you to her parents. And you
got [an adopted] French family in that way. [But] it wasn't necessary to
have love affairs [with them]. From time to time some *marraines de
guerre* fell in love with the soldiers they invited home. But generally, they
were only friendly relations.

Some of the French who had never seen a "black" man used to pay to
come and see us. [And the European soldiers] were making money selling
tickets. [They] used to take us to a hidden place and told us: "Stay here. We
are going to bring some Frenchmen who have never seen 'black' people
before." [But] we didn't know they were making money in that way.

   [And after they] got the money, they used to bring the *Tubabs*[3] to
look at us. And [they] said: "This one is a Senegalese, this one is a Soma-
lian, [and so forth]." And the *Tubabs* were touching us, and peeking,
creeping very close to us because we [looked so different].

[Return]

One day [we were on] the ship that brought us back to Senegal from
Bordeaux. . . . There were [many] Senegalese soldiers [aboard, and
sometimes] they got into arguments with some of the "white" men who
treated them like "dirty niggers." . . . And one of these soldiers—a citizen from Goree—was [called] a "*sale nègre*" by a "white" man. . . . I
think maybe the [French]man was not well educated, or perhaps he was
drunk. [And the soldier hit] him hard . . . and [they] started fighting.
[And] we all [joined in] and started to give our friend some help. And we
beat [the Frenchman] badly until he asked to be forgiven. He was crying
and said that he would never do it again.

   [3] Europeans. [Ed.]

So what happened [afterwards]? Nothing! We were within our rights, because discrimination between people [was no longer tolerated] at that time, [and] we were French citizens like anybody else. [If] the "white" man wanted to start acting like that, we [could retaliate] and nothing happened. [But] if the same thing had happened before the war, [we] would not have done the same thing. Because we had less power then, and [we] were treated badly like this [by the French] all the time.

[The parents of those who had been killed] knew the number of soldiers who went to the war together, and they [also] knew the number of soldiers who came back. So no one [had to tell] them that their sons were dead; they guessed it [on their own]. [But afterward], we told them how they died. Those [of us who] knew their sons had died explained to their families [what had happened to them]. . . . [I had to do this once.] . . . A son [from my grandfather's family] was lost in Champagne. . . . And [they] knew that we went [to the war] together. But when I came back, they didn't see him. And after a while, they began to ask me where he was. And I told them: "He is dead; you have to make the sacrifices."

[After the War]

We went to France, we fought for France, and the French took us by force to fight for them. [But] we learned nothing [there] — [not] even the French language. They only taught us some rudimentary [commands], [in order] to use us in the war. But they didn't care about teaching us the structure and the sound of their language. So [although we] went to the war, [we] came back here without any real knowledge of the French language.

I received many lasting things from the war. I demonstrated my dignity and courage, and [I] won the respect of the people and the [colonial] government. And whenever the people of the village had something to contest [with the French] — and they didn't dare do it [themselves] because they were afraid of them — I used to do it for them. And many times when people had problems with the government, I used to go with my decorations and arrange the situation for [them]. Because whenever the *Tubabs* saw your decorations, they knew that they [were dealing with] a very important person. . . . And I gained this ability — of obtaining justice over a *Tubab* — from the war.

The war changed many, many things. At first, when we joined the army, when you had an argument or a problem with a "white" man, what happened? You were wrong; you were [always] wrong. But later, those things changed. [Then] they looked into the matter and determined who was wrong or right. [But] before that time, the "black" man didn't mean anything. So that [change] was something [very important]. [And] the respect we gained [from] the war [continued] increasing; it never [diminished]. [And this] respect [continued] increasing day to day—up until [it culminated in] the Independence Day.

6

V. I. LENIN

War and Revolution, 1917

One of the great casualties of the First World War was the Russian Empire, including the czar, his family, many of the members of their class, and its centuries-old autocratic system. The burden of war was simply too much for Russian society to bear. The disillusionment in the army and civilian society, along with the overwhelming costs of war, fueled uprisings among civilians and the army, and Czar Nicholas II was forced to abdicate in February of 1917. The government that emerged, under Alexander Kerensky, proved unable to satisfy the growing demands of peasants, veterans, and urban workers for "land, peace, and bread," a slogan that V. I. Lenin (1870–1924) and the communists exploited, successfully seizing power from the moderate parliamentarians in October of that year.

As a Marxist, Lenin believed that he could establish a socialist society in Russia, but he argued that Russian conditions (such as economic underdevelopment; the devastation of war; the opposition of Europe, the United States, and Russian nobles to the revolution) made a democratic transition impossible. According to Lenin, a self-appointed government acting in the interests of the working class was the only way to a socialist Soviet Union. Lenin called this government "the dictatorship of the proletariat." Lenin delivered his "War and Revolution" address in May of 1917, during the fateful summer that followed the liberal February revolution and preceded the Bolshevik revolution in October. How did Lenin view the First World War and Russia's continued participation in it? What did he hope to accomplish in the summer of 1917? How did he hope to accomplish it? The most important news for Russia's allies, England and France, in the summer of 1917 was the United States' entry into the war on their behalf. What was Lenin's reaction to this development?

Source: V. I. Lenin, *Collected Works*, 4th English ed. (Moscow: Progress Publishers, 1964), 24:398–421.

THINKING HISTORICALLY

According to Lenin, what were the causes of the First World War? What did he believe to be the main cause of the Russian revolution that occurred in February? What were the consequences of that revolution? What did he think would be the causes of a new revolution in Russia?

What we have at present is primarily two leagues, two groups of capitalist powers. We have before us all the world's greatest capitalist powers—Britain, France, America, and Germany—who for decades have doggedly pursued a policy of incessant economic rivalry aimed at achieving world supremacy, subjugating the small nations, and making threefold and tenfold profits on banking capital, which has caught the whole world in the net of its influence. That is what Britain's and Germany's policies really amount to. . . .

These policies show us just one thing—continuous economic rivalry between the world's two greatest giants, capitalist economies. On the one hand we have Britain, a country which owns the greater part of the globe, a country which ranks first in wealth, which has created this wealth not so much by the labour of its workers as by the exploitation of innumerable colonies, by the vast power of its banks which have developed at the head of all the others into an insignificantly small group of some four or five super-banks handling billions of rubles, and handling them in such a way that it can be said without exaggeration that there is not a patch of land in the world today on which this capital has not laid its heavy hand, not a patch of land which British capital has not enmeshed by a thousand threads. . . .

On the other hand, opposed to this, mainly Anglo-French group, we have another group of capitalists, an even more rapacious, even more predatory one, a group who came to the capitalist banqueting table when all the seats were occupied, but who introduced into the struggle new methods for developing capitalist production, improved techniques, and superior organization, which turned the old capitalism, the capitalism of the free-competition age, into the capitalism of giant trusts, syndicates, and cartels. This group introduced the beginnings of state-controlled capitalist production, combining the colossal power of capitalism with the colossal power of the state into a single mechanism and bringing tens of millions of people within the single organization of state capitalism. Here is economic history, here is diplomatic history, covering several decades, from which no one can get away. It is the one and only guide-post to a proper solution of the problem of war; it leads you to the conclusion that the present war, too, is the outcome of the policies of the classes who have come to grips in it, of the two supreme giants, who, long before the war, had caught the whole world, all countries, in the net of financial exploitation and economically divided the globe up among themselves. They were bound to clash, because a redivision of this supremacy, from the point of view of capitalism, had become inevitable. . . .

The present war is a continuation of the policy of conquest, of the shooting down of whole nationalities, of unbelievable atrocities committed by the Germans and the British in Africa, and by the British and the Russians in Persia — which of them committed most it is difficult to say. It was for this reason that the German capitalists looked upon them as their enemies. Ah, they said, you are strong because you are rich? But we are stronger, therefore we have the same "sacred" right to plunder. That is what the real history of British and German finance capital in the course of several decades preceding the war amounts to. That is what the history of Russo-German, Russo-British, and German-British relations amounts to. There you have the clue to an understanding of what the war is about. That is why the story that is current about the cause of the war is sheer duplicity and humbug. Forgetting the history of finance capital, the history of how this war had been brewing over the issue of redivision, they present the matter like this: Two nations were living at peace, then one attacked the other, and the other fought back. All science, all banks are forgotten, and the peoples are told to take up arms, and so are the peasants, who know nothing about politics. . . .

What revolution did we make? We overthrew Nicholas. The revolution was not so very difficult compared with one that would have overthrown the whole class of landowners and capitalists. Who did the revolution put in power? The landowners and capitalists — the very same classes who have long been in power in Europe. . . . The [February] Russian revolution has not altered the war, but it has created organizations which exist in no other country and were seldom found in revolutions in the West. . . . We have all over Russia a network of Soviets of Workers', Soldiers', and Peasants' Deputies. Here is a revolution which has not said its last word yet. . . .

In the two months following the revolution the industrialists have robbed the whole of Russia. Capitalists have made staggering profits; every financial report tells you that. And when the workers, two months after the revolution, had the "audacity" to say they wanted to live like human beings, the whole capitalist press throughout the country set up a howl.

On the question of America entering the war I shall say this. People argue that America is a democracy, America has the White House.

I say: Slavery was abolished there half a century ago. The anti-slave war ended in 1865. Since then multimillionaires have mushroomed. They have the whole of America in their financial grip. They are making ready to subdue Mexico and will inevitably come to war with Japan over a carve-up of the Pacific. This war has been brewing for several decades. All literature speaks about it. America's real aim in entering the war is to prepare for this future war with Japan. The American people do enjoy considerable freedom and it is difficult to conceive them standing for compulsory military service, for the setting up of an army pursuing any aims of conquest—a struggle with Japan, for instance. The Americans have the example of Europe to show them what this leads to. The American capitalists have stepped into this war in order to have an excuse, behind a smoke-screen of lofty ideals championing the rights of small nations, for building up a strong standing army. . . .

Tens of millions of people are facing disaster and death; safeguarding the interests of the capitalists is the last thing that should bother us. The only way out is for all power to be transferred to the Soviets, which represent the majority of the population. Possibly mistakes may be made in the process. No one claims that such a difficult task can be disposed of offhand. We do not say anything of the sort. We are told that we want the power to be in the hands of the Soviets, but they don't want it. We say that life's experience will suggest this solution to them, and the whole nation will see that there is no other way out. We do not want a "seizure" of power, because the entire experience of past revolutions teaches us that the only stable power is the one that has the backing of the majority of the population. "Seizure" of power, therefore, would be adventurism, and our Party will not have it. . . .

Nothing but a workers' revolution in several countries can defeat this war. The war is not a game, it is an appalling thing taking a toll of millions of lives, and it is not to be ended easily.

. . . The war has been brought about by the ruling classes and only a revolution of the working class can end it. Whether you will get a speedy peace or not depends on how the revolution will develop.

Whatever sentimental things may be said, however much we may be told: Let us end the war immediately—this cannot be done without the development of the revolution. When power passes to the Soviets the capitalists will come out against us. Japan, France, Britain—the governments of all countries will be against us. The capitalists will be against, but the workers will be for us. That will be the end of the war which the capitalists started. There you have the answer to the question of how to end the war.

ROSA LUXEMBURG

The Problem of Dictatorship, 1918

Events moved very quickly in Russia in 1917. In May, Lenin insisted that the February revolution was incomplete. Remaking Russian society could not be achieved by a seizure of the state alone, but would also require mobilizing the support of a majority of the country's workers. The new Soviets, or workers' organizations, were to provide the foundation for this grassroots revolution. Futher, Lenin believed that workers throughout Europe needed to be liberated through revolution before peace and stability could be attained. The realities of the October revolution, however, obscured many of these original ideas. By the fall, Lenin and his Bolshevik party seized power without majority support while civil war still raged in Russia. The success of the Bolshevik revolution in October required a new revolutionary ideology.

Rosa Luxemburg (1870–1919) was born in Russian Poland, but at the age of nineteen fled to Switzerland, where she earned a doctorate in law and political science. At twenty-five she migrated to Germany where, as a journalist and theorist, she became an impassioned and influential voice in the German democratic socialist movement. She criticized its bureaucratic leadership and excoriated its submission to war hysteria. Her opposition to the war led to frequent imprisonment. While Luxemburg was imprisoned, Lenin seized power, and she composed her thoughts on the Russian Revolution in 1918.

As a cofounder of the German Spartacus League (which later became the German Communist Party), Luxemburg believed that the Bolshevik Revolution could mean the liberation of working people throughout Russia, then Germany and the rest of Europe. But since 1904 she disagreed with Lenin's ideas of centralized control and party discipline. What objections does she make to Lenin's revolution? What do you think of her arguments?

Ironically, the apparent success of Lenin's strategy in Russia led many in the German Spartacus League to agitate for a similar seizure of power in Germany at the end of the war. Rosa Luxemburg tried to dissuade them, believing it to be suicidal. Outvoted, she joined their uprising in Berlin in January 1919 and was subsequently arrested and murdered by the police.

Source: Rosa Luxemburg, *The Russian Revolution and Leninism or Marxism?* (Ann Arbor: The University of Michigan Press, 1961), 68–72. Introduction by Bertram D. Wolfe.

THINKING HISTORICALLY

Causes and consequences are often different sides of the same event. We might say that the First World War was a cause of the Russian Revolution or, conversely, that the Russian Revolution was a consequence of the First World War. Lenin argued that one of the consequences of the First World War was the particular sort of revolution he advocated, on the grounds that a democratic revolution was impossible under the circumstances. What do you think of that argument? Rosa Luxemburg disagreed that such draconian measures were necessary, and she argued that Lenin's revolutionary strategy would have its own consequences. Why did she think a dictatorial revolution could only lead to a dictatorial society?

Freedom only for the supporters of the government, only for the members of one party—however numerous they may be—is no freedom at all. Freedom is always and exclusively freedom for the one who thinks differently. Not because of any fanatical concept of "justice" but because all that is instructive, wholesome and purifying in political freedom depends on this essential characteristic, and its effectiveness vanishes when "freedom" becomes a special privilege.

The Bolsheviks themselves will not want, with hand on heart, to deny that, step by step, they have to feel out the ground, try out, experiment, test now one way now another, and that a good many of their measures do not represent priceless pearls of wisdom. Thus it must and will be with all of us when we get to the same point—even if the same difficult circumstances may not prevail everywhere.

The tacit assumption underlying the Lenin-Trotsky theory of dictatorship is this: that the socialist transformation is something for which a ready-made formula lies completed in the pocket of the revolutionary party, which needs only to be carried out energetically in practice. This is, unfortunately—or perhaps fortunately—not the case. Far from being a sum of ready-made prescriptions which have only to be applied, the practical realization of socialism as an economic, social and juridical system is something which lies completely hidden in the mists of the future. What we possess in our program is nothing but a few main signposts which indicate the general direction in which to look for the necessary measures, and the indications are mainly negative in character at that. Thus we know more or less what we must eliminate at the outset in order to free the road for a socialist economy. But when it comes to the nature of the thousand concrete, practical measures, large and small, necessary to introduce socialist principles into economy, law and all social relationships, there is no key in any socialist party program or textbook. That is not a shortcoming but rather the very thing that makes scientific socialism superior to the utopian varieties.

The socialist system of society should only be, and can only be, an historical product, born out of the school of its own experiences, born in the course of its realization, as a result of the developments of living history, which — just like organic nature of which, in the last analysis, it forms a part — has the fine habit of always producing along with any real social need the means to its satisfaction, along with the task simultaneously the solution. However, if such is the case, then it is clear that socialism by its very nature cannot be decreed or introduced by *ukase*. It has as its prerequisite a number of measures of force — against property, etc. The negative, the tearing down, can be decreed; the building up, the positive, cannot. New Territory. A thousand problems. Only experience is capable of correcting and opening new ways. Only unobstructed, effervescing life falls into a thousand new forms and improvisations, brings to light creative new force, itself corrects all mistaken attempts. The public life of countries with limited freedom is so poverty-stricken, so miserable, so rigid, so unfruitful, precisely because, through the exclusion of democracy, it cuts off the living sources of all spiritual riches and progress. (Proof: the year 1905 and the months from February to October 1917.)[1] There it was political in character; the same thing applies to economic and social life also. The whole mass of the people must take part in it. Otherwise, socialism will be decreed from behind a few official desks by a dozen intellectuals.

Public control is indispensably necessary. Otherwise the exchange of experiences remains only with the closed circle of the officials of the new regime. Corruption becomes inevitable. (Lenin's words, Bulletin No. 29) Socialism in life demands a complete spiritual transformation in the masses degraded by centuries of bourgeois rule. Social instincts in place of egotistical ones, mass initiative in place of inertia, idealism which conquers all suffering, etc., etc. No one knows this better, describes it more penetratingly; repeats it more stubbornly than Lenin. But he is completely mistaken in the means he employs. Decree, dictatorial force of the factory overseer, draconian penalties, rule by terror — all these things are but palliatives. The only way to a rebirth is the school of public life itself, the most unlimited, the broadest democracy and public opinion. It is rule by terror which demoralizes.

---

[1] In both 1905 and February/March of 1917, uprisings could not become revolutions because democracy was so thin. Only authoritarian regimes could carry out a revolution, as Lenin did in October/November 1917. [Ed.]

Syrian Congress Memorandum, 1919

As it became clear that the Allies would defeat the Central Powers, they began considering the nature of the peace and how they would construct the postwar world. On the issue of how to treat a defeated Germany after the war, the insistence of the French on stiff financial retribution fanned the embers for the next generation. Almost as important in the eyes of the victors was how to treat the defeated Ottoman Empire. In January, 1918, President Woodrow Wilson gave a speech to the U.S. Congress in which he listed "Fourteen Points" intended to ensure a just and lasting peace. An overall theme was the need for "national self-determination."

Point XII began: "The Turkish portions of the present Ottoman Empire should be assured a secure sovereignty, but the other nationalities which are now under Turkish rule should be assured an undoubted security of life and an absolutely unmolested opportunity of autonomous development." The Arabs of the Middle East constituted at least one of these "other nationalities," and many of them expected their independence after the war. Instead the Paris Peace Conference instituted a system of "mandates" by which the victorious European powers maintained control over enemy colonies, including the Ottoman Arab territories, until the Europeans determined the colonies were prepared for independence.

This selection details the Syrians' objections to this arrangement, sent as a memorandum to the King-Crane Commission, the body responsible for overseeing the transfer of Ottoman territory. What were their objections? What evidence did they give to support their position? What did they want?

THINKING HISTORICALLY

Do you think this conflict could have been an expected consequence of the First World War? Do you think Wilson's Fourteen Points made the Syrian demands more likely? Do you think the European powers expected this response? What were the consequences of the failure of the Allies to settle these grievances?

W e the undersigned members of the General Syrian Congress, meeting in Damascus on Wednesday, July 2nd 1919, . . . provided with credentials

---

Source: "The King-Crane Commission Report," in *Papers Relating to the Foreign Relations of the United States: Paris Peace Conference, 1919* (Washington, DC: GPO, 1947), 12:780–81.

and authorizations by the inhabitants of our various districts, Muslims, Christians, and Jews, have agreed upon the following statement of the desires of the people of the country who have elected us to present them to the American Section of the International Commission; the fifth article was passed by a very large majority; all the other articles were accepted unanimously.

1. We ask absolutely complete political independence for Syria within these boundaries. The Taurus System on the North; Rafah and a line running from Al Jauf to the south of the Syrian and the Hejazian line to Akaba on the south; the Euphrates and Khabur Rivers and a line extending east of Abu Kamal to the east of Al Jauf on the east; and the Mediterranean on the west.

2. We ask that the Government of this Syrian country should be a democratic civil constitutional Monarchy on broad decentralization principles, safeguarding the rights of minorities, and that the King be the Emir Feisal, who carried on a glorious struggle in the cause of our liberation and merited our full confidence and entire reliance.

3. Considering the fact that the Arabs inhabiting the Syrian area are not naturally less than other more advanced races and that they are by no means less developed than the Bulgarians, Serbians, Greeks, and Romanians at the beginning of their independence, we protest against Article 22 of the Covenant of the League of Nations, placing us among the nations in their middle stage of development which stand in need of a mandatory power.

4. In the event of the rejection by the Peace Conference of this just protest for certain considerations that we may not understand, we, relying on the declarations of President Wilson that his object in waging war was to put an end to the ambition of conquest and colonization, can only regard the mandate mentioned in the Covenant of the League of Nations as equivalent to the rendering of economical and technical assistance that does not prejudice our complete independence. And desiring that our country should not fall a prey to colonization and believing that the American Nation is furthest from any thought of colonization and has no political ambition in our country, we will seek the technical and economical assistance from the United States of America, provided that such assistance does not exceed 20 years.

5. In the event of America not finding herself in a position to accept our desire for assistance, we will seek this assistance from Great Britain, also provided that such assistance does not infringe the complete independence and unity of our country and that the duration of such assistance does not exceed that mentioned in the previous article.

6. We do not acknowledge any right claimed by the French Government in any part whatever of our Syrian country and refuse that she should assist us or have a hand in our country under any circumstances and in any place.

7. We oppose the pretensions of the Zionists to create a Jewish commonwealth in the southern part of Syria, known as Palestine, and oppose Zionist migration to any part of our country; for we do not acknowledge their title but consider them a grave peril to our people from the national, economical, and political points of view. Our Jewish compatriots shall enjoy our common rights and assume the common responsibilities.

8. We ask that there should be no separation of the southern part of Syria, known as Palestine, nor of the littoral western zone, which includes Lebanon, from the Syrian country. We desire that the unity of the country should be guaranteed against partition under whatever circumstances.

9. We ask complete independence for emancipated Mesopotamia and that there should be no economic barriers between the two countries.

10. The fundamental principles laid down by President Wilson in condemnation of secret treaties impel us to protest most emphatically against any treaty that stipulates the partition of our Syrian country and against any private engagement aiming at the establishment of Zionism in the southern part of Syria; therefore we ask the complete annulment of these conventions and agreements.

The noble principles enunciated by President Wilson strengthen our confidence that our desires emanating from the depths of our hearts, shall be the decisive factor in determining our future; and that President Wilson and the free American people will be our supporters for the realization of our hopes, thereby proving their sincerity and noble sympathy with the aspiration of the weaker nations in general and our Arab people in particular.

We also have the fullest confidence that the Peace Conference will realize that we would not have risen against the Turks, with whom we had participated in all civil, political, and representative privileges, but for their violation of our national rights, and so will grant us our desires in full in order that our political rights may not be less after the war than they were before, since we have shed so much blood in the cause of our liberty and independence.

We request to be allowed to send a delegation to represent us at the Peace Conference to defend our rights and secure the realization of our aspirations.

■ REFLECTIONS

By studying causes and consequences of world events, we learn how things change; more important, we learn how to avoid repeating past mistakes. History is full of lessons that breed humility as well as confidence. In *The Origins of the First World War*,[1] historian James Joll points out how unprepared people were for the war as late as

---

[1] James Joll, *The Origins of the First World War* (London: Longman, 1992), 200.

the summer of 1914. Even after the Austrian ultimatum to Serbia was issued on July 23 (almost a month after the assassination of the Archduke Franz Ferdinand on June 28), diplomats across Europe left for their summer holidays. By August, all of Europe was at war, though the expectation was that it would be over in a month.

We could make a good case for diplomatic blundering as an important cause of the First World War. It is safe to say that few statesmen had any inkling of the consequences of their actions in 1914. And yet, if we concentrate on the daily decisions of diplomats that summer, we may pay attention only to the tossing of lit matches by people sitting on powder kegs rather than on the origins of the powder kegs themselves.

President Wilson blamed secret diplomacy, the international system of alliances, and imperialism as the chief causes of the war. On the importance of imperialism, Wilson's conclusion was the same as that of Lenin, though he certainly did not share Lenin's conviction that capitalism was the root cause of imperialism, and in 1919 neither alliances nor imperialism was regarded as un-American or likely to end anytime soon. Still, Wilson's radical moral aversion to reviving Old World empires might have prevented a new stage of imperialism, as it developed in the mandate system. One of the consequences of a Wilsonian peace might have been the creation of independent states in the Middle East and Africa a generation earlier.

The principle of the "self-determination of nations" that Wilson espoused, however, was a double-edged sword. The fact that the war had been "caused" by a Bosnian Serb nationalist assassin in 1914 might have been a warning that national self-determination could become an infinite regress in which smaller and smaller units sought to separate themselves from "foreign" domination.

The rise of nationalist movements and the rise of international organizations were only two consequences of the First World War. Historians have attributed many other aspects of the twentieth century to the war. Stephen O'Shea offers a striking list of cultural changes:

> It is generally accepted that the Great War and its fifty-two months of senseless slaughter encouraged, or amplified, among other things: the loss of a belief in progress, a mistrust of technology, the loss of religious faith, the loss of a belief in Western cultural superiority, the rejection of class distinctions, the rejection of traditional sexual roles, the birth of the Modern [in art], the rejection of the past, the elevation of irony to a standard mode of apprehending the world, the unbuttoning of moral codes, and the conscious embrace of the irrational.[2]

Evidence of any of these consequences is only barely visible in the accounts of a chapter that ends in 1920, but many of the developments described in the next few chapters were consequences of World War I as well.

---

[2] Stephen O'Shea, *Back to the Front: An Accidental Historian Walks the Trenches of World War I* (New York: Avon Books, 1996), 9.

25

World War II and Mass Killing

Germany, the Soviet Union, Japan, and the United States, 1926–1945

■ HISTORICAL CONTEXT

In some ways World War II resembled World War I. At the European core, England and France again fought Germany and Austria. As in World War I, the United States eventually came to the aid of England and France, playing a decisive role. In both conflicts Russia also fought against Germany, only until the Soviet revolution in 1917, but fiercely and at great cost as the Soviet Union from 1941 to 1945. By contrast, Japan, an enemy of Germany in World War I, became an important German ally in World War II, and the pro-German Ottoman Empire of World War I was an independent, neutral Turkey in World War II.

While the main combatants were aligned on the same sides, and both wars ended in the defeat of Germany and its allies, the causes and consequences of the two wars were significantly different. The causes of World War II are clearer than those of World War I. German aggression was a factor in both wars, but in the buildup to World War I, there was much blame to go around. World War II, on the other hand, followed the aggressive conquests of Japan and Germany. Both countries had been militarized by extreme nationalist regimes. Similar "fascist" movements took power in Italy and Eastern Europe, partly in response to the economic hardship of the Great Depression of the 1930s. These movements, like the German Nazi Party, were led by demagogues — Hitler in Germany, Mussolini in Italy — who called for dictatorial power, the expulsion or conquest of foreigners, colonial expansion, and aggressive, violent solutions to social and economic problems. Similarly, the military party that took power in Japan sought an empire in China and Southeast Asia to ensure its economic prosperity.

The aggressions of Germany and Japan unleashed forces of violence that also distinguished World War II from World War I. New technologies of warfare (machine guns, biplanes, and gas in World War I) that had been directed almost entirely at soldiers in trenches were transformed by World War II into missiles and warheads that rained down on civilian populations. Even the victorious Allies directed previously unheard of violence against civilian populations in the firebombing of cities like Dresden and Tokyo and the use of nuclear bombs on Hiroshima and Nagasaki.

Despite the pounding barbarity of the Western Front, the era of World War I still contained features of earlier gentlemanly conflict. Like chivalric jousters, aristocratic World War I pilots displayed colorful scarves and saluted their falling rivals. But the extreme nationalist and racist movements of the interwar years instilled a hatred of the enemy that eviscerated any possibility of compassion or fellow feeling. Totalitarian governments indoctrinated mass citizen armies with a hatred that sometimes made the new technologies of violence redundant. Millions of newly designated enemies—neighbors as well as foreigners—were murdered by hand.

This chapter begins with selections on Nazi Germany: excerpts from Hitler's *Mein Kampf*, a Nazi speech on the extermination of Jews, and a description of the workings of one death camp, Treblinka. Then a recent historical essay places the holocaust of German Jews in a larger perspective. An even larger global view of the war and genocide brings us to Dr. Robert Wilson's letters about Japanese atrocities in China. We conclude this chapter on the war that killed so many millions by reflecting on its ending in mass death by a new weapon of far greater magnitude. We ask how, amidst the greatest technological progress the world had ever seen, the lives of ordinary people became so cheap.

■ **THINKING HISTORICALLY**

Thinking about the Unthinkable

To be able to think about the unthinkable is to be able to understand without excusing. Occasionally when we learn of something horrendous, we simply say, "I don't believe it." Our disbelief harbors two feelings: first, our sense of outrage and anger, a rejection of what was done; second, our unwillingness to believe that such a thing could happen or did happen. Our choice of words expresses the difficulty we have making sense of the senseless.

We must try, however, to understand such catastrophes so that we can help to prevent similar horrors in our own time. Understanding reprehensible acts requires a level of empathy that is often difficult to arouse. As you read these selections, you will be encouraged to understand and explain events that are easier to not think about. To understand what is offensive is not to excuse it, but to be better prepared to avoid it in the future.

1

ADOLF HITLER
Mein Kampf, 1926

Hitler (1889–1945) wrote *Mein Kampf* (My Struggle) in prison where he was jailed after an unsuccessful attempt to take over the German government in Munich in 1923. As he wrote in the Epilogue, included at the end of this selection, the German National Socialist Labor (Nazi) Party, banned after the attempted coup in 1923, was revived by 1926 to become a force in German politics.

We read from this rambling 700-page book today because of what happened in the years after its publication in 1926. In the context of the global depression after 1929, the Nazi party grew to be the largest party in the German Parliament by 1932 with 37 percent of the popular vote. In January 1933 Hitler was appointed chancellor by President Paul von Hindenburg. He proceeded to concentrate all power in his hands as *Fuhrer* (Dictator), militarize the German economy, and mobilize for war. In 1938, while the rest of Europe stood by, he annexed his native Austria and German-speaking regions of Czechoslovakia. In March 1939, he added the rest of Czechoslovakia. On September 1, 1939, the German invasion of Poland triggered World War II in Europe.

During the same period the Nazi regime imposed increasingly discriminatory restrictions on German Jews. As early as 1933, Jews were banned from government service, law practice, some medical careers and some schools, and Dachau, the first concentration camp in Germany, was built. In 1935 the Nuremburg laws outlawed any civic life for Jews and any sexual contact between Jews and non-Jews. In the next couple of years Jews were banned from all other occupations, Jewish children were banned from public schools, and German properties were seized. With the outbreak of war, Jews in Germany and in German-occupied countries were rounded up and put in concentration

Source: Adolf Hitler, *Mein Kampf*, translated by Ralph Manheim (Boston: Houghton Mifflin, 1999), 11–13, 15, 20–21, 34, 51–52, 56–58, 65, 78, 126, 134–36.

camps where they were forced to work in factories for private corporations or government producers of war materials. In 1941 the Nazis began building extermination camps, first in Poland, to annihilate Jews, Poles, and other enemies of the Nazis. These included communists, socialists, political dissenters, homosexuals, Romani (Gypsies), Slavs, and other ethnic and religious minorities. By 1945, upwards of 11 million Jews and other "undesirables" had been killed.

It would be a mistake to try to see all of this in embryo in a young artist in Vienna twenty years before, or even in the vitriolic ruminations of a prison inmate ten years later, but what do these selections suggest to you about Hitler's motivations and the roots of Nazism?

THINKING HISTORICALLY

To understand the unthinkable it is necessary to resist the temptation to demonize. To call someone a "Devil" or "Evil Incarnate" obviates the need to understand and learn. The English word *understand* is equivalent to the German word *verstehen*, which social scientists have used to connote empathetic knowledge: relating to another human, putting oneself in their shoes. This is a technique to gain knowledge; it has nothing to do with excusing or forgiving. Try this with probably the hardest subject in history: How did that aspiring art student become Hitler? What went wrong? How did his background, environment, and experience produce a future monster?

In the House of My Parents

Today it seems to me providential that Fate should have chosen Braunau on the Inn as my birthplace. For this little town lies on the boundary between two German states which we of the younger generation at least have made it our life work to reunite by every means at our disposal.

German-Austria must return to the great German mother country, and not because of any economic considerations. No, and again no: even if such a union were unimportant from an economic point of view; yes, even if it were harmful, it must nevertheless take place. One blood demands one Reich. Never will the German nation possess the moral right to engage in colonial politics until, at least, it embraces its own sons within a single state. Only when the Reich borders include the very last German, but can no longer guarantee his daily bread, will the moral right to acquire foreign soil arise from the distress of our own people. Their sword will become our plow, and from the tears of war the daily bread of future generations will grow. . . .

I, too, while still comparatively young, had an opportunity to take part in the struggle of nationalities in old Austria. Collections were taken for the *Südmark*[1] and the school association; we emphasized our convictions by wearing corn-flowers[2] and red, black, and gold colors; 'Heil' was our greeting, and instead of the imperial anthem we sang '*Deutschland über Alles*,' despite warnings and punishments. In this way the child received political training in a period when as a rule the subject of a so-called national state knew little more of his nationality than its language. It goes without saying that even then I was not among the lukewarm. In a short time I had become a fanatical 'German Nationalist,' though the term was not identical with our present party concept.

This development in me made rapid progress; by the time I was fifteen I understood the difference between dynastic '*patriotism*' and folkish '*nationalism*'; and even then I was interested only in the latter. . . .

Did we not know, even as little boys, that this Austrian state had and could have no love for us Germans?

Our historical knowledge of the works of the House of Habsburg was reinforced by our daily experience. In the north and south the poison of foreign nations gnawed at the body of our nationality, and even Vienna was visibly becoming more and more of an un-German city. The Royal House Czechized wherever possible, and it was the hand of the goddess of eternal justice and inexorable retribution which caused Archduke Francis Ferdinand, the most mortal enemy of Austrian-Germanism, to fall by the bullets which he himself had helped to mold. For had he not been the patron of Austria's Slavization from above! . . .

Years of Study and Suffering in Vienna

When after the death of my mother I went to Vienna for the third time, to remain for many years, the time which had meanwhile elapsed had restored my calm and determination. My old defiance had come back to me and my goal was now clear and definite before my eyes. I wanted to become an architect, and obstacles do not exist to be surrendered to, but only to be broken. I was determined to overcome these obstacles, keeping before my eyes the image of my father, who had started out as the child of a village shoemaker, and risen by his own efforts to be a government official. I had a better foundation to build on, and hence my possibilities in the struggle were easier, and what then seemed to be the harshness of Fate, I praise today as wisdom and Providence. While the

[1] Another term for Austria. Apparently devised in imitation of the old imperial Marks by the *Verein für Deutschtum im Ausland*, founded in 1881 to defend the endangered nationality of Germans in the border territories.

[2] The corn-flower was the emblem of Germans loyal to the imperial House of Hohenzollern and of the Austrian Pan-Germans.

Goddess of Suffering took me in her arms, often threatening to crush me, my will to resistance grew, and in the end this will was victorious.

I owe it to that period that I grew hard and am still capable of being hard. And even more, I exalt it for tearing me away from the hollowness of comfortable life; for drawing the mother's darling out of his soft downy bed and giving him 'Dame Care' for a new mother; for hurling me, despite all resistance, into a world of misery and poverty, thus making me acquainted with those for whom I was later to fight.

In this period my eyes were opened to two menaces of which I had previously scarcely known the names, and whose terrible importance for the existence of the German people I certainly did not understand: Marxism and Jewry. . . .

In the years 1909 and 1910, my own situation had changed somewhat in so far as I no longer had to earn my daily bread as a common laborer. By this time I was working independently as a small draftsman and painter of watercolors. Hard as this was with regard to earnings—it was barely enough to live on—it was good for my chosen profession. Now I was no longer dead tired in the evening when I came home from work, unable to look at a book without soon dozing off. My present work ran parallel to my future profession. Moreover, I was master of my own time and could apportion it better than had previously been possible.

I painted to make a living and studied for pleasure. . . .

Today it is difficult, if not impossible, for me to say when the word 'Jew' first gave me ground for special thoughts. At home I do not remember having heard the word during my father's lifetime. I believe that the old gentleman would have regarded any special emphasis on this term as cultural backwardness. In the course of his life he had arrived at more or less cosmopolitan views which, despite his pronounced national sentiments, not only remained intact, but also affected me to some extent.

Likewise at school I found no occasion which could have led me to change this inherited picture.

At the *Realschule*, to be sure, I did meet one Jewish boy who was treated by all of us with caution, but only because various experiences had led us to doubt his discretion and we did not particularly trust him; but neither I nor the others had any thoughts on the matter.

Not until my fourteenth or fifteenth year did I begin to come across the word 'Jew,' with any frequency, partly in connection with political discussions. This filled me with a mild distaste, and I could not rid myself of an unpleasant feeling that always came over me whenever religious quarrels occurred in my presence.

At that time I did not think anything else of the question.

There were few Jews in Linz. In the course of the centuries their outward appearance had become Europeanized and had taken on a human look; in fact, I even took them for Germans. The absurdity of this idea did not dawn on me because I saw no distinguishing feature but the strange religion. The fact that they had, as I believed, been persecuted on this account sometimes almost turned my distaste at unfavorable remarks about them into horror.

Thus far I did not so much as suspect the existence of an organized opposition to the Jews.

Then I came to Vienna.

Preoccupied by the abundance of my impressions in the architectural field, oppressed by the hardship of my own lot, I gained at first no insight into the inner stratification of the people in this gigantic city. Notwithstanding that Vienna in those days counted nearly two hundred thousand Jews among its two million inhabitants, I did not see them. In the first few weeks my eyes and my senses were not equal to the flood of values and ideas. Not until calm gradually returned and the agitated picture began to clear did I look around me more carefully in my new world, and then among other things I encountered the Jewish question. . . .

Once, as I was strolling through the Inner City, I suddenly encountered an apparition in a black caftan and black hair locks. Is this a Jew? was my first thought.

For, to be sure, they had not looked like that in Linz. I observed the man furtively and cautiously, but the longer I stared at this foreign face, scrutinizing feature for feature, the more my first question assumed a new form:

Is this a German?

As always in such cases, I now began to try to relieve my doubts by books. For a few hellers I bought the first anti-Semitic pamphlets of my life. Unfortunately, they all proceeded from the supposition that in principle the reader knew or even understood the Jewish question to a certain degree. Besides, the tone for the most part was such that doubts again arose in me, due in part to the dull and amazingly unscientific arguments favoring the thesis.

I relapsed for weeks at a time, once even for months.

The whole thing seemed to me so monstrous, the accusations so boundless, that, tormented by the fear of doing injustice, I again became anxious and uncertain.

Yet I could no longer very well doubt that the objects of my study were not Germans of a special religion, but a people in themselves; for since I had begun to concern myself with this question and to take cognizance of the Jews, Vienna appeared to me in a different light than before. Wherever I went, I began to see Jews, and the more I saw, the more sharply they became distinguished in my eyes from the rest of humanity. Particularly the Inner City and the districts north of the Danube Canal swarmed with a people which even outwardly had lost all resemblance to Germans. . . .

What had to be reckoned heavily against the Jews in my eyes was when I became acquainted with their activity in the press, art, literature, and the theater. All the unctuous reassurances helped little or nothing. It sufficed to look at a billboard, to study the names of the men behind the horrible trash they advertised, to make you hard for a long time to come. This was pestilence, spiritual pestilence, worse than the Black Death of olden times, and the people were being infected with it! . . .

If, with the help of his Marxist creed, the Jew is victorious over the other peoples of the world, his crown will be the funeral wreath of humanity and this planet will, as it did thousands of years ago, move through the ether devoid of men.

Eternal Nature inexorably avenges the infringement of her commands.

Hence today I believe that I am acting in accordance with the will of the Almighty Creator: *by defending myself against the Jew, I am fighting for the work of the Lord.* . . .

Political Reflections Arising out of My Sojourn in Vienna

The Western democracy of today is the forerunner of Marxism which without it would not be thinkable. It provides this world plague with the culture in which its germs can spread. In its most extreme form, parliamentarianism created a 'monstrosity of excrement and fire,' in which, however, sad to say, the 'fire' seems to me at the moment to be burned out. . . .

Munich

In the spring of 1912 I came at last to Munich. . . .

. . . A *German* city! What a difference from Vienna! I grew sick to my stomach when I even thought back on this Babylon of races. In addition, the dialect, much closer to me, which particularly in my contacts with Lower Bavarians, reminded me of my former childhood. . . .

Assuredly at a certain time the whole of humanity will be compelled, in consequence of the impossibility of making the fertility of the soil keep pace with the continuous increase in population, to halt the increase of the human race and either let Nature again decide or, by self-help if possible, create the necessary balance, though, to be sure, in a more correct way than is done today. But then this will strike all peoples, while today only those races are stricken with such suffering which no longer possess the force and strength to secure for themselves the necessary territories in this world. For as matters stand there are at the present time on this earth immense areas of unused soil, only waiting for the men to till them. But it is equally true that Nature as such has not reserved this soil for the future possession of any particular nation or race; on the contrary, this soil exists for the people which possesses the force to take it and the industry to cultivate it.

Nature knows no political boundaries. First, she puts living creatures on this globe and watches the free play of forces. She then confers the master's right on her favorite child, the strongest in courage and industry.

When a people limits itself to internal colonization because other races are clinging fast to greater and greater surfaces of this earth, it will be forced to have recourse to self-limitation at a time when the other peoples are still continuing to increase. . . .

For us Germans the slogan of 'inner colonization' is catastrophic, if for no other reason because it automatically reinforces us in the opinion that we have found a means which, in accordance with the pacifistic tendency, allows us 'to earn' our right to exist by labor in a life of sweet slumbers. Once this doctrine were taken seriously in our country, it would mean the end of every exertion to preserve for ourselves the place which is our due. Once the average German became convinced that he could secure his life and future in this way, all attempts at an active, and hence alone fertile, defense of German vital necessities would be doomed to failure. In the face of such an attitude on the part of the nation any really beneficial foreign policy could be regarded as buried, and with it the future of the German people as a whole.

Taking these consequences into account, it is no accident that it is always primarily the Jew who tries and succeeds in planting such mortally dangerous modes of thought in our people. He knows his customers too well not to realize that they gratefully let themselves be swindled by any gold-brick salesman who can make them think he has found a way to play a little trick on Nature, to make the hard, inexorable struggle for existence superfluous, and instead, sometimes by work, but sometimes by plain doing nothing, depending on how things 'come out,' to become the lord of the planet.

It cannot be emphasized sharply enough *that any German internal colonization must serve to eliminate social abuse particularly to withdraw the soil from widespread speculation, but can never suffice to secure the future of the nation without the acquisition of new soil.*

If we do not do this, we shall in a short time have arrived, not only at the end of our soil, but also at the end of our strength. . . .

Conclusion

On November 9, 1923, in the fourth year of its existence, the National Socialist German Workers' Party was dissolved and prohibited in the whole Reich territory. Today in November, 1926, it stands again free before us, stronger and inwardly firmer than ever before.

All the persecutions of the movement and its individual leaders, all vilifications and slanders, were powerless to harm it. The correctness of its ideas, the purity if its will, its supporters' spirit of self-sacrifice, have caused it to issue from all repressions stronger than ever.

If, in the world of our present parliamentary corruption, it becomes more and more aware of the profoundest essence of its struggle, feels itself to be the purest embodiment of the value of race and personality and conducts itself accordingly, it will with almost mathematical certainty some day emerge victorious from its struggle. Just as Germany must inevitably win her rightful position on this earth if she is led and organized according to the same principles.

A state which in this age of racial poisoning dedicates itself to the care of its best racial elements must some day become lord of the earth.

May the adherents of our movement never forget this if ever the magnitude of the sacrifices should beguile them to an anxious comparison with the possible results.

2

HEINRICH HIMMLER
Speech to the SS, 1943

Heinrich Himmler (1900–1945) was one of the most powerful leaders of Nazi Germany. He was the head of the SS, or *Schutzstaffel,* an elite army that was responsible for, among other things, running the many concentration camps. Hitler gave Himmler the task of implementing the "final solution of the Jewish question": attempted genocide of the Jewish population of Germany and the other countries the Nazis occupied. The horror that resulted is today often referred to by the word *holocaust* (literally, holy burnt offering).

The following reading is an excerpt from a speech Himmler gave to SS leaders on October 4, 1943. What was Himmler's concern in this speech? What kind of general support for the extermination of the Jews does this excerpt suggest existed?

THINKING HISTORICALLY

Psychiatrists say that people use various strategies to cope when they must do something distasteful. We might summarize these strategies as

Source: Heinrich Himmler, "Secret Speech at Posen," in *A Holocaust Reader*, ed. Lucy S. Dawidowicz (New York: Behrman House, 1976), 132–33.

denial, distancing, compartmentalizing, ennobling, rationalizing, and scapegoating. *Denial* is pretending that something has not happened. *Distancing* removes the idea, memory, or reality from the mind, placing it at a distance. *Compartmentalizing* separates one action, memory, or idea from others, allowing one to "put away" certain feelings. *Ennobling* makes the distasteful act a matter of pride rather than guilt, nobility rather than disgrace. *Rationalizing* creates "good" reasons for doing something, while *scapegoating* puts blame on someone else.

What evidence do you see of these strategies in Himmler's speech? Judging from the speech, which of these strategies do you think his listeners used to justify their actions?

I also want to make reference before you here, in complete frankness, to a really grave matter. Among ourselves, this once, it shall be uttered quite frankly; but in public we will never speak of it. Just as we did not hesitate on June 30, 1934, to do our duty as ordered, to stand up against the wall comrades who had transgressed,[1] and shoot them, so we have never talked about this and never will. It was the tact which I am glad to say is a matter of course to us that made us never discuss it among ourselves, never talk about it. Each of us shuddered, and yet each one knew that he would do it again if it were ordered and if it were necessary.

I am referring to the evacuation of the Jews, the annihilation of the Jewish people. This is one of those things that are easily said. "The Jewish people is going to be annihilated," says every party member. "Sure, it's in our program, elimination of the Jews, annihilation — we'll take care of it." And then they all come trudging, 80 million worthy Germans, and each one has his one decent Jew. Sure, the others are swine, but this one is an A-1 Jew. Of all those who talk this way, not one has seen it happen, not one has been through it. Most of you must know what it means to see a hundred corpses lie side by side, or five hundred, or a thousand. To have stuck this out — excepting cases of human weakness — to have kept our integrity, that is what has made us hard. In our history, this is an unwritten and never-to-be-written page of glory, for we know how difficult we would have made it for ourselves if today — amid the bombing raids, the hardships, and the deprivations of war — we still had the Jews in every city as secret saboteurs, agitators, and demagogues. If the Jews were still ensconced in the body of the German nation, we probably would have reached the 1916–17 stage by now.[2]

---

[1] A reference to the "Night of the Long Knives," when Hitler ordered the SS to murder the leaders of the SA, a Nazi group he wished to suppress. [Ed.]

[2] Here Himmler is apparently referring to the stalemate on Germany's Western Front in World War I. [Ed.]

The wealth they had we have taken from them. I have issued a strict order, carried out by SS-Obergruppenfuhrer Pohl, that this wealth in its entirety is to be turned over to the Reich as a matter of course. We have taken none of it for ourselves. Individuals who transgress will be punished in accordance with an order I issued at the beginning, threatening that whoever takes so much as a mark of it for himself is a dead man. A number of SS men—not very many—have transgressed, and they will die, without mercy. We had the moral right, we had the duty toward our people, to kill this people which wanted to kill us. But we do not have the right to enrich ourselves with so much as a fur, a watch, a mark, or a cigarette, or anything else. Having exterminated a germ, we do not want, in the end, to be infected by the germ, and die of it. I will not stand by and let even a small rotten spot develop or take hold. Wherever it may form, we together will cauterize it. All in all, however, we can say that we have carried out this heaviest of our tasks in a spirit of love for our people. And our inward being, our soul, our character has not suffered injury from it.

3

JEAN-FRANÇOIS STEINER

Treblinka, 1967

Treblinka, in Poland, was one of several Nazi extermination camps (see Map 25.1). In these "death factories," the Nazis murdered millions of Jews as well as Roma and Sinti, communists, socialists, Poles, Soviet prisoners of war, and other people. Extermination of Jews became official Nazi policy in 1942. Extermination camps were built to supplement earlier concentration camps used to contain political prisoners, Jews, and other forced laborers (many of whom also died there). In this selection, Steiner describes some of the elaborate study and preparation that went into the design of an extermination camp, focusing on the work of Kurt Franz, whom the prisoners called Lalka. What were the problems the Nazis faced in building an extermination camp? How did they solve them? What does this level of efficiency and scientific planning tell you about the Nazi regime or the people involved?

THINKING HISTORICALLY

Try to imagine what went through the mind of Lalka as he designed the extermination process at Treblinka. How did concerns for

Source: Jean-François Steiner, *Treblinka* (New York: Simon & Schuster, 1967), 153–54, 155–58, 159–60.

Map 25.1 Major Nazi Concentration Camps in World War II.

969

efficiency and humanity enter into his deliberations? Do you think he found his work distasteful? If so, which of the strategies mentioned in the previous selection did he adopt?

What would it have been like to be a sign-painter, guard, or hair-cutter at Treblinka? What do you imagine went through the minds of the victims?

Each poorly organized debarkation [of deportees from trains arriving at Treblinka] gave rise to unpleasant scenes—uncertainties and confusion for the deportees, who did not know where they were going and were sometimes seized with panic.

So, the first problem was to restore a minimum of hope. Lalka had many faults, but he did not lack a certain creative imagination. After a few days of reflection he hit upon the idea of transforming the platform where the convoys [trains] arrived into a false station. He had the ground filled in to the level of the doors of the cars in order to give the appearance of a train platform and to make it easier to get off the trains. . . . On [a] wall Lalka had . . . doors and windows painted in gay and pleasing colors. The windows were decorated with cheerful curtains and framed by green blinds which were just as false as the rest. Each door was given a special name, stencilled at eye level: "Stationmaster," "Toilet," "Infirmary" (a red cross was painted on this door). Lalka carried his concern for detail so far as to have his men paint two doors leading to the waiting rooms, first and second class. The ticket window, which was barred with a horizontal sign reading, "Closed," was a little masterpiece with its ledge and false perspective and its grill, painted line for line. Next to the ticket window a large timetable announced the departure times of trains for Warsaw, Bialystok, Wolkowysk, etc. . . . Two doors were cut into the [wall]. The first led to the "hospital," bearing a wooden arrow on which "Wolkowysk" was painted. The second led to the place where the Jews were undressed; that arrow said "Bialystok." Lalka also had some flower beds designed, which gave the whole area a neat and cheery look. . . .

Lalka also decided that better organization could save much time in the operations of undressing and recovery of the [deportees'] baggage. To do this you had only to rationalize the different operations, that is, to organize the undressing like an assembly line. But the rhythm of this assembly line was at the mercy of the sick, the old, and the wounded, who, since they were unable to keep the pace, threatened to bog down the operation and make it proceed even more slowly than before. . . . Individuals of both sexes over the age of ten, and children under ten, at a maximum rate of two children per adult, were judged fit to follow the complete circuit,[1] as long as they did not show serious wounds or marked disability. Victims who did not correspond to the norms were to be conducted to the "hospital" by members of the blue commando and turned over to the Ukrainians [guards] for special treatment. A bench was built all around the ditch of the "hospital" so that the victims would fall of their own weight after receiving the bullet in the back of the head. This bench was to be used only when Kurland[2] was swamped with work. On the platform, the door which these victims took was surmounted by the Wolkowysk arrow. In the Sibylline language of Treblinka, "Wolkowysk" meant the bullet in the back of the neck or the injection. "Bialystok" meant the gas chamber.

Beside the "Bialystok" door stood a tall Jew whose role was to shout endlessly, "Large bundles here, large bundles here!" He had been nicknamed "Groysse Pack." As soon as the victims had gone through, Groysse Pack and his men from the red commando carried the bundles at a run to the sorting square, where the sorting commandos immediately took possession of them. As soon as they had gone through the door came the order, "Women to the left, men to the right." This moment generally gave rise to painful scenes.

While the women were being led to the left-hand barracks to undress and go to the hairdresser,[3] the men, who were lined up double file, slowly entered the production line. This production line included five stations. At each of these a group of "reds" shouted at the top of their lungs the name of the piece of clothing that it was in charge of receiving. At the first station the victim handed over his coat and hat. At the second, his jacket. (In exchange, he received a piece of string.) At the third he sat down, took off his shoes, and tied them together with the string he had just received. Until then the shoes were not tied together in pairs, and since the yield was at least fifteen thousand pairs of shoes per day, they were all lost, since they could not be matched up again. At the fourth station the victim left his trousers, and at the fifth his shirt and underwear.

After they had been stripped, the victims were conducted, as they came off the assembly line, to the right-hand barracks and penned in until the women had finished: ladies first. However, a small number, chosen from among the most able-bodied, were singled out at the door to carry the clothing to the sorting square. They did this while running naked between two rows of Ukrainian guards. Without stopping once

[1] The "complete" circuit was getting off the train, walking along the platform through the door to the men's or women's barracks, undressing, and being led to the gas chamber "showers." [Ed.]

[2] Kurland was a Jew assigned to the "hospital," where he gave injections of poison to those who were too ill or crippled to make the complete circuit. [Ed.]

[3] Haircutter. [Ed.]

they threw their bundles onto the pile, turned around, and went back for another.

Meanwhile the women had been conducted to the barracks on the left. This barracks was divided into two parts: a dressing room and a beauty salon. "Put your clothes in a pile so you will be able to find them after the shower," they were ordered in the first room. The "beauty salon" was a room furnished with six benches, each of which could seat twenty women at a time. Behind each bench twenty prisoners of the red commando, wearing white tunics and armed with scissors, waited at attention until all the women were seated. Between haircutting sessions they sat down on the benches and, under the direction of a *kapo* [prisoner guard] who was transformed into a conductor, they had to sing old Yiddish melodies.

Lalka, who had insisted on taking personal responsibility for every detail, had perfected the technique of what he called the "Treblinka cut." With five well-placed slashes the whole head of hair was transferred to a sack placed beside each hairdresser for this purpose. It was simple and efficient. How many dramas did this "beauty salon" see? From the very beautiful young woman who wept when her hair was cut off, because she would be ugly, to the mother who grabbed a pair of scissors from one of the "hairdressers" and literally severed a Ukrainian's arm; from the sister who recognized one of the "hairdressers" as her brother to the young girl, Ruth Dorfman, who, suddenly understanding and fighting back her tears, asked whether it was difficult to die and admitted in a small brave voice that she was a little afraid and wished it were all over.

When they had been shorn the women left the "beauty salon" double file. Outside the door, they had to squat in a particular way also specified by Lalka, in order to be intimately searched. Up to this point, doubt had been carefully maintained. Of course, a discriminating eye might have observed that . . . the smell was the smell of rotting bodies. A thousand details proved that Treblinka was not a transient camp, and some realized this, but the majority had believed in the impossible for too long to begin to doubt at the last moment. The door of the barracks, which opened directly onto the "road to heaven," represented the turning point. Up to here the prisoners had been given a minimum of hope, from here on this policy was abandoned.

This was one of Lalka's great innovations. After what point was it no longer necessary to delude the victims? This detail had been the subject of rather heated controversy among the Technicians. At the Nuremberg trials, Rudolf Höss, Commandant of Auschwitz, criticized Treblinka where, according to him, the victims knew that they were going to be killed. Höss was an advocate of the towel distributed at the door to the gas chamber. He claimed that this system not only avoided disorder, but was more humane, and he was proud of it. But Höss did not invent this "towel technique"; it was in all the manuals, and it was utilized at Treblinka until Lalka's great reform.

Lalka's studies had led to what might be called the "principle of the cutoff." His reasoning was simple: Since sooner or later the victims must realize that they were going to be killed, to postpone this moment was only false humanity. The principle "the later the better" did not apply here. Lalka had been led to make an intensive study of this problem upon observing one day completely by chance, that winded victims died much more rapidly than the rest. The discovery had led him to make a clean sweep of accepted principles. Let us follow his industrialist's logic, keeping well in mind that his great preoccupation was the saving of time. A winded victim dies faster. Hence, a saving of time. The best way to wind a man is to make him run — another saving of time. Thus Lalka arrived at the conclusion that you must make the victims run. A new question had then arisen: At what point must you make the victims run and thus create panic (a further aid to breathlessness)? The question had answered itself: As soon as you have nothing more to make them do. Franz located the exact point, the point of no return: the door of the barracks.

The rest was merely a matter of working out the details. Along the "road to heaven" and in front of the gas chambers he stationed a cordon of guards armed with whips, whose function was to make the victims run, to make them rush into the gas chambers of their own accord in search of refuge. One can see that this system is more daring than the classic system, but one can also see the danger it represents. Suddenly abandoned to their despair, realizing that they no longer had anything to lose, the victims might attack the guards. Lalka was aware of this risk, but he maintained that everything depended on the pace. "It's close work," he said, "but if you maintain a very rapid pace and do not allow a single moment of hesitation, the method is absolutely without danger." There were still further elaborations later on, but from the first day, Lalka had only to pride himself on his innovation: It took no more than three quarters of an hour, by the clock, to put the victims through their last voyage, from the moment the doors of the cattle cars were unbolted to the moment the great trap doors of the gas chamber were opened to take out the bodies. . . .

But let us return to the men. The timing was worked out so that by the time the last woman had emerged from the left-hand barracks, all the clothes had been transported to the sorting square. The men were immediately taken out of the right-hand barracks and driven after the women into the "road to heaven," which they reached by way of a special side path. By the time they arrived at the gas chambers the toughest, who had begun to run before the others to carry the bundles, were just as winded as the weakest. Everyone died in perfect unison for the greater satisfaction of that great Technician Kurt Franz, the Stakhanovite [model worker] of extermination.

4

TIMOTHY SNYDER

Holocaust: The Ignored Reality, 2009

The mass killing of Jews was a policy of the Nazis fueled by long-standing anti-Semitism, aggravated by German economic collapse and propaganda that linked Jews to both communist laborer agitation and the bankers at the upper levels of finance capitalism. This anti-Semitism was not limited to Germany, however. It was especially pervasive throughout Eastern Europe, where most Jews lived. Thus, it would be a mistake, according to the author of this selection, to think of the Holocaust solely in terms of Germany and German Jews. What are the broader dimensions of the Holocaust that the author describes? Further, if the Holocaust refers only to the killing of Jews, how might a focus on this genocide alone minimize the scale of civilian casualties in World War II?

THINKING HISTORICALLY

The process of understanding without excusing is a struggle between the intellect and the emotions. No historical study can be entirely divorced from the emotions, but subjects like mass slaughter make it harder than many other subjects to be objective. Other factors might inhibit the historian's ability to get to the truth. One difficulty, for instance, lies with sources. What limitations does Snyder see in the sources that have been available to understand the Holocaust? How representative are survivors? What can we learn from the perpetrators? How do statistics help and hinder our understanding? What is gained, and lost, by distinguishing between such events as holocaust, genocide, war crimes, massacres, civilian casualties, and "collateral damage"?

Though Europe thrives, its writers and politicians are preoccupied with death. The mass killings of European civilians during the 1930s and 1940s [see Map 25.2] are the reference of today's confused discussions of memory, and the touchstone of whatever common ethics Europeans may share. The bureaucracies of Nazi Germany and the Soviet Union turned individual lives into mass death, particular humans into quotas of those to be killed. The Soviets hid their mass shootings in dark woods and falsified the records of regions in which they had

Source: Timothy Snyder, "Holocaust: The Ignored Reality," *New York Review of Books* 56, no. 12 (July 16, 2009), http://www.nybooks.com/articles/22875.

Map 25.2 Eastern Europe, c. 1942.

Source: Courtesy of the New York Review of Books.

975

starved people to death; the Germans had slave laborers dig up the bodies of their Jewish victims and burn them on giant grates. Historians must, as best we can, cast light into these shadows and account for these people. This we have not done. Auschwitz, generally taken to be an adequate or even a final symbol of the evil of mass killing, is in fact only the beginning of knowledge, a hint of the true reckoning with the past still to come.

The very reasons that we know something about Auschwitz warp our understanding of the Holocaust: we know about Auschwitz because there were survivors, and there were survivors because Auschwitz was a labor camp as well as a death factory. These survivors were largely West European Jews, because Auschwitz is where West European Jews were usually sent. After World War II, West European Jewish survivors were free to write and publish as they liked, whereas East European Jewish survivors, if caught behind the iron curtain, could not. In the West, memoirs of the Holocaust could (although very slowly) enter into historical writing and public consciousness.

This form of survivors' history, of which the works of Primo Levi[1] are the most famous example, only inadequately captures the reality of the mass killing. *The Diary of Anne Frank* concerns assimilated European Jewish communities, the Dutch and German, whose tragedy, though horrible, was a very small part of the Holocaust. By 1943 and 1944, when most of the killing of West European Jews took place, the Holocaust was in considerable measure complete. Two thirds of the Jews who would be killed during the war were already dead by the end of 1942. The main victims, the Polish and Soviet Jews, had been killed by bullets fired over death pits or by carbon monoxide from internal combustion engines pumped into gas chambers at Treblinka, Be zec,[2] and Sobibor in occupied Poland.

Auschwitz as symbol of the Holocaust excludes those who were at the center of the historical event. The largest group of Holocaust victims—religiously Orthodox and Yiddish-speaking Jews of Poland, or, in the slightly contemptuous German term, *Ostjuden*[3]—were culturally alien from West Europeans, including West European Jews. To some degree, they continue to be marginalized from the memory of the Holocaust. The death facility Auschwitz-Birkenau was constructed on territories that are today in Poland, although at the time they were part of the German Reich. Auschwitz is thus associated with today's Poland by anyone who visits, yet relatively few Polish Jews and almost no Soviet Jews died there. The two largest groups of victims are nearly missing from the memorial symbol.

[1] Primo Levi (1919–1987), Italian chemist, poet, essayist, novelist. Author of the memoir *Survival in Auschwitz*. [Ed.]

[2] Also rendered as Belzec. [Ed.]

[3] Eastern Jews (from Eastern Europe). [Ed.]

An adequate vision of the Holocaust would place Operation Reinhardt, the murder of the Polish Jews in 1942, at the center of its history. Polish Jews were the largest Jewish community in the world, Warsaw the most important Jewish city. This community was exterminated at Treblinka, Be zec, and Sobibor. Some 1.5 million Jews were killed at those three facilities, about 780,863 at Treblinka alone. Only a few dozen people survived these three death facilities. Be zec, though the third most important killing site of the Holocaust, after Auschwitz and Treblinka, is hardly known. Some 434,508 Jews perished at that death factory, and only two or three survived. About a million more Polish Jews were killed in other ways, some at Chelmno, Majdanek, or Auschwitz, many more shot in actions in the eastern half of the country.

All in all, as many if not more Jews were killed by bullets as by gas, but they were killed by bullets in easterly locations that are blurred in painful remembrance. The second most important part of the Holocaust is the mass murder by bullets in eastern Poland and the Soviet Union. It began with SS Einsatzgruppen shootings of Jewish men in June 1941, expanded to the murder of Jewish women and children in July, and extended to the extermination of entire Jewish communities that August and September. By the end of 1941, the Germans (along with local auxiliaries and Romanian troops) had killed a million Jews in the Soviet Union and the Baltics. That is the equivalent of the total number of Jews killed at Auschwitz during the entire war. By the end of 1942, the Germans (again, with a great deal of local assistance) had shot another 700,000 Jews, and the Soviet Jewish populations under their control had ceased to exist.

There were articulate Soviet Jewish witnesses and chroniclers, such as Vassily Grossman. But he and others were forbidden from presenting the Holocaust as a distinctly Jewish event. Grossman discovered Treblinka as a journalist with the Red Army in September 1944. Perhaps because he knew what the Germans had done to Jews in his native Ukraine, he was able to guess what had happened there, and wrote a short book about it. He called Treblinka "hell," and placed it at the center of the war and of the century. Yet for Stalin, the mass murder of Jews had to be seen as the suffering of "citizens." Grossman helped to compile a *Black Book* of German crimes against Soviet Jews, which Soviet authorities later suppressed. If any group suffered especially under the Germans, Stalin maintained wrongly, it was the Russians. In this way Stalinism has prevented us from seeing Hitler's mass killings in proper perspective.

In shorthand, then, the Holocaust was, in order: Operation Reinhardt, Shoah[4] by bullets, Auschwitz; or Poland, the Soviet Union, the rest. Of the 5.7 million or so Jews killed, roughly 3 million were prewar Polish citizens, and another 1 million or so pre-war Soviet citizens:

[4] Mass murder. [Ed.]

978 ■ 25 / World War II and Mass Killing

taken together, 70 percent of the total. (After the Polish and Soviet Jews, the next-largest groups of Jews killed were Romanian, Hungarian, and Czechoslovak. If these people are considered, the East European character of the Holocaust becomes even clearer.)

Yet even this corrected image of the Holocaust conveys an unacceptably incomplete sense of the scope of German mass killing policies in Europe. The Final Solution, as the Nazis called it, was originally only one of the exterminatory projects to be implemented after a victorious war against the Soviet Union. Had things gone the way that Hitler, Himmler, and Göring expected, German forces would have implemented a Hunger Plan in the Soviet Union in the winter of 1941–1942. As Ukrainian and south Russian agricultural products were diverted to Germany, some 30 million people in Belarus, northern Russia, and Soviet cities were to be starved to death. The Hunger Plan was only a prelude to Generalplan Ost, the colonization plan for the western Soviet Union, which foresaw the elimination of some 50 million people.

The Germans did manage to carry out policies that bore some resemblance to these plans. They expelled half a million non-Jewish Poles from lands annexed to the Reich. An impatient Himmler ordered a first stage of Generalplan Ost implemented in eastern Poland: ten thousand Polish children were killed and a hundred thousand adults expelled. The Wehrmacht[5] purposefully starved about one million people in the siege of Leningrad, and about a hundred thousand more in planned famines in Ukrainian cities. Some three million captured Soviet soldiers died of starvation or disease in German prisoner-of-war camps. These people were purposefully killed: as with the siege of Leningrad, the knowledge and intention to starve people to death was present. Had the Holocaust not taken place, this would be recalled as the worst war crime in modern history.

In the guise of anti-partisan actions, the Germans killed perhaps three quarters of a million people, about 350,000 in Belarus alone, and lower but comparable numbers in Poland and Yugoslavia. The Germans killed more than a hundred thousand Poles when suppressing the Warsaw Uprising of 1944. Had the Holocaust not happened, these "reprisals" too would be regarded as some of the greatest war crimes in history. In fact they, like the starvation of Soviet prisoners of war, are scarcely recalled at all beyond the countries directly concerned. German occupation policies killed non-Jewish civilians in other ways as well, for example by hard labor in prison camps. Again: these were chiefly people from Poland or the Soviet Union.

The Germans killed somewhat more than ten million civilians in the major mass killing actions, about half of them Jews, about half of them non-Jews. The Jews and the non-Jews mostly came from the same part of Europe. The project to kill all Jews was substantially realized;

[5] German Army. [Ed.]

the project to destroy Slavic populations was only very partially implemented.

Auschwitz is only an introduction to the Holocaust, the Holocaust only a suggestion of Hitler's final aims. Grossman's novels *Forever Flowing* and *Life and Fate* daringly recount both Nazi and Soviet terror, and remind us that even a full characterization of German policies of mass killing is incomplete as a history of atrocity in mid-century Europe. It omits the state that Hitler was chiefly concerned to destroy, the other state that killed Europeans en masse in the middle of the century: the Soviet Union. In the entire Stalinist period, between 1928 and 1953, Soviet policies killed, in a conservative estimate, well over five million Europeans. Thus when one considers the total number of European civilians killed by totalitarian powers in the middle of the twentieth century, one should have in mind three groups of roughly equal size: Jews killed by Germans, non-Jews killed by Germans, and Soviet citizens killed by the Soviet state. As a general rule, the German regime killed civilians who were not German citizens, whereas the Soviet regime chiefly killed civilians who were Soviet citizens. Soviet repressions are identified with the Gulag, much as Nazi repressions are identified with Auschwitz. The Gulag,[6] for all of the horrors of slave labor, was not a system of mass killing. If we accept that mass killing of civilians is at the center of political, ethical, and legal concerns, the same historical point applies to the Gulag as to Auschwitz. We know about the Gulag because it was a system of labor camps, but not a set of killing facilities. The Gulag held about 30 million people and shortened some three million lives. But a vast majority of those people who were sent to the camps returned alive. Precisely because we have a literature of the Gulag, most famously Aleksandr Solzhenitsyn's *Gulag Archipelago*, we can try to imagine its horrors—much as we can try to imagine the horrors of Auschwitz.

Yet as Auschwitz draws attention away from the still greater horrors of Treblinka, the Gulag distracts us from the Soviet policies that killed people directly and purposefully, by starvation and bullets. Of the Stalinist killing policies, two were the most significant: the collectivization famines of 1930–1933 and the Great Terror of 1937–1938. It remains unclear whether the Kazakh famine of 1930–1932 was intentional, although it is clear that over a million Kazakhs died of starvation. It is established beyond reasonable doubt that Stalin intentionally starved to death Soviet Ukrainians in the winter of 1932–1933. Soviet documents reveal a series of orders of October–December 1932 with evident malice and intention to kill. By the end, more than three million inhabitants of Soviet Ukraine had died.

[6] A system of Soviet labor camps, many in remote locations, where political prisoners were sent and sometimes disappeared. [Ed.]

What we read of the Great Terror[7] also distracts us from its true nature. The great novel and the great memoir are Arthur Koestler's *Darkness at Noon* and Alexander Weissberg's *The Accused*. Both focus our attention on a small group of Stalin's victims, urban Communist leaders, educated people, sometimes known in the West. This image dominates our understanding of the Great Terror, but it is incorrect. Taken together, purges of Communist Party elites, the security police, and military officers claimed not more than 47,737 lives.

The largest action of the Great Terror, Operation 00447, was aimed chiefly at "kulaks," which is to say peasants who had already been oppressed during collectivization.[8] It claimed 386,798 lives. A few national minorities, representing together less than 2 percent of the Soviet population, yielded more than a third of the fatalities of the Great Terror. In an operation aimed at ethnic Poles who were Soviet citizens, for example, 111,091 people were shot. Of the 681,692 executions carried out for alleged political crimes in 1937 and 1938, the kulak operation and the national operations accounted for 633,955, more than 90 percent of the total. These people were shot in secret, buried in pits, and forgotten.

The emphasis on Auschwitz and the Gulag understates the numbers of Europeans killed, and shifts the geographical focus of the killing to the German Reich and the Russian East. Like Auschwitz, which draws our attention to the Western European victims of the Nazi empire, the Gulag, with its notorious Siberian camps, also distracts us from the geographical center of Soviet killing policies. If we concentrate on Auschwitz and the Gulag, we fail to notice that over a period of twelve years, between 1933 and 1944, some 12 million victims of Nazi and Soviet mass killing policies perished in a particular region of Europe, one defined more or less by today's Belarus, Ukraine, Poland, Lithuania, and Latvia. More generally, when we contemplate Auschwitz and the Gulag, we tend to think of the states that built them as systems, as modern tyrannies, or totalitarian states. Yet such considerations of thought and politics in Berlin and Moscow tend to overlook the fact that mass killing happened, predominantly, in the parts of Europe between Germany and Russia, not in Germany and Russia themselves.

The geographic, moral, and political center of the Europe of mass killing is the Europe of the East, above all Belarus, Ukraine, Poland, and the Baltic States, lands that were subject to sustained policies of atrocity by both regimes. The peoples of Ukraine and Belarus, Jews above all but not only, suffered the most, since these lands were both part of the Soviet Union during the terrible 1930s and subject to the worst of the German

---

[7] Period in 1930s of Stalin's purges of political rivals and anyone who voiced criticism. Here refers to 1937–1938. [Ed.]

[8] Soviet policy from 1928 to 1940 to end private property in farmland and create large farming communes. Forced collectivization of peasant kulaks led to mass starvation. [Ed.]

repressions in the 1940s. If Europe was, as Mark Mazower[9] put it, a dark continent, Ukraine and Belarus were the heart of darkness.

Historical reckonings that can be seen as objective, such as the counting of victims of mass killing actions, might help to restore a certain lost historical balance. German suffering under Hitler and during the war, though dreadful in scale, does not figure at the center of the history of mass killing. Even if the ethnic Germans killed during flight from the Red Army, expulsion from Poland and Czechoslovakia in 1945–1947, and the firebombings in Germany are included, the total number of German civilians killed by state power remains comparatively small. . . .

The main victims of direct killing policies among German citizens were the 70,000 "euthanasia" patients and the 165,000 German Jews. The main German victims of Stalin remain the women raped by the Red Army and the prisoners of war held in the Soviet Union. Some 363,000 German prisoners died of starvation and disease in Soviet captivity, as did perhaps 200,000 Hungarians. At a time when German resistance to Hitler receives attention in the mass media, it is worth recalling that some participants in the July 1944 plot to kill Hitler were right at the center of mass killing policies: Arthur Nebe, for example, who commanded Einsatzgruppe B in the killing fields of Belarus during the first wave of the Holocaust in 1941; or Eduard Wagner, the quartermaster general of the Wehrmacht, who wrote a cheery letter to his wife about the need to deny food to the starving millions of Leningrad.

It is hard to forget Anna Akhmatova: "It loves blood, the Russian earth." Yet Russian martyrdom and heroism, now loudly proclaimed in Putin's Russia, must be placed against the larger historical background. Soviet Russians, like other Soviet citizens, were indeed victims of Stalinist policy: but they were much less likely to be killed than Soviet Ukrainians or Soviet Poles, or members of other national minorities. During World War II several terror actions were extended to eastern Poland and the Baltic states, territories absorbed by the Soviet Union. In the most famous case, 22,000 Polish citizens were shot in 1940 at Katyn and four other sites; tens of thousands more Poles and Balts died during or shortly after deportations to Kazakhstan and Siberia. During the war, many Soviet Russians were killed by the Germans, but far fewer proportionately than Belarusians and Ukrainians, not to mention Jews. Soviet civilian deaths are estimated at about 15 million. About one in twenty-five civilians in Russia was killed by the Germans during the war, as opposed to about one in ten in Ukraine (or Poland) or about one in five in Belarus.

Belarus and Ukraine were occupied for much of the war, with both German and Soviet armies passing through their entire territory twice, in attack and retreat. German armies never occupied more than a small portion of Russia proper, and that for shorter periods. Even taking into

---

[9] Historian, author of *The Dark Continent: Europe's Twentieth Century* (2000). [Ed.]

account the siege of Leningrad and the destruction of Stalingrad, the toll taken on Russian civilians was much less than that on Belarusians, Ukrainians, and Jews. Exaggerated Russian claims about numbers of deaths treat Belarus and Ukraine as Russia, and Jews, Belarusians, and Ukrainians as Russians: this amounts to an imperialism of martyrdom, implicitly claiming territory by explicitly claiming victims. This will likely be the line propounded by the new historical committee appointed by President Dmitri Medvedev to prevent "falsifications" of the Russian past. Under legislation currently debated in Russia, statements such as those contained in this paragraph would be a criminal offense.

Ukrainian politicians counter Russia's monopolization of common suffering, and respond to Western European stereotypes of Ukrainians as Holocaust collaborators, by putting forward a narrative of suffering of their own: that millions of Ukrainians were deliberately starved by Stalin. President Viktor Yushchenko does his country a grave disservice by claiming ten million deaths, thus exaggerating the number of Ukrainians killed by a factor of three; but it is true that the famine in Ukraine of 1932–1933 was a result of purposeful political decisions, and killed about three million people. With the exception of the Holocaust, the collectivization famines were the greatest political disaster of the European twentieth century. Collectivization nevertheless remained the central element of the Soviet model of development, and was copied later by the Chinese Communist regime, with the predictable consequence: tens of millions dead by starvation in Mao's Great Leap Forward.[10]

The preoccupation with Ukraine as a source of food was shared by Hitler and Stalin. Both wished to control and exploit the Ukrainian breadbasket, and both caused political famines: Stalin in the country as a whole, Hitler in the cities and the prisoner-of-war camps. Some of the Ukrainian prisoners who endured starvation in those camps in 1941 had survived the famine in 1933. German policies of starvation, incidentally, are partially responsible for the notion that Ukrainians were willing collaborators in the Holocaust. The most notorious Ukrainian collaborators were the guards at the death facilities at Treblinka, Be zec, and Sobibor. What is rarely recalled is that the Germans recruited the first cadres of such men, captured Soviet soldiers, from their own prisoner-of-war camps. They rescued some people from mass starvation, one great crime in the east, in order to make them collaborators in another, the Holocaust.

Poland's history is the source of endless confusion. Poland was attacked and occupied not by one but by both totalitarian states between 1939 and 1941, as Nazi Germany and the Soviet Union, then allies, exploited its territories and exterminated much of its intelligentsia at

---

[10] Chinese communist collectivization (1958–1961) under Mao Zedong, which failed. [Ed.]

that time. Poland's capital was the site of not one but two of the major uprisings against German power during World War II: the ghetto[11] uprising of Warsaw Jews in 1943,[12] after which the ghetto was leveled; and the Warsaw Uprising of the Polish Home Army in 1944, after which the rest of the city was destroyed. These two central examples of resistance and mass killing were confused in the German mass media in August 1994, 1999, and 2004, on all the recent five-year anniversaries of the Warsaw Uprising of 1944, and will be again in August 2009.

If any European country seems out of place in today's Europe, stranded in another historical moment, it is Belarus under the dictatorship of Aleksandr Lukashenko. Yet while Lukashenko prefers to ignore the Soviet killing fields in his country, wishing to build a highway over the death pits at Kuropaty, in some respects Lukashenko remembers European history better than his critics. By starving Soviet prisoners of war, shooting and gassing Jews, and shooting civilians in anti-partisan actions, German forces made Belarus the deadliest place in the world between 1941 and 1944. Half of the population of Soviet Belarus was either killed or forcibly displaced during World War II: nothing of the kind can be said of any other European country.

Belarusian memories of this experience, cultivated by the current dictatorial regime, help to explain suspicions of initiatives coming from the West. Yet West Europeans would generally be surprised to learn that Belarus was both the epicenter of European mass killing and the base of operations of anti-Nazi partisans who actually contributed to the victory of the Allies. It is striking that such a country can be entirely displaced from European remembrance. The absence of Belarus from discussions of the past is the clearest sign of the difference between memory and history.

Just as disturbing is the absence of economics. Although the history of mass killing has much to do with economic calculation, memory shuns anything that might seem to make murder appear rational. Both Nazi Germany and the Soviet Union followed a path to economic self-sufficiency, Germany wishing to balance industry with an agrarian utopia in the East, the USSR wishing to overcome its agrarian backwardness with rapid industrialization and urbanization. Both regimes were aiming for economic autarky in a large empire, in which both sought to control Eastern Europe. Both of them saw the Polish state as a historical aberration;[13] both saw Ukraine and its rich soil as indispensable. They defined different groups as the enemies of their designs, although the German plan to kill every Jew is unmatched by any Soviet policy in the totality of its aims. What is crucial is that the ideology that legitimated mass death

[11] Ghettos were urban areas in which Jews were forced to live, apart from the rest of the society. [Ed.]

[12] Revolt of Polish Jews in April 1943 in opposition to removal to Treblinka. Crushed by German troops in May. [Ed.]

[13] Polish territory had often been part of one or more larger states. [Ed.]

was also a vision of economic development. In a world of scarcity, particularly of food supplies, both regimes integrated mass murder with economic planning.

They did so in ways that seem appalling and obscene to us today, but which were sufficiently plausible to motivate large numbers of believers at the time. Food is no longer scarce, at least in the West; but other resources are, or will be soon. In the twenty-first century, we will face shortages of potable water, clean air, and affordable energy. Climate change may bring a renewed threat of hunger.

If there is a general political lesson of the history of mass killing, it is the need to be wary of what might be called privileged development: attempts by states to realize a form of economic expansion that designates victims, that motivates prosperity by mortality. The possibility cannot be excluded that the murder of one group can benefit another, or at least can be seen to do so. That is a version of politics that Europe has in fact witnessed and may witness again. The only sufficient answer is an ethical commitment to the individual, such that the individual counts in life rather than in death, and schemes of this sort become unthinkable.

The Europe of today is remarkable precisely in its unity of prosperity with social justice and human rights. Probably more than any other part of the world, it is immune, at least for the time being, to such heartlessly instrumental pursuits of economic growth. Yet memory has made some odd departures from history, at a time when history is needed more than ever. The recent European past may resemble the near future of the rest of the world. This is one more reason for getting the reckonings right.

5

DR. ROBERT WILSON

Letters from Nanking, 1937–1938

In 1946 the American-led International Military Tribunal for the Far East brought charges against the defeated Iwane Matsui, former Commander of the Japanese Shanghai Expeditionary Forces, for what was already being called "the Rape of Nanking." Matsui was charged with leading an army that systematically killed 200,000 defenseless Chinese civilians, committed 20,000 cases of rape, and stole or burned much of the property in the city.

Source: *Documents on the Rape of Nanking*, ed. Timothy Brook (Ann Arbor: University of Michigan Press, 1999), 210–11, 214–17, 250–54.

Dr. Robert Wilson was one of three American medical doctors, and the only surgeon, who remained at the University Hospital in Nanking when the Chinese defenders retreated and Japanese troops occupied the city in December, 1937. He wrote these letters to his family, even after he realized he wouldn't be able to mail them, as a kind of diary of events between December 1937 and March 1938.

What does Wilson's diary tell you about the Japanese occupation of Nanking? What does it tell you about Japanese forces? What are "war crimes" in the midst of war?

THINKING HISTORICALLY

It would be difficult to get into the shoes, much less the minds, of these Japanese troops from the viewpoint of a single American observer. Nevertheless, how might Robert Wilson account for their behavior? How do you make sense of it?

Tuesday, December 14

. . . On Monday morning the 13th, exactly four months after the trouble started in Shanghai, the Japanese entered the city by several gates at once. Some came in Hoping Men [Gate] in the north and some in Hansi and Kwanghua Mens in the west and south-east respectively. By night they had complete control of the city and numerous Japanese flags flew from various places including their former embassy.

The entire remaining population of Nanking, some 150 or 200 thousand individuals, were crowded into the zone I have described earlier as the refugee zone. The International Committee[1] are doing a tremendous job with them and there is no doubt but that they have saved thousands of lives by their efforts. At the last moment thousands of Chinese soldiers threw away their uniforms and equipment and donned looted civilian clothes and crowded into the zone. Handling them is a grave problem in itself. Doubly grave has it become since the Japanese have not been fooled and are rounding them up by the hundreds and shooting them, putting their bodies in the conveniently handy dugouts built for air-raid protection.

Any civilian who shows no signs of fear and goes quietly about his business in the daytime seems relatively safe. Nobody is safe at night. Last night Mr. Chi, architect for the university and left behind to look after the buildings as best he could, was only saved from shooting by the intervention of Charlie Riggs, who stoutly maintained that Chi was his

---

[1] The European (including German) and North American governors of the International Zone (non-Asian). [Ed.]

coolie.[2] They then came over to our place with another Chinese University staff man, Mr. Ku, and all three stayed the night on some cots we put up in the living room. Steele of the *Chicago Daily News* also slept there and we totalled eleven people sleeping on the main floor and up, and I completely lost track of the innumerable Chinese that slept in the basement. The servants are rightly scared to death. To finish this paragraph more or less as it began, any civilian that shows signs of fear or tries to run away is promptly bayonetted. I sewed up one severed trachea this afternoon and we have had several dozen cases of bayonetting.

This morning we were treated to a thorough though unofficial inspection by thirty or so Japanese troops with fixed bayonets. They poked into everything. [Dr. James] McCallum, [Dr. C. S.] Trimmer and I showed them around and they would jabber away in Japanese while we would jabber away in both Chinese and English and neither had any idea what the other was saying. They lined up some of the nurses and took away their pens, flashlights and wrist watches. They did a pretty good job of looting the nurses' dormitory, taking all kinds of petty things. So far there has been no physical violence done to any of our staff.

Wednesday, December 15

. . . The slaughter of civilians is appalling. I could go on for pages telling of cases of rape and brutality almost beyond belief. Two bayonetted cases are the only survivors of seven street cleaners who were sitting in their headquarters when Japanese soldiers came in without warning or reason and killed five of their number and wounded the two that found their way to the hospital. I wonder when it will stop and we will be able to catch up with ourselves again.

Saturday, December 18

Today marks the sixth day of the modern Dante's Inferno, written in huge letters with blood and rape. Murder by the wholesale and rape by the thousands of cases. There seems to be no stop to the ferocity, lust and atavism of the brutes. At first I tried to be pleasant to them to avoid arousing their ire but the smile has gradually worn off and my stare is fully as cool and fishy as theirs.

Tonight as I came back from supper to stay here for the night I found three soldiers had ransacked the place. Miss [Iva] Hynds had accompanied them to the back gate. Two of them arrived and the other had disappeared. He must be hiding somewhere around the place. I motioned

[2] Word used for usually Chinese workers. [Ed.]

to the others outside stating in no uncertain terms that this was a Bei-koku Byoyen [American hospital]. How do you like that? The two that were there allowed themselves to be led out. They had taken Miss Hynds' watch and several other watches and fountain pens as well.

Let me recount some instances occurring in the last two days. Last night the house of one of the Chinese staff members of the university was broken into and two of the women, his relatives, were raped. Two girls about 16 were raped to death in one of the refugee camps. In the University Middle School where there are 8,000 people the Japs came in ten times last night, over the wall, stole food, clothing, and raped until they were satisfied. They bayonetted one little boy, killing him, and I spent an hour and a half this morning patching up another little boy of eight who had five bayonet wounds including one that penetrated his stomach, a portion of omentum was outside the abdomen. I think he will live.

I just took time out because the third soldier had been found. He was on the fourth floor of the nurses' dormitory where there were fifteen nurses. They were scared within an inch of their lives. I don't know how much he had done before I arrived but he didn't do anything afterwards. He had a watch or two and was starting off with one of the girls' cameras. I motioned for him to give it back to her and to my surprise he obeyed. I then accompanied him to the front door and bade him a fond farewell. Unfortunately he didn't get the swift kick that I mentally aimed at him. One of the earlier ones was toying around with a rather formidable looking pistol which I'm thankful he didn't use.

One man I treated today had three bullet holes. He is the sole survivor of a group of eighty, including an eleven year old boy, who were led out of two buildings within the so-called safety zone and taken into the hills west of Tibet Road and there slaughtered. He came to after they had left and found the other seventy-nine dead about him. His three bullet wounds are not serious. To do the Japanese justice there were in the eighty a few ex-soldiers.

One girl I have is a half-wit with some sort of birth injury, I believe. She didn't have any more sense than to claw at a Japanese soldier who was taking away her only bedding. Her reward was a bayonet thrust that cut half the muscles of one side of her neck.

Another girl of seventeen has a terrific gash in her neck and is the only survivor of her family, the rest of them were finished off. She was employed by the International Export Company.

As I left the hospital for supper after finishing my rounds on the 150 cases now under my care, the full moon was rising over Purple Mountain and was indescribably beautiful, and yet it looked down on a Nanking that was more desolate than it has been since the Taiping Rebellion [1853–64]. Nine-tenths of the city are totally deserted by Chinese and contain only roving bands of plundering Japanese. The remaining tenth contains almost two hundred thousand terrified citizens.

Last night [Plumer] Mills, [Lewis] Smythe and [George] Fitch went over in Fitch's car to escort Mills to Ginling [College]. Minnie [Vautrin] holds the fort there with several thousand women. When they got to the front gate they were held up by a patrol of Japanese soldiers under command of a pugnacious, impudent lieutenant. He lined the men on one side and Miss Vautrin, Mrs. Chen [Shui-fang] and Mrs. [deWitt] Twinem on the other side. He snatched the hats off the men and ordered everyone off the place including the women. Fitch told him he didn't have a place for them to stay but he insisted. They just got into the car when he ordered them back again and again harangued them for some minutes, finally sending the men back where they came from. Later we learned that while this was going on some Japanese soldiers had climbed over the wall and helped themselves to sixteen women.

The population faces famine in the near future and there is no provision for winter's fuel. It is not a pleasant winter that we look forward to. It is too bad that the newspaper reporters left on the day they did instead of two days or so later when they could have been more detailed in their reports of the Reign of Terror.

Another interruption to usher two Japanese soldiers off the premises.

As I probably won't get much sleep tonight I had better turn in dressed to get what I can.

Thursday, February 10

[. . .] The proportion of medical [to] surgical cases at the hospital is steadily increasing so that now Trim has about 50 patients to my 100. Today for the first time I went to our regular surgical clinic at 2 p.m., starting my operative schedule at 3:30. I shall try to continue that as the clinic certainly needs a guiding hand and there have been a lot of complaints about the way people are being treated there. This afternoon a woman came in with her face badly burned. She had returned to her home, on the orders of the Japanese, four days ago. Several Japanese soldiers promptly visited the house and demanded girls. She had only one 11 year old and one 12 year old and as these did not satisfy the soldiers they set fire to her house burning up the 11 year old girl in the building.

We are getting a large number of women from 16 to 30, most of them nice looking girls who are ridden with venereal disease from frequent raping. All of them have gonorrhea, most have syphilis and a large proportion have chancroid as well. That aspect of the clinic is certainly a heartbreaking one. It doesn't take long for any remote respect for the Japanese soldiers to evaporate permanently.

When our two cases of beri-beri showed up the other day we got immediate action and a boat is starting from Shanghai tomorrow with 100 tons of green beans. We hope to cut down any further incidence.

Yesterday I tried my first heterogeneous skin graft using pinch grafts from a father to his daughter. The graft looked fine today but it is much too early to tell. This afternoon I admitted a horribly burned little girl who has all the skin off her lower abdomen and anterior thighs. It happened six days ago and the mother had put on a concoction of mice boiled in oil and ground up. I had to give the child a general anaesthesia to clean it up. Her father had been shot offhand by the Japs about a month ago and the mother had not been able to give the child the attention she wanted to.

We get up to the tune of Jap airplanes and hear them all day long. Every now and then we think some Chinese planes come to the outskirts but we have no direct confirmation except occasional radio reports from Hankow. [. . .]

Sunday, February 13

[. . .] Last night we finally had the members of the Japanese Embassy to dinner. Three of the four came, the fourth having celebrated the previous day too vigorously. The previous day was the Anniversary of the founding of the Empire. Mssrs. Fukui, Fukuda and Kasuya were the guests. We put our excellent radio upstairs and played some classical records for them. We settled the problem of what to talk about by finding that two of them played bridge so that a bridge game was quickly organized. Fitch and Fukuda playing Riggs and Fukui. Unfortunately they stayed until ten-fifteen so that we didn't get any of the news broadcasts. Ordinarily we listen to Manila at 8:50, Hongkong at 9:30 and Shanghai at 10:10. Occasionally London at 6:00 and now and then Melbourne or some other place that happens to be giving the news.

Another cheerful tale came to my attention yesterday. Two weeks ago six Japanese soldiers entered the town of Liulangchiao some miles southwest of our town. They proceeded with their usual system of rape and looting. Some of the men in the town organized some resistance and killed three of the soldiers, the other three getting away. The three soon returned with several hundred who quickly threw a cordon around the town. A town of 500 inhabitants, it had only about 300 at the time. These 300 were all tied together in groups of six to eight and thrown in the icy river. They then leveled the town so that there wasn't a wall standing. The story was told me by a man who had gone from Nanking to Tanyangchen, a village just beyond Liulangchiao. He talked with the few terrified inhabitants of the surrounding territory and saw the ruins. Coming back he passed two soldiers on sentry duty at Yuhwatai just outside of South Gate. He was with his wife and child. They had passed the sentries about fifty yards when one of them casually shot in their direction, the bullet going through his flank but fortunately not entering the peritoneum. He is anxious to get out and return to Tanyangchen.

Only tonight four Jap soldiers came in and robbed several people in the University Library at the point of pistols of several hundred dollars. I guess the millennium is not here yet.

March 7

[. . .] The fall of Nanking on December 13 was immeasurably hastened by the incompetence and defection of T'ang Sheng-chih who was supposed to coordinate the defence. I shall not go into details on that here but will some day when the opportunity affords. If anyone had mentioned to us on December 12 that the entry of the Japanese would be the signal for a reign of terror almost beyond description we would have laughed at their fears. We had urged our Chinese staff to stay in the firm belief that, once the much vaunted Japanese Imperial army had taken control, lives would be safe and, while there might be some interference in the conduction of affairs, it would be only petty annoyances and that we need not be overconcerned.

When the mass murder, rapine, looting and arson began shortly after the entry of the Japanese troops we at first could not believe our eyes but were effectively convinced in a very short time. We had experienced no trouble whatever at the hands of Chinese soldiers even during the night of December 12 when tens of thousands of them streamed northward through the city to their slaughter at Hsia Kwan. It is true that they had burned some of the buildings just outside of the city walls in preparation for a defence of the walls that was never made, but outside of that and the burning of the Ministry of Communications, which burned on December 12th and therefore was presumably burned by Chinese, no destruction was carried out.

The Red Swastika Society[3] has for the last month been feverishly burying bodies from all parts of the city outside the zone and from the surrounding countryside. A conservative estimate of the number of people slaughtered in cold blood is somewhere about 100,000, including of course thousand of soldiers that had thrown down their arms. A few pitiful survivors of many of the mass murders managed to get to the hospital to tell their tale. I will record only one incident to illustrate.

At the University where the haphazard registration was going on of the twenty thousand people occupying the new library and compound and the main University buildings and compound, speeches were made urging all those that had been connected with the military to acknowledge it. They were promised that if they did so they would be made into labor gangs and their lives would be spared. If they did not acknowledge it and for any reason the Japanese suspected they had been connected

[3] Nazi German imitation of Red Cross Society. [Ed.]

with the military they would be summarily shot. About two hundred came forward and gave themselves up. I treated several survivors of that group. They were separated into several gangs and joined with hundreds of others picked up elsewhere. One bunch was taken into the hills beyond Ginling College, a few machine guns sprayed on them, several gallons of gasoline doused over their heads and they were set afire. Two survivors later died in the hospital burned almost beyond recognition, one not even having been hit by the machine guns, and the other having his jaw torn open.

6

President Truman's Announcement of the Dropping of an Atom Bomb on Hiroshima, 1945

In World War II the aerial bombing of civilian populations became increasingly common. A war that began for the British in a Nazi blitzkrieg of bombs and missiles on London, and that began for the United States in a Japanese air attack on the naval base at Pearl Harbor, came to a conclusion with an increased intensity of allied aerial attacks on the populated cities of Germany and Japan. In February of 1945, 1,300 U.S. and British bombers dropped 3,900 tons of explosives on the medieval German city of Dresden, unleashing a firestorm that claimed tens of thousands of lives. Tokyo was bombed throughout the war, but in March of 1945, a single bombing run of 179 new long-range B-29s took well over a hundred thousand lives. By the end of the war 50 percent of Tokyo, the most densely populated city in the world, had been leveled, an area that had once housed one and a half million people. By the summer of 1945, a new kind of weapon was about to harness the atom for even greater destruction.

The U.S. effort to make an atomic bomb had been a secret wartime project, begun initially by President Franklin D. Roosevelt out of fear that Germany was already developing one. Work continued in 1945, despite the death of Roosevelt in April and the surrender of Germany in May, as the United States and its allies turned their attention to defeating the Japanese in the Pacific. President Truman was also interested in the propaganda value of the bomb to ward off possible Soviet

Source: "Statement by the President Announcing the Use of the A-Bomb at Hiroshima," Truman Library, http://www.trumanlibrary.org/calendar/viewpapers.php?pid=100.

intentions in China and Japan. On August 6, 1945, the United States dropped the world's first atomic bomb on the city of Hiroshima, Japan. Three days later, a second atomic bomb was dropped on the Japanese city of Nagasaki. On August 15, Japan surrendered.

This selection is President Truman's address after the bombing of Hiroshima. What reasons does he give for the use of such a weapon? How does he relate the atomic bomb to the use of other weapons of war? How does he relate it to the issue of peace?

THINKING HISTORICALLY

President Truman was aware there would be controversy about the use of an atomic bomb. He had received a petition from atomic scientists urging him to first demonstrate the power of the weapon to the Japanese by exploding it in an uninhabited area. He heard his secretary of war Stimson compare the army's imprecise bombing and high civilian casualties to Nazi atrocities. On the very day he gave the order to drop the bomb, July 25, 1945, he wrote in his diary: "I have told the Sec. of War, Mr. Stimson, to use it so that military objectives and soldiers and sailors are the target and not women and children. . . . The target will be a purely military one."[1] However, the order contained no such language.

What signs do you see in this announcement of an effort to counter some of these concerns? How might Truman have shielded himself from recognizing some of the consequences of his decision?

Sixteen hours ago an American airplane dropped one bomb on Hiroshima, an important Japanese Army base. That bomb had more power than 20,000 tons of T.N.T. It had more than two thousand times the blast power of the British "Grand Slam" which is the largest bomb ever yet used in the history of warfare.

The Japanese began the war from the air at Pearl Harbor. They have been repaid many fold. And the end is not yet. With this bomb we have now added a new and revolutionary increase in destruction to supplement the growing power of our armed forces. In their present form these bombs are now in production and even more powerful forms are in development.

It is an atomic bomb. It is a harnessing of the basic power of the universe. The force from which the sun draws its power has been loosed against those who brought war to the Far East.

Before 1939, it was the accepted belief of scientists that it was theoretically possible to release atomic energy. But no one knew any practical

[1] Truman quoted in Robert H. Ferrell, *Off the Record: The Private Papers of Harry S. Truman* (New York: Harper and Row, 1980), 55–56.

method of doing it. By 1942, however, we knew that the Germans were working feverishly to find a way to add atomic energy to the other engines of war with which they hoped to enslave the world. But they failed. We may be grateful to Providence that the Germans got the V-1's and the V-2's late and in limited quantities and even more grateful that they did not get the atomic bomb at all.

The battle of the laboratories held fateful risks for us as well as the battles of the air, land and sea, and we have now won the battle of the laboratories as we have won the other battles.

Beginning in 1940, before Pearl Harbor, scientific knowledge useful in war was pooled between the United States and Great Britain, and many priceless helps to our victories have come from that arrangement. Under that general policy the research on the atomic bomb was begun. With American and British scientists working together we entered the race of discovery against the Germans.

The United States had available the large number of scientists of distinction in the many needed areas of knowledge. It had the tremendous industrial and financial resources necessary for the project and they could be devoted to it without undue impairment of other vital war work. In the United States the laboratory work and the production plants, on which a substantial start had already been made, would be out of reach of enemy bombing, while at that time Britain was exposed to constant air attack and was still threatened with the possibility of invasion. For these reasons Prime Minister Churchill and President Roosevelt agreed that it was wise to carry on the project here. We now have two great plants and many lesser works devoted to the production of atomic power. Employment during peak construction numbered 125,000 and over 65,000 individuals are even now engaged in operating the plants. Many have worked there for two and a half years. Few know what they have been producing. They see great quantities of material going in and they see nothing coming out of these plants, for the physical size of the explosive charge is exceedingly small. We have spent two billion dollars on the greatest scientific gamble in history—we won.

But the greatest marvel is not the size of the enterprise, its secrecy, nor its cost, but the achievement of scientific brains in putting together infinitely complex pieces of knowledge held by many men in different fields of science into a workable plan. And hardly less marvelous has been the capacity of industry to design, and of labor to operate, the machines and methods to do things never done before so that the brain child of many minds came forth in physical shape and performed as it was supposed to do. Both science and industry worked under the direction of the United States Army, which achieved a unique success in managing so diverse a problem in the advancement of knowledge in an amazingly short time. It is doubtful if such another combination could be got together in the world. What has been done is the greatest achievement of organized science in history. It was done under high pressure and without failure.

We are now prepared to obliterate more rapidly and completely every productive enterprise the Japanese have above ground in any city. We shall destroy their docks, their factories, and their communications. Let there be no mistake; we shall completely destroy Japan's power to make war.

It was to spare the Japanese people from utter destruction that the ultimatum of July 26 was issued at Potsdam.[2] Their leaders promptly rejected that ultimatum.[3] If they do not now accept our terms they may expect a rain of ruin from the air, the like of which has never been seen on this earth. Behind this air attack will follow sea and land forces in such numbers and power as they have not yet seen and with the fighting skill of which they are already well aware.

The Secretary of War, who has kept in personal touch with all phases of this project, will immediately make public a statement giving further details.

His statement will give facts concerning the sites of Oak Ridge near Knoxville, Tennessee, and at Richland near Pasco, Washington, and an installation near Santa Fe, New Mexico. Although the workers at the sites have been making materials to be used in producing the greatest destructive force in history they have not themselves been in danger beyond that of many other occupations, for the utmost care has been taken of their safety.

The fact that we can release atomic energy ushers in a new era in man's understanding of nature's forces. Atomic energy may in the future supplement the power that now comes from coal, oil, and falling water, but at present it cannot be produced on a basis to compete with them commercially. Before that comes there must be a long period of intensive research.

It has never been the habit of the scientists of this country or the policy of the Government to withhold from the world scientific knowledge. Normally, therefore, everything about the work with atomic energy would be made public.

But under present circumstances it is not intended to divulge the technical processes of production or all the military applications, pending further examination of possible methods of protecting us and the rest of the world from the danger of sudden destruction. I shall recommend that the Congress of the United States consider promptly the establishment of an appropriate commission to control the production and use of atomic power within the United States. I shall give further consideration and make further recommendations to the Congress as to how atomic power can become a powerful and forceful influence towards the maintenance of world peace.

[2] Potsdam proclamation called for immediate unconditional surrender or "complete and utter destruction." [Ed.]

[3] Japan wanted the condition that it could keep the emperor (which the Allies later allowed). [Ed.]

AKIHIRO TAKAHASHI

Memory of Hiroshima, 1945/1986

The author of this selection, Akihiro Takahashi, was fourteen years old on August 6, 1945, when the United States bombed Hiroshima. He was standing in line with other students in the courtyard of the Hiroshima Municipal Junior High School. His and other survivors' recollections of that day and its aftermath were recorded, transcribed, and translated some forty years later by a Japanese peace project called "The Voice of Hibakusha."[1] How do you weigh the experience of Akihiro Takahashi against the reasons given by President Truman for dropping the bomb?

THINKING HISTORICALLY

One of the difficulties in thinking about the unthinkable is remembering the details we want to forget. Trauma victims often repress memories that are too painful to bear. In some cases time revives memories as well as heals. Akihiro Takahashi's recollections display both a prodigious and courageous memory. How might this process of remembering and telling be helpful to him? How might it be helpful to others?

. . . [W]e saw a B-29 approaching and about fly over us. All of us were looking up the sky, pointing out the aircraft. Then the teachers came out from the school building and the class leaders gave the command to fall in. Our faces were all shifted from the direction of the sky to that of the platform. That was the moment when the blast came. And then the tremendous noise came and we were left in the dark. I couldn't see anything at the moment of explosion just like in this picture. We had been blown by the blast. Of course, I couldn't realize this until the darkness disappeared. I was actually blown about 10 m. My friends were all marked down on the ground by the blast just like this. Everything collapsed for as far as I could see. I felt the city of Hiroshima had disappeared all of a sudden. Then I looked at myself and found my clothes had turned into rags due to the heat. I was probably burned at the back of the head, on my back, on both arms and both legs. My skin was peeling and hanging like this. Automatically I began to walk heading west

---

[1] Japanese term for the victims of Hiroshima and Nagasaki: literally, the "explosion-affected people."

Source: "The Voice of Hibakusha," Testimony of Akihiro Takahashi in Atomic Archive, http://www.atomicarchive.com/Docs/Hibakusha/Akihiro.shtml.

because that was the direction of my home. After a while, I noticed somebody calling my name. I looked around and found a friend of mine who lived in my town and was studying at the same school. His name was Yamamoto. He was badly burnt just like myself. We walked toward the river. And on the way we saw many victims. I saw a man whose skin was completely peeled off the upper half of his body and a woman whose eye balls were sticking out. Her whole body was bleeding. A mother and her baby were lying with a skin completely peeled off. We desperately made away crawling. And finally we reached the river bank. At the same moment, a fire broke out. We made a narrow escape from the fire. If we had been slower by even one second, we would have been killed by the fire. Fire was blowing into the sky, becoming 4 or even 5 m high. There was a small wooden bridge left, which had not been destroyed by the blast. I went over to the other side of the river using that bridge. But Yamamoto was not with me any more. He was lost somewhere. I remember I crossed the river by myself and on the other side, I purged myself into the water three times. The heat was tremendous. And I felt like my body was burning all over. For my burning body the cold water of the river was as precious as a treasure. Then I left the river, and I walked along the railroad tracks in the direction of my home. On the way, I ran into another friend of mine, Tokujiro Hatta. I wondered why the soles of his feet were badly burnt. It was unthinkable to get burned there. But it was an undeniable fact that the soles were peeling and red muscle was exposed. Even though I myself was terribly burnt, I could not go home ignoring him. I made him crawl using his arms and knees. Next, I made him stand on his heels and I supported him. We walked heading toward my home repeating the two methods. When we were resting because we were so exhausted, I found my grandfather's brother and his wife, in other words, great uncle and great aunt, coming toward us. That was quite a coincidence. As you know, we have a proverb about meeting Buddha in Hell. My encounter with my relatives at that time was just like that. They seemed to be the Buddha to me wandering in the living hell.

Afterwards I was under medical treatment for one year and half and I miraculously recovered. Out of sixty junior high school classmates, only ten of us are alive today. Yamamoto and Hatta soon died from the acute radiation disease. The radiation corroded their bodies and killed them. I myself am still alive on this earth suffering after-effects of the bomb. I have to see regularly an ear doctor, an eye doctor, a dermatologist and a surgeon. I feel uneasy about my health every day. Further, on both of my hands, I have keloids.[2] My injury was most serious on my right hand and I used to have terrible keloids right here. I had them removed by surgery in 1954, which enabled me to move my wrist a little

---

[2] Scars. [Ed.]

bit like this. For my four fingers are fixed just like this, and my elbow is fixed at one hundred twenty degrees and doesn't move. The muscle and bones are attached [to] each other. Also the fourth finger of my right hand doesn't have a normal nail. It has a black nail. A piece of glass which was blown by the blast stuck here and destroyed the cells of the base of the finger. That is why a black nail continues to grow and from now on, too, it will continue to be black and never become normal. Anyway I'm alive today together with nine of my classmates for this forty years. I've been living believing that we can never waste the deaths of the victims. I've been living on, dragging my body full of sickness, and from time to time I question myself; I wonder if it is worth living in such hardship and pain and I become desperate. But it's time I manage to pull myself together and I tell myself once my life was saved, I should fulfill my mission as a survivor; in other words, it has been and it is my belief that those who survived must continue to talk about our experiences. To hand down the awful memories to future generations representing the silent voices of those who had to die in misery. Throughout my life, I would like to fulfill this mission by talking about my experience both here in Japan and overseas.

■ REFLECTIONS

Short of war, the world community has adopted three strategies to counter genocide and the mass killing of civilians. The first is the trial of war criminals. At the conclusion of World War II, the victorious Allies conducted war-crime trials of leading Nazi and Japanese officials. Twelve high Nazi officials and seven Japanese leaders, including Iwane Matsui for the "Rape of Nanking," were sentenced to death. Many others served prison sentences. Critics argued that some of the alleged crimes ("wars of aggression" and "crimes against peace") were vague and that the victorious Allies might be guilty of these as well. Other charges—specifically "war crimes" and "crimes against humanity"— were devised as a response to the trials, an ex post facto (after the fact) violation of standard procedure where prosecution must be based on criminal statutes.

The problem was that the technology and practice of warfare had largely outrun international agreements. The first Geneva Conventions, dating from 1864, were mainly concerned with the treatment of the wounded and prisoners. Therefore, the second strategy was developing and refining international laws regarding human rights and the protection of civilians. In 1948, the "Universal Declaration of Human Rights" passed by the United Nations, itself a shaper and guardian of international law, offered a recognized standard and continuing process for defining and preventing genocide, mass murder, and "crimes against humanity." A fourth Geneva Convention in 1949 added the destruction of civilian populations in time of war to the list of war crimes for which a country would be held responsible. In addition, the precedent of the "International Military Tribunal" that tried Nazi and Japanese officials led to the creation of international laws and courts for the prosecution of war crimes and mass murder. The legacy continues. In 2002, the United Nations' International Court of Criminal Justice in the Hague, Netherlands, brought President Milošević of Yugoslavia to trial for the "ethnic cleansing" of Muslims in Kosovo and Bosnia, and (at this writing) the court continues with the prosecution of others. An International Tribunal for Genocide in Rwanda is similarly trying Hutu Rwandans charged with the mass murder of Tutsi fellow citizens in 1994.

A third strategy has emerged in recent years, largely where human rights abuses or civilian casualties have occurred within a national population. Often without the benefit of international courts or agencies, governments seeking to put past grievances aside, rather than prosecute offenders, have created "truth and reconciliation" commissions. In 1995, after decades of racist violence, the new South African government under Nelson Mandela established such a commission. Former white officials were guaranteed immunity from prosecution in return for complete and remorseful testimony of their crimes. Similarly, in El Salvador after a decade of violence in the 1980s, a new government established a Truth Commission in 1992 with United Nations assistance.

Finding the truth is the beginning of any strategy toward renewal. To promote understanding, archives must be opened, press and Internet censorship must be challenged, and laws such as the Freedom of Information Act must be used aggressively. But in addition, we must develop sensitivity to the plight of victims, knowledge of the victimizers' motives, and understanding about the ways that the horrendous can happen.

26

The Cold War and the Third World

Vietnam, Cuba, Argentina, and Afghanistan, 1945–1989

■ HISTORICAL CONTEXT

The United States and the Union of Soviet Socialist Republics (USSR or Soviet Union) were allies during World War II. Meetings between the heads of state could be strained, but the Allies cooperated in the war and reached many agreements on the peace that followed, including the division of Europe and the creation of the United Nations and other international organizations. The Cold War developed within these agreements about postwar Europe and in the debates of the new international organizations, but it also festered from prewar ideological differences and antagonisms. U.S. troops were sent to fight "communist" Latin American regimes throughout the first half of the century; the Soviets never forgot Western efforts to reverse the Russian Revolution of 1917, and they never imagined that capitalism would outlast socialism.

World War II ended with the devastation of Germany and Japan and the exhaustion of England and France. One of the casualties turned out to be the colonial system that had fed and served the imperial powers. Some German colonies in Africa and Japanese colonies in Asia were turned over to the Allies after the war, but the postwar decades eventually brought an end to English and French colonies as well: British India as early as 1947, French Vietnam (Indochina) in 1954, and most of Africa by the early 1960s.

Although the Soviet Union had suffered enormous losses, it emerged with the United States as one of the two great "superpowers" of the postwar world. Both countries hoped to build a new world in which they would play a dominant role. Both professed opposition to imperialism, by which the Soviets meant the capitalist commercial and military expansion that they believed caused two world wars and by which the Americans meant the expansion of Soviet military power in Eastern Europe and communist governments in China and beyond. Both the United States and the Soviet Union championed the emergence of new independent nations from the ashes of colonialism, but neither wanted these new states to ally with the other power. In response, leaders of some of these new states declared themselves "noncommitted" to communism or capitalism—they were members of a "Third World" caught between the first two. Many Third World leaders were nationalists who sought help where they could find it, and some found the road to independence blockaded at either end. The Cold War had much to do with the effort by the United States and the Soviet Union to woo these new nations to capitalism or communism and into American or Soviet spheres of influence.

■ THINKING HISTORICALLY

Detecting Ideological Language

The great enemy of clear language is insincerity. When there is a gap between one's real and one's declared aims, one turns as it were instinctively to long words and exhausted idioms, like a cuttlefish spurting out ink. In our age there is no such thing as "keeping out of politics." All issues are political issues, and politics itself is a mass of lies, evasions, folly, hatred, and schizophrenia.

—George Orwell, "Politics and the English Language"

In his 1946 essay, George Orwell flagged the Big Lies of Hitler, Stalin, and fascist dictatorships, but he also ruminated on the ways that political language served the interest of the ruling political belief system (for "ideology") rather than the truth. The result of language that deluded the speaker as well as the audience was poor, often self-defeating policy.

Since Orwell confronted the political distortions of language in the period of the developing Cold War, a term he coined, we will use our study of the Cold War as an opportunity to examine the use of ideological language. It was an era of new mass media like television; government efforts to control public opinion through pollsters, advertisers, and public relations; and a competitive struggle between superpowers to win the "hearts and minds" of the world. Thus, many of the efforts of political writers were devoted to propaganda. But propagandists were not the only ones to choose their words for political purposes. Political practitioners did so as well, and often without realizing that the words they chose trapped them in dogma, fantasy, or fog.

1

HEONIK KWON

Origins of the Cold War, 2010

Heonik Kwon is a modern specialist on Korean and Cold War history. He is one of a growing number of Cold War scholars who are examining the many "hot wars" that were caused by the "cold" conflict between the United States and the Soviet Union. In this selection he mentions the Korean War, but he is mainly concerned with examining the causes of the Cold War. How, according to Kwon, does the establishment of a beginning date and cause of the Cold War become a moral issue? What alternate starting dates for the Cold War does Kwon discuss? Which of these do you find most convincing? How do the ideas of George Kennan and J. Edgar Hoover help us understand the causes of the Cold War?

THINKING HISTORICALLY

One goal of propaganda is to convert rational analysis into powerful emotions, frequently fear. How do the writings included here of Kennan, Hoover, and Eisenhower do this? The line between propaganda and self-delusion can be very thin. Do you think these important people believed what they said? How did the Cold War psychology become so pervasive?

The story of the cold war, like that of any other war in human history, begins somewhere and ends somewhere. There is no consensus about the question of beginning. The origin of the cold war is an unsettled issue that continues to engender instructive debate among historians. Reflecting on the diverse ways to think about the origin of the cold war means rethinking the political history of the twentieth century and therefore considering the changing conditions of the contemporary

Source: Heonik Kwon, *The Other Cold War* (New York: Columbia University Press, 2010), 1–3, 70–73.

world in new historical perspectives. However, this openness to historical reasoning and imagining does not extend to the other end of the story. There is a strong consensus in contemporary literature that the end of the cold war is a fait accompli, a universal historical reality. The question of the end has no room for diversity and generates no such positive interpretive controversies like those about the origin. The story of the cold war we tell ourselves today, therefore, has an open-ended beginning and a closed ending.

The term *cold war* refers to the prevailing condition of the world in the second half of the twentieth century, divided into two separate paths of political modernity and economic development. In a narrower sense, it means the contest of power and will between the two dominant states, the United States and the Soviet Union, that (according to George Orwell, who coined the term in 1945) set out to rule the world between them under an undeclared state of war, being unable to conquer one another. In a wide definition, however, the global cold war also entails the unequal relations of power among the political communities that pursued or were driven to pursue a specific path of progress within the binary structure of the global order. The "contest-of-power" dimension of the cold war has been an explicit and central element in cold war historiography; in contrast, the "relation-of-domination" aspect has been a relatively marginal, implicit element. The debates about the origins of the cold war contribute to disclosing how complex the great bifurcation in the project of modernity has been for both nations and communities. The origin of the cold war is not merely a question of time but also, in significant measure, a moral question: Which side of the bipolarized human community was more responsible for bringing about the global order and engendering political and military crises? The moral question is intertwined with the chronological one, and their connectedness is more apparent in places where the bipolar conflict was waged in a violent form.

Imagining the political future of Korea, for example, is inseparable from locating the origin of the Korean War. For people who date the origin of the war to 1950, the culpability for the devastating civil war rests unquestionably with the northern Communist regime, which launched, with endorsement and support from Mao Zedong and Joseph Stalin, an all-out surprise offensive against the southern territory in June of that year. For those who trace the war's origin to earlier years, the blame is apportioned equally to the belligerent, strongly anti-Communist southern regime, which instigated a series of border skirmishes and crushed domestic radical nationalist forces in a ruthless manner from 1947 to 1950. The latter measure provoked the outbreak of armed partisan activities in parts of the southern territory, which were effectively in a state of war from 1948 on. For those who associate the origin of the Korean

War with the end of the Pacific War in 1945, however, the main responsibility for the civil war lies instead with the United States and the Soviet Union, which partitioned and separately occupied the postcolonial nation after the surrender of Japan. (And we should add to these divergent views the official position taken by North Korea, which continues to paint its part in the war as an act of self-defense against the unprovoked aggression from South Korea, orchestrated by the United States, despite a wealth of evidence that points to the contrary.) These diverse perspectives on the origin of one of the first violent manifestations of the bipolar global order are not merely matters of scholarly debate. They are also deeply ingrained in the society that endured what was at once a civil war and an international war, provoking heated public debate and developing conflicting political voices and forces. In this context, the origin of the cold war is largely the origin of the war-induced wounds felt in the society, thereby making the very concept of a "cold" war somewhat contradictory, so that claiming a particular version of the origin is simultaneously an act of asserting a particular vision of the nation's history and future.

In the wider terrain, too, the cold war's temporal identity continues to be revised as to the question of its origin. Conventional knowledge associates the origin of the cold war with the end of World War II and the breakdown of the wartime alliance between the Western powers and the Soviet state. However, several scholars have challenged this conventional view. For example, Melvyn Leffler retraces the origin to the period following the Russian Revolution of 1917, whereas William Appleman Williams famously argues that the seeds of the cold war were sown much earlier, during the nineteenth-century contest for global supremacy between the established European imperial powers and the newly rising American power. Each of these revisions of the cold war's origin is simultaneously an attempt to reinterpret the meaning of the global conflict in modern history. Leffler's scheme foregrounds the importance of ideology (the antagonistic view to communism as a radically alien way of life incompatible with the market-based liberal world) in the construction of the cold war global order, whereas Williams shows how the perception of the alien ideological other mirrored for the United States at the turn of the twentieth century the nation's own ideological self-image defined in terms of so-called Manifest Destiny—the idea that America, as a sole benevolent and progressive power, confronts the backward and confused world infested with imperialist excess and colonial miseries. . . .

Two important documents of the early cold war show how the ideological "other" was imagined both from within and from without. George Kennan, an American diplomat considered the "father of containment policy," wrote in his famous "Long Telegram" sent from the U.S. Embassy in Moscow to the U.S. State Department in February 1946:

> At bottom of [the] Kremlin's neurotic view of world affairs is the traditional and instinctive Russian sense of insecurity. Originally, this was the insecurity of a peaceful agricultural people trying to live on a vast exposed plain in the neighborhood of fierce nomadic peoples. To this was added, as Russia came into contact with the economically advanced West, fear of more competent, more powerful, more highly organized societies in that area. . . . For this reason they have always feared foreign penetration, feared direct contact between [the] Western world and their own, feared what would happen if Russians learned the truth about the world without or if foreigners learned the truth about the world within. And they have learned to seek security only [in] a patient but deadly struggle for total destruction of rival power, never in compacts and compromises with it.

In September of the same year, J. Edgar Hoover, director of the U.S. Federal Bureau of Investigation, spoke at the San Francisco Conference of the American Legion:

> During the past five years, American Communists have made their deepest inroads upon our national life. In our vaunted tolerance for all peoples the Communist has found our "Achilles' heel." . . . The Communist Party in this country is not working for the general welfare of all our people—it is working against our people. It is not interested in providing for the common defense. It has for its purpose the shackling of America and its conversion to the Godless, Communist way of life. . . . We, of this generation, have faced two great menaces in America—Fascism and Communism. Both are materialistic; both are totalitarian; both are anti-religious; both are degrading and inhuman. In fact, they differ little except in name. Communism has bred Fascism and Fascism spawns Communism. Both are the antithesis of the American belief in liberty and freedom. If the peoples of other countries want Communism, let them have it, but it has no place in America.

Kennan highlighted the "traditional and instinctive Russian sense of insecurity": just as their "neurotic" leaders ruthlessly destroyed all domestic oppositions to their rule, he argued, so would they act in a similar fashion toward their defined enemies abroad. Kennan's "Long Telegram" was mainly about the threats to the West's security in the international sphere, and it was Hoover who epitomized the flip side of the "two-pronged policy of containment"—the commitment to containing communism both at home and abroad. In his book A *Study of Communism*, Hoover explored what he called the biggest mystery of his time: "How anyone who enjoys the rights and privileges of

American citizenship [can] bring himself to join a [Communist] movement which is such an outspoken foe of our entire way of life."

As the views of these influential state officials were circulated and were becoming a consensus in policy circles and public opinion, by the end of 1946 "the basic Cold War psychology" was taking hold of the U.S. administration. The Soviet maneuvers in northern Iran and incursions to the Turkish border in 1946 strengthened the belief in the United States that the Russians were hell bent on expansion and that only a united, preponderant counterforce could stop it. At the same time, Stalin encouraged the idea of encirclement by hostile Western forces to justify his brutal terror campaigns against his own population. The rise of the so-called cold war security culture was to a large measure, according to Mary Kaldor, a reciprocal action between opposing powers and had an "inertial logic" of mutually reinforcing external threats and internal fears. She argues that the construction of the cold war was thus a "joint venture" between the contending political blocs.

Hoover stated that "if the peoples of other countries want Communism, let them have it, but it has no place in America." It is argued in recent studies that American foreign politics in the mid–twentieth century was based on a broad bipartisan compromise between the Republican-dominated militancy against domestic labor and civil rights unrests and the largely Democrat-led initiatives to aggressively counter Communist threats in foreign soils. These studies show that although the U.S. administration perceived the threats of communism to be coming both from within the society and from overseas, the formulation of security threats was initially complicated by bipartisan politics in which contending groups lay emphasis on either the domestic dimension or the foreign dimension of containment. These two dimensions of perceived Communist threats gradually merged into a rhetorical whole; the polemics against the enemy within (such as Hoover's) and the polemics against the external enemies (such as Kennan's) became increasingly indistinguishable. In the beginning of the 1960s, therefore, Hoover advocated radical measures against overseas Communist threats to Asia and Europe, whereas Kennan lamented the lack of spiritual vigilance and moral solidarity against communism within the Western world. Hence, we should add to Kaldor's idea of "joint venture" another dimension — how the vision of the ideological enemy inside and the vision of the enemy outside colluded with each other, thereby augmenting the intensity of anti-Communist politics.

Dwight D. Eisenhower aptly summed up the emerging Manichean worldview in his inaugural speech in 1953: "The forces of good and evil are massed and armed and opposed as rarely before in history. Freedom is pitted against slavery; lightness against the dark." This anti-Communist worldview drew on an epidemiological model of society as a vulnerable organism. Hoover saw communism as "a condition akin to disease that spreads like an epidemic and like an epidemic a quarantine is necessary to keep it from infecting the nation." In 1950, an important report from the U.S. National Security Council known as *NSC-68* described the Soviet Union as aiming to "contaminate" the Western world by means of its preferred technique of infiltrating "labor unions, civic enterprises, schools, churches, and all media for influencing opinion." The document argued that, in parallel with the urgency to stop domestic contagion, there was a need internationally "to quarantine a growing number of [states] infected [by the disease of communism]."

2

The Vietnamese Declaration of Independence, 1945

Although this document may predate the Cold War, it demonstrates the importance of the anticolonial struggle to create new states at the end of World War II. Vietnam had been part of French Indochina from 1887 until World War II, when it was occupied by Japan. This Declaration of Independence represented an effort by Vietnamese nationalists to prevent the French from retaking the country from the defeated Japanese.

The author of the declaration, Ho Chi Minh (1890–1969), is a prime example of the kind of new national leader torn between the appeals of Washington and Moscow. A founder of the French Communist Party in 1921 as well as the Vietnamese Communist Party in 1930, he was also the leader of the Viet Minh, the Vietnamese nationalist movement, even enjoying the secret help of the United States during World War II in the battle against Japan.

What, according to Ho Chi Minh, were the effects of French colonialism in Vietnam? What reasons does he give for Vietnamese independence?

THINKING HISTORICALLY

Since this document was intended as a declaration of Vietnamese nationalism, delivered in Vietnamese to the Vietnamese people, one is struck by the use of ideological language from both the U.S. Declaration of Independence and the French Declaration of the Rights of Man and Citizen. What other signs do you see that Ho Chi Minh may have been interested in attracting the favor of a U.S. or French audience? What purpose would such a strategy serve?

Source: *Ho Chi Minh, Selected Works* (Hanoi, 1960–1962), 3:17–21.

"All men are created equal. They are endowed by their Creator with certain inalienable rights, among these are Life, Liberty, and the pursuit of Happiness."

This immortal statement was made in the *Declaration of Independence* of the United States of America in *1776*. In a broader sense, this means: All the peoples on the Earth are equal from birth, all the peoples have a right to live, to be happy and to be free.

The Declaration of the *French Revolution* made in *1791* on *the Rights of Man and the Citizen* also states: "All men are born free and with equal rights, and must always remain free and have equal rights."

Those are undeniable truths.

Nevertheless, for more than eighty years, the French imperialists, abusing the standard of *Liberty, Equality, and Fraternity*,[1] have violated our Motherland and oppressed our fellow-citizens. They have acted contrary to the ideals of humanity and justice. In the field of politics, they have deprived our people of every democratic liberty.

They have enforced inhuman laws; they have set up three distinct political regimes in the North, the Center and the South of Vietnam in order to wreck our national unity and prevent our people from being united.

They have built more prisons than schools. They have mercilessly slain our patriots—they have drowned our uprisings in rivers of blood. They have fettered public opinion; they have practised obscurantism against our people. To weaken our race they have forced us to use opium and alcohol.

In the fields of economics, they have fleeced us to the backbone, impoverished our people, and devastated our land.

They have robbed us of our rice fields, our mines, our forests, and our raw materials. They have monopolised the issuing of bank-notes and the export trade. They have invented numerous unjustifiable taxes and reduced our people, especially our peasantry, to a state of extreme poverty.

They have hampered the prospering of our national bourgeoisie; they have mercilessly exploited our workers.

In the autumn of 1940, when the Japanese Fascists violated Indochina's territory to establish new bases in their fight against the Allies, the French imperialists went down on their bended knees and handed over our country to them.

Thus, from that date, our people were subjected to the double yoke of the French and the Japanese. Their sufferings and miseries increased. The result was that from the end of last year to the beginning of this year, from Quang Tri province to the North of Vietnam, more than two

---

[1] This was the rallying cry of the French Revolution of 1789. (*Fraternity* means brotherhood.) [Ed.]

million of our fellow-citizens died from starvation. On March 9, the French troops were disarmed by the Japanese. The French colonialists either fled or surrendered, showing that not only were they incapable of "protecting" us, but that, in the span of five years, they had twice sold our country to the Japanese.

On several occasions before March 9, the Vietminh League urged the French to ally themselves with it against the Japanese. Instead of agreeing to this proposal, the French colonialists so intensified their terrorist activities against the Vietminh members that before fleeing they massacred a great number of our political prisoners detained at Yen Bai and Cao Bang.

Notwithstanding all this, our fellow-citizens have always manifested toward the French a tolerant and humane attitude. Even after the Japanese putsch of March 1945, the Vietminh League helped many Frenchmen to cross the frontier, rescued some of them from Japanese jails, and protected French lives and property.

From the autumn of 1940, our country had in fact ceased to be a French colony and had become a Japanese possession.

After the Japanese had surrendered to the Allies, our whole people rose to regain our national sovereignty and to found the Democratic Republic of Vietnam.

The truth is that we have wrested our independence from the Japanese and not from the French.

The French have fled, the Japanese have capitulated, Emperor Bao Dai has abdicated. Our people have broken the chains which for nearly a century have fettered them and have won independence for the Fatherland. Our people at the same time have overthrown the monarchic regime that has reigned supreme for dozens of centuries. In its place has been established the present Democratic Republic.

For these reasons, we, members of the Provisional Government, representing the whole Vietnamese people, declare that from now on we break off all relations of a colonial character with France; we repeal all the international obligation that France has so far subscribed to on behalf of Vietnam and we abolish all the special rights the French have unlawfully acquired in our Fatherland.

The whole Vietnamese people, animated by a common purpose, are determined to fight to the bitter end against any attempt by the French colonialists to reconquer their country.

We are convinced that the Allied nations which at Tehran and San Francisco have acknowledged the principles of self-determination and equality of nations, will not refuse to acknowledge the independence of Vietnam.

A people who have courageously opposed French domination for more than eighty years, a people who have fought side by side with the Allies against the Fascists during these last years, such a people must be free and independent.

For these reasons, we, members of the Provisional Government of the Democratic Republic of Vietnam, solemnly declare to the world that Vietnam has the right to be a free and independent country and in fact it already has been so. The entire Vietnamese people are determined to mobilise all their physical and mental strength, to sacrifice their lives and property in order to safeguard their independence and liberty.

3

EDWARD LANSDALE

Report on CIA Operations in Vietnam, 1954–1955

France did not cede independence to Vietnam in 1945; nor did the United States support the Viet Minh against the French. The newly declared Democratic Republic of Vietnam controlled only the north while French forces controlled the south. Ho Chi Minh and the Viet Minh forces continued their struggle against the French, finally defeating them at the battle of Dien Bien Phu in 1954. An international peace conference at Geneva called for a temporary division of northern and southern Vietnam to be followed in two years by a national election for a unified government. However, in the wake of the Chinese communist victory in China in 1949 and the American fear of its further spread in the Korean War (1950–1953), the United States increasingly saw Ho Chi Minh and the Viet Minh as part of the expansion of communism rather than a national independence movement. In 1954 President Eisenhower voiced belief in a "falling domino" theory in which the loss of Vietnam would lead to communist victories throughout Southeast Asia and beyond. Fearing that Ho Chi Minh would win 80 percent of the vote in a general Vietnamese election, Eisenhower created a separate South Vietnamese government and army in violation of the Geneva Accords, and he sent U.S. advisors and resources to make this division along the 17th parallel permanent. But one of the problems was that many pro-French Catholics lived in the north where the Viet Minh were strongest, and many Viet Minh lived and operated in the south. Thus, the creation of a southern Republic of Vietnam required large-scale population transfers as well as efforts to bolster the resources and legitimacy of an untried southern government and army.

Source: Edward Lansdale, "Report on CIA Operations in Vietnam, 1954–55," in *The Pentagon Papers*, abr. ed., ed. George C. Herring (New York: McGraw-Hill, 1993), 23–36.

In this selection, Edward Lansdale informs his CIA superiors of some of the activities of one of the teams of advisors sent by the United States to accomplish these tasks. Lansdale was a legendary early CIA operative, known for his work in defeating a similar communist and nationalist movement in the Philippines. What did Lansdale's team attempt to do in the north? What was the purpose of the first rumor campaign? How would you judge the tactics and success of the Saigon Military Mission (SMM) team in the north? What did the CIA do in the south? How successful were its efforts?

THINKING HISTORICALLY

What do you make of Lansdale's quotation marks around "cold war"? What does Lansdale's use of the word *team* suggest to you? What does Lansdale mean by "the Geneva Agreements . . . imposed restrictive rules on all official Americans"? Notice how Lansdale uses terms such as *Vietminh* and *Vietnamese*, the "government," and "security forces." How might others use these terms? What do you think of Lansdale's praise of American reporters for giving "the U.S. an objective account of events in Vietnam"? How does Lansdale describe the differences between the Viet Minh and the "Vietnamese national army"? What conclusions does he draw from the differences between those two armies? What different conclusions could one draw?

Foreword

. . . It was often a frustrating and perplexing year, up close. The Geneva Agreements signed on 21 July 1954 imposed restrictive rules upon all official Americans, including the Saigon Military Mission. An active and intelligent enemy made full use of legal rights to screen his activities in establishing his stay-behind organizations south of the 17th Parallel and in obtaining quick security north of that Parallel. The nation's economy and communications system were crippled by eight years of open war. The government, including its Army and other security forces, was in a painful transition from colonial to self rule, making it a year of hot-tempered incidents. Internal problems arose quickly to points where armed conflict was sought as the only solution. The enemy was frequently forgotten in the heavy atmosphere of suspicion, hatred and jealousy.

The Saigon Military Mission received some blows from allies and the enemy in this atmosphere, as we worked to help stabilize the government and to beat the Geneva time-table of Communist takeover in the north. However, we did beat the time-table. The government did become stabilized. The Free Vietnamese are now becoming unified and learning how to cope with the Communist enemy. We are thankful that we had a chance to help in this work in a critical area of the world, to be positive and constructive in a year of doubt. . . .

Highlights of the Year

a. Early Days

. . . Working in close cooperation with George Hellyer, USIS[1] Chief, a new psychological warfare campaign was devised for the Vietnamese Army and for the government in Hanoi. Shortly after, a refresher course in combat psywar was constructed and Vietnamese Army personnel were rushed through it. A similar course was initiated for the Ministry of Information. Rumor campaigns were added to the tactics and tried out in Hanoi. It was almost too late.

The first rumor campaign was to be a carefully planted story of a Chinese Communist regiment in Tonkin taking reprisals against a Vietminh village whose girls the Chinese had raped, recalling Chinese Nationalist troop behavior in 1945 and confirming Vietnamese fears of Chinese occupation under Vietminh rule; the story was to be planted by soldiers of the Vietnamese Armed Psywar Company in Hanoi dressed in civilian clothes. The troops received their instructions silently, dressed in civilian clothes, went on the mission, and failed to return. They had deserted to the Vietminh. . . .

Ngo Dinh Diem[2] arrived on 7 July, and within hours was in despair as the French forces withdrew from the Catholic provinces of Phat Diem and Nam Dinh in Tonkin.[3] . . . The Tonkinese had hopes of American friendship and listened to the advice given them. Governor [name illegible] died, reportedly by poison. Tonkin's government changed as despair grew. On 21 July, the Geneva Agreement was signed. Tonkin was given to the Communists. Anti-Communists turned to SMM[4] for help in establishing a resistance movement and several tentative initial arrangements were made. . . .

---

[1] United States Information Service, the overseas offices of the United States Information Agency (USIA), which was created by President Eisenhower in 1953 to project a positive image of the United States in the world. [Ed.]

[2] Ngo Dinh Diem (1901–1963), a Catholic, became a favorite of the United States while in exile. He returned to Vietnam in 1954 and became first president of South Vietnam as the French withdrew; he was deposed and killed in a coup in 1963. [Ed.]

[3] Area of northern Vietnam. French Indochina consisted of Cambodia, Laos, and three areas now making up Vietnam: Tonkin in the north, Annam in the center, and Cochinchina in what is now southernmost Vietnam. [Ed.]

[4] Saigon Military Mission, the group run by Lansdale. [Ed.]

b. August 1954

An agreement had been reached that the personnel ceiling of U.S. military personnel with MAAG[5] would be frozen at the number present in Vietnam on the date of the cease-fire, under the terms of the Geneva Agreement. In South Vietnam this deadline was to be 11 August. It meant that SMM might have only two members present, unless action were taken. General O'Daniel agreed to the addition of ten SMM men under MAAG cover, plus any others in the Defense pipeline who arrived before the deadline. A call for help went out. Ten officers in Korea, Japan, and Okinawa were selected and rushed to Vietnam.

SMM had one small MAAG house. Negotiations were started for other housing, but the new members of the team arrived before housing was ready and were crammed three and four to a hotel room for the first days. Meetings were held to assess the new members' abilities. None had had political-psychological warfare experience. Most were experienced in paramilitary and clandestine intelligence operations. Plans were made quickly, for time was running out in the north; already the Vietminh had started taking over secret control of Hanoi and other areas of Tonkin still held by French forces.

Major Conein was given responsibility for developing a paramilitary organization in the north, to be in position when the Vietminh took over. . . . [His] . . . team was moved north immediately as part of the MAAG staff working on the refugee problem. The team had headquarters in Hanoi, with a branch in Haiphong. Among cover duties, this team supervised the refugee flow for the Hanoi airlift,[6] organized by the French. One day, as a CAT C-46[7] finished loading, they saw a small child standing on the ground below the loading door. They shouted for the pilot to wait, picked the child up and shoved him onto the aircraft, which they promptly taxied out for its takeoff in the constant air shuffle. A Vietnamese man and woman ran up to the team, asking what they had done with their small boy, whom they'd brought to say goodbye to relatives. The chagrined team explained, finally talked the parents into going south to Free Vietnam, put them in the next aircraft to catch up with their son in Saigon. . . .

c. September 1954

. . . Towards the end of the month, it was learned that the largest printing establishment in the north intended to remain in Hanoi and

---

[5] Military Assistance Advisory Group: military advisors sent to Vietnam by President Truman beginning in 1950 to train a Vietnamese national army for South Vietnam. [Ed.]

[6] To fly Catholics from the northern city of Hanoi to South Vietnam. [Ed.]

[7] A plane; Civil Air Transport was established in Shanghai in 1946 as a Chinese airline and was owned and used by the CIA after 1950. The C-46 was a military transport and cargo plane made by the Curtiss-Wright Company. [Ed.]

do business with the Vietminh. An attempt was made by SMM to destroy the modern presses, but Vietminh security agents already had moved into the plant and frustrated the attempt. This operation was under a Vietnamese patriot whom we shall call Trieu; his case officer was Capt. Arundel. Earlier in the month they had engineered a black psywar strike in Hanoi: leaflets signed by the Vietminh instructing Tonkinese on how to behave for the Vietminh takeover of the Hanoi region in early October, including items about property, money reform, and a three-day holiday of workers upon takeover. The day following the distribution of these leaflets, refugee registration tripled. Two days later Vietminh currency was worth half the value prior to the leaflets. The Vietminh took to the radio to denounce the leaflets; the leaflets were so authentic in appearance that even most of the rank and file Vietminh were sure that the radio denunciations were a French trick. . . .

d. October 1954

Hanoi was evacuated on 9 October. The northern SMM team left with the last French troops, disturbed by what they had seen of the grim efficiency of the Vietminh in their takeover, the contrast between the silent march of the victorious Vietminh troops in their tennis shoes and the clanking armor of the well-equipped French whose Western tactics and equipment had failed against the Communist military-political-economic campaign.

The northern team had spent the last days of Hanoi in contaminating the oil supply of the bus company for a gradual wreckage of the engines in the buses, in taking the first actions for delayed sabotage of the railroad (which required teamwork with a CIA special technical team in Japan who performed their part brilliantly), and in writing detailed notes of potential targets for future paramilitary operations. (U.S. adherence to the Geneva Agreement prevented SMM from carrying out the active sabotage it desired to do against the power plant, water facilities, harbor, and bridge.) The team had a bad moment when contaminating the oil. They had to work quickly at night, in an enclosed storage room. Fumes from the contaminant came close to knocking them out. Dizzy and weak-kneed, they masked their faces with handkerchiefs and completed the job.

Meanwhile, Polish and Russian ships had arrived in the south to transport southern Vietminh to Tonkin under the Geneva Agreement. This offered the opportunity for another black psywar strike. A leaflet was developed by Binh with the help of Capt. Arundel, attributed to the Vietminh Resistance Committee. Among other items, it reassured the Vietminh they would be kept safe below decks from imperialist air and submarine attacks, and requested that warm clothing be brought; the warm clothing item would be coupled with a verbal rumor campaign that Vietminh were being sent into China as railroad laborers. . . .

f. December 1954

. . . Till and Peg Durdin of the N.Y. Times, Hank Lieberman of the N.Y. Times, Homer Bigart of the N.Y. Herald-Tribune, John Mecklin of Life-Time and John Roderick of Associated Press, have been warm friends of SMM and worked hard to penetrate the fabric of French propaganda and give the U.S. an objective account of events in Vietnam. The group met with us at times to analyze objectives and motives of propaganda known to them, meeting at their own request as U.S. citizens. These mature and responsible news correspondents performed a valuable service for their country. . . .

g. January 1955

The Vietminh long ago had adopted the Chinese Communist thought that the people are the water and the army is the fish. Vietminh relations with the mass of the population during the fighting had been exemplary, with a few exceptions; in contrast, the Vietnamese National Army had been like too many Asian armies, adept at cowing a population into feeding them, providing them with girls. SMM had been working on this problem from the beginning. Since the National Army was the only unit of government with a strong organization through the country and with good communications, it was the key to stabilizing the situation quickly on a nation-wide basis. If Army and people could be brought together into a team, the first strong weapon against Communism could be forged. . . .

4

TIME MAGAZINE

Nikita Khrushchev: "We Will Bury You," November 26, 1956

The first years of the Cold War pitted former World War II allies Soviet Premier Joseph Stalin and Presidents Roosevelt, Truman, and Eisenhower against each other. Stalin died in 1953, to be followed by two inconsequential leaders[1] and then longtime Communist Party leader Nikita Khrushchev, premier from 1955 to 1964. Khrushchev initiated the Soviet space and missile program, but he attempted to reduce the size of the army and strengthen the consumer sector of the

---

[1] Georgy Malenkov and Nikolai Bulganin.

Source: "We Will Bury You!" *Time*, November 26, 1956.

economy. In February 1956, Khrushchev startled party members with a speech denouncing Stalin as a brutal dictator. The speech expressed long suppressed grievances, especially in the dependent Soviet satellite states of Poland, East Germany, Romania, and Hungary.

Hungarians opposed to continued Soviet rule saw an opportunity in the new climate and took to the streets in protest in October 1956. On November 1 their leader Imre Nagy declared an independent Hungarian government and asked for UN recognition. On November 4 Soviet troops invaded Hungary, crushing the revolution by November 10. This selection is a *Time* magazine report of a routine event the following week.

On November 17 Khrushchev attended a reception at the Polish Embassy hosted by visiting Polish communist leader Wladyslaw Gomulka, who also invited representatives of Western countries. At the reception, Khrushchev compared Soviet troops in Hungary and Eastern Europe with Western troops in two areas. What are these areas? What do you think of these comparisons? What was Khrushchev's attitude toward the United States and Western capitalist countries? What was his attitude toward colonialism?

THINKING HISTORICALLY

No four words better raised the fear of a Soviet threat for Americans during the Cold War than Khrushchev's "We will bury you." Numerous American political leaders, commentators, and citizens referred to that quote in the following years to underscore Soviet aggressive intentions. With those four words, the reformist premier who de-Stalinized Kremlin policy and later traveled through the United States arguing for nuclear disarmament and peaceful coexistence could be pictured as a dangerous belligerent.

What do you think Khrushchev meant by those four words? Why do you think *Time* magazine chose them to headline the article? How else might you summarize the evening at the Polish Embassy? What would be your headline?

At the final reception for Poland's visiting Gomulka, stubby Nikita Khrushchev planted himself firmly with the Kremlin's whole hierarchy at his back, and faced the diplomats of the West, and the satellites, with an intemperate speech that betrayed as much as it threatened.

"We are Bolsheviks!" he declared pugnaciously. "We stick firmly to the Lenin precept—don't be stubborn if you see you are wrong, but don't give in if you are right." "When are you right?" interjected First Deputy Premier Mikoyan—and the crowd laughed. Nikita plunged on, turning to the Western diplomats. "About the capitalist states, it doesn't depend on you whether or not we exist. If you don't like us, don't accept our invitations, and don't invite us to come to see you. Whether you like it or not, history is on our side. We will bury you!"

Just the day before, ambassadors of twelve NATO nations had walked out on a Khrushchev tirade that lumped Britain, France and Israel as bandits. Now Khrushchev was off again.

The Kremlin men cheered. Gomulka laughed. Red-faced and gesticulating, Nikita rolled on: "The situation is favorable to us. If God existed, we would thank him for this. On Hungary—we had Hungary thrust upon us. We are very sorry that such a situation exists there, but the most important thing is that the counterrevolution must be shattered. They accuse us of interfering in Hungary's internal affairs. They find the most fearful words to accuse us. But when the British, French and Israelis cut the throats of the Egyptians,[2] that is only a police action aimed at restoring order! The Western powers are trying to denigrate Nasser,[3] although Nasser is not a Communist. Politically, he is closer to those who are waging war on him, and he has even put Communists in jail."

"He had to," offered Soviet President Kliment Voroshilov.[4] Khrushchev turned on him and said: "Don't try to help me."

"Nasser is the hero of his nation, and our sympathies are on his side. We sent sharp letters to Britain, France and Israel—well, Israel, that was just for form, because, as you know, Israel carries no weight in the world, and if it plays any role, it was just to start a fight. If Israel hadn't felt the support of Britain, France and others, the Arabs would have been able to box her ears and she would have remained at peace. I think the British and French will be wise enough to withdraw their forces, and then Egypt will emerge stronger than ever."

Turning again to the Westerners, Khrushchev declared: "You say we want war, but you have now got yourselves into a position I would call idiotic" ("Let's say delicate," offered Mikoyan) "but we don't want to profit by it. If you withdraw your troops from Germany, France and Britain—I'm speaking of American troops—we will not stay one day in Poland, Hungary and Rumania." His voice was scornful as he added: "But we, Mister Capitalists, we are beginning to understand your methods."

By this time, the diplomats—who, in turn, have come to understand Mister Khrushchev's methods—had already left the room.

---

[2] On November 5, 1956, combined British and French forces invaded Egypt in retaliation for Egyptian nationalization of the Suez Canal, while Israel occupied the Egyptian Sinai Peninsula. [Ed.]

[3] Gamal Abdel Nasser (1918–1970), nationalist leader and president of Egypt, 1956–1970. Nasser was a socialist, a leader of neutral "nonaligned nations," and sought help from the United States, Soviet Union, and China. [Ed.]

[4] Chairman of the Presidium of the Supreme Soviet, the head of state but a largely symbolic office compared to the premier or the head of the Communist Party, both of which positions Khrushchev held. [Ed.]

5

NEW YORK TIMES

"Khrushchev Tirade Again Irks Envoys,"
November 19, 1956

The day after the Polish reception in Moscow described in document 4, the *New York Times* published the following story. Why did the Western diplomats walk out? Notice how the *Times* account emphasizes the conflict in the Middle East more than that in Eastern Europe. Notice how the Soviets wanted to talk about the Middle East while the Westerners wanted to talk about Hungary. What accounts for these different agendas?

THINKING HISTORICALLY

Notice the different words Khrushchev and the Westerners use to describe the military action in Egypt by the British, French, and Israelis. Why do these verbal differences cause so much trouble? How would you characterize the attitude of the reporter from the *New York Times*? In what ways is this report similar to that of *Time* magazine? How is it different? What is missing from the *New York Times* account? How might you explain this omission?

Special to the New York Times

MOSCOW, Nov. 18—Envoys from nations of the North Atlantic pact and Israel walked out of a reception here for the second time in twenty-four hours, because of a speech by Nikita S. Khrushchev, Soviet Communist leader.

The reason for the walkout was remarks by the party secretary that, among other things, charged the British, French and Israelis with having "cut the throats of the Egyptians" while pretending that their attack on Egypt was a police action aimed at restoring order.

As a sign of respect for the Poles, at whose embassy the reception was being held, the Western and Israeli envoys did not leave the building, but merely moved into another room, where Mr. Khrushchev's voice was inaudible. The Soviet leader was scornful about the origin of the attack on Egypt. In his mention of the contention by the British and French that they had gone into Egypt to restore order, he said:

Source: "Khrushchev Tirade Again Irks Envoys," *New York Times*, November 19, 1956.

"What kind of order is this? It is the order of colonizers, the order of enslavement, domination of the strong over the weak."

Mr. Khrushchev apologized to Wladyslaw Gomulka, Polish Communist leader, for "making such a speech on the territory of a foreign state." The reception marked the conclusion of a new Polish-Soviet Government and party accord.

The Western powers are trying to "defame" President Gamal Abdel Nasser of Egypt, Mr. Khrushchev said, adding:

"Actually Nasser is not a Communist and politically he is closer to those waging war on him."

Nasser Is Chided

"He has even put Communists in jail," he continued, in what is nowadays unusual Soviet criticism of the Egyptian leader.

"He had to," said Marshal Kliment Y. Voroshilov, in an apparent allusion to the Soviet contention that Egypt had been dominated by the anti-Communist Western powers until recently.

"Don't try to help me," Mr. Khrushchev admonished the elderly chief of the Soviet state, and continued:

"But Nasser is fighting for national independence, he is the hero of his nation and our sympathies are on his side."

Mr. Khrushchev reserved his most scathing sallies for Israel, which "carries no weight in the world and if it plays any role it is to start a fight."

The Soviet Union protested to Israel "just for form," he said, at the time it called on Britain and France to halt the war in Egypt.

Without British-French backing, Mr. Khrushchev continued, Israel would have had her "ears boxed" by the Arabs and peace would have been preserved.

Mr. Khrushchev promised that the Soviet Union would seek a Middle East settlement because it realized the situation in Egypt was serious and "the fire must be put out."

Withdrawal Urged

He predicted Britain and France would be "wise enough" to withdraw their troops from the Suez Canal zone and Egypt would emerge stronger than ever. He ignored Moscow's threat to send "volunteers" to help the Egyptians.

Mr. Khrushchev's estimate of the outlook was considerably more conciliatory and optimistic than anything heard here in recent days.

"We must seek a rapprochement," the party leader said. "We must seek a settlement so coexistence can be peaceful and advantageous."

Admitting the seriousness of the crisis he said the Soviet leaders were "realists" and would not seek to exploit it for their own purposes. He said the new Soviet disarmament proposals attested to Moscow's desire for peace.

The Soviet press reported this morning that Egypt had not requested Chinese Communist "volunteers" because of her "belief" that the United Nations resolutions on the withdrawal of troops would be carried out.

Mistakes Conceded

MOSCOW, Nov. 18 (AP) — Mr. Khrushchev told the Western envoys at the Polish Embassy tonight:

"It you don't like us, don't accept our invitations and don't invite us to come to see you."

The Soviet Communist party chief said many mistakes had been made in building socialism in the Soviet Union because of the lack of examples and the lack of personnel.

He continued:

"If we could have the revolution over again, we would carry it out more sensibly and with smaller losses. But history does not repeat itself. The situation is favorable for us. If God existed, we would thank Him for this."

6

WELLES HANGEN

"Pravda Modifies Khrushchev Slur," November 20, 1956

The day after its article about a second walkout at the Polish Embassy because of a speech by Soviet leader Nikita S. Khrushchev (document 5), the *New York Times* published a follow-up article on the Polish reception. The ostensible rationale for another article was to examine and critique the coverage of the event in the official Soviet communist newspaper, *Pravda*. The *Times* often showed how *Pravda* misinformed its readers, especially by omission of important news. But how, according to the *Times*, did *Pravda* change the tone of

Source: Welles Hangen, *"Pravda* Modifies Khrushchev Slur," *New York Times*, November 20, 1956.

Khrushchev's remarks? Why might *Pravda* want to do that? What was the "Khrushchev slur" that *Pravda* modified? What other reason might the *Times* have for the follow-up piece?

THINKING HISTORICALLY

The *Times* publishes daily, *Time* magazine weekly. Reporters often discussed their stories before they were published. Notice the paragraph below that begins: "For example." What does it suggest to you about the evolving story described in documents 4, 5, and 6? What, if anything, did that paragraph add to the charge of distortion by *Pravda*? What value did that paragraph have for the *Times*? If this article is an accurate rendition of Khrushchev's remarks, what did he likely mean? What Soviet ideological belief did Khrushchev's words affirm? What American ideological belief did *Time* magazine affirm?

Special to the New York Times

MOSCOW, Nov. 19—The biting remarks of Nikita S. Khrushchev that caused Western diplomats to leave a Polish reception last night were presented to the Soviet public today as a judicious call for coexistence.

The remarks of the First Secretary of the Soviet Communist Party were published in expurgated form by Pravda, Communist party newspaper.

Correspondents who heard Mr. Khrushchev make scathing comments about the West last night had difficulty recognizing the Pravda version.

For example, in commenting on coexistence last night Mr. Khrushchev said communism did not have to resort to war to defeat capitalism. "Whether you like it or not, history is on our side," he said. "We will bury you."

Missing from the Pravda account was any biting sallies on the part of Mr. Khrushchev. Attacks on Western "imperialism" made by the party leader last night were omitted. So were criticisms by Anastas I. Mikoyan, a First Deputy Premier; Marshal Kliment Y. Voroshilov, Soviet chief of state, and other Soviet leaders.

On the political level the party chief's charge that British, French and Israelis were out to "cut the throats of the Egyptians" was turned into a simple accusation of "aggression" in the Pravda account.

The "sharp letters" that Mr. Khrushchev said Moscow had sent to Britain, France and Israel became just "fairly candid" in Pravda's version.

Mr. Khrushchev's ridicule of Israel as a Western puppet whose only role was to start a fight was omitted entirely. His hope that the Arabs could have "boxed her ears" was absent.

Similarly, the party chief's remark that Gamal Abdel Nasser, President of Egypt, had imprisoned Communists and was closer to the West politically than to the Soviet Union was expunged.

The West, Pravda said, finds itself in a "very, very embarrassing situation"—this instead of the "idiotic predicament" Mr. Khrushchev described last night.

The comments published in Pravda contained nothing unusually offensive—at least by Mr. Khrushchev's standards—and might be used by Soviet propagandists in denouncing the envoys' departure. The new version also spares President Nasser's feelings and Arab sympathies for the Soviet Union at a time when Moscow wishes to pose as the Arabs' best friend.

Even when Mr. Khrushchev spoke about relations among the Communists, all of whom are presumably accustomed to blunt talk, Pravda's editors found it necessary to recast his comments. For example, Mr. Khrushchev's apparently inadvertent reference to the "Yugoslavian" brand of communism was deleted to conform with sharp criticism of Marshal Tito, Yugoslav President, appearing on another page of Pravda.

7

Soviet Telegram on Cuba,
September 7, 1962

On January 1, 1959, Cuban revolutionaries under Fidel Castro overthrew the government of U.S.-backed dictator Fulgencio Batista. The Castro government increasingly faced opposition from the United States and relied on the support of the Soviet Union. U.S. efforts to depose Castro included a failed CIA-sponsored invasion by Cuban exiles at the Cuban Bay of Pigs, April 17–19, 1961, three months after John F. Kennedy came into office. Expecting further U.S. attempts at toppling the regime, the Castro government received from the Soviet Union midrange nuclear missiles. President Kennedy learned of their existence on October 14, 1962. He demanded they be withdrawn and ordered a naval blockade of

Source: Telegram of Soviet Ambassador to Cuba A. I. Alekseev to the USSR Ministry of Foreign Affairs (MFA), 7 September 1962 at Woodrow Wilson International Center for Scholars, Cold War International History Project, Virtual Archive: http://www.wilsoncenter. org/index.cfm?topic_id=1409&fuseaction=va2.document&identifier=5034DA8F-96B6-175C-97D258B27DC3A0E6&sort=Collection&item=Cuban%20Missile%20Crisis. [Source: Archive of Foreign Policy of the Russian Federation (AVP RF), Moscow, copy courtesy of National Security Archive (NSA), Washington, DC; translation by Mark H. Doctoroff.]

Cuban ports. The confrontation, known as the Cuban Missile Crisis, October 18–29, came dangerously close to erupting into a nuclear war. The crisis ended with Khrushchev withdrawing the missiles and the United States pledging not to invade Cuba and to withdraw American missiles from Turkey.

This document reveals Cuban and Soviet attitudes shortly after the Cuban receipt of the missiles but a month before the crisis. The document is a telegram, dated September 7, 1962, from the Soviet ambassador in Cuba to the Soviet Foreign Ministry in Moscow. In it he informs Moscow about recent events on the island. What seems to be happening? What conclusions does the Soviet ambassador draw? What does the ambassador want the Soviet government to do? How well informed does the ambassador seem to be about events in Cuba, the United States, and Latin America? Do you think President Kennedy would have been less alarmed if he had read this telegram?

THINKING HISTORICALLY

How are the words that the Soviet ambassador uses to describe the situation in Cuba different from the way Americans would understand it? How significant were the Soviet missiles for the ambassador? Why are the charges of aggressive activity by the United States against Cuba more believable in this document than they would be in a magazine article or a public speech?

Recently, the ruling circles of the USA have noticeably activated a policy of provocation against Cuba;[1] military preparations and its political isolation. Nearly every day, the air space and territorial waters of Cuba are violated by American airplanes, submarines and ships trying to establish permanent control over the territory of Cuba and diverting passenger and transport ships bound for Cuba. The landing of counter-revolutionary bands of spies and arms has been increased.

The constant acts of provocation are carried out from the territory of the USA base at Guantanamo, most often in the form of shooting at Cuban patrols. Especially noteworthy among all these provocations are far reaching acts like the August 24 shelling of the hotel in which mainly live Soviet specialists, and also the lies published by the Kennedy Administration about the alleged August 30 attack, in international

[1] In November 1961, President Kennedy initiated Operation Mongoose, a secret plan to stimulate a rebellion in Cuba, bring Cuban exiles into the U.S. army for training, undermine the regime, and assassinate Castro. General Edward Lansdale was put in charge of operations. The program was stepped up in the spring of 1962. The CIA also continued to support internal resistance to Castro and engaged the assistance of organized crime figures who had interests in Cuba to assassinate Castro. [Ed.]

waters, on an American airplane from two small Cuban ships. In the USA government's announcement, it is noted that in the event of a repeat of "an incident of this type," the armed forces of the United States "will take all necessary retaliatory measures." It is entirely evident that this carries a great danger for Cuba, since it gives the most reactionary anti-Cuban authorities in the USA an opening at any moment to organize a provocation and unleash aggressive actions against Cuba.

In regard to the above two last actions undertaken by the USA, the government of Cuba came forward with corresponding official declarations signed by Fidel Castro. Both of these declarations were circulated as official documents to the UN. The goal of these declarations is to attract the attention of the appropriate international organizations and all of world public opinion to the provocative and far-reaching acts of the USA, to unmask the aggressive schemes of the United States in relation to Cuba, and to ward them off. In these declarations the government of Cuba precisely makes the point that the anti-Cuban actions and schemes of the USA present a threat not only to Cuba, but to the whole world.

The series of provocations is now accompanied by a whipped up, broad anti-Cuba campaign in the USA press, striving with all its might to convince the population of the United States of the alleged presence in Cuba of large contingents of Soviet troops and of the fact that Cuba has turned into a military base of "world Communism" which presents a grave threat to the USA and all Latin American countries. Under this pretext, the press, certain American senators and other public figures demand of the Kennedy administration the revival of the Monroe Doctrine,[2] establishment of a sea and air blockade of Cuba, the bringing into force of the Treaty of Rio de Janeiro,[3] and the military occupation of Cuba.

Following the signing in Moscow of the Soviet-Cuban communiqué in which the agreement of the Soviet government to provide assistance in strengthening its armed forces is noted, Kennedy in a public statement on September 4 pointed to the defensive nature of Cuba's military preparations and noted that Soviet military specialists are in Cuba to teach the Cubans how to use defensive equipment presented by the Soviet Union. Several USA press agencies, commenting on that part of Kennedy's statement, underline the evidence of the fact that the president of the USA obviously preferred an attempt to calm down those circles in the USA which are supporting quick, decisive actions against Cuba. Along with this, in Kennedy's statement there are contained insinuations of purported aggressive Cuban schemes regarding influence on the American continent and a threat to use "all necessary means" to "defend" the continent.

[2] The Monroe Doctrine (1823) warned European nations that any efforts by them to interfere in affairs of the Americas would be viewed as aggression requiring U.S. intervention. [Ed.]

[3] The Inter-American Treaty of Reciprocal Assistance (1947) held that any attack on one nation of the Americas would be viewed as an attack on them all. [Ed.]

According to certain information, the USA State Department through its ambassadors notified the governments of Latin American countries that they can expect changes in the situation in the Caribbean basin "if Castro's government does not come to its senses." More probably, in the near future the USA, using the pretext of an allegedly growing threat to the Western hemisphere, will embark on a long process of increasing the pressure on governments of the Latin-American countries and will probably convene a meeting of foreign ministers of the member-countries of the OAS[4] to work out supplementary sanctions against Cuba. One can also assume that the most wildly aggressive powers in the USA (the Pentagon, the Cuban external counter-revolution,[5] and others) will continue to exert pressure on Kennedy in order to realize the most decisive actions against Cuba.

The campaign of anti-Cuban hysteria has been conveyed via American propaganda to Latin American countries too. There the publication of articles and transmissions of radio programs of anti-Cuban and anti-Soviet content is constantly encouraged, while the external Cuban counter-revolution and local reaction put constant pressure on the governments of those countries, conduct loud demonstrations and terrorize individuals and organizations which speak out in defense of the Cuban revolution, and by means of bribery and blackmail get a range of people who have visited Cuba to make anti-Cuban statements, and so forth.

Simultaneously, the USA continues actively to conduct purely military preparations,[6] aimed at repressing possible centers of the national-liberation movement in Latin America, and, given the appropriate circumstances, the Cuban revolution itself. This is shown by such facts as the organization by the United States of schools for instruction in methods of street-fighting and anti-partisan struggle in many Latin American countries (in Panama, Peru, Colombia, Equador, Bolivia, and others); continuing intensive instruction of Cuban counter-revolutionaries in camps located on the territory of the USA, in Puerto Rico and in several Central American countries; many inspection trips to these bases, schools, and camps by responsible American military officials and the heads of the Cuban counter-revolution, including Miro Cardona;[7]

---

[4] Organization of American States. A State Department memo dated May 17, 1962, lists Operation Mongoose "Task 1" as "obtain some special and significant action within the OAS organization against the Castro-Communist regime." For this and following U.S. security memos, see http://www.globalsecurity.org/intell/library/reports. [Ed.]

[5] "External counter-revolution" refers to Cuban exiles in the United States and elsewhere, including veterans of the Bay of Pigs, who were still organized to topple Castro. [Ed.]

[6] Whether President Kennedy was willing to mount another military operation is uncertain, but active preparations were made to train exiles, prepare a blockade, and consider all options, including military. [Ed.]

[7] Jose Miro Cardona (1902–1974): briefly prime minister of Cuba in 1959; went into exile and led anti-Castro Cubans in the United States. Was to be president if Bay of Pigs invasion succeeded. [Ed.]

unflagging efforts of the USA aimed at strengthening the unity of the external Cuban counter-revolution and unity in the action of counter-revolutionary organizations active in Cuba itself, etc.

At the same time, the USA is actively continuing to conduct its efforts towards the political isolation of Cuba, particularly in Latin America. The USA is concentrating on putting pressure on the governments of Mexico and Brazil,[8] which continue to express their support for the principle of non-interference and self-determination of peoples. This pressure is applied through economic means, and also by exploiting the domestic reaction. The realization of Kennedy's visit to Mexico, following which he was to have quickly visited Brazil too (this visit was put off to the last months of the year), served the goals of determining the likelihood of attracting these two countries to the anti-Cuban plans of the USA.

Until now none of the attempts of the USA to attract Brazil and Mexico to its anti-Cuban adventures has had any success.

Under pressure from the USA, in a majority of Latin American countries the local authorities are applying the harshest measures aimed at forbidding or tightly limiting visits of any groups or individuals to Cuba, and also their contacts with Cuban delegations in third countries. People who visit Cuba or make contact with Cuban delegations in third countries are subject to arrest, repression, investigations upon return to their homeland. The USA does not lack means for organizing broad and loud provocations against Cuban delegations taking part in international quorums, as took place recently in Finland[9] and Jamaica.

Referring to the decision taken at the meeting at Punta-del-Este about the exclusion of Cuba from the OAS, the USA is undertaking all measures to deny Cuba participation in any organizations connected with the inter-American system. In particular, they recently undertook an attempt to secure the exclusion of Cuba from the Pan American Health Organization (PAHO). The unlawful denial of Cuba's application to join the so-called Latin American Free Trade Association is another example.[10] In response to the American policy towards Cuba of provocation, military threats, and political isolation, the Cuban government is intensifying its efforts on strengthening its own armed forces, struggling with the internal counter-revolution, unmasking before world public opinion the aggressive designs of the USA, and broadening its anti-American propaganda in

[8] Mexico and Brazil were thought particularly important propaganda targets by the United States. [Ed.]

[9] U.S. State Department memo, June 27, 1962: "it is important to work with the forthcoming youth festival in Helsinki (where there will be 2,000 Latin American students) to take the festival away from the Communists and ensure a good amount of anti-Communist propaganda emanating from this support." [Ed.]

[10] Memo from Lansdale on Operation Mongoose, July 5, 1962: "State reports that diplomatic efforts are being made to block Cuba's application for accreditation to the European Economic Community. Similarly, efforts are being made to exclude Cuba from the proposed Latin American Free Trade area." [Ed.]

Latin America. At the end of August, taking into account the activization of provocative actions by the USA and the possible increase in the unleashing of counter-revolutionary bands and manifestations of domestic counter-revolution, preventive arrests were carried out in the country and strengthened control was established over many registered [known] counter-revolutionary elements and the places where they gather.

The Cuban leaders are paying serious attention to the question of strengthening the devotion to the revolution of the cadres of its diplomatic missions, particularly in Latin American countries; they are taking every opportunity, as was the case with their presentation at the Latin American Free Trade Association, to widen the sphere of their activity in Latin America; they are strengthening their connections with the Latin American peoples by inviting to Cuba society delegations and individual Latin American officials; in timely fashion and aggressively, they speak at international organizations, unmasking the aggressive schemes and actions of the USA; they are striving to take part in any international forums at which there is a possibility to expose the aggressive character of American imperialism; they are strengthening Cuba's ties with African and Asian countries, etc.

The Cuban leadership believes, however, that the main guarantee of the development of the Cuban Revolution under conditions of possible direct American aggression is the readiness of the Soviet government to provide military assistance to Cuba and simultaneously to warn the USA of that fact. From this position, the joint Soviet-Cuban communiqué about [Ernesto "Che"] Guevara's visit to Moscow was greeted by the Cuban leaders and the vast majority of the Cuban people with great enthusiasm and gratitude. The Cuban leadership and Fidel Castro himself suggest that these warnings will help to prevail against those forces in the USA that are warning of the outbreak now of a world conflict, and are staving off a direct American attack on Cuba in the near future.

In our opinion, in the near future the ruling circles of the USA will continue to expand the attacks on Cuba by all the above-mentioned means: provocations, the propaganda campaign, military preparations, and actions of the domestic counter-revolution, political isolation, and so forth. Their success in drawing the Latin American countries into their aggressive actions will most depend on the positions of the governments of Mexico and Brazil.

We also suggest that the question of direct American actions against Cuba will be decided by the correlation of forces in American ruling circles which have differing approaches to questions of war and peace in the present period, and the struggle between them on these issues.

The mood of the overwhelming majority of the Cuban people is defiant, and regardless of the reality of the threat of intervention, no panic or fear before the threat which is hanging over Cuba is observed in the masses of the people. The American provocations make possible an ever-tighter unity of the Cuban workers and raise the political consciousness of the masses.

Regarding the provocations, the influence of the Soviet Union in Cuba has grown as never before, and our cooperation with the Cuban leaders has been strengthened even more.

In the interest of future productive work with our Cuban friends it would be desirable to receive from you for dispatch to the Cuban leaders information which we have about the plans of the USA government toward Cuba.

8

U.S. Government Meeting Transcript and Telegram on Military Coup in Argentina, 1976

On March 24, 1976, a right-wing military coup d'état led by General Jorge Videla overthrew the government of President Isabel Perón of Argentina. Even before the coup, right-wing generals in the Argentine military had secretly joined forces with other extreme anti-leftists in Uruguay, Bolivia, Brazil, Peru, and Chile in "Operation Condor." Named after the national bird of Chile, Operation Condor was run by the Chilean dictator Augusto Pinochet, who in 1973 had led a military coup against the government of Salvatore Allende, the first legally elected socialist president in South America. Condor enabled Pinochet to seek out, abduct, torture, and kill those Chilean socialists and their allies who were able to escape Chile in the aftermath of his coup and bloody repression. Generals and right-wing politicians in other "Southern Cone" countries of South America, especially in Argentina and Uruguay, participated in the alliance in order to get rid of leftists in their own countries. These countries, internally divided by huge economic disparities, had given birth to various socialist, communist, and guerilla movements, including the Tupamaros of Uruguay and the ERP (People's Revolutionary Army) in Argentina. The communist ERP launched a guerilla campaign in 1969 against a previous military dictatorship, continuing their attacks on the military and carrying out bank robberies and kidnappings of the wealthy, including foreign business executives well into the 1970s.

In the "Dirty War" of state terrorism that followed, the police and military targeted not only communists but students, pacifists,

Source: Documents posted at The National Security Archive, The George Washington University. http://www.gwu.edu/~nsarchiv/NSAEBB/NSAEBB185/index.htm

academics, critics, and everyone on the left who they believed supported the web of terrorism. In October 1975 the coup-leader General Jorge Videla promised that "in order to guarantee the security of the state all the necessary people will die," defining "subversives" as "anyone who opposed the Argentine way of life."[1] Estimates of the dead and "disappeared" from 1975 to 1978 vary between 22,000 and 30,000.

Based on these two documents from March 1976, what seems to be the attitude of the United States toward the coup and the military government? What appeared to be the concerns and interests of the United States? Would you call the United States involved or detached? Does it appear that the United States was globalizing the Cold War or that the Argentine right wing was using the United States to accomplish its own objectives?

THINKING HISTORICALLY

The Dirty War of "disappearing" Argentines had already begun before the coup. To some degree, the coup occurred because Isabel Perón was not sufficiently compliant with military requests to ratchet up the violent response to the ERP. At the State Department Staff Meeting, what concerns does the prospect of greater violent repression raise? How thoroughly do Secretary of State Henry Kissinger and the twenty men at the meeting discuss this? How do they decide to deal with that prospect?

In the telegram from U.S. Ambassador to Argentina Robert C. Hill, the subject line reads: "Videla's Moderate Line Prevails." What does Ambassador Hill mean by that, and how do the contents of the telegram support that judgment? What, according to Hill, are the two sides that Videla was moderating? What signs do you see of Hill's support for the military coup? What words, phrases, or passages in the telegram strike you as euphemisms that downplay the military violence? What examples of ideological language can you find in this and the previous document?

Secret Staff Meeting Transcript, Secretary of State Henry Kissinger, Chairman, March 26, 1976

SECRETARY KISSINGER　Bill?

MR. ROGERS　The chief negotiator in Panama has resigned. It looks as though for personal reasons he's going to be succeeded, in all probability, by Guerra, who's a former Foreign Minister.

---

[1] John Simpson and Jana Bennett, *The Disappeared and the Mothers of the Plaza* (New York: St. Martin's, 1985), 75–76.

Secretary Kissinger   I don't think Tack[2] is such a great loss, is he?

Mr. Rogers   No, sir. It wouldn't seem that way—even in Panama.

In Argentina, although the junta[3] has had some pretty good success, we're trying to make whatever estimates we can about what's going to happen. We've asked both the Mission and Washington to do their own visualizations—to compare them. But I think the preliminary estimate has got to be that it's going to go downhill. This junta is testing the basic proposition that Argentina is not governable, so they're going to succeed where everybody else has failed. I think that's a distinctly odds-on choice.

I think we're going to look for a considerable effort to involve the United States—particularly in the financial field. I think we're going to see a good deal—

Secretary Kissinger   Yes, but that's in our interest.

Mr. Rogers   If there's a chance of it succeeding and if they're not asking us to put too much up on the table. What we're going to try to do, when and if they come up with such a plan, is what we were prepared to do about six months ago. We had worked out as intermediaries a sensible program for international assistance, using the private banks and monetary institutions.

Whether we can pull that off again, I don't know; but I think we're going to hear from them very early on in terms of financial programs.

I think also we've got to expect a fair amount of repression, probably a good deal of blood, in Argentina before too long. I think they're going to have to come down very hard not only on the terrorists but on the dissidents of trade unions and their parties.

Secretary Kissinger   But—

Mr. Rogers   The point I'm making is that although they have good press today, the basic line of all the interference was they had to do it because she[4] couldn't run the country. So I think the point is that we ought not at this moment to rush out and embrace this new regime—that three–six months later will be considerably less popular with the press.

Secretary Kissinger   But we shouldn't do the opposite either.

Mr. Rogers   Oh, no; obviously not.

Mr. McCloskey   What do we say about recognition?

---

[2] Panamanian foreign minister Juan Antonio Tack; in 1974 he negotiated an agreement with Secretary of State Henry Kissinger on eight principles to serve as a guide for a new treaty on the Panama Canal to eliminate increasing conflict between Panamanian nationalists and the United States. [Ed.]

[3] Government of military officers who seized power in a coup. [Ed.]

[4] President Isabel Perón of Argentina. [Ed.]

MR. ROGERS Well, we're going to recognize this morning a formal note in response to their request for recognition—as have virtually all the other countries of Latin America. But beyond that, Hill will keep his mouth shut.

SECRETARY KISSINGER Yes, but what does that mean concretely? Whatever chance they have, they will need a little encouragement from us. What is he telling them?

MR. ROGERS What? Oh, nothing. He has not been talking with them yet. He has not been invited to talk with them. He's ready to go in and talk with them when and if they request a meeting. But the Generals who are now presently occupying the Ministerial positions are there very temporarily—probably for the week—until the junta can make its final decisions as to whom they're going to appoint. They will make decisions on who they will appoint within a week. We think we know who's the Foreign Minister—which is the key appointment.

SECRETARY KISSINGER Who?

MR. ROGERS Probably a fellow named Vanek, who we have worked with in the past. And if he is appointed, then I think we're in a position to work with him.

SECRETARY KISSINGER But can I see some instructions on what you're going to tell Hill if somebody should come in—

MR. ROGERS Yes.

SECRETARY KISSINGER —because I do want to encourage them. I don't want to give the sense that they're harassed by the United States.

MR. ROGERS No. What I was basically concerned about in the first instance was the public posture.

SECRETARY KISSINGER I agree with that. . . .

Telegram from U.S Ambassador to Argentina, Robert C. Hill, to Secretary of State Henry Kissinger, March 30, 1976

1. *Summary*: It is too early to make any firm predictions concerning final success of the experiment in govt undertaken by the Armed Forces on Mar 24. Even so, with Videla now named Pres and his new cabinet now named, it is perhaps a convenient moment to report several short-term conclusions: a) Videla is at least for the time being in a strong enough position to keep the hardliners in check and impose a moderate approach; b) *The terrorists are likely to keep a relatively low profile for the next few weeks*, especially in view of the fact that the Armed Forces have launched a massive drive against them; c) The new govt has not yet presented its full economic program, but the approach evidenced so far is encouragingly pragmatic and deliberate, and d) Once the govt begins

to impose an austerity program, labor reaction may stiffen, but so far it has been almost nonexistent; indeed, absenteeism reportedly ceased to be a problem almost the day after the coup. The USG[5] of course should not become overly identified with the Junta, but so long as the new govt can hew to a moderate line the USG should encourage it by examining sympathetically any requests for assistance. *End Summary.*

2. The *coup d'etat* which culminated during the early hours of Mar 24 can now definitely be judged as moderate in character. In their first statements the three members of the Junta indicated they had taken power only to save the country and that their takeover was not directed at any group or sector. They did not attack the memory of Gen Peron, nor did they say anything derogatory about Peronism or any other party. They have arrested some high officials such as Raul Lastiri, Julio Gonzalez and Gov Carlos Menem who are believed to be guilty of malfeasance or abuse of power and they have rounded up a good number of suspected terrorists. But it is now clear that there have been no massive arrests. No one has been put against a wall and no one has been pulled in simply because they happened to be a Peronist or because they served in the last govt. Most congressmen, governors and other deposed officials have simply been told to go home. Mrs. Peron herself is in custody but clearly the Junta does not intend to make a martyr of her. If there is an investigation of her questionable activities, it will probably be a fair one, and if she is convicted, her sentence is likely to be nothing more than exile. Indeed, many in the military would like to put her on a plane to Madrid even without an investigation.

3. Several extreme left-wing parties, mostly Trotskyite and Maoist in orientation, have been banned, but the charters of other parties, including the orthodox Communist Party (PCA), remain in force. Political activity is suspended temporarily and the various parties have had to remove signs and slogans from their headquarters. Their organizations are intact, however, and several of the Embassy's sources within the parties have expressed hope that limited political activity may resume within six months or so.

4. Prior to the coup, there had been fears that hardline commanders in the field might exceed their orders and arbitrarily shoot or arrest any labor leader, Peronist or leftist they did not like. As indicated above, however, this did not happen. Videla and his moderate colleagues kept the hawks[6] in line. Further, the smoothness with which the coup was carried out and the way in which it was accepted by the people did much to enhance Videla's image. Probably at least for the next several months, therefore, his position relative to that of the hardliners will be overpowering. It is most unlikely that any of them would try to move against him. If they did, they would lose. Thus, for now, Videla's moderate policies seem safe.

---

[5] United States Government. [Ed.]
[6] Those favoring more violent repression of labor and leftists. [Ed.]

5. If fending off the hawks was Videla's first concern, coming to grips with the terrorists was his second. Indeed, in order of importance the second outranks the first, but the new govt needed a firm political base in order effectively to confront the terrorists and thus its first thought had to be for institutional unity. With that now assured, at least for the time being, the Armed Forces have launched a nationwide effort against the terrorists. Many suspected terrorists have been rounded up. Widespread searches are being conducted and shifting roadblocks have resulted in the capture of several guerrillas in Cordoba and elsewhere.

6. For their part, the guerrillas are likely to continue some hit-and-run operations such as *today's assassination* of a *Police Commissioner*, but they will probably keep a fairly low profile for the next few weeks. Tactically, they will probably want to get the lay of the land and wait for the military to drop its guard. Strategically, they probably hope popular opinion will begin to swing against the military govt within a few weeks. That would be the time to move. They may have some recalculating to do, however, for so far the military have not behaved in the repressive way the terrorists seem to have expected. If Videla can hold to his moderate course, the guerrillas may be surprised to find several weeks from now that the govt continues to enjoy popular support.

7. Equally as pressing as the terrorist problem is that of the economy. The govt has not yet had a chance to present its plan, but the economic team is now in place and looks impressive. The contacts the Embassy has had so far with Econ Min Martinez de Hoz and some of his assistants indicate they have a firm grasp of the problems and hopefully will have a practical approach to their solution. Detailed analysis of economic program will follow ASAP.

8. As encouraging as the new govt's own performance so far has been public reaction to it. Most Argentines were glad to be rid of Mrs. Peron's pathetically incompetent govt. But they did not rush into the streets to cheer the Armed Forces or jeer the Peronists. They approve of what the Armed Forces have done, but they have some healthy reservations. They have seen military govts start off well before, only to fail further down the road. They hope this one will be different and at this point are willing to give it their support. But no one seems to expect miracles, and that is one of the most mature phenomenon about this coup.

9. Even Labor so far is quiescent. Absenteeism, for example, disappeared as a major problem on Mar 25. Many labor leaders have made their peace with the military and are willing to cooperate. For its part, the Junta has handled Labor intelligently and with prudence. Some of the more corrupt labor leaders have been arrested, but most leaders have been left alone. The CGT[7] is intervened but most unions within it are functioning more or less normally. The crunch, however, has not yet

---

[7] General Confederation of Labor; includes most unions and workers. [Ed.]

come and will not until the govt introduces its econ program and begins to impose austerity measures.

10. *US Position.* This was probably the best executed and most civilized coup in Argentine history. It was unique in other ways too. The US has not been accused of being behind it, except by *Nuestra Palabra*,[8] the organ of the PCA. The Embassy hopes to keep it that way. Clearly, we should not become overly identified with the Junta. That would not be good for them or for us. Nonetheless, Argentina's best interests, and ours, lie in the success of the moderate govt now led by Gen Videla. He has a chance of pulling Argentina together again, stopping terrorism and getting the economy going. His govt, moreover, has promised to solve quickly our various investment problems (Exxon, Chase Manhattan, Standard Electric, etc.) and to bring about a better climate in general for foreign investment. Should Videla's govt fail, that might on the one hand open the door to the hardliners, who would return Argentina to the polarization of the past and who, being more nationalistically inclined than the moderates, would not take as favorable an attitude toward the US and US investments. On the other side, Videla's failure could also bring about conditions under which the extreme left might have an opportunity to make a bid for power, which would clearly run contrary to all our interests.

11. Thus, while we should move discreetly and keep our distance, we should also, so long as the Videla govt sticks to a moderate course, look sympathetically on any requests for assistance it may direct to us.

[8] Argentine Communist Party periodical. [Ed.]

9

Telephone Transcript: Soviet Premier and Afghan Prime Minister, 1979

The Soviet war in Afghanistan (1979–1989), which eventually contributed to the dissolution of the Soviet Union itself, began, like the American war in Vietnam, with seemingly small steps on behalf of a client who lacked widespread support. This document reveals one of the first of those steps. The Soviet client was Nur Mohammed Taraki, a leader of the communist movement in Afghanistan who came to the Afghan presidency as a result of a military coup in April 1978.

Source: Transcript of telephone conversation between Soviet premier Alexei Kosygin and Afghan prime minister Nur Mohammed Taraki, March 18, 1979. Cold War International History Project Bulletin, Issues 8–9, Winter 1996/1997, 145–46. Available at http://wilsoncenter.org/topics/pubs/ACF193.pdf.

His ambitious program of radical social reform alienated tribal and religious leaders. After only a year of an Afghan communist experiment, he was seeking aid from Moscow—an effort captured in this document. It is a transcript of a telephone conversation between the Soviet premier Alexei Kosygin and the Afghan prime minister Nur Mohammed Taraki on March 18, 1979, about six months before the Soviets sent troops into Afghanistan. Alexei Kosygin succeeded Khrushchev as Soviet premier, serving from 1964 to 1980.

It was common in the Cold War period to speak of clients of the big powers, like Taraki, as "puppets," but historians have since recognized that such collaborators had considerable power. What are the different powers that Kosygin and Taraki exert in this conversation? How are their differences expressed and resolved?

THINKING HISTORICALLY

Notice that Kosygin uses different words than Taraki to describe the Afghan people. What are these differences, and how do you explain them? How did Soviet ideology hinder Soviet policy?

KOSYGIN   Ask Comrade Taraki, perhaps he will outline the situation in Afghanistan.

TARAKI   The situation is bad and getting worse.

KOSYGIN   Do you have support among the workers, city dwellers, the petty bourgoisie, and the white collar workers in Herat? Is there still anyone on your side?

TARAKI   There is no active support on the part of the population. It is almost wholly under the influence of Shiite slogans—follow not the heathens, but follow us. The propaganda is underpinned by this.

KOSYGIN   Are there many workers there?

TARAKI   Very few—between 1,000 and 2,000 people in all.

KOSYGIN   What are the prospects?

TARAKI   We are convinced that the enemy will form new units and will develop an offensive.

KOSYGIN   Do you not have the forces to rout them?

TARAKI   I wish it were the case.

KOSYGIN   What, then, are your proposals on this issue?

TARAKI   We ask that you extend practical and technical assistance, involving people and arms.

KOSYGIN   It is a very complex matter.

TARAKI   Iran and Pakistan are working against us, accordingly to the same plan. Hence, if you now launch a decisive attack on Herat, it will be possible to save the revolution.

KOSYGIN   The whole world will immediately get to know this. The rebels have portable radio transmitters and will report it directly.

TARAKI   I ask that you extend assistance.

KOSYGIN   We must hold consultations on this issue. Do you not have connections with Iran's progressives? Can't you tell them that it is currently the United States that is your and their chief enemy? The Iranians are very hostile toward the United States and evidently this can be put to use as propaganda. What foreign policy activities or statements would you like to see coming from us? Do you have any ideas on this question, propaganda-wise?

TARAKI   Propaganda help must be combined with practical assistance. I suggest that you place Afghan markings on your tanks and aircraft and no one will be any the wiser. Your troops could advance from the direction of Kushka and from the direction of Kabul. In our view, no one will be any the wiser. They will think these are Government troops.

KOSYGIN   I do not want to disappoint you, but it will not be possible to conceal this. Two hours later the whole world will know about this. Everyone will begin to shout that the Soviet Union's intervention in Afghanistan has begun. If we quickly airlift tanks, the necessary ammunition and make mortars available to you, will you find specialists who can use these weapons?

TARAKI   I am unable to answer this question. The Soviet advisers can answer that.

KOSYGIN   Hundreds of Afghan officers were trained in the Soviet Union. Where are they all now?

TARAKI   Most of them are Moslem reactionaries. We are unable to rely on them, we have no confidence in them.

KOSYGIN   Can't you recruit a further 50,000 soldiers if we quickly airlift arms to you? How many people can you recruit?

TARAKI   The core can only be formed by older secondary school pupils, students, and a few workers. The working class in Afghanistan is very small, but it is a long affair to train them. But we will take any measures, if necessary.

KOSYGIN   We have decided to quickly deliver military equipment and property to you and to repair helicopters and aircraft. All this is for free. We have also decided to deliver to you 100,000 tons of grain and to raise gas prices from $21 per cubic meter to $37.

TARAKI   That is very good, but let us talk of Herat. Why can't the Soviet Union send Uzbeks, Tajiks, and Turkmens in civilian clothing? No one will recognize them. We want you to send them. They could drive tanks, because we have all these nationalities in Afghanistan. Let them don Afghan costume and wear Afghan badges and no one will recognize them. It is very easy work, in our view. If Iran's and Pakistan's experience is anything to go by, it is clear that it is easy to do this work, they have already shown how it can be done.

KOSYGIN   You are, of course, oversimplifying the issue. It is a complex political and international issue, but, irrespective of this, we will hold consultations again and will get back to you.

TARAKI   Send us infantry fighting vehicles by air.

KOSYGIN   Do you have anyone to drive them?

TARAKI   We will find drivers for between 30 and 35 vehicles.

KOSYGIN   Are they reliable? Won't they flee to the enemy, together with their vehicles? After all, our drivers do not speak the language.

TARAKI   Send vehicles together with drivers who speak our language — Tajiks and Uzbeks.

KOSYGIN   I expected this kind of reply from you. We are comrades and are waging a common struggle and that is why we should not stand on ceremony with each other. Everything must be subordinate to this.

■ REFLECTIONS

The Cold War used to be ancient history. It ended at such breathtaking speed and with such pronounced results that few imagined tomorrow would have anything to do with yesterday. The Soviet Union collapsed in 1991, like the Berlin Wall in 1989, into an irretrievable heap of rubble. Commissars became capitalists, the USSR awoke as Russia, Leningrad turned back into St. Petersburg, and the red flag with hammer and sickle was exchanged for a French-like tricouleur of red, white, and blue stripes. Shoppers replaced placeholders as waiting lines disappeared; shelves of pricey foreign delicacies appeared fully stocked.

Whole countries cracked off along the periphery of what had been a great empire. Baltic city-states breathed their own air and minted their own money. Newly independent Central Asian countries built mosques and elected new dictators. These non-Soviet "stans" sent Russians back to Russia, from which they emigrated by the millions to Toledo and Tel Aviv. Some of those who stayed turned nationalized industries into personal possessions. Others lost their jobs, their savings, their homes, and half their life expectancies. New classes emerged — the "Russian mafia" from the KGB, the plutocrats from the bureaucrats — except they were often the same people in better clothes.

So too the view from America. Reagan's "Evil Empire" of 1983 became a partner in peace. In 1990 Mikhail Gorbachev received the Nobel Prize for ending the Cold War. *Time* magazine — the same magazine that brought America the Cold War — named Gorbachev "Man of the Year." Ex-president Nixon — the same Nixon who had made a career of anticommunism, coming into national prominence in a "kitchen debate" with Khrushchev in 1959—said Gorbachev should have been "Man of the Decade." Times had changed.

But the New World Order of nuclear disarmament, shrunken military budgets, and global cooperation that Gorbachev and Reagan envisioned never quite arrived. A CIA director became president of the United States, shortly followed by his son, and a KGB secret policeman from the old USSR became president of the new Russia. George W. Bush, the son, said he looked into the eyes of Vladimir Putin, the KGB man, and saw his soul. Putin saw a partner. That was in June 2001. In the following years, the United States became more militarized and chose to show it could fight two major wars (in Iraq and Afghanistan) at the same time, while Putin, as president and prime minister, closed down the budding democracy of Russia faster than one could say Ivan the Terrible.

From the vantage point of 2012, the Cold War has certainly not returned. But its history has become more current. Russia and the United States are more often at variance in choosing friends and at odds over global issues than they were in the halcyon 1990s. The United States has lessons to learn from the old Soviet Union's misadventures in Afghanistan. And if Russia is a shadow of its Soviet self, China has become a giant. The give and take of superpowers may not be far ahead. One hopes the lessons will not lag too far behind.

27

New Democracy Movements

The World, 1977 to the Present

■ HISTORICAL CONTEXT

One of the most striking developments in world history has been the recent rise in the number of democracies and the increasing consensus that democracy is desirable and achievable. Before 1945, democracy was limited to a few Western countries, many of which ruled colonial empires like despots. The end of World War II brought an end to those colonial empires. But the newly created independent states of Asia and Africa did not always opt for democracy. India, which became independent in 1947, did create what is still called today "the world's largest democracy," but elsewhere many newly independent regimes established single-party dictatorships to replace colonial rule.

In some ways the Cold War made things worse. The United States and the Soviet Union demanded loyalty above all from their client states. For the Soviet Union that meant the domination of puppet Communist Parties in Eastern Europe. For the United States, the desired loyalty was to vigorous anticommunism at home and abroad. Dictators delivered better than democrats, who were often too sympathetic to popular forces, communists and socialists included. Consequently the Cold War superpowers extinguished budding national democracies and democratic movements. At least for the duration of the conflict, nondemocratic regimes in Eastern Europe, Latin America, and even much of Africa were rewarded with financial and military assistance that enabled them to continue old feuds, social conflicts, or civil wars, as long as they remained loyal to their patron.

As the Cold War came to an end in the late 1980s, the exhausted and indebted former enemies cared less about who governed in Poland, South Africa, or Argentina, thus allowing new democratic movements to rise and rule. After the Soviet Union was replaced by the Russian

Federation in 1991, independent states mushroomed throughout the Baltic region and Eastern Europe. Similarly, in Latin America, military dictatorships were replaced by democratic governments, some of which even called themselves "socialist." Before 1991, it was inconceivable that Russian or American governments would ever have allowed such a change.

In a perverse way, the Cold War had undermined the popular legitimacy of democratic movements. Since both the United States and the Soviet Union claimed to be democratic, while subverting democratic movements abroad, nationalist leaders, especially in Africa, derided democracy as an imperialist ideology. But since 1991, it has become easier to see democracy and human rights as universal goals.

Our chapter spans the Cold War and post–Cold War periods. This allows us to see how democratic movements developed in the context of the Cold War and have thrived since its end. During the last decade of the Cold War, demands for democracy were voiced *against* the clients of the Soviet Union and the United States, as we see in the protests of the "Mothers of the Plaza de Mayo" in Argentina, and *by* the leaders of those superpowers, as we see in Mikhail Gorbachev's policy of *Perestroika*. After the Cold War, countries like East Germany or South Africa were freed by their patrons to pursue their own destinies, as indicated here in the address by Nelson Mandela that is included in the chapter.

In recent years, democracy movements have continued to develop in Eastern Europe and Latin America, but the newest breakthroughs have been in the Middle East. These began in Tunisia in December 2010, when a young street vendor set himself on fire after his goods had been taken and he had been denied a hearing by government authorities. Massive street protests followed, bringing down the ruler of the country, forcing him, his family, and aides into exile. The example of Tunisia sparked popular protests in Egypt against President Mubarak in January 2011, resulting in his resignation by February. As similar movements for popular government broke out in Bahrain, Yemen, and Libya, these and other Arab countries were swept up in what was called an "Arab Spring." This is perhaps most remarkable because the Middle East had been for so long dominated by oil-rich autocratic sheiks, super-privileged royal families, and, as a consequence of the Cold War and the creation of Israel, United States–supplied military regimes: Iran and Iraq at various times and Egypt throughout.

Whether the Arab Spring turns into a truly democratic summer is complicated by continued high unemployment, remaining members of the old ruling class, sectarian conflicts, and global politics, but the hunger for popular representation and responsive government, once tasted, is unlikely to disappear. A powerful model, the Arab Spring has raised democratic aspirations from China to Chile.

■ THINKING HISTORICALLY

Using Connections and Context to Interpret the Past

When historians ask about causes, as they frequently do, they look to connections with past events and the general context in which the event takes place. These are two different ways of understanding the causes of anything. To take an example from our discussion of the Arab Spring, we might ask to what extent the events in Egypt in early 2011 were connected to (that is, a continuation of or influenced by) the events in Tunisia, and to what extent the Egyptian revolution was a product of the Egyptian context (its unique problems, politics, etc.). Obviously both played a role; that is why historians frequently study connections and context together, but it is always valuable to understand which, if either, was more important.

In this chapter we will search the primary source documents for signs of connections to earlier events and for the impact of the local and immediate context of the events under discussion. An explanation of an historical event that ignores either outside influences or the internal context is almost always incomplete. We may or may not be able to conclude which was more important, but we will learn to look in both directions.

1

HEBE DE BONAFINI AND MATILDE SÁNCHEZ

The Madwomen at the Plaza de Mayo, 1977/2002

The history of Latin America is pockmarked by the rule of caudillos, generals, and military juntas. During the Cold War, with the blessings of the United States, anticommunist military dictatorships ruled throughout Central and South America. Since the end of the Cold War, democracies have created a new Latin America. We might date

Source: Hebe de Bonafini and Matilde Sánchez, "The Madwomen at the Plaza de Mayo," trans. Patricia Owen Steiner in *The Argentina Reader: History, Culture, Politics*, eds. Gabriela Nouzeilles and Graciela Montaldo (Durham: Duke University Press, 2002), 430–37.

the origins of these new democracies to the protests against the military juntas of the Cold War. Under some of the most brutal of these terrorist states, dedicated to repress any opposition, some people found the strength to say "no."

In the previous chapter, we looked at the impact of the military coup and Dirty War in Argentina (document 8). Between 1975 and 1978, 22,000–30,000 people were killed by the military. In addition to hundreds of communist revolutionaries who had already declared war on the military, tens of thousands of ordinary citizens were rounded up, interrogated, tortured, and ultimately "disappeared" with a bullet in the back of the head or the drop of a broken body into the Atlantic Ocean from an army helicopter. Infants were taken from their condemned parents and given to their torturers to be raised as their own. Students left one day for school, and never returned. And so it was the mothers of teenagers and the grand-mothers of infants suddenly disappeared who began asking for an accounting. As the women began to gather in the Plaza de Mayo of Buenos Aires, the police mocked them as the "Madwomen" of the Plaza, insinuating that they had been driven mad by misbehaved children who ran away from home. But the constant presence of these women, each Thursday afternoon in the Plaza, allowed the world to see the Mothers for who they were and listen to their stories.

Hebe de Bonafini was one of these "Madwomen," having lost two sons to the repression. Here, with the help of journalist Matilde Sánchez, Hebe de Bonafini tells what happened after she was denied informa-tion about her eldest son Jorge Omar in March 1977. What enabled her and the other Mothers to challenge the junta? Of course, the women were not asking for democracy *per se*; they were demanding the return of their children and at the very least they wanted informa-tion. But how did these demands grow to challenge an antidemo-cratic regime?

THINKING HISTORICALLY

We read nothing here to suggest that Hebe de Bonafini read past democratic theorists or borrowed ideas of democracy from historical sources. In fact, she says nothing about democracy. The eruption of the force of the Mothers sprang from the specific context of Argen-tina: foremost the military dictatorship and the state terrorism against leftists. But as we indicated in the previous chapter, the Argentine coup had connections to military planners throughout the hemisphere. Further, on a personal level, women made connections with each other. How did the forging of these connections among the women contribute to the strength of the protest? And how did connections to outside observers provide a stage and an audience much larger than could be gathered in the Plaza de Mayo?

I was beginning to notice that the faces were repeating themselves in the courts and police stations of La Plata. But I didn't say hello to the other women. And it was obvious that what had happened to me had happened to them because after a time I had exhausted all the possibilities in La Plata and absolutely had to go to Buenos Aires, where I began to run into those same faces in the courts, in the Ministry of the Interior, which was located at the time in the Casa Rosada itself. But we gave each other only shy, sideways glances. For my part, at first there was only a disguised effort to fish for a little information. Since we were all standing in the same lines, there was no need to ask questions. Each of us had to repeat her own story of the crime dozens of times to the changing faces at the little windows.

It was in April, I believe, when I first started to talk with some of the women. Our conversations were limited to the habeas corpus petitions[1] and the best way of writing them and of identifying the judges that weren't granting them. But I didn't give any of the women my name or my telephone number. We were anonymous, distrustful people, united by the paperwork and the lives we were trying to recover. Faces of mothers without children, wives without husbands or brothers. Women looking for other people, we were a precarious company in the aloneness of bureaucracy. . . .

On the train from La Plata to Buenos Aires, one of those faces that I used to see in those days in the offices of the capital was already approaching its dreadful destiny. That afternoon my steps and my itinerary matched those of that gray-haired woman with the dark circles under her eyes whom I had spotted days before on the train when I went to the First Army Corps. We both made the change to the subway at Constitutión and rode together to the Plaza de Mayo, to the offices of Interior Minister Albano Harguindeguy. I greeted her. We didn't meet again for two weeks.

"We could go back on a bus if that seems like a good idea to you," the woman finally said one afternoon when we saw each other again. "It's a little more expensive, but it's a much more comfortable ride."

I agreed. We sat down in the back of the bus. We were silent. Then I began to ask myself why I had accepted her invitation if I intended to remain mute. In reality, I was wondering if she had a child missing. Perhaps her child might be sharing the cell and some meals with my son while we were sharing the bus seat, mute, not knowing how to get to know each other under such circumstances. She was the one who spoke. She didn't give her name. She was looking for her twenty-four-year-old daughter. They had taken her away five months ago. She was pregnant.

---

[1] The women were encouraged to file petitions of "habeas corpus," which would release a prisoner from unlawful detention, but the petitions were routinely denied without explanation. [Ed.]

I was overwhelmed by astonishment: her case seemed unbelievable. How could that woman go on living if her daughter was a prisoner and about to give birth? I refused to believe that things were really so harsh, so crude. I didn't know the woman's name, but I began to feel a tremendous sense of solidarity with her pain. I was beginning to think that my case was not as serious, although it was my own case that was hurting me. Yet as the bus sped along—probably late because it was leaving lines of passengers standing at every stop—I felt a bond of sisterhood with that woman. I felt understood. She went on talking about her daughter, about the paperwork she had done. But although she sounded sad, she seemed a little released from her own suffering, as if she had gotten past the moments of confusion that I was now living through myself. "We are many more than you believe," she finally said, "and we are beginning to work."

"To work?" I asked. I had no idea what that could mean in this case The woman responded that a group of mothers were doing their paperwork together and were arranging for interviews with influential people who could help them. I asked her if my presence would do any good. . . .

The woman smiled; that initial distance between us had evaporated. She said that next Thursday afternoon a group of mothers would be getting together at the Plaza de Mayo. They were going to sign a petition or meet with a priest. It wouldn't be a bad idea to come—"the more mothers, the better." I said that I'd think it over (something in me was still asking if we weren't creating too much of a scandal over nothing, over some confusion that would surely be cleared up sooner or later). The woman stood up and shook hands with me and began to walk down the aisle of the bus.

"Don't forget. Thursday at two, on the dot." . . .

I walked around; it wasn't two o'clock yet. I hadn't seen the woman from the train with the dark circles under her eyes. I was feeling nervous; I wanted to be sure she would be in the Plaza before I arrived. Suddenly I asked myself why I was afraid: what was wrong, when you came right down to it, with my joining those women? The billboards on Bolívar Street proclaimed the official slogan, "The country is advancing," in sky-blue letters on a white background, like the national flag. I followed that street back to the Plaza.

Some women were already there, near the obelisk, on the right, standing together beside a bench. There were no more than ten: the woman from the train hadn't arrived yet, but another woman walked toward me. She had brown hair and strong, attractive features. She was short, with strong arms and workers' hands, and her body made you think of a great fortress. The weather was cool for April, but she was wearing a loose cotton T-shirt. I tried to explain who I was and how I happened to be there: "A lady from La Plata told me on the bus." It was all very vague, but the woman began to smile. "Ah! Yes." she said at last. "She mentioned you. She said you'd be here. Come on over."

They all appeared extremely rushed. They were talking quickly, softly, their voices bumping into one another. They were passing around a piece of paper. "By chance we managed to get hold of a typewriter," the woman whispered to me. "We wrote a letter to President Videla pleading for our children. Now we're signing it, before we deliver it to the secretary. Sign it if you want.". . . .

The women continued passing around the paper and explaining what it was about to the latest women to arrive. Behind us, the city kept on at its rhythm; it didn't seem to realize that we were there. Men were hurrying because the banks were closing; some retired men, completely indifferent, were lying in the sun. We women might well be alumnae of some school, meeting to arrange another reunion. Most of us were about my age or somewhere in their fifties; Azucena moved quickly, like a young woman, but she was a little older. She and I became friends. I agreed with the petition, and I signed. I did it with a large, clear signature so that the president would read my name and it would be engraved on his eyes. Also, so that he would know that my son's name gave me no shame.

We left saying that we would see each other again the following Thursday in the Plaza. At that time, none of us thought that our waiting without children would be longer than a couple of months or that the initial search would someday be transformed into this painful story. . . .

Toward the end of September 1977, we are already more than fifty women, and our feelings grow closer with our growing numbers. Every time there are more of us. Every time we feel stronger and less afraid. Every time we feel safer together. But every time there are more children missing. At the benches on the side of the Plaza we feel defiant, almost invincible for a few minutes. The truth is, they don't know what to do with us. If there is anything left in their hearts, it is the line from all those macho tangos about "my poor old lady." That keeps us safe for the moment. They think that we are crazed by grief, that we'll last until we get tired of standing there with all our varicose veins or until one of us has a heart attack. . . .

They dispatch the police. "This is a demonstration, and the country is under a state of siege. Move on, ladies, move on." We begin to walk together in pairs, arm in arm. Then they make us walk separately.

The Plaza is big, the pairs break up, nobody can make us out from the other women who are just out for a walk. We know that the most important thing is to keep closing the circle, but imperceptibly, a little closer to the obelisk each time, so that they don't have time to realize it. There are more of them all the time; but every Thursday there are more of us, and the police bring reinforcements. They stand in front of the obelisk and keep us from getting close to it. We walk around talking in pairs, watching the necks of the pair of mothers in front of us. . . .

September 1977: . . . Azucena said it would be a good idea for all of us to join the annual pilgrimage to Luján "because people talk a lot on the way and we can stand out." We agreed: besides, there were also many Catholic mothers with us who wanted to go to pray the rosary. The problem is that not all of them wanted to go on foot: some would meet in Haedo, others in Moreno or Castelar. "We all have to agree clearly on where we'll meet."

"I know," said Eva, a mother who usually preferred to keep quiet. "We have to wear something that can be spotted from far away so we can find each other. A kerchief on our heads, for example."

"Or a mantilla. But we don't all have mantillas. Better a kerchief."

"Yes," says another woman. "Or better still a baby diaper; it looks like a kerchief, but it'll make us feel better, closer to our children.". . .

The husbands come along that day, but they always keep a little to the side. As soon as they enter the crowd, they see many other white-headed women like their wives. The diapers leap out at the sun in the sea of people walking along: we begin to come together, first two, then three. Further on, we come across another small group. The diapers multiply and stun the rest of the pilgrims who have already ceased to see them as a coincidence. When we get to the plaza across from the basilica in Luján, we're a good-sized group. Fifteen or twenty of us come together, and, standing in a circle, we pray the rosary for the children who no longer are. For the children who have disappeared.

Naturally the word *disappeared* bursts out. What does it mean? someone asks. The term is explicit: only someone who didn't want to understand could fail to understand. The word is multiplied many times by our mouths. It is repeated with the Ave Marias of the rosary. It embraces all the impunity of the situation. One woman, then another, comes over to talk with us. Their children are also "disappeared," they want to see us again, to pray with us, even with diapers on their heads. People look on, listening to the rosary in the plaza. In the basilica, in front of the altar, some of the devoted women are taking communion or praying for world peace. We are, in some way, the horrible worm that has wriggled out of a shining Argentina "that is advancing." Advancing toward what? Toward those graves without crosses. Toward the bottom of the river. . . .

A few days before the World Cup, a final blow struck "our family." On 25 May, in the afternoon, military forces abducted a group of women in a pastry shop in Lomas de Zamora. One of them was María Elena Bugnone, who was looking for her husband, her brother-in-law Raúl, her sister, and her sister's husband. Not one of that group of women ever returned. Later information from released prisoners indicated that María Elena was held for two years in the prison at Ezeiza. . . .

We know that the World Cup will fill the country with tourists and media professionals from all over the world. I said, "The question is how do we take advantage of those TV cameras for our own cause, to ask for our children and produce a juicy scandal for the government."

"But we don't know how to talk very well, Hebe. We know how to keep house, and we have learned how to do the paperwork, but what are we going to answer if they ask us something in English?"

"It's easy, Clarita," said a mother who had just joined but had plenty of energy. "You look at the journalist, and you say, 'We want our children. We want them to tell us where they are.'"

Our slogans and our rallying cries were being born: later on, they would shatter our silent circling of the obelisk at the center of the Plaza. But for the month of May they wouldn't let us circle: the police were there waiting punctually at three o'clock and charged whenever they saw more than three women together. But we fought them as long as we could. They threw us out one side, and we slipped back in the other. They dragged us out of one flower bed, and, after going around the block, we turned up next to the other. This game of cat and mouse that so exasperated them had for us the almost symbolic objective of occupying the obelisk, the center of the Plaza. From there people would see us better.

And the World Cup began: Argentine flags, confetti thrown from every office window. This meant the indifference of others, of all those Argentines who didn't want to know anything about death but preferred to celebrate to the end the mad fiesta power had offered them, stuffing themselves full with the four TV channels until they were sick or thoroughly brainwashed.

Meanwhile, we women worked to spread the news about our group. We sent hundreds of letters to foreign politicians, and we sought interviews with different world TV networks. Those men listened to us wide-eyed, some became indignant, and all considered us news. We had made it.

2

MIKHAIL GORBACHEV

Perestroika and Glasnost, 2000

Mikhail Gorbachev (b. 1931) was the head (General Secretary) of the Communist Party of the Soviet Union (1985-1991) and president of the Soviet Union (1988-1991). He led the party and the state through the wrenching changes of its liberalization, democratization, and demise. Beginning in 1985, Gorbachev envisioned the democratic reform

Source: Gorbachev, *On My Country and the World* (New York: Columbia University Press, 2000), 55–61.

of the party and state. His formula was *perestroika* (restructuring) and *glasnost* (opening). In this selection from his memoir, he describes that effort.

In what ways was the democratization of the Soviet Union, as described here, different from that of Argentina (see chapter 26, document 8 and the previous document)?

THINKING HISTORICALLY

In what ways does Gorbachev connect his democratization with the ideas and efforts of others? In what ways does he attribute it to the particular context of the Soviet Union and the world in the late 1980s?

There has been a continuing debate over when reform actually began in our country. Politicians and journalists have been trying to locate the exact point at which all our dramatic changes began. Some assert that reforms in Russia did not really begin until 1992.

The basis for reform was laid by Khrushchev.[1] His break with the repressive policies of Stalinism was a heroic feat of civic action. Khrushchev also tried, though without much success, to make changes in the economy. Significant attempts were made within the framework of the so-called Kosygin reforms. Then came a long period of stagnation and a new attempt by Yuri Andropov[2] to improve the situation in our society. An obvious sign that the times were ripe for change was the activity of the dissidents. They were suppressed and expelled from the country, but their moral stand and their proposals for change (for example, the ideas of Andrei Sakharov[3]) played a considerable role in creating the spiritual preconditions for perestroika.

Of course external factors were also important. Thus the Prague Spring of 1968 sowed the seeds of profound thought and reflection in our society. The invasion of Czechoslovakia, dictated by fear of the "democratic infection," was not only a crude violation of the sovereignty and rights of the Czechoslovak people. It had the effect, for years, of putting the brakes on moves toward change, although change was long overdue both in our country and throughout the so-called socialist camp. I should also acknowledge the role of such phenomena as Willy Brandt's[4]

---

[1] Nikita Khrushchev, First Secretary of the Communist Party of the Soviet Union from 1953 to 1964; responsible for early de-Stalinization reforms. See chapter 26, selections 4, 5, and 6. [Ed.]

[2] General Secretary of the Communist Party of the Soviet Union from November 1982 until February 1984. [Ed.]

[3] Soviet nuclear scientist who became a human rights activist. [Ed.]

[4] Mayor of West Berlin 1957–1966, Chancellor of West Germany 1969–1974, and leader of the socialist Social Democratic Party of Germany (SPD) 1964–1987. His Eastern policy was an effort to improve relations with communist East Germany, Poland, and the Soviet Union. [Ed.]

"Eastern policy" and the search for new avenues toward social progress by those who were called Euro-Communists. All this contributed to deeper reflection in our country, reflection on the values of democracy, freedom, and peace and the ways to achieve them.

Thus we see that attempts at change were made, quite a few of them in fact. But none of them produced results. This is not surprising: After all, none of these attempts touched the essence of the system—property relations, the power structure, and the monopoly of the party on political and intellectual life. The suppression of dissidence continued in spite of everything.

Clearly what was needed was not particular measures in a certain area, even if they were substantial, but rather an entirely different policy, a new political path. Since early 1985, especially after the April plenum of the CPSU Central Committee,[5] this kind of policy began to be formulated. A new course was taken.

Today, in retrospect, one can only be amazed at how quickly and actively our people, the citizens of our country, supported that new course. Apathy and indifference toward public life were overcome. This convinced us that change was vitally necessary. Society awakened.

Perestroika was born out of the realization that problems of internal development in our country were ripe, even overripe, for a solution. New approaches and types of action were needed to escape the downward spiral of crisis, to normalize life, and to make a breakthrough to qualitatively new frontiers. It can be said that to a certain extent perestroika was a result of a rethinking of the Soviet experience since October.[6]

The vital need for change was dictated also by the following consideration. It was obvious that the whole world was entering a new stage of development—some call it the postindustrial age, some the information age. But the Soviet Union had not yet passed through the industrial stage. It was lagging further and further behind those processes that were making a renewal in the life of the world community possible. Not only was a leap forward in technology needed but fundamental change in the entire social and political process.

Of course it cannot be said that at the time we began perestroika we had everything thought out. In the early stages we all said, including myself, that perestroika was a continuation of the October revolution. Today I believe that that assertion contained a grain of truth but also an element of delusion.

The truth was that we were trying to carry out fundamental ideas that had been advanced by the October revolution but had not been realized: overcoming people's alienation from government and property, giving

[5] The Central Committee of the Communist Party of the Soviet Union was the governing body between party congress meetings. [Ed.]

[6] October 1917, the Bolshevik Revolution. [Ed.]

power to the people (and taking it away from the bureaucratic upper echelons), implanting democracy, and establishing true social justice.

The delusion was that at the time I, like most of us, assumed this could be accomplished by improving and refining the existing system. But as experience accumulated, it became clear that the crisis that had paralyzed the country in the late 1970s and early 1980s was systemic and not the result of isolated aberrations. The logic of how matters developed pointed to the need to penetrate the system to its very foundations and change it, not merely refine or perfect it. We were already talking about a gradual shift to a social market economy, to a democratic political system based on rule of law and the full guarantee of human rights.

This transition turned out to be extremely difficult and complicated, more complicated than it had seemed to us at first. Above all, this was because the totalitarian system possessed tremendous inertia. There was resistance from the party and government structures that constituted the solid internal framework of that system. The nomenklatura encouraged resistance. And this is understandable: Since it held the entire country in its hands, it would have to give up its unlimited power and privileges. Thus the entire perestroika era was filled with struggles—concealed at first and then more open, more fully exposed to public view—between the forces for change and those who opposed it, those who, especially after the first two years, simply began to sabotage change.

The complexity of the struggle stemmed from the fact that in 1985 the entire society—politically, ideologically, and spiritually—was still in the thrall of old customs and traditions. Great effort was required to overcome these traditions, as mentioned above. There was another factor. Destroying the old system would have been senseless if we did not simultaneously lay the foundations for a new life. And this was genuinely unexplored territory. The six-year perestroika era was a time filled with searching and discovery, gains and losses, breakthroughs in thought and action, as well as mistakes and oversights. The attempted coup in August 1991 interrupted perestroika. After that there were many developments, but they were along different lines, following different intentions. Still, in the relatively short span of six years we succeeded in doing a great deal. The reforms in China, incidentally, have been going on since 1974, and their most difficult problems still remain unsolved.

What specifically did we accomplish as a result of the stormy years of perestroika? The foundations of the totalitarian system were eliminated. Profound democratic changes were begun. Free general elections were held for the first time, allowing real choice. Freedom of the press and a multiparty system were guaranteed. Representative bodies of government were established, and the first steps toward a separation of powers were taken. Human rights (previously in our country these were only "so-called," reference to them invariably made only in scornful quotation marks) now became an unassailable principle. And freedom of conscience was also established.

Movement began toward a multistructured, or mixed, economy providing equality of rights among all forms of property. Economic freedom was made into law. The spirit of enterprise began to gain strength, and processes of privatization and the formation of joint stock companies got under way. Within the framework of our new land law, the peasantry was reborn and private farmers made their appearance. Millions of hectares of land were turned over to both rural and urban inhabitants. The first privately owned banks also came on the scene. The different nationalities and peoples were given the freedom to choose their own course of development. Searching for a democratic way to reform our multinational state, to transform it from a unitary state in practice into a national federation, we reached the threshold at which a new union treaty was to be signed, based on the recognition of the sovereignty of each republic along with the preservation of a common economic, social, and legal space that was necessary for all, including a common defense establishment.

The changes within our country inevitably led to a shift in foreign policy. The new course of perestroika predetermined renunciation of stereotypes and the confrontational methods of the past. It allowed for a rethinking of the main parameters of state security and the ways to ensure it. . . .

In other words, the foundations were laid for normal, democratic, and peaceful development of our country and its transformation into a normal member of the world community.

These are the decisive results of perestroika. Today, however, looking back through the prism of the past few years and taking into account the general trends of world development today, it seems insufficient to register these as the only results. Today it is evidently of special interest to state not only *what* was done but also *how* and *why* perestroika was able to achieve its results, and what its mistakes and miscalculations were.

Above all, *perestroika would have been simply impossible if there had not been a profound and critical reexamination not only of the problems confronting our country but a rethinking of all realities — both national and international.*

Previous conceptions of the world and its developmental trends and, correspondingly, of our country's place and role in the world were based, as we have said, on dogmas deeply rooted in our ideology, which essentially did not permit us to pursue a realistic policy. These conceptions had to be shattered and fundamentally new views worked out regarding our country's development and the surrounding world.

This task turned out to be far from simple. We had to renounce beliefs that for decades had been considered irrefutable truths, to reexamine the very methods and principles of leadership and action, indeed to rethink our surroundings entirely on a scientific basis (and not according to schemes inherited from ideological biases).

The product of this effort was the new thinking, which became the basis for all policy—both foreign and domestic—during perestroika. The point of departure for the new thinking was an attempt to evaluate everything not from the viewpoint of narrow class interests or even national interests but from the broader perspective: that of giving priority to the interests of all humanity with consideration for the increasingly apparent wholeness of the world, the interdependence of all countries and peoples, the humanist values formed over centuries.

The practical work of perestroika was to *renounce stereotypical ideological thinking and the dogmas of the past. This required a fresh view of the world and of ourselves with no preconceptions, taking into account the challenges of the present and the already evident trends of the future in the third millennium.*

During perestroika, and often now as well, the initiators of perestroika have been criticized for the absence of a "clear plan" for change. The habit developed over decades of having an all-inclusive regimentation of life. But the events of the perestroika years and of the subsequent period have plainly demonstrated the following: *At times of profound, fundamental change in the foundations of social development it is not only senseless but impossible to expect some sort of previously worked out "model" or a clear-cut outline of the transformations that will take place. This does not mean, however, the absence of a definite goal for the reforms, a distinct conception of their content and the main direction of their development.*

All this was present in perestroika: a profound democratization of public life and a guarantee of freedom of social and political choice. These goals were proclaimed and frequently reaffirmed. This did not exclude but presupposed the necessity to change one's specific reference points at each stage as matters proceeded and to engage in a constant search for optimal solutions.

An extremely important conclusion follows from the experience of perestroika: Even in a society formed under totalitarian conditions, democratic change is possible by *peaceful evolutionary means.* The problem of revolution and evolution, of the role and place of reforms in social development, is one of the eternal problems of history. In its inner content perestroika of course was a revolution. But in its form it was an evolutionary process, a process of reform.

Historically the USSR had grown ripe for a profound restructuring much earlier than the mid-1980s. But if we had not decided to begin this restructuring at the time we did, even though we were quite late in doing so, an explosion would have taken place in the USSR, one of tremendous destructive force. It would certainly have been called a revolution, but it would have been the catastrophic result of irresponsible leadership.

In the course of implementing change we did not succeed in avoiding bloodshed altogether. But that was a consequence solely of resistance by the opponents of perestroika in the upper echelons of the nomenklatura. On the whole the change from one system to another took place peacefully and by evolutionary means. Our having chosen a policy course that was supported from below by the masses made this peaceful transition possible. And our policy of glasnost played a decisive role in mobilizing the masses and winning their support.

Radical reforms in the context of the Soviet Union could only have been initiated from above by the leadership of the party and the country. This was predetermined by the very "nature" of the system—supercentralized management of all public life. This can also be explained by the inert condition of the masses, who had become used to carrying out orders and decisions handed down from above.

From the very beginning of the changes our country's leadership assigned primary importance to open communication with the people, including direct disclosure in order to explain the new course. Without the citizens' understanding and support, without their participation, it would not have been possible to move from dead center. That is why we initiated the policies of perestroika and glasnost simultaneously.

Like perestroika itself, glasnost made its way with considerable difficulty. The nomenklatura on all levels, which regarded the strictest secrecy and protection of authorities from criticism from below as the holy of holies of the regime, opposed glasnost in every way they could, both openly and secretly, trampling its first shoots in the local press. Even among the most sincere supporters of perestroika, the tradition over many years of making everything a secret made itself felt. But it was precisely glasnost that awakened people from their social slumber, helped them overcome indifference and passivity and become aware of the stake they had in change and of its important implications for their lives. Glasnost helped us to explain and promote awareness of the new realities and the essence of our new political course. In short, without glasnost there would have been no perestroika.

The question of the relation between ends and means is one of the key aspects of politics and of political activity. If the means do not correspond to the ends, or, still worse, if the means contradict the ends, this will lead to setbacks and failure. The Soviet Union's experience is convincing evidence of this. When we began perestroika as a process of democratic change, we had to ensure that the means used to carry out these changes were also democratic.

In essence, glasnost became the means for drawing people into political activity, for including them in the creation of a new life, and this, above all, corresponded to the essence of perestroika. Glasnost not only created conditions for implementing the intended reforms but also made it possible to overcome attempts to sabotage the policy of change.

We are indebted to glasnost for a profound psychological transformation in the public consciousness toward democracy, freedom, and the humanist values of civilization. Incidentally, this was one of the guarantees that the fundamental gains of this period would be irreversible.

Perestroika confirmed once again that the normal, democratic development of society rules out universal secrecy as a method of administration. Democratic development presupposes glasnost—that is, openness, freedom of information for all citizens and freedom of expression by them of their political, religious, and other views and convictions, freedom of criticism in the fullest sense of the word.

Why, then, did perestroika not succeed in achieving all its goals? The answer primarily involves the question of "harmonization" between political and economic change.

The dominant democratic aspect of perestroika meant that the accent was inevitably placed on political reform. The dialectic of our development during those years was such that serious changes in the economic sphere proved to be impossible without emancipating society politically, without ensuring freedom—that is, breaking the political structures of totalitarianism. And this was accomplished. But economic change lagged behind political change, and we did not succeed in developing economic change to the full extent.

3

NELSON MANDELA
Nobel Peace Prize Address, 1993

Democracy for South Africa meant racial democracy: political equality for all South Africans regardless of the color of their skin. It meant the end of apartheid, a system of legal racial segregation in jobs, housing, and access to the political process. It meant the end of the political domination of the 80 percent of South Africans who were black by the 10 percent who were white. In practice, it meant the defeat of the white-supremacist National Party that had ruled South Africa since 1948 and the victory of the mainly black African National Congress party, led by Nelson Mandela despite his imprisonment from 1962 to 1990.

A change of this magnitude was made even more momentous by the fact that it occurred relatively peacefully when National Party

Source: Acceptance Speech of the President of the African National Congress, Nelson Mandela, at the Nobel Peace Prize Award Ceremony: Oslo, Norway. December 10, 1993. At http://www.nobelprize.org/nobel_prizes/peace/laureates/1993/mandela-lecture.html

leader and South African president F. W. de Klerk released Mandela from prison in 1990 and scheduled elections that would include the previously outlawed African National Congress for 1994. As a consequence, the Noble Peace Prize committee awarded the 1993 prize jointly to Mandela and de Klerk.

The Nobel Peace Prize is not, of course, a democracy prize. Still, the realization of a political democracy in black-majority South Africa is what the Nobel committee celebrated. Mandela humbly accepted the prize, knowing the challenges that lay ahead in creating a democratic state in South Africa. What did he see as the elements of the democracy he hoped to create? What were his goals? What, if any, elements of democracy did he not include? How was his vision of democracy different from that of Gorbachev?

THINKING HISTORICALLY

The end of institutional racism in South Africa came about after domestic protests, starting in the black township of Soweto in 1976, attracted international attention. Western campaigns to boycott South African goods and investments gained support during the following decade. By the end of the Cold War, the support of anti-communist white South Africa by the United States became unnecessary as well as untenable. Thus, the Nobel Peace Prize acknowledged both a national and an international achievement. How does Mandela recognize the national context of the South African democratic revolution? How does he connect the arrival of democracy in South Africa with the global development of democracy and human rights?

Your Majesty the King,
Your Royal Highness,
Honourable Prime Minister,
Madame Gro Brundtland,
Ministers,
Members of Parliament and Ambassadors,
Esteemed Members of the Norwegian Nobel Committee,
Fellow Laureate, Mr. F. W. de Klerk,
Distinguished guests,
Friends, ladies and gentlemen:

I am indeed truly humbled to be standing here today to receive this year's Nobel Peace Prize.

I extend my heartfelt thanks to the Norwegian Nobel Committee for elevating us to the status of a Nobel Peace Prize winner.

I would also like to take this opportunity to congratulate my compatriot and fellow laureate, State President F. W. de Klerk, on his receipt of this high honour.

Together, we join two distinguished South Africans, the late Chief Albert Luthuli and His Grace Archbishop Desmond Tutu, to whose seminal contributions to the peaceful struggle against the evil system of apartheid you paid well-deserved tribute by awarding them the Nobel Peace Prize.

It will not be presumptuous of us if we also add, among our predecessors, the name of another outstanding Nobel Peace Prize winner, the late African-American statesman and internationalist, the Rev. Martin Luther King Jr.

He, too, grappled with and died in the effort to make a contribution to the just solution of the same great issues of the day which we have had to face as South Africans.

We speak here of the challenge of the dichotomies of war and peace, violence and non-violence, racism and human dignity, oppression and repression and liberty and human rights, poverty and freedom from want.

We stand here today as nothing more than a representative of the millions of our people who dared to rise up against a social system whose very essence is war, violence, racism, oppression, repression and the impoverishment of an entire people.

I am also here today as a representative of the millions of people across the globe, the anti-apartheid movement, the governments and organisations that joined with us, not to fight against South Africa as a country or any of its peoples, but to oppose an inhuman system and sue for a speedy end to the apartheid crime against humanity.

These countless human beings, both inside and outside our country, had the nobility of spirit to stand in the path of tyranny and injustice, without seeking selfish gain. They recognised that an injury to one is an injury to all and therefore acted together in defence of justice and a common human decency.

Because of their courage and persistence for many years, we can, today, even set the dates when all humanity will join together to celebrate one of the outstanding human victories of our century.

When that moment comes, we shall, together, rejoice in a common victory over racism, apartheid and white minority rule.

That triumph will finally bring to a close a history of five hundred years of African colonisation that began with the establishment of the Portuguese empire.

Thus, it will mark a great step forward in history and also serve as a common pledge of the peoples of the world to fight racism wherever it occurs and whatever guise it assumes.

At the southern tip of the continent of Africa, a rich reward is in the making, an invaluable gift is in the preparation, for those who suffered in the name of all humanity when they sacrificed everything—for liberty, peace, human dignity and human fulfilment.

This reward will not be measured in money. Nor can it be reckoned in the collective price of the rare metals and precious stones that rest in the bowels of the African soil we tread in the footsteps of our ancestors. It will and must be measured by the happiness and welfare of the children, at once the most vulnerable citizens in any society and the greatest of our treasures.

The children must, at last, play in the open veld, no longer tortured by the pangs of hunger or ravaged by disease or threatened with the scourge of ignorance, molestation and abuse, and no longer required to engage in deeds whose gravity exceeds the demands of their tender years.

In front of this distinguished audience, we commit the new South Africa to the relentless pursuit of the purposes defined in the World Declaration on the Survival, Protection and Development of Children.

The reward of which we have spoken will and must also be measured by the happiness and welfare of the mothers and fathers of these children, who must walk the earth without fear of being robbed, killed for political or material profit, or spat upon because they are beggars.

They too must be relieved of the heavy burden of despair which they carry in their hearts, born of hunger, homelessness and unemployment.

The value of that gift to all who have suffered will and must be measured by the happiness and welfare of all the people of our country, who will have torn down the inhuman walls that divide them.

These great masses will have turned their backs on the grave insult to human dignity which described some as masters and others as servants, and transformed each into a predator whose survival depended on the destruction of the other.

The value of our shared reward will and must be measured by the joyful peace which will triumph, because the common humanity that bonds both black and white into one human race, will have said to each one of us that we shall all live like the children of paradise.

Thus shall we live, because we will have created a society which recognises that all people are born equal, with each entitled in equal measure to life, liberty, prosperity, human rights and good governance.

Such a society should never allow again that there should be prisoners of conscience nor that any person's human rights should be violated.

Neither should it ever happen that once more the avenues to peaceful change are blocked by usurpers who seek to take power away from the people, in pursuit of their own, ignoble purposes.

In relation to these matters, we appeal to those who govern Burma that they release our fellow Nobel Peace Prize laureate, Aung San Suu Kyi, and engage her and those she represents in serious dialogue, for the benefit of all the people of Burma.

We pray that those who have the power to do so will, without further delay, permit that she uses her talents and energies for the greater good of the people of her country and humanity as a whole.

Far from the rough and tumble of the politics of our own country, I would like to take this opportunity to join the Norwegian Nobel Committee and pay tribute to my joint laureate, Mr. F. W. de Klerk.

He had the courage to admit that a terrible wrong had been done to our country and people through the imposition of the system of apartheid.

He had the foresight to understand and accept that all the people of South Africa must, through negotiations and as equal participants in the process, together determine what they want to make of their future.

But there are still some within our country who wrongly believe they can make a contribution to the cause of justice and peace by clinging to the shibboleths that have been proved to spell nothing but disaster.

It remains our hope that these, too, will be blessed with sufficient reason to realise that history will not be denied and that the new society cannot be created by reproducing the repugnant past, however refined or enticingly repackaged.

We live with the hope that as she battles to remake herself, South Africa will be like a microcosm of the new world that is striving to be born.

This must be a world of democracy and respect for human rights, a world freed from the horrors of poverty, hunger, deprivation and ignorance, relieved of the threat and the scourge of civil wars and external aggression and unburdened of the great tragedy of millions forced to become refugees.

The processes in which South Africa and Southern Africa as a whole are engaged, beckon and urge us all that we take this tide at the flood and make of this region a living example of what all people of conscience would like the world to be.

We do not believe that this Nobel Peace Prize is intended as a commendation for matters that have happened and passed.

We hear the voices which say that it is an appeal from all those, throughout the universe, who sought an end to the system of apartheid.

We understand their call, that we devote what remains of our lives to the use of our country's unique and painful experience to demonstrate, in practice, that the normal condition for human existence is democracy, justice, peace, non-racism, non-sexism, prosperity for everybody, a healthy environment and equality and solidarity among the peoples.

Moved by that appeal and inspired by the eminence you have thrust upon us, we undertake that we too will do what we can to contribute to the renewal of our world so that none should, in future, be described as the wretched of the earth.

Let it never be said by future generations that indifference, cynicism or selfishness made us fail to live up to the ideals of humanism which the Nobel Peace Prize encapsulates.

Let the strivings of us all prove Martin Luther King Jr. to have been correct, when he said that humanity can no longer be tragically bound to the starless midnight of racism and war.

Let the efforts of us all, prove that he was not a mere dreamer when he spoke of the beauty of genuine brotherhood and peace being more precious than diamonds or silver or gold.

Let a new age dawn!

Thank you.

4

GENE SHARP

From Dictatorship to Democracy, 1993

Gene Sharp (b. 1928) is the founder of The Albert Einstein Institution and author of numerous books on nonviolent political struggle. His theoretical and "how to" writings have been instrumental in new democracy movements in Southeast Asia and Eastern Europe. These have included the peaceful "Orange Revolution" in Ukraine in 2004–2005 and similar successful nonviolent democratic movements in Serbia, Georgia, Belarus, and the Baltic countries.

During the "Arab Spring" of 2011, the *New York Times* and *London Daily Telegraph* (among others) published articles that claimed this "unknown professor" was behind the democratic revolutions shaking the Arab world. Many Egyptians disputed this, along with Sharp himself who insisted that the Egyptian revolution showed that Egyptians could do it themselves, without the intervention of Western actors.

Nevertheless, Sharp's study of nonviolent revolutions has led him to an analysis of the exercise of state power that would be useful to many democratic revolutionaries. He challenges the more popular view that nonviolence is rarely successful and that violence is always the most powerful weapon. He argues instead that nonviolence is always *tactically* (as well as morally) preferable against superior power. What do you think of his argument? What does he teach you about fighting dictators? How might this argument be more persuasive in our contemporary age than it would have been in the past?

THINKING HISTORICALLY

How does Sharp undermine the arguments of those who seek to export democracy? How does he support them? How does he show the importance of every particular context? How does he show the value of connections to history?

Centers of Democratic Power

One characteristic of a democratic society is that there exist independent of the state a multitude of nongovernmental groups and institutions.

Source: Gene Sharp, *From Dictatorship to Democracy: A Conceptual Framework for Liberation*, 4th U.S. edition (Boston: The Albert Einstein Institution, 2010), pp. 21–23, 31–34, 62–64, 69.

These include, for example, families, religious organizations, cultural associations, sports clubs, economic institutions, trade unions, student associations, political parties, villages, neighborhood associations, gardening clubs, human rights organizations, musical groups, literary societies, and others. These bodies are important in serving their own objectives and also in helping to meet social needs.

Additionally, these bodies have great political significance. They provide group and institutional bases by which people can exert influence over the direction of their society and resist other groups or the government when they are seen to impinge unjustly on their interests, activities, or purposes. Isolated individuals, not members of such groups, usually are unable to make a significant impact on the rest of the society, much less a government, and certainly not a dictatorship.

Consequently, if the autonomy and freedom of such bodies can be taken away by the dictators, the population will be relatively helpless. Also, if these institutions can themselves be dictatorially controlled by the central regime or replaced by new controlled ones, they can be used to dominate both the individual members and also those areas of the society. However, if the autonomy and freedom of these independent civil institutions (outside of government control) can be maintained or regained they are highly important for the application of political defiance. The common feature of the cited examples in which dictatorships have been disintegrated or weakened has been the courageous *mass* application of political defiance by the population and its institutions. . . .

During the Hungarian Revolution of 1956–1957 a multitude of direct democracy councils emerged, even joining together to establish for some weeks a whole federated system of institutions and governance. In Poland during the late 1980s workers maintained illegal Solidarity unions and, in some cases, took over control of the official, Communist-dominated, trade unions. Such institutional developments can have very important political consequences. . . .

Methods of Nonviolent Struggle

In contrast to military means, the methods of nonviolent struggle can be focused directly on the issues at stake. For example, since the issue of dictatorship is primarily political, then political forms of nonviolent struggle would be crucial. These would include denial of legitimacy to the dictators and noncooperation with their regime.

Noncooperation would also be applied against specific policies. At times stalling and procrastination may be quietly and even secretly practiced, while at other times open disobedience and defiant public demonstrations and strikes may be visible to all. On the other hand, if the dictatorship is vulnerable to economic pressures or if many of the popular grievances against it are economic, then economic action, such as boycotts or strikes, may be appropriate resistance methods. The dictators' efforts to exploit the economic system might be met with limited general strikes, slowdowns, and refusal of assistance by (or disappearance of) indispensable experts. Selective use of various types of strikes may be conducted at key points in manufacturing, in transport, in the supply of raw materials, and in the distribution of products.

Some methods of nonviolent struggle require people to perform acts unrelated to their normal lives, such as distributing leaflets, operating an underground press, going on hunger strike, or sitting down in the streets. These methods may be difficult for some people to undertake except in very extreme situations. Other methods of nonviolent struggle instead require people to continue approximately their normal lives, though in somewhat different ways. For example, people may report for work, instead of striking, but then deliberately work more slowly or inefficiently than usual. "Mistakes" may be consciously made more frequently. One may become "sick" and "unable" to work at certain times. Or, one may simply refuse to work. One might go to religious services when the act expresses not only religious but also political convictions.

One may act to protect children from the attackers' propaganda by education at home or in illegal classes. One might refuse to join certain "recommended" or required organizations that one would not have joined freely in earlier times. The similarity of such types of action to people's usual activities and the limited degree of departure from their normal lives may make participation in the national liberation struggle much easier for many people.

Since nonviolent struggle and violence operate in fundamentally different ways, even limited resistance violence during a political defiance campaign will be counterproductive, for it will shift the struggle to one in which the dictators have an overwhelming advantage (military warfare). Nonviolent discipline is a key to success and must be maintained despite provocations and brutalities by the dictators and their agents. . . .

Openness, Secrecy, and High Standards

Secrecy, deception, and underground conspiracy pose very difficult problems for a movement using nonviolent action. It is often impossible to keep the political police and intelligence agents from learning about intentions and plans. From the perspective of the movement, secrecy is not only rooted in fear but contributes to fear, which dampens the spirit of resistance and reduces the number of people who can participate in a given action. It also can contribute to suspicions and accusations, often unjustified, within the movement, concerning who is an informer or agent for the opponents.

Secrecy may also affect the ability of a movement to remain nonviolent. In contrast, openness regarding intentions and plans will not only have the opposite effects, but will contribute to an image that the resistance movement is in fact extremely powerful. The problem is of course more complex than this suggests, and there are significant aspects of resistance activities that may require secrecy. A well informed assessment will be required by those knowledgeable about both the dynamics of nonviolent struggle and also the dictatorship's means of surveillance in the specific situation.

The editing, printing, and distribution of underground publications, the use of illegal radio broadcasts from within the country, and the gathering of intelligence about the operations of the dictatorship are among the special limited types of activities where a high degree of secrecy will be required. . . .

Planning Political Defiance

During the planning and implementation of political defiance and non-cooperation, it is highly important to pay close attention to all of the dictators' main supporters and aides, including their inner clique, political party, police, and bureaucrats, but especially their army.

The degree of loyalty of the military forces, both soldiers and officers, to the dictatorship needs to be carefully assessed and a determination should be made as to whether the military is open to influence by the democratic forces. Might many of the ordinary soldiers be unhappy and frightened conscripts? Might many of the soldiers and officers be alienated from the regime for personal, family, or political reasons? What other factors might make soldiers and officers vulnerable to democratic subversion?

Early in the liberation struggle a special strategy should be developed to communicate with the dictators' troops and functionaries. By words, symbols, and actions, the democratic forces can inform the troops that the liberation struggle will be vigorous, determined, and persistent. Troops should learn that the struggle will be of a special character, designed to undermine the dictatorship but not to threaten their lives. Such efforts would aim ultimately to undermine the morale of the dictators' troops and finally to subvert their loyalty and obedience in favor of the democratic movement. Similar strategies could be aimed at the police and civil servants.

The attempt to garner sympathy from and, eventually, induce disobedience among the dictators' forces ought not to be interpreted, however, to mean encouragement of the military forces to make a quick end to the current dictatorship through military action. Such a scenario is not likely to install a working democracy, for (as we have discussed) a coup d'état does little to redress the imbalance of power relations between the populace and the rulers. Therefore, it will be necessary to plan how sympathetic military officers can be brought to understand that neither a military coup nor a civil war against the dictatorship is required or desirable. Sympathetic officers can play vital roles in the democratic struggle, such as spreading disaffection and noncooperation in the military forces, encouraging deliberate inefficiencies and the quiet ignoring of orders, and supporting the refusal to carry out repression.

Military personnel may also offer various modes of positive nonviolent assistance to the democracy movement, including safe passage, information, food, medical supplies, and the like. The army is one of the most important sources of the power of dictators because it can use its disciplined military units and weaponry directly to attack and to punish the disobedient population.

Defiance strategists should remember that it will be exceptionally difficult, or impossible, to disintegrate the dictatorship if the police, bureaucrats, and military forces remain fully supportive of the dictatorship and obedient in carrying out its commands. Strategies aimed at subverting the loyalty of the dictators' forces should therefore be given a high priority by democratic strategists.

The democratic forces should remember that disaffection and disobedience among the military forces and police can be highly dangerous for the members of those groups. Soldiers and police could expect severe penalties for any act of disobedience and execution for acts of mutiny. The democratic forces should not ask the soldiers and officers that they immediately mutiny. Instead, where communication is possible, it should be made clear that there are a multitude of relatively safe forms of "disguised disobedience" that they can take initially. For example, police and troops can carry out instructions for repression inefficiently, fail to locate wanted persons, warn resisters of impending repression, arrests, or deportations, and fail to report important information to their superior officers. Disaffected officers in turn can neglect to relay commands for repression down the chain of command. Soldiers may shoot over the heads of demonstrators. Similarly, for their part, civil servants can lose files and instructions, work inefficiently, and become "ill". . .

Escalating Freedom

Combined with political defiance during the phase of selective resistance, the growth of autonomous social, economic, cultural, and political institutions progressively expands the "democratic space" of the society and shrinks the control of the dictatorship. As the civil institutions of the society become stronger vis-à-vis the dictatorship, then, whatever the dictators may wish, the population is incrementally building an independent society outside of their control. If and when the dictatorship intervenes to halt this "escalating freedom," nonviolent struggle can be applied in defense of this newly won space and the dictatorship will be faced with yet another "front" in the struggle.

In time, this combination of resistance and institution building can lead to *de facto* freedom, making the collapse of the dictatorship and the formal installation of a democratic system undeniable because the power relationships within the society have been fundamentally altered.

5

WAEL GHONIM

Revolution 2.0, 2012

Wael Ghonim (b. 1980) was an Egyptian computer engineer working for Google in the Middle East when in June 2010 a friend posted pictures on his Facebook Wall of the bloody body of a young man, Khaled Said, who had been beaten to death by Egyptian police. Unable to stop crying at an image that crystallized for him the police state that had developed under Hosni Mubarak, Ghonim decided to devote all of his computer and marketing ability to bring justice for Khaled Said. He created a Facebook page called *Kullena Khaled Said* ("We are all Khaled Said") and within two minutes 300 had joined the page. Within an hour it had grown to 3,000. In the following weeks, Ghonim used the page to engage supporters and then promote peaceful demonstrations, the first of which was a Silent Stand along the banks of the Nile in both Alexandria and Cairo. By the end of June there were 100,000 members, many of whom were young people who had never done anything political.

In *Revolution 2.0*, Ghonim captures the next eight months of what became, in no small part thanks to his efforts and those who joined him, the Arab Spring of democratic revolution. This selection is drawn from the end of the book. It describes the last days of massive peaceful protest in Tahrir Square Cairo, as Ghonim, recognized as the administrator of the Facebook page and imprisoned for eleven days, is called by the minister of the interior to negotiate on behalf of the people in Tahrir. *Kullena Khaled Said* then had 1,650,000 members.

Source: Wael Ghonim, *Revolution 2.0* (Boston: Houghton Mifflin Harcourt, 2012), 282–94.

Ghonim is promised a meeting with Mubarak but after a long wait he drives home. He picks up the story there.

From the title of his book to the epilogue, Ghonim displays the power of technology: television as well as social media on the Internet (though he also mentions the power of Friday prayers and sermons). How important were these new technologies, perhaps especially new media, to the protests in Egypt? In what ways was this Revolution 2.0? Is Revolution 2.0 easier than Revolution 1.0?

THINKING HISTORICALLY

Ghonim writes about the importance of connections to foreigners and events outside of Egypt. He also writes with a great deal of national pride and knowledge of conditions in Egypt. In explaining the fall of Mubarak, how do you balance the impact of these connections with the immediate Egyptian context? What foreign connections were important? To what extent was this Egyptian revolution a continuation of events in Tunisia? To what extent was it a distinctly Egyptian event?

Everyone in Tahrir Square was cheering, and news channels started asking people there to comment on the to-be-confirmed news that Mubarak was stepping down. Al Arabiya[1] asked me for a phone interview to congratulate the Egyptian people. I said we had finally succeeded in realizing the objective of the president's resignation and it was now time to go home and think of rebuilding Egypt. . . .

After speaking to Al Arabiya, I decided to watch the resignation speech from Tahrir Square. I had spoken to many people there who were very happy with the news and eagerly awaiting the speech.

Mubarak began his speech much later than expected, and a wave of suspense washed over us as we waited. But he spoke in his traditional manner. He reminded us of his role in war and in peace, and of his achievements and history. And although he spent a moment offering condolences for the lives of the martyrs, it wasn't half as emotional as the moment when he expressed his pain at Tahrir Square's depiction of him. He even referred to the martyrs as "your martyrs," unwittingly reinforcing his clear disconnection from the square. Mubarak invited everyone to give precedence to Egypt's interests over everything else. He said he had lived on Egyptian soil and would die on Egyptian soil. Then, during the final thirty seconds of the speech, Mubarak said he delegated his authority to Vice President Omar Soliman. It was not actually a resignation from power.

---

[1] Saudi-owned Arabic television channel. [Ed.]

In Tahrir Square, thousands of disappointed yet determined people started chanting, "Leave means go, in case you did not know!" A group of people in the square gathered around me. "What will we do? This is unbelievable. Don't these people understand?" they exclaimed. I had nothing to say to them except that we were the stronger ones and would not give up until our goal was reached. We desired a real resignation and not a murky delegation of power. Disappointed, I left Tahrir with a friend who drove me home.

Two surprising pieces of news surfaced when I met my friends to discuss our next steps. The first was that the Middle East News Agency reported that I had issued a statement inviting all Egyptians at Tahrir to return to their homes following the president's speech. The second was that hundreds of angry protesters had begun marching from Tahrir Square toward the presidential palace to force the president to step down. It was an extremely dangerous development. Everyone was talking about how this could lead to a bloodbath. The presidential guard would attack anyone who approached the palace. I was devastated by this news and extremely apprehensive about the consequences. . . .

I received a call from the TV host Amr al-Laithy, who asked that I call in during his show and declare my opinion of events and of the president's decision. I accepted.

On the air, I clarified that I had not made any statements and that, like everyone else, I was not happy with Mubarak's speech. The president was not resigning but delegating authority to his vice president while remaining president. Amr al-Laithy asked . . . me to say something to the people marching toward the palace. I said that it was not for me to address the protesters and asked him and others to stop trying to influence them, because the protesters were not watching television. My final comment was that I would formulate my position after completing an opinion poll on the Facebook page, asking members how they evaluated the events on the ground, as I had done before.

A huge burden of responsibility lay on my shoulders. It was true that my statements might not influence the masses and that rallying through the Facebook page might not be as effective as it had been, since heroes on the ground were now the ones who controlled the course of events. Yet I still sensed — for the first time — that my computer keyboard had become a machine gun, firing bullets with every keystroke. I felt a new sense of responsibility for everything I wrote, and I became very tense.

I designed a questionnaire to canvass people's reactions to the president's speech and find out what they thought the next steps should be, including the idea of marching toward the palace. My plan was to base my own decision on the majority's opinion. We would then all shoulder the responsibility for our actions, even if the result was gunfire from the presidential guard that claimed the lives of hundreds of young Egyptians.

Moments after posting the questionnaire, the polling service that I had been using for months stopped working. The main server that hosted the service suddenly froze because of a burst of user traffic. Thousands, or maybe tens of thousands, of website visitors wanted to participate and share their opinions, which created more traffic than their server could handle. I tried several times to revive the server, without success. I announced the failure of the polling service on the page as some members accused me of cowardice, lies, and deception. At that point I was physically worn out beyond imagination. I decided to go home, not knowing what I would post next. . . .

I entered my family home with my emotions transparent on my face. My mother asked our relatives, who lived in the same building, to come to my room and try to talk to me, but I asked everyone to leave me alone. Then I vented through the Facebook page.

> Dear God, you know our intentions best and that we are seeking our rights and our freedom . . . Dear God, inspire us to do what is right and increase the strength of each and every one of us.
>
> 👍 15,095 Likes　　　💬 19,690 Comments　　1,405,565 Views

I tried to think as I lay down in bed, but before I knew it I was fast asleep, after a day full of unexpected events. For the first time since my release from detainment, I slept for more than seven hours. When I woke up, I was no longer confused. I was determined—and angry. I was angry that we had been used to broadcast an image of "dialogue" to undermine the revolution. I was angry that my name had been used in a press statement to dissuade the protesters from continuing their sit-in. Once again I expressed my complete support for the revolution and its demands on the Facebook page.

> I'm with all of you, I'm with our rights and our freedom. I'm with taking all the corrupt people to justice. I'm with ending over 30 years of violation of the basic rights of Egyptians and their dignity.
>
> 👍 6,632 Likes　　　💬 2,540 Comments　　1,538,294 Views

Mostafa al-Nagar called and said that we must make a media appearance to tell the story of our deception the night before. He suggested appearing with the famous TV host Hafiz al-Mirazi on Al Arabiya.

Later Mostafa arrived at my house with a formal statement he and other political activists had prepared for the army, containing a number of demands. The statement was based on the army's announcement the day before. It began by saluting the SCAF's[2] involvement and went on to outline our demands: confirmation of the complete resignation of the president and his irrevocable removal from power; dissolution of the National Democratic Party and the free formation of political parties; removal of the restrictions placed on candidate nominations for presidential elections; immediate suspension of the emergency law; new rounds of parliamentary elections in all the constituencies in which the court had ruled the previous ballot results illegitimate; monitoring of all elections by local and international civil society, as well as facilitation of the voting process by allowing all resident citizens to use their national ID card and allowing expatriate Egyptians to vote from abroad; the release of all arrested protesters from detainment; the bringing to justice of all the murderers responsible for crimes against Egyptian youth; the bringing to justice of corrupt politicians and the confiscation of all assets stolen from the Egyptian people; and re-creation of the security apparatus on a base of transparency that would prevent monstrous acts of torturing and terrorizing the citizens.

On our way to Al Arabiya, we learned that the numbers at the presidential palace were still limited but increasing as the time for Friday prayers approached. Meanwhile, Tahrir was flooded with hundreds of thousands of protesters and a march had taken off toward the state television building, which was guarded by army forces to prevent it from being raided. By the time my Al Arabiya interview began, I was angrier than I had ever been. I told Hafiz al-Mirazi, the interviewer, that Egypt was experiencing an immense crisis of trust. I said that the country was like a girl who had been raped continually for thirty years, and as soon as she had obtained a knife to fight back, her rapist was begging her to "dialogue" and give up revenge. I read our statement of demands aloud. Mostafa al-Nagar declared that complying with these demands was necessary because martyrs' blood had been shed.

I told the interviewer how Mostafa had held a dying protester in his arms after the man had been shot in the chest. "Mostafa, are we on the right side?" he had asked. "Will I die a martyr?" Speaking through tears as he held him, Mostafa had replied, "Yes, of course." Then the wounded man let out his last breath.

Then my voice rose. "Our tears are not tears of weakness but a sign of strength. Our tears are stronger than the bullets to our chests from Omar Soliman and his men. I am stronger than Omar Soliman and stronger than Hosni Mubarak." Although I ended my statement in the first person, to me it felt as if the protesters had just uttered those words. There was no way we were going to give up our dream, especially not because of fear.

[2] Supreme Council of Egyptian Armed Forces.

Outside on the street after the interview, people crowded around us once again. I wanted to depart quickly to follow the updates and access the Facebook page. The scene at Tahrir Square was magnificent that Friday. It was clear evidence that the majority of Jan 25 protesters had not been satisfied by Mubarak's mere delegation of powers to his vice president. I soon discovered that national television had broadcast the army's approval of the protesters' demands. They even mentioned specific demands, including the ones in our statement. We became hopeful once again.

Message to the regime: The people on the streets raise the level of their demands with every passing hour. The current demand that needs to be fulfilled as fast as possible is for the president to step down and leave Egypt.

👍 5,514 Likes　　　💬 5,030 Comments　　　1,013,841 Views

At about 5 p.m., television stations announced that an important statement would be broadcast "shortly." After the experience of the previous night, anything was possible. So we decided not to celebrate just yet.

This time Vice President Omar Soliman appeared on national television, looking very serious. "In the name of God, most gracious, most merciful," Soliman read, "my fellow citizens, in the difficult circumstances our country is experiencing, President Muhammad Hosni Mubarak has decided to give up the office of the president of the republic and instructed the Supreme Council of the Armed Forces to manage the affairs of the country. May God guide our steps."

I could not believe it. The dream had been realized. What was impossible for years had been achieved in eighteen days. I went around hugging everyone in the vicinity: my mother, sister, brother, aunt, and friends. We all started singing the national anthem, raising our voices high. I called my wife and said, "You won't believe it! Mubarak is gone!"

"Are you serious?"

"Yes!" I exclaimed. "He's gone! He's gone! He's gone!" I kept repeating it hysterically.

One minute later I updated the Facebook page:

Congratulations, Egypt! This is the historical moment we have been longing to witness!

👍 15,190 Likes　　　💬 10,832 Comments　　　968,496 Views

. . . The rejoicing and celebrations in the streets were incredible. Car horns, fireworks, screams, chants, and applause were heard everywhere. It was a defining moment of Egypt's modern history. The will of the people vanquished the will of the rulers.

I went out on the street surrounded by neighbors and friends. Together we stopped the passing cars and chanted with all our might, "Mubarak is gone! The Egyptian people are free!" Celebrations continued throughout the night. We began at Mostafa Mahmoud Square in Mohandeseen and moved all the way to Tahrir Square, which was now filled with people as never before. There I got on the main stage and recited the opening chapter of the Qur'an, "Al-Fatihah," in tribute to the martyrs, and I called on a young Christian to lead a prayer for the martyrs as well. Everyone started chanting, "Muslims and Christians, we are all Egyptians!". . .

I returned home after midnight with my head held high. I updated the *"Kullena Khaled Said"* page before I went to bed:

Proud to be Egyptian!

👍 9,413 Likes   💬 2,539 Comments   655,359 Views

Epilogue

. . . Something changed when Egyptians stood up to the Mubarak regime. That change is not limited to our country or to our revolution—it is happening in many countries in the Middle East and on the streets of many cities around the world. Now that so many people can easily connect with one another, the world is less hospitable to authoritarian regimes. Humanity will always be cursed with power-hungry people, and the rule of law and justice will not automatically flourish in all places at all times. But thanks to modern technology, participatory democracy is becoming a reality. Governments are finding it harder and harder to keep their people isolated from one another, to censor information, and to hide corruption and issue propaganda that goes unchallenged. Slowly but surely, the weapons of mass oppression are becoming extinct.

The Egyptian revolution showed us that the great mass of people who are normally risk-averse, aren't normally activists, can become extraordinarily brave and active when they unite together as one. It was like an offline Wikipedia, with everyone anonymously and selflessly contributing efforts toward a common goal. . . .

Revolutions of the past have usually had charismatic leaders who were politically savvy and sometimes even military geniuses. Such revolutions followed what we can call the Revolution 1.0 model. But the revolution in Egypt was different: it was truly a spontaneous movement led by nothing other than the wisdom of the crowd. One day revolution seemed utterly impossible, and there were just a few people dreaming of change. And then, after the brave people of Tunisia ignited a fire that had been smoldering in the hearts of Egyptians and many other Arab people, the impossible quickly became possible. People who would only post comments in cyberspace became willing to stand in public; then those protesters, among many others, made the great leap to become marchers and chanters, and grew into a critical mass that toppled a brutal and tyrannical regime.

6

China's "Charter 08," 2008

In 1979 the Chinese Communist Party began to introduce markets and open the Chinese economy to national and foreign capitalists. But the Party maintained a tight grip on all political offices and public media, sometimes brutally silencing criticism. Various efforts at political liberalization, like the China Democracy Movement in 1989, were met by fierce military suppression and efforts to substitute material well-being for political participation and freedom of expression. The exponential growth of the Chinese economy since then was largely successful in pacifying the population. But critics did not disappear.

This 2008 Chinese democratic manifesto was originally signed by 350 Chinese human rights activists, lawyers, artists, writers, intellectuals, and even some former communist officials. Today over 10,000 have signed. It was immediately banned in China and many of the signers were harassed or jailed. One of the authors, Liu Xiaobo, was awarded the Nobel Peace Prize in 2010 while in a Chinese prison, where he remains as of this writing.

What does the fact that these ideas and demands were so threatening tell you about the struggle for democracy in China today? How would the realization of these demands create a democratic China?

THINKING HISTORICALLY

The name given to this democratizing effort, "Charter 08," recognized a similar set of demands signed by prominent citizens of

---

Source: "Charter 08," translated by "Human Rights in China." http://www.hrichina.org/crf /article/3203

Czechoslovakia in 1977 called "Charter 77." Many of the signers of Charter 77 were active in the Velvet Revolution of 1989 in which the Czechoslovakian Communist Party relinquished power. Making a connection to that earlier event was evidently important to the drafters of Charter 08 in China. In addition, the authors make a point of connecting their charter with earlier Chinese reform movements. Beyond that, many of the statements and demands of Charter 08 reflect an emerging global consensus about human rights and democracy. As such, they form a connection to other charters, constitutions, and revolutionary pronouncements going back to the Enlightenment. On the other hand, some of the demands reflect the specific context of contemporary China. Which passages in the document are connected to earlier, foreign, or universal issues? Which stem from a particular Chinese context?

Preamble

This year marks 100 years since China's [first] Constitution, the 60th anniversary of the promulgation of the *Universal Declaration of Human Rights*,[1] the 30th anniversary of the birth of the Democracy Wall,[2] and the 10th year since the Chinese government signed the *International Covenant on Civil and Political Rights*.[3] Having experienced a prolonged period of human rights disasters and challenging and tortuous struggles, the awakening Chinese citizens are becoming increasingly aware that freedom, equality, and human rights are universal values shared by all humankind, and that democracy, republicanism, and constitutional government make up the basic institutional framework of modern politics. A "modernization" bereft of these universal values and this basic political framework is a disastrous process that deprives people of their rights, rots away their humanity, and destroys their dignity. . . .

The tremendous historic changes of the mid-19th century exposed the decay of the traditional Chinese autocratic system and set the stage for the greatest transformation China had seen in several thousand years. The Self-Strengthening Movement [1861–1895] sought improvements in China's technical capability by acquiring manufacturing techniques, scientific knowledge, and military technologies from the West;

[1] List of individual rights adopted by the UN General Assembly, December 1948. [Ed.]
[2] Brick wall in Beijing where political statements were posted in the Chinese democracy movement of 1978. [Ed.]
[3] Treaty adopted by UN General Assembly, December 1966, in force in 1976, signed by China in 1998. [Ed.]

China's defeat in the first Sino-Japanese War [1894–1895] once again exposed the obsolescence of its system; the Hundred Days' Reform [1898] touched upon the area of institutional innovation, but ended in failure due to cruel suppression by the die-hard faction [at the Qing court]. The Xinhai Revolution [1911], on the surface, buried the imperial system that had lasted for more than 2,000 years and established Asia's first republic. But, because of the particular historical circumstances of internal and external troubles, the republican system of government was short lived, and autocracy made a comeback.

The failure of technical imitation and institutional renewal prompted deep reflection among our countrymen on the root cause of China's cultural sickness, and the ensuing May Fourth [1919] and New Culture Movements[4] [1915–1921] under the banner of "science and democracy." But the course of China's political democratization was forcibly cut short due to frequent civil wars and foreign invasion. The process of a constitutional government began again after China's victory in the War of Resistance against Japan [1937–1945], but the outcome of the civil war between the Nationalists and the Communists plunged China into the abyss of modern-day totalitarianism. The "New China" established in 1949 is a "people's republic" in name, but in reality it is a "party domain." The ruling party monopolizes all the political, economic, and social resources. It has created a string of human rights disasters, such as the Anti-Rightist Campaign, the Great Leap Forward, the Cultural Revolution, June Fourth,[5] and the suppression of unofficial religious activities and the rights defense movement, causing tens of millions of deaths, and exacting a disastrous price from both the people and the country.

The "Reform and Opening Up" of the late 20th century extricated China from the pervasive poverty and absolute totalitarianism of the Mao Zedong era, and substantially increased private wealth and the standard of living of the common people. Individual economic freedom and social privileges were partially restored, a civil society began to grow, and calls for human rights and political freedom among the people increased by the day. . . . In 2004, the National People's Congress amended the Constitution to add that "[the State] respects and guarantees human rights." And this year, the government has promised to formulate and implement a "National Human Rights Action Plan." But so

---

[4] Chinese turn from Confucianism to embrace Western democratic values as universal. [Ed.]

[5] First three were campaigns of Mao Zedong against capitalism, the middle class, and political and personal enemies. The Great Leap Forward was also a campaign by Mao to radically collectivize the economy. It failed, causing much hardship instead. June 4th is the Chinese term for the democracy movement in 1989 called in the West the Tiananmen Square protest and massacre. [Ed.]

far, this political progress has largely remained on paper: there are laws, but there is no rule of law; there is a constitution, but no constitutional government; this is still the political reality that is obvious to all. The ruling elite continues to insist on its authoritarian grip on power, rejecting political reform. This has caused official corruption, difficulty in establishing rule of law, the absence of human rights, moral bankruptcy, social polarization, abnormal economic development, destruction of both the natural and cultural environment, no institutionalized protection of citizens' rights to freedom, property, and the pursuit of happiness, the constant accumulation of all kinds of social conflicts, and the continuous surge of resentment. . . .

Our Fundamental Concepts

At this historical juncture that will decide the future destiny of China, it is necessary to reflect on the modernization process of the past hundred and some years and reaffirm the following concepts:

Freedom: Freedom is at the core of universal values. The rights of speech, publication, belief, assembly, association, movement, to strike, and to march and demonstrate are all the concrete expressions of freedom. Where freedom does not flourish, there is no modern civilization to speak of.

Human Rights: Human rights are not bestowed by a state; they are inherent rights enjoyed by every person. Guaranteeing human rights is both the most important objective of a government and the foundation of the legitimacy of its public authority; it is also the intrinsic requirement of the policy of "putting people first." . . . People are the mainstay of a nation; a nation serves its people; government exists for the people.

Equality: The integrity, dignity, and freedom of every individual, regardless of social status, occupation, gender, economic circumstances, ethnicity, skin color, religion, or political belief, are equal. The principles of equality before the law for each and every person and equality in social, economic, cultural, and political rights of all citizens must be implemented.

Republicanism: Republicanism is "joint governing by all, peaceful coexistence," that is, the separation of powers for checks and balances and the balance of interests; that is, a community comprising many diverse interests, different social groups, and a plurality of cultures and faiths, seeking to peacefully handle public affairs on the basis of equal participation, fair competition, and joint discussion.

Democracy: The most fundamental meaning is that sovereignty resides in the people and the government elected by the people. Democracy has the following basic characteristics: (1) The legitimacy of political power comes from the people; the source of political power is the people. (2) Political control is exercised through choices made by the people. (3) Citizens enjoy the genuine right to vote; officials in key positions at all levels of government must be the product of elections at regular intervals. (4) Respect the decisions of the majority while protecting the basic human rights of the minority. In a word, democracy is the modern public instrument for creating a government "of the people, by the people, and for the people."

Constitutionalism: Constitutionalism is the principle of guaranteeing basic freedoms and rights of citizens as defined by the constitution through legal provisions and the rule of law, restricting and defining the boundaries of government power and conduct, and providing appropriate institutional capability to carry this out. In China, the era of imperial power is long gone, never to return; in the world at large, the authoritarian system is on the wane; citizens ought to become the true masters of their states. The fundamental way out for China lies only in dispelling the subservient notion of reliance on "enlightened rulers" and "upright officials," promoting public consciousness of rights as fundamental and participation as a duty, and putting into practice freedom, engaging in democracy, and respecting the law.

Our Basic Positions

Thus, in the spirit of responsible and constructive citizens, we put forth the following specific positions regarding various aspects of state administration, citizens' rights and interests, and social development:

1. **Constitutional Amendment:** Based on the aforementioned values and concepts, amend the Constitution, deleting clauses in the current Constitution that are not in conformity with the principle that sovereignty resides in the people, so that the Constitution can truly become a document that guarantees human rights and allows for the exercise of public power, and become the enforceable supreme law that no individual, group, or party can violate, establishing the foundation of the legal authority for democratizing China.

2. **Separation of Powers and Checks and Balances:** Construct a modern government that separates powers and maintains checks and balances among them, that guarantees the separation of legislative, judicial, and

executive powers. Establish the principle of statutory administration and responsible government to prevent excessive expansion of executive power; government should be responsible to taxpayers; . . . the central power must be clearly defined and mandated by the Constitution, and the localities must exercise full autonomy.

3. **Legislative Democracy:** Legislative bodies at all levels should be created through direct elections; maintain the principle of fairness and justice in making law; and implement legislative democracy.

4. **Judicial Independence:** The judiciary should transcend partisanship, be free from any interference, exercise judicial independence, and guarantee judicial fairness; it should establish a constitutional court and a system to investigate violations of the Constitution, and uphold the authority of the Constitution. . . .

5. **Public Use of Public Instruments:** Bring the armed forces under state control. Military personnel should render loyalty to the Constitution and to the country. Political party organizations should withdraw from the armed forces; raise the professional standards of the armed forces. All public employees including the police should maintain political neutrality. Abolish discrimination in hiring of public employees based on party affiliation; there should be equality in hiring regardless of party affiliation.

6. **Human Rights Guarantees:** Guarantee human rights in earnest; protect human dignity. Set up a Commission on Human Rights, responsible to the highest organ of popular will, to prevent government abuse of public authority and violations of human rights, and, especially, to guarantee the personal freedom of citizens. No one shall suffer illegal arrest, detention, subpoena, interrogation, or punishment. Abolish the Reeducation-Through-Labor system.

7. **Election of Public Officials:** Fully implement the system of democratic elections to realize equal voting rights based on "one person, one vote." Systematically and gradually implement direct elections of administrative heads at all levels. Regular elections based on free competition and citizen participation in elections for legal public office are inalienable basic human rights.

8. **Urban-Rural Equality:** Abolish the current urban-rural two-tier household registration system to realize the constitutional right of equality before the law for all citizens and guarantee the citizens' right to move freely.

9. **Freedom of Association:** Guarantee citizens' right to freedom of association. Change the current system of registration upon approval for community groups to a system of record-keeping. Lift the ban on political parties. Regulate party activities according to the Constitution and law; abolish the privilege of one-party monopoly on power; establish the principles of freedom of activities of political parties and fair competition for political parties; normalize and legally regulate party politics.

10. **Freedom of Assembly:** Freedoms to peacefully assemble, march, demonstrate, and express [opinions] are citizens' fundamental freedoms stipulated by the Constitution; they should not be subject to illegal interference and unconstitutional restrictions by the ruling party and the government.

11. **Freedom of Expression:** Realize the freedom of speech, freedom to publish, and academic freedom; guarantee the citizens' right to know and right to supervise [public institutions]. Enact a "News Law" and a "Publishing Law," lift the ban on reporting, repeal the "crime of inciting subversion of state power" clause in the current *Criminal Law*, and put an end to punishing speech as a crime.

12. **Freedom of Religion:** Guarantee freedom of religion and freedom of belief, and implement separation of religion and state so that activities involving religion and faith are not subjected to government interference. Examine and repeal administrative statutes, administrative rules, and local statutes that restrict or deprive citizens of religious freedom; ban management of religious activities by administrative legislation. Abolish the system that requires that religious groups (and including places of worship) obtain prior approval of their legal status in order to register, and replace it with a system of record-keeping that requires no scrutiny.

13. **Civic Education:** Abolish political education and political examinations that are heavy on ideology and serve the one-party rule. Popularize civic education based on universal values and civil rights, establish civic consciousness, and advocate civic virtues that serve society.

14. **Property Protection:** Establish and protect private property rights, and implement a system based on a free and open market economy; guarantee entrepreneurial freedom, and eliminate administrative monopolies; set up a Committee for the Management of State-Owned Property, responsible to the highest organ of popular will; launch reform of property rights in a legal and orderly fashion, and clarify the ownership of property rights and those responsible; launch a new land movement,

advance land privatization, and guarantee in earnest the land property rights of citizens, particularly the farmers.

15. **Fiscal Reform:** Democratize public finances and guarantee taxpayers' rights. Set up the structure and operational mechanism of a public finance system with clearly defined authority and responsibilities, and establish a rational and effective system of decentralized financial authority among various levels of government; carry out a major reform of the tax system, so as to reduce tax rates, simplify the tax system, and equalize the tax burden. Administrative departments may not increase taxes or create new taxes at will without sanction by society obtained through a public elective process and resolution by organs of popular will. Pass property rights reform to diversify and introduce competition mechanisms into the market; lower the threshold for entry into the financial field and create conditions for the development of privately-owned financial enterprises, and fully energize the financial system.

16. **Social Security:** Establish a social security system that covers all citizens and provides them with basic security in education, medical care, care for the elderly, and employment.

17. **Environmental Protection:** Protect the ecological environment, promote sustainable development, and take responsibility for future generations and all humanity; clarify and impose the appropriate responsibilities that state and government officials at all levels must take to this end; promote participation and oversight by civil society groups in environmental protection.

18. **Federal Republic:** Take part in maintaining regional peace and development with an attitude of equality and fairness, and create an image of a responsible great power. Protect the free systems of Hong Kong and Macau. On the premise of freedom and democracy, seek a reconciliation plan for the mainland and Taiwan through equal negotiations and cooperative interaction. Wisely explore possible paths and institutional blueprints for the common prosperity of all ethnic groups, and establish the Federal Republic of China under the framework of a democratic and constitutional government.

19. **Transitional Justice:** Restore the reputation of and give state compensation to individuals, as well as their families, who suffered political persecution during past political movements; release all political prisoners and prisoners of conscience; release all people convicted for their beliefs; establish a Commission for Truth Investigation to find the truth of historical events, determine responsibility, and uphold justice; seek social reconciliation on this foundation.

Occupy Wall Street, 2011

In the wake of a global financial crisis in 2008 and the following "Great Recession" that in some countries duplicated the effects of the Great Depression of the 1930s, a number of movements sprang up in opposition to what were seen as the progenitors of the crisis: Wall Street, corporations, crony capitalism, government support of big money, and economic inequality. One of the most visible of these protests, because of its location, was Occupy Wall Street. But similar groups sprang up in cities in the United States and throughout the world. Here we see a declaration from the New York group as well as images from protests on both Wall Street and in Adelaide, New Zealand.

Critics of the protests frequently said that it was not clear what the protesters wanted. What does the New York document tell you about the demands of the protesters? Do they seem to be all over the map, or is there a unifying theme? In what ways would the realization of these goals increase democracy? How are these economic demands different from the more political demands of previous movements documented in this chapter?

Finally, look at the two photos. Do they suggest diverse protests across the globe or a considerable degree of consensus? Are these images from opposite sides of the world distinct or interchangeable?

THINKING HISTORICALLY

The demands in the New York declaration spring from the specific context of the financial crisis in the United States. Yet the authors reach out to connect with movements throughout the world. How does a national context become a global context? What phrases or stylistic features connect this document to other declarations or manifestos of the past?

Declaration of the Occupation of New York City

This document was accepted by the NYC General Assembly on September 29, 2011.

As we gather together in solidarity to express a feeling of mass injustice, we must not lose sight of what brought us together. We write so that all people who feel wronged by the corporate forces of the world can know that we are your allies.

Source: http://www.nycga.net/resources/declaration/ or http://occupywallst.org/forum /first-official-release-from-occupy-wall-street/

As one people, united, we acknowledge the reality: that the future of the human race requires the cooperation of its members; that our system must protect our rights, and upon corruption of that system, it is up to the individuals to protect their own rights, and those of their neighbors; that a democratic government derives its just power from the people, but corporations do not seek consent to extract wealth from the people and the Earth; and that no true democracy is attainable when the process is determined by economic power. We come to you at a time when corporations, which place profit over people, self-interest over justice, and oppression over equality, run our governments. We have peaceably assembled here, as is our right, to let these facts be known.

- They have taken our houses through an illegal foreclosure process, despite not having the original mortgage.
- They have taken bailouts from taxpayers with impunity, and continue to give Executives exorbitant bonuses.
- They have perpetuated inequality and discrimination in the workplace based on age, the color of one's skin, sex, gender identity and sexual orientation.
- They have poisoned the food supply through negligence, and undermined the farming system through monopolization.
- They have profited off of the torture, confinement, and cruel treatment of countless animals, and actively hide these practices.
- They have continuously sought to strip employees of the right to negotiate for better pay and safer working conditions.
- They have held students hostage with tens of thousands of dollars of debt on education, which is itself a human right.
- They have consistently outsourced labor and used that outsourcing as leverage to cut workers' healthcare and pay.
- They have influenced the courts to achieve the same rights as people, with none of the culpability or responsibility.
- They have spent millions of dollars on legal teams that look for ways to get them out of contracts in regards to health insurance.
- They have sold our privacy as a commodity.
- They have used the military and police force to prevent freedom of the press.
- They have deliberately declined to recall faulty products endangering lives in pursuit of profit.
- They determine economic policy, despite the catastrophic failures their policies have produced and continue to produce.
- They have donated large sums of money to politicians, who are responsible for regulating them.
- They continue to block alternate forms of energy to keep us dependent on oil.

- They continue to block generic forms of medicine that could save people's lives or provide relief in order to protect investments that have already turned a substantial profit.
- They have purposely covered up oil spills, accidents, faulty book-keeping, and inactive ingredients in pursuit of profit.
- They purposefully keep people misinformed and fearful through their control of the media.
- They have accepted private contracts to murder prisoners even when presented with serious doubts about their guilt.
- They have perpetuated colonialism at home and abroad.
- They have participated in the torture and murder of innocent civilians overseas.
- They continue to create weapons of mass destruction in order to receive government contracts.

To the people of the world,

We, the New York City General Assembly occupying Wall Street in Liberty Square, urge you to assert your power.

Exercise your right to peaceably assemble; occupy public space; create a process to address the problems we face, and generate solutions accessible to everyone.

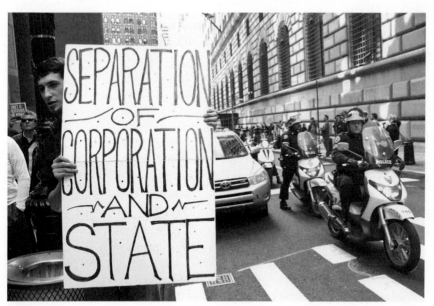

Figure 27.1 Occupy Wall Street, 2011.
Source: Tomas Abad/Alamy.

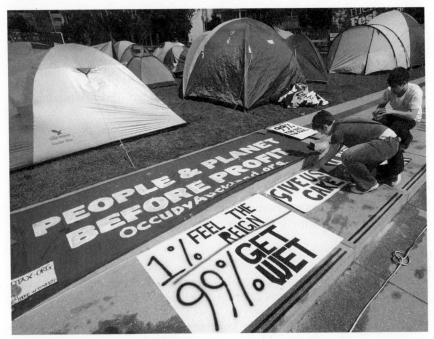

Figure 27.2 Occupy Aukland, New Zealand, 2011.
Source: EPA/Kim Ludbrook/Landov.

To all communities that take action and form groups in the spirit of direct democracy, we offer support, documentation, and all of the resources at our disposal.

Join us and make your voices heard!

8

WILLIAM MOSS WILSON

Just Don't Call Her Che, 2012

This piece from the *New York Times* is interesting in a number of ways. As a media phenomenon: Camila Vallejo, a striking unknown becomes a global media sensation. It is also interesting in that it turns our study of new democracy movements full circle since many of the

Source: William Moss Wilson, "Just Don't Call Her Che" (*New York Times*, January 29, 2012), SR 5.

democratic movements since 1977 were related to the fall of communism in the Soviet Union and its satellites, and this woman declares
herself a communist. Further, Chile is already perceived as something
of a democratic success story: The age of dictator Augusto Pinochet
has been discredited, and democratic elections have brought new
leaders from the socialist party that elected Salvador Allende in 1970.
And yet, as Wilson writes, Chile is still the thirteenth most unequal
country in the world and that inequality manifests itself glaringly in
the meager state support for public education.

So this article raises some important questions in Chile that might
be asked in the United States and other countries that have already
experienced democratic revolutions. How important is education to
democracy? How important is equal access to education? What is
the impact of high fees, heavy loans, private institutions for the
wealthy, separate educational tracks for rich and poor? Is education
a human right? Is equal access to education a necessary ingredient of
democracy in the modern knowledge economy?

THINKING HISTORICALLY

Asking about connections and context (or what is borrowed from elsewhere and what is invented in the local context) in a political movement
is difficult enough when we have a primary source to draw on. Here we
have only the journalist's account. Nevertheless, what in Wilson's description of this movement suggests possible connections to Gene Sharp
or Wael Ghonim? What strikes you as more likely local or Chilean?

Late last month the British newspaper *The Guardian* asked readers to
vote for its person of the year. The candidates included household names
like German Chancellor Angela Merkel, the Egyptian techno-revolutionary
Wael Ghonim and the Burmese pro-democracy leader Daw Aung San Suu
Kyi. All placed far behind a striking, nose-ringed student from Chile
named Camila Vallejo.

Though far from a familiar face in the United States, the 23-year-old
Ms. Vallejo has gained rock-star status among the global activist class.
Since June she has led regular street marches of up to 200,000 people
through Santiago's broad avenues — the largest demonstrations since the
waning days of the Pinochet regime in the late 1980s. Under her leadership, the mobilization, known as the Chilean Winter, has gained nation-
wide support; one of its slogans, "We are the 90 percent," referred to its
approval rating in late September.

Ms. Vallejo's charismatic leadership has led commentators to make
the obligatory comparisons to other Latin American leftist icons like
Subcomandante Marcos and Che Guevara. Yet "Commander Camila,"
as her followers call her, has become a personality in her own regard.

She skewers senators in primetime TV debates and stays on message with daytime talk-show hosts hungry for lurid details about her personal life, while her eloquence gives her a preternatural ability to connect with an audience far beyond her left-wing base.

In perhaps the most poignant set piece in the year of the protester, Ms. Vallejo addressed a dense ring of photographers and reporters in August while kneeling within a peace sign made of spent teargas shells, where she calmly mused about how many educational improvements could have been bought with the $100,000 worth of munitions at her feet.

Ms. Vallejo, like many of her fellow student leaders, is an avowed communist. But while she has publicly commended other regional leftists like Presidents Evo Morales of Bolivia and Rafael Correa of Ecuador, she and her generation have little in common with the older left of Fidel Castro or Hugo Chávez. They are less ideological purists than change-seeking pragmatists, even if that means working within the existing political order.

Still, there's no question that the movement is upending Chilean society. True, it is centered on a policy question, namely reforming an educational system that disproportionally favors the children of wealthy families. But the earth-shaking Paris protests in 1968 also began with calls for university reform — before spiraling into street battles between radicalized students and truncheon-wielding gendarmes, opposing symbols in the culture war between old and new France.

The same process is under way in Chile. As the protests increasingly devolve into rock and tear-gas exchanges between students and the police, it's becoming clear that more than education policy is at stake: a nonviolent social revolution in which disaffected, politically savvy youth are trying to overthrow the mores of an older generation, one they feel is still tainted by the legacy of Pinochet. It is not just about policy reform, but also about changing the underlying timbers of Chilean society.

It's no surprise that the movement should be led by someone as charismatic as Ms. Vallejo. Paris 1968 had its celebrity protesters, handsome faces that brought hundreds of thousands into the streets, photogenic young men like Jacques Sauvageot and Daniel Cohn-Bendit. Chile has Ms. Vallejo.

Chile is perhaps Latin America's greatest success story. After decades of authoritarian rule, it has spent the last 20 years building a thriving economy with a renewed democratic culture and a booming, educated middle class. But it is also confronting a dangerous imbalance: While the liberalization of higher education has led to improvements in access, tuition has consistently outpaced inflation and now represents 40 percent of the average household's income.

At the same time, protesters say that wealthy students from private and expensive, co-pay charter schools have unfair access to elite universities, while the rest struggle to meet entrance standards at under-financed public institutions.

Criticism of the university system has been growing for years, but it was only in April that, energized by protests against a dam in Patagonia, students finally took to the streets. The protests grew over the winter; by the first press conference held by the national confederation of student unions, known as the Confech, Ms. Vallejo had emerged as its leader.

Echoing 1960s street activism, the Chilean Winter dabbled in the absurd, but with a high-tech, social-media twist. Thousands gathered in front of the presidential palace in June dressed as zombies, then broke into a choreographed dance to Michael Jackson's "Thriller." In July, students again gathered in front of the palace for a huge "kiss-in."

Though the ideas came, said Giorgio Jackson, former student president of Chile's Catholic University, from "everywhere, absolutely every local space," the movement's success hinged on the leadership's ability to channel such creativity while maintaining a unified front to government and the media. The organization used a Web site to gather ideas and disseminate content for placards and posters. And it has used Ms. Vallejo's 300,000-plus Twitter followers to quickly initiate huge "cacerolazos," a form of dictatorship-era protest where people walk the streets banging on pots and pans.

While they vow to continue until all their lofty demands are met, the students have already scored some political victories. The government's proposed 2012 budget has a $350 million increase for higher education, with promises to finance scholarships for qualifying students from families up to the 60th percentile in household income. Meanwhile, the year began with the naming of Chile's third education minister in six months.

It was only a matter of time, perhaps, before the movement's focus on education began to broaden. As more support for the movement came from outside the universities, its interests changed accordingly. "This year we have already started talking about political reforms and tax reforms, and we think the students and youth in general play an important role in profound reforms in the country," said Noam Titelman, the new student president at Catholic University.

Tax reform is, not coincidentally, now at the top of the government's agenda. And rightly so: though it has the largest economy in Latin America, Chile is the 13th most unequal country in the world.

"Something very powerful that has come out of the heart of this movement is that people are really questioning the economic policies of the country," Ms. Vallejo said. "People are not tolerating the way a small number of economic groups benefit from the system. Having a market economy is really different from having a market society. What we are asking for, via education reform, is that the state take on a different role."

The movement has also begun to spread regionally. Ms. Vallejo lent her star power to Brazilian student protests in August, while in November students demonstrated in France, Germany and several other countries in support of Confech's Latin American March for Education.

"The student movement here is permanently connected to other student movements, principally in Latin America, but also in the world," Ms. Vallejo said. "We believe this reveals something fundamental: that there is a global demand for the recovery and defense of the right to education."

But the students clearly have a lot to learn about real-world politics. Ms. Vallejo and other student leaders spent weeks lobbying in Parliament, only to be left out of the final budget negotiations.

Frustration with Ms. Vallejo's strategy propelled a rival leftist, Gabriel Boric, to challenge her in the latest round of student-government elections. On Dec. 7, national TV news crews lingered past 5 a.m. outside the University of Chile to cover a stunning defeat for the world's most famous student leader.

Yet even in her early-morning concession speech, Ms. Vallejo claimed victory, recognizing that the movement was greater than any one figure. Indeed, her rise has barely broken stride. She just left for a speaking tour in Europe, while her first book, a collection of her speeches and essays for the last year, is rising through the best-seller ranks. And she is being heavily courted by the Communist Party to run at the top of its list for the Chilean Congress in the 2013 elections.

For all its recent stumbles, the movement's prospects of getting a woman under 26 elected to Congress would help fulfill one of its underlying aims, to kindle young people's interest in traditional politics. This may be Ms. Vallejo's greatest contribution: to restore faith in a discredited system by showing a new generation that politics can be responsive to the people's demands.

▪ REFLECTIONS

This chapter has argued that democracy is new and spreading, especially in recent years and decades. But any argument has to bear the burden of a counterargument. How might we counter the argument of this chapter?

First we might point out that a claim for recent years or decades is always subject to the near-sightedness of the present. Recent events and movements that seem important now may well disappear from the longer view a hundred or five hundred years from now. A century from now, will the six years of Gorbachev's reform become a blip, possibly like the Russian Revolution of 1905 or even that of 1917, in a long history of continued Czarism from Saint Vladimir I's rule during the tenth century through Putin VI's rule in the twenty-second century? Will the Arab Spring seem like the seasonal change the term implies rather than the beginning of a new age? Has Egypt seen its last pharaoh or was Mubarak only the most recent?

This line of questioning rests, I think too much, on a belief that the past is far more continuous than it is. Many other fifty-year periods of the past experienced as many protests as our own age. Many other historical periods produced protests of the have-nots against the haves. But the ideas and vocabulary of democracy are certainly new at least to recent centuries. No peasant uprising of the ancient or medieval world called for elected representatives, universal suffrage, equality before the law, the people as source of the law, freedom of expression, belief, and religion, universal education, social justice, and human rights. These are all principles and practices that have evolved and developed over the last couple of centuries. They all have earlier roots, but taken together they form a set of hopes, expectations, and experiences that are distinctly modern. Times *do* change.

A second line of criticism might run like this. Even if democracy is a modern idea and experience, how can we certify a flowering in a couple of protests, many of which have been thwarted or defeated? Gorbachev's democratization, after all, occurred twenty-five years ago and even Russians do not remember it fondly. Some of the democratic gains that were won by Gorbachev by 1991 receded in the following years under Boris Yeltsin, first President of the Russian Federation (1991–1999), and Vladimir Putin (president and prime minister since 1999). To take one indicator of glasnost—press freedom—since 1993 over 200 Russian journalists have been murdered, making Russia the third most dangerous country in the world for a free press. Gorbachev today calls for a new wave of democratic protests in Russia: something like the Arab Spring. And what about the Arab Spring? Only a year after 2011 the optimism of the Arab Spring has soured for many Egyptians who thrilled to the prospect of a liberal civic society for all Egyptians— Christian and Muslim—as the Muslim Brotherhood Party's struggle against the unyielding military squeezes out secular democrats. In more secular Tunisia, the achievement of democratic revolution, one Tunisian recently quipped, is that now "everyone is above the law."[1] In Libya, the revolution that deposed Gaddafi reverted to tribal war, the uprising in Syria led to sectarian conflict and civil war, and those of Bahrain and Yemen were crushed (with some U.S. support).

To this argument, I would respond that the Arab revolution is definitely a work in progress. It occurs in a part of the world where democracy was least expected. The same might be said of the former Soviet Union. Gorbachev started a process that unleashed democratic and national independence movements throughout the former Soviet dominions. Some of these continue to be controlled by single parties or strong men, but not all. Czechoslovakia managed a peaceful Velvet Revolution and then a peaceful divorce between the Czech Republic

---

[1] Quoted by Michael J. Totten, Dispatches, April 18, 2012, at http://www .worldaffairsjournal.org/blogs/michael-j-totten.

and Slovakia. Poland and Hungary have become viable democracies. The Baltic states—Estonia, Lithuania, and Latvia—are independent republics. Many of the former Soviet states like Ukraine, Belarus, and "the stans" are independent. And, perhaps most remarkably of all, the former East Germany became independent, then part of a unified German state, one of the most democratic in Europe. One can carp about backsliding in Russia and the rise of supernationalists in Hungary, but there is no way to dismiss the numbers of people or countries who now govern themselves. Their example and the example of even temporarily successful democratic revolutions from the Philippines to Paraguay have buttressed the expectation that self-government in a free society is the right of all.

Democracy is not a light turned on, or off. It is a process that advances, or recedes. Still the advances are more contagious and longer lasting, at least in the mind. Few want to return to the conditions of dictatorship. But the process is rarely smooth. There are those in any society who lose privilege or power in a democratic revolution. And they are, by definition, the privileged and powerful.

The Mothers of the Disappeared still gather around the Plaza de Mayo; they still seek a full accounting for the acts of state terrorism under the military junta of the 1970s. Students in Chile are fighting battles fought by their parents and grandparents. Latin Americans celebrate democratic and independence movements that go back hundreds of years, but that have still not been fully realized. Indeed, in the Americas and the rest of the world the goalposts have moved since the days when democratic states accepted enslaved Africans, invisible Indians, and colonial subjects. Recent claims for human rights, freedom from sexual or gender discrimination, international jurisdiction over war crimes and genocide are all extensions of our democratic expectations. Failure or retrenchment can be seen as the setting of the next battle rather than a sign that democracy failed or, worse, that it doesn't work.

Democratic demands in the twenty-first century reach further than ever before. Likewise, the conditions for achieving democracy have also expanded. A democracy that was limited to white men of the propertied class could function with an educational system that ignored everyone else. A mass democracy requires a mass citizenry educated to think and participate intelligently. It requires what Franklin D. Roosevelt called "freedom from want" to allow all citizens the time and resources to participate. And it requires the level playing field, unencumbered by special interests with private agendas. The early years of modern liberal democracy heard the call for the separation of church and state. Today we hear the call for the separation of corporations and the state. The effort to create the public space where citizens can create their common world continues.

28

Globalization

The World, 1990 to the Present

■ HISTORICAL CONTEXT

Globalization is a term used by historians, economists, politicians, religious leaders, social reformers, business people, and average citizens to describe large-scale changes and trends in the world today. It is often defined as a complex phenomenon whereby individuals, nations, and regions of the world become increasingly integrated and interdependent, while national and traditional identities are diminished. Although it is a widely used term, *globalization* is also a controversial and widely debated topic. Is globalization really a new phenomenon, or is it a continuation of earlier trends? Is it driven by technological forces or economic forces, or both? Does it enrich or impoverish? Is it democratizing or antidemocratic? Is it generally a positive or negative thing?

Some limit the definition of globalization to the global integration driven by the development of the international market economy in the last twenty to forty years. Worldwide integration dates back much further, however, and has important technological, cultural, and political causes as well. In fact, all of human history can be understood as the story of increased interaction on a limited planet. Ancient empires brought diverse peoples from vast regions of the world together under single administrations. These empires, connected by land or maritime routes, interacted with each other through trade and exploration, exchanging goods as well as ideas. The unification of the Eastern and Western hemispheres after 1492 was a major step in the globalization of crops, peoples, cultures, and diseases. The industrial revolution joined countries and continents in ever vaster and faster transportation and communication networks. The great colonial empires that developed during the eighteenth and nineteenth centuries integrated the populations of far-flung areas of the world. The commercial aspects of these developments cannot be divorced from religious zeal, technological innovations, and political motives, which were often driving factors.

The current era of economic globalization is largely a product of the industrial capitalist world, roughly dating back to the middle of the nineteenth century. We might call the period between 1850 and 1914 the first great age of globalization in the modern sense. It was the age of ocean liners, mass migrations, undersea telegraph cables, transcontinental railroads, refrigeration, and preserved canned foods, when huge European empires dramatically reduced the number of sovereign states in the world. The period ended with World War I, which not only dug trenches between nations and wiped out a generation of future migrants and visitors, but also planted seeds of animosity that festered for decades, strangling the growth of international trade, interaction, and immigration.

Since the conclusion of World War II in 1945, and increasingly since the end of the Cold War in 1989, political and technological developments have enabled economic globalization on a wider scale and at a faster pace than occurred during the previous age of steamships and telegraphs. The collapse of the Soviet Union and international communism unleashed the forces of market capitalism as never before. Jet travel, satellite technology, mobile phones, and the World Wide Web have revived global integration and enabled the global marketplace. The United States, the World Bank, and the International Monetary Fund led in the creation of regional and international free-trade agreements, the reduction of tariffs, and the removal of national trade barriers, touting these changes as agents of material progress and democratic transformation. Yet these changes have also elicited wide-ranging resistance in peaceful protests, especially against the West's economic dominance, and violent ones against the West's political and cultural domination, such as the terrorist attacks on September 11, 2001.

Multinational companies are now able to generate great wealth by moving capital, labor, raw materials, and finished products through international markets at increasing speeds and with lasting impact. This economic globalization has profound cultural ramifications; increasingly the peoples of the world are watching the same films and television programs, speaking the same languages, wearing the same clothes, enjoying the same amusements, and listening to the same music. Whether free-market capitalism lifts all boats, or only yachts, is a hotly debated issue today.

■ THINKING HISTORICALLY

Understanding Process

What are the most important ways in which the world is changing? What are the most significant and powerful forces of change? What is the engine that is driving our world? These are the big questions raised at the end of historical investigation. They also arise at the beginning, as the assumptions that shape our specific investigations. *Globalization* is one of the words most frequently used to describe the big changes that are occurring in our world. All of the readings in this chapter assume or describe some kind of global integration as a dominant driver of the world in which we live. This chapter asks you to think about large-scale historical processes. It asks you to examine globalization as one of the most important of these processes. It asks you to reflect on what globalization means, and what causes it. How does each of these authors use the term? Do the authors see this process as primarily commercial and market-driven, or do they view it as a matter of culture or politics? Does globalization come from one place or many, from a center outwards, or from one kind of society to another? Is globalization linear or unidirectional, or does it have differing, even opposite effects? What do these writers, thinkers, and activists believe about the most important changes transforming our world? And what do you think?

1

SHERIF HETATA

Dollarization, 1998

Sherif Hetata is an Egyptian intellectual, novelist, and activist who was originally trained as a medical doctor. He and his wife, the prominent feminist writer Nawal El-Saadawi, have worked together to promote reform in Egypt and the larger Arab world. In this presentation given at a conference on globalization, Hetata outlines the global economy's homogenizing effects on culture. Through what historic lens does Hetata view globalization? What links does he make between globalization and imperialism? What do you think of his argument?

Source: Sherif Hetata, "Dollarization, Fragmentation, and God," in *The Cultures of Globalization*, ed. Fredric Jameson and Masao Miyoshi (Durham, NC: Duke University Press, 1998), 273–74, 276–80.

THINKING HISTORICALLY

What, according to Hetata, is the main process that is changing the world? Does he think the engine of world change is primarily techno-logical, commercial, or cultural?

As a young medical student, born and brought up in a colony, like many other people in my country, Egypt, I quickly learned to make the link between politics, economics, culture, and religion. Educated in an English school, I discovered that my English teachers looked down on us. We learned Rudyard Kipling by heart, praised the glories of the British Empire, followed the adventures of Kim in India, imbibed the culture of British supremacy, and sang carols on Christmas night.

At the medical school in university, when students demonstrated against occupation by British troops it was the Moslem Brothers who beat them up, using iron chains and long curved knives, and it was the governments supported by the king that shot at them or locked them up.

When I graduated in 1946, the hospital wards taught me how poverty and health are linked. I needed only another step to know that poverty had something to do with colonial rule, with the king who supported it, with class and race, with what was called imperialism at the time, with cotton prices falling on the market, with the seizure of land by foreign banks. These things were common talk in family gatherings, expressed in a simple, colorful language without frills. They were the facts of everyday life. We did not need to read books to make the links: They were there for us to see and grasp. And every time we made a link, some-one told us it was time to stop, someone in authority whom we did not like: a ruler or a father, a policeman or a teacher, a landowner, a *maulana* (religious leader or teacher), a Jesuit, or a God.

And if we went on making these links, they locked us up.

For me, therefore, coming from this background, cultural studies and globalization open up a vast horizon, one of global links in a world where things are changing quickly. It is a chance to learn and probe how the economics, the politics, the culture, the philosophical thought of our days connect or disconnect, harmonize or contradict.

Of course, I will not even try to deal with all of that. I just want to raise a few points to discuss under the title of my talk, "Dollarization, Fragmentation, and God." Because I come from Egypt, my vantage point will be that of someone looking at the globe from the part we now call South, rather than "third world" or something else.

A New Economic Order: Gazing North at the Global Few

Never before in the history of the world has there been such a concentration and centralization of capital in so few nations and in the hands of so few people. The countries that form the Group of Seven,[1] with their 800 million inhabitants, control more technological, economic, informatics, and military power than the rest of the approximately 4.3 billion who live in Asia, Africa, Eastern Europe, and Latin America.

Five hundred multinational corporations account for 80 percent of world trade and 75 percent of investment. Half of all the multinational corporations are based in the United States, Germany, Japan, and Switzerland. The OECD (Organisation for Economic Cooperation and Development) group of countries contributes 80 percent of world production. . . .

A Global Culture for a Global Market

To expand the world market, to globalize it, to maintain the New Economic Order, the multinational corporations use economic power and control politics and the armed forces. But this is not so easy. People will always resist being exploited, resist injustice, struggle for their freedom, their needs, security, a better life, peace.

However, it becomes easier if they can be convinced to do what the masters of the global economy want them to do. This is where the issue of culture comes in. Culture can serve in different ways to help the global economy reach out all over the world and expand its markets to the most distant regions. Culture can also serve to reduce or destroy or prevent or divide or outflank the resistance of people who do not like what is happening to them, or have their doubts about it, or want to think. Culture can be like cocaine, which is going global these days: from Kali in Colombia to Texas, to Madrid, to the Italian mafiosi in southern Italy, to Moscow, Burma, and Thailand, a worldwide network uses the methods and the cover of big business, with a total trade of $5 billion a year, midway between oil and the arms trade.

At the disposal of global culture today are powerful means that function across the whole world: the media, which, like the economy, have made it one world, a bipolar North/South world. If genetic engineering gives scientists the possibility of programming embryos before children are born, children, youth, and adults are now being programmed after

---

[1] Canada, France, Germany, Italy, Japan, the United Kingdom, and the United States meet as the G7. [Ed.]

they are born in the culture they imbibe mainly through the media, but also in the family, in school, at the university, and elsewhere. Is this an exaggeration? an excessively gloomy picture of the world?

To expand the global market, increase the number of consumers, make sure that they buy what is sold, develop needs that conform to what is produced, and develop the fever of consumerism, culture must play a role in developing certain values, patterns of behavior, visions of what is happiness and success in the world, attitudes toward sex and love. Culture must model a global consumer.

In some ways, I was a "conservative radical." I went to jail, but I always dressed in a classical, subdued way. When my son started wearing blue jeans and New Balance shoes, I shivered with horror. He's going to become like some of those crazy kids abroad, the disco generation, I thought! Until the age of twenty-five he adamantly refused to smoke. Now he smokes two packs of Marlboros a day (the ones that the macho cowboy smokes). That does not prevent him from being a talented film director. But in the third-world, films, TV, and other media have increased the percentage of smokers. I saw half-starved kids in a marketplace in Mali buying single imported Benson & Hedges cigarettes and smoking.

But worse was still to come. Something happened that to me seemed impossible at one time, more difficult than adhering to a leftwing movement. At the age of seventy-one, I have taken to wearing blue jeans and Nike shoes. I listen to rock and reggae and sometimes rap. I like to go to discos and I sometimes have other cravings, which so far I have successfully fought! And I know these things have crept into our lives through the media, through TV, films, radio, advertisements, newspapers, and even novels, music, and poetry. It's a culture and it's reaching out, becoming global.

In my village, I have a friend. He is a peasant and we are very close. He lives in a big mud hut, and the animals (buffalo, sheep, cows, and donkeys) live in the house with him. Altogether, in the household, with the wife and children of his brother, his uncle, the mother, and his own family, there are thirty people. He wears a long *galabeya* (robe), works in the fields for long hours, and eats food cooked in the mud oven.

But when he married, he rode around the village in a hired Peugeot car with his bride. She wore a white wedding dress, her face was made up like a film star, her hair curled at the hairdresser's of the provincial town, her finger and toe nails manicured and polished, and her body bathed with special soap and perfumes. At the marriage ceremony, they had a wedding cake, which she cut with her husband's hand over hers. Very different from the customary rural marriage ceremony of his father. And all this change in the notion of beauty, of femininity, of celebration, of happiness, of prestige, of progress happened to my peasant friend and his bride in one generation.

The culprit, or the benevolent agent, depending on how you see it, was television.

In the past years, television has been the subject of numerous studies. In France, such studies have shown that before the age of twelve a child will have been exposed to an average 100,000 TV advertisements. Through these TV advertisements, the young boy or girl will have assimilated a whole set of values and behavioral patterns, of which he or she is not aware, of course. They become a part of his or her psychological (emotional and mental) makeup. Linked to these values are the norms and ways in which we see good and evil, beauty and ugliness, justice and injustice, truth and falseness, and which are being propagated at the same time. In other words, the fundamental values that form our aesthetic and moral vision of things are being inculcated, even hammered home, at this early stage, and they remain almost unchanged throughout life.

The commercial media no longer worry about the truthfulness or falsity of what they portray. Their role is to sell: beauty products, for example, to propagate the "beauty myth" and a "beauty culture" for both females and males alike and ensure that it reaches the farthest corners of the earth, including my village in the Delta of the Nile. Many of these beauty products are harmful to the health, can cause allergic disorders or skin infections or even worse. They cost money, work on the sex drives, and transform women and men, but especially women, into sex objects. They hide the real person, the natural beauty, the process of time, the stages of life, and instill false values about who we are, can be, or should become.

Advertisements do not depend on verifiable information or even rational thinking. They depend for their effect on images, colors, smart technical production, associations, and hidden drives. For them, attracting the opposite sex or social success or professional achievement and promotion or happiness do not depend on truthfulness or hard work or character, but rather on seduction, having a powerful car, buying things or people. . . .

Thus the media produce and reproduce the culture of consumption, of violence and sex to ensure that the global economic powers, the multinational corporations can promote a global market for themselves and protect it. And when everything is being bought or sold everyday and at all times in this vast supermarket, including culture, art, science, and thought, prostitution can become a way of life, for everything is priced. The search for the immediate need, the fleeting pleasure, the quick enjoyment, the commodity to buy, excess, pornography, drugs keeps this global economy rolling, for to stop is suicide.

PHILIPPE LEGRAIN

Cultural Globalization Is Not Americanization, 2003

Philippe Legrain, an economist, journalist, and former advisor to the
World Trade Organization, takes aim at what he calls the myths of
globalization in the following article. What, according to him, are
these myths? What are the consequences of globalization according
to Legrain? What evidence does he cite to support his argument?
How does his view differ from that of Hetata?

THINKING HISTORICALLY

Does Legrain believe the driving force of globalization is economic
or cultural? How important does he think globalization is? How,
according to the author, is globalization changing the world?

Fears that globalization is imposing a deadening cultural uniformity are
as ubiquitous as Coca-Cola, McDonald's, and Mickey Mouse. Europeans
and Latin Americans, left-wingers and right, rich and poor—all of them
dread that local cultures and national identities are dissolving into a
crass All-American consumerism. That cultural imperialism is said to
impose American values as well as products, promote the commercial at
the expense of the authentic, and substitute shallow gratification for
deeper satisfaction.

. . . If critics of globalization were less obsessed with "Cocacoloniza-
tion," they might notice a rich feast of cultural mixing that belies fears
about Americanized uniformity. Algerians in Paris practice Thai boxing;
Asian rappers in London snack on Turkish pizza; Salman Rushdie de-
lights readers everywhere with his Anglo-Indian tales. Although—as
with any change—there can be downsides to cultural globalization, this
cross-fertilization is overwhelmingly a force for good.

The beauty of globalization is that it can free people from the tyranny of geography. Just because someone was born in France does not
mean they can only aspire to speak French, eat French food, read French
books, visit museums in France, and so on. A Frenchman—or an American, for that matter—can take holidays in Spain or Florida, eat sushi or
spaghetti for dinner, drink Coke or Chilean wine, watch a Hollywood
blockbuster or an Almodóvar, listen to bhangra or rap, practice yoga or

Source: Philippe Legrain, "Cultural Globalization Is Not Americanization," *Chronicle of
Higher Education* 49, no. 35 (May 9, 2003): B7.

kickboxing, read *Elle* or *The Economist*, and have friends from around the world. That we are increasingly free to choose our cultural experiences enriches our lives immeasurably. We could not always enjoy the best the world has to offer.

Globalization not only increases individual freedom, but also revitalizes cultures and cultural artifacts through foreign influences, technologies, and markets. Thriving cultures are not set in stone. They are forever changing from within and without. Each generation challenges the previous one; science and technology alter the way we see ourselves and the world; fashions come and go; experience and events influence our beliefs; outsiders affect us for good and ill.

Many of the best things come from cultures mixing: V. S. Naipaul's Anglo-Indo-Caribbean writing, Paul Gauguin painting in Polynesia, or the African rhythms in rock 'n' roll. Behold the great British curry. Admire the many-colored faces of France's World Cup–winning soccer team, the ferment of ideas that came from Eastern Europe's Jewish diaspora, and the cosmopolitan cities of London and New York. Western numbers are actually Arabic; zero comes most recently from India; Icelandic, French, and Sanskrit stem from a common root.

John Stuart Mill was right: "The economical benefits of commerce are surpassed in importance by those of its effects which are intellectual and moral. It is hardly possible to overrate the value, for the improvement of human beings, of things which bring them into contact with persons dissimilar to themselves, and with modes of thought and action unlike those with which they are familiar. . . . It is indispensable to be perpetually comparing [one's] own notions and customs with the experience and example of persons in different circumstances. . . . There is no nation which does not need to borrow from others."

It is a myth that globalization involves the imposition of Americanized uniformity, rather than an explosion of cultural exchange. For a start, many archetypal "American" products are not as all-American as they seem. Levi Strauss, a German immigrant, invented jeans by combining denim cloth (or "serge de Nîmes," because it was traditionally woven in the French town) with Genes, a style of trousers worn by Genoese sailors. So Levi's jeans are in fact an American twist on a European hybrid. Even quintessentially American exports are often tailored to local tastes. MTV in Asia promotes Thai pop stars and plays rock music sung in Mandarin. CNN en Español offers a Latin American take on world news. McDonald's sells beer in France, lamb in India, and chili in Mexico.

In some ways, America is an outlier, not a global leader. Most of the world has adopted the metric system born from the French Revolution; America persists with antiquated measurements inherited from its British-colonial past. Most developed countries have become intensely secular, but many Americans burn with fundamentalist fervor—like

Muslims in the Middle East. Where else in the developed world could there be a serious debate about teaching kids Bible-inspired "creationism" instead of Darwinist evolution?

America's tastes in sports are often idiosyncratic, too. Baseball and American football have not traveled well, although basketball has fared rather better. Many of the world's most popular sports, notably soccer, came by way of Britain. Asian martial arts—judo, karate, kickboxing—and pastimes like yoga have also swept the world.

People are not only guzzling hamburgers and Coke. Despite Coke's ambition of displacing water as the world's drink of choice, it accounts for less than 2 of the 64 fluid ounces that the typical person drinks a day. Britain's favorite takeaway is a curry, not a burger: Indian restaurants there outnumber McDonald's six to one. For all the concerns about American fast food trashing France's culinary traditions, France imported a mere $620 million in food from the United States in 2000, while exporting to America three times that. Nor is plonk[1] from America's Gallo displacing Europe's finest: Italy and France together account for three-fifths of global wine exports, the United States for only a twentieth. Worldwide, pizzas are more popular than burgers, Chinese restaurants seem to sprout up everywhere, and sushi is spreading fast. By far the biggest purveyor of alcoholic drinks is Britain's Diageo, which sells the world's best-selling whiskey (Johnnie Walker), gin (Gordon's), vodka (Smirnoff), and liqueur (Baileys).

In fashion, the ne plus ultra is Italian or French. Trendy Americans wear Gucci, Armani, Versace, Chanel, and Hermès. On the high street and in the mall, Sweden's Hennes & Mauritz (H&M) and Spain's Zara vie with America's Gap to dress the global masses. Nike shoes are given a run for their money by Germany's Adidas, Britain's Reebok, and Italy's Fila.

In pop music, American crooners do not have the stage to themselves. The three artists who were featured most widely in national Top Ten album charts in 2000 were America's Britney Spears, closely followed by Mexico's Carlos Santana and the British Beatles. Even tiny Iceland has produced a global star: Björk. Popular opera's biggest singers are Italy's Luciano Pavarotti, Spain's José Carreras, and the Spanish-Mexican Placido Domingo. Latin American salsa, Brazilian lambada, and African music have all carved out global niches for themselves. In most countries, local artists still top the charts. According to the IFPI, the record-industry bible, local acts accounted for 68 percent of music sales in 2000, up from 58 percent in 1991.

One of the most famous living writers is a Colombian, Gabriel García Márquez, author of *One Hundred Years of Solitude*. Paulo Coelho,

---

[1] British slang for cheap, low-quality alcohol. [Ed.]

another writer who has notched up tens of millions of global sales with *The Alchemist* and other books, is Brazilian. More than 200 million Harlequin romance novels, a Canadian export, were sold in 1990; they account for two-fifths of mass-market paperback sales in the United States. The biggest publisher in the English-speaking world is Germany's Bertelsmann, which gobbled up America's largest, Random House, in 1998.

Local fare glues more eyeballs to TV screens than American programs. Although nearly three-quarters of television drama exported worldwide comes from the United States, most countries' favorite shows are homegrown.

Nor are Americans the only players in the global media industry. Of the seven market leaders that have their fingers in nearly every pie, four are American (AOL Time Warner, Disney, Viacom, and News Corporation), one is German (Bertelsmann), one is French (Vivendi), and one Japanese (Sony). What they distribute comes from all quarters: Bertelsmann publishes books by American writers; News Corporation broadcasts Asian news; Sony sells Brazilian music.

The evidence is overwhelming. Fears about an Americanized uniformity are over-blown: American cultural products are not uniquely dominant; local ones are alive and well.

3

MIRIAM CHING YOON LOUIE

Sweatshop Warriors: Immigrant Women Workers Take On the Global Factory, 2001

Sherif Hetata and Philippe Legrain highlight the impact of globalization on consumers, but it is also important to examine how it affects workers. Free-trade policies have removed barriers to international trade, with global consequences. An example of such change can be witnessed along the border between Mexico and the United States, especially in the export factories, or *maquiladoras,** that are run by international corporations on both the U.S. and Mexican sides of the border. In the following excerpt, Miriam Ching Yoon Louie, a writer

* mah kee lah DOH rahs

Source: Miriam Ching Yoon Louie, *Sweatshop Warriors: Immigrant Women Workers Take On the Global Factory* (Cambridge, MA: South End Press, 2001), 65–71, 87–89.

and activist, interviews Mexican women who work in these factories and explores both the challenges they face and the strength they show in overcoming these challenges. What is the impact of liberalized trade laws on women who work in the *maquiladoras*? What is neoliberalism, and how is it tied to globalization? Why are women particularly vulnerable to these policies?

THINKING HISTORICALLY

According to Louie, how far back do neoliberalism and economic globalization date? How does Louie's assessment of economic globalization differ from the views expressed by Legrain? How might they both be right?

Many of today's *nuevas revolucionarias*[1] started working on the global assembly line as young women in northern Mexico for foreign transnational corporations. Some women worked on the U.S. side as "commuters" before they moved across the border with their families. Their stories reveal the length, complexity, and interpenetration of the U.S. and Mexican economies, labor markets, histories, cultures, and race relations. The women talk about the devastating impact of globalization, including massive layoffs and the spread of sweatshops on both sides of the border. *Las mujeres*[2] recount what drove them to join and lead movements for economic, racial, and gender justice, as well as the challenges they faced within their families and communities to assert their basic human rights. . . .

Growing Up Female and Poor

Mexican women and girls were traditionally expected to do all the cooking, cleaning, and serving for their husbands, brothers, and sons. For girls from poor families, shouldering these domestic responsibilities proved doubly difficult because they also performed farm, sweatshop, or domestic service work simultaneously. . . .

Petra Mata, a former seamstress for Levi's whose mother died shortly after childbirth, recalls the heavy housework she did as the only daughter:

> Aiyeee, let me tell you! It was very hard. In those times in Mexico, I was raised with the ideal that you have to learn to do everything — cook, make tortillas, wash your clothes, and clean the house — just the way they wanted you to. My grandparents were very strict. I always

---

[1] New revolutionaries. [Ed.]
[2] moo HAIR ace The women. [Ed.]

had to ask their permission and then let them tell me what to do. I was not a free woman. Life was hard for me. I didn't have much of a childhood; I started working when I was 12 or 13 years old.

Neoliberalism and Creeping Maquiladorization

These women came of age during a period of major change in the relationship between the Mexican and U.S. economies. Like Puerto Rico, Hong Kong, South Korea, Taiwan, Malaysia, Singapore, and the Philippines, northern Mexico served as one of the first stations of the global assembly line tapping young women's labor. In 1965 the Mexican government initiated the Border Industrialization Program (BIP) that set up export plants, called *maquiladoras* or *maquilas*, which were either the direct subsidiaries or subcontractors of transnational corporations. Mexican government incentives to U.S. and other foreign investors included low wages and high productivity; infrastructure; proximity to U.S. markets, facilities, and lifestyles; tariff loopholes; and pliant, pro-government unions. . . .

Describing her quarter-century-long sewing career in Mexico, Celeste Jiménez ticks off the names of famous U.S. manufacturers who hopped over the border to take advantage of cheap wages:

> I sewed for twenty-four years when I lived in Chihuahua in big name factories like Billy the Kid, Levi Strauss, and Lee *maquiladoras*. Everyone was down there. Here a company might sell under the brand name of Lee; there in Mexico it would be called Blanca García.

Transnational exploitation of women's labor was part of a broader set of policies that critical opposition movements in the Third World have dubbed "neoliberalism," i.e., the new version of the British Liberal Party's program of laissez faire capitalism espoused by the rising European and U.S. colonial powers during the late eighteenth and nineteenth centuries. The Western powers, Japan, and international financial institutions like the World Bank and International Monetary Fund have aggressively promoted neoliberal policies since the 1970s. Mexico served as an early testing ground for such standard neoliberal policies as erection of free trade zones; commercialization of agriculture; currency devaluation; deregulation; privatization; outsourcing; cuts in wages and social programs; suppression of workers', women's, and indigenous people's rights; free trade; militarization; and promotion of neoconservative ideology.

Neoliberalism intersects with gender and national oppression. Third World women constitute the majority of migrants seeking jobs as maids, vendors, *maquila* operatives, and service industry workers. Women also pay the highest price for cuts in education, health and housing programs, and food and energy subsidies and increases in their unpaid labor. . . .

The deepening of the economic crisis in Mexico, especially under the International Monetary Fund's pressure to devaluate the peso in 1976, 1982, and 1994, forced many women to work in both the formal and informal economy to survive and meet their childbearing and household responsibilities. María Antonia Flores was forced to work two jobs after her husband abandoned the family, leaving her with three children to support. She had no choice but to leave her children home alone, *solitos,* to look after themselves. Refugio Arrieta straddled the formal and informal economy because her job in an auto parts assembly *maquiladora* failed to bring in sufficient income. To compensate for the shortfall, she worked longer hours at her *maquila* job and "moonlighted" elsewhere:

> We made chassis for cars and for the headlights. I worked lots! I worked 12 hours more or less because they paid us so little that if you worked more, you got more money. I did this because the schools in Mexico don't provide everything. You have to buy the books, notebooks, *todos, todos* [everything]. And I had five kids. It's very expensive. I also worked out of my house and sold ceramics. I did many things to get more money for my kids.

In the three decades following its humble beginnings in the mid-1960s, the *maquila* sector swelled to more than 2,000 plants employing an estimated 776,000 people, over 10 percent of Mexico's labor force. In 1985, *maquiladoras* overtook tourism as the largest source of foreign exchange. In 1996, this sector trailed only petroleum-related industries in economic importance and accounted for over U.S. $29 billion in export earnings annually. The *maquila* system has also penetrated the interior of the country, as in the case of Guadalajara's electronics assembly industry and Tehuacán's jeans production zones. Although the proportion of male *maquila* workers has increased since 1983, especially in auto-transport equipment assembly, almost 70 percent of the workers continue to be women.

As part of a delegation of labor and human rights activists, this author met some of Mexico's newest proletarians[3] — young indigenous women migrant workers from the Sierra Negra to Tehuacán, a town famous for its refreshing mineral water springs in the state of Puebla, just southeast of Mexico City. Standing packed like cattle in the back of the trucks each morning the women headed for jobs sewing for name

---

[3] Workers, especially exploited ones (a Marxist term derived from Latin for lower classes). [Ed.]

brand manufacturers like Guess?, VF Corporation (producing Lee brand clothing), Gap, Sun Apparel (producing brands such as Polo, Arizona, and Express), Cherokee, Ditto Apparel of California, Levi's, and others. The workers told U.S. delegation members that their wages averaged U.S. \$30 to \$50 a week for 12-hour work days, six days a week. Some workers reported having to do *veladas* [all-nighters] once or twice a week. Employees often stayed longer without pay if they did not finish high production goals.

Girls as young as 12 and 13 worked in the factories. Workers were searched when they left for lunch and again at the end of the day to check that they weren't stealing materials. Women were routinely given urine tests when hired and those found to be pregnant were promptly fired, in violation of Mexican labor law. Although the workers had organized an independent union several years earlier, Tehuacán's Human Rights Commission members told us that it had collapsed after one of its leaders was assassinated.

Carmen Valadez and Reyna Montero, long-time activists in the women's and social justice movements, helped found Casa de La Mujer Factor X in 1977, a workers' center in Tijuana that organizes around women's workplace, reproductive, and health rights, and against domestic violence. Valadez and Montero say that the low wages and dangerous working conditions characteristic of the *maquiladoras* on the Mexico-U.S. border are being "extended to all areas of the country and to Central America and the Caribbean. NAFTA represents nothing but the '*maquiladorization*' of the region."

Elizabeth "Beti" Robles Ortega, who began working in the *maquilas* at the age of fourteen and was blacklisted after participating in independent union organizing drives on Mexico's northern border, now works as an organizer for the Servicio, Desarrollo y Paz, AC 520 (SEDEPAC) [Service, Development and Peace organization]. Robles described the erosion of workers' rights and women's health under NAFTA:

> NAFTA has led to an increase in the workforce, as foreign industry has grown. They are reforming labor laws and our constitution to favor even more foreign investment, which is unfair against our labor rights. For example, they are now trying to take away from us free organization which was guaranteed by Mexican law. Because foreign capital is investing in Mexico and is dominating, we must have guarantees. The government is just there with its hands held out; it's always had them out but now even more shamelessly. . . . Ecological problems are increasing. A majority of women are coming down with cancer—skin and breast cancer, leukemia, and lung and heart problems. There are daily deaths of worker women. You can see and feel the contamination of the water and the air. As soon

as you arrive and start breathing the air in Acuña and Piedras Negras [border cities between the states of Coahuila and Texas], you sense the heavy air, making you feel like vomiting.

Joining the Movement

Much of the education and leadership training the women received took place "on the job." The women talked about how much their participation in the movement had changed them. They learned how to analyze working conditions and social problems, who was responsible for these conditions, and what workers could do to get justice. They learned to speak truth to power, whether this was to government representatives, corporate management, the media, unions, or co-ethnic gatekeepers. They built relations with different kinds of sectors and groups and organized a wide variety of educational activities and actions. Their activism expanded their world view beyond that of their immediate families to seeing themselves as part of peoples' movements fighting for justice. . . .

Through her participation in the movement, [María del Carmen Domínguez] developed her skills, leadership, and awareness:

> When I stayed at work in the factory, I was only thinking of myself and how am I going to support my family—nothing more, nothing less. And I served my husband and my son, my girl. But when I started working with La Mujer Obrera I thought, "I need more respect for myself. We need more respect for ourselves." (laughs) . . .
> . . . I learned about the law and I learned how to organize classes with people, whether they were men or women like me.

4

BENJAMIN BARBER
Jihad vs. McWorld, 1995

Not everyone views the world as coming together, for better or worse, under the umbrella of globalization. Benjamin Barber, a political scientist, uses the terms *Jihad* and *McWorld* to refer to what he sees as the two poles of the modern global system. *McWorld* is the force of Hollywood, fast-food outlets, jeans, and Americanization. *Jihad* (the

Source: Benjamin Barber, *Jihad vs. McWorld: How Globalism and Tribalism Are Reshaping the World* (New York: Ballantine, 1995), 3–9, 17–20.

Arab word for "struggle") is used to symbolize all the nationalist, fundamentalist, ethnocentric, and tribal rejections of McWorld. Barber's argument is that these forces have largely shaped modern culture and that despite their opposition to each other, they both prevent the development of civic society and democracy. According to Barber, in what ways do both Jihad and McWorld stymie this development? What do you think of his argument? Can the world really be divided into these two groups? What sort of future does Barber predict?

THINKING HISTORICALLY

Barber argues that Jihad originated in opposition to McWorld and that the two play off each other in a way that gives them both substance and support. Which is a greater force toward globalization? Does Barber see Jihad and McWorld as primarily cultural or economic forces? How is Barber's idea of the process of global change different from that of the previous authors?

History is not over.[1] Nor are we arrived in the wondrous land of techné[2] promised by the futurologists. The collapse of state communism has not delivered people to a safe democratic haven, and the past, fratricide and civil discord perduring, still clouds the horizon just behind us. Those who look back see all of the horrors of the ancient slaughterbench reenacted in disintegral nations like Bosnia, Sri Lanka, Ossetia, and Rwanda and they declare that nothing has changed. Those who look forward prophesize commercial and technological interdependence—a virtual paradise made possible by spreading markets and global technology—and they proclaim that everything is or soon will be different. The rival observers seem to consult different almanacs drawn from the libraries of contrarian planets.

Yet anyone who reads the daily papers carefully, taking in the front page accounts of civil carnage as well as the business page stories on the mechanics of the information superhighway and the economics of communication mergers, anyone who turns deliberately to take in the whole 360-degree horizon, knows that our world and our lives are caught between what [Irish poet] William Butler Yeats called the two eternities of race and soul: that of race reflecting the tribal past, that of soul anticipating the cosmopolitan future. Our secular eternities are

---

[1] This is a response to the argument of Francis Fukuyama in "The End of History" (1989) that with the downfall of communism, there were no more fundamental conflicts to challenge the universalization of liberal democracy. [Ed.]

[2] Technology. [Ed.]

corrupted, however, race reduced to an insignia of resentment, and soul sized down to fit the demanding body by which it now measures its needs. Neither race nor soul offers us a future that is other than bleak, neither promises a polity that is remotely democratic.

The first scenario rooted in race holds out the grim prospect of a retribalization of large swaths of humankind by war and bloodshed: a threatened balkanization of nation-states in which culture is pitted against culture, people against people, tribe against tribe, a Jihad in the name of a hundred narrowly conceived faiths against every kind of interdependence, every kind of artificial social cooperation and mutuality: against technology, against pop culture, and against integrated markets; against modernity itself as well as the future in which modernity issues. The second paints that future in shimmering pastels, a busy portrait of onrushing economic, technological, and ecological forces that demand integration and uniformity and that mesmerize peoples everywhere with fast music, fast computers, and fast food—MTV, Macintosh, and McDonald's—pressing nations into one homogenous global theme park, one McWorld tied together by communications, information, entertainment, and commerce. Caught between Babel and Disneyland, the planet is falling precipitously apart and coming reluctantly together at the very same moment.

Some stunned observers notice only Babel, complaining about the thousand newly sundered "peoples" who prefer to address their neighbors with sniper rifles and mortars; others—zealots in Disneyland—seize on futurological platitudes and the promise of virtuality, exclaiming "It's a small world after all!" Both are right, but how can that be?

We are compelled to choose between what passes as "the twilight of sovereignty" and an entropic end of all history, or a return to the past's most fractious and demoralizing discord; to "the menace of global anarchy," to [John] Milton's capital of hell, Pandaemonium; to a world totally "out of control."

The apparent truth, which speaks to the paradox at the core of this book, is that the tendencies of both Jihad *and* McWorld are at work, both visible sometimes in the same country at the very same instant. Iranian zealots keep one ear tuned to the mullahs urging holy war and the other cocked to [Australian media mogul] Rupert Murdoch's Star television beaming in *Dynasty*, *Donahue*, and *The Simpsons* from hovering satellites. Chinese entrepreneurs vie for the attention of party cadres in Beijing and simultaneously pursue KFC franchises in cities like Nanjing, Hangzhou, and Xian where twenty-eight outlets serve over 100,000 customers a day. The Russian Orthodox church, even as it struggles to renew the ancient faith, has entered a joint venture with California businessmen to bottle and sell natural waters under the rubric Saint Springs Water Company. Serbian assassins wear Adidas sneakers and listen to Madonna on Walkman headphones as they take aim through their gunscopes at scurrying Sarajevo civilians looking to fill family watercans. Orthodox Hasids and brooding neo-Nazis have both turned to rock music to get their traditional messages out to the new generation, while fundamentalists plot virtual conspiracies on the Internet.

Now neither Jihad nor McWorld is in itself novel. History ending in the triumph of science and reason or some monstrous perversion thereof (Mary Shelley's Doctor Frankenstein) has been the leitmotiv of every philosopher and poet who has regretted the Age of Reason since the Enlightenment. [W. B.] Yeats lamented "the center will not hold, mere anarchy is loosed upon the world," and observers of Jihad today have little but historical detail to add. The Christian parable of the Fall and of the possibilities of redemption that it makes possible captures the eighteenth-century ambivalence—and our own—about past and future. I want, however, to do more than dress up the central paradox of human history in modern clothes. It is not Jihad and McWorld but the relationship between them that most interests me. For, squeezed between their opposing forces, the world has been sent spinning out of control. Can it be that what Jihad and McWorld have in common is anarchy: the absence of common will and that conscious and collective human control under the guidance of law we call democracy?

Progress moves in steps that sometimes lurch backwards; in history's twisting maze, Jihad not only revolts against but abets McWorld, while McWorld not only imperils but re-creates and reinforces Jihad. They produce their contraries and need one another. My object here then is not simply to offer sequential portraits of McWorld and Jihad, but while examining McWorld, to keep Jihad in my field of vision, and while dissecting Jihad, never to forget the context of McWorld. Call it a dialectic[3] of McWorld: a study in the cunning of reason that does honor to the radical differences that distinguish Jihad and McWorld yet that acknowledges their powerful and paradoxical interdependence.

There is a crucial difference, however, between my modest attempt at dialectic and that of the masters of the nineteenth century. Still seduced by the Enlightenment's faith in progress, both [G. W. F.] Hegel and [Karl] Marx believed reason's cunning was on the side of progress. But it is harder to believe that the clash of Jihad and McWorld will issue in some overriding good. The outcome seems more likely to pervert than to nurture human liberty. The two may, in opposing each other, work to the same ends, work in apparent tension yet in covert harmony, but democracy is not their beneficiary. In East Berlin, tribal communism has yielded to capitalism. In Marx-Engelsplatz, the stolid, overbearing

---

[3] Interaction; *dialectic* is a term borrowed from the German philosopher G. W. F. Hegel and the philosopher and revolutionary Karl Marx that described historical change as the product of competing systems—of ideas for Hegel, and of social-economic systems for Marx. [Ed.]

statues of Marx and [Friedrich] Engels face east, as if seeking distant solace from Moscow: but now, circling them along the streets that surround the park that is their prison are chain eateries like T.G.I. Friday's, international hotels like the Radisson, and a circle of neon billboards mocking them with brand names like Panasonic, Coke, and GoldStar. New gods, yes, but more liberty?

What then does it mean in concrete terms to view Jihad and McWorld dialectically when the tendencies of the two sets of forces initially appear so intractably antithetical? After all, Jihad and McWorld operate with equal strength in opposite directions, the one driven by parochial hatreds, the other by universalizing markets, the one recreating ancient subnational and ethnic borders from within, the other making national borders porous from without. Yet Jihad and McWorld have this in common: They both make war on the sovereign nation-state and thus undermine the nation-state's democratic institutions. Each eschews civil society and belittles democratic citizenship, neither seeks alternative democratic institutions. Their common thread is indifference to civil liberty. Jihad forges communities of blood rooted in exclusion and hatred, communities that slight democracy in favor of tyrannical paternalism or consensual tribalism. McWorld forges global markets rooted in consumption and profit, leaving to an untrustworthy, if not altogether fictitious, invisible hand issues of public interest and common good that once might have been nurtured by democratic citizenries and their watchful governments. Such governments, intimidated by market ideology, are actually pulling back at the very moment they ought to be aggressively intervening. What was once understood as protecting the public interest is now excoriated as heavy-handed regulatory browbeating. Justice yields to markets, even though, as [New York banker] Felix Rohatyn has bluntly confessed, "there is a brutal Darwinian logic to these markets. They are nervous and greedy. They look for stability and transparency, but what they reward is not always our preferred form of democracy." If the traditional conservators of freedom were democratic constitutions and Bills of Rights, "the new temples to liberty," [literary critic and philosopher] George Steiner suggests, "will be McDonald's and Kentucky Fried Chicken."

In being reduced to a choice between the market's universal church and a retribalizing politics of particularist identities, peoples around the globe are threatened with an atavistic return to medieval politics where local tribes and ambitious emperors together ruled the world entire, women and men united by the universal abstraction of Christianity even as they lived out isolated lives in warring fiefdoms defined by involuntary (ascriptive) forms of identity. This was a world in which princes and kings had little real power until they conceived the ideology of nationalism. Nationalism established government on a scale greater than the tribe yet less cosmopolitan than the universal church and in time gave birth to those intermediate, gradually more democratic institutions that would come to constitute the nation-state. Today, at the far end of this history, we seem intent on re-creating a world in which our only choices are the secular universalism of the cosmopolitan market and the everyday particularism of the fractious tribe.

In the tumult of the confrontation between global commerce and parochial ethnicity, the virtues of the democratic nation are lost and the instrumentalities by which it permitted peoples to transform themselves into nations and seize sovereign power in the name of liberty and the commonweal are put at risk. Neither Jihad nor McWorld aspires to re-secure the civic virtues undermined by its denationalizing practices; neither global markets nor blood communities service public goods or pursue equality and justice. Impartial judiciaries and deliberate assemblies play no role in the roving killer bands that speak on behalf of newly liberated "peoples," and such democratic institutions have at best only marginal influence on the roving multinational corporations that speak on behalf of newly liberated markets. Jihad pursues a bloody politics of identity, McWorld a bloodless economics of profit. Belonging by default to McWorld, everyone is a consumer; seeking a repository for identity, everyone belongs to some tribe. But no one is a citizen. Without citizens, how can there be democracy? . . .

Jihad is, I recognize, a strong term. In its mildest form, it betokens religious struggle on behalf of faith, a kind of Islamic zeal. In its strongest political manifestation, it means bloody holy war on behalf of partisan identity that is metaphysically defined and fanatically defended. Thus, while for many Muslims it may signify only ardor in the name of a religion that can properly be regarded as universalizing (if not quite ecumenical), I borrow its meaning from those militants who make the slaughter of the "other" a higher duty. I use the term in its militant construction to suggest dogmatic and violent particularism of a kind known to Christians no less than Muslims, to Germans and Hindis as well as to Arabs. The phenomena to which I apply the phrase have innocent enough beginnings: identity politics and multicultural diversity can represent strategies of a free society trying to give expression to its diversity. What ends as Jihad may begin as a simple search for a local identity, some set of common personal attributes to hold out against the numbing and neutering uniformities of industrial modernization and the colonizing culture of McWorld. . . .

McWorld is a product of popular culture driven by expansionist commerce. Its template is American, its form style. Its goods are as much images as matériel, an aesthetic as well as a product line. It is about culture as commodity, apparel as ideology. Its symbols are Harley-Davidson motorcycles and Cadillac motorcars hoisted from the roadways, where they once represented a mode of transportation, to the marquees of global market cafés like Harley-Davidson's and the Hard Rock where they become icons of lifestyle. You don't drive them, you feel their vibes and rock to the images they conjure up from old movies and new celebrities, whose personal appearances are the key to the wildly popular international café chain Planet Hollywood. Music, video, theater, books, and theme parks—the new churches of a commercial civilization in which malls are the public squares and suburbs the neighborless neighborhoods—are all constructed as image exports creating a common world taste around common logos, advertising slogans, stars, songs, brand names, jingles, and trademarks. Hard power yields to soft, while ideology is transmuted into a kind of videology that works through sound bites and film clips. Videology is fuzzier and less dogmatic than traditional political ideology: it may as a consequence be far more successful in instilling the novel values required for global markets to succeed.

McWorld's videology remains Jihad's most formidable rival, and in the long run it may attenuate the force of Jihad's recidivist tribalisms. Yet the information revolution's instrumentalities are also Jihad's favored weapons. Hutu or Bosnian Serb identity[4] was less a matter of real historical memory than of media propaganda by a leadership set on liquidating rival clans. In both Rwanda and Bosnia, radio broadcasts whipped listeners into a killing frenzy. As *New York Times* rock critic Jon Pareles has noticed, "regionalism in pop music has become as trendy as microbrewery beer and narrowcasting cable channels, and for the same reasons."[5] The global culture is what gives the local culture its medium, its audience, and its aspirations. Fascist pop and Hasid rock are not oxymorons; rather they manifest the dialectics of McWorld in particularly dramatic ways. Belgrade's radio includes stations that broadcast Western pop music as a rebuke to hard-liner Milosevic's supernationalist government and stations that broadcast native folk tunes laced with antiforeign and anti-Semitic sentiments. Even the Internet has its neo-Nazi bulletin boards and Turk-trashing Armenian "flamers" (who assail every use of the word *turkey*, fair and fowl alike, so to speak), so that the abstractions of cyberspace too are infected with a peculiar and rabid cultural territoriality all their own.

The dynamics of the Jihad-McWorld linkage are deeply dialectical. Japan has, for example, become more culturally insistent on its own traditions in recent years even as its people seek an ever greater purchase on McWorld. In 1992, the number-one restaurant in Japan measured by

---

[4] This is a reference to the attempted genocide of Tutsis by Hutus in Rwanda (1994) and of Muslim Bosnians by Serbian Bosnians in what was Yugoslavia (1992–1995). In both cases the "other" was so indistinguishable that the perpetrators demanded identity cards. [Ed.]

[5] Jon Pareles, "Striving to Become Rock's Next Seattle," *The New York Times*, July 17, 1994, Section 2, p. 1.

volume of customers was McDonald's, followed in the number-two spot by the Colonel's Kentucky Fried Chicken. In France, where cultural purists complain bitterly of a looming Sixième République ("la République Américaine"),[6] the government attacks "franglais" even as it funds EuroDisney park just outside of Paris. In the same spirit, the cinema industry makes war on American film imports while it bestows upon Sylvester Stallone one of France's highest honors, the Chevalier des arts et lettres. Ambivalence also stalks India. Just outside of Bombay, cheek by jowl with villages still immersed in poverty and notorious for the informal execution of unwanted female babies or, even, wives, can be found a new town known as SCEEPZ—the Santa Cruz Electronic Export Processing Zone—where Hindi-, Tamil-, and Mahratti-speaking computer programmers write software for Swissair, AT&T, and other labor-cost-conscious multinationals. India is thus at once a major exemplar of ancient ethnic and religious tensions and "an emerging power in the international software industry."[7] To go to work at SCEEPZ, says an employee, is "like crossing an international border." Not into another country, but into the virtual nowhere-land of McWorld.

More dramatic even than in India, is the strange interplay of Jihad and McWorld in the remnants of Yugoslavia. In an affecting *New Republic* report, Slavenka Drakulic recently told the brief tragic love story of Admira and Bosko, two young star-crossed lovers from Sarajevo: "They were born in the late 1960's," she writes. "They watched Spielberg movies; they listened to Iggy Pop; they read John le Carré; they went to a disco every Saturday night and fantasized about traveling to Paris or London."[8] Longing for safety, it seems they finally negotiated with all sides for safe passage, and readied their departure from Sarajevo. Before they could cross the magical border that separates their impoverished land from the seeming sanctuary of McWorld, Jihad caught up to them. Their bodies lay along the riverbank, riddled with bullets from anonymous snipers for whom safe passage signaled an invitation to target practice. The murdered young lovers, as befits émigrés to McWorld, were clothed in jeans and sneakers. So too, one imagines, were their murderers.

Further east, tourists seeking a piece of old Russia that does not take them too far from MTV can find traditional Matryoshka nesting dolls (that fit one inside the other) featuring the nontraditional visages of (from largest to smallest) Bruce Springsteen, Madonna, Boy George, Dave Stewart, and Annie Lennox.

[6] "Sixth Republic"; the present French government is the Fifth Republic. [Ed.]

[7] National Public Radio, *All Things Considered,* December 2, 1993, from the broadcast transcription.

[8] Slavenka Drakulic, "Love Story: A True Tale from Sarajevo," *The New Republic,* October 26, 1993, pp. 14–16.

In Russia, in India, in Bosnia, in Japan, and in France too, modern history then leans both ways: toward the meretricious inevitability of McWorld, but also into Jihad's stiff winds, heaving to and fro and giving heart both to the Panglossians and the Pandoras,[9] sometimes for the very same reasons. The Panglossians bank on EuroDisney and Microsoft, while the Pandoras await nihilism and a world in Pandaemonium. Yet McWorld and Jihad do not really force a choice between such polarized scenarios. Together, they are likely to produce some stifling amalgam of the two suspended in chaos. Antithetical in every detail, Jihad and McWorld nonetheless conspire to undermine our hard-won (if only half-won) civil liberties and the possibility of a global democratic future. In the short run the forces of Jihad, noisier and more obviously nihilistic than those of McWorld, are likely to dominate the near future, etching small stories of local tragedy and regional genocide on the face of our times and creating a climate of instability marked by multimicrowars inimical to global integration. But in the long run, the forces of McWorld are the forces underlying the slow certain thrust of Western civilization and as such may be unstoppable. Jihad's microwars will hold the headlines well into the next century, making predictions of the end of history look terminally dumb. But McWorld's homogenization is likely to establish a macropeace that favors the triumph of commerce and its markets and to give to those who control information, communication, and entertainment ultimate (if inadvertent) control over human destiny. Unless we can offer an alternative to the struggle between Jihad and McWorld; the epoch on whose threshold we stand—postcommunist, postindustrial, postnational, yet sectarian, fearful, and bigoted—is likely also to be terminally postdemocratic.

[9] Extreme optimists and pessimists, respectively. [Ed.]

5

THE WORLD BANK

World Development Report: Gender and Development, 2012

The World Bank and its sister organization, The International Monetary Fund, were created by the United States and European Allies in 1944 as World War II was coming to an end. Its purpose was to

Source: The World Bank, *2012 World Development Report: Gender and Development,* chapter 6: "Globalization's impact on gender equality: What's happened and what's needed," 255–72.

promote international trade. In recent decades it has concentrated on problems of the developing countries, looking to finance projects to reduce poverty, child mortality, illiteracy, and gender inequality. In this regard, the bank issues reports like the one selected here from 2012.

What according to the authors is the relationship between globalization and gender inequality? In what ways does globalization improve the lives of women?

THINKING HISTORICALLY

For the purposes of this report, what does the World Bank mean by "globalization"? How does their definition correspond to, and differ from, others in this chapter?

The world is becoming more and more integrated. What started with greater trade openness is translating into growing global economic integration and interdependence, as transnational movements of people and capital accelerate and information becomes ever more accessible. Technological developments are rapidly changing the way people learn, work, and communicate. And the world population is concentrating in medium and large cities.

The new forces associated with globalization—understood as the combination of economic integration, technological diffusion, and greater access to information—have operated through markets, formal institutions, and informal institutions to lift some of the constraints to greater gender equality.

First, trade openness and the diffusion of new information and communication technologies (ICTs) have translated into more jobs and stronger connections to markets for many women, increasing their access to economic opportunities. In some countries and sectors, women's wages have also increased relative to those of men.

Second, gender inequality has more costs in an integrated world. It can diminish countries' ability to compete internationally—particularly for countries with export potential in goods and services with high female employment. And given growing global awareness of women's rights, continued gender inequality can also hurt a country's international standing. These factors strengthen the incentives for policy action toward gender equality around the world.

Third, greater access to information has allowed many in developing countries to learn about life and mores in other parts of the world, including those pertaining to the role of women, possibly affecting attitudes and behaviors. A shift toward more egalitarian gender roles and norms has also been facilitated and, in some cases, reinforced by women's economic empowerment.

But in the absence of public policy, globalization alone cannot and will not reduce gender inequality. Despite significant increases in agency and in access to economic opportunities for many women in many countries, the rising tide has not lifted everybody. Those often left behind are women for whom the existing constraints are most binding. That is why public action aimed at closing existing gender gaps in endowments, agency, and access to economic opportunities is necessary for countries to fully capitalize on the potential of globalization as a force for development and greater gender equality. . . .

Female Workers Wanted

The early years of trade liberalization were mainly characterized by the move of textile and information technology manufacturing from developed to developing countries. New employment in manufacturing often consisted of labor-intensive assembly line jobs, and the initial gains in manufacturing employment were greatest in countries with abundant unskilled labor and a comparative advantage in producing basic manufactures.

This shift in geographic location of production promoted female labor force participation and the feminization of employment in manufacturing in developing countries—particularly in Asia and Central America. . . .

In the past 15 years, the spread of ICTs has expanded trade in services and has, to a lesser extent, promoted the growth of ICT sectors in developing countries. As a result employment shifted from manufacturing, where jobs could be automated, to services. In the process, demand for nimble fingers on the assembly line gave way to demand for computer literacy as the tasks became more sophisticated and direct interaction with clients and customers more common.

As technology advanced, low-skilled women in light manufacturing were often displaced by men. . . .

New ICT-enabled jobs in services—particularly information processing in banking, insurance, printing, and publishing—were mainly taken up by women, but not the same women who lost their manufacturing jobs, because the new jobs required a different set of skills, including keyboarding, English, and sometimes French. Female employment in data entry and processing was initially highest in Barbados, Jamaica, and the Philippines. Later, ICT-related jobs were concentrated in software, call centers, and geographical information systems, and clustered in Malaysia and India, particularly in Delhi and Mumbai, where call centers employ more than 1 million people, most of them women.

In both manufacturing and service exports, growth in female employment was faster than ever before and faster than in other sectors. And although exports in many countries initially accounted for a small fraction of total female employment, their importance grew over time as a result of rapid employment growth. . . .

But the feminization of employment through exports appears to be less common in agricultural economies. Growth in traditional agricultural exports has benefited men more than women because women are less likely to work on commercial crops and are crowded out of traditionally female-intensive crops when these corps become commercial. . . .

Higher female employment in exports has often (but not always) been accompanied by wage gains. Transnational and exporting companies may be able to pay higher wages than locally owned firms and firms producing for the domestic market. They also may be better able to insulate their workers from economic cycles—and their workers may be better protected by labor legislation and are more likely to be unionized and thus eligible for benefits. That is why female wages are frequently higher and the gender wage gap is lower in exports than in other sectors, even after controlling for worker characteristics. . . .

More Connected and Better Informed—ICTs Have Increased Women's Access to Markets

ICTs can improve access to markets and increase participation in market work by reducing transaction costs associated with time and mobility constraints. They facilitate the gathering and transmission of price and other information and increase the flexibility in where and when economic activities can occur. Because women often face more restrictions than men in their mobility and available time, they stand to benefit more from these developments. . . .

Cell phone access and use can alleviate time and mobility constraints for women by increasing the ability to coordinate their family and work lives, reducing the cost of money transfers, and cutting down the physical labor or travel required to discover information (including avoiding fruitless trips to get supplies or meet customers). In Senegal, female fishmongers report that access to cell phones facilitates communication with their clients and suppliers, reducing travel time and costs, and with their families while they are away from home. Similarly, 41 percent of women interviewed in Bolivia, the Arab Republic of Egypt, India, and Kenya declared that owning a mobile phone had increased their income and their access to economic opportunities. . . .

In many cases, women, particularly rural women, were willing to reduce expenditures on other items to have access to a mobile phone, suggesting that the perceived benefits outweighed the costs, which averaged 3.5 percent of household income among those surveyed. . . .

The picture is quite different for the Internet. Low private access in the developing world, especially in rural areas, has severely limited its impact on access to economic opportunities—beyond the impact of ICTs on out-sourcing and service export employment discussed earlier. Governments and development agencies have set up village "telecenters" for public use, generally as a fee for service, to increase access to basic ICT services among underserved populations. These centers generally offer computers linked to the Internet and are available for word processing and graphics work, faxes, e-mail, photocopying, and phone lines. They may also feature train-ing on the equipment, and some incorporate radio broadcasts or video resources. . . .

Adapt or Miss the Boat

Trade openness, technological diffusion, and access to information have fundamentally changed the way countries interact and compete with each other in the global economy. Because gender (and other) inequality has more costs in a globalized world, these changes could translate into stronger incentives for both firms and governments to move toward gender equality. Specifically in countries with a comparative advantage in female goods, gender differences in access to market work and persis-tent employment segregation by gender could severely undermine the country's capacity to compete internationally and ultimately hamper economic growth.

Added to this economic reality is growing international pressure for countries to grant and enforce formal rights for women. International action in this area has translated into agreements sponsored by international organizations, primarily the International Labour Organization (ILO) and the United Nations (UN), followed by strong international pressure on countries to formally adhere to these agreements either directly or indirectly as part of broader trade and other economic agreements. . . .

Pressure from media and consumers in developed countries can also lead multinational firms to offer better working conditions to their workers in developing countries. For instance, both wages and nonwage working conditions (such as hours worked, accidents, contractual characteristics, work environment, and other benefits) among formal workers (most of them women) in the export textile and apparel indus-tries in Cambodia, El Salvador, and Indonesia were found to be at or above the average in the rest of the economy. Similarly, antisweatshop campaigns in Indonesia led to large wage increases in foreign-owned and export firms, with some costs to the firms in the form of reduced invest-ment, falling profits, and increased probability of closure for smaller plants, but no significant impact on employment. . . .

Globalization Could Also Promote More Egalitarian Gender Roles and Norms

The changes unleashed by globalization—especially the greater access to economic opportunities and information among women—could also influence existing gender roles and norms, ultimately promoting more egalitarian views. . . .

Women turned income earners may be able to leverage their new position to change gender roles in their households by influencing the allocation of time and resources among household members, shifting relative power within the households, and more broadly exercising stronger agency. In fact, women appear to gain more control over their income by working in export-oriented activities, although the impact on well-being and agency is more positive for women working in manufacturing and away from their male relatives than for those working in agriculture. Women in factories feel their status has improved. They are more likely to marry and have their first baby later than other women of similar socioeconomic status and to have better quality housing and access to modern infrastructure. They also report greater self-esteem and decision-making capacity, with benefits extending to other family members. In contrast, women in agriculture have not experienced significant changes in decision-making capacity or agency as a result of commercialization and higher export orientation, even when typical "women's crops" are promoted.

Beyond the economic sphere, increased access to information, primarily through higher exposure to television and the Internet, has also exposed many in developing countries to the roles women play in other parts of the world, which may affect gender roles and outcomes. For instance, in Brazil, a country where soap opera watching is ubiquitous and cuts across social classes, the presence of the Globo signal (a television channel that offers many popular Brazilian soap operas) has led to lower fertility, measured as the number of live births for women ages 15–49. . . .

Access to economic opportunities has also brought change in the public sphere. In Bangladesh, the employment of hundreds of thousands of women in the ready-made garment industry feminized the urban public space, creating more gender-equitable norms for women's public mobility and access to public institutions. In the process, Bangladeshi women had to redefine and negotiate the terms of *purdah*, typically reinterpreting it as a state of mind in contrast to its customary expression as physical absence from the public space, modest clothing, and quiet demeanor. . . .

Is The Glass Half Full or Half Empty?
The Need for Public Action

What, then, are we to conclude from the discussion in this chapter? The evidence suggests that employment in the export sector represents an attractive option for a large number of women in the developing world. These jobs enable women to contribute to household income, increase their economic empowerment within the household, and allow for greater social participation. . . .

But persistent gender differences in endowments, time availability, access to productive inputs and agency, and pervasive employment segregation by gender, mean that not all women have fully benefited from the economic opportunities brought about by globalization. And even among women who did benefit, remaining gaps, primarily in wages and working conditions, still need to be closed.

As long as these differences persist, globalization alone cannot—and will not—make gender inequality go away. Public action to close gender gaps is therefore critical for countries to fully capitalize on the potential of globalization as a force for development and greater gender equality. Such action is also urgent in light of the rising costs of gender inequality in a globalized world.

6

Cartoons on Globalization, 2000s

The following are editorial cartoons. Each addresses economic components of globalization, and each in some way addresses the relationship between those in the most developed part of the world and those in the developing world.

Figure 28.1, "As an Illegal Immigrant," raises questions about increased labor and capital mobility, allowing the import of migrant workers and the export of capital for foreign factories. What is the point of the cartoon? How would you describe its attitude toward globalization?

Figure 28.2, "Help Is on the Way, Dude," focuses on an irony of some well-intentioned efforts to protect the environment and exploited foreign laborers. What is the irony? How might you solve the problem posed by the cartoon?

Figure 28.3, "Cheap Chinese Textiles," explores the problem of low-cost manufacturing countries flooding global markets with cheap

Figure 28.1 "As an Illegal Immigrant."

Source: Gary Markstein.

Figure 28.2 "Help Is on the Way, Dude."

Source: By permission of Chip Bok and Creators Syndicate, Inc.

Figure 28.3 "Cheap Chinese Textiles."

Source: Patrick Chappatte/Globe Cartoon.

Figure 28.4 "Keep the Europeans Out."

Source: Bruce MacKinnon/artizans.com.

Figure 28.5 "I Don't Mean to Hurry You."

Source: J. McGillen/Cartoonstock.com.

products. What is the meaning of the comment by the representative of the European Union (EU)? What is the meaning of the cartoon?

Figure 28.4, "Keep the Europeans Out," examines a concern of North American farmers, here expressed on a placard of a Canadian farmer. What is that concern, and what is the farmer's solution? What is the point of the cartoon? What does this cartoon say about the use of tariffs, quotas, or other protectionist barriers to limit global competition? Compare this cartoon to the previous one on this issue.

Figure 28.5, "I Don't Mean to Hurry You," asks about the wishes of people in the developing world. What is the point of the cartoon? Compare the cartoon with the analysis of Barber.

THINKING HISTORICALLY

All of these cartoonists explore a process of economic globalization. What are the economic forces that bring about the globalization depicted in these cartoons? To what extent does the humor in these cartoons depend on a realization that globalization is inevitable? To what extent is that attitude shared by the authors of the other selections in this chapter?

■ REFLECTIONS

Globalization is not one process, but many. It is as technological as the Internet, smart phones, and the latest flu vaccine. It is as cultural as international film festivals, sushi, and disappearing languages. It is as political as the United Nations, time zones, and occupying armies. Perhaps most important, it is economic. People migrate for jobs, factories move for cheaper labor, and neither consumers nor corporations care about country of origin. Since the end of communism, the entire world has become a single market.

Is this a good thing? It depends on whom you ask. Sherif Hetata sees overcommercialization undermining national traditions. Philippe Legrain applauds the new menu of possibilities. Life is clearly hard for the women working in the sweatshops of international corporations, as Miriam Ching Yoon Louie points out; but is economic globalization responsible for their suffering, or does it provide women like them with new opportunities? Benjamin Barber explains why some choose jihad in response to the effects of world trade. More than any of the other authors, he is skeptical of the inevitability of globalization, but his prognosis is not pretty. The World Bank offers a way forward, but acknowledges that only with public action will global inequalities change.

It is the duty of citizens, not historians, to decide what outcomes are good or bad, better or worse. But historians can help us decide by showing us where we are—by deepening the temporal dimension of our awareness.

Understanding the process of change is the most useful "habit of mind" we gain from studying the past. Although the facts are many and the details overwhelming, the historical process appears to us only through the study of the specifics. And we must continually check and revise our interpretations to conform to new information. But like a storyteller without a plot, we are lost without some overall understanding of how our world is changing.

More important, understanding change does not mean that we have to submit to it. Of the processes of globalization discussed in this chapter—trade and technological transfers, cultural homogenization and competition, commercialization and market expansion—some may seem inevitable, some strong, some even reversible. Intelligent action requires an appreciation of the possible as well as the identification of the improbable.

History is not an exact science. Fortunately, human beings are creators, as well as subjects, of change. Even winds that cannot be silenced can be deflected, harnessed, or made to chime. Which way is the world moving? What are we becoming? What can we do? What kind of world can we create? These are questions that can only be answered by studying the past, both distant and recent, and trying to understand the overarching changes that are shaping our lives. Worlds of history converge upon us, but only one world will emerge from our wishes, our wisdom, and our will.

Acknowledgments

Chapter 15

1   Nicholas D. Kristof. "1492: The Prequel" from the *New York Times Magazine*, June 6, 1999. All rights reserved. Used by permission and protected by the Copyright Laws of the United States. The printing, copying, redistribution, or retransmission of this Content without express written permission is prohibited.

2   Ma Huan. From *The Overall Survey of the Ocean Shores*, ed. and trans. Feng Ch'eng Chun, originally published by Hakluyt Society, 1970. Reprinted by permission of David Higham.

4   Christopher Columbus. "Letter to King Ferdinand and Queen Isabella" from *The Four Voyages of Columbus*, ed. Cecil Jane, Dover, 1988.

5   Kirkpatrick Sale. Excerpt from *The Conquest of Paradise*. Copyright © 1990 by Kirkpatrick Sale. Used by permission of The Joy Harris Literary Agency.

Chapter 16

1   Bernal Díaz. Excerpt from *The Conquest of New Spain*, trans. J. M. Cohen, Penguin UK, 1963. Reprinted by permission of Penguin UK.

2   From *The Broken Spears: The Aztec Account of the Conquest of Mexico*, ed. Miguel Leon-Portilla, trans. Lysander Kemp, Beacon Press, 1990.

3   Bartolomé de Las Casas. From *The Devastation of the Indies: A Brief Account*, trans. Herma Briffault. Copyright © 1974. Reproduced with permission of Continuum Publishing Company in the format Textbook via Copyright Clearance Center.

5   Nzinga Mbemba. "Appeal to the King of Portugal" from *The African Past*, ed. Basil Davidson. Copyright © 1964 by Basil Davidson. Reprinted by permission of Curtis Brown, Ltd.

7   J. B. Romaigne. From *Journal of a Slave Ship Voyage*, Dover Publications. Reprinted by permission of the publisher.

Chapter 17

1   Jonathan D. Spence. From *Emperor of China*, copyright © 1974, copyright renewed 2002 by Jonathan D. Spence. Used by permission of Alfred A. Knopf, a division of Random House.

2   From *Japan: A Documentary History*, ed. David J. Lu (Armonk, NY: M. E. Sharpe, 1997), pp. 219–20. English translation copyright © 1997 by David J. Lu. Reprinted with permission from M. E. Sharpe, Inc.

3   Abdul Qadir Bada'uni. From *Muntakhab-ut-Tawarikh*, Volume 2, by G. S. A. Ranking and W. H. Lowe. Copyright © Columbia University Press. Reprinted with permission of the publisher.

5   Benjamin J. Kaplan. *Divided by Faith: Religious Conflict and the Practice of Toleration in Early Modern Europe,* pp. 28–32, 100–03, Cambridge, Mass.: The Belknap Press of Harvard University Press. Copyright © 2007 by Benjamin J. Kaplan. Reprinted by permission of Harvard University Press.

Chapter 18

1   Miu Family of Guangdong Province. "Family Instructions for the Miu Lineage," trans. Clara Yu, from *Chinese Civilization: A Sourcebook,* Second Edition, ed. Patricia Ebrey, Free Press, 1993.

2   Pu Songling. "The Lady Knight-Errant" from Liao-chai chih-i, translated by Lorraine S. Y. Lieu, Y. W. Ma and Joseph S. M. Lau, from *Traditional Chinese Stories: Themes and Variations,* ed. Y. W. Ma and Joseph S. M. Lau, copyright © 1986 by Cheng & Tsui Company, Inc. Originally published by Columbia University Press in 1978. Used by permission of Cheng & Tsui Company, Inc.

4   Anna Bijns. "Unyoked Is Best! Happy the Woman without a Man," trans. by Kristiaan P. G. Aercke, from *Women and Writers of the Renaissance and Reformation,* ed. Katharina M. Wilson, The University of Georgia Press, 1987.

6   Countess de Rochefort. "Diary of the Countess de Rochefort" from *Not in God's Image,* eds. Julia O'Faolain and Lauro Martines, HarperCollins Publishers. Used by permission of the author.

7   "Court Case on Marriage in High Court of Aix" from *Not in God's Image,* eds. Julia O'Faolain and Lauro Martines, HarperCollins Publishers. Used by permission of the author.

8   Mary Jo Maynes and Ann Waltner. "Childhood, Youth, and the Female Life Cycle: Women's Life-Cycle Transitions in a World-Historical Perspective: Comparing Marriage in China and Europe" from *Journal of Women's History* 12:4. Copyright © 2001 Journal of Women's History. Reprinted with permission of The Johns Hopkins University Press.

Chapter 19

1   Jack Goldstone. Excerpt from *Why Europe? The Rise of the West in World History 1500–1850.* Copyright © 2009 by Jack Goldstone. Reprinted with the permission of The McGraw-Hill Companies, Inc.

4   Bonnie S. Anderson and Judith P. Zinsser. From *A History of Their Own: Women in Europe from Prehistory to the Present,* Volume I. Copyright © 1988 by Bonnie S. Anderson and Judith Zinsser. Reprinted by permission of HarperCollins Publishers.

6   Lynda Norene Shaffer. "China, Technology, and Change" from *World History Bulletin* 4, no. 1 (Fall/Winter 1986–1987) pages 1–6.

7   Sugita Gempaku. From *Japan: A Documentary History,* ed. David J. Lu (Armonk, NY: M. E. Sharpe, 1997), pp. 219–20. English translation copyright © 1997 by David J. Lu. Reprinted with permission from M. E. Sharpe, Inc.

Chapter 20

7 Toussaint L'Ouverture. "Letter to the Directory, November 5, 1797" from *The Black Jacobins*, ed. C.L.R. James, Vintage Books, 1989. Reproduced with permission of Curtis Brown Group Ltd., London on behalf of the Estate of C.L.R. James. Copyright © The Estate of C.L.R. James.

9 Chakrabarty, Dipesh. From *Provincializing Europe*. © 2000 Princeton University Press. Reprinted by permission of Princeton University Press.

Chapter 21

1 Arnold Pacey. *Technology in World Civilization: A Thousand-Year History*, pp. 128–35, copyright © Massachusetts Institute of Technology, by permission of The MIT Press.

5 Peter N. Stearns. Excerpt from *The Industrial Revolution in World History*. Copyright © 1993 Stearns, Peter N. Reprinted by permission of Westview Press, a member of the Perseus Books Group.

7 Samuel L. Bailey and Franco Ramella. *One Family, Two Worlds: An Italian Family's Correspondence Across the Atlantic*. Copyright © 1988 by Rutgers, the State University. Reprinted by permission of Rutgers University Press.

Chapter 22

1 George Orwell. From *Burmese Days*, copyright © 1934 by George Orwell and renewed 1962 by Sonia Pitt-Rivers, reprinted by permission of Houghton Mifflin Harcourt Publishing Company. All rights reserved.

3 "An Image of Africa: Racism in Conrad's *Heart of Darkness*" from *Hopes and Impediments* by Chinua Achebe. Copyright © 1988 by Chinua Achebe, used by permission of The Wylie Agency LLC.

4 Chinua Achebe. From *Things Fall Apart*, 1958. Reprinted by permission.

Chapter 23

1 Theodore von Laue, Excerpt from *The World Revolution of Westernization: The Twentieth Century in Global Perspective*, Oxford University Press, 1987.

2 Fukuzawa Yukichi. From *Japan: A Documentary History*, ed. David J. Lu (Armonk, NY: M. E. Sharpe, 1997), pp. 351–53. English translation copyright © 1997 by David J. Lu. Reprinted with permission from M. E. Sharpe, Inc.

6 Mohandas K. Gandhi. Excerpt from *Hind Swaraj*, Navajivan, 1938. Reprinted by permission of The Navajivan Trust.

Chapter 24

1 David Fromkin. From *Europe's Last Summer: Who Started the Great War in 1914?* Copyright © 2004 by David Fromkin. Used by permission of Alfred A. Knopf, a division of Random House, Inc.

Chapter 25

Chapter 26

6   Welles Hangen. "*Pravda* Modifies Khrushchev Slur," the *New York Times,* November 20, 1956. All rights reserved. Used by permission and protected by the Copyright Laws of the United States. The printing, copying, redistribution, or retransmission of this Content without express written permission is prohibited.

8a Secret Staff Meeting Transcript, Secretary of State Henry Kissinger, Chairman, March 26, 1976. These materials are reproduced from www.nsarchive.org with the permission of the National Security Archive.

8b Telegram from U.S Ambassador to Argentina, Robert C. Hill, to Secretary of State Henry Kissinger, March 30, 1976. These materials are reproduced from www.nsarchive.org with the permission of the National Security Archive.

9   "Transcript of telephone conversation between Soviet Premier Alexei Kosygin and Afghan Prime Minister Nur Mohammad Taraki" (March 18, 1979) from *Cold War International History Project Bulletin* 8–9 (Winter 1996/1997): 145–46. Available at www.CWIHP.org.

Chapter 27

1   Hebe de Bonafini and Matilde Sánchez. "The Madwomen at the Plaza de Mayo," excerpted from *The Argentina Reader: History, Culture, Politics* (Durham: Duke University Press, 2002). Reprinted by permission of the authors.

2   Mikhail Gorbachev. From *On My Country and the World*. Copyright © Columbia University Press. Reprinted with permission of the publisher.

3   Nobel Peace Prize Address by Nelson Mandela. © The Nobel Foundation 1993. Used by permission.

4   Gene Sharp. Excerpt from "Dictatorship to Democracy," The Albert Einstein Institution.

5   Wael Ghonim. Excerpt from *Revolution 2.0: The Power of the People is Greater than the People in Power*. Copyright © 2012 by Wael Gohnim. Reprinted by permission of Houghton Mifflin Harcourt Publishing Company. All rights reserved.

6   "Charter 08," http://www.hrichina.org/crf/article/3203.

7   General Assembly of Occupy Wall Street. "Declaration of the Occupation of New York City."

8   William Moss Wilson. "Just Don't Call Her Che," the *New York Times*, January 29, 2012. All rights reserved. Used by permission and protected by the Copyright Laws of the United States. The printing, copying, redistribution, or retransmission of this Content without express written permission is prohibited.

Chapter 28

1   Sherif Hetata. "Dollarization, Fragmentation, and God" from *The Cultures of Globalization*, eds. Frederic Jameson and Masasao Miyoshi. Copyright © 1998 Duke University Press. All rights reserved. Reprinted by permission of the publisher. www.dukepress.edu.

About the Author

Kevin Reilly is a professor of humanities at Raritan Valley College and has taught at Rutgers, Columbia, and Princeton Universities. Cofounder and first president of the World History Association, Reilly has written numerous articles on the teaching of history and has edited works including *The Introductory History Course* for the American Historical Association. A specialist in immigration history, Reilly incorporated his research in creating the "Modern Global Migrations" globe at Ellis Island. His work on the history of racism led to the editing of *Racism: A Global Reader*. He was a Fulbright scholar in Brazil and Jordan and an NEH fellow in Greece, Oxford (UK), and India. Awards include the Community College Humanities Association's Distinguished Educator of the Year and the World History Association's Pioneer Award. He has also served the American Historical Association in various capacities, including the governing council. He is currently writing a global history of racism.

About the Cover Images

Spring Scything in China, 1974 (left), and Candido Portinari, *Coffee*, 1935 (right). The agricultural revolution five thousand years ago was one of the most important events in human history. While agricultural processes have changed over time, so too have they endured, as these images of workers in a rice field in China and coffee-pickers in Brazil attest.